The Little Brainwaves investigate...
ANIMALS

Illustrated by
Lisa Swerling and Ralph Lazar

LONDON, NEW YORK,
MELBOURNE, MUNICH, and DELHI

Written and edited by Caroline Bingham
Designed by Jess Bentall

Illustration Lisa Swerling & Ralph Lazar
Picture researcher Rob Nunn
Production editor Siu Chan
Creative director Jane Bull
Category publisher Mary Ling
Consultant Kim Bryan

First published in Great Britain in 2010 by
Dorling Kindersley Limited, 80 Strand, London WC2R 0RL

2 4 6 8 10 9 7 5 3 1
175935 – 04/10

A CIP catalogue record for this book
is available from the British Library
ISBN 978-1-40535-179-9
Colour reproduction by MDP, UK
Printed and bound by Toppan, China

Discover more at
www.dk.com

is a trademark
of Lisa Swerling
& Ralph Lazar

The Little Brainwaves investigate...

ANIMALS

Illustrated by
Lisa Swerling and Ralph Lazar

Contents

Spot the Little Brainwaves!

The Little Brainwaves are little people with big ideas. With their help, this fascinating book takes an extremely informative look at the amazing world of animals. Each of the colourful characters below appear on every page of the book. Have fun spotting them!

Ed the explorer

Vince the vet

Mop & Bop, the zoo keeper twins

Goobie

Naughty Ned

Mr Strong

Hidden Harry

Brianwave

What is an animal?

All living things fall into two main groups. They are either an animal or a plant. They all grow, feed, and have young. But animals can do something plants can't do – they can move (or at least most of them can)! Join the Little Brainwaves to find out more.

WHAT KIND OF ANIMAL?

Animals can be split into two groups: the largest group are the invertebrates (or creepy crawlies), while vertebrates (animals with *backbones*) can be divided into mammals, birds, fish, reptiles, and amphibians.

Vertebrates

MAMMALS
We are mammals. So are lions and tigers and mice and whales and seals. Mammal mothers feed their young with milk.

BIRDS
Birds can be found everywhere and their songs are often heard at dawn. Birds have feathers and most can fly.

REPTILES
Most reptiles lay eggs. They have dry skin that is covered with protective scales or horny plates. Snakes are reptiles.

AMPHIBIANS
Amphibians have soft skin and must keep it moist. Most amphibians breathe air as adults, but begin their life in water.

FISH
Fish spend their lives in water. They have fins and a protective covering of scales. Most breathe using gills.

IT'S A FOOD CHAIN!

Everything that's alive needs energy, and this energy has to come from somewhere. A plant gets its energy from the Sun. When the plant is eaten by an animal, it passes its energy to that animal. If that animal is eaten, it passes on the energy. This is called a food chain.

The Sun's energy allows plants to grow.

A top predator, such as an eagle, feeds on the snake.

Small animals feed on plants and their seeds.

Carnivores, such as snakes, prey on the small animals.

What kind of animal can't move?

Coral. Find out more on page 42

Invertebrates

INSECTS
Butterflies, moths, flies, beetles, mosquitoes... insects are everywhere. In fact, more than one million types of insect are known.

ARACHNIDS
Did you know that ticks and mites are related to spiders? They all have eight legs, and they are all arachnids.

OTHERS
From the snails in your garden to sponges in the sea, there are lots of groups of invertebrates. They are incredibly varied.

Latin, anybody?

All animals have a Latin name, so that scientists working anywhere in the world (and therefore speaking different languages) can identify them. They may be known by different local names, but the Latin name is always the same.

An American robin is *Turdus migratorius*. The European robin is *Erithacus rubecula*.

There are so many invertebrates!

What are mammals?

There are around 5,000 species of mammal, from tiny shrews and bats to huge, water-based mammals such as the blue whale. Certain features set mammals apart from other animals.

THEY HAVE LIVE BABIES

Most mammals give birth to live babies. Many of these babies look like their parents and are fully developed, but they are miniature versions and require a lot of care before they are ready to survive on their own.

Whales and dolphins don't have fur, though some have bristles around their mouths.

What mammals don't have fur?

The blue whale is a marine mammal. Learn more about marine mammals on page 22-23.

(BUT SOME LAY EGGS!)

There are five egg-laying mammals: four species of echidnas, and the duck-billed platypus. (The echidna is also known as the spiny anteater.) These mammals lay eggs with soft, leathery shells.

A BONY INSIDE

Mammals have a bony skeleton with a backbone, like all vertebrates. However, mammal skeletons have a jaw hinged to the skull and a lower jaw that is one bone. These things make the jaw good for cutting or slicing and chewing food.

A FUR COAT

Most, though not all, mammals have fur. It provides a protective, warm coat. Fur can also help an animal to hide – from prey or from a predator.

STAYING WARM

Mammals are warm blooded. That means that they make their own body heat, using the food they have eaten as fuel.

IT'S TIME FOR YOUR MILK!

Mammals suckle their young, the mother producing milk to nourish the baby. Most mammal babies suckle the milk through teats on the mother's chest.

Mothers and babies

Mammals (or at least most of them) give birth to live babies. Humans are mammals, and lots of other mammal mothers take care of their babies as we do – feeding them, keeping them warm, and teaching them how look after themselves in the world.

TIME FOR NURSING

A mother rabbit may have up to nine babies at a time. They are born blind and without fur, but use their sense of smell to find food – milk from their mother. The mother usually has enough teats to allow all her young to feed at once.

DANGEROUS GRUB

Like other mammals, baby meerkats feed on milk. As they get older, they move onto insects. These can be poisonous and dangerous to eat, so a pup's mother (and other meerkats in the group) show it how to catch and kill and feed safely.

Baby rabbits are called kits.

MARINE MAMMAL MUMMY

Dolphins are mammals that live in water. A dolphin breathes air through nostrils on top of its head, and females give birth in water. As soon as her baby is born, she helps it to the surface to breathe.

Rabbits nibble all sorts of plants.

They like carrots because carrots taste sweet.

IT'S A BABY KOALA

A koala baby, a joey, is smaller than your little finger at birth. And, like rabbit kits, it is bald and blind. But it can still drag itself into its mother's pouch where it drinks milk, keeps warm, and grows.

Is it an ape or a monkey?

Monkeys and apes belong to a large group of mammals called primates. Primates are good climbers, and some spend their whole life in trees. They have strong arms and legs, and long, grasping fingers. Many are playful and intelligent. But how do you tell an ape from a monkey?

Chimpanzees have a large brain and are among the most intelligent of all animals.

APES USE TOOLS

Few animals use tools, but chimpanzees will regularly pick up a stick, strip off its bark, and use it to poke a termite nest. They can then pick off the termites to eat. They will also use stones to crack open nuts. Other apes have been seen to use tools – but only two species of monkey.

Gorillas are the largest apes.

WHAT MAKES AN APE?

There are 21 species of ape. Chimpanzees are apes. So are gibbons. And human beings.
* Most are larger than monkeys.
* They have no tail.
* The forelimbs are longer than the hindlimbs (except humans).
* Chests more rounded.

ONLY MONKEYS HAVE TAILS

Most monkeys have long tails, and some have tails they can use to grasp as they move through the trees. It's a bit like having an extra arm, and very useful – it is known as a "prehensile" tail. Not all monkeys have a prehensile tail. This one doesn't.

TIME FOR GROOMING

One thing that apes and monkeys all love to do is to groom. Regular grooming helps to keep a primate's coat clean, and helps the animals to bond.

Mona monkeys belong to a group known as "old world monkeys".

WHAT MAKES A MONKEY?

There are about 248 species of monkey. Monkeys include baboons and macaques.
* Most have tails.
* All four limbs are a similar length.
* They rarely walk on two limbs.
* Monkeys have flat chests.

MONKEYS WALK ON ALL FOURS

Most monkeys will use all four limbs for walking, while apes can more easily walk on two. Monkeys are so well adapted to walking in this way that they can easily run along branches that are high above the ground.

13

Look closer: orang-utan

The orang-utan is one of the great apes, and is the largest tree-dwelling mammal in the world. It is perfectly adapted to tree life, with arms that have a long reach and grasping feet. These are the only apes that live in Asia.

Orang-utans have eyes set at the front of their face, just like we do. They have good vision, and see in colour.

HOW OLD DO THEY GET?

Wild orang-utans can live to the ripe old age of 45 years. Most of the time they live alone, but young orang-utans are dependent on their mothers until they are about five.

I CAN DO THAT, TOO

Orang-utans are intelligent. In captivity, they will copy the actions of their keepers. In the wild they build nightly nests from leaves and sticks, and will also use sticks as tools.

IT'S A BOY!

A male orang-utan looks very different from a female. He grows a moustache and beard, and has much larger cheek pads as well as a big throat pouch.

FINGERS AND THUMBS
Like other primates, including humans, orang-utans have opposable thumbs. This means they can touch their little finger with their thumb. Unlike us, orang-utans have opposable toes on their feet as well, with their big toe acting like a thumb. It helps them to grip and grab when in the trees.

The orang-utan has incredibly flexible joints that allow it to turn, bend, and reach further than any other primate. It is a master climber!

All orang-utans have red hair.

An orang-utan's arms are much stronger than its legs.

I'M HUNGRY!
Orang-utans love to eat fruit, peeling off the skin just like we do, but they will also tuck into leaves and flowers, insects, and even an egg (if they find a nest).

LIVING IN THE TREETOPS
The word orang-utan means "person of the forest" in Malay. This is a fitting name as wild orang-utans spend nearly all their lives in the treetops. Only the males tend to venture down to the forest floor. The females even give birth in the treetops!

I CAN REACH IT!
Orang-utans have amazingly long arms. Males can have an arm span of more than 2 metres (6½ ft), which is longer than they are tall. That's a useful stretch when they are reaching for particularly tasty fruits.

Big cat, little cat

Cats are efficient hunters. Big or small, they have sharp canine teeth, whiskers that are incredibly sensitive to touch, keen night sight, and fur that provides good camouflage when they stalk their prey.

GOING HUNTING

A wild cat will prey on what it can catch. Depending on the cat's size, this may be anything from rodents and birds to deer, wild pigs, and cattle. A pet cat hunts instinctively, catching mice, birds, and frogs. Both wild cats and pet cats hunt by crouching and movng slowly.

All cats will take the time to stretch their bodies after a nap. It helps to wake up their muscles.

The largest wild cat is the tiger. An adult tiger can eat up to 40 kg (88 lb) at one meal.

A lion's roar can be heard up to 8 km (5 miles) away.

TEAM WORK

The only cats to hunt in groups are lions. These groups are called prides, and they can number up to 35 animals. The females do most of the work. The male's job is to protect the pride's territory.

All cats have:

*Five toes on the front paws and four toes on the back feet
*A long, flexible tail
*A rounded face and short muzzle
*Curved, retractable claws
*Pads on the soles of their feet
*Large, forward facing eyes
*Large, mobile ears
*Long whiskers
*A preference for being alone (except for the lion)
*Keen senses and excellent night vision.
*Attentive mothers
*Long, sharp canines

SLEEP EASY

All cats, no matter what their size, like to sleep. Most will spend about 20 hours a day asleep or resting.

Look closer: family life

You learn from your parents, and so do many other animals. Parents across the animal kingdom protect, teach, and feed their babies. Female elephants make particularly attentive parents.

Newborn elephants may drink more than 11 litres (20 pints) of milk a day.

FAMILY GROUPS

Elephant herds contain related females and their young, with the largest female (known as the "matriarch") in charge. Males leave the herd once they are old enough to look after themselves.

A calf will suckle its mother until it is four or five years old.

LIFE'S LESSONS

All the skills a baby elephant needs to survive in the wild are learned from its mother, aunts, and older siblings. This tight family group all help to look after the youngest elephants, which allows the mothers the time to find the food they need.

Elephants are herbivores: they eat plant matter.

EARLY YEARS
Elephants have one calf, which is usually born at night. The first couple of years of a calf's life are the most dangerous, and it needs its mum to help it find its way around and teach it to find food and water.

An elephant can reach the age of 70

Males leave the herd between the ages of 12 and 15

When one of the herd dies, the other elephants show signs of sadness and loss.

HUGGED BY A NOSE
An elephant communicates with her calf, and her herd, using sound and with constant body contact and the trunk plays a big part in this. On meeting, elephants use their trunks to smell each other. Quite often, one will place its trunk tip in the other's mouth.

I'LL USE MY TRUNK!
The trunk is used to suck, gather food, throw dust over the elephant's back, dig, to reassure other elephants, to smell, and as a hand... in fact, its uses are almost infinite.

A trunk has more than 40,000 muscles.

Now I see you!

Many mammals are masters of disguise. Whether they are hunters, needing to creep up on prey, or the hunted, needing to hide, their appearance helps them to disappear, and it can make a difference between life or death.

A seal pup's fluffy white coat helps to hide it from the polar bears that would like to eat it.

Why doesn't it just swim away?

Pups don't float well and they have to learn to swim.

HIDE AND SEEK
A polar bear crouches by an air hole in the ice, pale against the white snow. A newborn deer lies in dry grass, its brown coat helping to hide it. The way an animal can disappear into its background is seen throughout the animal world. It is called camouflage.

It's summer!

I FANCY A CHANGE

Some animals change colour with the seasons. The Arctic fox has a white coat in the autumn and winter, while in spring and over the summer it turns brownish grey. The colours help the fox hunt its prey more easily.

It's winter!

They look very different – it's bigger in winter. Is it the same fox?

An Arctic fox's winter coat is thicker than its summer coat.

TRICKS WITH PATTERNS

Why is a zebra striped? Lions, who hunt zebra, are colour blind, so a crowd of striped zebra blends into the background, giving more protection to the zebras that stay close to the herd.

21

Mammals at sea

Our planet's largest mammals (whales!) don't walk on land; they swim in the sea. Many whales are huge. An adult blue whale is the size of a large truck, while a humpback's flipper is the length of a family car.

Sperm whales have the largerst brain of any animal.

A dolphin is a toothed whale.

DOES IT HAVE TEETH?
Whales can be split into two groups: those that have teeth and those that don't. Toothed whales like this sperm whale have teeth that are all the same shape.

Baleen plates

Barnacles

Barnacles attach themselves to the skin of some whales. This doesn't harm the whale.

Barnacles are small shellfish.

HOW DO TOOTHLESS WHALES EAT?

Whales without teeth are called "baleen" whales. They sift tiny shrimp-like creatures from the sea through baleen plates. These are rows of stiff hairs that grow down from their top jaw. The northern right whale, shown here, is a baleen whale.

THE WOLF OF THE SEA

The orca, or killer whale, is an efficient hunter. This toothed whale hunts fish, squid, penguins, and sea lions, as well as young blue whales.

Other sea mammals

More mammals than you might think live in (or depend on) the sea. They include:

* Bottlenose dolphins are perhaps the best-known of all 36 different types of marine dolphin.

* Sea otters spend most of their time in water – they even sleep on their backs at sea.

* Dugongs are also known as "sea cows" because they graze on sea grass.

* Walruses are protected from the icy waters of the Arctic ocean by a thick layer of blubber.

Inside a beaver's lodge

Beavers are rodents – they are related to rats and mice, but they are far larger. Like rats and mice they have teeth made for gnawing. However, their teeth can gnaw through thick tree trunks, providing them with the branches they need to build a home.

A BEAVER'S HOME

Beavers build dens on river banks, or they may build a lodge in a lake. For this, they drag sticks to their chosen site and build up a large mound. They then chew an underwater entry and create a dry chamber. An outer coating of mud freezes in the winter, providing a hard, protective surface.

I'VE FELLED ANOTHER TREE!

Beavers have incredibly strong front teeth that never stop growing and are perfect for cutting through wood. In fact, they need to keep gnawing to stop their teeth from getting too long. And gnaw they do. One beaver can take down 200 trees a year!

There will usually be two dens, one for drying off, one a dry area.

CHANGES TO THE LANDSCAPE

A beaver family may dam a river to create a pond for a lodge. Two beavers can build a basic dam in a few days, but will then build it up. Some dams reach amazing sizes - a large one can be the height of two cars piled on top of each other.

The dam makes a wetland, changing the area it's in and attracting birds and animals that wouldn't otherwise be there.

A PLACE OF SAFETY

A lodge provides a safe home because it is impossible for predators to enter as the entrance and exit are underwater. Once inside, the North American beaver is safe from the bears, wolves, and coyotes that might choose it as prey.

What is a bird?

Birds are the only animals that have feathers. They also have bills (but they don't have teeth!). There are about 10,000 different species of birds around the world, in an amazing array of colours. Most can fly.

Family groups

Birds are divided into groups of similar kinds. Here are some of them:

* Water birds, such as pelicans and their relatives, are strong swimmers. Some eat plants, some eat fish.

* Flightless birds include penguins. Although they can't fly, penguins can speed though water chasing their next meal.

* Birds of prey include eagles and vultures. These hunt during the day, killing, or feeding on animals that are already dead.

* Owls are birds of prey too, but they usually hunt at night. They swoop down silently on their prey, catching it in their sharp talons.

* Passerines, or perching birds, such as this robin are known for their songs. Most bird species are passerines.

This peregrine falcon is one of the fastest birds in the world.

When it dives on prey, a peregrine can travel at more than 160 kph (100 mph).

BILL TALK
Birds have bills, instead of jaws with teeth. These are different shapes, depending on what they are used for. Seed eaters have short, cone-shaped bills, while birds of prey have sharp, hooked bills.

Penguins are one of the few birds that cannot fly.

FEATHERY FACTS

Believe it or not, feathers are made from the same material as your hair: keratin. (It is also found in a reptile's scales.) Birds constantly clean and oil their feathers to keep them in good shape. This is known as preening.

This is what a feather looks like under a microscope.

A bird's feathers help to shape its wing so air flows around it and gives the bird lift.

Many birds have feathers that weigh more than their skeleton!

A STARLING'S SKELETON

Many scientists now believe that birds are related to dinosaurs.

A bird's wide breast bone acts as an anchor for the flight muscles.

HOLLOW BONES

A bird's bones are full of holes! This makes them light in weight – if the bones were solid, the bird wouldn't be able to fly.

27

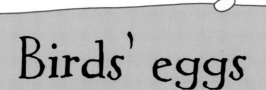

Birds' eggs

All birds lay eggs. Depending on the species, these can be as small as a pea or as large as a melon. A chick grows inside a fertilized egg. When it's big enough, it pecks its way out. Cheep!

WHAT'S IN A SHAPE?

Some birds lay eggs that are almost round. Others lay long eggs. Many seabirds lay eggs that are pointy. This is helpful because some seabirds lay eggs on cliff faces. The shape means that if the egg rolls, it rolls round in a circle and doesn't crash into the sea below.

LITTLE AND LARGE

The smallest egg is laid by the world's smallest bird, the bee hummingbird. This tiny creature is little bigger than a bee, and buzzes like one when it flaps its wings. Its egg is pea-sized. The largest egg belongs to the ostrich. You could fit more than 4,000 bee hummingbird eggs into one ostrich egg.

It's a bee hummingbird's egg.

It's tiny!

Seabirds' eggs come in lots of different patterns so parents can recognize their own eggs among the thousands on the cliff.

COLOUR WAYS

Birds lay their eggs out in the open, or in holes, or in nests. Eggs laid in the open tend to be speckled so they blend in with the surroundings. But eggs laid in holes tend to be bright white or blue so the parent birds can find them.

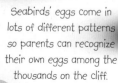

HERE I COME!

Chickens grow inside their shells for 21 days before pecking their way out. Hatching is an exhausting process for a chick, as it has to peck at the shell hundreds of times to make a hole. Just before they are ready to come out, chicks will often begin to cheep to their mother from inside the egg.

Eggs are laid big end first.

A chicken can lay an egg a day.

Supermarket eggs aren't fertilized, so they can't turn into chicks.

LET'S TAKE A LOOK INSIDE AND WATCH A CHICK GROW.

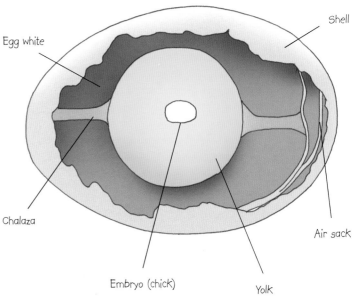

Egg white

Shell

Chalaza

Air sack

Embryo (chick)

Yolk

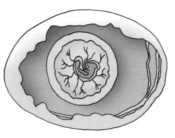

DAY 4 The embryo develops quickly and there are already buds for the legs and wings. The yolk provides the chick's food.

DAY 10 The head develops at the larger end of the egg. The chick now looks like a bird, with a beak. It still uses the yolk for food.

DAY 20 By now, the chick has little room and is in position to break out of the egg, using a special egg tooth. Hatching occurs on day 21.

Birds' nests

From hollows made in sand to simple cup-shaped dwellings to shared nests that engulf telegraph poles, there are an amazing variety of birds' nests. Take a look at some of them with the Little Brainwaves.

WHY BUILD A NEST?

Birds lay eggs, and they need a safe place to lay those eggs and a warm place in which the eggs can develop. A nest is perfect for this. However, not all nests provide this protection – some birds simply scrape a shallow dip on the ground.

WHAT SHALL I USE?

Nests may be built from materials that range from stones to mud to twigs to found items such as string. Some birds, such as swallows, use saliva to glue their mud nests together. Feathers and lichen are then often used to line a nest for warmth and softness.

The masked weaver bird builds its nest from green grasses.

This songbird has built a cup-shaped nest in the fork of a tree branch.

Long-tailed tits use cobwebs to hold their moss nests together.

Some birds lay directly on the ground, using no nest.

Types of nest

This model of an ovenbird's mud nest has an open top to show the nest's interior.

Woodpeckers drill holes into tree trunks, hollowing out a space for a nest.

This Steller's sea eagle has built an immense platform nest at the top of a tree. The nest is called an aerie.

African sociable weavers build massive communal nests. Up to 100 families may share a nest.

I CAN'T BE BOTHERED

Owls are not good nest builders. Instead, depending on the species, they will choose a hole in a tree trunk or a cavity in a log. Some nest close to, or at, ground level. Others move into abandoned burrows.

What is a reptile?

If asked to name a reptile, most people will mention a crocodile or a snake. There are actually around 9,000 species (types) of reptile. All have features in common. Can you name the most noticeable? It's their scaly bodies!

WE HAVE SCALY SKIN

Reptiles are covered with a protective layer of scaly skin. The scales actually contain the same substance as is in your fingernails, which gives them strength. (It's called keratin.) Learn more about how this skin is regularly replaced on pages 34-35.

Cameleons belong to the lizard group of reptiles.

A reptile's scales are waterproof.

Family groups

Reptiles can be divided into four main groups:

* Snakes and lizards
* Crocodiles
* Tortoises and turtles
* Tuataras

Baby ball python

Paraguayan (common) caiman

These turtles are warming themselves in the Sun's rays.

BASKING IN THE SUN

Reptiles cannot make their own heat – they are cold blooded. That doesn't mean that their blood is cold. It means their body temperature depends on their surroundings. So sometimes reptiles will lie in sunlight to warm up, moving into shade if it becomes too hot.

A chameleon's tail can be used to grasp branches.

THEY LAY EGGS!

Many reptiles are egg layers (some reptiles give birth to live young). Most reptile eggs have a tough, leathery shell, and they will be laid in burrows or in dead plant matter. Reptile young are usually left to look after themselves from birth.

A new skin

We lose millions of dead skin cells each day, but as we don't have to shed skin in large pieces, we don't see it happening. Reptiles are different. Their scales don't grow, so a reptile has to shed its skin in order to grow.

IS IT GOING TO SHED?

Shortly before a snake is ready to lose (or slough off) its skin, it will change colour, often becoming duller, while its eyes will appear cloudy. Snakes usually don't eat around this time. To break the skin, it will rub its head against a rock or tree trunk.

The scales that appear beneath the shed layer are larger.

Is it possible to tell from a shed skin what snake it came from?

Yes, sometimes! A snake's body patterns may leave clues or markings on the shed piece.

A new skin

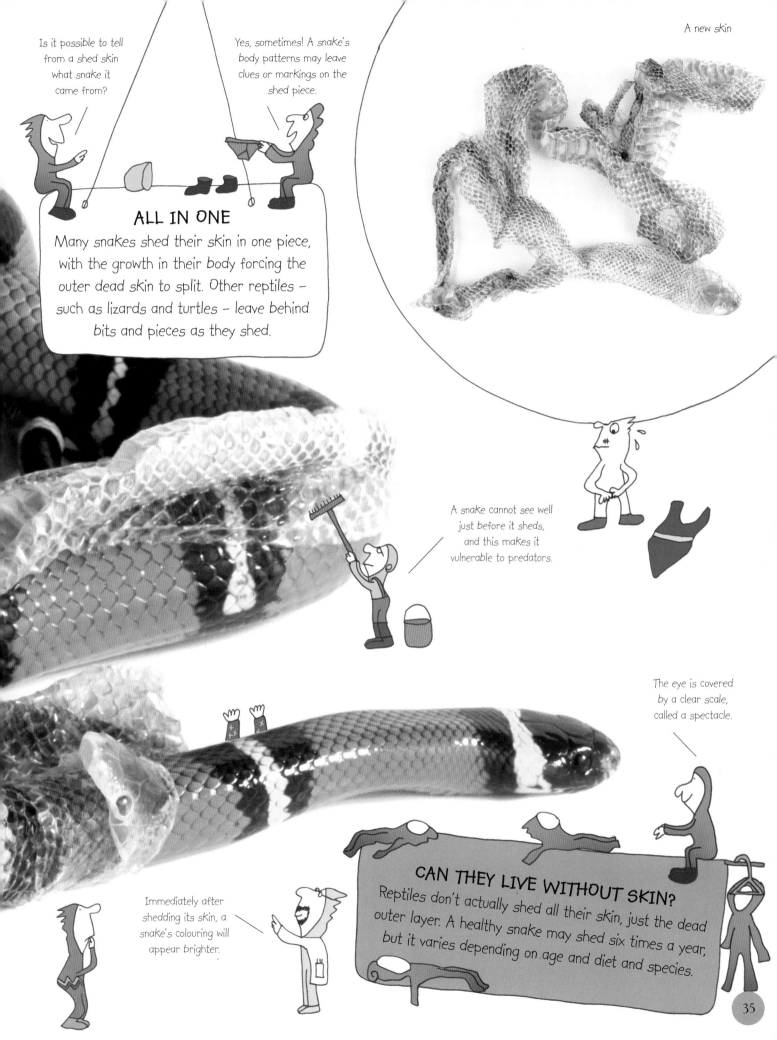

ALL IN ONE

Many snakes shed their skin in one piece, with the growth in their body forcing the outer dead skin to split. Other reptiles – such as lizards and turtles – leave behind bits and pieces as they shed.

A snake cannot see well just before it sheds, and this makes it vulnerable to predators.

The eye is covered by a clear scale, called a spectacle.

Immediately after shedding its skin, a snake's colouring will appear brighter.

CAN THEY LIVE WITHOUT SKIN?

Reptiles don't actually shed all their skin, just the dead outer layer. A healthy snake may shed six times a year, but it varies depending on age and diet and species.

35

What is an amphibian?

Like reptiles, amphibians are cold blooded, but their skin has no scales and is usually soft and moist (some toads have skin that is as tough as leather!). Most amphibians live in damp surroundings, which helps to keep it this way.

Around 380 species of salamander have no lungs at all!

How do they breathe?

Some through their skin and mouth. Others have external gills.

FROM WATER TO LAND TO WATER

Most amphibians spend part of their life in water and part on land. The majority begin life as larvae in water, and move onto land as adults. However, they always remain near water, as they dry out quickly if they do not stay damp.

Family groups

There are three main groups of amphibians: frogs and toads, newts and salamanders, and worm-like caecilians.

Great plains toad

Ringed caecilian

Red-spotted newt

Caecilians are rarely seen because they live in soil burrows or underwater.

TAKE A BREATH

Although they have lungs, some amphibians (such as this frog) are also able to breathe through their skin (that's very useful for a frog when it dives underwater). Some can even take in oxygen through the roof of their mouth.

FIRE SALAMANDER

What is an amphibian?

DO THEY GET EATEN?

If their skin is so soft, how do amphibians protect themselves from predators. Well, they can't always, but all amphibians have poison glands in their skin, and many taste highly unpleasant. Predators learn to avoid them. Many are also well camouflaged and therefore hard to find.

An adult frog is carnivorous: it catches and feeds on live prey.

Amphibians have been around for at least 370 million years!

I know! But did you know that they evolved from fish?

PERFECT COLOURS

Some amphibians have brightly patterned skin and that warns predators they are poisonous. Others change colour to change their body temperature or to match their background for camouflage.

An amphibian's skin is not waterproof.

37

Tadpole to frog

All amphibians undergo a body change known as metamorphosis. Most begin life as an egg that develops into a larva. The Little Brainwaves are going to take a look at this process in a common frog.

ONE

Frogs (and toads) start life as eggs. These have a jelly-like coating, and clump together on a pond's surface as frog spawn. Each egg contains an embryo. A common frog will lay up to 2,000 eggs at one time.

TWO

After about six days, if conditions have been right, the eggs hatch and tadpoles emerge. The tadpoles breathe through external gills and feed on green algae.

THREE

At six weeks, the tadpoles have budding hind legs. Their gills are now internal. As well as algae, the tadpoles will begin to feed on dead insects.

FOUR

At nine weeks, the frog's rear legs are fully formed, while the front legs have appeared.

What happens to the tadpole's tail?

It's absorbed by the body.

FIVE

At 12 weeks, the froglet has lost its gills and can breathe with its lungs and through its skin. The tail has disappeared. Now they just have to grow to reach adult size - the body will reach about 8 cm (3 in).

Learn about insect metamorphosis on pages 50-51.

39

What is a fish?

More than half of all vertebrate (animals with backbones) species are fishes. These animals are built for life in water, most having gills and a body covered with smooth, protective scales.

Fish are cold blooded.

MADE FOR LIFE UNDER WATER

A fish's stream-lined shape helps the animal to slip through the water, while gills allow it to breathe under the water.

The first vertebrates were primitive fishes.

When did they appear?

More than 450 million years ago!

EARLY LIFE

All fishes begin life as eggs. Some are laid in the water and hatch as larvae, others as tiny adults. Others, such as sharks, develop inside the body and are born as live young.

A bony flap protects the fish's gills.

Fish go to school!

No, they swim in schools! There's safety in numbers when they all swim together.

Brown trout eggs

FLEXIBLE FINS

Most fish swim using fins, but some use their fins for more than swimming. Some use their fins for walking along the sea bed, while flying fish use theirs to glide briefly above the water's surface. Mudskippers use their front fins to crawl across mud.

Mudskipper

Fish scales form a protective layer.

HOW DOES A FISH BREATHE?

Fish use gills to remove oxygen from water to breathe (apart from lungfishes that can breathe directly from the air). What are gills? They are feathery structures found along the sides of the head, often protected by a bony flap.

Unusual fishes

* Sea horses may not look like fish, but they are. They have tiny fins and tails that can grip onto plants or corals.

* Eels are long, and snake-like in their appearance and behaviour. Many eels have sharp teeth to grab prey.

* Rays have a flattened shape. Some are able to stun their prey – smaller fish – with a charge of electricity.

On the coral reef

The warm, shallow waters of a tropical coral reef are home to some of the most unusual and colourful fish in the world. Many of these swim together in schools of hundreds of fish.

SAFETY IN NUMBERS
These blue-striped snapper fish swim skilfully together, all heading in the same directions and turning at the same time. This makes it difficult for an enemy (a predator) to pick out a single fish to eat.

WHAT'S CORAL?
Coral is a type of tiny sea animal. Its home is a stony cup that it builds around itself. When the coral dies, the cup stays behind. Coral lives in huge colonies, with new animals making their cups on top of the ones that have died. Over time they form coral reefs.

TIME TO GET BIGGER

Pufferfish have big ideas when it comes to escaping from an enemy. When threatened, they quickly fill their bodies with water, growing in size. When the danger has passed, they push the water out and go back to normal.

Why so colourful?

There's lots of colour on a coral reef – animals and plants are bursting with it. They use it as camouflage, so they can hide from enemies, or to confuse enemies. Or they use it to signal to other fish.

* This copperband butterfly fish has a false eyespot to confuse predators.

* This trumpet fish changes colour to match the fish it is swimming with.

* This little flasher wrasse flashes brilliant colours to attract a female.

LET'S GET CLEANED UP

Fish are covered in dead skin and scales as well as tiny animals called parasites. Sometimes they need a clean! So they go to cleaning stations on the reef, where cleaner fish eat away the debris.

Killing machine

Sharks are feared by many, yet they rarely attack people. So why do they make people nervous? It's because of their teeth... in some species, all 3,000 of them. They are sharp, and perfectly shaped for cutting and tearing.

OPEN WIDE!

Let's peep into the mouth of a great white shark, with its sharp, jagged-edged teeth arranged in three rows. When the shark loses a tooth, there is always another ready to move forward and take its place.

Instead, sharks tear off chunks of flesh and swallow it straight down.

Sharks can't chew their food. They don't have grinding teeth like us (our back teeth).

You're more likely to be struck by lightning than eaten by a shark.

Don't eat me!

SHARP TEETH

A closer look at a great white shark's tooth shows its jagged, or serrated, edge. This tooth is designed to cut and tear. Not all sharks have serrated teeth.

Egg-laying sharks lay their eggs in a protective pouch.

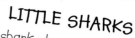

Killing machine

LITTLE SHARKS

Lots of sharks lay eggs, but most give birth to live young (called pups). A shark can have one to one hundred pups at a time, depending on what kind of shark it is. Sharks do not care for their eggs or pups. In fact many sharks would eat their own pups if they swam too close.

WHAT'S FOR DINNER?

Sharks never sleep. They spend their time hunting. Some, such as the tiger shark, eat anything – from turtles, seals, and squid to tin cans, clothes, car tyres and number plates! Others are fussier – they take a bite, check the flavour, and swim away if it is not to their taste.

Different sharks

There are more than 300 kinds of sharks. Let's take a look at a few of these.

* The shortfin mako is the fastest shark in the ocean. It can swim at 97 kph (60 mph).

* Angel sharks are flat (like a stingray) and bury themselves under sand to lie in wait for prey.

* Hammerhead sharks have eyes on the ends of their wide, flattened, hammer-shaped heads.

* Goblin sharks have long, pointy snouts and are rarely seen as they patrol deep waters.

* Whale sharks are the world's largest shark. They can grow to be as long as a bus.

45

What is an invertebrate?

At least ninety-five per cent of the known animal kingdom are invertebrates. These are animals that have no backbone or internal skeleton. From simple worms and sea sponges to insects that live in communities (such as bees), invertebrates are fun to watch and study.

Types of invertebrate

There are so many different types of invertebrates that they are classified into large groups. Here are a few of these groups (there are actually more than 30 of them).

* Annelida... include earthworms, leeches, and bristleworms. These invertebrates have bodies that are divided into segments.

* Arthopods... form the largest group of animals. They have a hard outer covering and jointed limbs. Insects and crustaceans are arthropods

* Cnidaria... include jellyfish and corals. All the animals in this group have tentacles with stinging cells with which they catch their food.

* Echinodermata... live largely on the sea floor. Many have a prickly body. Sea stars, sea urchins, and sea cucumbers belong in this group.

* Porifera... the sponges. These are the simplest of all living animals. Adult sponges spend their lives in one place, fixed to a rock on the sea floor.

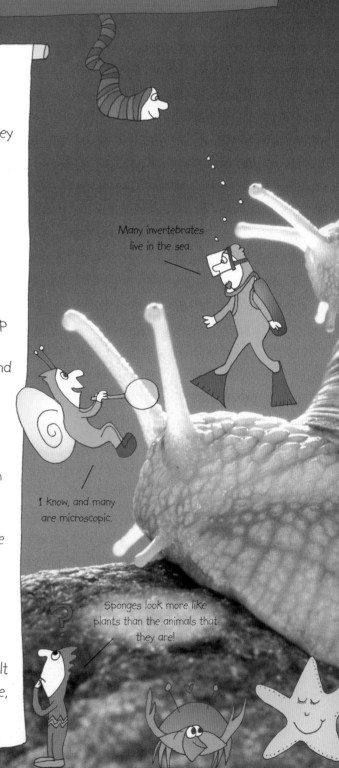

Many invertebrates live in the sea.

I know, and many are microscopic.

Sponges look more like plants than the animals that they are!

HUMAN SPINE
Human beings have skeletons with a backbone made up from bones called vertebrae. Invertebrates don't have bony skeletons, and they lack a backbone.

CLOSE RELATIONS
Snails are molluscs. These invertebrates have an amazing array of body shapes. Squids and octopuses are also molluscs.

What is an insect?

There are more than a million different kinds of insects. But what IS an insect? Join the Little Brainwaves to find out. (The main things to remember are that an insect has three parts to its body and six legs.)

HOW IT WORKS

An insect's body is made up of its head at one end, thorax in the middle, and abdomen at the other end. Its six legs are attached to the thorax. Its brain is in its head and its digestive system is in its abdomen.

There's an incredible variety of insects. What am I pretending to be?

You're an ant! Did you know that lots of insects have wings. Flies are insects.

Family groups

Insects can be split into groups of similar insects (too many to list here). They include:

The five largest groups:
*Beetles
*Bugs
*Flies
*Wasps, ants, and bees
*Butterflies and moths

as well as:
*Termites
*Earwigs
*Cockroaches
*Dragonflies
*Grasshoppers and crickets

Hoverfly (Eristalis)

Earwig (Dermaptera)

Abdomen

Insects hatch from eggs

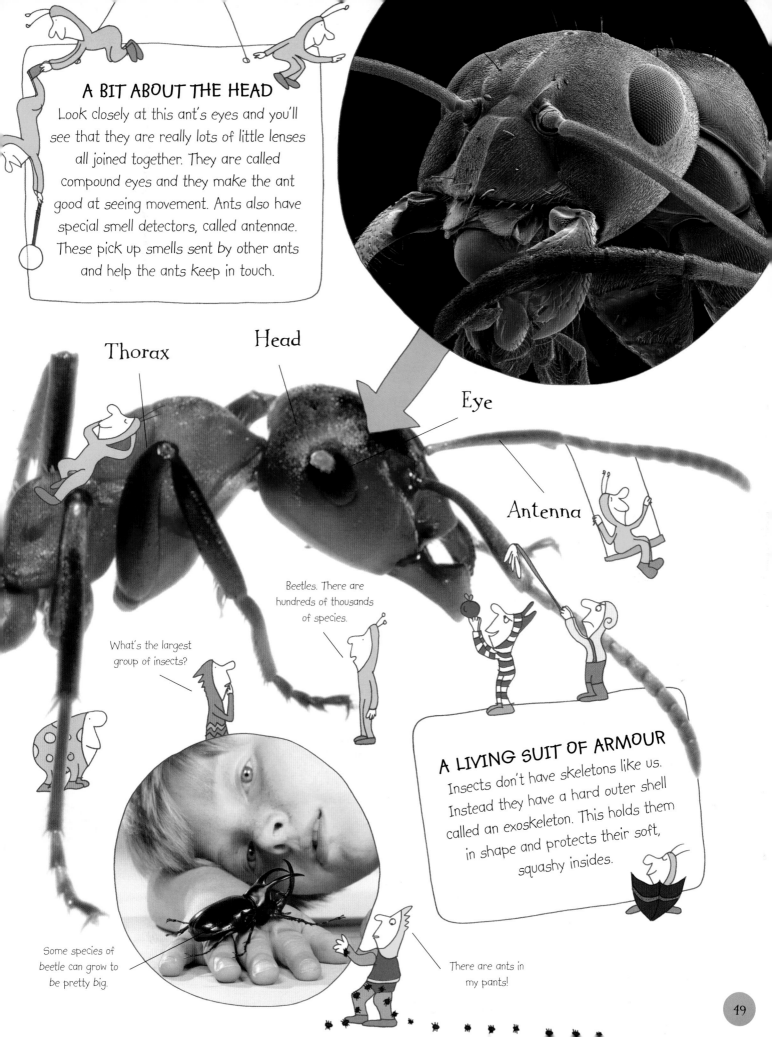

A BIT ABOUT THE HEAD

Look closely at this ant's eyes and you'll see that they are really lots of little lenses all joined together. They are called compound eyes and they make the ant good at seeing movement. Ants also have special smell detectors, called antennae. These pick up smells sent by other ants and help the ants keep in touch.

Thorax

Head

Eye

Antenna

What's the largest group of insects?

Beetles. There are hundreds of thousands of species.

A LIVING SUIT OF ARMOUR

Insects don't have skeletons like us. Instead they have a hard outer shell called an exoskeleton. This holds them in shape and protects their soft, squashy insides.

Some species of beetle can grow to be pretty big.

There are ants in my pants!

A butterfly emerges

Insects start life as an egg and then undergo different stages before reaching their adult form. Many undergo a complete change in appearance. It's known as "metamorphosis". One example of metamorphosis is the butterfly.

ONE
Butterfly eggs are laid on leaves or stems, usually on or near the intended caterpillar food.

An empty chrysalis is a sign a butterfly has emerged.

TWO
The caterpillar's job is to eat and grow, and avoid being eaten. A caterpillar (or larva) often has a pattern of stripes or patches that help it to hide. Some have spine-like hairs. As it grows, it sheds its skin four or more times so as to enclose its rapidly growing body.

THREE

A chrysalis (or pupa) is the stage when the caterpillar changes. Inside this hard case, the caterpillar's tissues break down and the adult insect forms. Most butterflies have a brown or green chrysalis, to blend into the background.

Chrysalis

After it breaks out of its chrysalis, a butterfly has to let its wings dry before it can fly.

FOUR

The adult (the "imago") can both fly and reproduce. The adults spend their time looking for a mate and laying eggs. Some butterflies travel a long way after they emerge.

Look closer: bees

Busy bees. They buzz around the garden and can inflict a nasty sting. But don't worry, bees are actually the good guys – especially if you are a flower.

Bees carry pollen in baskets on their back legs.

A BEE'S WORK

The bee is a flower's best friend. Bees transfer pollen from flower to flower and that allows the flowers to reproduce.

They take the pollen back to the hive to feed their young.

SO MUCH TO DO

A bee will visit between 50 and 100 flowers on each flying trip. It takes the nectar from two million flowers to make 500 g (1 lb) of honey. No wonder honeybees are so busy.

A single honeybee will produce just one-twelfth of a teaspoon of honey in its lifetime!

Bees are furry, which is how you can tell them from wasps. Bumblebees are hairier than honeybees.

OUCH!

Bees only sting if they are attacked or upset. Worker honeybees have a barbed sting, which is left in your skin after stinging. This results in the honeybee dying. Bumblebees don't die after stinging, and some bees don't sting at all.

Bee facts

* Bee head. The *bee's* sensitive antennae sit between its compound eyes, which are made up of more than 4,000 lenses.

* Food source. Bees visit flowers for the sweet nectar, which they eat. While collecting the nectar, the flower's pollen sticks to the *bee*.

* Waggledance. Want directions to a new flower? The dance performed by honeybees tells the others how far it is and which way to go.

* Home fields. Farmers and *beekeepers* work together, using *bees* to pollinate crops and make honey. Some *beekeepers* move their hives onto farms.

WHY DOES IT BUZZ?

Bees fly at an average speed of 22.5 km/h (14 mph). They beat their wings about 180 times a minute when they're flying. This is what makes the buzzing sound.

Look closer: grasshoppers

There are about 10,000 species of grasshopper. They belong to the same family as crickets, but there are lots of differences between the two. For a start, grasshoppers are active in the day, while crickets come out at night.

THEY SING!

Stand in a field of grass and you will probably soon hear a grasshopper's song. They sing by rubbing a row of little pegs on their long hind legs against the side of their wings. Only the males sing – they do it to attract a female. Different species sing different songs.

Do grasshoppers have "ears" in their knees?

No, those are crickets. Grasshoppers have "ears" on the side of their bodies.

YUM TUM

Like most crickets, this one eats just about anything – from grass to maggots and insects. Grasshoppers on the other hand will only eat plant matter.

When a grasshopper is picked up, it spits a brown liquid.

Scientists think this is protection against ant attacks.

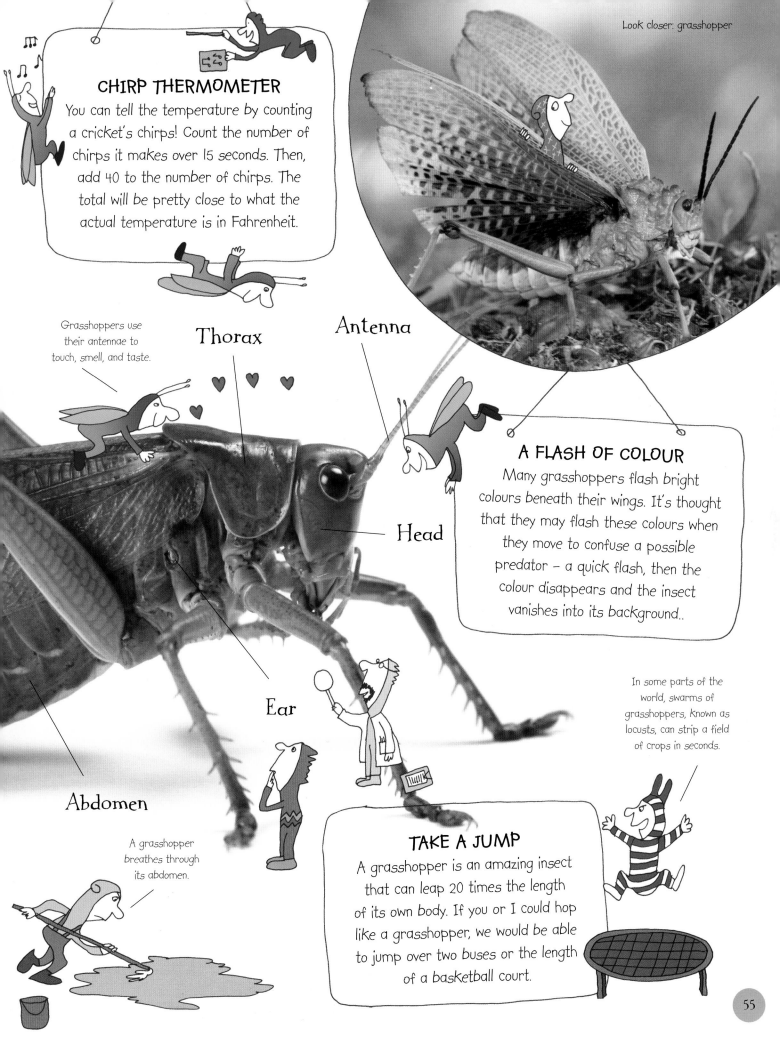

CHIRP THERMOMETER
You can tell the temperature by counting a cricket's chirps! Count the number of chirps it makes over 15 seconds. Then, add 40 to the number of chirps. The total will be pretty close to what the actual temperature is in Fahrenheit.

Grasshoppers use their antennae to touch, smell, and taste.

Thorax

Antenna

Head

A FLASH OF COLOUR
Many grasshoppers flash bright colours beneath their wings. It's thought that they may flash these colours when they move to confuse a possible predator – a quick flash, then the colour disappears and the insect vanishes into its background..

In some parts of the world, swarms of grasshoppers, Known as locusts, can strip a field of crops in seconds.

Ear

Abdomen

A grasshopper breathes through its abdomen.

TAKE A JUMP
A grasshopper is an amazing insect that can leap 20 times the length of its own body. If you or I could hop like a grasshopper, we would be able to jump over two buses or the length of a basketball court.

What is an arachnid?

This massive group of arthropods includes spiders and scorpions, as well as tiny ticks and mites. How do you tell something is an arachnid? For a start, nearly all arachnids have eight legs and two main body parts.

The eight legs are attached to the front part of an arachnid's body.

GOING HUNTING!

Lots of arachnids hunt living prey, biting or stinging to kill or paralyse. They use limb-like mouthparts called pedipalps to hold their food. Ticks, however, stab into their prey and suck up blood.

Pedipalp

DRIBBLE, DRIBBLE

Most arachnids have small mouths and cannot chew food. They get around this by dribbling digestive fluid onto their prey to dissolve it into a pulp. They can then suck up the juices.

All arachnids are flesh (or blood) eaters, though mites often feed on plants.

WE ARE THE BIGGEST!

Spiders form the largest group of arachnids. There are more than 40,000 known species of spider.

No arachnid has wings or antennae.

What am I then?

You're an insect!

What is an arachnid?

The sting has a pair of venom glands at its base.

A SCORPION

Pedipalp

Most arachnids live on land.

SCORPION ALERT!
Scorpions are the among the most ancient of all arachnids. Their pincer pedipalps are used to catch and hold their prey, while the end of the tail delivers a venomous sting to paralyse the scorpion's victim.

Eeeeek... I'm scared of spiders!

Say hello to Mr Spider!

Did you know...?

... that ticks and mites are related to spiders? They are arachnids, too.

* Ticks are blood suckers. They swell as they take in blood.

* Mites are all around us, but they are tiny and go unseen.

IT'S GOT TOO MANY LEGS!
Some people are scared of spiders and other arachnids. Being scared of spiders is called arachnophobia.

Amazing animals

Scientists believe there may be more than ten million species, or types, of animals, but fewer than two million have been described. Take a look at some of the amazing facts that help to make the world of animals so incredible.

THE SIBERIAN TIGER
This tiger, *Panthera tibris altaica*, is the largest member of the cat family. An adult male can reach the weight of about twelve nine-year-old children.

FOOD TALK
Do you eat three times a day? Many animals eat far less frequently, especially reptiles. A crocodile needs a good meal just once a week and can go without food for longer if necessary!

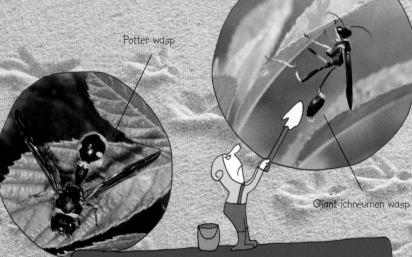

Potter wasp

Giant ichneumon wasp

HUNGRY LION
An adult male lion will eat the equivalent of some 650 sausages at one meal. An adult female will eat quite a bit less – the equivalent of about 375 sausages.

THAT'S A POTTER WASP... THAT'S A GIANT ICHNEUMON! THERE ARE THOUGHT TO BE UP TO 140,000 SPECIES OF WASP!

MOST POISONOUS VERTEBRATE

The GOLDEN poison FROG (*Phyllobates terribilis*) is the most poisonous of all vertebrates: the poison contained within just one frog could kill up to 20 people. Most animals know to avoid it – but one species of frog-eating snake is resistant to the poison.

DON'T STICK OUT YOUR TONGUE!

A giant anteater will flick out its tongue 150 times a minute when it's feeding at an ant's nest.

I SMELL LUNCH

A shark can detect a few drops of blood in an area of water the size of a Olympic-sized swimming pool.

A FULLY GROWN BLUE WHALE, THE WORLD'S LARGEST ANIMAL, IS AS LONG AS 19 DIVERS SWIMMING HEAD TO FOOT.

SMALLEST BIRD

The smallest bird in the world, the bee hummingbird, is tiny enough to perch happily on top of a pencil. It weighs just 2 g ($\frac{1}{16}$th oz).

A little bit of history!

c. 4th century BCE ARISTOTLE (384 to 322 BCE) divided living things into two groups: plants and animals. He divided animals into three groups according to how they moved - walking, flying, or swimming. This system was used until the 1600s.

In the 18th century, Swedish scientist Carolus Linnaeus (1707-1778) divided living things into two kingdoms: plants and animals, and divided each kingdom into small groups called genera. Genera were divided into species. His system gave each living thing a unique name.

1859 Charles Darwin (1809-1882) published *On the Origin of Species*, which changed the way people saw the natural world.

Glossary

AMPHIBIAN: An animal that may live on land or in the water and lays shell-less eggs.

ANTENNA (plural **ANTENNAE**): One of a pair of long sense organs, found on an arthropod's head. They are used to feel, taste, and smell, as well as to pick up vibrations.

ARACHNID: A group of invertebrates that have eight legs.

ARTHROPOD: An invertebrate with a hard body casing (exoskeleton) and jointed legs.

CAMOUFLAGE: A colour or pattern that helps an animal blend into its background, so it can't be seen.

CARNIVORE: An animal that eats meat.

CHRYSALIS: The protective case of a pupa.

COLD BLOODED: An animal that cannot maintain its body temperature, and has to rely on the Sun's heat to warm up, or find shade in which to cool down.

COMPOUND EYE: An eye made up of hundreds of tiny units, each of which makes a separate image.

EGG TOOTH: A horny growth on a chick's bill, which is used to break through the shell to allow the chick to hatch. The egg tooth soon disappears.

EMBRYO: An animal in the very early stages of its growth, before it has hatched or been born.

EXOSKELETON: An arthropod's hard outer skeleton.

FOOD CHAIN: The transfer of energy from the Sun to a plant to the animal that eats it, and so on.

GILLS: Feathery structures on the side of a fish's head. Fish use gills to take oxygen from water in order to breathe.

GNAW: To bite or nibble continuously.

HERBIVORE: An animal that eats only plants and their fruits and seeds.

INSECT: A group of invertebrates that have six legs and three body parts.

INVERTEBRATE: Animals without a backbone. Molluscs are invertebrates.

KERATIN: A tough protein found in hair, nails, claws, hooves, and horns.

LARVA (plural **LARVAE**): The young stage of an insect, amphibian, or cnidarian. Larvae look very different from the adults.

MAMMAL: An animal that feeds its young on milk.

METAMORPHOSIS: The change in body form that some animals, such as amphibians and butterflies, undergo before becoming an adult.

NECTAR: A sugary liquid made by plants.

PEDIPALPS: An arachnid's limb-like appendages, positioned by its mouth.

POLLEN: A dust-like powder produced by flowers.

PREDATOR: An animal that kills and eats other animals.

PREENING: The way a bird cleans and oils its feathers with its beak.

PREHENSILE TAIL: A tail that can grasp.

PREY: The animal that is killed and eaten by a predator.

PRIDE: A group of lions.

PRIMATE: A mammal, such as an ape or monkey, with forward facing eyes and opposable thumbs.

RODENT: A group of mammals, including rats and mice, that have a pair of sharp front teeth for gnawing.

SPECIES: A group of living things that can breed together in the wild.

STALK: The creeping behaviour of a predator approaching its prey.

SUCKLE: The means by which a baby mammal takes milk from its mother by sucking a teat.

TALONS: The claws of a bird of prey such as an eagle.

VENOM: A harmful liquid produced by some animals (such as snakes) and delivered by a bite or a sting.

VERTEBRATE: Animals with a backbone. Apes are vertebrates.

Index

Clydebank Public Library.

LENDING DEPARTMENT.

This Book must be returned to the Library not later than **two weeks** from the date of issue; but it may be taken out again, if not wanted by another reader.

A fine of One Penny will be stringently exacted for every three days the book is kept beyond the time allowed.

Each book will be carefully examined when returned, and readers will be held responsible for any damage a book may have sustained while in their possession. Writing or drawing on any part of a book with pen or pencil, or doubling down the leaves, will be treated as serious damage.

Readers are requested to give notice of any defect or disfigurement they find in a book when they receive it.

This book cannot be returned on the day of issue.

Immediate notice is to be given to the Librarian of loss of book or of ticket, and of change of address.

It is requested that borrowers who can exchange their books during the day will do so rather than wait until evening.

In the event of infectious disease occurring, books and borrowers' tickets are to be handed to the Officer of the Sanitary Authority, **not** returned to the Library.

Borrowers should carefully read and observe the Bye-Laws and Regulations.

No. 72891

H. G. PINCOTT, Librarian.

Contemporary Europe

Contemporary Europe

A Study of National, International, Economic, and Cultural Trends

A Symposium

By

René Albrecht-Carrié, Ph.D.
Howard Becker, Ph.D.
Lynn M. Case, Ph.D.
Oscar G. Darlington, Ph.D.
Huntley Dupre, Ph.D.
R. Ernest Dupuy, Lt. Col., U. S. Army
Chester Verne Easum, Ph.D.
John C. Engelsman, M.A.
R. E. Falconer
Michael T. Florinsky, Ph.D.
J. Marshall Gersting, Ph.D.
James L. Glanville, Ph.D.
Wilson Leon Godshall, Ph.D.
Frederick E. Graham, Ph.D.
Ernst C. Helmreich, Ph.D.

John Weldon Hoot, Ph.D.
Harry N. Howard, Ph.D.
Thorsten V. Kalijarvi, Ph.D.
Elmer Louis Kayser, Ph.D.
Tibor Kerekes, Ph.D.
Hans Kohn, D.Jur.
William L. Kolb, M.A.
Loren C. MacKinney, Ph.D.
George S. Pettee, Ph.D.
Joseph Remenyi, Ph.D.
Joseph S. Roucek, Ph.D.
S. Harrison Thomson, Ph.D.
Margaret H. Warren, Ph.D.
Roland L. Warren, Ph.D.
Gerald Wendt, Ph.D.

LONDON

CHAPMAN & HALL, LTD.

11 Henrietta Street, W.C. 2

PRINTED IN THE U. S. A.
THE PLIMPTON PRESS, NORWOOD, MASS.

Authors

Joseph S. Roucek, EDITOR

Associate Professor of Political Science and Sociology, Hofstra College

René Albrecht-Carrié

Howard Becker
Professor of Sociology
University of Wisconsin

Lynn M. Case
Assistant Professor of European History, Louisiana State University

Oscar G. Darlington
Associate Professor of History
Hofstra College

Huntley Dupre
Professor of History
University of Kentucky

R. Ernest Dupuy
Lieutenant Colonel, Field Artillery
United States Army

Chester Verne Easum
Associate Professor of History
University of Wisconsin

John C. Engelsman
Assistant in History
Louisiana State University

R. E. Falconer

Michael T. Florinsky
Lecturer in Economics
Columbia University

J. Marshall Gersting
Associate Professor of Economics
Miami University

James L. Glanville
Professor of History
Southern Methodist University

Wilson Leon Godshall
Associate Professor of Diplomatic History and International Relations, Lehigh University

Frederick E. Graham
Professor of European History
San Jose State College

Ernst C. Helmreich
Associate Professor of History and Government, Bowdoin College

John Weldon Hoot
Assistant Professor of Economics
Wharton School, University of Pennsylvania

Harry N. Howard
Professor of History
Miami University

Thorsten V. Kalijarvi
Professor and Head of Department of Government, University of New Hampshire

Elmer Louis Kayser
Dean of University Students and Professor of European History, George Washington University

Tibor Kerekes
Chairman, Department of History, The Graduate School, Georgetown University

Hans Kohn
Sydenham Clark Parsons Professor of History, Smith College

William L. Kolb
Instructor of Sociology, Oklahoma Agricultural and Mechanical College

Loren C. MacKinney
Professor of History
University of North Carolina

George S. Pettee
Instructor in Government
Harvard University

Joseph Remenyi
Assistant Professor of Comparative Literature, Western Reserve University

S. Harrison Thomson
Professor of History
University of Colorado

Margaret H. Warren

Roland L. Warren
Assistant Professor of Philosophy
Hofstra College

Gerald Wendt
(Formerly) Dean, School of Chemistry and Physics, Pennsylvania State College

To Božena

Preface

What are the main causes of world unrest? Why, in spite of all the earnest desire of millions of people for peace, have we drifted into another world war? Are Hitler, Mussolini and Stalin the ones to be blamed, or are the British and their allies the responsible devils?

These are just a few of the many questions that confront all of us. The present work does not try to answer them all, but it does try earnestly to supply the much-needed background for an understanding of post-war Europe in its political, economic and social aspects within the framework of world relationships.

A question may be asked: why another book on Europe's history? There is a vast literature of monographs and specialized studies in almost every field; the specialist cannot keep up with them and the man in the street is overwhelmed by them. It becomes necessary occasionally to pause and to synthesize the available material, to interpret it, to sift the important from the unimportant, and to put new constructions on the historical events in the light of recent events. History today needs more architects than bricklayers; it needs specialists to present their patient researches in readable form. It has become to some extent traditional in American scholarship to evaluate books as a contribution to knowledge in terms of their contribution to the discovery of some hitherto unknown fact or facts, or in terms of their presentation of facts within the framework of the ideology of the moment. But, while it is not difficult to uncover new facts, given patience and a modicum of training in the use of source material, it is difficult to interpret to thousands of students those co-related facts in terms of their credits and requirements. Facts are innumerable but they are useless unless they make a coherent pattern.

This coherent pattern is the foundation of this work which aims to synthesize the genetic development of Europe in its political, economic and cultural aspects from 1918 to the present time. Each chapter, prepared by an authority in its field is designed to bring into sharp focus the facts in each field and their bearing upon related fields — to give a comprehensive introduction to each particular topic. No apology is needed for the fact that the book is a symposium of outstanding authorities. Insulation from the findings of specialists was a normal matter only a few decades ago but today the student can hardly be led through a period of history or through the confines of a continent on a string fashioned out of the mere rewriting of numberless books. Hence, the cooperation of this group of outstanding specialists who have provided individual chapters on the basis of a framework outlined by the editor in consultation with numerous scholars in the field. The editor has received useful aid from Mr. Anthony Netboy, who has done much to clarify the expression and unify the presentation of the book. Thanks are also due Anita Arbeitel, Francine Sanborne, Richard Francis, LeRoy Millard, Myron Robbins, and Daniel Rubin for their systematic help in the development of the whole project.

A definite effort has been made to integrate the work, and references at the end of each chapter will permit teachers to assign additional specialized work to the student for more intensive reading or for additional research.

The tasks of an editor are extremely difficult but in this case these tasks have brought a superb reward. The cooperation of the authors will never be forgotten and their helpful and useful suggestions will be in large measure responsible for the success of the book. The editor is sincerely grateful to them and it is hoped that by the mutual cooperation of all who have contributed to this enterprise, the present work will be found a readable and informative introduction to what has happened in Europe since 1918 by the college and university student as well as by the lay reader. Our understanding of Europe as a great cultural unit, and of its component parts, should contribute to our comprehension of the present-day forces moving the world, and thus elucidate the role which the United States is playing in the history of the world of today.

JOSEPH S. ROUCEK

NEW YORK, N.Y.

June, 1941

Contents

Contents

A Note on the Maps

Considerable thought and study have gone into these maps. The effort throughout has been to maintain a maximum of simplicity. I have endeavored to furnish a key to the text which will identify in the mind of the student dates and essential changes.

Shifts in territorial boundaries are presently important. The unconventional method employed in breaking Europe apart, thereby establishing the limits of the several maps, is based on the need for a clarified exposition of these recent changes. In addition, there are two maps devoted to recent German and Russian organizations.

Place names assume a secondary importance. No attempt has been made to classify the cities according to size. It was felt that, for the purpose of this work, the simple appearance of the important cities should be sufficient. The world is flooded with maps of Europe which show classifications of population.

Again, no attempt has been made to turn the material presented herewith into war maps. Such an attempt would fall of its own weight, since armed forces move so swiftly under the new rules of warfare. It will be observed that what was yesterday merely a wide space in a camel trail is today a town of major military importance and tomorrow a devastated name among a hundred others in the history of a campaign.

The economic and population work has been geared to the limits of the topographic maps. The reason for this duplication of area is that it was decided that such treatment would quicken the student's grasp of the essential comparisons involved. For instance, it will be noted at once that, generally, population density decreases exactly as the elevation increases; and that the areas of greatest concentration of people are inevitably the areas of industrial concentration. A comparison of these maps with the charts relating to mineral resources will at once explain the population density of the western European plains.

It is felt that the scheme of relating one type of map to another, and these to a series of charts which develop the clarity of the whole, forms a somewhat different approach to the difficult problem of furnishing cartographic illustrations for a textbook of this type.

The cartographer is indebted to the editors for numerous valuable suggestions relating to the project, and for a degree of cooperation hitherto outside his experience.

R. E. Falconer

New York, N. Y.
June 1941

Maps

CHAPTER I

Outlines of a New Era

No one can escape the realization that he is living through one of the greatest crises of civilization. Certain landmarks loom out of the past to point the zigzag course of human history; the coming of the barbarians and the fall of the Roman Empire; the Dark Ages; the Renaissance of the twelfth century and the Reformation; the political revolutions of the eighteenth century and the industrial revolution of the nineteenth.

Certainly ours is a period of transition. Never since the moving finger began to write have the pages of the chronicle been so crowded as during the past two decades. This revolution can be traced directly to forces long developing which resulted in the world-wide struggle of 1914–1918. The issues were fought in that slaughterhouse of the world, Europe, a continent whose political, economic, cultural, and social importance has been such in modern times that its upheavals have had immediate repercussions elsewhere on the globe.

The Treaty of Versailles. The First World War formally ended on January 10, 1920 with the ratification of the Versailles Treaty, a document which certainly was not satisfactory to everybody, being a hodgepodge of quite contradictory concepts. The idealists were championed by President Wilson, who was convinced that the new order would ensure an enduring peace — a peace which was "to be planted upon the tested foundation of political liberty." But Wilson's idealism could hardly be reconciled with the special desires and needs of the victorious states. The interests of the Allies, as expressed in the secret agreements, conflicted with the higher goals set forth in the Fourteen Points. After all, the leading statesmen of the Paris Peace Conference, unlike the diplomats of the previous century, were responsible for their actions to peoples who, wearied by the deadly struggle, demanded a peace of vengeance.

Confronted with the idealism of the Fourteen Points on the one hand and the Bismarckian politics of Clemenceau on the other, the Conference finally evolved a peace which pleased few and displeased most. Germany was punished, but not punished enough to provide complete security for *la Patrie.* The victors got some of the spoils, but not all they wanted, and what they got was wrapped up in such fine phrases as "mandates." A peace which seemed to establish the new world order was prepared,

This chapter by Joseph S. Roucek, Associate Professor of Political Science and Sociology, Hofstra College.

but certainly this was not the kind of order which could abolish wars forever.

The Versailles Treaty was not, however, the source of all the evils of the post-war period. This point must be noted here in view of Hitler's propaganda. The constantly reiterated denunciation of Versailles has served Hitler's purposes, but it is not historically correct. The argument that if Great Britain and France had been wiser and more generous at the Peace Conference the Second World War would have been avoided is pure supposition.

The Myth of Peace. The Versailles Treaty must be considered as but one of the causes which led to the disintegration of the new European order instituted by the Peace Treaties of 1919–1923. The complexity of the events leading to the tragedy of 1939 is such that no single explanation can be found. The failure of all the efforts to promote peace needs to be studied in its highly complicated ramifications, including a sudden reversal of policy of the United States from active participation in European affairs to isolation, the efforts of the Soviet Union to undermine the capitalist order of western Europe, and Japan's emergence on a path of imperialistic expansion.

To what extent countless additional factors must bear responsibility for the failure of the peace settlements will long remain a topic of controversy. We thus hear that "bad men" led Europe and that they failed to right wrongs and remedy evils, that economic policies — new and higher tariff walls, staggering national debts, unsound international capital movements, and the manipulation of currencies — helped to defeat all peace efforts. The fact remains that these theories contain some truth, but not the whole truth. Obviously, history, in order to be worthy of its task, must show how the most important of these factors operated in conjunction with all other factors in the European drama.

Let us look at some of the leading forces which were in operation at the end of the First World War and which have led to the Second World War.

Note, first of all, that whereas the Paris Conference attracted representatives from all corners of the earth, Europe was subsequently left to face its own problems. But paradoxically enough, the peace treaties of 1919–1923 really did not bring peace. Little wars cropped up in the immediate post-war years with maddening regularity. Obviously, "the war to end war" did not accomplish its purpose. The scene of battle was merely shifted from the Franco-German front, and from the military to economic fronts.

But the masses of Europe refused to admit such realities; suffering humanity pinned its hopes on the reconstruction of the world on permanent foundations of peace. The victors as well as losers wanted to be convinced that four years of misery and suffering would be succeeded by an era of peace and prosperity. The war had been fought to " make the world safe for democracy," and mankind placed its faith in that magic phrase.

To the victors the peace meant revenge, and at least reparation for the damages and outrages perpetrated by the losers. In Germany, hope for a peace based on Wilson's Fourteen Points sustained those struggling to prevent the masses from seeking in Communism a solution of their problems. For the nations liberated and consolidated on the ruins of the Austro-Hungarian, Russian, and Turkish Empires the peace meant the liberty of shaping their national lives. Throughout the continent exploited masses, not understanding very well but appreciating the attractive slogans of democratic or Communist propaganda, were sure that *their* generation was to find salvation in the promises of the " new order," symbolized by that magic word " democracy."

The Real Consequences of the First World War. At the time of the armistice the pre-war era seemed remote and unreal. Men had endured the agony of centuries in four years. Nothing would ever be as it was in 1914. All aspects of life were transformed. One age had died on the battlefields of Europe and the Near East; a new age had dawned in which men placed their hopes of a better life but which, as this book will show, deceived them cruelly. The war revolutionized all forms of social life and altered the thinking of all social classes. Such an upheaval could not end with the formal declaration of an armistice and the signing of peace treaties. There was " peace," yet the world was in uproar. The old ideals which had led the nations into blood and fire were now discredited; within a few years patriots were to put freedom into a coffin and spike it down. The younger generation was cynical, desperate, pleasure-mad, critical and contemptuous of the " older " generation.

World Revolution in the Making. The war spirit had not died. Unemployed ex-soldiers, restless and violent youngsters for the most part, liked to wear resplendent uniforms and swagger about the streets, armed with clubs or revolvers. Led by bold men, they carried on in civil life the warfare so well learned on the Eastern and Western Fronts. They really did not know what they wanted, but in Germany and Italy two corporals were eventually to give direction to their goalless strife. One summer evening in 1919, Infantry Corporal Hitler, a lonely, unhappy, and frustrated man of thirty, who hated the republic, the Socialists and the Jews, became the seventh member of an obscure organization in a Munich beer hall, which was to become the National Socialist — or Nazi — Party. About the time that Hitler joined the Nazi Party, Benito Mussolini in Italy was forming the first detachment of Fascist Blackshirts. Europe offered, unfortunately, fertile soil for the two corporals and their imitators, for those who sought a solution of mankind's difficulties in violence, sadism, and terror.

Violence and terror increased as post-war difficulties grew. The sweet reasonableness of the pre-1914 days was gone. Everything was in turmoil. The soldiers who had fought the war could scarcely revere the moral, ethical, and religious teachings which they had imbibed as youths. Indeed, why should they? The war was over — the statesmen and politicians said. But the psychological, economic, and social damage could not be repaired. Even the fundamental necessities of life were unavailable, particularly in central Europe. In short, the First World War aggravated old problems and created new ones. The post-war years could not bring the much-advertised and prayed-for "normalcy." There was no longer any balance and harmony within or among the nations.

The False Democracies. Post-war Europe saw a resurgence of democracy, a spread of representative government and parliamentary forms. Yet, how illusory the glittering phrases of constitutionalism and parliamentarism were to prove in the early breakdown of democratic machinery in Poland, Lithuania, and Yugoslavia, later in Germany, and in the general trend toward a stronger executive in the other states, culminating in the ultimate rejection of parliamentarism throughout most of Europe.

Many of the seeds which destroy most democracies were sown in the post-war constitutions themselves. The ardent republicans often neglected the realities of politics. In many instances they seemed too intent upon attaining juridical perfection at the expense of political expediency, and provided, as a result, for some institutions which the state could not assimilate. In many cases, there was no socio-political background for the successful operation of the imported parliamentary institutions.[1] The democrats of the new states forgot that the English parliamentary system had taken centuries to establish itself, that it assumed its form by the method of trial and error. As Chapter XXV points out, nothing could have been more remote from the social climate of British parliamentarism than the conditions prevailing in the Eastern and Balkan countries where enthusiastic political theorists were permitted to copy the fundamental features of English, French, and Belgian governments. The results were, of course, disastrous, and various brands of dictatorships soon began to crop up.

The general trend of the post-war years, however, favored the lower classes. Governments introduced differential scales of taxation, old-age pensions, various kinds of social insurance, factory laws, limitation of the hours of work, and other reforms. The upper classes, and particularly the landowners, were in some countries deprived of their former privileges. In central and eastern Europe, in particular, the large estates were confiscated, with or without compensation, and divided among small peasant holders. This movement reached its climax in Soviet Russia, where class relationships were twisted beyond recognition, and where the former propertied and ruling classes were liquidated.

The general democratization of society influenced the relations of the sexes. While women were granted the full-suffrage only in Norway and Finland before 1914, during and after the war this was extended to Great Britain, Germany, Russia, all of Scandinavia, the Netherlands, Spain, and most of the new states of eastern and central Europe. The weaker sex during the war had replaced the men called to arms in many occupations; when the war ended many women retained their positions in commerce, industry, and the professions, although the later dictatorships tried to reverse this tendency by urging them to pay attention to *Kinder, Kirche, und Küchen:* that is, " raising children, attending church, and cooking."

The Upsurge of Socialism. The spread of democratic governments immediately after the First World War exerted tremendous influence on the Socialist movement, a movement which had been somewhat inactive during the great conflict and which was discredited by the willingness of the German Social Democrats to support the war. In the early post-war years nearly all the Social-Democratic parties increased their memberships; some acquired power. At the same time, the Second International had been weakened by the departure of the extreme Left Wing parties as a result of the Russian revolution. The Third International was formed in Moscow, which became the headquarters of the international revolutionary movement.

The course of events was to show, however, that ideologies and political systems cannot be transplanted successfully, and that varied economic, political, and social conditions, national characteristics and mentalities, and contrasting historical traditions, nearly always determine the direction of political evolution. The downfall of the Bolshevik republics in Hungary and Bavaria, and the fate of the Communist movement in Bulgaria, Italy, and elsewhere, offered proof of this truism.

The failure of the extreme Leftist movements did not alter the fact that there were, in the immediate post-war years, general improvements in the living conditions of the laboring classes. The passing of old-age and health insurance laws, the enactment of an eight-hour working day in a majority of states, the creation of the International Labor Office, were far-reaching accomplishments. But the desire of the masses to participate in the government had its darker aspects, especially where the inauguration of the democratic institutions was not based on high educational levels, political and moral traditions, and lofty economic standards. There appeared numerous instances within the democratic states where both capital and labor placed narrowly conceived class interests above those of the national welfare. Many labor leaders and intellectuals lost all confidence in capitalistic democracy and turned to the U.S.S.R. as an example of a new heaven on earth. Certainly, the Third International made a powerful appeal to many liberals and radicals. But the menace of Communism, fancied or real, led the conservative and middle classes to support Fascist revolutions in Italy, and later in Germany and Spain, and produced an internal cleavage in Britain, France, and elsewhere.

The New Role of Government. The new states, as well as the old ones, faced enormous problems in 1918. During the war, states had undertaken tasks which left no aspect of civilian life untouched. In many countries these tasks continued to be performed by the states after the war, and to them more were added. Incapacitated soldiers had to be cared for. Cities and devasted areas needed to be rebuilt. Production figures for steel skyrocketed and the problem of urbanization became one of the most glaring and difficult to solve. Private loans, largely from America, helped to stabilize currencies in a large part of Europe and undoubtedly prevented immediate social upheavals in many countries.

While the Western democracies and the United States had the resources to pay for the new responsibilities of government without destroying private property and limiting private initiative, elsewhere the established state forms, unable to provide the citizens with either freedom or security, began to succumb to Fascism. Thus *laissez faire* had vanished in many countries long before the great depression. With it collapsed the vitally important concept of the "Economic Man." The proof that the economic freedom of the individual does not automatically lead to social equality was to shake the capitalist world to its foundations. Orthodox economists may argue that the Russian, German, and Italian economic systems defy "economic law," but the European masses, no longer willing to accept institutions simply because they serve economic ends, appeared quite willing to endure the restrictions of the new totalitarian systems for the sake of their material benefits.[2] In Italy, Germany, and Russia, increasing wealth was eventually to be superseded by increasing impoverishment. But in all these countries "unemployment" has been banished, and the masses have attained some measure of security. Non-economic satisfactions have taken the place of economic ones.

Internationalism versus Egoistic Nationalism. The hysterical revulsion against the horror of war, the hope that Europe could now sit back and enjoy peace and brotherhood, gave birth in the 'twenties and 'thirties to pacifistic movements which appealed vigorously to conscience, humanitarianism, courage, and the highest interests of humanity. These movements had many forms. Thus the Youth movement in many countries consecrated itself to the philosophy of peace, international culture, and a profound concern for the preservation of individual and social values. The League of Nations, the International Labor Office, and the World

Court arose out of similar desires. The League was born of the hope that peace could be maintained by international cooperation. Wilson based his faith on the hope that international democracy would be assured by " public opinion," that watchword of parliamentary reformers. Hence the newly created League of Nations would have for its backbone the rule of international law, which in the last analysis would be the rule of world opinion.

The pacifists believed that peace could be safeguarded by signing covenants, treaties, and international agreements. Thus the members of the League of Nations were covenanted to settle their disputes peacefully. To reassure themselves, the leading European states signed the Locarno Treaties as the final guarantee of enduring peace and, to make the reassurance " quite sure," outlawed war " forever " by the Kellogg-Briand Pact of 1928. The futility of these efforts will become apparent in the following chapters.

Revival of Economic Nationalism. Post-war trends in international trade and monetary policy created obstacles for the pacifists and idealists. With the steady export of gold from Europe to the United States, the European states found it exceedingly difficult to achieve financial stability. Germany's experience with inflation brought the same dismal results in Austria and Poland. Various inflationary and deflationary measures were tried, as we shall see, by other countries, with the result that fundamental recovery was even more retarded everywhere. Concurrently, the states were finding it more and more impossible to carry successfully the load of international indebtedness. Needing to import heavily from the United States, governments were forced to build up favorable trade balances by the reduction of imports. But since not only the United States, but all European states, were raising their tariffs seeking to protect their warborn industries as well as their new national independence, a kind of mercantile anarchy began to creep over Europe, characterized by the efforts of all nations to import only the most necessary raw materials and commodities.

These fundamental facts of the new mercantilism were not, however, to show their terrifying reality until the world plunged into the depression of the 'thirties. The reckoning had been postponed, on the surface, from 1925 to 1929. But since 1918 a whole arsenal of devices of economic nationalism, fostering domestic prosperity at the expense of the foreign producer, was thrown into action. The prosperity of the boom years was proven artificial, precarious, and unevenly distributed.

A strange paradox confronted Europe during this period. Although millions of able workers had been killed and hundreds of thousands incapacitated, the dragon of unemployment soon began to raise its head, in spite of the tremendous reconstruction activities. Here, not only the invention of labor-saving machinery and the general economic trends just noted, but the closing of frontiers played its part. In the nineteenth century the pressure of European population was relieved by migration to less populated continents. Labor was plentiful, and so was capital; the expansion of markets assured the profitable operation of a vast industrial machine. But after 1870 a mad scramble began for colonies and overseas markets. Migration to the United States, which had assumed vast proportions in the previous half century, virtually ceased after the passage of the Immigration Act of 1929. These were the symptoms of the shrinking economic frontier.

After the First World War, economic opportunities declined further. Production increased, but at the expense of labor. Machines displaced human beings. The conversion of the world from a relatively free trade basis to nationalistic mercantilism promoted world tensions. The resulting economic difficulties only intensified the mechanization and rationalization of industry, a process which helped to precipitate, toward the end of the 'twenties, probably the most serious economic crisis which the world ever faced. Millions were doomed to inactivity and dependence on private and especially state relief. The state budgets, already overburdened with the costs of the late war and its consequences, now had to include enormous items for the support of the unemployed.

The Curse of Minorities. National, racial, and religious minorities also helped to undermine central European states. The peacemakers of 1919 believed that they had solved one of Europe's most persistent problems by international protection of minorities.

In 1919, the liberated nationalities, while talking about the right of self-determination, gave every indication that the minorities in their newly formed states would not be granted equal rights. The difficulties were enhanced by the obvious impossibility either of granting the right of self-determination to every nationality, or of drawing frontiers which would dispose of all minorities. As a matter of fact, experiments in self-determination by the Peace Conference revealed some of the serious limitations of this principle.[3] How, indeed, can we hope for the establishment of stable international order if, at any moment, minorities may destroy the territorial unity of states by invoking an unlimited right of succession? It is plain that limitation must be imposed on the right of a minority to self-determination. Sometimes a people may be too small to stand alone; sometimes, as in parts of the Balkans, the mixture of people may defy separation.

The utter impossibility of solving this problem left central and eastern Europe strewn with minorities dwelling on the wrong side of frontiers, with the result that self-determination, somewhat dormant during the first post-war decade, was to become an explosive doctrine, which blew, as it were, the map of Europe to pieces. In short, the system of the international protection of minorities failed because of the unwillingness of the aggressive European states to be bound by legalistic contracts, and because the democratic spirit retreated under the attacks of intolerant authoritarian movements.

Progress through War. The outstanding political characteristic of the present age has been the tendency to expand the power of the state. Even the democracies which have survived have had to grant more power to the state.

The tragedy of recent European history has been that, by rendering all human values subservient to the political, social institutions tended to become subordinated to politics. The main function of politics is to equalize and adjust social conflicts. But as all creative forms of human life were in flux, governments could not function smoothly. The resulting social uncertainties produced regimes which were anything but peaceful — additional symptoms of the critical age.

The chief contribution of Mussolini and Hitler was the autocratic state which depends upon force for its existence. In modern dictatorships the dominating mentality is the war mentality. The state is permanently mobilized, life is on a war footing, the party system is discarded and the historic liberties of the individual are destroyed. The national interest as interpreted by the Leader is the sole criterion at all times. Sacrifice is the badge of patriotism, as in wartime among free peoples.

It is not accidental that the dictators use a militarist vocabulary to describe actions which in free countries are regarded as peaceful. Democracies stimulate wheat growing by bounties and tariffs, but dictators fight the Battle of Wheat. Democracies build tractor factories, but dictatorships hurl their Shock Brigades into trenches on the Tractor Front. The autocratic state is always on the lookout for the enemy within and outside its gates.

Post-war autocracy, therefore, created military states which, superficially at least, had singleness of purpose, and remarkable efficiency and discipline accompanied by censorship, despotism, and impoverishment culminating finally in war.

The Achilles heel of the totalitarian state is war. It can " banish " unemployment but cannot rid itself of internal strife and the ever-present specter of war. Not that the dictatorships can profit from successful war, but they cannot continue to exist unless they find new scapegoats to attack and new " grievances " to satisfy, both at home and abroad. The tragedy of the European democracies was that they failed to understand that the dictatorial states could not be appeased since the satisfaction of any " grievance " only led to new demands. With Mussolini, Hitler, and Stalin in the saddle, Europe was in a state of armed truce.

The Phenomenon of Propaganda. Knowledge of the " irrationality " of the masses has been extensively and diabolically utilized by the totalitarian governments. The need for general public approval, in order to carry on modern warfare, made the widespread use of propaganda in the First World War inevitable, although the word " propaganda " was then hardly known to students of politics. Today no word is of more frequent occurrence whenever public affairs are discussed. This modern phenomenon was called into being by the democratization of society, by the same economic and social conditions which have made mass opinion supremely important in politics, and by trained publicity men who learned their art while advertising consumer goods. The radio, film, and popular press are the supreme instruments of propaganda.

In the nineteenth century, the philosophers of *laissez faire* believed that public opinion, like trade, ought to be free from all controls. The war taught the belligerents that psychological weapons must accompany military weapons, and propaganda, spreading Wilson's slogans, played a considerable part in the Allied victory. Thereafter the Soviet government utilized propaganda as a regular instrument of international politics; in fact, Soviet Russia was the first modern state to establish, in the form of the Communist International, a large-scale international propaganda organization.[4] Meanwhile men like Wilson and Lord Cecil stressed the utilization of the " organized opinion of mankind " for the support of the League of Nations, whereby the governments would be forced to make their decisions according to the enlightened international opinion. Unfortunately, overenthusiastic appeals to slogans like " peace " and " disarmament " meant little since each had different and often contradictory meanings to different states. The result was that " throughout the 1920's this fallacy of an effective international public opinion was being gradually exposed." [5] The fallacious belief that international propaganda could be divorced from power politics became especially evident in the 'thirties, when Fascism utilized propaganda on an unprecedented scale, on Hitler's famous assumption that " By clever persistent propaganda, even heaven can be represented to a people as hell, and the most wretched life as paradise."

It is true that, in theory, democracies are supposed to follow mass opinion, while the totalitarian states enforce conformity to the notions of the leaders. But in practice, the distinctions are less clear-cut: totalitarian rulers profess to represent the will of the masses, while democracies frequently shape their policies to conform to the demands of an influential group. Even in peace, propaganda has become a regular instrument of the foreign policy of aggressive states, and the radio, in particular, the most popular and convenient instrument for conducting propaganda in foreign countries.

The Crumbling of European Civilization. Europe before 1914 had a sort of common spiritual foundation. The leading countries regarded the teachings of the Christian Church as basic, took capitalism for granted, set a high value on free speech, a free press and scientific inquiry, promoted international trade and exalted the democratic process. Most enlightened peoples believed in liberalism, democracy, parliamentarism, and humanitarianism. If some nations had not reached that stage, it was believed that they would attain it quickly and surely. Only isolated individuals dared to question these commonly accepted principles.

Some nineteenth-century thinkers deduced from the rapid political and inductrial progress of their day that evolution always implied progress. But in the post-war years there arose such pessimists as Oswald Spengler, whose *Decline of the West* became a best seller. The " West " shows many symptoms of " decline "; new " élites " are emerging. It took a man of great faith, indeed, to face the years between the outbreak of the First and Second World Wars with unshaken confidence in rationalism and progress. Today Europe has no common front. There is no single belief which has not been proclaimed as heretical. All the pillars of the world's culture are weakened. The only common feeling left is fear of the future, since there is little hope that Europe will recapture its former leadership of the world.

In 1914, civil and religious liberty, at least in western Europe, seemed to be safe from attack. In no civilized country at that time would a man have been persecuted for his beliefs. Persons and goods moved freely across national boundaries and currencies maintained a more or less stable purchasing power. Twenty-five years later, civil and religious liberty was denied to millions of people, and countries still faithful to liberal institutions were wondering whether these very institutions would not lead them to disaster.

In much of Europe today, as well as in other parts of the world, democracy is considered the government of weaklings — a sort of prelude to national suicide. Instead of government by discussion there is government by coercion; to dissent from the tyrant's opinion is to jeopardize one's life. Revolvers and machine guns are the instruments of government, not debate and argumentation.

Today many European thinkers are laughing at humanitarianism. Concurrently, they are attacking Christianity, one of the pillars of Western civilization. In the nineteenth century, agnostics believed that if Christianity were overthrown the golden age would follow. Now, Christianity is in eclipse in the Nazi countries and a new paganism has appeared with the Swastika as its symbol. But the golden age has not arrived.

The Tempo of Change. The outstanding characteristic of the story of the two post-war decades, told in the following pages, is the fact that changes have occurred with heartbreaking speed. That in itself indicates that European civilization is in transition. We must remember that all transitions from one social system to another have been accompanied by periods of unrest, by anarchistic decades. The old order is being destroyed; the forms of the new cannot be discerned as yet. We know only that in the last quarter-century the world was not " made safe for democracy."

The transition of all forms of European civilization is the *Leitmotif* of this book. Europe is breaking up under our very eyes, as the Roman Empire did in the fourth and fifth centuries A.D. Ideologies and nations are at war. Individualism grapples with collectivism; democracy is in mortal combat with Fascism and Nazism; Christianity fights for its life against the new paganism.

This conflict is becoming more dangerous every day. Whether Germany wins the war or not, we need not despair, if we are willing to take a long-range view. When the barbarians overran the Roman Empire, or when Parisian mobs stormed the Bastille, the world seemed to have reached an end. But actually it was just a beginning. Today the pillars of Western civilization are being shattered, but new pillars will arise. The Dark Ages have returned to Europe, but they must give way, some day, to ages of light.

The ferment of Europe should be closely studied by Americans. In spite of all legislative and other pronouncements, the United States did not live in isolation in the spring of 1941. The airplanes arriving constantly from Europe, the news printed or broadcast, and the never-ending output of books devoted to European affairs testified to that. Our democracy has survived only because it is based on enlightened discussion and free speech. The fate of Europe holds lessons in responsible citizenship for us. This point cannot be overemphasized.

The present chapter has attempted to sketch the broad outlines of the history of Europe since 1918, to give the reader some points of orientation. The remaining chapters of the book, presented by scholars who have collected and digested an enormous amount of widely scattered material, will fill in the details.

REFERENCES

1 J. S. Roucek, *The Politics of the Balkans*, New York: McGraw-Hill, 1939, p. 11.

2 See P. F. Drucker, *The End of Economic Man*, New York: John Day, 1939, for an excellent analysis of this thesis.

3 J. S. Roucek, "Minorities — A Basis of the Refugee Problem," *The Annals*, May, 1939, CCIII: 1–17.

4 See E. H. Carr, *Propaganda in International Politics*, Pamphlet on World Affairs, No. 16, New York: Farrar and Rinehart, 1939.

5 *Ibid.*, p. 16.

SELECTED BIBLIOGRAPHY

Barnes, H. E., *The History of Western Civilization*, New York: Harcourt, Brace, 1935, Vol. II.

Beneš, Edward, *Democracy: Today and Tomorrow*, New York: Macmillan, 1939.

Benns, F. L., *European History since 1870*, New York: Crofts, 1940.

Ford, G. S., ed., *Dictatorship in the Modern World*, Minneapolis: Univ. of Minnesota Press, 1939.

Gunther, John, *Inside Europe*, New York: Harper, 1940.

Jackson, J. H., *A Short History of the World since 1918*, Boston: Little, Brown, 1939.

Langsam, W. C., *The World since 1914*, New York: Macmillan, fourth edition, 1940.

——, ed., with the assistance of Eagan, J. M., *Documents and Readings in the History of Europe since 1914*, New York: Lippincott, 1939.

Orton, W. A., *Twenty Years' Armistice: 1918–1938*, New York: Farrar and Rinehart, 1938.

Robb, D. M. and Garrison, J. J., *Art in the Western World*, New York: Harper, 1935.

Schuman, F. L., *Europe on the Eve*, New York: Knopf, 1939.

Sharp, W. R. and Kirk, Grayson, *Contemporary International Politics*. New York: Farrar and Rinehart, 1940.

Shean, Vincent, *Not Peace but a Sword*, Garden City, N. Y.: Doubleday, Doran, 1939.

Slocombe, G. E., *A Mirror to Geneva: Its Growth, Grandeur and Decay*, New York: Holt, 1938.

Snell, Lord, Steed, Wickham, Temperley, A. C., Tabouis, Genevieve, Crossman, R. H. S., and Morrison, Herbert, *New Tyrannies for Old*, New York: Macmillan, 1939.

Steiner, H. A., *Principles and Problems of International Relations*, New York: Harper, 1940.

Speier, Hans and Kahler, Alfred, eds., *War in Our Times*, New York: Norton, 1939.

Waller, Willard, ed., *War in the Twentieth Century*, New York: Dryden Press, 1940.

CHAPTER II

The Post-War Settlements: 1919–1923

The Eve of Versailles

Armistice. At five o'clock on the morning of November 11, 1918, in Marshal Foch's private railway car in Compiègne Forest, representatives of the German High Command signed an armistice presented to them by the Allies, thus terminating fifty-two months of hostilities that had involved all the principal powers of the world. Negotiations had been under way since October 4, when the German Chancellor, Prince Max of Baden, at the urgent request of Generals Ludendorff and Hindenburg, and with the consent of the Kaiser, had communicated to President Wilson the desire of the German government for an armistice. Several notes had been exchanged between Wilson and the Central Powers. Germany had expressed hope that the arrangements would be in accordance with the Fourteen Points which Wilson, in addresses to Congress on January 8 and September 27, 1918, had set forth as the conditions of a fair and lasting peace.

Wilson's Fourteen Points. Briefly stated, the Fourteen Points were: (I) Open covenants of peace, openly arrived at; (II) Absolute freedom of navigation upon the seas, outside territorial waters, alike in peace and in war; (III) Removal, so far as possible, of all economic barriers and the establishment of an equality of trade conditions among all the nations consenting to the peace; (IV) Adequate guarantees given and taken that national armaments will be reduced to the lowest point consistent with domestic safety; (V) A free, open-minded, and absolutely impartial adjustment of all colonial claims, based upon a strict observance of the principle that in determining all such questions of sovereignty the interests of the populations concerned must have equal weight with the equitable claims of the government whose title is to be determined; (VI) Such a settlement of all questions concerning Russia as will secure the best and freest cooperation of the other nations . . . in obtaining for her an unhampered and unembarrassed opportunity for the independent determination of her own political development and national policy and assure her of a sincere welcome into the society of free nations under institutions of her own choosing; (VII) Belgium . . . must be evacuated and restored; (VIII) All French territory should be freed and the invaded portions restored, and the wrong done to France by Prussia of 1871 in the matter of

This chapter by S. Harrison Thomson, Professor of History, University of Colorado.

Alsace-Lorraine . . . righted; (IX) A readjustment of the frontiers of Italy should be effected along clearly recognizable lines of nationality; (X) The peoples of Austria-Hungary . . . should be accorded the freest opportunity of autonomous development; (XI) Rumania, Serbia, and Montenegro should be evacuated; occupied territories restored; Serbia accorded free and secure access to the sea; and the relations of the several Balkan states to one another determined by friendly counsel along historically established lines of allegiance and nationality; (XII) The Turkish portions of the present Ottoman Empire should be assured a secure sovereignty, but the other nationalities which are now under Turkish rule should be assured an undoubted security of life and an absolutely unmolested opportunity of autonomous development; (XIII) An independent Polish state should be erected which should include the territories inhabited by indisputably Polish populations, which should be assured a free and secure access to the sea; (XIV) A general association of nations must be formed under specific covenants for the purpose of affording mutual guarantees of political independence and territorial integrity to great and small states alike.

Military Terms of the Armistice. The Allied governments agreed to an armistice on this general basis, and the military terms were drawn up by Marshal Foch. These called for withdrawal of German troops to the east bank of the Rhine, the surrender of large quantities of matériel, all of Germany's submarines and most of her surface naval craft. Allied prisoners were to be set free, whereas German prisoners would be released only at the Allies' discretion. The Allied blockade was to be maintained, but necessary food and provisions would be allowed to pass through. In effect, Germany agreed to a virtual surrender *in toto*.

These were harsh terms, but by November 11 Germany had no alternative. Turkey had signed an armistice on October 31, Austria-Hungary had followed suit on November 3. On that same day mutinies had broken out in the German navy at Kiel. On November 9, Kaiser Wilhelm had abdicated and fled to Holland, leaving his country on the verge of revolution. There is some legal ground for contending that Germany sued for peace under certain conditions, but, on the other hand, there was no doubt at all in the minds of the German General Staff that Germany was completely defeated and would have been obliged to surrender unconditionally if the Allies had so demanded.[1]

War Aims. The most devastating war thus far known to human history was over. But peace would have to be rebuilt. It could not, at a single gesture, spring majestically from the war-torn fields of France and Belgium or from the unmarked graves of the sea. Almost ten million soldiers and sailors had lost their lives in the long months since August, 1914. For what?

During the war the real aims of the belligerents had been so vaguely expressed that an uninitiated observer would have thought that every participant in the struggle was fighting for truth, justice, honor, human liberty, and true religion. It is perhaps wise to pass swiftly over these lofty protestations, and consider instead the way the peace was built. Whatever the aims of the Central Powers may have been, they were not achieved. The Allied and Associated Powers, because they were victorious, may be presumed to have come closer to attaining their ends.

Wilson's Fourteen Points and the Allies. The armistice had been based upon acceptance by all concerned of Wilson's Fourteen Points and subsequent clarifications. Much negotiation would be necessary before they could be translated from the realm of theory to that of fact. Great Britain had made a specific reservation concerning the second point, the freedom of the seas, and France insisted that " reparations for damages to civilians " should be exacted from Germany. It was indeed no secret that the French government regarded the Wilsonian plan as rather unrealistic, and greatly in need of the concrete interpretation which France, because of her great suffering in the war and her experience of two German invasions within fifty years, could give best.[2] But in spite of these deviations, the broad principles of the prospective peace may be considered as formally agreed upon. The determination of their ultimate, specific applications was another and more difficult matter. That was to be the task of the Peace Conference of 1919.

A Changed Europe. The Conference had to deal with a Europe radically different from the Europe of August, 1914. When the war began, the balance of power was maintained by two great alliances: the Triple Entente of Great Britain, France and Russia, and the Triple Alliance of Germany, Austria-Hungary and Italy. Associated with the latter group were its Balkan satellites, Bulgaria and the Ottoman Empire. When the war was over, three great absolute monarchies had disappeared: Russia was in the throes of a revolution which had begun in the spring of 1917; Austria-Hungary had disintegrated into its component nations; and the Hohenzollerns had fled from a Germany which faced social revolution and economic collapse. Italy, having found the aims of Germany and Austria-Hungary contrary to the conditions of her alliance with them, had entered the war in 1915 on the side of France and Great Britain. The United States had joined the Allies in 1917, and now the United States, by reason of its decisive part in the victory, would have for the first time in history a prominent voice in shaping the internal affairs of Europe. The events of the last four years had left men very much confused. On the eve of the Peace Conference, the future, to those who honestly sought its meaning, looked even more confused.

Preparations for the Conference. The victorious nations did not come to the conference table unprepared. Early in the war France had set up

several commissions to study the inevitable problems which the end of the conflict would bring. One of these commissions, the "Comité d'Etudes," under the direction of the eminent historian, Professor Lavisse, organized relevant historical, territorial, and ethnographic information. A second group under Senator Morel paid particular attention to the economic factors of European life. The third, under André Tardieu, was created in December, 1918, to assimilate the findings of the two previous committees as a basis for concrete French proposals to the Conference.[3] Great Britain, perhaps in a less formal fashion, had been doing the same thing, and the British experts at the Conference were as well informed as the French. Shortly after our entry into the war, President Wilson had instructed Colonel House to organize a commission of historians, economists, statisticians, geographers, and experts in international law and politics, to collect data of all kinds and put it into usable shape. Of all the Allied groups, the American experts were perhaps the most objective in their approach to the delicate problems before the Conference. Indeed, never before in history did a peace conference have at its disposal so much information, so many qualified experts, and such copious means of adjusting international affairs. How conscientiously these aids were used may well be another question.

Paris as a Meeting Place. The choice of Paris as a site for the Conference was made only after some debate. The Belgians hoped that Brussels would be selected. London, Geneva, Rome, and Berlin were suggested and discarded for one reason or another. The French felt that justice would be served if the peace treaty marking the defeat of the German Empire were to be signed in the same room — the Hall of Mirrors of the palace at Versailles — in which William I had been crowned Emperor of Germany in 1871. This, coupled with the central location of Paris, finally determined its choice.

From some points of view, at least in retrospect, it would appear to have been an unfortunate selection. All the delegates were sensible of the great psychological pressure brought to bear on them in Paris. The French press, subject to governmental influence, did not hesitate to criticize directly any attitude or action which would have softened the terms of peace delivered to a prostrate foe. The sufferings of France were repeatedly brought to the attention of the plenipotentiaries. The delegates would have been superhuman indeed had they been able under these circumstances to maintain any appreciable measure of detachment.[4]

The Plenipotentiaries

Early Trends of the Conference. Delegates and experts from the participating victorious countries trickled into Paris from November, 1918 to

February, 1919, supplementing representatives already on hand. The first plenary session of the Conference was held on January 18. It was opened by the President of the French Republic, Raymond Poincaré, and presided over by Georges Clemenceau, Premier of France. Twenty-seven large and small countries, the Allies and their associates, were represented. There was no suggestion that the four defeated powers be invited to send delegates to discuss provisions of the peace treaty they would be called upon to sign.

Moreover, it was evident from this first meeting that the lesser powers would have little real voice in the determination of either the broad principles or significant details of the settlement. Clemenceau's brusque and imperious manner left no doubt in anybody's mind that the real decisions would be made by the great powers, and that the lesser nations would be allowed merely the privilege of assent. The latter, pointing to Wilson's lofty pronouncements concerning the inviolable sovereignty of free and independent states, were bitterly resentful of the arbitrary disregard of their future interests as well as of their recent sacrifices in a common cause during the long war. Wilson's prestige, at its height about the middle of January, 1919, declined in the remaining months of the Conference. His initial mistake of not insisting that the small nations participate in decisions affecting their sovereignty, territory, and claims to just reparations, was a tangible cause of his loss of influence. Confidence in the American President's ideals was shaken, never again to be recovered. This failure of Wilson's moral influence was one of the tragedies of the Conference — the scene of a number of tragedies.[5]

The Big Ten. Before the Peace Conference opened, there had already been held on January 12, 1919 the first meeting of a group afterward known as the Big Ten. It included the two leading delegates from each of the five principal powers: for France, Clemenceau and Paul Pichon, Minister of Foreign Affairs; for Great Britain, Prime Minister David Lloyd George and A. F. Balfour, Foreign Secretary; for the United States, President Wilson and Robert Lansing, Secretary of State; for Italy, Premier Orlando and Baron Sonnino, Foreign Minister; and for Japan, Ambassadors Makino and Matsui.

Division of the Council. This Council of Ten held almost eighty meetings between January 12 and July 12. On March 24 it was divided into two councils, the Big Four (or Supreme Council) consisting of Wilson, Clemenceau, Lloyd George, and Orlando, and the Little Five consisting of the five foreign ministers, Pichon, Balfour, Lansing, Sonnino, and one of the Japanese diplomats. The Little Five occupied themselves with matters of detail or review delegated to them by the Council of Four. The Japanese were not interested in most of the European settlements and preferred to remain silent members of the Councils.[6]

The Races
of
EUROPE
Boundaries Given As
post-Versailles:

Portuguese

Italian

OSLO

Portuguese

Italian

HELSINKI

STOCKHOLM

TALLINN

RIGA

MOSCOW

KAUNAS

COPENHAGEN

BERLIN

WARSAW

PRAGUE

VIENNA

BUDAPEST

BUCHAREST

BELGRADE

SOFIA

ME

TIRANA

ANKARA

ATHENS

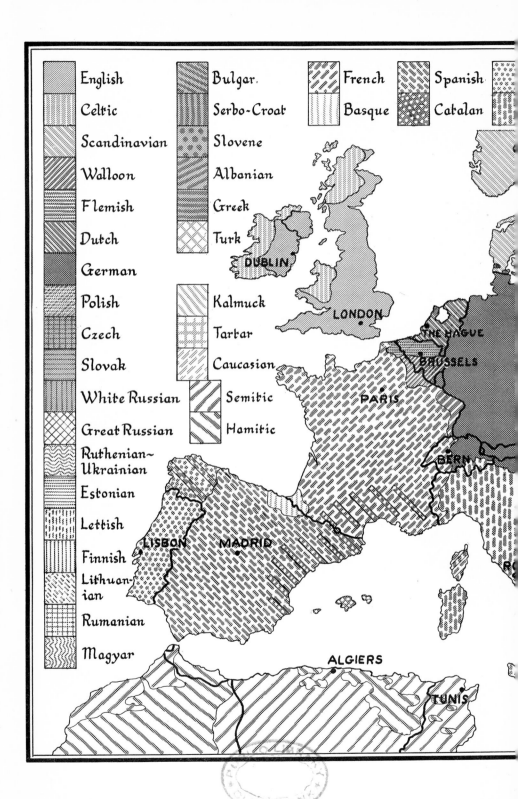

English
Celtic
Scandinavian
Walloon
Flemish
Dutch
German
Polish
Czech
Slovak
White Russian
Great Russian
Ruthenian~
Ukrainian
Estonian
Lettish
Finnish
Lithuan-
ian
Rumanian
Magyar

Bulgar.
Serbo-Croat
Slovene
Albanian
Greek
Turk

Kalmuck
Tartar
Caucasian
Semitic
Hamitic

French
Basque

Spanish
Catalan

DUBLIN
LONDON
THE HAGUE
BRUSSELS
PARIS
BERN
LISBON
MADRID
ALGIERS
TUNIS

The Big Four: Clemenceau. The peace was to be largely the work of Clemenceau, Lloyd George, and Wilson. Clemenceau was at this time in his late seventies. He had lived through the Franco-Prussian War of 1870–1871, and most of his subsequent journalistic and political career was directed toward wiping out the stigma of that defeat. Clemenceau had earned the nickname of " Tiger " by his reputation as a fierce parliamentary debater. His firmness, resourcefulness, and single-minded devotion to France had guided her to victory in 1918. Many delegates at the Conference thought him cruelly sarcastic, despotic, and brutal to representatives of the smaller powers. Nevertheless, he was the most tenacious, clever, and successful negotiator of the Big Four. He was suave, patient, and seemingly solicitous of others' opinions. Only occasionally would his brusqueness or his patriotic fervor get the better of him. In the smaller councils the conversations were in both French and English. Since Orlando did not know English, and Lloyd George and Wilson had but an elementary knowledge of French, Clemenceau, knowing both languages well, held a distinct advantage in the give and take of informal discussion. Even the presence of the official interpreter did not lessen Clemenceau's control of the Council. The peace as finally written, save for the Covenant of the League of Nations, was largely Clemenceau's peace. His technique was simple: to make consistently high demands, patiently wear down the opposition by an eloquent appeal to the devastation wrought by German arms in France, and finally make minor concessions which his colleagues Wilson and Lloyd George would be glad to accept.[7]

President Wilson. Woodrow Wilson was, as he said of himself, a man " with a one-track mind." His all-absorbing aim was to guide the delegates in fashioning a League of Nations, a mechanism by which " a single overwhelming powerful group of nations . . . shall be the trustees of the peace of the world." [8] In Rome on January 3, 1919 Wilson told the Italian people: " Our task at Paris is to organize the friendship of the world, to see to it that all the moral forces that make for right and justice and liberty are united and are given a vital organization to which the peoples of the world will readily respond. . . . I am happy to say that in my dealings with the distinguished gentlemen who lead your nation and those who lead France and England I feel that atmosphere gathering, that desire to do justice, that desire to establish friendliness, that desire to make peace rest upon right." [9] Few delegates at the Conference, incidentally, would have admitted finding among the leaders at Paris the altruism of which he spoke so confidently. Of Wilson's sincere idealism there can be no question. But his judgment of his fellows and their motives was sometimes fallible. His colleagues were impressed by his lofty moral tone and his idealism, but they found him uninformed about many phases of European history and politics. Wilson had come to Paris directly against the advice of many Americans who were fully versed in international affairs, and during the Conference he paid less attention, seemingly, to his experts than Lloyd George and Clemenceau did to theirs. Indeed, many of the defects of the final settlements can be traced to Wilson's combination of idealism, ineptitude in negotiation and ignorance.

David Lloyd George. The British Prime Minister, David Lloyd George, was a dynamic parliamentarian, agile of mind, buoyant in temperament, but fundamentally lacking in either the vindictive doggedness of Clemenceau or the altruism of Wilson. Lloyd George's parliamentary training, however, had not given him the gift of consistency, nor allowed him time to acquire a wide knowledge of continental politics. Had he not been wise enough to rely on Balfour's guidance and the assistance of the British experts, he would have appeared in a worse light than he did. As it was, both London and Paris accused him of vacillation and opportunism. Lloyd George would have preferred a treaty infinitely less punitive than was turned out under Clemenceau's dictation. As the representative of a great commercial empire, his primary concern was to allow Germany to recover sufficiently to buy, sell, and produce goods. For when world commerce came to life again Britain would be sure to profit. Lloyd George would have helped Wilson win many a decision that was lost to Clemenceau, if Wilson had had the vision and fortitude to hold out for his own more reasonable proposals. But Wilson was deftly overridden by Clemenceau, and Lloyd George was not a man to stand alone.[10]

Signor Orlando. Vittorio Emmanuele Orlando had a judicial, exact, logical, tempered mind. But he participated in the discussions less than the others, partly because he spoke no English. Besides, Italy's interests were limited, since she had no claims on Germany at all. In political outlook and method the Italian Premier was no opportunist, and could not be called a politician in the sense of Clemenceau and Lloyd George who were trained and adept parliamentarians. His mission at the Conference was to gain for Italy what Great Britain and France had promised her in the secret Treaty of London of April, 1915: the Dalmatian coast and the Brenner frontier. Orlando made the tactical error of assuming that Wilson would support the addition of Fiume (which was 90 per cent Italian) on the basis of nationality. Instead, Wilson was alienated because Italy sought to combine this claim with those based on the secret pact. After Wilson went over the heads of Orlando and Sonnino and appealed to the Italian people to moderate their demands, the two Italian delegates left the Conference in protest, on April 24, but returned on May 6 when their anger had cooled. Orlando was the least influential member of the Big Four, partly because of his temperament and his inability to speak English, but mainly because Italy had had but a minor share in winning the victory.

Lesser Lights. Many other striking and influential personalities attended the Conference. The Greek Premier, Venizelos, a lifelong rebel against Turkish misrule of Greek minorities, belied his lurid past by his sweet persuasiveness, gentle smile, and pleasant demeanor. His black skull cap, white mustache, and pointed beard gave him an air of venerable benevolence which turned out to be very effective in gaining territory for Greece. Edward Beneš, the young Foreign Minister of the new State of Czechoslovakia, earnest, well-informed, a genius at negotiation, presented the case for his country on the wide basis of the natural tendency of general European polity. Generals Botha and Smuts of South Africa were men of sterling integrity and detached judgment. Both believed that the final treaty was too severe to establish a permanent peace. Robert Lansing, the American Secretary of State, disagreed with Wilson on many points, both in principle and in detail. As a result, little use was made by Wilson of Lansing's fine judicial mind, unfortunately, perhaps, for everyone concerned.

The Conference at Work

Preliminary Organization. General preliminary organization of the Conference was arranged by the French. Clemenceau early in January asked Tardieu to draw up a plan of procedure which divided the work for the delegates under five general headings: (1) Guiding principles; (2) Territorial problems; (3) Financial problems; (4) Economic problems; (5) Promotion of the League of Nations. The French proposals, however, were considered too formal, so the delegates decided to proceed by committees and commissions consisting of representative diplomats and experts chosen from the five large powers. These groups were to hold hearings, confer together, and make recommendations to the Councils when asked.[11] It soon became evident, however, that the great powers were determined to keep absolute control of these committees and commissions.

Work of the Committees. The lesser diplomats and technical experts did an enormous amount of work. Their 58 committees held a total of 1646 meetings. Any accredited representative of a political or ethnic group embraced by the Conference could have a hearing, and most of them did. The committees were almost swamped by reports, briefs, notes, statistics, maps, and speeches. Some delegates spoke good French, some did not. The meetings were a physical and mental ordeal of no mean proportions, and it was small wonder that some tempers were frayed. Yet the general atmosphere was one of honest industriousness.[12]

Difficulties of the Conference. In spite of the great effort to create an efficient organization, there was a noticeable lack of coordination. Much of the conscientious work of the numerous committees proved unnecessary and was eventually disregarded. There are many recorded instances where the Big Ten or the Big Four asked for a detailed report from a committee of experts and then pigeonholed it. The minor European states, such as Belgium, Serbia, Greece, and Rumania, who during the war had suffered comparatively as much as France and perhaps more than England, bitterly resented the disproportionate role they were assigned in writing the peace treaties. They could be heard, but they could not make their influence felt on the real arbiters of peace, the great powers. To an early protest from a representative of one of these lesser countries, Clemenceau replied that the big nations, who had put twelve million soldiers into the field, were going to make the peace. Indignation against such arrogance ran high, but the smaller nations could do little about it. The fact that the final terms gave them much territory and new rights could hardly offset the hurt to their pride.[13]

On February 14, Wilson returned to America to report on the progress of the Conference and to approve or veto bills which awaited his signature. While he was gone, an attempt was made (February 19) to assassinate Clemenceau, but the old statesman soon was back at his desk.

The Communist regime of Béla Kun in Hungary, disorders on the eastern Polish frontier, the Spartacist uprisings in Germany, the clamor of the Italian press for Fiume and of the French press for the left bank of the Rhine, radical differences of opinion among the Big Four — these and many other problems kept the Conference in such turmoil that only sage counsel and herculean patience enabled it to keep running.

Germany Accepts. After more than three months of constant deliberation, the Conference on April 18 invited the German government to send plenipotentiaries to Versailles to receive the preliminary text of the peace treaty. The German delegation was headed by Count Brockdorff-Rantzau, a diplomat of the Imperial school, Foreign Minister of the new Socialist republic. The treaty of peace was presented to the German delegates on May 7 at the Trianon Palace Hotel in a short and dramatic ceremony. The Germans were allowed fifteen days for written observations, and notes on details of the treaty passed back and forth between Clemenceau and Brockdorff-Rantzau. A short extension was granted and several delegates returned to Germany to confer with the government. Counterproposals were made by the German plenipotentiaries, but except for some very minor points all were rejected. On June 20 the Scheidemann cabinet resigned in protest against the severity of the Versailles Treaty, but a new cabinet was quickly formed and it agreed (June 23) to sign. This historic ceremony took place in the Hall of Mirrors at Versailles on June 28. The two Chinese delegates refused to append their signatures, as a protest against the award of Shantung-Kiao-chow to Japan.[14]

Separate treaties were arranged for Austria, Hungary, Turkey, and Bulgaria.

The Versailles Treaty. The Versailles Treaty, as finally signed by the representatives of the twenty-seven Allied and Associated Powers and Germany, contained 440 articles divided into fifteen parts. The most important are: (I) the Covenant of the League of Nations; (II) and (III) establishing the new boundaries of Germany and contiguous states; (IV) depriving Germany of her overseas colonies; (V) the disarmament of Germany; (VIII–X) reparations and general economic readjustments; (XII) changes in the control of certain rivers, ports, and railways; (XIII) the organization of an international bureau of labor. The sections of the Treaty dealing with financial and economic problems are just as important as the political and territorial settlements, but will be discussed in Chapters III and IV.

The League, Wilson, and French Security. The Covenant of the League of Nations forms the first part of all the peace treaties. In the form finally approved by Wilson, it was largely the work of Balfour. Without delving too deeply into the details of the Covenant, it is important to note that several points gave rise to bitter controversies.

The conquered states, although compelled to sign the treaties, were not invited to become members of the League. Furthermore, the Covenant organized the League with two separate bodies, a Council representing only the principal powers, and an Assembly representing all the rest. Thus the League perpetuated the same peremptory discrimination that had denied the small nations any real voice in the Paris negotiations and had enabled Clemenceau to dictate the terms of peace. Moreover, this distinction ran counter to the great body of international law, which heretofore had assumed the equality of every state regardless of size or might. The lesser powers reluctantly accepted their disappointing status in the League, which, we may note, destroyed the last shreds of Wilson's prestige. A third handicap for the new League was contributed by the Peace Conference in postponing certain problems apparently impossible of solution at the time.

We may assume that when Wilson gave in to Clemenceau on treaty provisions that clearly violated some of his Fourteen Points, he was hoping that the League would rectify the injustices of the treaties. Wilson was obliged to admit that in spite of his extraordinary confidence in the League it might not be able to guarantee France against future German aggression. Clemenceau wanted tangible protection, and in order to gain his support for the League Wilson and Lloyd George agreed that England and the United States would guarantee France their military support if she were again attacked by Germany. Clemenceau was quite aware of the fact that Wilson could not constitutionally make any such military guarantee without the consent of Congress, but if Wilson's pledge failed to materialize Clemenceau could not be held responsible. In general it must be said that Wilson's negotiations for the Covenant were sometimes lacking in wisdom, consistency, and political astuteness. It is not unjust to lay this charge at his door, since the League was his main objective and, by his own profession, America's great contribution to world peace.

Territorial Adjustments of the Versailles Treaty

Germany: the West. We may now consider the principal territorial changes involved in the treaties.

In 1914 continental Germany, with a population of over 65 million, embraced 185,000 square miles. By the terms of the Versailles Treaty she lost 26,000 square miles (about 14 per cent of her territory) and about 6.5 million people. Alsace and Lorraine, acquired in 1871, were restored to France. In these two provinces a majority of the people spoke a Germanic dialect, but sentiment was overwhelmingly anti-German and pro-French. In Alsace and Lorraine Germany lost 58 per cent of its iron output and a considerable source of coal. Eupen, Malmédy, and Moresnet, small but rich mining areas, were ceded to Belgium on the basis of some ancient and obscure claim.[15] In compensation for losses suffered by France when the Germans flooded the coal mines of northern France, the Saar mines were to become French property for fifteen years, the territory to be administered by a League Commission. A plebiscite was then to determine its disposition. The Saar Commission was strongly pro-French, and French military occupation was allowed. World opinion was soon convinced of the injustice of the Saar arrangements, and on this issue, at least, France had no outside support. The plebiscite held in 1935, after powerful propaganda had been disseminated from Berlin, voted overwhelmingly for reunion with Germany.[16]

Germany: the South and East. On the southern border of Germany only slight territorial changes were made. A very small strip of territory in Upper Silesia was ceded to Czechoslovakia. At the eastern frontier, however, considerable alterations occurred. A large part of Upper Silesia, comprising 4300 square miles and inhabited by almost 2 million people, was claimed by Poland. Taken as a whole, the population of the district was about two-thirds Polish and one-third German. Upper Silesia had great economic importance since it produced, before the war, 23 per cent of Germany's coal, 34 per cent of its lead, and 81 per cent of its zinc. After a plebiscite conducted by the League, the southern and eastern sections of the province were awarded to Poland (October 20, 1921). The new border followed ethnographic lines quite closely, but Poland received the greater portion of the mineral and industrial wealth of the area. Poland also annexed five-sixths of the province of Posen, which had been appropriated by Prussia in the Second Partition of 1793. Here the population, mostly agricultural, was predominantly Polish. Poland received a large slice of West Prussia as a corridor to the sea. This territory, whose population was mostly Slavic, was fifty miles wide and about one hundred miles long, extending along the Vistula to the Gulf of Danzig. The port of Danzig, situated at the mouth of the Vistula, was a natural outlet for Poland, but its German majority of over 90 per cent precluded its inclusion within a Polish state. Danzig and a small tributary territory was therefore made a Free City and incorporated into the Polish customs union under the administrative control of the League of Nations. For hundreds of years of its history Danzig had been a Free City so that there was some historical justification for this arrangement. The difficulties inherent in separating West and East Prussia — a separation to which Germany never became reconciled — were lightened somewhat by assuring Germany of transportation facilities across the Corridor. Poland claimed Marienwerder and Allenstein on the southern and western borders of East Prussia, but these regions voted by overwhelming majorities to remain under German rule.[17]

Germany: the North. The question arose of returning Schleswig, taken from Denmark after the Prusso-Danish War of 1864, to its former sovereign. In the intervening half-century, the process of Germanization had been carried on so thoroughly as to make the southern part of Schleswig largely German. Denmark was reluctant to claim this region, having no desire to acquire a troublesome minority. Schleswig was divided into three plebiscite zones, but Denmark requested that the southernmost area be left to Germany intact. Of the two remaining zones, the northern voted for Denmark (February 10, 1920) and the southern for Germany (March 14, 1920). The final boundary was drawn at a safe distance from the Kiel Canal. The island of Heligoland, which had been ceded to Germany by England in 1890, was demilitarized.[18]

German Colonies. In 1914 Germany ruled over about 13 million people in Africa: in Togoland, the Cameroons, German East Africa, and German Southwest Africa. French, British, South African, and Belgian forces had conquered these territories during the war. In the Versailles Treaty Germany renounced her claims to this extensive empire as well as to her Pacific islands and Kiaochow. The administration of these areas was distributed among the victorious states as mandatories of the League of Nations. Under Article XXII of the Covenant of the League, freedom of religion was guaranteed, the slave trade and the arms and liquor traffic were outlawed. The mandates of Togoland and the Cameroons were divided between

Great Britain and France; German East Africa was mandated to Great Britain, save for a strip along the northern shore of Lake Tanganyika which was attached to the administration of the Belgian Congo; German Southwest Africa was mandated to the Union of South Africa.[19] Australia became the mandatory for Papua and other German Pacific islands; New Zealand for Samoa; Japan for the Marshall and Marianne islands, and for Kiaochow.

Execution of Territorial Clauses. All the cessions of German territory, either explicit in the Treaty of Versailles or resulting from plebiscites, were carried out with as much expedition as could be reasonably expected. By 1923 the last Boundary Commission had reported to the Conference of Allied Ambassadors sitting at Paris. With her boundaries fixed, Germany faced the task of adjusting her national life to her shrunken proportions.

Treaties with Austria, Hungary, Bulgaria, and Turkey

Disintegration of Austria-Hungary. The polyglot State of Austria-Hungary had been crumbling for a long time; its ultimate collapse was inevitable. Even before the armistice the Czechs and Slovaks had formed a national state and were recognized by the Allies on October 15, 1918; the Croat Diet had announced the existence of an independent Serb-Croat-Slovene state on October 29. Hungary, which had been straining for years at the dynastic bonds that held it to Austria, proclaimed itself an independent republic on November 16. Thus, instead of one diplomatic and political unit, the Conference at Paris had to deal with at least four: Czechoslovakia, Austria, Hungary, and Yugoslavia (the Serb-Croat-Slovene State). Other parts of the mighty Hapsburg Empire were acquired by Poland, Italy, and Rumania.[20]

The New Austria. On November 12, 1918 the Provisional Assembly in Vienna declared the existence of a republic. Delegates of this republic signed the peace treaty presented to them at St. Germain-en-Laye, near Paris, on September 10, 1919. Although the Treaty of St. Germain followed the Versailles Pact in broad outline, it was in many respects more severe. Austria was reduced from a nation of 30 million to one of 6.5 million, of whom nearly a third lived in Vienna. Austria was all head and no body, and the economic consequences of this foreshortening were appalling. Vienna, the industrial capital of pre-war Austria, was deprived of its markets, its access to raw materials, and to an adequate food supply. The reconstruction of post-war Austria, therefore, was perhaps more difficult than that of any other defeated nation.

The peacemakers partitioned Austria-Hungary thoroughly, in some instances recognizing rebellious minorities who had taken advantage of the Central Powers' defeat to declare their independence, in others making rather arbitrary awards of territory to satisfy the demands of Italy, Rumania, Poland, and Yugoslavia.   Thus Bohemia, Moravia, and most of Austrian Silesia, containing over 3 million Austrian Germans, became part of Czechoslovakia.   Bosnia, Herzegovina, and the Dalmatian coastline were incorporated into Yugoslavia.   Galicia was ceded to Poland, and Bukovina to Rumania.   Italy received Istria, Trieste, and the southern Tyrol.   For the last, only strategic reasons could be advanced, as the population was almost wholly Austrian.   On her eastern frontier, where the Hungarian border was only a few miles from Vienna, the Treaty gave Austria a strip of Hungary known as the " kitchen garden of Vienna." Austria needed this hinterland for food, and Hungary was not disposed to question the matter.   This, by the way, was the only instance at the Conference where substantial territory was taken from one enemy and given to another.   With this minor exception, the boundary of Austria was essentially that which the succession states themselves had set either by military occupation or political control.   The city of Klagenfurt in Carinthia, claimed by Austria and Yugoslavia, was awarded to the former after a plebiscite.

With her greatly reduced population and shrunken resources Austria could not be expected to assume her pre-war debts, and the Treaty judiciously obliged the succession states to share these obligations.[21]   But the stupidity of the Hapsburgs and their underlings had made cooperation between the various national groups impossible.   Hard hit when the partition finally came, the Austrian and Hungarian peoples were paying for the blind maladministration of the famously incompetent Hapsburgs.   The Dual Monarchy, which had already fallen to pieces, was divided into several small, and, in some cases, mutually antagonistic units.   Although the principle of self-determination of minorities was invoked, the final territorial settlements in many instances violated this guiding rule.   To cite some outstanding examples: Czechoslovakia acquired about two million Austrians and one million Germans in the Sudetenland, and Italy undertook to govern the preponderantly Austrian Tyrol.

Anschluss Rejected.   A state so reduced in size as Austria was bound to have a difficult time.   The peacemakers, warned of this by the experts, faced two alternatives: they could permit a customs union or even a political union with Germany (*Anschluss*), or give Austria economic aid which would of necessity be pure charity.   Anschluss, the first alternative, would have increased the size of Germany and given her a foothold on the Danube.   Neither the Allies nor the succession states could permit that, so the second alternative of continued loans and economic support was adopted.[22]

Bulgaria.   The treaty with Bulgaria was signed at Neuilly-sur-Seine on November 27, 1919.   It deprived Bulgaria of 2,750 square miles of territory, inhabited by 300,000 people. A slice of western Bulgaria was ceded to Yugoslavia in order to strengthen the latter's frontier. The cession to Greece of Western Thrace with its Aegean coastline was not only a heavy blow to Bulgaria but gave Greece control of Moslem and Bulgarian minorities who would be difficult to rule. Bulgaria was guaranteed trading privileges on the Aegean, but her pride was deeply wounded and she never renounced her claims to this territory, which had been won by the Bulgars in the Balkan Wars. The fundamental reason for the transfer of Western Thrace to Greece was the Allies' desire not only to aggrandize Greece but to keep the Dardanelles in the possession of a friendly power.[23]

Hungary. The armistice stipulations of November 3, 1918 between the Allies and Hungary had called for an almost unconditional surrender. In the ensuing months Hungary was so thoroughly shaken by social and political revolutions, aggressive military action by Rumania in the east and the Czechoslovaks in the north, that the Peace Conference found it impossible to carry on satisfactory negotiations with any Hungarian government. The Bolshevik regime of Béla Kun was more or less in power from March to August 1, 1919. The Rumanians had been at war with Hungary since July; on August 8 they entered Budapest. In the meantime, the drastically curtailed boundaries of Hungary had been announced at Paris (June 13), and immediately hatred for the Allies ran high among the proud Magyars. The Allies, however, were able to effect the formation of a Hungarian government under Admiral Horthy that was willing to deal with them, and the peace treaty was finally signed at the Trianon Palace in Versailles on June 4, 1920.

Like Austria, Hungary emerged as a sadly shrunken state, with only one-third of her pre-war territory and about 40 per cent of her pre-war population. Some effort had been made to draw ethnographic frontiers, but so intricate was the mingling of nationalities that this became impossible. Of the 21 million people in pre-war Hungary no more than 9.5 million could safely be called Magyar. The rest consisted of approximately 2 million Slovaks in the north, 500,000 Ruthenians in the northeast, 3 million Rumanians in Transylvania and the Banat of Temesvar, 2.5 million Croats and Slovenes in the west, 2 million Germans, and one million Jews.

The Trianon Treaty placed 3 million Magyars in neighboring states. Slovakia and Sub-Carpathian Ruthenia became part of Czechoslovakia. Croatia, including the Adriatic coast and Fiume, Slavonia, and the western third of the Banat, were ceded to Yugoslavia. Rumania acquired the large and prosperous province of Transylvania, whose population was almost 60 per cent Rumanian, and the eastern two-thirds of the Banat of Temesvar, on the northern bank of the Danube.[24]

The " Crime " of Trianon. Of all the treaties, the Trianon Pact gave rise to the greatest racial disturbances and animosities. There is little doubt

that it was excessively severe, although territorial adjustments equitable
to all nations would have taxed the ingenuity of men far wiser and more
dispassionate than the leading spirits at the Paris Conference. The Allies
were influenced by the scandalous treatment Hungary had accorded
her minorities throughout her history, and to a certain extent, therefore, were trying to rectify ancient wrongs, even at the cost of commit-
ting an injustice in the other direction. No one was satisfied with the
result.

Disarming the Central Powers. The military clauses of the four treaties
were substantially alike. Germany was deprived of her navy and allowed
to maintain a professional volunteer army of only 100,000 officers and
men, the latter to be enlisted for twelve years. Austria lost her navy and
was permitted an army of 30,000. The Hungarian army was reduced to
35,000, the Bulgarian to 33,000, including frontier guardsmen. By contrast,
the succession allied states were allowed to maintain relatively large armies:
in 1921 Greece had 210,000 men under arms, Italy 300,000, Rumania 160,-
000, Czechoslovakia 147,000, and Yugoslavia 200,000.

Turkey: Defeat and Reconstruction. Turkey, the remaining member of
the defeated Quadruple Alliance, had ruled in 1914 over a vast empire of
many peoples, in Europe, Asia Minor, Palestine, and Arabia. Before the
armistice, the Allies had parcelled out Turkish territories among themselves in a number of secret treaties. Russia was to have received the greatest spoils: all of European Turkey and Constantinople. The Bolshevik revolution in 1917 cancelled this plan.

The Treaty of Sèvres, signed on August 10, 1920 — the last treaty
written by the Paris Conference — reduced the Turkish Empire to two-
thirds of its pre-war territory and population. Syria was mandated to
France, Palestine and Mesopotamia (Iraq) to Great Britain, while Greece,
the great enemy of the Turks, was given a mandate over Smyrna and surrounding territory for five years, pending a plebiscite. Armenia, the perpetual victim of Turkish cruelty, in a vague fashion was given her freedom.
In Arabia there was already an independent Kingdom of the Hedjaz, supported by Great Britain. Constantinople was to remain in Turkish hands,
but the Straits were internationalized. The great Ottoman Empire was
thus remorselessly partitioned by the victors.

The Treaty of Sèvres, which the impotent Sultan had signed, was destined to be discarded, like the equally severe Treaty of Brest-Litovsk imposed on Russia by Germany in March, 1918. Angered by the Treaty,
the renascent Turkish nationalists, ably led by Mustapha Kemal, seized
control of the government. Once firmly in the saddle, Kemal ignored
the Treaty of Sèvres, and the Allies did not attempt to enforce it, being
in no mood to make war on Turkey. On October 2, 1921 France recognized the new government, renounced her sphere of influence in southern

Asia Minor, and returned to Turkey a strip of territory north of Syria which included the important Bagdad railway. Only the Greeks refused to recognize the new regime, and declared war on the Turks in July, 1921. Unassisted by the Allies, the Greek armies were at first successful, but the Turks defeated them decisively in the autumn of 1922. The Greeks were forced to abandon Asia Minor, and thereafter the Allies were glad to modify radically the terms of the unworkable Treaty of Sèvres. A new Treaty was signed at Lausanne on July 23, 1923. Of all World War treaties, this alone represented a negotiated, not an imposed, peace. Turkey recovered all the territory it had lost in Europe and Asia Minor since 1914. Only the Arab states were taken from her. Aside from provisions for the protection of minorities under League of Nations guarantees, Turkey's sovereignty as to her military establishments and her economic autonomy remained untouched.[25]

Had it been possible to negotiate the other treaties in a similar spirit of justice and good will, much grief and disappointment might have been spared the world in the next two decades.

Eastern Europe and the Baltic States

Russia and Rumania. The rise of the new Baltic states and the establishment of the final eastern frontiers of Rumania and Poland were scarcely influenced by the Allies or the Paris Peace Conference, but rather by the course of events in Russia. Imperial Russia collapsed in 1917, and the peoples on her western borders took advantage of the catastrophe to form independent national states. For several generations prior to the war, unrest had been growing more vocal among the Rumanians in Bessarabia, which Russia had ruled since 1812. On February 6, 1918 the Sfat (Council) proclaimed the independence of the Moldavian Republic. But since so small a state could not survive in the face of Bolshevik and Ukrainian hostility, the Sfat voted on April 8 for the union of Bessarabia with Rumania on condition of limited autonomy. This enlargement of its territory was some consolation to Rumania after the humiliating Peace of Bucharest which the Central Powers had forced her to sign on May 7, 1918. Rumania re-entered the war on November 9; Germany was obliged to renounce the Treaty of Bucharest; and the Paris Conference assigned to Rumania both Bessarabia and Bukovina on ethnic, historical, and geographic grounds. This, added to the acquisitions of Transylvania and the Banat, made Rumania one of the principal beneficiaries of the war. Rumania's territory was more than doubled, and its population rose from 7 to 17 millions. At the end of 1919 nearly every Rumanian would have avowed that the war had been an eminently good investment, even though the Rumanian armies had met disastrous defeat.[26]

Russia and Poland. At the Peace Conference the Poles demanded the boundaries of Poland as they existed before the First Partition of 1772, extending from the Baltic almost to the Black Sea. This was clearly impossible, but the Allies allowed generous frontiers to the new state, creating a country of 30 million people.

Poland's western frontier was fixed by the Paris Conference, but her eastern border was settled by the trial of arms. Dissatisfied with their eastern boundaries, and taking advantage of the struggle between the Reds and Whites, the Poles, led by Marshal Pilsudski, invaded Russia early in 1920 and advanced as far as Kiev. A Bolshevik counterattack hurled them back to the gates of Warsaw. Here Pilsudski with the aid of General Weygand, hurriedly summoned from Paris, reorganized his shattered army and soundly defeated the Russians. By the Treaty of Riga, signed March 18, 1921, Poland added a large slice of western Russia to her eastern frontier.[27]

Lithuania and Memel. While Russia was enmeshed in revolution and counter-revolution, Germany had encouraged the Baltic peoples to revolt. Germany planned to displace Russia as the dominant power in the Baltic region by controlling or absorbing the small nations along the coast: Lithuania, Latvia, Estonia, and Finland. The armistice of November 11, 1918, having spelled defeat for Germany, found these small states struggling for some sort of national existence. A dispute between Poland and her northern neighbor, Lithuania, over Vilna was won by Poland. The decisive fact was military occupation by General Zeligowski in October, 1920. The Conference of Ambassadors in Paris found it expedient to recognize this on March 15, 1923. The German city of Memel, at the mouth of the Niemen River, was given to Lithuania as compensation by the Allies.

Latvia. Latvia (ancient Livonia) declared her independence on November 18, 1918. For a time it was the battle-ground between German free-lance forces under General von der Goltz and a Bolshevik army. The Latvians with Allied help finally overpowered both Germans and Bolsheviks, and the Latvian Republic was recognized by Russia on August 11, 1920, and by the Allies on January 26, 1921.

Estonia. Estonia, on the southern shore of the Gulf of Bothnia, had long sought autonomy from the Czars. German troops were called in to help the natives oust the Bolsheviks in December, 1917, and an independent republic was declared on February 24, 1918. But Russia greatly desired this outlet to the Baltic, and there were sporadic hostilities between Estonian and Bolshevik forces for almost two years before a definitive peace treaty between the two countries was signed on February 2, 1920. The Allies gave *de jure* recognition to the Estonian government on January 26, 1921; the United States followed suit on July 28, 1924.

Finland. The Duchy of Finland was the largest and most advanced of the Russian Baltic provinces. Throughout her long history, Finland had been

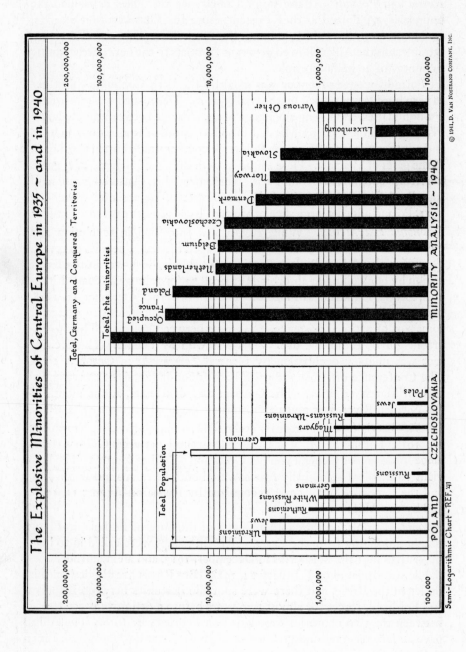

The Explosive Minorities of Central Europe in 1935 ~ and in 1940

MINORITY ANALYSIS ~ 1940

Total, Germany and Conquered Territories

Total, the minorities

Various Other
Luxembourg
Slovakia
Norway
Denmark
Czechoslovakia
Belgium
Netherlands
Poland
Occupied France

CZECHOSLOVAKIA

Poles
Jews
Russians–Ukrainians
Magyars
Germans

POLAND

Russians
Germans
White Russians
Ruthenians
Jews
Ukrainians

Total Population

200,000,000
100,000,000
10,000,000
1,000,000
100,000

Semi-Logarithmic Chart ~ REF. '41

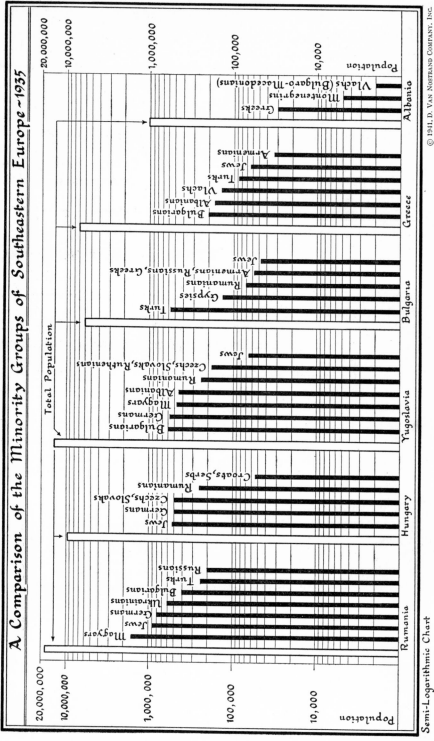

A Comparison of the Minority Groups of Southeastern Europe ~1935

Semi-Logarithmic Chart

a battle-ground between Sweden and Russia. Since 1809 she had been a
semi-autonomous Duchy under the Czar, but the demand for complete
freedom became ever more insistent. After the Bolshevist revolution the
Finnish Diet renounced its allegiance to Russia (December 6, 1917), and
the Treaty of Brest-Litovsk confirmed Finnish independence. Hostilities
between the Bolsheviks and Finns, however, continued for two years. A
Finnish Republic with a new constitution came into being in the summer of
1919, and satisfactory peace terms were finally arranged in the Treaty of
Dorpat, signed October 14, 1920. Finland received an ice-free port, Petsamo, on the Arctic coast; minor boundary disputes were gradually settled.
Sweden claimed the strategic Aaland Islands. But the League of Nations,
although admitting that the inhabitants were mostly Swedish, awarded the
islands to Finland (June 24, 1921).[28]

The Minorities Treaties

The Maze of European Minorities. In the early months of the Peace Conference the problem of assuring maximum security to racial minorities in
both the new and enlarged states was regarded as at once urgent and delicate. In several instances national groups formerly enjoying sovereignty
had come under the political domination of peoples whom they regarded as
inferior — for example, the Germans in Poland, the Austrians in Czechoslovakia, and the Magyars in Rumania. These and other new minorities
belonged to races which have sovereign states that might rise to defend
their blood relatives if the latter were persecuted. In other instances,
such as the Jews in Poland and Ruthenians in Czechoslovakia, the minorities had no national state to summon to their defense. The problem of
safeguarding minorities was therefore exceedingly knotty. This complicated the work of the Conference in providing for minorities in general,
as it introduced a different kind of minority. The Japanese delegates proposed an amendment declaring the equality of all nationalities. So radical
a suggestion, however, was unacceptable to the British, who ruled over
many different nationalities, and as religion and nationality had thus been
brought together, the whole section had to be dropped.[29]

Minorities in Poland. Nevertheless, protection of specific minorities had
to be provided for. The representatives of the various Jewish groups in
Europe and America had formed a united front, and were determined to
use the opportunity of Poland's imminent recognition to obtain a clear-cut
statement of minority, particularly Jewish, rights. Wilson was sympathetic to their cause, and the Conference appointed a New States Committee to hear all sides of the minority issues and formulate acceptable articles as fairly as possible for the Polish and subsequent treaties. The New
States Committee had not finished its work when the Versailles Treaty was

submitted to Germany on May 7. Poland, however, promised to agree in principle to whatever decision the Supreme Council (Big Four) might make. The New States Committee was forced to steer a course which would, on the one hand, avoid giving so much autonomy to minorities as to constitute them states within states, or, on the other hand, providing so little protection for them that their position might become precarious.

Polish and Rumanian Protests. Poland — and Rumania when its turn came — objected to the fact that it was singled out as a state requiring special minority guarantees. The Polish and Rumanian representatives pointedly observed that neither Germany nor Italy was asked to give such guarantees. But the Great Powers replied that their military success had made the establishment of a Polish state possible, and in the last analysis their military power would be called upon to preserve peace. Hence equitable guarantees for minorities were regarded as necessary in order to remove causes of friction that might lead to war. To this argument there was no effective answer.

The explicit provisions for the Polish minorities as well as those of other countries will be dealt with in more detail in the next chapter. Here we may briefly note that the Treaty as finally accepted by Poland promised to admit to full citizenship all nationals not subjects of other nations, guaranteed equality of all nationals before the law, freedom of worship, and government support of education in their native languages for non-Polish nationals. The minorities were placed under the protection of the League of Nations. This document was signed June 28, the day on which the German delegates affixed their signatures to the Versailles Treaty.

Other Minorities Treaties. Other minorities treaties were signed by the Allies with Czechoslovakia, September 10, 1919; Austria and Yugoslavia, September 10, 1919; Bulgaria, November 27, 1919; Rumania, December 9, 1919; Hungary, June 4, 1920; Greece, August 10, 1920; Armenia, August 10, 1920; and Turkey, July 24, 1923. These states accepted treaties which amounted to a restriction of their sovereignty with varying attitudes. Beneš on May 20, 1919 presented to the New States Committee a Czechoslovakian minority program more liberal in its assurances of rights and privileges than the Committee would have required.[30] But Rumania and Yugoslavia were more difficult to convince. They felt keenly the implication that the Great Powers anticipated that the minorities in these states had been or might be mistreated. Greece, under Venizelos' guidance, was anxious to show her good will, and made no serious objections. Naturally, each country presented special problems for which allowances had to be made in the respective treaties. Rumania, for example, had a larger proportion of Jews than Yugoslavia or Czechoslovakia. Czechoslovakia acquired Sudeten Germans and Ruthenians. Bulgaria, Greece, and Yugoslavia contained sizable Mohammedan groups whose presence raised delicate issues. Negotiation and counterproposals in every case brought compromises that seemed to be partially satisfactory. In general, the Polish Pact served as a model for all the minorities treaties, and their underlying principles were practically identical.

Supplementary Treaties. Pacts were signed between contiguous states, such as Poland and Czechoslovakia, with mutual minority or frontier problems, giving more precision to the minorities clauses in the general peace treaties. These supplementary treaties came explicitly under the supervision of the League of Nations which, in this matter, as in so many others, was designated as the organization through which the decisions of the victorious powers should be carried out.[31]

Post-war Awareness of Minorities. The agitation of national or racial minorities for independence or union with their parent states had been one of the roots of the war. It is therefore not strange that from 1919 onwards the feeling grew in certain quarters that this was the most pressing political problem of post-war Europe, and that if it were solved at least one prominent cause of war would be eliminated. Certainly more thought was given at the Peace Conference to the political aspects of the minorities question than to its purely humanitarian aspects.

Results of the Treaties. In conclusion it may be said that although the actual rectifications were as great as could be expected amid the lingering passions of war and the overcharged atmosphere that pervaded the Peace Conference, the ethnic readjustments were often unscientific, and in some cases ill-advised. Before the war, over 80 million people in Europe were governed by races other than their own; after the peace, the minorities were reduced to less than 30 million. Given the factors of geography, economic ties, and ethnic complexities, it would have been difficult to reduce the number of subjugated peoples beyond the point reached by the Peace Conference. Although solemn treaties were signed to protect the minorities, this did not guarantee the coming of an era of complete racial and religious tolerance. Too often, as subsequent chapters of this book will recount, only lip service was paid to the treaties. Nations long oppressed became oppressors when they acquired sovereignty. Irredentism did not cease.

Summary

The legal justification for the severe peace terms imposed on Germany was embodied in Article 231 of the Versailles Treaty, the "war guilt" clause:

" The Allied and Associated Governments affirm and Germany accepts the responsibility of Germany and her allies for causing all the loss and damage to which the Allied and Associated Governments and their nationals have been subjected as a consequence of the war imposed upon them by the aggression of Germany and her allies."

The making of a constructive peace in the twentieth century turned out to be a more complicated matter than the making of a destructive war. After an indisputable military decision had been reached in November, 1918, there were two broad phases of the readjustment that had to be worked out: territorial and economic. The vastly involved economic problems arising out of the war settlement are treated elsewhere in this book. In this chapter we have traced the broad lines of the territorial adjustments. When the Treaty of Versailles is bitterly criticized as a large factor in bringing on the Second World War, as it is even today in certain quarters, it must be pointed out that the economic clauses with their alleged pronouncement of a judgment of German war guilt and consequent responsibility for " just reparations," are at the root of that criticism and of German resentment. At the same time it cannot be too clearly stated that German publicists have systematically distorted the meaning and intent of these clauses of the Treaty, and in so doing have not only convinced the German people but also many well-meaning people in the Allied countries that Article 231 placed sole responsibility for the war upon Germany. It does nothing of the sort. Germany was obliged to admit responsibility for war-damages caused by her aggression. Of the fact that Germany was the first power to invade foreign territory in 1914 there has never been any question. And this priority of military action and invasion has been frequently defined as "aggression" in subsequent international agreements, some of which bear Germany's signature.

As compared with the economic provisions of the Treaty, the territorial adjustments cannot be so harshly judged. Compared with the terms of the Treaty of Brest-Litovsk which Germany herself imposed upon a prostrate Russia in March, 1918,[32] and the Treaty of Bucharest which Rumania had to sign in May, 1918, the territorial as well as the economic clauses of the Versailles Treaty were dictated by brotherly love and sweet reasonableness. The fact that for two decades the German people have been incited to regard as an unbearable humiliation to a great people a treaty considerably more moderate than two treaties which they themselves had imposed on two defeated foes, should not be lost sight of in our judgment of the justice or injustice of the Treaty of Versailles. Indeed the broad principle of racial and national self-determination, upon which, as we have seen, the territorial adjustments were based, was readily accepted by the Germans, though objections were made to specific applications of that principle by the peacemakers. Within rather wide limits, in spite of opportunism and occasional mistakes, the peacemakers must be given credit for having made an effort to do justice in setting political borders that might remove the need for war from the international scene.[33] With all its faults — and of the recognition of their existence by the Conference, the establishment of the League of Nations with ample provisions for adjustment is the simple proof — the peace settlements of 1919–1923 made two great contributions to the peaceful development of Europe: the League of Nations and the implemented principle of the freedom of national, racial or religious minorities to freedom within the law. The fact that twenty years later we find these two grand instruments in eclipse does not lessen the greatness of the ideas which gave them birth. Rather does the present darkness make it more necessary for us to appreciate their grandeur and demand that in our generation we strive to recapture the fineness of spirit and high determination which launched so hopefully in 1920 a New Europe.

REFERENCES

[1] For details of the armistice negotiations see *Preliminary History of the Armistice* (documents); H. W. V. Temperley, *A History of the Peace Conference at Paris*, London, Froude (6 vols., 1920–1924, hereafter referred to as *HPC*); André Tardieu, *The Truth about the Treaty*, pp. 27–76; Mermeix, *Les Negotiations secrètes et les quatres armistices.*

[2] J. M. Keynes, *Economic Consequences of the Peace*, New York: Harcourt, Brace, 1920, p. 33. Evidence of this general opinion was widespread in the French press. See also G. B. Noble, *Policies and Opinions at Paris*, New York: Macmillan, 1935, pp. 30 ff., 41 ff.

[3] Tardieu, *op. cit.*, p. 77 ff. For the preparations in general see *HPC*, I: 236 ff.; Harold Nicolson, *Peacemaking, 1919*, pp. 24–29; C. H. Haskins and R. H. Lord, *Some Problems of the Peace Conference*, p. 21 ff.; Gabriel Hanotaux, *Le Traité de Versailles*, Paris: Plon, 1919, p. 157 ff. Professor Hanotaux, one of the leading French experts, has published many of the opinions he submitted to the French delegates.

[4] Noble, *op. cit.*, p. 1 ff.; E. J. Dillon, *The Inside Story of the Peace Conference*, pp. 1–44.

[5] Nicolson, *op. cit.*, p. 241 ff.; K. F. Nowak, *Versailles*, p. 149 ff.; Noble, *op. cit.*, p. 67 ff.

[6] Nicolson, *op. cit.*, p. 232 ff.; Robert Lansing, *The Peace Negotiations, A Personal Narrative*, p. 213 ff. A useful chronology of events from June, 1914 to August, 1920 is given in *HPC*, III: 1–41. It has been generally followed throughout this chapter.

[7] Keynes, *op. cit.*, p. 27 ff., calls it a " Carthaginian Peace " and says that, " In so far as the main economic lines of the Treaty represent an intellectual idea, it is the idea of France and of Clemenceau." For French reaction to Keynes' book see R. G. Levy, *La juste paix ou la vérité sur le traité de Versailles*, Paris: Plon, 1920.

[8] *HPC*, III: 58 ff.

[9] *HPC*, III: 60.

[10] Lansing, in his *Big Four and Others at the Peace Conference*, Boston: Houghton Mifflin, 1921, gives excellent characterizations of the leading personalities.

[11] Tardieu, *op. cit.*, pp. 88–91.

[12] Nicolson, *op. cit.*, Book II, *passim;* Haskins and Lord, *op. cit.*, pp. 24–33; Tardieu, *op. cit.*, pp. 91–94.

[13] Dillon, *op. cit.*, pp. 184–263; Nicolson, *op. cit.*, pp. 184 ff., 122 ff.

[14] *HPC*, II: 1–20 and 420–447; see also *The Germans at Versailles, 1919*, London: William and Norgate, 1930, by Victor Schiff, member of the German delegation.

[15] Haskins and Lord, *op. cit.*, pp. 75–116; *HPC*, II: 159–175.

[16] John Macintosh, *The Paths That Led to War: Europe 1919–39*, p. 248 ff. The French position is briefly stated by Tardieu, *op. cit.*, pp. 250–279. The literature on the Saar is immense, but see M. T. Florinsky, *The Saar Struggle.*

[17] I. F. D. Morrow, *The Peace Settlements in the German-Polish Borderlands; HPC*, II: 207–215; Haskins and Lord, *op. cit.*, pp. 153–200; R. L. Buell, *Poland: Key to Europe*, New York: Knopf, 1939, pp. 56–74; Robert Machray, *Poland, 1914–1931*, London: Allen and Unwin, 1932.

[18] *HPC*, II: 197–206; Haskins and Lord, *op. cit.*, pp. 37–47.

[19] *HPC*, II: 216–245; G. L. Beer, *African Questions at the Paris Peace Conference*, New York: Macmillan, 1923.

[20] Oscar Jaszi in *The Dissolution of the Hapsburg Empire*, Chicago: University of Chicago Press, 1929, analyzes the deeper forces that made collapse inevitable; *HPC*, IV: 89–119, 141–157, 389–411.

[21] *HPC*, IV: 368–411, 462–484.

[22] A. J. Toynbee, *Survey of International Affairs 1920–1923*, p. 311 ff.

[23] *HPC*, IV: 444–461.

[24] *HPC*, IV: 415–428, 485–498. Sir Robert Ronald presents the case for Hungary in *The Tragedy of Trianon*, London: Butterworth, 1928. See also Count Stephen Bethlen, *The Treaty of Trianon and European Peace;* Count Albert Apponyi *et al, Justice for Hungary.*

25 *HPC,* IV: 1–192, 602–616.
26 *HPC,* IV: 213–236; R. W. Seton-Watson, *History of the Rumanians,* New York: Macmillan, 1934, pp. 526–564.
27 R. L. Buell, *Poland: Key to Europe,* pp. 74–84.
28 For the Baltic states see *HPC,* VI: 284–310.
29 For the minorities problem see C. A. Macartney, *National States and National Minorities; J. S. Roucek, The Working of the Minorities System under the League of Nations,* Prague: Orbis, 1928; L. P. Mair, *The Protection of Minorities,* London: Christophers, 1928; M. O. Hudson, " The League of Nations and the Protection of Inhabitants of Transferred Territories," *Annals of the American Academy,* July, 1921, LXXXVI: 77–83.
30 Macartney, *op. cit.,* p. 241 ff.
31 Macartney, *op. cit.,* pp. 268–272.
32 J. W. Wheeler-Bennett, *The Forgotten Peace, Brest-Litovsk,* New York: Morrow, 1939.
33 The mass of anti-Versailles literature is appalling, most of it best forgotten. It has taken time and the shock of a Second World War to bring us back to sanity so that we can see the Treaty in its true perspective. A succinct and reasoned restatement of the problem will be found in René Albrecht-Carrié, " Versailles Twenty Years After " in *Political Science Quarterly,* Vol. 55, March, 1940, pp. 1–24.

SELECTED BIBLIOGRAPHY

The most important single work dealing with the peace settlements is the *History of the Peace Conference,* edited by H. W. V. Temperley, with the collaboration of numerous experts. Published under the auspices of the Institute of International Affairs by the Oxford University Press, London, 1920–1924, its six ample volumes deal with almost every phase of the peacemaking. Most of the actual treaties are included.

Aside from the *Parliamentary Papers* for the years 1919–1923, the *League of Nations, Treaty Series,* for the same years, and the publications of the foreign offices of the various countries, the following list comprises the most important monographs that discuss the issues of the peace, the aims, methods, personalities, and results of the Paris Conference and related negotiations.

Albrecht-Carrié, Réné, " Versailles Twenty Years After," *Political Science Quarterly,* Vol. 55 March, 1940.
Baker, Ray Stannard, *Woodrow Wilson and the World Settlement,* New York: Doubleday, Doran, 1922–1923, 3 vols. A fervid defense of Wilson at Paris, with much original documentation.
Bethlen, Count Stephen, *The Treaty of Trianon and European Peace,* London: Longmans, Green, 1934. Presents the official Hungarian view of the Treaty of Trianon.
Birdsall, Paul, *Versailles Twenty Years After,* New York: Reynal and Hitchcock, 1941.
Dillon, E. J., *The Inside Story of the Peace Conference,* New York: Harper, 1920. Dr. Dillon was not on the " inside," but merely a well-informed journalist. His account portrays the atmosphere of the Conference.
Ebray, Arcide, *A Frenchman Looks at the Peace,* New York: Knopf, 1927. An informed Frenchman opposes the Treaty on the grounds of its severity and impracticability.
Haskins, C. H. and Lord, R. H., *Some Problems of the Peace Conference,* Cambridge: Harvard Univ. Press, 1920. Two leading American territorial experts at the Conference present a picture of the settlement.
House, E. M. and Seymour, Charles, *What Really Happened at Paris,* New York: Scribner, 1921. A defense of the work of the American delegation.
Lansing, Robert, *The Peace Negotiations, A Personal Narrative,* Boston: Houghton Mifflin, 1921. Wilson's Secretary of State presents his side of the radical disagreements between himself and the President.

Lloyd George, David, *Memoirs of the Peace Conference*, 2 vols., London: Gollancz, 1938 (New Haven: Yale Univ. Press, 1939). The importance of these two volumes cannot be exaggerated, although they are naturally a defense of Lloyd George.

Macartney, C. A., *National States and National Minorities*, New York: Oxford Univ. Press, 1934. Thorough and objective.

Mermeix, *Le Combat des trois. Notes et documents sur la conférence de la paix*, Paris: Ollendorff, 1922.

Morrow, Ian F. D., *The Peace Settlement in the German Polish Borderlands*, Oxford: Oxford Univ. Press, 1936. Thorough treatment of the intricate racial and linguistic problems of the southern Baltic region.

Nicolson, Harold, *Peacemaking, 1919*, New York: Houghton Mifflin, 1933. The reflections of a diplomatic member of the British delegation, written fourteen years after the event.

Nitti, Francesco, *Peaceless Europe*, London: Cassell, 1922. An Italian liberal expresses his dissatisfaction with the punitive nature of the Treaty.

Nowak, Karl Friedrich, *Versailles*, New York: Payson and Clarke, 1929. A reputable German historian discusses the German view.

Seymour, Charles, ed., *The Intimate Papers of Colonel House*, 4 vols., New York: Houghton Mifflin, 1926–1928. A defense of House's role at Paris, with interesting sidelights on his relationship with Wilson.

Tardieu, André, *The Truth about the Treaty*, Indianapolis: Bobbs-Merrill, 1921. One of the most important single works on the Conference. An able defense of Clemenceau.

Toynbee, A. J., *Survey of International Affairs*, 1920–1923, Oxford: Oxford Univ. Press, 1924. Factual chronicle of the early post-war European political scene.

Chapter III

The Labyrinth of Peace Efforts
1919–1930

Political Reconstruction

Among the Allied war aims, as formulated by France and Russia in 1914, was the political reconstruction of Europe. This objective was endorsed by President Wilson in his Fourteen Points, which, it was confidently expected, would guide the Peace Conference in making a lasting settlement of the problems of Europe. Secret inter-Allied commitments,[1] combined with the intense pressure of numerous ethnic groups, prevented the realization of President Wilson's dream, although, of course, thoroughgoing application of the principle of self-determination was impossible and perhaps undesirable. Had Wilson's ideas been carried to their logical conclusion many tiny nationalistic islands would have been created which could not maintain themselves politically or economically.

The territorial settlements created or perpetuated racial antagonisms which boded ill for the peace of Europe. Some of the new governments aligned themselves against others, like the Little Entente of Czechoslovakia, Rumania, and Yugoslavia, which was directed against Hungary. Determined to prevent the restoration of the Hapsburgs, France openly abetted any scheme which might be utilized to that end, and negotiated an imposing array of political alliances designed to " freeze " the new status quo. Within a few years of the peace settlements, however, it became evident that Central Europe dwelt in an atmosphere of suspicion and hostility, and the high purposes of certain of the peacemakers had virtually come to naught. Possibly too many small states, consumed by petty jealousies and exaggerated territorial ambitions, had been carved from the empires of Austria-Hungary, Germany, Russia, and Turkey. In a world dominated by power politics, the small countries are likely to become mere pawns and ultimate victims of rapacious neighbors.

To reconcile nationalistic demands with the interests of the victorious powers, the Peace Conference resorted to three devices: plebiscites, assignments, and protective minorities treaties.

Plebiscites. Elections were held, under presumably impartial auspices, such as the Supreme War Council, the Conference of Ambassadors, or the

---

This chapter by Wilson Leon Godshall, Associate Professor of Diplomatic History and International Relations, Lehigh University.

Council of the League of Nations, to ascertain local opinion as a basis for fixing boundaries. In nine instances disposition of territory was guided by the results of the plebiscite.[2] In some cases, however, popular will was ignored. Vorarlberg voted on May 11, 1919 for annexation to Switzerland, but the Supreme War Council granted this region to Austria. The Aaland Islanders, as already noted, preferred to be ruled by Sweden, but the Council of the League assigned them to Finland. In Upper Silesia a majority of the inhabitants voted on March 20, 1921 for annexation to Germany, but the Conference of Ambassadors imposed an " adjustment ": the region was divided so as to permit Poland to procure valuable industrial territory.

Assignments. In some instances projected plebiscites were abandoned, as in Teschen, where the Conference of Ambassadors arbitrarily fixed the Polish-Czechoslovak boundary on July 28, 1920 in such a way as to favor Czechoslovakia. This act created almost indelible hostility between Czechs and Poles. In September, 1919 Gabriele d'Annunzio's irregular army occupied Fiume in flagrant disregard both of the wishes of the population and the Supreme War Council. An Italo-Yugoslav Treaty (November 12, 1920) recognized the free status for the city but as that arrangement proved unsatisfactory, Italian sovereignty was conceded by Yugoslavia on January 27, 1924.

Minorities Treaties. The third device used by the Peace Conference to preserve the New Order in Europe was the negotiation or imposition of treaty guarantees. The Treaties of St.-Germain, Neuilly, Trianon, and Lausanne contained clauses protecting the rights of minorities.[3] Articles 63 and 69 of the Treaty of St.-Germain are representative:

" Austria undertakes to assure full and complete protection of life and liberty to all inhabitants . . . without distinction of birth, nationality, language, race or religion. . . . Austria agrees that the stipulations . . . constitute obligations of international concern and shall be placed under the guarantee of the League of Nations."

Special pacts of the same kind were concluded by the Allies with the new states. In addition to provisions identical with the above, the Czechoslovak Treaty, which may be taken as a model, stipulated that:

" All persons born in Czecho-Slovak territory who are not born nationals of another state shall *ipso facto* become Czecho-Slovak nationals . . . equal before the law. . . . No restriction shall be imposed on the free use by any Czecho-Slovak national of any language in private intercourse, in commerce, in religion, in the press or publication of any kind, or at public meetings. . . . Czecho-Slovak nationals who belong to racial, religious, or linguistic minorities shall enjoy the same treatment and security . . . as the other Czecho-Slovak nationals." [4]

The stipulations of the minority treaties were to be recognized as fundamental laws of the land. Germany, on May 29, 1919, agreed to conform to these treaty standards, and similar declarations were filed by Albania, Estonia, Finland, Latvia, and Lithuania. It is noteworthy that the Allied Powers did not consider it necessary to give the same guarantees.

This system for protecting minorities under the guarantee of the League of Nations worked, in a way, during the first post-war decade. But in the long run the problem of minorities could not be solved by international guarantees because the nations were unwilling to be bound by the legalistic interpretation of the treaties. Professor Roucek poses a series of questions which illustrate the complications involved in the situation:

" Is the Jew of Czechoslovakia, born and living there for some centuries, a ' race,' ' religion,' ' nationality,' or ' language ' minority? Or is a Slovak, speaking a dialect of the Czech language, a ' language ' minority? . . . Are the Ukrainians a ' Ukrainian ' or a ' Polish ' or a ' Russian ' minority in Poland? . . . Is the Catholic Croat, resentful of the ruling Greek Orthodox Serb, a minority in Yugoslavia? . . . Is it possible to find one minority acknowledging that ' adequate ' facilities have been granted to it? Or is there a majority state not emphasizing that it has granted ' more than adequate ' facilities? " [5]

Exchange of Minorities. An important arrangement for the reconciliation of frontiers and nationalities was the Turco-Greek plan of 1914 for exchanging minorities in both states. This scheme was revived by the Treaty of Lausanne which ordered a compulsory exchange of populations. Ultimately more than one million Greeks were transplanted from Turkish lands to Greece, and over 400,000 Turks were repatriated from Greece. This extraordinary migration was not accomplished without tremendous human suffering. Some Turks were permitted to remain in Western Thrace and some Greeks were allowed to reside in Turkey. Whatever success has attended the experiment may be attributed to the fact that seven years of war in the Balkans (two Balkan Wars and the World War) had accustomed the people to sudden migrations and unmitigated hardships.

The inability of European states to face squarely the complex problems of minorities is one of the keys to the failure of the peace settlements, although it must be recognized that the difficulties involved seem almost, if not entirely, insurmountable. Only perhaps by the amalgamation of European nations into a few great empires will the minorities finally be prevented from periodically disturbing the peace of the continent. The attempt to integrate frontiers and nationalities, as was urged in 1918 by Professor Zimmern,[6] may be futile and unsound, but peaceful adjustments will require generous forbearance, unusual tolerance, and unprecedented abandonment of intense nationalism.

Reparations and Debts

President Wilson's Fourteen Points, accepted by the Allies and Germany in November, 1918 as the basis of peace, insisted not only upon the evacuation and restoration of invaded territories, but on the payment of compensation " by Germany for all damage done to the civilian population of the Allies and to their property." The French and British delegates wished to add the costs of the war to the damage to the civilian population. But Wilson stood by the pre-armistice agreement with the defeated powers, and Lloyd George, Clemenceau, and Orlando were forced to agree that " Germany's reparation obligations should be limited to what might be called actual damage, the costs of the war being excluded. A single exception was made in the case of Belgium; Germany was to pay all of her war costs down to the signing of the armistice." [7] Moral justification for this step was provided in the war guilt clause of the Versailles Treaty which placed the onus of aggression squarely on Germany and her allies.

Fixing and Distribution of Reparations. It was relatively easy to decide upon the principle of reparations; to fix a reasonable sum proved more difficult. The Allies could not agree on how much Germany should pay. The estimates ranged from 10 to 120 billion dollars, but no stated sum was fixed by the Peace Conference, Lloyd George and Clemenceau fearing the political vengeance of their enemies at home if the bill seemed too little. The final sum was to be determined by a reparations commission. The Allies at a conference at Spa, July 5–16, 1920, decided upon the following apportionment of collections:

France	52	per cent
Great Britain	22	" "
Italy	10	" "
Belgium	8	" "
Greece, Rumania, and Yugoslavia	6.5	" "
Japan and Portugal	1.5	" "
	100.0	per cent

The Reparations Commission. The United States was expected to accept membership on the Reparations Commission and lend its influence to soften French determination to weaken Germany beyond possibility of recovery. When the Senate declined to authorize ratification of the Versailles Treaty and refused to join the League of Nations, thus nullifying Wilson's guarantee of French frontiers, France's reparations policy stiffened immediately.

The 1921 Bill. On January 29, 1921 the Allies decided that Germany should pay an indemnity of $56,500,000,000 in a series of forty-two fixed annuities. The Germans were outraged at this astronomical sum, and even Allied experts declared that it was clearly beyond Germany's capacity to pay. Upon invitation to submit counterproposals the Germans suggested a total bill of $7,500,000,000 based upon certain relaxations in the Versailles Treaty.

This suggestion was greeted with derision in the Allied countries. On March 8, French troops occupied Düsseldorf, Duisburg, and Ruhrort on the right bank of the Rhine in order to show Germany that the Allies were determined to make her pay. On April 28, 1921 the Reparations Commission submitted a reduced bill of $32,000,000,000 (132,000,000,000 gold marks), or thrice the sum recommended by the experts at the Peace Conference. This figure was accepted by Germany on May 11 under the threat of extended Allied occupation of the Ruhr. Payments were to be made in annuities of $500,000,000 plus 26 per cent of annual German exports.

Germany's Default. Allied refusal to lessen the reparations burden, and Germany's inability to pay, brought about the collapse of German currency and credit in 1922.[8] Following a partial moratorium on reparation payments in March, 1922 the German government on July 12 requested a total moratorium for two and one-half years. A six-month respite from cash payments was conceded on August 31, 1922 but on November 14 Germany demanded a moratorium for three or four years and credit to stabilize the mark. Great Britain was disposed to grant this request in order to aid German recovery and thereby create a demand for British goods in Germany, but France, having spent large sums on pensions and reconstruction, was determined to exact its pound of flesh.

Occupation of the Ruhr. On October 20, 1922 France had asked the Reparations Commission to declare default of German deliveries of timber, and on January 11, 1923 French and Belgian troops marched into the Ruhr, the industrial heart of Germany. The Germans met French occupation with a campaign of passive resistance. The government terminated all deliveries of reparation commodities; it forbade the inhabitants of the Ruhr to pay customs duties or taxes to the French, or to assist the army of occupation in any way. Those who lost their jobs by the paralysis of Ruhr industries were given state aid. French and Belgian reprisals took the form of a ban on exports of Ruhr manufactures; leading citizens were expelled, others fined or interned; the press was censored and private property was seized. Bloody clashes occurred between Allied troops and Germans.

This state of siege had disastrous consequences for Germany. The halting of Ruhr industries caused unemployment not only in the Ruhr but in other parts of the country dependent upon products from this region. Relief payments to Ruhr inhabitants, coupled with other financial burdens, severely strained the German treasury and caused the mark to decline precipitously.   On August 8, 1923 it reached 5 million to the dollar. Chancellor Cuno's die-hard government was finally replaced by a conciliatory Cabinet headed by Gustav Stresemann, a statesman who inaugurated a new and happier era of Franco-German relations.   On September 26 the German government abandoned passive resistance; two days later the ban on reparation deliveries was lifted.   France was victorious.

The occupation of the Ruhr had far-reaching results.   It mitigated German stubbornness in regard to collaboration with France, but at the same time it proved to France that the coercion of a hapless foe did not bring monetary gain.   The costs of the Allied occupation almost equalled the sums exacted from the Ruhr.

The Dawes Plan.   The intense strain was finally relieved by French acquiescence to a suggestion, first advanced in December, 1922 by Secretary of State Hughes, that committees of financial and economic experts be appointed to investigate Germany's capacity to pay.   One committee, headed by the American banker Charles G. Dawes, studied the stabilization of German currency.   Another, headed by the Englishman Reginald McKenna, was " to consider the means of estimating the amount of German exported capital and bringing it back to Germany."   The Dawes Committee met in Paris on January 14, 1924 and reported its conclusions on April 9, 1924.   Although the consultants were not authorized to determine a maximum reparations bill, they recommended a series of annual payments starting in 1925–1926 at $250,000,000 (1,000,000,000 gold marks) and rising gradually to $625,000,000 (2,500,000,000 gold marks) in 1927–1928; thereafter payments would be determined by " an index of German prosperity."   The Committee recommended a foreign loan of $200,000,000 — of which $110,000,000 was later subscribed by the United States — to meet the gold reserve of a new Reichsbank which would undertake to stabilize the mark.   The directorate of the bank was to consist of seven Germans and seven foreigners.   The Dawes Report urged the speedy evacuation of the Ruhr in order to restore Germany's economic sovereignty and permit the new plan to operate without delay.   Again France hesitated, but by August 30, 1924 it was agreed that future defaults could be declared only by unanimous vote of the Reparations Commission. The Dawes Plan went into effect on September 1, 1924 under the supervision of an American Agent-General, S. Parker Gilbert.   The last French and Belgian troops left the Ruhr July 31, 1925.

The Young Plan.   The absence of a reasonable debt total which Germany could aspire to pay was a formidable psychological barrier to the successful fulfilment of the Dawes Plan.   Indeed, it soon became apparent that Germany could not meet the annuities, even with American loans.   Her request for an examination of capacity to pay resulted in the designation of another committee which met in Paris on February 11, 1929 under the chairmanship of Owen D. Young. The Young Plan, accepted by the powers on June 9, 1929, scaled down the reparations account to $26,500,-000,000 (106,000,000,000 gold marks), payable in varying annuities in 58 years and integrated with Allied debt payments to the United States (discussed in the next chapter); German remittances were to equal 65 per cent of these payments. The index of prosperity was abandoned and the Reparations Commission was abolished. A Bank for International Settlements was established at Basle, Switzerland, to act as trustee for the creditors.[9] Germany recovered financial autonomy and the Allies agreed to final evacuation of the Rhineland by June 30, 1930, five years before the date stipulated in the Versailles Treaty. By this time the Young Plan was in operation.

Termination of Reparations. The world economic crisis caused the final breakdown in the payment of reparations and inter-Allied war debts to which they were linked. American loans to Germany ceased in 1930. In 1931 there was a financial panic in Germany, and the powers accepted President Hoover's suggestion for a moratorium on inter-governmental debts and reparation payments beginning with July 1, 1931. An international conference at Lausanne in June–July 1932 decided to abolish reparations altogether, contingent upon "the solution of the debt problem with relation to the United States." But the United States refused to wipe out the war debts. Some of the Allied states continued to make payments on their debts to the United States until 1933. Reparations were dead, and so in effect were the war debts.

The total payments made by Germany under the various schemes, including deliveries in kind, aggregated about 17,000,000,000 marks ($4,-250,000,000), a fraction of the total Allied war costs. This sum was more than offset by American, British, and other Allied loans to Germany from 1924 to 1930, which, including short-term deposits, totaled 27,000-000,000 marks ($4,750,000,000). Neither the principal nor interest on these loans has been paid since 1931.

Although the reparations system, like the territorial settlements, was based on the desire to promote international amity, the planning and execution of the successive debt plans provoked considerable rancor and animosity. Debts of any nature are not conducive to friendship, among individuals or nations. Default both embitters the creditor and kindles within the debtor a feeling of estrangement. The post-war experiences of Europe and America have amply demonstrated this truism.

The Search for Security

The League of Nations. The League of Nations represented the most conspicuous international effort to preserve peace since the Holy Alliance.

Its proponents were convinced that the League would inspire international cooperation, cow aggressors, and safeguard small as well as Great Powers. As President Wilson said in his report to the Peace Conference of February 14, 1919:

" Armed forced is in the background of this programme, but it is in the background, and if the moral force of the world will not suffice, the physical force of the world shall. But that is the last resort, because this is intended as a constitution of peace, not as a league of war. . . . It is a definite guarantee by word against aggression. . . . It is a League which can be used for cooperation in any international matter." [10]

The League and the Powers. At its zenith in 1927 the League had 56 members, of which 45 were small powers. The Great Powers — France, Germany, Great Britain, Italy, and Japan — dominated the League: that is, approximately 20 per cent of the sovereign members in 1927 exerted a controlling influence. This inequality was frankly recognized in the Covenant, for example in Article IV, which conceded to the Great Powers permanent seats in the Council. Inequality was generally tolerated because the weaker states had few policies in common and were united only in regarding the League as an instrument for preserving their security. Their very weakness prevented the acceptance or assignment of responsibilities by the League. Without the Great Powers, the League would be a mere debating society. When the powers agreed upon any matter, the handling of it was simple; when they disagreed, the united opposition of the small states was futile. Those who would have to bear the brunt of action shaped the League's policies.

Inherent Weaknesses of the League. We have already touched upon some of the inherent weaknesses of the League. The renowned Article X, in which

" the Members of the League undertake to respect and preserve as against external aggression the territorial integrity and existing political independence of all Members " [11]

constituted in practice a moral, not legal, obligation. Article XI, which announced that

" Any war or threat of war, whether immediately affecting any of the Members of the League or not, is hereby declared a matter of concern to the whole League, and the League shall take any action that may be deemed wise and effectual to safeguard the peace of nations "

was narrowly construed in that " any action that might be deemed wise and effectual " which the League should take in the event of international friction was limited to peaceful measures. The threat of sanctions (embodied in Article XVI) against any member of the League who should "resort to war in disregard of its covenants" depended in actuality not on the League as a body but on the independent decision of each member state. Delegates to the Council and Assembly were unable to commit their governments, which reserved complete freedom of action. The political effectiveness of the League, therefore, was measured only by the extent to which the home governments were willing to instruct their delegates to take strong positions at Geneva.

In 1923 the League Assembly adopted a Draft Treaty of Mutual Assistance which branded aggressive war as an international crime and authorized regional alliances; the British Empire was conspicuous in its opposition to this measure. In 1924 the Geneva Protocol for the Pacific Settlement of International Disputes was accepted by about twenty states. Arbitration was integrated with security, and an aggressor was defined as a state resorting to force without first seeking peaceful settlement.[12] Again Great Britain interposed objections, partly on the ground that the United States would not be bound because it did not belong to the League, and partly because it was not anxious to accept additional responsibilities. From these and other instances in which the Great Powers showed reluctance to increase their obligations, we may conclude that the basic difficulty was to be found not in the phraseology or interpretation of the Covenant but in the absence of sincere devotion to the principles upon which the League was founded.

The United States and the League. It has frequently been asserted that the failure of the United States to abide by Wilson's commitments to the Peace Conference devitalized the League from the very beginning.[13] This implies that the United States is responsible for the weaknesses of the League. But while it may be true that American membership would have contributed a spirit of detachment and moderation to the Geneva deliberations, it is difficult to prove that our presence would have sufficed to overcome the Great Powers' reluctance to rely upon collective security. Moreover, although the United States did not join the League, it participated in its social and humanitarian activities.[14] In addition, the United States accepted full membership in the International Labour Organization.

Locarno. Outside the League numerous bilateral and multilateral agreements were signed by the powers to bolster the status quo and preserve the fabric of peace. Much hope was reposed in the Locarno Treaties of October 16, 1925 which guaranteed the Franco-German and German-Belgian frontiers. These states solemnly declared "that they will in no case attack or invade each other or resort to war against each other" except in "the exercise of the right of legitimate defense," in "pursuance of Article 16 of the Covenant," or other action to implement League policy. France agreed to aid Czechoslovakia and Poland in circumstances arising " from a failure to observe the undertakings " between them and Germany. Four arbitration treaties were signed by Germany: with Belgium, Czechoslovakia, France, and Poland. Great Britain and Italy served as blanket guarantors. Germany expressed satisfaction with her western frontiers, but refused to commit herself at Locarno to a pact fixing her eastern boundaries. The Locarno Treaties paved the way for Germany's admission to the League on September 9, 1926. After considerable wrangling by Brazil, Poland, and Spain, all of whom aspired to the same honor, Germany was granted a permanent seat on the Council. This incident was a direct cause for Brazil's withdrawal from the League on June 13, 1928. Poland was persuaded to accept a semi-permanent place in the Council, and Spain was caressed into silence.

The World Court. President Wilson regarded the creation of a World Court as a necessary adjunct of the League of Nations. In 1907, at the Second Hague Conference, Theodore Roosevelt's hopes for a Permanent Court of Arbitral Justice had been frustrated by the inability of the small and Great Powers to agree upon a basis of representation. That difficulty was circumvented by the Permanent Court of International Justice established at The Hague in January, 1921. The World Court utilized an ingenious scheme for selecting jurists from both the members of the Permanent Court of Arbitration (Hague Tribunal) and the League of Nations. The jurisdiction of the Court comprises all cases which the parties refer to it and all matters specially provided for in treaties and conventions. The jurists are guided in their decisions by international customs, international conventions, the general principles of international law, and judicial decisions of national courts.[15]

About sixty states have adhered to the Statute of the Court; about forty have accepted, with more or less reservation, compulsory jurisdiction in disputes embracing " (a) the interpretation of a treaty; (b) any question of international law; (c) the existence of any fact which, if established, would constitute a breach of an international obligation." [16] Advisory opinions may be requested by the League. All questions are decided by a majority of the judges, with no appeal from their verdict. The United States refused to accept membership in this useful agency of international peace. It is pleasant to relate that the Court's judgments and advisory opinions have been accepted in good faith and only rarely have the judges been accused of placing national prejudices above juridical logic.

European Pacts. That the nations doubted the efficacy of the League and the Court in providing security against aggression is disclosed by the additional machinery and protective devices which were set up during the decade 1920–1930. When the United States and Great Britain refused to ratify the Guarantee Treaty of 1919, France turned for security to a deliberate program of converting the League into an instrument of its foreign policy. The French government foresaw clearly that a rejuvenated Germany would demand annexation of Austria and recovery of the Germanic lands incorporated into Czechoslovakia and Poland. Growing constantly more powerful, the Reich would menace both French and European security. Until Great Britain and the United States recognized this situation, and were prepared to use the League machinery to maintain the peace of Europe and compel observance of international obligations, France was resolved to find other means of attaining her ends. She formed a *cordon sanitaire*, or series of alliances with Belgium, Czechoslovakia, Poland, Rumania, and Yugoslavia, designed to " encircle " Germany and prevent disturbance of the status quo.

Russia and the Baltic states entered into numerous conferences and pacts; Italy, Turkey, and the Balkan countries not enmeshed in the French system made similar arrangements.[17]

British Imperial Conferences. Related to this European search for security were the British Imperial Conferences, beginning with the London Conference of June 20–August 5, 1920, in which it was agreed that the Dominions should participate in the formulation of Imperial foreign policy. Traditional British reluctance to assume responsibilities on the continent of Europe was now endorsed by the Dominions' insistence that no obligations be accepted without their prior consent. This, in fact, was consistent with the basic tenet of British foreign policy: to maintain a balance of power in Europe, with substantial parity between opposing groups. At the second Imperial Conference of 1923 it was decided

" that any of the Governments of the Empire contemplating the negotiation of a treaty should give due consideration to its possible effect upon other Governments and should take steps to inform Governments likely to be interested of its intention." [18]

The Conference of 1926 adopted the Balfour Report which declared that Great Britain and the Dominions

" are autonomous Communities within the British Empire, equal in status, in no way subordinate one to another in any respect of their domestic or external affairs, though united by a common allegiance to the Crown. . . . And, though every Dominion is now, and must always remain, the sole judge of the nature and the extent of its cooperation, no common cause will, in our opinion, be thereby imperilled." [19]

The new status of the Dominions was legalized in the Statute of Westminster passed by the British Parliament on December 11, 1931.

The Briand-Kellogg Pact. On April 6, 1927, the anniversary of our entry into the World War, Aristide Briand, French Foreign Minister, gave a significant interview to the Associated Press correspondents in Paris.

" Ten years have passed [he said] since the American nation, with magnificent enthusiasm, associated itself with the Allied Nations for the defense of imperilled liberty. . . . France would be willing to subscribe publicly with the United States to any mutual engagement tending to outlaw war, to use an American expression, as between these two countries." [20]

On June 20 the American Ambassador in Paris transmitted to Washington a French draft of a proposed treaty, but the American government was not receptive to a bilateral commitment. On December 27, 1927 Secretary of State Kellogg suggested to France

" that the two Governments . . . might make a more signal contribution to world peace by joining in an effort to obtain the adherence of all of the principal powers of the world to a declaration denouncing war as an instrument of national policy." [21]

France, although hoping to enroll the United States in her efforts to prop up the status quo, marshaled an array of objections to Kellogg's proposals, based upon her obligations under the Covenant of the League. Secretary Kellogg retorted that if League members could negotiate bilateral pacts, as proposed by France, surely they could expand them into multilateral agreements. At length Briand agreed to suggest immediately to the German, British, Italian, and Japanese governments that they join in a contemplated new treaty, restricted to the outlawing of wars of aggression. The responses of the other governments contained reservations similar to Great Britain's suggestion that the Pact be restricted to " certain regions of the world the welfare and integrity of which constitute a special and vital interest for our peace and safety." The Kellogg-Briand Pact was formally signed at Paris on August 27, 1928 by Belgium, Czechoslovakia, France, Germany, Great Britain, Italy, Japan, Poland, and the United States. By July 1, 1935 sixty-one countries had ratified the obligation " to condemn recourse to war for the solution of international controversies, and renounce it as an instrument of national policy in their relations with one another." [22]

By its obvious phraseology, this treaty was designed to close the " gaps " in Article XV of the League Covenant which failed to make specific provision for states that refused to comply with the Council's recommendations in the settlement of any dispute. The United States Senate in approving the Pact added a reservation which sapped its strength: " The treaty does not provide sanctions, express or implied. Should any signatory violate the terms . . . there is no obligation . . . upon the other signers . . . to engage in punitive or coercive measures." [23] Thus the Kellogg-Briand Pact had a purely negative meaning, and implementation of its high-sounding aims depended solely on the moral fiber of the signatories. The Kellogg-Briand Pact indeed became but a straw in the gale of aggression which beset the world in the 1930's. Its sole effect, perhaps, was to dispense with declarations of war, since no adherent to the Pact wished to be stigmatized as an aggressor.

The Limitation of Armaments

The Treaties of Peace, 1919. In the Peace Treaties of 1919 the Allies assumed that the Central Powers were the arch-villains of European society. Restoration and preservation of peace could be achieved only by drastically disarming those who were allegedly responsible for the war. The need for universal limitation of armaments was reaffirmed in Article VIII of the League Covenant:

" The maintenance of peace requires the reduction of national armaments to the lowest point consistent with national safety and the enforcement by common action of international obligations. The Council, taking account of the geographical situation and circumstances of each State, shall formulate plans for such reduction for the consideration and action of the several Governments." [24]

The manufacture and distribution of munitions and implements of war were deplored, and members of the League undertook to exchange full and frank information concerning their respective armaments and convertible industries.

We already have alluded to the military restrictions imposed upon the defeated powers, including the demilitarization of the Rhineland, while at the same time the victors and their satellite states were permitted to retain large armaments. This discrimination, in fact, demonstrated to Germany the fundamental insincerity of such Allied assertions as were embodied in Article VIII.

The Washington Conference. To forestall another armaments race like that preceding the World War, the powers gladly availed themselves of the United States' invitation to attend a disarmament conference at Washington. It was hoped to discuss all forms of armaments at the sessions which began on November 11, 1921 but the experience of the Temporary Mixed Commission in 1920 and 1921 had proven that it was impossible to achieve agreement in the matter of land forces. In his opening address Secretary of State Hughes presented a specific agenda which took the British and Japanese delegates somewhat aback: he suggested

" 1. That all capital ship building programs, either actual or projected, should be abandoned;
2. That further reduction should be made through the scrapping of certain of the older ships;

3. That, in general, regard should be had to the existing naval strength of the powers concerned;

4. That the capital ship tonnage should be used as the measurement of strength for navies and a proportionate allowance of auxiliary combatant craft prescribed." [25]

Proceeding to details, Hughes listed the ships which Great Britain, Japan, and the United States should scrap. This bold proposal was accepted after much wrangling. Great Britain, the United States, and Japan agreed on a ratio of 5:5:3 respectively for capital ships (battleships). France and Italy accepted ratios of 1.67 each. It proved impossible to agree on the limitation of auxiliary craft, such as submarines, cruisers, destroyers, and smaller combatant types, chiefly because of the conflicting claims of Great Britain and France as to their needs of such vessels in guarding their commercial ships in time of war. France demanded a submarine fleet of 90,000 tons. With this fleet so near the shores of England, the latter reserved the right to build any auxiliary craft necessary to deal with the situation. Japan could accept the smaller ratio because, as noted below, British and American promises not to build naval bases close to her shores gave her supremacy in eastern Asiatic waters. France, though sensitive to the fact that she was allotted a smaller ratio, accepted it because it represented considerably greater tonnage than she possessed at the time. Italy demanded only parity with France.

The strength of nations depends upon incalculable factors fully as much as on material elements which can be stated in an equation. Hence even the 5:5:3:1.67:1.67 ratios could not be applied exactly. Great Britain actually retained 558,950 tons in fifteen capital ships, whereas the American figure was 527,850 tons for fifteen ships, the difference being conceded to the British navy because some of its craft were slightly older than ours. By 1929 the discrepancy was 76,250 tons in Britain's favor, but by 1942 absolute parity was expected.

The Treaty signed in 1922 fixed 35,000 tons as the maximum standard displacement for capital ships, none of which should carry guns in excess of 16 inches. Japan was allotted 315,000 tons; France and Italy 175,000 tons apiece. Aircraft carriers were limited to 135,000 tonnage each for Great Britain and the United States, 60,000 for France and Italy, and 81,000 for Japan, with individual ships restricted to 27,000 tons and 8-inch guns. A specific exception was made to accommodate the U.S.S. *Saratoga* and the U.S.S. *Lexington*, each of 33,000 tons. The Washington Treaty sanctioned the status quo with regard to existing fortifications and naval bases in the Pacific Ocean, but permitted expansion of facilities in Japan, Alaska, Hawaii, the Panama Canal Zone, Hongkong, Canada, Australia, New Zealand, Formosa, and the Kurile, Bonin, Loochoo, and Pescadores Islands. The use of poison gas was prohibited, but a ban on submarines as commerce raiders was balked by France. A ten-year holiday in the construction of capital ships was accepted by all signatories.

In the Four Power Treaty concluded at the Washington Conference (December 13, 1921), France, Great Britain, Japan, and the United States pledged themselves to respect each other's rights in the Pacific for a period of ten years. A Nine Power Pact was signed on February 6, 1922 by Belgium, China, France, Great Britain, Italy, Japan, the Netherlands, Portugal, and the United States to respect " the sovereignty, independence, and territorial and administrative integrity of China " and

" to provide the fullest and most unembarrassed opportunity to China to develop and maintain for herself an effective and stable government; to use their influence for the purpose of effectually establishing and maintaining the principle of equal opportunity for the commerce and industry of all nations throughout the territory of China; to refrain from taking advantage of conditions in China in order to seek special rights or privileges." [26]

The United States and Britain thus allowed Japan naval supremacy in eastern Asia in return for a Japanese promise to preserve the territorial integrity of China.

The Washington Conference was the most successful of all post-war disarmament conferences, chiefly because it took place when memories of the World War were fresh, and when Britain, France, Japan, and Italy, economically exhausted, welcomed a respite in the construction of expensive ships. Yet the only achievement of the Conference was in limiting capital ship construction, and although this was important, it was in time to be nullified by the resumption of competitive building in the unrestricted classes and by the growth of air power as a factor in warfare.

The Geneva Conference. In order to extend the limitation to other categories of naval vessels than capital ships, President Coolidge issued invitations to a conference which convened at Geneva on June 20, 1927. France and Italy declined to participate, the former on the pretext that outside conferences would hinder the disarmament efforts of the League, the latter on the ground that her exposed geographical position permitted of no further naval limitation. Japan acted as an interested observer in the highly technical Anglo-American discussions of cruisers, tonnage, and gun-caliber. The British emphasized their need for small, fast cruisers carrying 6-inch ordnance, particularly adaptable for servicing by a network of naval bases throughout the world. The Americans preferred large cruisers of about 10,000 tons, carrying 8-inch guns and having a larger range of operation from widely scattered bases. The Conference adjourned on August 5 without agreement. Its unique achievement was to focus public attention on the futility of expecting naval experts, in the capacity of delegates, to abandon their professional convictions or abolish their jobs.

Disarmament Efforts of the League. In accordance with Article IX of the Covenant, the League Council in 1920 appointed a Permanent Advisory Commission of military, naval, and air corps experts to advise upon reduction of armaments and investigate the armament status of applicants for League membership. This procedure elicited from Salvador de Madariaga the penetrating comment that: " It was as foolish to expect a disarmament convention from such a commission as a declaration of atheism from a commission of clergymen."

The Temporary Mixed Commission. Upon the recommendation of the First Assembly in September, 1920 a new commission of sixteen civilians and six experts drawn from the Permanent Advisory Commission was created, and the secretariats of the two commissions were incorporated into the Disarmament Section of the League Secretariat. During 1922 the League studied Lord Esher's Plan for Standing Armies, under which land and air forces would be organized in units of 30,000 men and assigned to countries according to their geographical position and resources. For example, France would have six units; Italy and Poland four; and Belgium three. Reserve classes and colonial troops would be excluded from this calculation. The Plan was rejected as impractical.

Acting upon the French thesis that security must precede disarmament, the Third Assembly adopted Resolution XIV in September, 1922:

" In the present state of the world many Governments would be unable to accept the responsibility for a serious reduction of armaments unless they received in exchange a satisfactory guarantee of the safety of their country." [27]

The problem of effecting a satisfactory guarantee was referred to the Temporary Mixed Commission, which in turn followed some suggestions of Lord Robert Cecil in submitting to the Fourth Assembly in 1923 a Draft Treaty of Mutual Assistance for victims of aggression. This treaty, like the subsequent Geneva Protocol of 1924, failed of adoption.

The Rome Conference of 1924, called to discuss the possibility of extending the principles of naval limitation adopted at Washington to all countries having capital ships, brought no tangible results, and the projected " International Conference for the Reduction of Armaments " scheduled to meet at Geneva in June, 1925 was called off after the Geneva Protocol failed of adoption.

The Preparatory Commission for the Disarmament Conference. Upon the suggestion of the Sixth Assembly in 1925, the Temporary Mixed Commission was replaced by the Preparatory Commission, membership in which was extended to Germany, Russia, and the United States. At the first session, May 18, 1926, the "security group" led by France and several continental states insisted that military and economic guarantees must precede disarmament; that all types of armament are interdependent and cannot be discussed separately; that any further naval limitation must be considered in global tonnage; that land reserves cannot be limited, and international supervision and control of armaments must be established. The "disarmament group" led by Great Britain and non-European states believed that excessive armaments foster insecurity; that the only feasible procedure is to approach naval, air, and land armaments separately; that trained land reserves must be limited, and reliance should be placed in the good faith of signatories, without supervision or control. The British and French draft proposals presented on March 21, 1927 agreed only on the need for centering efforts on limitation instead of reduction of armaments.

The Russian delegate, Maxim Litvinoff, on November 27, 1927 spectacularly proposed total disarmament within one year: the complete abolition of armed forces; destruction of all weapons, munitions and military supplies; discontinuance of military training, demolition of forts, bases, and war-industry plants; dismissal of general staffs and war ministries; and prohibition of war propaganda. Such forthright measures were entirely beyond the Commission's comprehension, and consideration of them was postponed until the fifth session in March 1928, on the pretexts that the time was inopportune and that they contravened the League Covenant which presumes the use of force. Furthermore, the British suspected Russia of an ulterior motive: total disarmament would remove the obstacles to world revolution.

On March 15, 1928 Litvinoff castigated the League for indulging in mere theoretical discussions and arguments about disarmament, and then formally presented a draft convention providing for a gradual reduction of armaments within four years; two categories of naval police forces; four categories of military police; prohibition of chemical and air armaments; reduction of defense budgets; and a Permanent International Commission of Control. The Preparatory Commission, with the exception of the German and Turkish delegates, quickly rejected Litvinoff's plan on the ground that it failed to take geography and degree of industrialization sufficiently into account.

Anglo-French Naval Accord. About the same time, conversations were initiated by Great Britain and France, in correlation with negotiations which culminated in the Kellogg-Briand Pact, regarding mutual concessions on naval tonnage and army reserves. France had urged total or global reduction, with each country free to apportion its allotment among large and small cruisers, destroyers, and submarines. Britain preferred limitations in category tonnage with specific allotments to each type of craft. An opportunity for compromise lay in the British desire to count army reserves with land forces, to which France objected.

Before announcing the Anglo-French naval accord, the British government desired to reach a preliminary agreement with the United States. The lid was blown off, however, on September 21, 1928 by Hearst's New York *American* which published a report of the secret Anglo-French conversations, procured by its correspondent J. T. Horan from a French journalist, Roger Deleplanque, who had been permitted by M. de Noblet of the Quai d'Orsay to read a copy of the accord. Horan is said to have paid $10,000 for the papers, the publication of which resulted in France's deportation of Hearst reporters and the hasty release by the Quai d'Orsay of the entire correspondence.

The Anglo-French naval accord provided for the limitation of capital ships and aircraft carriers of more than 10,000 tons, of other surface vessels carrying between 6- and 8-inch ordnance, and of submarines of over 600 tons. No limitation was placed on land reserves. The United States notified Great Britain on September 28, 1928 that

" This proposal is obviously incompatible with the American position at the Three-Power (Geneva) Conference. . . . It puts the United States at a decided disadvantage . . . (and) discards altogether the principle of limitation as applied to important combatant types of vessels. . . . Limitation of this type only would add enormously to the comparative offensive power of a nation possessing a large merchant tonnage on which preparation may be made in times of peace for mounting six inch guns." [28]

The Gibson Proposal. At the sixth session of the Preparatory Commission, on April 22, 1929, the American delegate, Hugh Gibson, advanced a suggestion for " tonnage transfer " as a concession to France. Upon due notice an agreed percentage of naval tonnage might be transferred from one category to another: i.e., suppose 300,000 tons were allotted respectively to Great Britain and the United States, 100,000 tons for large cruisers and 200,000 tons for small cruisers. A 25 per cent transfer allowance would permit the United States to build an additional 25,000 tons of large cruisers by reducing its small cruiser tonnage to 175,000. Likewise, the British navy could transfer 25,000 tons to small cruisers by cutting its large cruiser tonnage to 75,000. A system of index numbers was proposed as a measuring stick, embracing such factors as size, displacement, age, ordnance, speed, and cruising radius of vessels. For example, " 100 " would designate a 10,000-ton cruiser with 8-inch guns; " 70 " would represent a 7,000-ton cruiser with 6-inch guns, and " 55 " might be applied to the same cruiser when it became obsolete. The plan could be expanded to include naval bases, merchant marine, and oil reserves. Sir Austen Chamberlain, the British delegate, responded favorably, but the Commission recessed on May 6, in anticipation of the approaching naval conference, without taking action on the Gibson proposal.

The London Naval Conference of 1930. Following Anglo-American acceptance of the principle of naval parity, the British government issued invitations to a naval conference in London in January, 1930. President Hoover, on November 11, 1929, expressed our willingness to reduce naval strength in proportion to that of other powers. France accepted the invitation but rejected the prospect of parity with Italy, affirming that its naval needs were determined by Empire requirements and not by the Washington ratios. Italy unreservedly accepted the invitation, and Japan agreed to attend, hoping for a 70 per cent cruiser ratio and retention of submarines.

At the Conference the British delegation proposed the abolition of battleships, abolition or " humanization " of submarine warfare, and reduction in tonnage and size of aircraft carriers. The United States declined to consider the elimination of battleships, asserting that competition in new designs would follow, and that it was politically and economically expedient to retain existing types and postpone replacements. France and Japan objected to the abolition of submarines, and the United States was unwilling to reduce aircraft carrier tonnage below 135,000, of which the *Lexington* and *Saratoga* consumed 66,000.

France, on February 13, demanded a navy of 725,000 tons, in contrast to her 1930 total of 681,808 tons afloat and under construction. That in itself was not startling, but as Italy insisted upon parity with France the prospective total of 1,450,000 tons alarmed Great Britain, who would have to build more ships to maintain its policy of keeping abreast of the combined fleets of any two European powers. The United States and Great Britain had agreed upon parity; the 1930 British tonnage was 1,332,566. Japan finally compromised on a 67 per cent ratio with the United States.

The London Naval Treaty of 1930. In the London Naval Treaty signed on April 22, 1930 Great Britain, the United States, Japan, France, and Italy agreed to a holiday in capital ship construction until December 31, 1936. Great Britain promised to scrap five capital ships, the United States three, and Japan one, in accordance with the new ratio of 10:10:6.7. Guns on aircraft carriers were limited to 6.1 inches, submarines to 2,000 tons with 5.1-inch ordnance, except that each signatory was permitted to have not more than three 2,800-ton submarines with 6.1-inch guns.

Cruisers, destroyers, and submarines were allotted as follows:

	British Empire	United States	Japan
Cruisers with guns above 6.1-inch calibre:	15 (146,800 tons)	18 (180,000 tons)	12 (408,400 tons)
Cruisers with guns of less than 6.1-inch calibre:	192,200 tons	143,000 tons	100,450 tons
Destroyers:	150,000 tons	150,000 tons	105,000 tons
Submarines:	52,700 tons	52,700 tons	52,700 tons

Since France and Italy abstained from signing this part of the Treaty, the renowned Escalator Clause (Article XXI) was inserted permitting naval construction beyond established ratios if new ships were laid down by any other powers.

Before leaving the analysis of the Treaty, the problem of parity might be scrutinized. Due to relative factors, such as the ratio of distance from bases to the fighting strength of an adversary, parity is largely illusory. All American warships use oil, which affords a wider cruising radius than coal, and the fifteen American capital ships carried 64 more guns than the fifteen British. American anti-aircraft and anti-torpedo armor protection was regarded as superior to those on British ships, but the British *Hood*, *Nelson*, and *Rodney* were in 1930 the most powerful battleships afloat. In view of these facts, how can parity be attained?

The Final Session of the Preparatory Commission. In November, 1930 the Preparatory Commission ended its five years of labor with a resolution to submit to the Disarmament Conference a draft convention dealing only with methods of limitation. The discussions, however, had served to crystallize opinion, and ranged the powers in two divergent groups. One group held that it was necessary to limit armaments quantitatively. The other or qualitative group maintained that certain types of weapons are particularly adaptable in penetrating defense works and hence heavy artillery, large tanks, and long-range aircraft must be banned. These vital issues were passed on to the long-awaited General Disarmament Conference.

The General Disarmament Conference. February 2, 1932 was set for the opening of the Conference, and members of the League were asked to file armament data as a basis for discussion. On October 2, 1931 a proposal for an arms truce of one year was circulated, to which forty-seven nations subscribed, effective November 1, 1931.

The grouping of the fifty-seven participants in the Conference was similar to that of the Preparatory Commission. France, Belgium, Poland,

and the Little Entente deplored the steady deterioration of the League's efficacy and advocated an international police force with preventive and repressive functions. Only states willing to place their facilities at the League's disposal should be permitted to possess aggressive armaments. Germany, Italy, Russia, Spain, and Denmark advocated equality of armaments, and Russia again argued for total disarmament on the assumption that prohibition of weapons to all nations would be more conducive to security than increasing them under any controls that could be devised. Great Britain and the United States urged proportional reduction; Japan advocated reduction or abolition of weapons to which she was specially vulnerable, such as battleships, large aircraft carriers, poison gas, and airplanes.

After a recess from March 16 to April 11, Hugh Gibson introduced a proposal for the abolition of particularly aggressive weapons, which received British and Swiss support, but André Tardieu objected that aggressive weapons could not be defined, and Germany declared that the plan did not go far enough! Following another adjournment, President Hoover tried to revive the Conference by advocating

" the abolition of all tanks, all chemical warfare, and all large mobile guns. . . . We should accept for all nations a basic police component of soldiers proportionate to the average which was . . . allowed Germany [100,000 for approximately 65,000,000 people]. . . . There should be a reduction of one-third in the strength of all land armies over and above the police component. . . . All bombing planes [should] be abolished. . . . The treaty number and tonnage of battleships shall be reduced by one-third. . . . The treaty tonnage of aircraft carriers, cruisers, and destroyers shall be reduced by one-fourth . . . [and of] submarines . . . by one-third." [29]

This radical plan was approved only by Italy, and on April 29 a third recess began after the armaments truce was extended to March 1, 1933.

The German Withdrawals. Finding it impossible to persuade France and other states to recognize Germany's claim to arms equality on whatever basis the Conference might fix for all nations, the German Delegation served notice, on July 23, that its further participation would depend upon a satisfactory settlement of this issue. To forestall German withdrawal, the French Premier Herriot drafted a scheme for substituting militia for professional armies in countries defeated in the World War. Security would be enhanced by treaties of mutual assistance modeled on the Locarno Pacts, by compulsory arbitration agreements, and by thorough enforcement of League sanctions. Germany was promised equality of arms, and the Conference resumed its session on February 2, 1933. But in the meantime Adolf Hitler had acquired power and the success of the Conference became more problematical than ever. Great Britain was unwilling to assume the continental commitments embodied in the Herriot Plan, and espoused the MacDonald Plan of March 16, 1933 providing for a uniform short-term continental militia, the increase of German land forces to the French level, and abolition of the Versailles armament restrictions. President Franklin D. Roosevelt appealed on May 16 for " complete elimination of all offensive weapons," acceptance of the MacDonald Plan, and " a solemn and definite pact of non-aggression " which received Hitler's endorsement, but France persisted in seeking retention of existing armament levels under international supervision. When the German request for " token arms," or samples of small defensive tanks, pursuit planes, and anti-aircraft guns, was denied, the Germans summarily withdrew on October 14, 1933, announcing at the same time their intention to resign from the League of Nations in 1935. Since without German participation disarmament was unthinkable, the Conference had been dealt its death blow.

The Collapse of the Conference. Reconvening on October 16, the delegates found themselves devoid of enthusiasm or energy. The national plebiscite of November 12, 1933 had endorsed Hitler's policies, so that his government could declare on December 18 its intention to rearm Germany. On April 20, 1934 France informed the British government that further disarmament negotiations were impossible in the face of Germany's violations of treaties, and on May 29 the Conference adjourned indefinitely.

The London Naval Conference of 1935. With the approaching expiration of the ratios and limitations of 1922 and 1930, Japan demanded defensive equality which, in effect, would amount to superiority because of geographical and other factors. In the light of Japan's aggression in Manchuria, and her formulation of a " Monroe Doctrine " for eastern Asia, the other powers were less disposed than ever to concede her naval parity which would render them less able to challenge any further moves she might make toward domination of China and the Far East. Such a move would also confirm the status of Manchukuo, the puppet state that Japan had carved out of Manchuria, and would remove the League's stigma on the Manchurian invasion. Accordingly, the Japanese government tried to attach France and Italy to a joint denunciation of ratios, but France on December 1 and Italy on December 4, 1934 declined to hearken to Japan's plea unless all signatories indicated a similar desire. On December 29 Japan gave notice of her intention to renounce the 1930 Naval Treaty. Six months later Great Britain invoked the Escalator Clause. By this time the actual naval ratios were: Great Britain, 10; United States, 7.46; Japan, 6.62; France, 3.78; Italy, 3.01.

Another naval conference convened at London on December 9, 1935, consisting of delegates from the United States, Great Britain, Japan, France, and Italy. Each delegation reaffirmed its nation's previously stated attitudes. Japan withdrew on January 15, 1936, with the statement that existing naval treaties no longer afforded her security.

The London Naval Treaty of 1936. On March 25, 1936 Great Britain, France, and the United States signed a new naval treaty. Great Britain and the United States undertook to maintain the Washington ratio by the simple expedient of outbuilding Japan. Parity was not mentioned in the treaty, but was retained in a supplementary exchange of notes. The only constructive measures of the London Treaty of 1936 constituted an agreement about tonnage and the size of guns on warships. No capital ship of less than 17,500 tons would be laid down until January 1, 1943; this was to prevent the competition in new designs. The signatories agreed to exchange information annually and to give four months' notice of construction programs until the expiration of the Treaty on December 31, 1942.

A Protocol of June 30, 1938 was signed by France, Great Britain, and the United States raising the maximum size of battleships to 45,000 tons.

The Failure to Disarm. Fifteen years of discussions and numerous conferences failed to bring substantial reductions in the world's armaments. Political and economic insecurity, the specter of a rearmed Germany forcing other nations to disgorge their World War conquests, the expansion of Japan in Asia, the glaring impotence of the League — these and other factors account for the negligible results of the disarmament conferences.

The failure to disarm may be laid to the psychosis of insecurity which afflicted the victorious powers, both great and small, as they gradually became aware of the deception of peace and of the insubstantial results of the treaties fashioned in Paris in 1919. Hugh Gibson succinctly described the psychological aspects of disarmament in an address to the alumni of Yale University on June 17, 1930:

"Democracy has developed slowly, has never been perfected and needs constant watching to keep it in operation. The limitation of armaments is similarly of slow growth and its childhood needs constant nursing. I do not expect to see a final solution . . . in my life time, for it is a problem of human relations. . . . The only human problems that can be definitely disposed of are those concerned with the dead. . . . I have great sympathy with those who demand immediate and drastic action. I think I should enjoy dramatic achievements in the control of arms even more than they would, but they have never explained to my satisfaction how we are to force other nations to stop preparing to fight unless we are prepared to fight to make them stop it. . . . They may, after all, live under conditions which make it difficult for them to have the courage of our convictions."

Briand's Plea for a European Union

Along with other French leaders, Aristide Briand believed that the peace might best be promoted by a European Union or creation of intra-League machinery for regional collaboration in such things as intellectual activity, inter-parliamentary relations, foreign trade, public health, labor regulation, finance, and rationalization of industrial and agricultural production. A European Committee could be set up in which each member would have equal voting power, with complete freedom of action to agree or disagree with the resolutions adopted. The Assembly of the League created a Commission of Inquiry for European Union in 1930 but circumstances conspired against the plan, including the rise of National Socialism in Germany, the dismissal of Sir Austen Chamberlain as British Foreign Secretary in 1929, and the death of Briand in March, 1932. Although it was in no way proposed to form a European bloc outside the League, suspicion lurked in the minds of some statesmen that Briand's project was designed either to extend French influence in the League or subordinate the League to some other international agency. Great Britain was reluctant to expand her European contacts at the expense of the Dominions, particularly at the beginning of the depression, and the Briand plan was allowed to drop from view.[30]

Summary

Hopes for a new order ran high immediately after the World War. Oratorical praise for the motives and methods of international behavior eclipsed more sober warnings that the peace was a pipe dream. The governments of the Great Powers failed to frame and execute policies designed to alleviate the burdens of less fortunate states, with the result that these struggling nations began in time to take things into their own hands. International obligations were evaded or defaulted; peoples were persecuted; resentment and suspicion mounted. The Europe of 1920, with its opportunities for constructing a lasting peace and affording the masses a better life, evolved into the Europe of the 1930's, with its pervading gloom and despair. The fruits of the disastrous policies we have sketched in this chapter remain to be gathered.

REFERENCES

1 W. H. Cooke and E. P. Stickney, *Readings in International Relations since 1789*, New York: Harper, 1931, Document No. 100.

2 Schleswig, Allenstein and Marienwerder, Eupen, Malmédy and Moresnet, Klagenfurt, Odenburg (Sopron), and the Saar.

3 W. C. Langsam, *Documents and Readings in the History of Europe since 1918*, Philadelphia: Lippincott, 1939, Document No. 160.

4 *Ibid.*, Document No. 24.

5 J. S. Roucek, "Minorities — A Basis of the Refugee Problem," *Annals of the Academy of Political and Social Science*, May, 1939, pp. 7–8.

6 Alfred Zimmern, *Nationality and Government*, New York: McBride, 1918, p. 46.

7 F. L. Benns, *Europe since 1914*, New York: Crofts, 1939, p. 156.

8 The German mark sank from 56 to the dollar in July, 1922 to 435 to the dollar one year later.

9 W. H. Cooke and E. P. Stickney, *op. cit.*, Document No. 183.

10 W. C. Langsam, *op. cit.*, Document No. 13.

11 For the text of the Covenant see *ibid.*, Document No. 14.

12 W. H. Cooke and E. P. Stickney, *op. cit.*, Document No. 174.

13 P. Haile, "The League of Nations," in F. J. Brown, C. Hodges, and J. S. Roucek, eds., *Contemporary World Politics*, New York: Wiley, 1940, p. 444.

14 For a summary see U. P. Hubbard, "The Co-operation of the United States with the League of Nations and with the International Labour Organization," *International Conciliation*, November, 1931, No. 274, p. 10. Also, L. F. Schmeckebier, *International Organizations in Which the United States Participates*, Washington: Brookings Institution, 1935.

15 M. O. Hudson, *The Permanent Court of International Justice*, New York: Macmillan, 1934, ch. 11.

16 W. C. Langsam, *op. cit.*, Document No. 16.

17 For a complete list see F. H. Simonds and B. Emeny, *The Great Powers in World Politics*, New York: American Book Co., new ed. 1939.

18 W. H. Cooke and E. P. Stickney, *op. cit.*, Document No. 179.

19 W. C. Langsam, *op. cit.*, Document No. 98.

20 Quoted in J. T. Shotwell, *War as an Instrument of National Policy and Its Renunciation in the Pact of Paris*, New York: Harcourt, Brace, 1929, p. 41.

21 W. L. Godshall, *American Foreign Policy: Formulation and Practice*, Ann Arbor: Edwards, 1937, Document No. 383.

22 *Ibid.*, Document No. 386.

23 F. H. Simonds and B. Emeny, *op. cit.*, p. 585.

24 W. C. Langsam, *op. cit.*, Document No. 14.

25 *Ibid.*, Document No. 5.

26 W. H. Cooke and E. P. Stickney, *op. cit.*, Document No. 164(a).

27 B. H. Williams, *The United States and Disarmament*, New York: McGraw-Hill, 1931, p. 245.

28 W. L. Godshall, *op. cit.*, Document No. 397.

29 *Ibid.*, Document No. 410.

30 E. Herriot, *The United States of Europe*, New York: Viking, 1930.

SELECTED BIBLIOGRAPHY

Bergmann, K., *The History of Reparations*, Boston: Houghton Mifflin, 1927. An authoritative German view.

Conwell-Evans, T. P., *The League Council in Action*, London: Oxford, 1929. A careful and interesting study of 23 disputes.

De Madariaga, S., *Disarmament*, New York: Coward-McCann, 1927. A splendid presentation of the issues.

Howard-Ellis, C., *The Origin, Structure and Working of the League of Nations*, Boston: Houghton Mifflin, 1928. A complete and authoritative analysis.

Hudson, M. O., *The Permanent Court of International Justice*, New York: Macmillan, 1934. An authoritative account of the history, workings, and achievements of the Court.

Jessup, P. C., *International Security*, New York: Council for Foreign Relations, 1935. A scholarly analysis.

Lefebure, V., *Scientific Disarmament*, New York: Macmillan, 1931. A chemical-warfare expert's views.

Mitrany, D., *The Problem of International Sanctions*, London: Oxford, 1925. A brief treatment.

Moulton, H. G., and L. Pasvolsky, *War Debts and World Prosperity*, New York: Century, 1932. An excellent summary.

Myers, D. P., *The Reparation Settlement*, Boston: World Peace Foundation, 1930. A collection of documents related to the Young Plan.

Roucek, J. S., *The Working of the Minorities System under the League of Nations*, Prague: Orbis, 1929. A well-documented exposition.

Sprout, Harold and Margaret, *Toward a New Order of Sea Power*, Princeton: Princeton Univ. Press, 1940.

Stone, J., *International Guarantees of Minority Rights*, London: Oxford, 1932. A juridical examination.

Wheeler-Bennett, J., *The Disarmament Deadlock*, London: Routledge, 1934. A readable account.

CHAPTER IV

Economics in the Service of European Politics

The Costs of the War

Before the First World War, European nations vied with one another for the control of sources of raw materials and markets. But their economic systems followed mainly the *laissez-faire* tradition, in which the role of government was minimized in both domestic and foreign trade. The economic functions of production, exchange, and consumption were organized by private individuals or private groups. Governments were not conceived as supervisors of planned national economies, backing up their systems and interests by power politics on an international scale. The peacetime clashes of expanding nations were mere diplomatic skirmishes, quickly forgotten.[1]

Much of the current economic change can be understood as a reaction against the liberalism which has characterized social and economic development of the past two centuries. Philosophically the individual had declared himself free from the arbitrary restraints of church and state. In some parts of the world he had claimed the right to choose and control his government. Freedom of enterprise for the businessman, freedom of choice of occupation for the worker, and free choice among consumers were the economic results of liberalism. Since 1914, however, economic systems have rapidly undergone significant alterations. Many of these changes can be traced to influences generated by the First World War.

Economic Influences of the First World War. When the First World War began no nation expected it to last long. The prevailing attitude was " business as usual." But it presently became apparent that the war would be decided by the productive capacities of the economic systems of the various powers. The immense scale of operations consumed materials at an unprecedented rate. Fighting forces could be maintained only by devoting a maximum of productive capacity to war goods, and curtailing production of civilian goods to a minimum. In short, peacetime economies became war economies; national objectives were put ahead of the rights of individuals, military needs were given priority.

This chapter by John Weldon Hoot, Assistant Professor of Economics, Wharton School of Finance and Commerce, University of Pennsylvania, and J. Marshall Gersting, Associate Professor of Economics, Miami University, Oxford, Ohio.

Wartime Planning. Although the phrase was not then commonly used, *economic planning* had begun on a national and international scale. Governments undertook to control production for war purposes by allocating raw materials, shipping facilities, rail transport, and supplies of labor and capital to those industries considered most essential to the winning of the war. In foreign trade, imports were planned to secure war materials, and exports were so directed as to provide the means of paying for imports. The prices of a wide list of commodities and services were controlled, and such control, once begun, was necessarily increased. For example, if the price of a finished product is fixed, the costs of labor, materials, and capital that go into it must also be set. In this manner the role and influence of government were enlarged to a degree which had never before been considered.

War Costs and Finance. Tremendous financial stakes went into the war. The direct costs of the war totaled $186,000,000,000. This figure does not include indirect costs — losses due to destruction of property on land and sea, the capitalized value of the lost lives of soldiers and civilians, the losses of production opportunities, the cost of war relief, and loss to neutrals. If these are included the total costs amount to more than $340,000,000,000. Even this figure does not include the continuing post-war costs of veterans' care and pensions, and interest on public debts. Such items run into many additional billions.[2]

It must be remembered that most property in the warring countries was privately owned. Governments therefore had to buy their way into control of supply and production, and to do so, they had to acquire purchasing power. This they did in five general ways:

1. The issuance of unbacked or partially backed paper money.
2. Short-term borrowing from banks.
3. The sale of long-term bonds to individuals and financial institutions.
4. Increased taxation.
5. Loans from foreign countries, largely from Great Britain and the United States to the Allied Powers.

Post-war Indebtedness. Since wars could not be financed in any large degree by taxation, the cost of the war was represented mainly by increased national indebtedness. France's debt rose from 6 to 75 billion dollars, England's from 3 to 34 billion dollars, Russia's from 4.4 to 18 billion dollars before the revolution of 1917, and Italy's debt stood at 12 billion dollars by the end of the war. The Central Powers fared no better. The debt of Austria-Hungary increased from 4 to 25 billion dollars and led to serious inflation at the time of the armistice. German war expenditures totaled more than 40 billion dollars, most of which was represented by debt, since little effort was made to finance the war by additional taxation. These debts were accompanied by increasing issues of paper money and the loss of gold reserves. The resulting instability of foreign exchange and government credit contributed heavily to the political and economic disturbances that afflicted Europe in the 1920's and 1930's.[3]

From War Economy to Peace Economy

Economic Consequences of the Peace Treaties. Before 1914 the gradual development of international business had created a system which brought raw materials from the far corners of the world to the manufacturing nations of Europe. Manufactured goods flowed out in return. Because world-wide British commerce made it a recognized, dependable basis of exchange, the pound sterling became a kind of international currency. Old countries with surpluses of savings invested them in the economic enterprises of new countries and drew upon the profits earned by these investments for imports of food and other essentials. No major industrial country attempted to feed its population wholly with food produced at home. The well-being of most of Europe's population consequently came to depend upon the smooth flow of international trade. The wartime blockade demonstrated what serious effects a severe stoppage of this trade could have. Yet the Peace Treaty and various tariff-walls perpetuated the " blockade " to some extent in the post-war years.

The Versailles Treaty. The Versailles Treaty deprived Germany of 13 per cent of her population and 14 per cent of her land. The economic significance of these losses was much greater than these figures imply, because the ore deposits in Lorraine had accounted for three-quarters of Germany's pre-war supply of iron. As a student of post-war Germany puts it: " In terms of her 1913 production, Germany surrendered 19 per cent of her coke, 74.5 per cent of her iron ore, 26.6 per cent of her blast furnaces, 19.2 per cent of her raw iron and steel, 15.8 per cent of her rolling mills, 68.5 per cent of her zinc foundries, 12 per cent of her live stock, her entire ocean-going merchant marine, 5,000 locomotives and 40,000 boxcars." [4] The loss of her colonies was relatively unimportant, as they had entailed continuous subsidies and had contributed only one-half of one per cent to Germany's foreign trade. By comparison, the loss of the merchant marine was much more disastrous, since shipping operations had constituted an intangible " export " of services to pay for imports of needed materials.

In addition to these losses in productive capacity, the unstable German economy had to face the problem of paying $32,000,000,000 in reparations. Since this sum equalled one-third of Germany's pre-war national wealth, it represented a staggering burden. How this problem was met has been described at length in the preceding chapter.

Economic Problems of the 1920's. The first post-war decade witnessed an effort to revive economic and political liberalism in Europe. Democratic governments, responsible to the people, multiplied. Economically, liberalism took the form, except in the Soviet Union, of efforts to return to free enterprise and private initiative. The Soviets set about to create a socialized economy. The new nations hampered the development of efficient production and interchange of goods because they were formed chiefly on racial or national, instead of geographic or economic, lines.

Economic Readjustments. Many post-war economic problems were common to all countries. With the armistice, demands for war materials virtually ceased. The economies of the warring countries had been radically dislocated; millions of men had been taken out of productive employment; some industries were overstimulated, others depressed. To find jobs for millions of demobilized soldiers was a major problem. National governments took responsibility for these readjustments, and created new departments to plan and ease the transition from a war economy to a peace economy, but the inevitable result was still a large surplus of manpower and widespread unemployment. The trade union movement received an impetus because workmen tended to band together more eagerly than in the past, in order to protect themselves against severe competition. The influence of labor on government consequently increased. The necessity of restoring property destroyed by the war provided a temporary economic stimulus. While such destruction was not as great as is popularly supposed, it did create new and immediate demands for materials and labor. Railroads, machines, roads, and buildings, which had been allowed to deteriorate during the war, had to be restored to peacetime efficiency. As such replacements could be financed by long-term loans, they were soon undertaken. Expanding employment opportunities in construction work and heavy industries soon stimulated the demand for consumers' goods and assisted in recovery.

The compensation and care of veterans and their dependents plus the enormous debts left by the war forced governments generally to impose heavier taxes. While this resembled the taking of money from one pocket and putting it into another, it required financial operations which dwarfed pre-war fiscal efforts. On the average, annual expenditures of post-war national governments were four times as great as in 1914. For example, the British government's expenditures rose from £170,400,000 in 1913–1914 to £783,300,000 in 1931–1932.

Inflation and Deflation. During the war the belligerents, although maintaining stocks of gold, placed their money on an inconvertible paper basis and resorted to inflation. As a result, the purchasing power of money went down, and prices consequently went up until they had generally more than doubled at the end of the war. The following comparison indicates how inflation varied in the different countries. Taking the 1913 price level as 100, the index number for Great Britain rose to 220 early in 1919. In Germany it was 260 by 1919, and soared to about 1200 before the disastrous inflation of 1923. Italian prices quadrupled, and French prices rose to approximately five times the 1913 figure.

Fluctuation of Currencies. These rapid changes in the purchasing power of money tended to upset business calculations and production plans, thus delaying a return to prosperity. The rapid fluctuations encouraged wild currency speculation, which only accentuated economic instability. Since much of Europe's prosperity depends on the importation of raw materials and exportation of finished goods, on extensive international shipping services, and on tourist travel, such instability could lead only to continued disasters.

The efforts of individual nations to return to normal business operations had their counterpart internationally in attempts to achieve stable rates of exchange which would permit the easy flow of goods over national boundaries. This latter objective was not easily gained. Imports of goods and services must be paid for with gold or with exports of goods and services. A country that imports more than it exports requires sufficient quantities of gold to guarantee the payment of adverse trade balances. This guarantee was more difficult to make in the 1920's than in the pre-war period, because the United States had accumulated nearly half of the world's monetary gold supply and through its continued export surpluses kept on drawing Europe's gold.

All through the 1920's, American exports were stimulated in every possible way, through the efforts of the expanded Bureau of Foreign and Domestic Commerce and other public and private trade promotional organizations, as well as by tariff legislation, loans to Europe, and by the government's monetary policies.

Return to Gold. Great Britain in 1925 was the first major European country to return to the gold standard. The pound was revalued at par (1913 figure) of $4.87. Germany, after the war, had a seriously unbalanced budget, and an inflation of serious proportions soon began. Although the mark was temporarily stabilized in 1921, government expenses were so far ahead of income that the gap could be bridged only by borrowing, raising taxes, or printing money. Since Germany had no credit, and the government was afraid of unduly increasing taxes, the last expedient was resorted to. Soon prices began to soar, as people tried to exchange their depreciated marks for tangible goods. In 1923, when the inflation was halted with the aid of an international loan, the mark was worth but one-trillionth of its pre-war value. At this time the worthless paper money gave way to the new *Rentenmark*, guaranteed by a lien on real estate, with a gold value of 24 cents, the same as the old mark. France returned to the

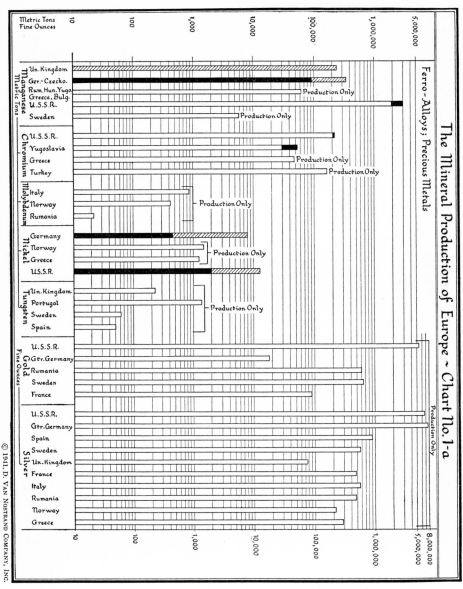

The Mineral Production of Europe ~ Chart No. 1-a

Ferro-Alloys; Precious Metals

© 1941, D. Van Nostrand Company, Inc.

COMPILED FROM LATEST AVAILABLE INFORMATION (1935–1940)

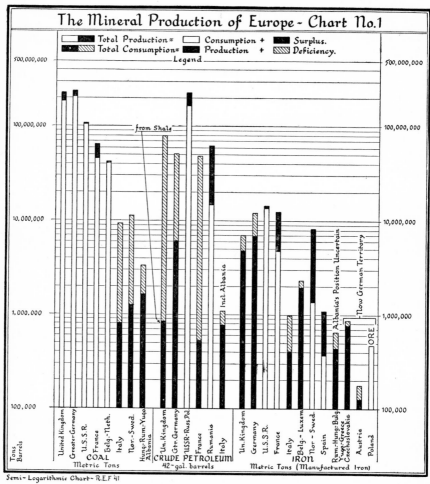

The Mineral Production of Europe - Chart No. 1

Legend

Total Production = Consumption + Surplus.
Total Consumption = Production + Deficiency.

from Shale

500,000,000 — 500,000,000
100,000,000 — 100,000,000
10,000,000 — 10,000,000
1,000,000 — 1,000,000
100,000 — 100,000

Tons
Barrels

United Kingdom | Greater Germany | U.S.S.R. | France | Belg.-Neth. | Italy | Nor.-Swed. | Hung.-Rum.-Yugo. Albania

COAL
Metric Tons

Un.Kingdom | Gtr.Germany | USSR-Russ.Pol. | France | Rumania | Italy *Incl.Albania*

CRUDE PETROLEUM
42-gal. barrels

Un.Kingdom | Germany | U.S.S.R. | France | Italy | Belg.-Luxem | Nor.-Swed. | Spain | Rum.-Hung.-Bulg.-Yugo.-Greece | Czechoslovakia | Austria | Poland

Albania's Position Uncertain | *Now German Territory* | ORE

IRON
Metric Tons (Manufactured Iron)

Semi-Logarithmic Chart - R.E.F 41

COMPILED FROM LATEST AVAILABLE INFORMATION (1935-1940)

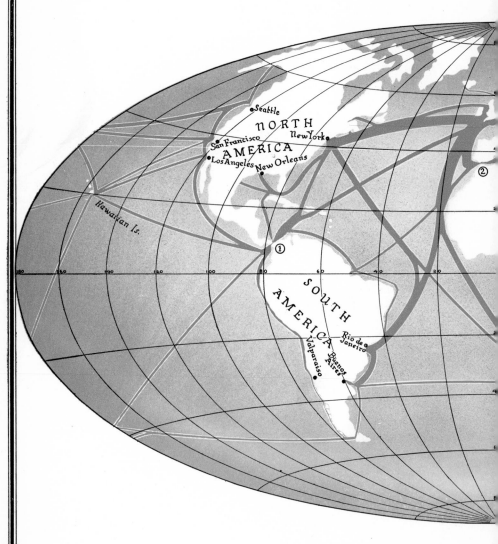

① Panama Canal
② Straits of Gibraltar
③ Dardanelles-Bosporus

The Major Trade
Showing the Strat
Aitoff's Equal-
(Width of Line is
to Volume

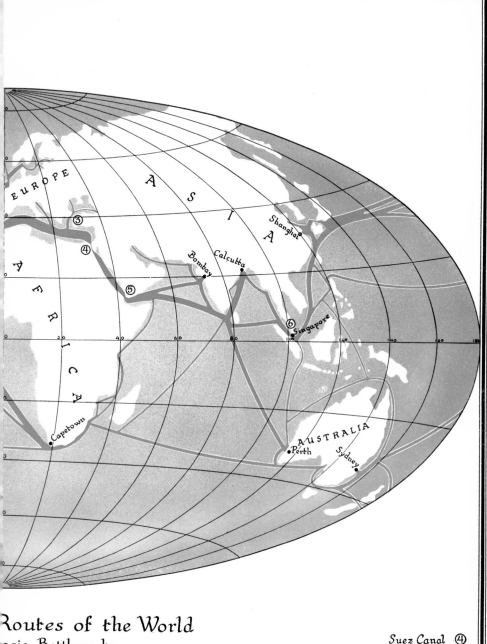

Routes of the World

egic Bottlenecks

Area Projection
oughly Proportional
f Traffic)

Suez Canal ④
Straits of Bab-el-Mandeb ⑤
Straits of Malacca ⑥

R.E. Falconer, 1940

gold standard in 1927 when the franc was devalued to 3.94 cents from the pre-war rate of 19.3 cents. Italy returned to the gold standard in 1928 with the aid of $100,000,000 borrowed in the United States. The lira was devalued from 19.3 to 5.25 cents.

Results of Inflation. These extraordinary changes in the value of currencies upset price levels and had profound economic effects. As prices rose a given amount of money could purchase less goods. People having property claims calling for payment in a fixed number of monetary units — for example, holders of bonds, mortgages, savings accounts, life insurance policies, and the like — lost purchasing power. A large part of the savings of the upper and middle classes in some countries, particularly Germany and Austria, was wiped out. Many aristocrats become paupers, and people of means were reduced to starvation. The story of the beneficiary of a life insurance policy for 5000 marks who, at the height of inflation, could not collect because the postage stamp would have cost 7500 marks, poignantly illustrates the havoc caused by inflation. A considerable number of Hitler's early supporters were middle-class citizens who had been ruined by inflation and hoped to recover their position in society when National Socialism triumphed.

One result of soaring price levels was the easing of debt burdens. Whereas those who had savings were wiped out, those who owed money, governments or corporations, could liquidate their debts with worthless marks and start life again debt-free. In France and Italy, where there was only moderate inflation as compared with Germany and Austria, debts were eased approximately in proportion to the rise in prices and devaluation of currencies. The Soviet Union repudiated entirely the debts of the Czarist government. Great Britain benefited least from the post-war inflation, since the pound was revalued at its former high level and the British depression of 1920–1921 had actually caused a fall in prices.

The economic nationalism of the 1920's and its attendant features appear to have led remorselessly to the depression of the 1930's and the outbreak of the Second World War in 1939. The economic history of "armistice years" may be divided into three periods: (1) from 1919 to 1929, (2) 1930 to 1933, and (3) 1934 to 1939.

The Struggle for Stability, 1919–1929

The concept which dominated the 1920's was the desirability of returning to free international commerce as it existed before 1914. Although this proved to be idealistic rather than practical, some progress was made in this direction. The first requisite for the restoration of " normal " international trade was a return to the gold standard. An international conference to discuss this desideratum was held in Brussels in 1920, and attended by representatives of most European countries. The conference concluded that national currencies should be returned as soon as possible to stable gold standards, and that barriers should not be raised to hamper the flow of goods among nations. These wise recommendations were confirmed by the Geneva International Conference in 1922.

The two chief barriers to normal trade were the Allied attempt to collect German reparations which has been described in the last chapter, and the enormous increases in tariffs.

Tariffs and Economic Nationalism. The new political boundaries often violated the simple principle of geographic specialization. They cut across and disrupted economic units, and became the bases upon which tariff walls, acting as peacetime blockades, were erected. For example, the economically balanced Dual Monarchy in which Austria provided the manufactured and Hungary the agricultural products was carved up into several parts, none of them economically self-sustaining. The Polish Corridor to the sea injured the German economy by separating East Prussia from the remainder of the country. Poland, on the other hand, lacked adequate ocean outlets. As Danzig, the Corridor port, was a free city, the Poles developed Gdynia in order to have a port under their full control. Germany, the most highly industrialized nation on the continent, needed food, raw materials, and a market for her goods. Many of these materials and markets were found in southeastern Europe, but tariffs erected by the new and enlarged states hampered the normal flow of goods. Czechoslovakia was not an economic unit in any useful sense. The Soviet Union, a potential source of raw materials, and a huge market for capital goods and other manufactures, was prevented from becoming an integral part of the post-war world economy because she could not get long-term loans and because she introduced the first Five-Year Plan in 1927 in an attempt to gain self-sufficiency.

Tariff Wars. These interferences with the exchange of goods and services would have been serious enough in normal times. But the decade of 1919–1929 was not, in an economic sense, a period of normalcy. Each nation strove to produce as much foodstuffs, raw materials, and manufactured goods as it consumed, and to depend on other nations less and less. To attain this goal, high tariffs were enacted. Once a nation raises any tariff barriers, retaliation is invited from countries discriminated against, since the exports of the latter suffer, and their trade balances are upset. They may lose gold, and their governments' credit is threatened. Self-interest therefore demands that energetic measures be taken to restore the balance of foreign trade by counter-tariffs.

An additional factor encouraging tariffs was the depreciation of currencies. If a nation's currency is devalued, exports are stimulated as long as customers in countries where currency is at par can purchase its goods

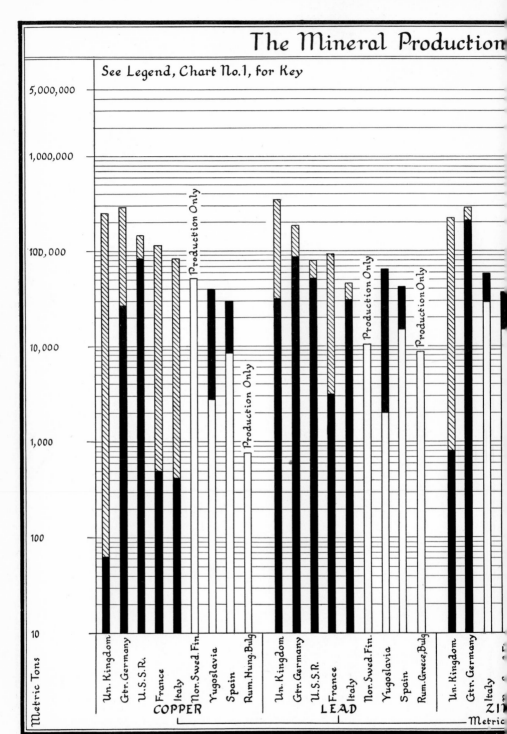

See Legend, Chart No.1, for Key

Metric Tons

5,000,000

1,000,000

100,000

10,000

1,000

100

10

COPPER
Un. Kingdom · Gtr. Germany · U.S.S.R. · France · Italy · Nor. Swed. Fin. · Yugoslavia · Spain · Rum. Hung. Bulg.

Production Only · Production Only

LEAD
Un. Kingdom · Gtr. Germany · U.S.S.R. · France · Italy · Nor. Swed. Fin. · Yugoslavia · Spain · Rum. Greece, Bulg.

Production Only · Production Only

ZIN
Un. Kingdom · Gtr. Germany · Italy

Metric

Semi-Logarithmic Chart ~ R.E.F., '41

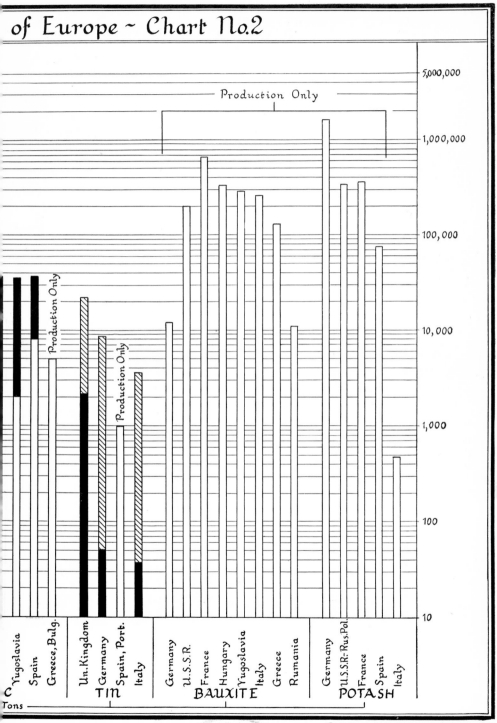

# of Europe ~ Chart No.2

Production Only

5,000,000

1,000,000

100,000

10,000

1,000

100

10

Production Only

Production Only

Yugoslavia
Spain
Greece, Bulg.

Un. Kingdom
Germany
Spain, Port.
Italy

Germany
U.S.S.R.
France
Hungary
Yugoslavia
Italy
Greece
Rumania

Germany
U.S.S.R.-Rus.Pol.
France
Spain
Italy

C
Tons

TIN

BAUXITE

POTASH

ABLE INFORMATION (1935–1940)

at a monetary advantage. For instance, when the franc was devalued American dollars could purchase more French goods and services than formerly. Furthermore, if the dollar fetches more in terms of the franc than of the pound, American customers will buy from France rather than England, assuming the desired goods are obtainable from either country. Because the pound was pegged at a high level, Britain, primarily a trading nation, suffered various disadvantages in competing with countries whose currencies were depreciated. This finally led her to abandon the gold standard on September 21, 1931.

The United States, regardless of its desire for isolation from world politics, was by no means isolated economically. Its investment status had changed from a net debtor position of approximately $3,000,000,000 in 1914 to a net creditor position in 1931 of about $14,100,000,000. The major creditor nation, it diminished payment of its claims in goods by raising its tariff barriers successively in 1921, 1922, and 1930. Agricultural over-expansion during the war brought great suffering to the American farmer in 1919–1920, and Congress was prompt in offering the time-honored cure of protection in the Tariff Act of 1921, preventing the dumping of foreign agricultural products. The Fordney-McCumber Tariff Bill of 1922 set a new high level of protection and drew a storm of protest both from within and without the country. Not only did the Act provide for general increases in duties, but it permitted the President to alter rates to meet rapidly changing economic conditions. These changes were generally upward. Normally an exporter of raw materials and food products, the United States found its European markets curtailed by retaliatory tariffs. Worse still, as already remarked, it financed its foreign customers by the purchases of foreign securities. For example, the aggregate new dollar loans made to Germany by the United States from 1924 to the end of 1935 totaled $1,364,000,000. Payments on these debts could be made ultimately only with imports. The United States' refusal to accept imports was tantamount to a refusal to recognize that it had become an integral member of the world economy.

The enormous increases in tariffs is seen in the following table despite the clear need of reductions as advised by the Brussels and Geneva Conferences and strongly reiterated by the Geneva World Economic Conference in 1927.

Examination of the table shows that in 1927 the average European tariff was up 25 per cent from the 1913 figure, although there was considerable difference of policy among the individual countries. By 1931 the average was over 90 per cent above that of 1913, or nearly doubled. Observe also that in the four intervening years every country had been forced into line and had raised its tariff above the 1913 level. Even Sweden and Poland, the only two countries which had not reached the 1913 figure, had increased their tariffs approximately 25 per cent above the 1927 rates. Comparison of these figures, therefore, fully reveals the cumulative effects of the tariff war.

The absence of Great Britain from the list is significant. Except for "key" industries and certain preferences in favor of the dominions, Britain followed her traditional policy of free trade until 1931. Up to 1932, 83 per cent of British imports were on the free list.

TABLE I

Europian Post-war Tariff Levels Compared with 1913 Levels [5]
(1913 = 100)

Country	1927 as % of 1913	1931 as % of 1913	Country	1927 as % of 1913	1931 as % of 1913
Germany	122.0	244	Sweden	72.5	97
France	97.5	160	Finland	91.0	134
Italy	112.0	195	Poland ‡	74.0	93
Belgium	77.5	122	Rumania	140.0	207
Switzerland	160.0	252	Hungary §	131.0	197
Austria *	77.0	158	Yugoslavia ‖	144.0	207
Czechoslovakia †	137.0	220	Bulgaria	296.0	420
			Spain	132.0	185

　* Austria 1913 = Austria-Hungary 1913
　† Czechoslovakia 1913 = Austria-Hungary 1913
　‡ Poland 1913 = Russia 1913
　§ Hungary 1913 = Austria-Hungary 1913
　‖ Yugoslavia 1913 = Serbia 1913

The decade of 1919–1929 also saw the development of what has been called the "commercialization of diplomacy." [6] The pre-war governments did not interfere greatly with international trade. In the post-war period governments were drawn, and also thrust themselves, into the promotion of international commerce. It seemed vital to France and Great Britain to maintain a *cordon sanitaire* or "protective ring" around Germany. This was accomplished not only through the usual treaties of alliance, but also by loans to the friendly governments of southeastern Europe. "Golden bullets" were thus used to enhance diplomatic efforts. Meanwhile the Soviet Union remained pretty much aloof economically, although greatly in need of capital goods. Repudiation of the Czarist debts had injured her credit, while her ability to export agricultural commodities and minerals had not been developed sufficiently to pay for large imports of capital. The fear of Communist propaganda also prevented the capitalist nations from resuming fulsome trade relations with Russia.

The Prosperity of 1925–1929. In spite of these barriers to international commerce, a fair degree of prosperity was restored to most European countries between 1925 and 1929. Economic problems, particularly unemployment, continued to dog the heels of statesmen, but production increased to satisfactory levels. In the industrial countries of Germany, Belgium, France, and Great Britain, private enterprise took new inspiration from the remarkable technological progress of the United States.   Production techniques were rationalized: that is, advanced types of machinery, new industrial processes, and scientific management were introduced. New power systems were developed; enterprises were coordinated or merged.   Public works took on new importance.   Slums were abolished and giant housing programs completed in Great Britain, Russia, Austria, and Germany.   In England, for example, one-third of the nation was re-housed during the decade after the war.   The municipal apartment buildings of Vienna became models of their kind.   The appearance of prosperity generated high hopes.   Even in Germany, despite the disastrous inflation of 1923 and the handicap of colossal reparations, the future looked roseate. " The road marked out for Germany through the coming decades," wrote a careful student in 1929, " is not easy, but is a road which climbs steadily upward, and at its end lies the prize of assured national strength and prosperity." [7]

The Great Depression, 1930–1933

The prosperity of Europe, however, was short-lived.   Indeed prosperity was partly fictitious because in many countries it depended too much upon loans from the United States and Great Britain.   Exports of capital (long- and short-term loans) from Great Britain and the United States between 1923 and 1930 were as follows: [8]

TABLE II

(Millions of Dollars)

	1923	1924	1925	1926	1927	1928	1929	1930
U. S. A.	—126*	409	622	140	170	1036	233	547
Great Britain	700	380	261	—29*	482	667	672	190

* A minus sign shows imports of capital.

When this pump priming dried up, trouble soon appeared.   By the middle of 1929, prices of agricultural products had begun to fall.   This meant that the farming countries of southeastern Europe had difficulty in meeting their foreign obligations.   The collapse of the New York stock market in October, 1929 disturbed confidence and created fear.   Panic soon spread around the world.   In two years the prices of agricultural products declined 50 per cent and industrial products 35 per cent.   Falling prices brought heavy losses and business failures, and the repercussions were felt in country after country until the whole world was involved.   Unemployment mounted and the familiar unbalanced government budgets reappeared.   With 1929 taken as 100, world trade fell 89 per cent for agricultural products and 58 per cent for finished or manufactured products by 1932.[9]

The Smoot-Hawley Tariff. Each nation, finding its exports diminishing, undertook to limit its imports as well. The result was a recrudescence of tariff wars as shown in Table I above. Leadership was taken by the United States in the Smoot-Hawley Tariff of 1930. While the sponsors of this bill promised a " return of prosperity in three months," it had quite opposite effects.[10]

While the Smoot-Hawley Bill was under consideration, thirty-three nations sent protests. After it was passed, retaliation began, partly from anger and dismay and partly from the growing necessity for each nation to reduce imports when its exports were curtailed.

The Quota System. France in 1931 unleashed a relatively new form of import control — the quota system — that was destined to spread to other European countries, to South America, and eventually even to the United States.[11] The quota system quickly demonstrated its greater effectiveness and flexibility in controlling imports as compared to the manipulation of tariff rates. Some imports might conceivably scale the highest tariff wall, but under the quota system the total volume of imports was fixed for given commodities. This permitted a country to balance its exports and imports if it so desired, and provided a means of bargaining with other countries for concessions. The tariff question was shoved into the background. Doubtless the appearance of the quota system can be ascribed to the pressure in Europe for increased protection to retaliate for the Smoot-Hawley Tariff Act.

The high tariff levels and quotas encouraged unstable currencies during the depression, because nations with imports in excess of exports found their currencies selling below par and began to lose gold to their creditors. Debtor nations, which included most of Europe, found it impossible to meet debts when exports were declining. The vicious downward spiral reached its end with the departure of England from the precarious gold standard. This was caused largely by an increasing import balance as a result of tariffs against British goods. Gold flowed out in payment of adverse balances in such volume that the gold standard had to be abandoned. The pound thereafter fell to less than $4.00. Nations in the " sterling area " — that is, those carrying on international trade in terms of the pound — likewise abandoned gold and allowed their currencies to depreciate. Such devaluation gave these countries temporary export advantages which, in turn, caused currencies in the " gold bloc " — France, Italy, Switzerland, Holland, Belgium, and the Scandinavian countries — to become unstable. Germany lost gold rapidly and soon resorted to divers devices to preserve her position. The international monetary mechanism which had provided a wide and fluid market for the settlement of trade balances was being smashed.

The erection of tariff walls continued throughout the depression. The British Tariff of March, 1932 imposed duties ranging from 10 to 33 per

cent on the value of imports. About 40 per cent of all imports were covered. France, as we have seen, introduced the quota and licensing systems which in 1933 embraced about 12,000 items or one-third the volume of her total imports. Germany found it increasingly difficult to make payments on reparations after 1930. The Hoover moratorium of 1931 temporarily relieved her of this obligation, and the Lausanne Conference in 1932 finally wiped out reparations. " Standstill " agreements were made on German private debts to foreign countries, and were renewed periodically. Briefly, these provided that interest and principal be paid into " blocked " accounts which could not be transferred abroad without government permission. Countries importing goods from Germany in excess of their exports to her promptly retaliated by refusing to allow their nationals to pay for German goods until domestic creditors had been satisfied.[12]

Despite this international conflict some rays of hope had appeared by 1933–1934. The fall of prices was checked. Commercial and banking failures were declining throughout the world. A World Monetary and Economic Conference was called in London for June, 1933 with the objective of taking effective measures for restoring trade and stabilizing currencies. Careful preparations had been made and the delegates were already assembled when word came from the President of the United States that his nation could make no commitments until domestic problems were solved. Since this implied that the dollar was to be devalued (as it was, in January, 1934), the conference abruptly adjourned, and the trade wars continued. Oddly enough, however, one of the first moves to curb this conflict came from the United States in 1934 with the adoption of Secretary Hull's policy of reciprocal trade agreements. Hull's aim was to reduce barriers to goods seeking markets in the United States provided other countries reduced barriers against American commodities. By the middle of 1940, twenty-one agreements had been negotiated by the State Department, nine of them with European countries. This was the first American step away from extreme protection, but it came too late to reverse the trend in Europe.[13]

Economic Policies and Approaching War, 1934–1939

Until 1935 the League of Nations, however inadequate, dominated international politics. This system of collective security stressed treaty obligations and opposed resort to war. The League succeeded in settling about forty disputes, mostly among smaller nations, but failed to prevent the outbreak of war between Paraguay and Bolivia over the Gran Chaco in 1928. The first serious break in the League system, however, occurred when Japan invaded Manchuria in 1931. As later events proved, Japan intended to drive the Occidentals from Asia and establish a political and economic hegemony over China by force rather than by peaceful measures.

Within Europe, two danger spots developed — Italy and Germany. Hitler became Chancellor in January, 1933 with the avowed purpose of smashing the League system and substituting German domination of the continent. After consolidating his power, Hitler took rapid strides to reach his objectives. The Versailles Treaty was repudiated, a German army recruited, the Rhineland militarized, and Germany's League membership was dropped. Anschluss with Austria was accomplished in March 1938. The Munich Accord of September, 1938 gave the Sudetenland to Germany, and the following March the balance of Czechoslovakia was incorporated into the Reich except for small areas ceded to Poland and Hungary. It became apparent that the system of collective security sponsored by the League and desired by England and France had broken down. Indeed, the strength of the League was sapped in 1935 when Italy conquered Ethiopia despite the imposition of economic sanctions — the refusal to sell vital goods to Italy — by the League members. When Italy defeated Ethiopia, however, the League was presented with a *fait accompli* which it was powerless to change.

The 1930's saw the appearance of new and radical devices in carrying on world trade. In 1934 the United States reduced the gold content of the dollar by approximately 40 per cent. The cheaper dollar would attract foreign customers to our goods and thereby raise demand, causing prices to rise somewhat. Of the profit resulting from devaluation, $2,000,-000,000 was set aside as a Stabilization Fund to protect the dollar in foreign exchange. England had established its Exchange Equalization Account [14] in 1931 when she abandoned the gold standard. Foreign exchange control enables a nation to regulate incoming and outgoing services and goods by manipulating exchange rates through stabilization funds, or by requiring all foreign currencies received in payment for exports to be sold to the government at a set rate. This currency is, in turn, made available to importers under such conditions as the government deems suitable. Since 1931 practically all European and American countries have adopted some measure of foreign exchange control.[15] This practice is defended on the ground that it helps to stabilize currencies. Furthermore, it is claimed, such control permits the government to acquire the exchange necessary to service its foreign debts, and thus maintain its credit standing. Exchange control also enables a country to provide importers of prime necessities with foreign currency at favorable rates. Such a system can also be used as a bargaining device in negotiating international trade agreements. Not the least advantage of exchange control is the profit that the government makes by selling foreign currency at a higher price than it pays to exporters. All in all, exchange control constitutes one of the leading barriers yet devised to the free flow of international trade.

When Germany and Italy became totalitarian military states, each government secured more or less complete power over labor and capital,

banking and foreign trade. No greater centralization of political and economic power has ever been witnessed before. Each country began to establish a war economy in 1935, the primary object of which was to achieve autarchy or maximum national self-sufficiency. In Germany, rearmament began on an immense scale. Raw materials essential to war industries took precedence over other imports. Supplies of foreign exchange were rationed and the production of consumers' goods was curtailed. Consumer complaints were overruled in the interest of national " needs." Agricultural production was stimulated and *ersatz* or substitute materials were feverishly developed.

" Power politics " required a German trade drive to finance exports with which to pay for necessary imports. This was done partly by " swapping " goods with European countries, particularly those with which Germany had favorable trade relations. Commodities were also bartered with South America. Evidence indicates that many barter agreements reacted to the disadvantage of countries dealing with Germany, since the latter frequently paid in " blocked " marks which could be spent only for German goods. For example, Hungary and Yugoslavia sold Germany their cereals and in return received blocked marks which they could not exhaust because their people, with extremely low standards of living, had little use for German manufactures.

German exports were subsidized by the government and nearly forty types of marks were created. Tourist marks, for instance, could be purchased at about half-price before the Second World War. The German trade drive attempted, with considerable success, to include Hungary, Yugoslavia, and Rumania within the German economy. A commercial treaty with Hungary in 1934 called for " adjusting portions of Hungarian agricultural production to German import needs." The treaty with Rumania (March, 1939) went much further and provided for the development of Rumanian agriculture and raw material sources by German technicians to suit German needs. The treaty described the specific products to be developed, such as bauxite, chrome, and manganese. Mixed Rumanian and German companies were to be formed for these purposes.

France and England did not remain idle in this trade war. In 1934 France tried to strengthen the " protective ring " around Germany by drawing up a plan of economic cooperation among the Little Entente — Czechoslovakia, Yugoslavia, and Rumania. The plan included financing and transportation of Czech manufactures for agricultural products and raw materials from the other countries, but it had little effect in combatting German encroachment.

The next step in this process was to change the character of international trade from multilateral, or many-sided, to bilateral, or two-sided, agreements. Great Britain and France, in meeting German competition, concluded numerous bilateral commercial treaties. Germany's effort was

to break down the free movement of goods between nations and, because she had little gold reserves, to convert her foreign trade increasingly into barter agreements. The major purpose of the Tripartite Agreement between Great Britain, France, and the United States in September, 1936 was to combat this tendency and sustain the use of gold as a medium of international exchange.[16]   The three governments agreed to work together to maintain a stable relationship between the pound, franc, and dollar. An invitation was extended to other countries to subscribe to the agreement, and subsequently Belgium, Holland, and Switzerland did so. On October 2, 1936 France devalued the franc, a move doubtless facilitated by support derived from the Tripartite Agreement. Less than a year later, however, on June 30, 1937, France was forced to abandon the gold standard. The operation of the Tripartite Agreement was cloaked in comparative secrecy, and its status since the collapse of France and occupation of Belgium and Holland in 1940 is uncertain.

Summary

By the beginning of the Second World War in 1939 governments dominated international trade relations. The totalitarian regimes took the lead in this trend, but the democracies found it necessary to follow their example in order to protect themselves. The economic systems of Europe were converted to war economies in the latter 1930's: in Germany by 1935, in England and France by 1938, and in other countries accordingly as alarm spread. Thus intense economic warfare preceded armed warfare.

Fundamental Changes during Two Decades. The rapid survey of two decades of European economic history presented in the preceding pages may be summarized in two statements:

1. The period of 1919–1939 saw a decline in the economic freedom and the power of private persons and groups. The attempted return to *laissez faire* after 1918 was not a success in most European countries, although it was more successful in domestic trade than in foreign commerce. As economic power was shifted from individuals to governments, the governments began to use their power for political ends.

2. In world trade a new form of mercantilism has developed in which national units enter into direct economic competition with one another. It seems improbable that free international trade will soon return. There is a growing tendency, however for nations to be grouped together in self-sufficient economic regions, as shown by German efforts to integrate the productive capacities of the continent [17] and by British organization of empire trade. Whatever the result, it will be born of intense travail and considerable experimentation, and of forces now locked in mortal combat in Europe, Africa, and Asia. The world economy is again in transition, as it has so often been in the past.

REFERENCES

1 There are no better descriptions of the operations of *laissez-faire* economics than the standard textbooks of pre-war origin. See, for example, Alfred Marshall, *Principles of Economics*, New York and London: eighth edition, and earlier editions. Also F. W. Taussig, *Principles of Economics*, New York: Macmillan, 1940. For a justification of competitive capitalist systems see T. N. Carver, *Essays in Social Justice*, Cambridge: Harvard Univ. Press, 1914. For criticism of competitive capitalism see John A. Hobson, *Work and Wealth*, New York: Macmillan, 1922.

2 On the costs of the war see Ernest L. Bogart, *Direct and Indirect Costs of the Great World War*, New York: Oxford Univ. Press, Carnegie Endowment for International Peace, 1919.

3 The commodities and services used to fight the modern war are produced by the generation living at the time of the war, but the debts remain a burdensome " financial hangover," because their payment may involve considerable redistribution of income, and because the government's ability to collect taxes may diminish. Post-war economic difficulties were due much more to economic dislocations than to destruction of wealth. See J. M. Clark, *The Costs of the World War to the American People*, Carnegie Endowment for World Peace; *Economic and Social History of the World War*, James T. Shotwell, general editor, American series, New Haven: Yale Univ. Press, 1931, especially chs. 5 and 6. See also S. H. Patterson and Karl W. H. Scholz, *Economic Problems of Modern Life*, New York: McGraw-Hill, 1937, third edition, ch. 14.

4 Robert A. Brady, *The Rationalization Movement in German Industry*, Berkeley: Univ. of California Press, 1933, p. xiv.

5 Some of the figures in the table are taken from H. Liepman, *Tariff Levels and the Economic Unity of Europe*, New York: Macmillan, 1938, p. 415. For the method of calculating the tariff levels, see the same source. See also the calculation for 1925 by the League of Nations, *Tariff Level Indices*, Geneva: League of Nations, 1927, p. 15.

6 J. B. Condliffe, *The Reconstruction of World Trade*, New York: Norton, 1940.

7 James W. Angell, *The Recovery of Germany*, New Haven: Yale Univ. Press, 1929, p. 361.

8 Data from G. D. H. Cole, *A Guide through World Chaos*, New York: Knopf, 1930, p. 64.

9 J. P. Day, *An Introduction to World Economic History since the Great War*, New York: Macmillan, 1939.

10 It is noteworthy that 1,080 American economists asked President Hoover to veto the bill. They pointed out that tariffs decrease exports as well as imports, and so diminish total world trade. Furthermore, it was contended that retaliation from foreign countries would inevitably follow. The argument that the bill would protect the wages of American labor was refuted by the fact that less than 10 per cent of the products of American industry entered into *direct* competition with foreign goods. This is the first instance in which American professional economists as a body publicly opposed governmental policy. History justified their opposition.

11 F. A. Haight, *French Import Quotas*, London: King, 1935.

12 On the political and economic maneuvers in Europe during this period see W. R. Sharp and Grayson Kirk, *Contemporary International Politics*, New York: Farrar and Rinehart, 1940.

13 P. H. Lohman, "Some Questions on the Alleged Success of the Reciprocal Trade Agreements Program," *Annalist*, October 5, 1938, Vol. 52, No. 1342, p. 463.

14 For a study of this agency see Leonard Waight, *The History and Mechanism of the Exchange Equalization Account*, Cambridge, England: Cambridge Univ. Press, 1939.

15 F. A. Southard, Jr., *Foreign Exchange Practice and Policy*, New York: McGraw-Hill, 1940.

16 Henry J. Tasca, *World Trading Systems*, Paris: International Institute of Intellectual Cooperation, League of Nations, 1939. This is a study devoted principally

to the United States and Great Britain, but is a useful explanation of changing trade relations. See also J. B. Condliffe, *op. cit.*

[17] Vera Micheles Dean, *Europe under Nazi Rule*, New York: Foreign Policy Association Report, October 15, 1940, Vol. XVI, No. 15.

SELECTED BIBLIOGRAPHY

Annals of the American Academy of Political and Social Science, Philadelphia, published bi-monthly. See, for example, *The World Trend toward Nationalism*, E. M. Patterson, ed., July, 1934.

Angell, James W., *The Recovery of Germany*, New Haven: Yale Univ. Press, 1929. Indispensable for the economic history of Germany from the end of the World War to 1928.

Bowden, Witt, Karpovich, M., and Usher, A. P., *An Economic History of Europe since 1750*, New York: American Book Company, 1937. See especially Part VI.

Carnegie Endowment for International Peace has published more than one hundred volumes on the Economic and Social History of the World War which are a mine of information. Among these are:

    Anderson, B. M., Jr., *Effects of the War on Money, Credit and Banking in France and the United States*, New York: Oxford Univ. Press, 1919.

    Baker, Charles Whiting, *Government Control and Operation of Industry in Great Britain and the United States during the World War*, New York: Oxford Univ. Press, 1921.

    Clark, J. M., *The Costs of the World War to the American People*, New Haven: Yale Univ. Press, 1931.

    Litman, Simon, *Prices and Price Control in Great Britain and the United States during the World War*, New York: Oxford Univ. Press, 1920.

    Lloyd, E. M. H., *Experiments in State Control* (at the War Office and the Ministry of Food), New York: Oxford Univ. Press, 1924.

Day, J. P., *An Introduction to World Economic History since the Great War*, New York: Macmillan, 1940.

Dickens, Paul D., *American Direct Investments in Foreign Countries, 1936*, Washington: U. S. Dept. of Commerce, Bureau of Foreign and Domestic Commerce, 1937.

Dietrich, Ethel B., *World Trade*, New York: Holt, 1939. This book attempts to show the necessity of foreign trade and the need for adjusting it to the social and political environment.

Einzig, Paul, *World Finance*, 1914–1935, New York: Macmillan, 1935.

——, *World Finance*, 1935–1937, New York: Macmillan, 1937.

——, *World Finance*, 1938–1939, New York: Macmillan, 1939.

——, *World Finance*, 1939–1940, New York: Macmillan, 1940.

——, *Bankers, Statesmen, and Economists*, London: Macmillan, 1935.

——, *Economic Warfare*, London: Macmillan, 1940.

    This author is a prolific writer on international economics and finance. While his opinions and interpretations give rise to controversy, the steady flow of books from his pen provides a running account of the economic history of Europe for the past fifteen years.

Ellsworth, P. T., *International Economics*, New York: Macmillan, 1938.

Foreign Policy Reports, published semi-monthly by the Foreign Policy Association, New York: see especially those on European countries by Vera M. Dean, John C. deWilde, and Mildred S. Wertheimer.

Heuser, Heinrich, *Control of International Trade*, Philadelphia: Blakiston, 1939. The causes, methods, and results of the regulation of foreign trade are examined.

Langsam, Walter C., *Documents and Readings in the History of Europe since 1918*, Philadelphia: Lippincott, 1939.

Lawley, F. E., *The Growth of Collective Economy*, 2 vols., London: King, 1938. A treatise on international cooperation and collectivization, arguing that collective economy is on its way nationally and internationally.

League of Nations annual survey of *World Economic Conditions.* To understand the
important role which the League played in international affairs in the decade
from 1920 to 1930 see *Ten Years of World Cooperation,* Geneva: The Secretariat
of the League of Nations, 1930.

Loucks, W. N. and Hoot, J. W., *Comparative Economic Systems,* New York: Harper,
1938.

Patterson, Ernest Minor, *The Economic Bases of Peace,* New York: McGraw-Hill,
1939.

Sharp, W. R. and Kirk, Grayson, *Contemporary International Politics,* New York:
Farrar and Rinehart, 1940.

Shotwell, James T., *What Germany Forgot,* New York: Macmillan, 1940. The Second World War is traced to the costs of the First World War which Germany
forgot.

Southard, Frank A., Jr., *Foreign Exchange Practice and Policy,* New York: McGraw-
Hill, 1940, see especially ch. 5, " Foreign Exchange Policy."   ..

Staley, Eugene, *World Economy in Transition,* New York: Council on Foreign Relations, 1939. The conflict between power and welfare economics is resolved
in favor of a " Mixed System " in which the best of *laissez faire* is combined with
the best in planned production.

Tasca, H. J., *World Trading Systems,* New York: Columbia Univ. Press, 1939.

Von Haberler, Gottfried, *The Theory of International Trade,* New York: Macmillan,
1937. An English translation of a comprehensive German work applying a theoretical analysis to every question arising from international trade policy.

Whittlesey, Charles R., *International Monetary Issues,* New York: McGraw-Hill, 1937.

CHAPTER V

Great Britain, Ireland, and the Empire

BEFORE THE SECOND WORLD WAR (1918–1939)

Great Britain

The Geographical Setting. The United Kingdom of Great Britain and Ireland, embracing the most important group of islands in the world, constitutes a well-defined geographic area. To the east the British Isles are separated from the continent of Europe by the North Sea, and on the south by the English Channel, only twenty-one miles wide at its narrowest point. To the north and west lie the vast expanse of the Atlantic Ocean. Great Britain, the largest of the islands, has an extraordinarily jagged coastline, the numerous indentations of which furnish good harbors. A number of rivers, navigable to small vessels, increase accessibility to the sea. In fact, no point in Great Britain is more than seventy miles from open water. Scotland comprises the mountainous northern part of Great Britain as well as the adjacent small islands; Wales consists of a small peninsula, also mountainous, on the west coast; and the balance of the island, for the most part low and rolling country, comprises England. Ireland, lying to the west of Great Britain and shaped somewhat like a saucer, with an irregular coastline, is a central plain surrounded by green hills which are massed along the shores. Despite the northern latitude, the climate of the British Isles is characterized by warm winters and cool summers, and by an abundance of rainfall and fog.

Influence of the Insular Location. In 1918 the United Kingdom consisted of four nations, once distinct and separate — England, Wales, Scotland, and Ireland. In the course of centuries the English, chiefly by conquest, had welded these nations into a single state. Wales was conquered in 1356 and Ireland in the seventeenth century; Scotland was united to England by the

---

This chapter by Frederick E. Graham, Professor of European History, San José State College.

the early days of the war he served as Minister of Munitions, becoming Prime Minister in December, 1916. In the dark years of strife his fertile imagination, infectious high spirits, native intuition, and gift for improvisation in the face of emergencies were invaluable assets to the nation. These traits, combined with a genuine sympathy for the underprivileged and an ardent patriotism, made him an ideal war Prime Minister. Although some distrusted Lloyd George's brilliance, suspecting him of superficiality, most Englishmen felt that no one was better fitted to cope with the difficulties of liquidating the war.

" It was a bewildering world with all the old, familiar landmarks disappearing, and change taking place so fast and furiously that no one could say when it was going to stop," says E. C. Winsfield-Stratford.[8] Nevertheless Lloyd George was confident that in a period of flux and uncertainty he could provide the necessary guidance. " Few men are capable of public office without the growth of a conviction that the State is unsafe in other hands than their own," says Philip Guedalla.[9] Lloyd George determined to remain in office despite some restlessness in the ranks of his ill-assorted Liberal and Conservative colleagues. Expansively optimistic, the Prime Minister proclaimed the dissolution of Parliament, eight years having elapsed since its election, and scheduled new elections for December 14, 1918.

The Elections of 1918. In the campaign that followed Lloyd George and his coalition offered the nation an attractive platform designed to appeal to a war-inflamed public: the punishment of German " war criminals "; the payment of Allied war costs by the defeated nations; protection for Great Britain's essential industries, especially against the dumping of goods produced abroad by cheap labor; improved labor and housing conditions; and a permanent settlement of the Irish question. In urging the country to continue their support of his coalition he assured the electorate that he would " win the peace " and that he would create in England " homes fit for heroes." A war-weary nation could hope for little more.

Earlier in the year Lloyd George had sponsored legislation which was calculated to strengthen his chances of victory at the polls. A champion of democracy he had lent his support to the Representation of the People Act which extended the franchise to 8,000,000 new voters. This act admitted to the electorate, with minor exceptions, all men who had attained twenty-one years of age and who could establish six months' residence or occupation of business premises, and all women thirty years of age who were electors in local government or wives of electors. There was a redistribution of Parliamentary seats on the basis of single-member constituencies. A large portion of the new voters could be reasonably expected to support the government which had granted them the franchise.

Herbert Asquith, Lloyd George's predecessor at 10 Downing Street,

the empire, had to be revived, if unemployment and misery were not to stalk the land. Industry and commerce, diverted to meet the requirements of war, had to be readjusted to the demands of a peaceful society. Places had to be found for millions of demobilized soldiers whose training and experience in many cases had unfitted them for civilian life. Society was in need of stabilization for the impoverishment of the aristocracy and the middle classes as a result of wartime taxation, the extensive employment of women, the breakdown of conventional manners and morals, had all contributed to its partial disintegration.[5]

Furthermore, Great Britain which had entered the conflict a creditor nation had emerged a debtor as a result of the tenfold expansion of the national debt, non-recoverable loans to her allies, and loans from the United States. War debts and currency stabilization were interrelated problems which had to be solved before prosperity could return. In addition certain problems, such as the Irish question, the status of India, and Imperial relations which had been temporarily shelved during the war, still had to be faced.

The Political System. Great Britain was almost unique among European powers in that it emerged from the war with its political structure unchanged. It remained a constitutional monarchy.[6] Although the king was nominally the source of authority, all official acts being signed by him, he was a mere figurehead, or as has been said, "a working hypothesis." Effective power rested in the hands of the Prime Minister and his Cabinet. This body, exercising chiefly legislative and administrative functions, derived its authority from the electorate and retained power only so long as it possessed a working majority in the House of Commons. Thus, in effect, the Commons expressed the will of the nation and dominated the state in contradistinction to the House of Lords, which was a vestigial reminder of an aristocratic oligarchy that had passed away.

The Conservatives, Liberals, and Laborites were the three principal parties. During the war, partisan rivalries had been held in abeyance, a truce being declared so as to cooperate in the task of winning the conflict. This virtual erasure of party lines and the consequent cessation of internecine strife enabled a coalition government under Lloyd George to rule rather dictatorially over a comparatively united nation until the achievement of victory in 1918.

The Ascendancy of Lloyd George. With the abrupt end of the war accompanied by the announcement of the armistice terms, Lloyd George's prestige stood at a level scarcely equaled by any statesman in British history.[7] Born in Wales in 1863, the son of poor parents, Lloyd George had made his way first as a lawyer, later as a Leftist member of the Liberal Party. When the Liberals came into power in 1905 he entered the Cabinet first as President of the Board of Trade, later as Chancellor of the Exchequer; in

Laborites advanced a moderately socialistic platform including a capital levy on fortunes of £5000 and over, the nationalization of mines and railways, better housing facilities, beneficial labor and industrial legislation, a broad pension system, and a revision of the Treaty of Versailles. Although the bulk of the electorate distrusted the more radical Labor proposals, such as the capital levy, many voted for its candidates, or for the Liberals in protest against Baldwin's protectionism. The Conservatives won 258 seats, the Laborites and Liberals 191 and 157 respectively.

Acknowledging defeat, Baldwin resigned. Although his party had more seats than either of its two rivals it lacked a workable majority. MacDonald backed by his own party and by the Liberals who preferred his mild socialism to Baldwin's protectionism, was invited to form the first Labor ministry in British history.

The First Labor Government. The advent of the Labor government scarcely inaugurated a millennium. Although the Laborites' ideology accepted class consciousness it rejected the principle of class warfare. Furthermore the Labor government was prevented from embarking on radical legislation by its devotion to legal methods and parliamentary practices. In MacDonald, a veteran politician and pacifist, it possessed a leader of commanding stature. He was an astute politician versed in all the subtleties of his profession. After becoming Prime Minister his radicalism, unkind critics whispered, disappeared in proportion to his success in gaining entree to aristocratic circles.

"The Labor Party," said Guedalla, "is an immediate creation of the industrial problem. It exists, say its friends, to solve it. It lives, say its enemies, by leaving it unsolved."[14] Dependent upon the support of the Liberals it was in no position to introduce the Socialist program. Instead, it contented itself with a few liberal measures. The McKenna war duties and the tax on cheap amusements were abolished; duties on tea, coffee, and chocolate were reduced; and through the Wheatley Bill the building of homes, aided by government subsidies, was encouraged. Inasmuch as unemployment remained at a high level the dole system, slightly modified, had to be continued. No attempt was made to introduce the capital levy and fears of a Socialist regime quickly evaporated.

MacDonald's government acquired its greatest prestige as a result of its foreign policies. The Prime Minister evinced a willingness to cooperate with the powers in reducing armaments and enhancing international security, he helped to pave the way for the acceptance of the Dawes Plan and the Locarno treaties. Ironically, MacDonald's policy of international cooperation contributed to the fall of his party. Desirous of securing British access to the Russian markets MacDonald granted *de jure* recognition to the Soviet government on February 1, 1924. In April an Anglo-Russian conference met in London to renew commercial relations and settle con-

economic reforms. The Conservatives gained a comfortable majority of
79. To the surprise of many the Laborites secured second place with 142
seats and thus supplanted the Liberals as His Majesty's Opposition. Lloyd
George's prestige, like that of the Liberals, was hopelessly shattered.

The Conservatives' triumph, however, was short-lived. Bonar Law's
Cabinet was no better than a " second eleven," for he had refused to include
those elder statesmen in the party who had stood by Lloyd George. Consequently with the exceptions of Lord Curzon as Foreign Minister and
Baldwin as Chancellor of the Exchequer, it was a thoroughly mediocre assembly. To make matters worse the intelligent and conscientious Prime
Minister, suffering from an incurable disease, was forced to retire in May,
1923.

The Settlement of the American Debt. Earlier in the year he had dispatched Baldwin to the United States to settle the English debts. Although
Great Britain favored the cancellation of both reparations and war debts,
it was impossible to get the United States to agree. Therefore, Baldwin
signed a funding agreement, reducing the debt from $4,715,310,000 to $3,-
788,470,000 and obligating England to make annual payments over a period
of sixty-two years at an average of 3.3 instead of 5 per cent interest. Baldwin's bargain received a favorable, if not enthusiastic reception, and raised
the prestige of the government. It did not, however, assure England that
her debtors would pay or that the stabilization of the American debt would
contribute to economic recovery.

The Rise of Baldwin. With the retirement of Bonar Law, Stanley Baldwin
became Prime Minister.[13] Although a wealthy magnate and a Cabinet
member he was comparatively unknown. Observers found it difficult to
assess his capabilities, one journalist inquiring somewhat plaintively: " Is
Mr. Baldwin the luckiest of incompetent politicians or the subtlest of competent statesmen? " Modest and hardworking, although perhaps a trifle
stodgy, he exemplified the traditional British spirit of " muddling through."
It was Baldwin's conviction that England must resort to protection to combat the depression. He held that a tariff on manufactured goods would
curb foreign competition, relieve unemployment, preserve wage levels, and
stabilize prices. In determining to sponsor protection, however, Baldwin
encountered considerable opposition. He decided, therefore, to take the
question to the people. Parliament was dissolved and new elections were
called for December 6, 1923.

The Defeat of the Conservatives. Baldwin's argument for a protective
tariff and his recommendation of Imperial preference failed to impress the
nation. The two wings of the Liberal Party, reuniting temporarily in defense of free trade, campaigned with considerable success against the government. More significant, however, was the opposition of the rapidly-
growing Labor Party. Under the leadership of J. Ramsay MacDonald the

ingness to come to terms. An Anglo-Russian trade agreement was signed on March 16, 1921. This provided for the resumption of commerce until a formal treaty should define more clearly the political relations of the two countries. Both signatory powers agreed to refrain from intrigue and propaganda in each other's realms. Neither the treaty nor the Bolsheviks were popular in England nor were Lloyd George's economic aspirations fulfilled.

Another step was taken in 1921 to rejuvenate British trade. An act was passed which levied a 33⅓ per cent duty on certain goods as well as a tax on imports from countries whose currencies were depreciated. These arrangements, it was hoped, would protect British industries and workers from cheap commodities produced abroad. They symbolized, however, the partial abandonment of the historic policy of free trade.

The Disintegration of the Coalition. By the autumn of 1922 Lloyd George's coalition was obviously disintegrating. The Conservatives who constituted the majority of his supporters were dissatisfied with the Prime Minister's Russian treaty as well as with his Irish policies discussed further on in this chapter. Although they approved of his partial adoption of protectionism they had, like many people, lost confidence in his ability to check the depression. Then, too, Lloyd George's foreign policy had gone on the rocks. His attempt to collaborate with France in a program of strict treaty enforcement and at the same time encourage German recovery, so as to benefit British industries, had proven a fiasco. Turkey's rout of the Greeks, who had been supported by Lloyd George, further undermined his prestige. In the spring of 1922 the Cabinet was on the verge of resigning because of internal dissension; in October, the Conservatives, led by Andrew Bonar Law and Stanley Baldwin, held a party meeting at which at was decided to withdraw from the coalition. With the defection of the Conservatives Lloyd George's workable majority vanished and he was compelled to resign on October 19, 1922. " The lumbering tortoise," says John Gunther, " tripped the bright sharp fox — and the era of Versailles was over." [12]

The Triumph of the Conservatives. Great Britain returned to single party government. Bonar Law organized a conservative ministry, dissolved Parliament, and scheduled new elections for November. He assured the electorate that his party, relying on traditional methods and solid virtues rather than Welsh wizardry, would lead the country back to prosperity. Lloyd George, backed by the National Liberals and a few Conservatives, made lavish promises in a vain effort to re-establish his hold on the nation. Asquith again headed the Independent Liberals, asserting that his group rather than Lloyd George's was the true heir of the pre-war Liberals. The Labor Party, expanding rapidly the cause of an influx of workers protesting against distressing economic conditions, agitated for extensive social and

denounced the government and organized the Independent Liberals. The Labor Party withdrew from the coalition and presented its program to the electorate. Certain irreconcilable Conservatives also went on their own, although the bulk of the party continued to support the Prime Minister. The Sinn Feiners, having virtually supplanted the Irish Nationalists, were interested primarily in Irish independence, and had little in common with the government. Nevertheless the electorate remained loyal to Lloyd George, whose coalition won 467 seats. The Independent Liberals and the insurgent Conservatives obtained but 28 and 23 seats respectively. The Labor Party increased its representation to 63 and the Sinn Feiners gained 73 seats but the Irish delegates refused to occupy them. Thus Lloyd George, enjoying an overwhelming majority, was enabled in January, 1919 to organize a predominantly Conservative Ministry.

Economic Unrest after the War. Its triumph at the polls notwithstanding, the government soon found itself overwhelmed by economic problems. A temporary revival of commerce and industry which immediately followed the war was accompanied by a terrific rise in prices and the resumption of class warfare.[10] Beginning in 1919 an epidemic of strikes in which the workers demanded higher wages, shorter hours, and improved labor conditions, threatened to demoralize economic life. Labor achieved some advances in the form of the eight-hour day and better wages. Toward the latter part of 1920, however, the boom collapsed. The impoverishment of England's European customers, the non-recognition of Soviet Russia which prevented the resumption of commerce with that country, serious competition from the American and German goods, and shifts in demand, especially away from coal and British-built vessels, contributed to the economic decline. In 1921 foreign trade fell 50 per cent and many years elapsed before the pre-war level was again attained.

There were grave repercussions. Unemployment mounted to nearly 2,000,000 by the end of 1921; and retail as well as wholesale prices dropped precipitously. The business stagnation was not only prolonged but general, affecting every major industry.

Lloyd George's Attempts to Revive Prosperity. Lloyd George acted to alleviate the suffering. The Unemployment Insurance Act of 1920 was modified to afford greater relief and the government set up a system of doles by means of which the unemployed would be kept from starvation. These measures were mere palliatives, however, and contributed little toward a solution of the economic dilemma.[11] Prosperity could not be restored until Britain's export trade was recaptured.

Russian leaders interested perhaps in developing closer contacts with the British workers and spreading Bolshevik propaganda among them were in a receptive mood when Lloyd George, hopeful of arresting the business recession through the re-establishment of Russian markets, evinced a will-

industrial establishment. Some progress was made along these lines in the chemical, electrical, tin-plate, and other industries. Out-of-date machinery was discarded in favor of labor-saving equipment. Unfortunately the gigantic costs involved discouraged corresponding advances in the older and more staple industries.

In 1929 Parliament for the first time since the First World War had lived out its full legal life of five years. In the elections of May 30, 1929 the economic problem was uppermost in the minds of the electorate. The Conservatives, as befitted their name, advocated the preservation of the status quo, contending that the rationalization of industry under private direction was the key to prosperity. Lloyd George, spokesman for the Liberals, recommended on the other hand a gigantic program of public works which, he asserted, would solve the unemployment problem and at the same time help Great Britain regain its ascendancy in world trade.

The Labor Party proposed to regenerate the nation by transforming the capitalist into a socialist system through parliamentary methods. It advocated the nationalization of the coal, power, and transport industries, the repeal of the Mines Act of 1926 and the Trades Disputes and Trades Union Act of 1927, and suggested reforms calculated to invigorate the economic system and eradicate unemployment. Furthermore, it favored a steeply graded inheritance tax in addition to supertaxes on high incomes.

The Second Labor Government. The Laborites obtained 289 seats to the Conservatives 259 and the Liberals 58. Baldwin promptly resigned and MacDonald on June 5, 1929 organized England's second Labor government.

MacDonald's second ministry fared little better than the first for the combined strength of the Conservatives and Liberals, exceeding that of the Laborites, was sufficient to prevent any Socialistic experimentation. During its tenure of two years the Labor government was compelled to content itself with such modest achievements as a bill which extended a weekly pension to about 500,000 widows unprovided for in earlier legislation; a new unemployment insurance act designed to safeguard 1,000,000 unemployed at any given time; a bill for the rehabilitation of the coal mining industry through price-fixing agreements, compulsory marketing methods, and possible amalgamation; and the creation of an Economic Advisory Council to advise the government on pertinent subjects. The recognition of Russia in December, 1929 upon her promise to abstain from subversive propaganda within the British Empire was followed in April, 1930 by a trade treaty. This provided for mutual most-favored-nation treatment, the inviolability of the Russian trade offices in Great Britain, and a credit of $150,000,000 to finance Russian purchases in Great Britain during the ensuing two years. MacDonald hoped that this agreement

a blow at the Labor Party which depended extensively on trade union funds.

Another consequence of the strike was the deterioration of relations with Russia. The close connections between the Third International and the British Communist Party had been revealed in 1925. During the coal strike the miners were subsidized to some extent by Russian funds and the Bolsheviks spread anti-capitalistic propaganda in England. Suspecting the Russian trade headquarters, Arcos, Ltd., of having purloined valuable documents from the War Office, Scotland Yard raided their offices on May 12, 1927. Although the documents sought were not found sufficient evidence of espionage and sabotage was uncovered to justify Parliament in severing relations with the Soviet regime shortly thereafter.

The Reforms of the Conservatives. Having gained a respite because of the temporary exhaustion of labor the Baldwin government sponsored a number of political and social reforms. A suffrage law passed in 1928 enlarged the electorate by 5,000,000 by extending the franchise to all women twenty-one years of age on an identical basis with men. A proposal to democratize the House of Lords and increase its political significance was balked by strong opposition from the Liberals and some Conservatives. An act providing pensions for widows, orphans, and over-age workers from a retirement fund contributed by the state, the employers, and the wage-earners, was calculated to increase social security. At sixty-five an insured worker could retire on his pension, but in the event of prior decease it would go to his widow and children. England's basic industries were benefited by a law which relieved them of about 75 per cent of their local tax burdens.

These attempts to foster recovery did not bring significant results.[16] Over 2,000,000 people were out of work in 1928 and their situation was becoming desperate. Some new industries had been founded in southern England, but they were capable of absorbing only a small number of workers. The decline of exports was chiefly responsible for England's economic plight. Yet in view of unsettled conditions and of foreign competition there was little prospect that Great Britain would soon recover her primacy in world trade.

Some form of planning, involving the unification, expansion, cooperation, and rationalization of basic industries, was vital if Great Britain was to meet competition from the United States, Germany, France, and elsewhere. Owing to the fact that the Industrial Revolution had developed there more recently, American factories had more modern equipment and superior organization, and employed newer techniques and production methods than the British factories. To cope with them Great Britain would have to " rationalize," that is to say, modernize a large part of her

ing deliveries of coal from Germany as partial reparation payments. Consequently the price of coal fell and British producers in an effort to reduce production costs asked the miners to accept a wage cut and a longer working day. When the miners refused, the operators on July 31, 1925 announced the termination of the existing wage schedule. The inability of the miners and the operators to cooperate created an impasse.

Alarmed at the possible consequences of a total cessation of operations the government decided to subsidize the coal industry temporarily. It demanded that the wage scale of June, 1925 be maintained until May 1, 1926 and handed nearly £20,000,000 to the operators for that purpose. A Royal Commission headed by Sir Herbert Samuel then conducted a thorough investigation. Its report of March 11, 1926 [15] recommended an extensive reorganization of the industry under government supervision. Inasmuch as 75 per cent of British coal was produced at a loss, it declared that wage reductions were imperative and recommended the abandonment of the subsidies. With operators and miners unable to come to an agreement the former notified the unions that the existing wage scale would terminate May 1.

The "General Strike" and Its Aftermath. A walkout of the miners on May 3 was accompanied by sympathetic strikes called by the Trades Union Congress in certain vital industries, such as the transport services and the printing trade. Since less than half the 6,000,000 trade union members were called out it was not really a general strike. Food, gas, electricity, sanitary and health services, and some transportation remained available, despite occasional difficulties. The government proclaimed a state of emergency and appealed for volunteers to maintain essential activities. A prompt response together with the hostility of the public, which regarded the walkout as an attempt to coerce the nation, contributed to the failure of the strike. On May 12 the general strike was called off. In July Parliament enacted legislation establishing an eight-hour day in the mines. The miners did not capitulate, however, till November 19, 1926 when they accepted a wage cut and longer hours. A permanent settlement of the difficulties in the coal industry has not been found and it took many years to allay the bitterness engendered by the strike of 1926.

The aftermath of the general strike was a determined offensive by the Conservatives against the labor unions. In 1927 Parliament passed the Trades Disputes and Trades Union Act which made a general strike illegal, forbade picketing, and prohibited the disciplining of union members for refusing to participate in walkouts. The exemption of trade unions from legal suits was abolished and their funds were declared subject to attachment by the attorney-general. Furthermore political levies on members could be made only if the latter gave written consent. This provision was

flicting claims. Whereas the British hoped to get Russia to acknowledge debts to the Czarist and Kerensky regimes aggregating over £1,000,000,-000, the Soviets were interested in procuring a loan of £60,000,000 for the purchase of manufactured goods. Two treaties evolved from the conference. One reopened the Russian market by according most-favored-nation treatment to British goods. The other stipulated that a joint commission should investigate the British debt claims and that the proposed loan should be contingent upon its findings. It was MacDonald's hope that the re-entry of British goods into the Russian market would aid in combatting the depression.

A storm of criticism greeted the treaties. The Liberals withdrew their support from the Laborites. Deprived thereby of his working majority MacDonald decided to take the issue to the people. Both Liberals and Conservatives condemned the recognition of Russia and warned of the danger of Communist influence in England. In the public mind the Labor Party became identified with the Red peril. The publication in October, 1924 of the Zinoviev letter — alleged by some to be a forgery — lent credence to the alarm, for it urged the workers to prepare for the impending revolution. Fear of Bolshevism, together with MacDonald's inability to stimulate economic recovery, caused the defeat of the Labor government in the Commons on October 8, 1924. The Conservatives were returned to power in the elections of October 29 with a majority of over 200 seats, while the representation of the Laborites and Liberals dwindled to 155 and 36 respectively. MacDonald resigned and was replaced by Baldwin.

Five Years of Conservative Rule. Five years of Conservative rule followed in which the dominant note in domestic politics was the struggle against the depression. Baldwin and his Chancellor of the Exchequer, Winston Churchill, hopeful of stabilizing national finances and of re-establishing British prestige so that " the pound . . . would be able once more to look the dollar in the face," restored England to the gold standard in 1925. Although generally hailed as a step toward recovery this move actually raised the prices of British exports so that they had to compete at a disadvantage in foreign markets. To protect the domestic market Baldwin secured the passage of an act authorizing certain tariff duties, subject to the approval of the Board of Trade and Parliament. Designed to curtail foreign competition the scheme failed to achieve signal success. On the contrary, the commercial and industrial stagnation persisted and unemployment tended to increase.

The Crisis in the Coal Industry. The coal industry was especially hard hit by the economic recession. Demand for coal had decreased because of the development of electricity, oil, and lignite as sources of power. France and Italy formerly dependent on British supplies were now receiv-

but exempted certain raw products and other materials. Later a special tariff commission was created which was authorized to raise duties as much as 100 per cent on imports from countries that discriminated against British goods. People were urged to " Buy British " and " Buy Empire," pay income taxes in advance, and turn in gold to counteract foreign gold withdrawals. Furthermore by using the protective tariff as a basis for bargaining Great Britain was able to negotiate reciprocal trade agreements with other countries, especially Germany, Argentina, Denmark, and Russia. The Imperial Economic Conference at Ottawa which met in 1932 arranged a system of Imperial preferences (favorable tariffs among the members of the British Commonwealth) but the net gains to England were relatively slight since the dominions wanted to protect their own markets.

Attempts were also made by the government to regenerate industry and agriculture. Devices somewhat resembling the American New Deal were adopted which provided for the obligatory fixing of wages and prices, the control of marketing, the scrapping of obsolete equipment, and the semi-official supervision of industry. Governmental subsidies were forthcoming in this process of rationalization. Agriculture was aided mainly through direct subsidies and processing taxes, as well as by protective tariffs and import quotas. Parliament passed a law which virtually guaranteed the British farmer $1.00 per bushel of wheat. One of the most notable of post-war reforms was a gigantic slum clearance and housing program. By the summer of 1935 some 2,500,000 houses had been built, of which approximately 1,000,000 were constructed after 1931.[19] About half were partly financed, directly or indirectly, by government subsidies. Retail business in certain parts of England was stimulated correspondingly. In certain areas, however, such as South Wales, the north of England and Scotland, the economic situation remained desperate despite the government's efforts to stimulate economic life through the construction of roads and railways, and the revival of business enterprises.[20]

During the first two years of the National government the number of unemployed rose steadily, reaching an all-time high of 3,000,000 at the end of 1932. The ensuing years, however, showed great improvement. In 1935 the number of unemployed fell below 2,000,000 for the first time since 1930; by 1937 it was down to 1,300,000. Then came a business recession with its invitable concomitant of increased unemployment. A vast rearmament program together with compulsory conscription in 1939 drained the ranks of the idle and by the summer of 1939 the unemployed totaled 1,200,000.

Balancing the budget was no easy task. Although the budget of 1931–1932 was balanced on paper it was necessary to persuade the citizenry to pay taxes in advance. By readjusting the government's loans and stopping war debt payments to the United States in 1933 British finances were im-

would benefit the export trade and thus contribute indirectly to the reduction of unemployment.

The Formation of a National Coalition. By 1931 the whole world was in the throes of a depression which was bound to affect the aggravated economic situation. Industrial production and the export trade sagged to lower levels; unemployment rose to 2,600,000, approximately two and one half times what it had been when the Labor Party took office in 1929; and the national budget strained by emergency demands became more seriously unbalanced. Gold began to flow out of London and British financial prestige was shaken.[17] Confronted by the danger of a general collapse MacDonald resigned on August 24 and the Labor government was at an end. The three parties then combined to form a National Coalition government headed by MacDonald. Many of MacDonald's Labor colleagues, who were opposed to his program of reduced doles and curtailed social services, refused to support the non-partisan regime. He and other Laborites who had joined the National government were read out of the party.[18]

The Search for Prosperity. In view of the gravity of the situation the National Coalition government adopted a vigorous course of action. Through increased taxes and rigid economies the budget was balanced. On September 21, 1931 the government, hoping to check the drain on its gold reserves and stimulate trade, abandoned the gold standard. This reduced the price of the pound below the gold prices prevailing abroad. The consequent disparity in price levels, it was hoped, would encourage home consumption of domestic products which would now be cheaper than imported goods. Imports would decline and exports increase since English producers would be in a position to undersell their competitors. Stimulation of industry as well as foreign trade, accompanied by a gradual rise in prices, was anticipated.

In addition the Conservatives demanded and MacDonald assented to a high tariff. Lloyd George's Liberals, as traditional free-traders, refused to support the measure. MacDonald therefore appealed to the nation for its support and scheduled new elections for October 27, 1931. Campaigning as Nationalists MacDonald's Conservative, National Liberal and National Labor supporters decisively defeated their opponents. The government secured a majority of nearly 500 in the Commons as its two rivals dwindled to 4 and 52 seats respectively. The Conservatives alone had 471 seats, making them the dominant element in the coalition.

During the next few years the Nationalists had to wrestle with three interrelated problems: the establishment of a favorable trade balance, unemployment, and balancing the budget. In tackling the first the government reverted to protection. On March 1, 1932 a tariff law was enacted which levied a 10 per cent *ad valorem* duty on manufactured goods

proved. Taxes were reduced and the salary cuts of government officials and employees restored. Dangerous international tension, however, compelled Great Britain in 1936 to launch an extensive naval building program, the first step toward comprehensive rearmament. These efforts to revamp the nation's defenses frustrated attempts to balance the budget, for despite increases in taxes large deficits began to pile up annually.[21]

The National Coalition retained the confidence of the nation. On June 7, 1935 MacDonald resigned on the grounds of ill-health and Stanley Baldwin became Prime Minister, retaining the same Cabinet with only a few changes. In October he dissolved Parliament and called for elections on November 14. Waging the campaign chiefly on the basis of his foreign policy which called for collaboration with the League of Nations — a poll of 10,000,000 voters had recently endorsed the League and its sanctions against Italy — the Baldwin government sailed to easy victory, although its majority was reduced from about 400 to 250. During the 1930's Sir Oswald Mosley organized a British Fascist Party which became increasingly anti-Communist and anti-Semitic. It never gained much public support despite the misery engendered by the depression.

The Dynastic Crisis. George V died on June 20, 1936, aged 70, and was succeeded by his son, Edward VIII. Before the date set for his coronation, however, Edward was compelled to renounce the throne and go into exile. The crisis arose because of the young king's determination against the advice of his ministers to marry Mrs. Wallis Simpson, twice-divorced American woman. It had become a question as to whether the will of the monarch should prevail over that of the government. Perceiving the impasse Edward abdicated on December 10 in favor of his brother, the Duke of York. On the following day Parliament passed the Abdication Act and regulated the succession of George VI to the throne.

The Chamberlain Government. In the Spring of 1937 Baldwin, too, disappeared from the public scene. Neville Chamberlain, next in line among Conservative leaders, was invited to form a new government.[22] His ministry, like that of Baldwin, was based on the National Coalition and, though predominantly Conservative, contained several Liberals and Laborites.

Chamberlain had to continue the fight against the depression for the slight business boom of 1936 and 1937 was followed by a serious recession. The adverse trade balances were the largest in British history in 1937 and 1938; unemployment was again on the rise; and the public debt despite higher taxes soared to an all-time high of £8,000,000,000 in 1938. Preoccupied by foreign problems as a result of German, Italian and Japanese aggression, Chamberlain could do little to solve domestic problems. Nevertheless the government in 1937 decided to nationalize the mines by 1942 and agreed to indemnify the 4000 owners to the extent of £66,450,-000. In 1937 Chamberlain announced a five-year plan of rearmament, involving expenditures of £300,000,000 annually, some of it to be defrayed by loans, but the bulk derived from an excess profits tax and higher income taxes. By 1939 the per capita tax burden in Great Britain was twice that of the United States while the enormous defense and war budgets brought great increase in the national debt.

The Rearmament Program. Preoccupation with defense and with foreign affairs forced Chamberlain to shelve after 1938 a number of projected social and economic reforms. The government concentrated most of its attention on the production of aircraft, warships, munitions, air-raid shelters, and other war material. Even before the outbreak of war in September, 1939, the British industrial structure was artificially stimulated and distorted as a consequence of preparedness. There was a slight increase in unemployment due to the dislocation of peace industries. The doubling of the Territorial Army by voluntary enlistment in March, 1939 and the adoption of universal conscription absorbed much of the available man power. In preparation for enemy air attacks the country on April 18, 1939 was divided into eighteen regional units each under a commissioner endowed with broad executive and administrative authority. On August 29 the Emergency Powers Act by endowing the government with full authority over industrial production, agriculture, transportation, communication, navigation, and prices, set up what was tantamount to a dictatorship in the event of war.

The Roots of British Foreign Policy. British foreign policy has been determined by geographic factors.[23] The British Isles, situated on the exposed flank of Europe, are in close proximity to, and economically dependent upon, that continent. In addition Great Britain is the center of a vast world empire. In modern times she has been confronted with the dual necessity of insuring her own defense, food supplies, and raw materials, and maintaining communications with her Imperial possessions. In other words Britain's primary interests have been, speaking broadly, independence and trade. To safeguard these interests is the chief responsibility of her diplomats and armed forces.

It is characteristic of British foreign policy not to look far ahead. Unlike most continental powers Britain is a satiated state. Possessing the world's largest empire, vast wealth, abundant resources, and strategic bases, she has advocated, naturally enough, preservation of the status quo. As a " have " power, in contradistinction to " have-not " states like Germany, Italy, and Japan, she has been mainly concerned with the retention rather than increase of her extensive possessions. In view of the multiplicity and variety of her interests and of those of her empire, Britain has been unable to work out a long-range or uniform course of action. Therefore she has had to muddle through to make compromises to fit changing conditions. This constant trimming of the sails to the wind, resulting in

frequent uncertainties, vacillation and occasional reversals of policy, has endowed British foreign relations with the quality of opportunism. The British have preferred to meet situations as they arise rather than follow a preconceived plan. As Frederick the Great remarked: " The English have no system."

The Balance of Power. Perhaps the only constant in British foreign policy is its devotion to the balance of power in Europe. In fact for the British, in view of the fact that a dominant state might exclude their goods from continental markets, it is almost a law of nature. Great Britain has championed the Open Door and the rights of small nations not simply out of altruism, but because it has feared the rise of a dominant continental power. Such a power might seize the strategic Channel ports and jeopardize British commerce. The British have therefore upheld the Western state system and fought any nation which threatened to subjugate its European neighbors. Hence England's historic opposition to Charles V, Louis XIV, Napoleon, William II, and Hitler.

" *Splendid Isolation.*" The foreign policy of Great Britain down to about 1900 has been described as " splendid isolation." Her insularity afforded complete immunity from invasion as well as a free hand in international relations. Great Britain could remain aloof from continental politics, if she so desired, or she could project herself into the European scene by diplomatic or military intervention, deftly avoiding long-term policies or continental commitments.

After 1900 Great Britain's isolation became less splendid as Europe was divided into two rival coalitions, both hostile to England. Thenceforth she was compelled to seek friends in order to protect her empire and her commerce. As a consequence she allied herself with Japan in 1902 and later with France and Russia in the diplomatic bloc known as the Triple Entente. After overthrowing its rival, the Triple Alliance, in the First World War, the Entente was dissolved. Thereupon the British, eschewing new continental commitments and suspicious of the post-war militarism of France and her allies, reverted to traditional isolation. Great Britain joined the League of Nations but many of her statesmen were frankly skeptical as to its capacity to foster collective security and disarmament. Eventually public opinion in the British Isles crystallized in favor of the League, as was revealed by the poll of 1935 in which an overwhelming number of voters signified their desire to cooperate with the League to restrain aggressor nations. By this time Great Britain had virtually abandoned isolation and stood forth as one of the chief protagonists of collective security. The dwindling of her own security as a result of the development of aircraft, submarines, and other instruments of war together with the rising menace of totalitarian states, such as Germany, Italy, and Japan, impelled Great Britain to enter into closer diplomatic

relations with the continental democracies. In entering into alliances with France and other countries Great Britain assumed mutual guarantees and continental responsibilities which signified the renunciation, perhaps permanently, of isolation.

The Tradition of Naval Supremacy. Great Britain's dependence on sea-going commerce, the variety and far-flung distribution of her Imperial possessions, and the corresponding problems of defense, made it imperative that she maintain a preponderance of seapower against any possible combination of enemies. Before 1914 she generally maintained a naval ratio of 2 to 1 as compared with the second ranking power, or to put it differently, a fleet equal to those of the second and third ranking powers combined. Although Great Britain's naval supremacy was indisputable, it annoyed only those who endeavored to challenge her primacy. After 1919 the financial burdens of maintaining such naval preponderance together with improved relations with the United States induced the British to accept parity with the Americans. This arrangement achieved at the Washington and London Naval conferences, to which we have already referred, signified the abandonment of traditional policy but it brought closer Anglo-American cooperation in the post-war years.

Devotion to the Status Quo. The economic recovery of Europe involving obviously peace, disarmament, and general security, was beneficial to the British for it would enable them to increase their continental trade and investments. Also, a conciliated Islamic world in the Near and Middle East was essential for a country which ruled so many Moslems. An orderly China and a prosperous Japan were likewise compatible with British interests. In fact the greater the prosperity of the world the brighter the prospects were for economic revival in the British Isles. Therefore the British were hostile to such disturbing movements as Communism, Fascism, and National Socialism calculated to destroy the status quo and by so doing weaken the international foundations upon which the fortunes of Great Britain and her empire rested. British statesmen in the years before the Second World War carried on a policy of appeasement in the dwindling hope of preserving peace for Great Britain had nothing to gain and everything to lose by war.

Natural Resources. Great Britain's natural economy has been largely determined by geographic considerations. In the first place the British Isles have an abundance of natural resources, particularly coal and iron. Professor H. S. Jevons predicted that coal reserves, which he estimated at 197,000,000,000 tons in 1915, would suffice for four or five centuries at the prevailing rate of production. The annual output was valued at about $900,000,000. Britain has ranked third in the world production of iron and steel. In addition there are sizable deposits of limestone, igneous rock, zinc and tin, and some copper. Oil shale is also found in Great Britain and

there are small seepages of oil, but petroleum production is negligible. Aside from mineral resources Great Britain has a climate suitable for farming, grazing, and cotton spinning. The highlands of Scotland, North Wales, and Cumberland in addition to the rivers of Lancashire, Yorkshire, and North Derbyshire have furnished power for steam turbines and electrical appliances. Finally Britain's insular location athwart the main trade routes, as stated before, has made accessible the raw materials, foodstuffs, and markets of the world.

Agriculture. Agriculture is the largest single industry in the country, affording employment to about 1,300,000 people. Over 45,000,000 of an approximated 56,343,000 available acres are ordinarily devoted to farming. In general cultivation is more intense in England than in other parts of the British Isles and more persons are supported there per acre. Wheat, barley, oats, potatoes and miscellaneous vegetables are the leading crops; the agricultural output totaled £275,000,000 in 1925. Stock raising is significant, cattle normally accounts for about 40 per cent of the annual output. The size and density of the population, however, is too great to enable domestic production to meet British needs. In normal years it is necessary to import 80 per cent of the breadstuffs and fruit, 50 per cent of the eggs, dairy products and meat, and 33 per cent of the vegetables and fish consumed in the British Isles. During both the First and the Second World Wars the area under cultivation was enlarged as unusual exertions were made to increase the food supply.

Industry. Manufacturing along with mining and foreign trade has been the backbone of British economic strength. An idea of its tremendous significance can be gained by noting the value of the outputs of various industries for a recent, normal year: food, drink, and tobacco, $3,163,-815,000; ships, vehicles, and other engineering products, $2,366,195,000; textiles, $2,220,000,000; public utilities, $1,700,000,000; iron and steel $1,400,000,000; chemicals, $950,000,000; building and contracting, $935,-000,000; paper and printing, $900,000,000; clothing, $860,000,000; non-ferrous metal, $520,000,000; clay and building materials, $520,000,000; timber, $340,000,000; leather, $165,000,000. In recent years there has been a decrease in the number of persons engaged in personal services, textile trades, especially cotton, and clothing, woodworking and building trades. On the other hand, there have been increases in metal and chemicals, engineering, shipbuilding, and housing industries as well as in government service, sports, and entertainment. Agriculture, although important, is dwarfed by manufacturing with respect to the volume and value of its products and the number of persons employed. Only the United States and Germany have shown comparable industrialization.

Foreign Trade. Dependence on foreign trade was the inevitable result of Great Britain's agricultural and industrial progress. The inadequacy of

minerals and foodstuffs as stated above necessitated large imports. Britain exchanged its manufactures, its shipping and banking securities for foodstuffs and vital raw materials, such as rubber, petroleum, cotton, and wool. Consequently overseas markets were indispensable since large-scale production created enormous surpluses which had to be sold. In other words, foreign trade was the life blood of the British economic system. During 1938 shipments of imports and exports combined reached the staggering total of 127,253,000 tons valued respectively at $4,199,965,000 and $2,300,-956, 000. It is not surprising, therefore, that the government, as we have seen, should devote much of its efforts to the protection and encouragement of foreign trade.

Social Problems. A number of social problems had arisen partly as a result of the economic situation.[24] One of these was the uneven distribution of property, 2 per cent of the population controlling 64 per cent of the wealth. Whereas a minority was rich or comparatively well off, the masses were very poor or destitute. If industry or commerce slackened many more would be thrown out of work. Thus the whole question of social security was closely related to the economic situation.

Furthermore, such problems as slum clearance, public hygiene, malnutrition, and unemployment derived from the maldistribution of wealth. Class consciousness was increasing, and in the eyes of some, this was a disturbing symptom, for it presaged class warfare. The government was endeavoring through beneficial legislation to solve some of these social problems, but the outbreak of war in 1939 necessitated the shelving of the reform program. What the future holds few have the temerity to predict.

Literature. The post-war period witnessed something of a revolution in English literature. Such stalwarts as George Bernard Shaw (1856–   ), H. G. Wells (1866–   ), G. K. Chesterton (1874–1936), and John Galsworthy (1867–1933) were still writing brilliant plays, novels, and essays, but their philosophy and approach to their art was essentially pre-war. Preoccupied with political and social issues, their works, despite the prevalence of subtlety, humor, satire, and insight into character, were not typical of the post-war era. Leading younger writers like Aldous Huxley (1894–   ), David Garnett (1892–   ), Richard Aldington (1892–   ), Robert Graves (1895–   ), and the three Sitwells (Sachaverell, Osbert, and Edith), were more in tune with the age. The horrors of the war had made them disillusioned and blasé, and their fiction and nonfiction contained biting satires on the frivolities and pretensions of English society. To them, ethics, moral ideas, the responsibilities of the individual, and concern with political and social problems, were manifestations of an outworn civilization. They preferred to assume that life was senseless and

farcical, that social and political problems were absurd, and that progress was an illusion.

There were other significant figures. D. H. Lawrence (1885–1930), neurotic and preoccupied with sex, exerted through his novels a potent influence on his contemporaries. So did Lytton Strachey (1880–1932), whose biographies of Victorian luminaries and of Queen Elizabeth, are masterpieces of iconoclasm and established a style which others tried to emulate. H. G. Wells, in his passion for leveling, also helped to dethrone historical heroes by showing that they were really but ordinary persons. What has been called his " little man complex " appealed to a disillusioned post-war generation which, if it could not climb to high places, could flatter its ego by dragging idols from their pedestals. To many, the Irishman, James Joyce (1882–1941), was the most significant figure in English letters. His *Ulysses*, depicting the sensuous and intellectual lives of average Dubliners, revealed not only remarkable originality of style and method, but summed up the disillusionment, the rejection of spiritual values, the emphasis on materialism, which marked the post-war generation. Of Joyce's hero one critic has remarked: " Here is the Smallest Man stripped naked, exposed in all his squalor, his meanness, his filth." [25]

In general, English literature after 1918, despite its cynicism, neuroticism, and lack of moderation, upheld the traditionally high level of previous eras. If there were fewer solid masterpieces than in the Victorian age, there was greater variety and perhaps a more realistic approach to the problems of life.

Art and Architecture. The painting of post-war Britain was not of commanding significance. The failure of British painters to produce outstanding works was due partly to an inferiority complex, the feeling that continental artists could not be excelled. As a contemporary wrote: " English form is normally a stone below French. At any given moment the best painter in England is unlikely to be better than a first-rate man in the French second class." [26] There were important painters, of whom Sir William Orpen (1878–1931) and Augustus John (1878–   ) are perhaps outstanding, but the source of their inspiration and style was mostly European. In etching and sculpture contemporary Britons rank among the greatest in the world. Jacob Epstein (1880–   ), an American domiciled in England, carries on the great traditions of Rodin; his busts and compositions have great strength and originality. Sir D. Y. Cameron (1865–   ), Sir Muirhead Bone (1876–   ), James McBey (1883–   ), and Dame Laura Knight, among others, have raised the art of line drawing and etching to a perfection never seen before in British art.

In architecture Great Britain has failed to participate in the fructifying movements emanating from the continent and the United States. Although many modernistic buildings have been built, most Englishmen, deeply individualistic and traditional, have resented them.

Music. Although rich in folk music and in musical forebears such as Henry Purcell (1658–1695) English music failed to keep pace with contemporaneous developments in Europe. It became intellectually bankrupt after Handel and there was a stagnation in taste as English composers slavishly imitated the works of Liszt, Mendelssohn, and others. It was not until the twentieth century that native genius showed signs of emancipation. By that time Sir Edward Elgar (1857–1934) through his symphonies and other works, had re-established the prestige of English music. His compositions did not display remarkable originality but they revealed a mastery of technique. Equally significant were the works of Ralph Vaughan Williams (1872–   ) and Gustav Theodore Holst (1874–1934) which displayed both independence of academic tradition and devotion to artistic originality. Frederick Delius (1862–1934) also achieved international recognition. The fertile technique and vigor of the works of these composers was evidence of a healthy, if somewhat belated, revival of English musical genius.[27]

Great Britain on the Eve of War. By 1939 Great Britain despite many vicissitudes seemed to have recovered from the First World War. Traditional liberties and established customs had been preserved. In contrast to the totalitarian states her educational system was free of militant ideologies and regimentation. All religious faiths were tolerated and although the Anglican Church was the official one, membership therein was not prescribed. At the outbreak of the Second World War Great Britain appeared in the eyes of contemporaries, friends and foe alike, as the chief European stronghold of democracy.

Ireland

The Irish Question. The emergence of an independent Ireland was one of the significant developments in the post-war British history.[28] The Irish question agitated the British Parliament for a century before the War. In 1914 Ireland was on the verge of revolution over the third Home Rule Bill. For religious and economic reasons the Protestants of Ulster preferred to fight rather than be united with Ireland. On the other hand the majority of the Irish people, who were Catholic, were equally determined that the island should be united under an Irish parliament. With the outbreak of war home rule was postponed. The Irish Nationalists, a party which inherited the liberal traditions of the nineteenth century, were content with home rule; but the extremely nationalistic Sinn Feiners were prepared to resort to violence in order to obtain complete independence.[29] The Easter Rebellion of 1916 led by the Sinn Feiners and aided by the

Germans resulted in the proclamation of a republic. It was promptly crushed, however, by the English and an armed peace persisted until the end of the War.

The Movement for Independence. In the elections of 1918 the question of independence was the major issue in Ireland. The Sinn Feiners, who now styled themselves the Irish Republican Party, secured 73 seats in the Commons as compared to 6 for the Nationalists. Instead of taking their seats in London the Irish Republicans proclaimed a republic and constituted themselves an Irish Parliament, the *Dail Eireann,* which met in Dublin on January 21, 1919. Delegates were sent to the Paris Peace Conference but they failed to secure admission. De Valera, a mathematician and patriot "who would no more have dreamed of compromising than he would of making polite concessions in the working of an equation," was elected President; a ministry was chosen, and Ireland found herself in a virtual state of war with Great Britain.

The Government of Ireland Act (1920). Lloyd George undertook in 1920 to solve the Irish question. He sympathized with Irish aspirations for home rule, but was unalterably opposed to full independence. Furthermore he was unwilling to compel the six Protestant counties to submit to union with the Catholic majority. Accordingly the Government of Ireland Act was promulgated on December 23, 1920 which separated Ulster from the rest of Ireland. Each was granted home rule and a Parliament but certain powers and Imperial services were reserved for the British Parliament in which the two sections of Ireland were to be represented. A Council of Ireland, elected by the two Irish Parliaments and designed to harmonize the relationships and interests of the two sections, was to be established. Ulster acquiesced in the new plan but the rest of Ireland rejected the arrangement and flared into revolt.

Establishment of the Irish Free State. Determined to liquidate the problem the British were willing to grant further concessions. Months of fighting and negotiations followed before the Sinn Feiners on December 6, 1921 accepted a treaty setting up the Irish Free State. This arrangement put Ireland, except for Ulster, on the same constitutional basis as the self-governing dominions. The six Protestant counties remained subject to the Act of 1920. A schism was provoked among the Sinn Feiners when the *Dail Eireann* approved the Anglo-Irish treaty. In protest De Valera resigned the presidency and was succeeded by Arthur Griffith. When the *Dail Eireann* was converted into the Parliament of the Free State De Valera's followers withdrew. A provisional government under the direction of Michael Collins continued to function and proceeded to the task of drafting a constitution.[30] Rather than submit to the new regime De Valera and other irreconcilables plunged the country into civil war which was crushed in the spring of 1923 only after bitter fighting.

The Irish Free State was something of an anomaly.[31] Having achieved dominion status by virtue of the Anglo-Irish Treaty of 1921 it began to organize a system of government. In September, 1922 a provisional Parliament met and elected William Cosgrave, a moderate, President and chairman of the provisional regime. Then on October 25 it adopted a constitution which acknowledged the nominal authority of the king who was to be represented in Dublin by a governor-general.[32] Real executive power, however, was vested in an executive council or ministry which was directly responsible to the *Dail* (the lower house of the legislature). The upper house or *Seanad Eireann* consisted of sixty members elected for twelve years; it had no authority to amend money bills and only a suspensive veto on other legislation. The *Dail* elected on a basis of universal suffrage and proportional representation was the dominant body with a position analogous to the British House of Commons. With the assent of the king the new constitution went into effect on December 6, 1922. In the first parliamentary elections held in August, 1923 the Free State Party headed by Cosgrave and Kevin O'Higgins gained 63 seats out of a total of 153, as compared to 44 for De Valera's Republicans. As a result, Cosgrave was enabled to remain in office.

Problems Confronting the Irish Free State. A number of difficult problems confronted the Irish Free State. One of these arose out of the refusal of De Valera's followers, who in protest against the Anglo-Irish Treaty had recently been in revolt against the Irish Free State, to take their seats or to cooperate with the government. Even after De Valera had made peace with the state many of his followers refused to do so. Instead, styling themselves the Irish Republican Army they freed themselves from De Valera's control and continued to agitate for a fully united and independent Ireland. They perpetrated a number of outrages, including assassinations, in their attempts to sabotage the Free State. In 1927 De Valera and his party took the oath of allegiance to the new regime and re-entered Irish politics.

Another vexatious question concerned the boundary between the Free State and Northern Ireland. The latter insisted on retaining the boundary prescribed by the Act of 1920. But the treaty of 1921 stipulated that a new boundary should be drawn by a commission of three, one each to be designated by the Free State, Northern Ireland, and Great Britain. Upon the refusal of Northern Ireland to select a member, the British appointed one for her. The situation along the border was so tense, however, that it seemed better to compromise. Accordingly the boundary of 1920 was retained, the approval of the Free State being won by canceling her share of the United Kingdom debt as of 1921.

Cosgrave's government in addition to restoring order enacted a number of needed reforms. The administrative system was revamped through

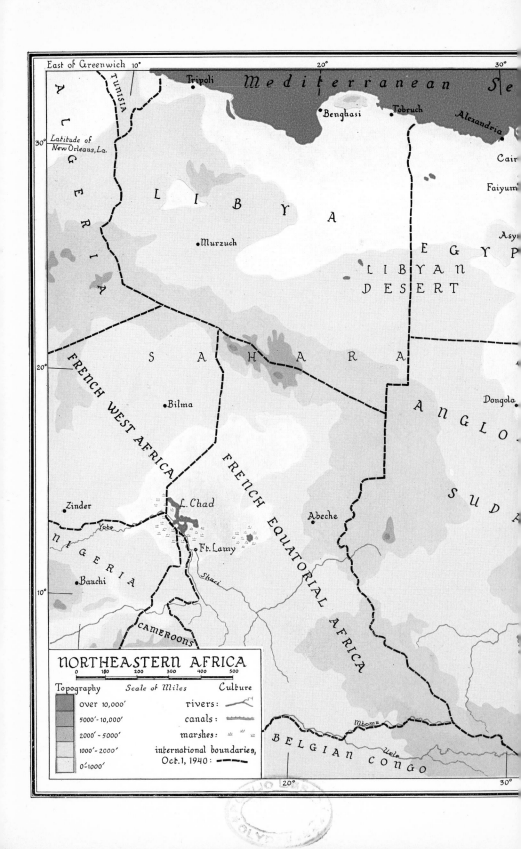

NORTHEASTERN AFRICA

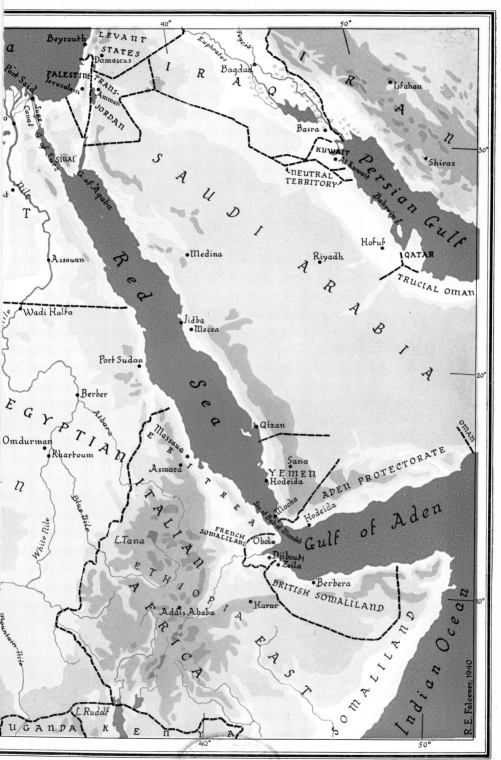

the consolidation of overlapping departments and services, and the reform and increased centralization of local government. The judiciary was reorganized, the police force reduced; the system of public relief remodeled, and the educational program modernized. Agriculture was benefited through additional land-purchase legislation, the sugar-beet industry was introduced, and a scheme for electrifying the Shannon River was adopted. Despite the expenditures involved in these achievements the national budget was balanced. As an expression of Irish nationalism the Gaelic language was revived and made compulsory for civil servants and lawyers; many family and place names were Gaelicized; and Gaelic appeared on the coins and postage stamps of the Free State. Its use did not become universal, however, for many were unable to comprehend it and continued to rely on English.

The Rise of De Valera. After 1930 the Free State, like the rest of the world, was engulfed by the great depression. As everywhere people blamed the government for their economic and social ills. Manufacturers denounced its unwillingness to enact a high tariff while farmers condemned its restrictions on agricultural exports. There were widespread demands for the cancelation of the land annuities and other obligations to the British. The Irish Republican Army and other anti-governmental bodies resumed their activities and frequently resorted to terroristic methods. Cosgrave's government replied in October, 1931 by outlawing the Irish Republican Army and eleven other organizations. A military tribunal was created to try persons accused of sedition and terrorism. Soon the jails were filled with malcontents but Cosgrave's popularity was destroyed as a result of these repressive measures. In the parliamentary elections of February, 1932 Cosgrave's followers secured only 65 seats as compared to 72 for De Valera's party, *Fianna Fail.* When the Laborites who held the balance of power threw their support to De Valera, he was elected President of the executive council.[33]

The Attempt to Sever British Ties. De Valera now undertook to carry out the platform which he had presented to the nation in the election campaign. Aiming at political and economic self-sufficiency for Eire it included the abolition of the oath of allegiance to the king, the retention by the Irish treasury of the land annuities due to the British, the creation of a protective tariff, and the repeal of the Public Safety Act of October, 1931. The suspension of the last named legislation permitting the release of many political prisoners and the resumption of drills by the Irish Republic Army was the first step in the realization of De Valera's program. After Anglo-Irish negotiations concerning land annuities had failed Ireland withheld the payment of £1,500,000 due on July 21, 1932. The British retaliated by levying a heavy duty on Irish imports and De Valera countered by prohibitive tariffs on British goods. A trade war followed which hit Ireland, 90 per cent of whose exports went to Great Britain, very hard. Since payments were not made they helped to balance the Irish budget. Approval of De Valera's policies was forthcoming in the parliamentary elections of January 24, 1933 which returned a clear-cut majority for the *Fianna Fail*.

De Valera was determined to sever the political connection with Great Britain. In May, 1933 the oath of allegiance was abolished; then the approval of the Governor-General of acts passed by the Irish Parliament was repudiated; and the right of appeal from Irish courts to the British Privy Council was abolished. Later foreign diplomats were instructed to present their credentials to the President rather than to the Governor-General; Free State instead of British citizenship was prescribed. The Free State officially ignored the twenty-fifth anniversary and the death of George V in 1936. No representative was sent to his funeral nor was Edward VIII or George VI proclaimed king in Dublin.

The attempts to achieve economic self-sufficiency through the encouragement of local industry were not successful. Instead they contributed to the serious decline of foreign trade, increased living costs, and large governmental deficits. In 1936 De Valera retreated to the extent of entering into a trade agreement with Great Britain. This reduced the duties on many British commodities, especially coal and cement, while London reciprocated with respect to livestock and meat.

Opposition to De Valera. Dissatisfaction with De Valera's policies soon crystallized in the founding of an organization headed by General Owen O'Duffy, known as the "Blue Shirts." Its ranks were recruited from the Cosgravites, from those who resented the Free State Treaty of 1921, or were embittered over the results of the trade war with Great Britain. The Blue Shirts frequently resorted to incendiarism and violence which necessitated strong-arm methods on the part of De Valera. He was forced to revive the Public Safety Act of 1931. All subversive organizations including the Blue Shirts and the Irish Republican Army were outlawed, and the jails were again filled with political agitators.

The Constitution of 1937. In April, 1937 De Valera presented the Free State with a new constitution. Proclaiming the independence and sovereignty of the Irish nation it made no mention of Great Britain or its king. Instead it provided for a President elected for a seven-year term by direct vote of the people who would be the nominal head of the state, henceforth known as Eire. Actual executive power was to be exercised by the Prime Minister and his Cabinet which were responsible to the *Dail*. The bicameral parliamentary system was retained. In the elections of July 1 the new constitution was approved by about 56 per cent of the voters and as a consequence went into operation on December 29. The elections destroyed De Valera's workable majority and again placed him in a position of dependence on the support of the Labor Party.

The Termination of Anglo-Irish Disputes.   Meanwhile the Irish President tried to adjust amicably the outstanding difficulties with Great Britain. After lengthy negotiations with Chamberlain three agreements were made on April 25, 1938. These provided for: (1) the withdrawal of British naval and military forces from Eire and the assumption by the latter of responsibility for her own defense; (2) the payment by Eire to Great Britain of £10,000,000 by November 30, 1938 as a final settlement of the land annuities; (3) annual payments of £250,000 until 1987 to Great Britain for certain property damages; (4) the cancellation of the retaliatory duties adopted by Great Britain and Eire during their trade war; and (5) a treaty designed to re-establish Anglo-Irish trade on mutually beneficial lines. These agreements seemed to have terminated the Anglo-Irish disputes but they left Eire's position with respect to the Empire uncertain and ill-defined.

The prestige accruing to De Valera from this settlement enabled him to strengthen his position. He dissolved the *Dail* and scheduled new elections for June 17, 1938. Public approval of his policies was registered to the extent of giving *Fianna Fail* a decisive majority. In order to heal the wounds lingering from recent internal strife De Valera and Cosgrave, as leaders of Eire's two largest political parties, agreed to offer the presidency to Douglas Hyde, a distinguished historian. The fact that he was a Protestant, although an ardent nationalist, was a gesture of reconciliation to Ulster, whose union with Eire was still sought. On May 4, 1939 Hyde, in default of any rival candidates, was chosen President by acclamation.

Eire at the Outbreak of War. New complications plagued Eire in 1939. The Irish Republican Army impatient at De Valera's failure to bring about the incorporation of Northern Ireland engaged in bombings and other disturbances, hoping to embarrass the authorities in Great Britain, Northern Ireland, and Eire. Officials in all three countries cooperated in the suppression of this lawlessness but their efforts were not altogether successful for the subterranean organization of the Irish Republican made it difficult to apprehend and punish them. On May 31, 1939 an Offenses Against the State Act was passed which legalized the death penalty and detention for treasonable acts. De Valera was still hopeful of uniting the two parts of Ireland but he preferred to accomplish this purpose by peaceful means.

The Dominions

The Extent of the Empire. The British Empire consists of territories aggregating about 12,000,000 square miles or almost one-fourth of the earth's surface. These are scattered throughout the globe, most of them in the temperate zones. The population of the British Empire was estimated in 1935 at 475,000,000, of whom only 68,000,000 were whites. The rest included the black, yellow, and brown races, besides millions of hybrids.

From the governmental and administrative points of view the Empire falls into several distinct divisions: [34] (1) Great Britain and Northern Ireland; (2) six self-governing dominions — Canada, Australia, New Zealand, South Africa, Eire, and Newfoundland; (3) self-governing colonies possessing wide but not unrestricted autonomy and not represented in the imperial conference; (4) crown colonies which, lacking responsible government, are under the supervision of the Secretary of State for Colonies in London; (5) protectorates and protected states which, while retaining varying degrees of autonomy, are under British supervision; (6) India which has a special status; and (7) the mandated territories which are not actually parts of the Empire. The form of control varies widely in these miscellaneous territories, but the most fundamental distinction among them is that between those which enjoy self-government and those which are under the direct jurisdiction of the Crown.

The Rise of the Dominions. In the post-war period the Empire has undergone a sweeping transformation. Six self-governing dominions each politically mature and conscious of its separateness emerged. They were recognized as quasi-international states by admittance to the League of Nations and by being permitted to exchange diplomatic representatives and enter into treaties with foreign powers. In 1921 the first official use of the term " British Commonwealth of Nations " recognized the fact that the Empire had ceased to be a centralized organism.

The tendency toward Imperial decentralization was further emphasized in 1925 when the Colonial Office in Downing Street was divided. At that time a Secretary of State for Dominions was created while the non-self-governing territories remained under the Colonial Office. At the Imperial Conference of 1926, as we have seen, the dominions were officially designated as " autonomous communities within the British Empire, equal in status, in no way subordinate one to another in any aspect of their domestic or external affairs, though united by a common allegiance to the British Crown." [35] In the absence of a written constitution the Crown was the chief bond of unity. Curiously, this tendency toward decentralization so far from weakening the empire seemed to strengthen it. In the words of General Smuts: " The Empire is the greatest paradox of all time in that it derives its strength at the centre from the weakness of its hold on the circumference." [36]

The Divergence of Imperial Interests. In some respects the interests of the dominions diverged from those of the Empire. Their desire for tariff protection was at variance with the traditional British free trade as was their insistence on preferential treatment for their agricultural products in British markets. At the Ottawa Conference in 1932 several bilateral treaties were signed between Great Britain and the dominions, and among the dominions themselves. These were designed through the crea-

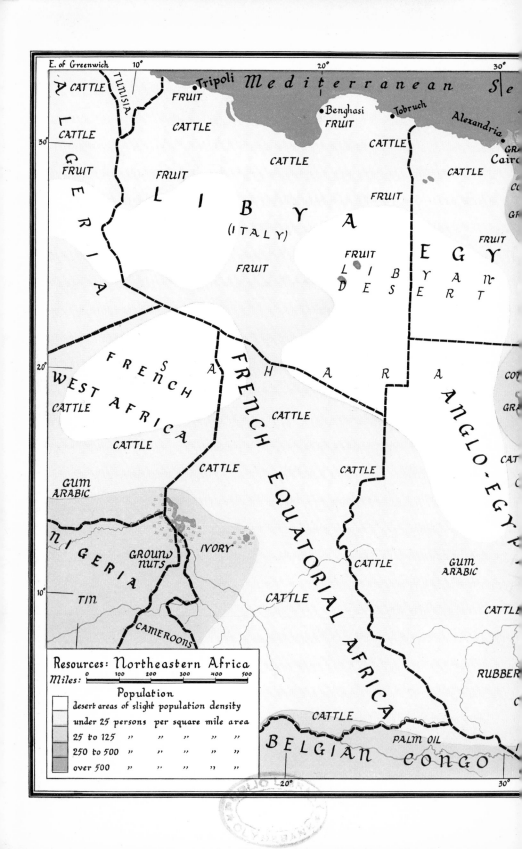

Resources: Northeastern Africa

Miles: 0   100   200   300   400   500

Population

desert areas of slight population density
under 25 persons per square mile area
25 to 125   "   "   "   "   "
250 to 500   "   "   "   "   "
over 500   "   "   "   "   "

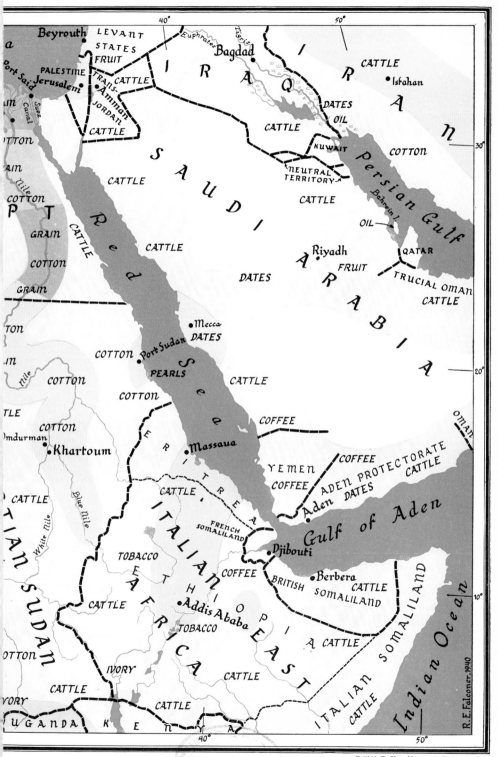

Beyrouth · LEVANT STATES · FRUIT
Port Said · PALESTINE · Jerusalem · Trans-Amman · JORDAN · CATTLE
Suez Canal
COTTON
GRAIN
COTTON
GRAIN
COTTON
TLE
COTTON
CATTLE
IVORY
CATTLE
IVORY
UGANDA

40°
Euphrates · Tigris
Bagdad
IRAQ
DATES
OIL
CATTLE
KUWAIT
NEUTRAL TERRITORY
CATTLE

50°
CATTLE
Isfahan
IRAN
COTTON
30°
OIL
Bahrein I.
QATAR
Persian Gulf

SAUDI
CATTLE
CATTLE
DATES
Riyadh
FRUIT
ARABIA
TRUCIAL OMAN
CATTLE
20°

Red Sea
Mecca · DATES
COTTON · Port Sudan
PEARLS
COTTON
CATTLE
COFFEE

Nile
COTTON
COTTON
Omdurman · Khartoum
CATTLE
Blue Nile
White Nile
ITALIAN SUDAN

ERITREA
Massaua
CATTLE
FRENCH SOMALILAND
ITALIAN EAST AFRICA
TOBACCO
CATTLE
Addis Ababa
TOBACCO
IVORY
CATTLE
ETHIOPIA
KENYA

YEMEN
COFFEE
COFFEE
COFFEE
Aden · ADEN PROTECTORATE · CATTLE
DATES
Gulf of Aden

OMAN

COFFEE
Djibouti
BRITISH SOMALILAND
Berbera · CATTLE
CATTLE
ITALIAN SOMALILAND
CATTLE
Indian Ocean
10°

R.E.Falconer, 1940

40°
50°

tion of preferential tariffs and special concessions to check alleged Russian dumping and to retaliate against the high-tariff policies of the United States. The Ottawa agreements although they accomplished their purpose to some extent, failed to convert the Empire into anything like a coordinated economic unit.

The Problem of India. Other factors acted as barriers to Imperial unity. India, whose status within the Empire had been somewhat anomalous since the war, was in a state of semi-rebellion. The Nationalists, under the leadership of Mahatma Gandhi, protested vehemently against British rule and demanded independence. As British concessions failed to keep pace with Indian demands there was intermittent civil strife. The Government of India Bill (1919) enlarged native control of local government and created a Legislative Assembly and Council of State. Composed mainly of natives, the legislation suggested by these bodies was to be subject to British approval. Since this " dyarchy," as it was called, did not go very far in the direction of home rule, it was widely denounced by the natives. Parliament supplanted it with a new constitution in 1935 but this, too, was unpalatable to India because it did not grant her even dominion status. Unrest persisted as strikes and hostile demonstrations were organized. The Nationalists were still demanding independence when the Second World War broke out, and were unwilling to support Great Britain against Germany unless they received specific pledges of independence. The white dominions, too, had offended the Indians by raising bars to Indian immigration and this fact made it difficult for India to cooperate with the rest of the Empire.

Difficulties in the Islamic World. British control over much of the Islamic world was not maintained without difficulties. The Moslems resented Great Britain's share in the dismemberment of Turkey, her alleged betrayal of the Pan-Arabic movement, and her sponsorship of the Zionist movement in Palestine. Here desire for raw commodities, particularly oil, had forced Britain to disregard the rights of Moslem peoples in Persia, Mosul, and elsewhere. On the other hand the granting of nominal independence to Egypt, the creation of a sovereign Iraq state, benevolence toward the Hedjaz, and the restriction of Jewish immigration in Palestine had partially placated the Moslems. Inasmuch as these areas are mandates and protectorates rather than integral parts of the Empire they need not concern us here, except to note that they help to keep the Empire in a state of unrest. In 1939 these areas, despite Italian attempts to foment dissatisfaction, were relatively stable and friendly to the Crown.

The Future of the Empire. The rise of nationalism in India and Ireland and the growing self-determination of the dominions created the belief that the Empire had reached its twilight state. Many Englishmen recommended, therefore, that these territories be permitted to secede painlessly and that Britain concentrate her attention on the less developed possessions. In short they wished to withdraw from enterprises which, with some exceptions, especially India, were no longer considered profitable.

Many, on the other hand, were convinced that the tendency toward Imperial solidarity was stronger than the movement toward independence. They advocated the strengthening of the bonds between the mother country and the Empire. It was their belief that the Empire with its common cultural heritage and interlocking political, economic, and defense interests could survive indefinitely as a British league of nations. As related elsewhere, however, the variety and complexity of the Empire's interests made it almost impossible to devise a coordinated foreign policy. The attempt of Great Britain to direct this vast array of peoples along a charted course has been compared to that of a man who tries to propel a number of sugar cubes along a given line by putting them end to end and pushing the hindermost. Therefore, Britain has preferred to meet Imperial problems as they arise rather than anticipate them by a long-range program. The dominions have been permitted some leeway in foreign affairs and they have revealed a strong predilection for collective security but for a minimum of other commitments. In recent years they have undertaken to provide for their own defense, thus further emphasizing their march toward complete freedom.

The Economic Importance of the Empire. To assess the economic importance of the Empire is not easy. Embracing one-fourth of the world's land area, one-fourth of its population, and producing one-fourth of its food supply and raw materials, the British Empire is the greatest concentration of lands, peoples, and resources ever incorporated in a single political framework. Since 1914 Great Britain has found herself increasingly dependent upon the Empire for raw materials, foodstuff, markets, and opportunities for investment. Whereas Britain's average share of world trade has been about 20 per cent since 1919, her share of Empire trade has averaged about 40 per cent. In general it would seem no exaggeration to say that Great Britain's future as a great power is bound inextricably with the fate of the Empire.

II: AFTER THE OUTBREAK OF THE SECOND WORLD WAR

Great Britain

Great Britain's entrance into the Second World War on September 3, 1939 resulted in profound and rapid social and economic changes. In fact the necessity of creating a war economy prompted the enactment of sweeping measures even before the outbreak of hostilities. Already the British government had set up the pattern of a regimented social order which in some respects was comparable to those of the totalitarian states. Corresponding political and social controls, however, were not introduced until after the start of the war.

Building a " War Front." Within a short time Great Britain found herself living under a form of wartime socialism. On September 29 the entire population was registered in order to furnish the government with an inventory of man power. A system for rationing food and fuel was set up as the authorities assumed full control of imports and exports. The state was empowered to allocate labor for defense work in accordance with agreements reached jointly with employers and trade unions. An attempt was made to curtail profiteering by means of a drastic arms profits tax. The introduction of blackouts for protection against air raids and the wholesale evacuation of children from threatened areas came early in the war. A censorship was created to prevent leakages of vital information to the enemy. Other customary civil liberties, however, were as far as possible preserved.

Financing the War. The defense budget for the year ending March, 1940 originally set at £580,000,000 was raised in July, 1939 to £730,000,000. By January 1, 1940 it was estimated that the conflict was costing Great Britain £6,000,000 daily. Special measures designed to facilitate loans and increase revenues were adopted to meet these mounting expenses. Foreseeing financial difficulties Parliament had already doubled the government's borrowing capacity in February, 1939. In September income taxes were raised 37½ per cent; estate duties 10 per cent; surtaxes and other levies were drastically increased. It was not until March 12, 1940, however, that the government placed on the market the first bond issue of £300,000,000 redeemable at par on October 15, 1959 and carrying 3 per cent interest. The rapidity with which the bonds were sold and the government's success in floating subsequent loans were indications of British financial strength and of public confidence in ultimate victory.[37]

The Party Truce. On September 22, 1939 a party truce was proclaimed and all parliamentary and municipal elections postponed until after the struggle. Chamberlain's National cabinet still predominantly Conservative was broadened into a non-partisan war ministry through the inclusion of Winston Churchill, Anthony Eden, and prominent Labor leaders. The Labor Party like other political organizations, pledged its support to the Prime Minister for the duration of the conflict. Complete harmony, however, was not achieved as was indicated in the abrupt dismissal in January, 1940 of Leslie Hore-Belisha, the Minister of War, whose notions of strategy and military reforms made him persona non grata in certain circles. Meanwhile public criticism of the government despite the censorship was not suppressed and was indicative of a waning confidence in its policies and methods.

The Ascendancy of Winston Churchill. After the debacle in Norway in April, 1940 Chamberlain's position became untenable and on May 10, 1940 he was succeeded by the fiery Winston Churchill, who was clothed with even wider powers than his predecessor. Churchill proceeded to broaden the political basis of his coalition so as to make it truly non-partisan. The new Prime Minister immediately organized an inner Cabinet, consisting of three Conservatives, himself, Chamberlain, and Lord Halifax, and two Laborites, Clement Attlee and Arthur Greenwood, to conduct the war more vigorously. Lord Beaverbrook, a newspaper magnate, was placed in charge of a newly created Ministry of Aircraft. War efforts in every field were stepped up as Churchill inspired a singleness of purpose and a unity of direction. The terrible defeat of the Allied armies in the Low Countries and in France in the Spring of 1940 did not break the English resolve to fight on to victory even though France had fallen by the wayside.

By this time not only the country's man power but its wealth, lands, factories, and in fact all its resources were at the disposal of the state. Those who obstructed the government's program, including Mosley's Fascists, German sympathizers, and other malcontents were silenced or jailed. The Irish Republican Army in protest against the division of Ireland sponsored a terroristic program throughout England in 1939–1940 which had only nuisance value. Consecrated to the single, compelling task of winning the war Great Britain seemed in the summer of 1940 more than ever a tight little island. Even when the Great German air attacks on London and other cities began in August, 1940 spreading indescribable horror and destruction, the national morale remained firm and unwavering.

Ireland

The Impact of the War. The outbreak of the Second World War placed Eire in a very difficult position. Deep-seated antipathy toward the British prevented the Irish from espousing their cause. On the other hand, there was little sympathy with the aims and aspirations of Germany. Therefore, De Valera proclaimed the neutrality of Eire and endeavored to prevent belligerent naval and air fleets from violating Irish territories. The strategic location of the island, however, made it a vital link in defending British trade routes; and inability to use its facilities complicated the problem of combating German submarine warfare. As a consequence, Eire had to consider the possibilities of being occupied by the British as a defensive precaution or by the Germans as a convenient base for the attack on Great Britain. The Irish were determined to prevent either contingency.

Eire was compelled, therefore, to adjust herself to the abnormal situation created by the war. De Valera launched a program of rearmament to which the British contributed cannon and anti-aircraft guns. The armed forces were increased and equipped with modern implements. Germany's amazing military successes in the Low Countries and France together with the fear that an attack on Great Britain possibly via Ireland, might be next on the agenda, prompted the Dublin government to order mobilization in June. A military invasion did not materialize in 1940, although the Germans dropped a few bombs on Irish soil. Relations between Eire and Germany remained outwardly cordial. The counter-blockades of the warring powers cut Eire off from most of her overseas markets, and made her more than ever dependent economically on Great Britain. An emergency measure was approved which authorized the Finance Minister to regulate transactions in gold, securities, and foreign exchange. Although no recruitment for British service was permitted on Irish territory, many Irishmen crossed the Channel to enlist. Despite Eire's earnest desire to remain neutral there was widespread fear of embroilment.

The Dominions

The Response to the War. When England declared war on Germany most of the Empire — the dominions, colonies, protectorates, dependencies, and even the mandated countries — rallied to her cause. Even in Eire public opinion favored Great Britain more than it did in 1914. In India, except for the powerful Union Congress, most political, economic, and religious groups affirmed their support of Great Britain. In South Africa Premier Hertzog's government was pro-German but it was soon supplanted by a loyalist regime under the veteran General Smuts. Before the end of October, 1939 representatives of the dominion governments and of India met in London to coordinate and intensify the war efforts of the Empire.

Canada. By pre-arranged decision Canada considered the British declaration of war as a signal for her own participation. The opposition of isolationists, nationalists, and French-Canadian separatists was immediately squashed by the dominion government under the premiership of Mackenzie King.[38] Nine days before the outbreak of hostilities the Canadian militia was called to guard the transportation facilities, industries, and merchant marine. In order to thwart attempts at espionage and sabotage, malcontents and foreigners, particularly the German minority in Saskatchewan, were placed under surveillance.

Little time was lost by Canada in building a "war front." The War Measures Act of September 4, 1939 endowed the government with extraordinary power following which a number of important steps were taken. The wartime budget was boosted, financed in part by an excess-profits tax levied on business transactions; the government assumed control over imports, exports, and foreign exchange transactions; and a censorship was put in force. All wheat and grain resources were reserved for Allied use and on October 12 the government announced its first war loan of $200,000,000. The Canadians were determined that not only should the flow of munitions, grain supplies, and soldiers to Great Britain be uninterrupted, but that this aid should be increased.

Apart from its significance as a source of raw materials and munitions Canada was to become a reservoir of military strength. In accordance with an agreement involving Great Britain and the dominions signed at Ottawa on December 17, 1939 Canada was designated as a principal Imperial center for the training of aircraft personnel. It was planned to train 5000 pilots and technicians in the first year, 10,000 in the second, and 20,000 in the third. The entire instructional staff was to be Canadian but Great Britain provided most of the training planes in the beginning. Of an estimated total cost of $600,000,000 by March 31, 1943 Canada was to contribute $350,000,000. In addition Canadian factories were to be geared to quantity-production of various types of war planes. On December 17, 1939 the first of two army divisions landed in Great Britain and assurances were given that more would follow. In the summer of 1940 a system of military conscription was adopted. Small increases in the fleet testified to Canada's determination to support the mother country on the sea as well as in the air and on land.

Australia. Like Canada Australia responded promptly to the emergency. A war Cabinet under the direction of Prime Minister Menzies launched an armament program for the purpose of expanding the navy, air force, and militia. Compulsory military service was re-established in January, 1940, all males between the ages of 15 and 64 having been registered the preceding August. It was decided to equip an expeditionary force for service in Europe. For her share in the Ottawa agreements Australia assumed the responsibility of training 10,400 pilots and 15,600 observers, wireless operators, and gunners. Meanwhile the state on August 28, 1939 had assumed control of overseas exchange transactions and had prohibited the export of gold.[39] A National Security Act approved in September clothed the government with dictatorial power. It was thus empowered to negotiate arrangements by which Great Britain agreed to take all the wool crop, the surpluses in butter, cheese, meat, eggs, canned and dried fruits, and wheat. Australia's importance as a source of man power and raw materials was bound to have cumulative significance if the war lasted long enough.

New Zealand. New Zealand's role in the conflict was in many respects similar to that of Australia except on a smaller scale. It proceeded to build up its armaments and develop its strategically located naval bases, of special value should the struggle spread to the Far East. Food and other raw materials as well as trained man power were obtainable here. Its government, too, was placed on an emergency basis.

The Union of South Africa. After some hesitation, the Union of South Africa assured Great Britain of her support. The new premier, General Smuts, immediately undertook to crush a pro-Nazi ring which was engaged in propagandist activities and sabotage. South Africa's value to the British cause was threefold: she produced enormous quantities of gold which would help finance the war; she had large agricultural surpluses, especially corn and dairy products which the British agreed to purchase; by virtue of an armament program she could stand guard over the whole southern portion of the African continent and by so doing relieve the British of much of the responsibility for its defense.

The Rest of the Empire. The remaining portions of the Empire had their special contributions to make to the war. In general they furnished not only supplies of food and vital raw materials, but also financial backing. Some, like Egypt, provided naval and air bases and thus helped to make the British blockade effective. Such diverse areas as India, Newfoundland, Malta, and Gibraltar performed functions and assumed responsibilities which were essential to the security of the British Commonwealth.

Summary

By 1940 a great deal of water had passed under the bridge since 1918. That day in November, 1918 when the firing of cannon, ringing of bells, waving of flags, and impromptu parading of joyous crowds hailed the armistice which ended the First World War seemed as remote as the pre-1914 world itself. Most of the twenty-one-year interval between the First and Second World Wars was dominated in the British Isles by attempts to solve the problems of the first conflict; the later years of this armistice period were occupied with endeavors to prepare for the ensuing combat. Nevertheless, as we have seen, there was a continuous march toward genuine democracy in which everyone should have equality of opportunity. This process was interrupted by the recurrence of war, in one year of which Great Britain's political order, society, and national economy were so distorted as to be almost unrecognizable. Yet her people despite military reverses, the collapse of Allies, and devastating air attacks remained steadfast, determined, and confident. For as H. G. Wells observed through one of his characters in *Mr. Britling Sees It Through:* " You think that John Bull is dead and a strange generation is wearing his clothes. I think you'll find very soon it's the old John Bull." [40]

REFERENCES

[1] For additional information on the evolution of English nationalism, see E. C. Wingfield-Stratford, *Foundations of British Patriotism*, London: Routledge, 1939. M. Demiashkevich, *National Mind*, New York: American Book Co., 1938, contains a stimulating analysis of what the author calls the "English mind."

[2] Quoted in M. Demiashkevich, *National Mind*, p. 3.

[3] For a good summary of this material, see C. S. Coon, *Races of Europe*, New York: Macmillan, 1939.

[4] E. F. Benson, *As We Are*, New York: Longmans, Green, 1932, is an interesting review of post-war English society.

[5] C. F. G. Masterman, *England After The War*, New York: Harcourt, Brace, 1923, is valuable for its treatment of society and culture.

[6] A stimulating analysis of the British political system is found in Harold Laski, *Parliamentary Government in England*, New York: Viking, 1938.

[7] There are no satisfactory biographies of Lloyd George. J. H. Edward's *David Lloyd George*, New York: Sears, 1929, is uncritical; C. E. Mallet's *Mr. Lloyd George: A Study*, New York: Dutton, 1930, is too partisan.

[8] E. C. Wingfield-Stratford, *Harvest of Victory, 1918–1926*, London: Routledge, 1935, p. 22.

[9] Philip Guedalla, *Gallery*, New York: Putnam, 1924, p. 216. Written in a satirical vein, this book contains a number of short biographical selections of recent British statesmen.

[10] G. D. H. Cole, *Short History of the British Working-Class Movement*, New York: Macmillan, 1938, is a standard work.

[11] A splendid study of the unemployment problem is contained in A. C. C. Hill, Jr. and I. Lubin, *The British Attack on Unemployment*, Washington: Brookings Institution, 1934. Also see the works by Davison cited in the Selected Bibliography.

[12] John Gunther, *Inside Europe*, New York: Harper, rev. ed., 1940, p. 217. This book, written in a journalistic vein, contains much entertaining data on contemporary British personalities.

[13] Wickham Steed, *The Real Stanley Baldwin*, London: Nisbet, 1930, is a fairly good interpretation, although by no means an exhaustive study.

[14] Guedalla, *op. cit.*, p. 105.

[15] For a detailed analysis of the coal question, see the *Report of the Royal Commission on the Coal Industry*, London: Oxford Univ. Press, 1925.

[16] For a searching investigation of Britain's economic situation by an eminent French scholar, see André Siegfried, *England's Crisis*, New York: Harcourt, Brace, 1931. R. Berkeley, *England's Opportunity*, London: Mundanus, 1931, is a reply to it.

[17] F. W. P. Lawrence, *This Gold Crisis*, London: Gollancz, 1931, is a good study by a competent financier.

[18] For the Labor Party's program, see Hugh Dalton, *Practical Socialism for Britain*, London: Routledge, 1935.

[19] See the *Encyclopedia Britannica*, fourteenth edition, article on Housing.

[20] For information on the depressed areas, see J. B. Priestley, *An English Journey*, New York: Harper, 1934.

[21] Ramsay Muir, *The Record of the National Government*, London: G. Allen, 1936, is hostile to the National Union.

[22] There are no satisfactory biographies of Neville Chamberlain.

[23] Additional information concerning British foreign policy may be found in Harold Nicolson, *Diplomacy*, New York: Harcourt, Brace, 1938; C. E. Sipple, *British Foreign Policy since the World War*, Iowa City: Univ. of Iowa Press, 1932; Arthur Willert, *Aspects of British Foreign Policy*, New Haven: Yale Univ. Press, 1928; and E. H. Carr, *Britain*, New York: Longmans, Green, 1939.

[24] G. D. H. Cole and Raymond Postgate, *The British Common People, 1746–1938*, New York: Knopf, 1939; A. Hutt, *The Postwar History of the British Working Class*, New York: Coward-McCann, 1938.

[25] Wingfield-Stratford, *op. cit.*, p. 271.

[26] C. Bell, *Since Cézanne*, New York: Harcourt, Brace, 1923, p. 190.

[27] David Ewen, *Twentieth-Century Composers*, New York: Crowell, 1937, contains biographical sketches of important modern English composers.

[28] W. A. Phillips, *Revolution in Ireland, 1906–1923*, New York: Longmans, Green, 2nd ed., 1926, attempts to present an impartial survey, but is unsympathetic to the Irish cause.

[29] For a vivid and well-informed account of the Sinn Fein movement see S. Desmond, *The Drama of Sinn Fein*, New York: Scribner, 1923.

[30] P. Beasley, *Michael Collins and the Making of New Ireland*, New York: Harper, 1927, is by a Sinn Feiner.

[31] D. R. Gwynn, *The Irish Free State, 1922–1927*, New York: Macmillan, 1928. A good survey of the early years of the Free State.

[32] N. Mansergh, *The Irish Free State*, New York: Macmillan, 1934, is useful for a study of Irish political life. W. Moss, *Political Parties in the Irish Free State*, New York: Columbia Univ. Press, 1933.

[33] D. R. Gwynn, *De Valera*, New York: Dutton, 1933. A scholarly and valuable biography.

[34] W. P. Hall, *Empire to Commonwealth*, New York: Holt, 1928, is a good history of the Empire in the twentieth century. See also E. Jenks, *Government of the British Empire*, Toronto: Carswell, fifth edition, 1937.

[35] Quoted in Wingfield-Stratford, *op. cit.*, p. 440. For additional information see P. J. N. Baker, *The Present Juridical Status of the British Dominions in International Law*, New York: Longmans, Green, 1929.

[36] Quoted in Richard Freund, *Zero Hour*, New York: Oxford Univ. Press, 1937, p. 325.

[37] On the subject of financing the war see Lionel Robbins, "How Britain Will Finance the War," in *Foreign Affairs*, XVIII, No. 3, April, 1940, pp. 525–534.

[38] M. Kirkconnell, *Canada, Europe, and Hitler*, New York: Oxford Univ. Press, 1940, contains interesting data on Canadian reactions to European crises.

[39] See E. R. Walker, *War-Time Economics with Special Reference to Australia*, Melbourne: Univ. Press, 1939, for additional data.

[40] H. G. Wells, *Mr. Britling Sees It Through*, Chicago: Donohue, 1916, p. 34.

SELECTED BIBILIOGRAPHY

Britain's Industrial Future. Report of the Liberal Industrial Inquiry. London: Benn, 1928. Very important.

Chamier, J. D., *A World to Make: A Survey of Post-War England*, New York: Longmans, Green, 1939. A critical and stimulating inquiry.

Clapham, J. H., *Economic History of Modern Britain*, New York: Macmillan, 1938, Vol. III. An authoritative study.

Cole, G. D. H., *Next Ten Years in British Social and Economic Policy*, New York: Macmillan, 1929. A significant analysis by a well-known scholar.

Davison, R. C., *British Unemployment Policy*, New York: Longmans, Green, 1938. This study covers the period after 1930.

——, *Unemployment, Old Policies and New*, New York: Longmans, Green, 1929. This book deals with the problem prior to 1929.

Dibelius, W., *England*, New York: Harper, 1930. A comprehensive study by a critical German scholar.

Elliott, W. Y., *The New British Empire*, New York: McGraw, 1932. An excellent work.

Hirst, F. W., *The Consequences of the War to Great Britain*, New Haven: Yale Univ. Press, 1934.

Keith, A. B., *Dominions as Sovereign States*, New York: Macmillan, 1938. An important work.

Liddell Hart, B. H., *Defense of Britain*, Toronto: Ryerson, 1939. A military study by a competent authority.

Macardle, D., *The Irish Republic,* Toronto: Ryerson, 1937. Detailed for the period 1916 to 1923.

Royal Institute of International Affairs, *British Empire,* second edition, New York: Oxford Univ. Press, 1938. Valuable.

——, *Political and Strategic Interests of the United Kingdom,* New York: Oxford Univ. Press, 1939. Important.

Salter, J. A., *Security, Can We Retrieve It?,* New York: Macmillan, 1939. An interesting investigation by a prominent scholar.

Snowden, P., *Autobiography,* London: Nicholson, 1934, 2 vols. An important source of information.

Viton, A., *Great Britain, An Empire in Transition,* New York: Day, 1940. A penetrating analysis.

Chapter VI

France and Her Empire

"LIBERTY, EQUALITY, FRATERNITY."
"FAMILY, TOIL, COUNTRY."

Post-War Conditions

Geography. The earth's largest continental group, Eurasia, tapers off at its northwestern extremity into a narrow arm of land called western Europe. Near the end of this peninsula is an area of 207,000 square miles called France, whose history and population have been greatly influenced by its geographical location. The movement of the peoples of Eurasia, like those of America, has been prevailingly westward. As they finally squeezed into the European bottleneck, France has had to absorb or repel the shocks of their invasions. As shock absorber France has enriched her racial strain with Celts, Romans, Visigoths, Vandals, Burgundians, Franks, and Normans. As shock repeller she has had to fight many a fierce war against Romans, Huns, Saracens, Normans, Englishmen, and Germans.

Nature has given France, however, many geographical advantages in repelling these invaders. In the northeast the Rhine River and the Vosges and Jura mountains do not form complete barriers, but to the southeast the Alps stand as powerful bulwarks of defense. In the southwest the Pyrenees mountains separate France from Spain. Nearly all the rest of France's borders are seacoasts touching the Mediterranean on the south, the Atlantic on the west, and the English Channel and North Sea on the north.

The lowlands along the Belgian frontier are France's most vulnerable boundary and explain her historical quest for a Rhine frontier. Belgium and northeastern France were bitterly contested by Louis XIV and the Spaniards in the seventeenth century, by Napoleon and the Austrians in the nineteenth century, and by the Allies and the Germans in the twentieth century. The construction of the heavily fortified Maginot Line was the latest, albeit unsuccessful, attempt to protect this French Achilles' heel.

France's mountainous frontiers have not always prevented foreign invasion nor acted as barriers to her own expansion. The armies of Charlemagne, Louis XIII, Louis XIV, Custine, and Napoleon poured over the Vosges and crossed the Rhine into Germany, and the German armies under

This chapter by Lynn M. Case, Assistant Professor of European History, Louisiana State University.

Blücher, the two Moltkes, and Hitler have marched into France on four different occasions during the last century and a half. To the southeast the armies of Hannibal, Pippin, Charlemagne, Charles VIII, Louis XII, Francis I, and Napoleon have pressed through the passes of the Alps into the Italian peninsula. On numerous occasions the French have crossed the Pyrenees into Spain, and just about as often the Spanish have invaded southwestern France.

While France is the land's end of the Eurasian continent, in western Europe she serves as the crossroads of commerce and culture. A large volume of trade and travel between northern Europe and the Mediterranean passes through her winding valleys on her rivers, canals, roads, and railroads; the products of her farms, shops, and factories have found outlets abroad. Scholars and artists from many lands have come to France for training and inspiration, and the seeds of her cultural influence have been " sown broadcast to all the winds." Her music, art, literature, manners, philosophy, politics, law, and science have been woven into the warp and woof of Europe's cultural fabric.

If France's seacoasts have a protective function, they also serve as windows which look out upon a wider world. The North Sea and north Atlantic have beckoned to the fishermen of Normandy, Brittany, and Gascony. From her western shores have gone explorers and colonists to Canada, Louisiana, and the West Indies. From her Mediterranean ports have embarked crusaders, missionaries, and merchants for the Near East, India, the Far East, and north Africa, where they built a vast colonial empire. For centuries the ships of France have sailed the seven seas, and a proud navy has guarded their far-flung lines of trade.

Ethnography. The people of France, who now number about 40 million, can be traced to the Iberians and Ligurians who were pushed southward (c. 425 B.C.) by the incursion of the Celts or Gauls. While the population after these Celtic incursions was largely a mixture of Celts, Iberians, and Ligurians, the Iberians or Basques remained predominant at the western end of the Pyrenees, retaining their peculiar physical characteristics and a language unrelated to any other linguistic group in Europe. The Ligurians also preserved their identity somewhat in southeastern France.

Not until the collapse of the Roman Empire were there important new admixtures to the racial stock of Gaul. Then, as Roman authority declined, barbarian German tribes began to overrun the region. The Visigoths came first (A.D. 406) and settled in southwestern France, east of the Basques. They were followed by the Burgundians (413) who took over the valleys of the Saône and Rhone. Finally the Franks moved in from the northeast and conquered all of Gaul by 536. While the Franks have given France her name, these various German tribes formed only a minority of the population; and as they intermarried with the Gauls, the Gallic

BRITISH
ISLES

SCOTLAND

Dundee

Firth of Forth

Glasgow   Edinburgh

Malin Head

North F. of Clyde

Tweed

Newcastle

Londonderry

Donegal

Donegal Bay

NORTHERN
IRELAND

Belfast

Dundalk

Middlesbrough

Solway Firth

I. of
Man

Middlesbrough

Leeds   Hull
Ouse

EIRE

Dublin

Galway

Irish
Sea

Blackpool   Manchester

Liverpool   Sheffield

Anglesey

ENGLAND

Nottingham

Limerick

Shrewsbury

Trent

Birmingham

Northampto

Carnsore Pt.

Cork

St. George's Chan.

WALES

Gloucester

Lon

Mizen Head

Swansea
Cardiff

Bristol   Reading Th

Bristol Chan.

Liverpool   Brighton

Southampton   Portsmouth
I. of Wight

Plymouth

Falmouth

Land's End

Lizard Head

English Channel

C. de la Hague

Cherbourg

Channel Is.
(Br.)

Caen

Atlantic Ocean

Brest

Pte. de S. Mathieu

Pte. de Raz

Rennes

Le Mo

Lorient

Loire   Angers

St. Nazaire

Nantes

Bay of
Biscay

La Rochelle

NORTHWESTERN EUROPE

| 0 | 50 | 100 | 150 |

Topography   Scale of Miles   Culture

over 12000'	rivers:
6000'-12000'	marshes:
3000'-6000'	canals:
1500'-3000'	boundaries, Oct. 1, 1940:
0'-1500'	other boundaries dated: June 1940

strain remained the strongest. In the sixth century the northwestern peninsula of France was settled by Celtic Britons who were fleeing from the
invading Anglo-Saxons. The region took the name of Brittany, and the
language of the inhabitants became the *Breton* dialect.

The German Franks in Gaul were in turn raided and pillaged by the
Northmen, especially in the lower valley of the Seine. Finally, by agreement (911) the "Normans" were allowed to settle in the region which
became the Duchy of Normandy.

Since the sixteenth century, conquests have brought some foreign people within French borders: Flemings in the Calais and Dunkerque region,
Germans in eastern Lorraine and Alsace, Italians northeast of Nice, and
some Catalans at the eastern end of the Pyrenees. These minorities, however, have enjoyed for centuries the rights and privileges of other French
citizens.[1]

Territorial Gains by the Versailles Treaty. By the Versailles Treaty
France regained Alsace and Lorraine with their 1,900,000 inhabitants and
valuable mineral and industrial resources. She also acquired title to the coal
mines of the Saar Basin whose output totaled 17 million tons a year. Along
with her former allies, France shared in the occupation of the Rhineland.
In Africa and Asia she gained about 244,000 square miles of colonial territories with a population of about 6 million.[2]

The war cost France the lives of 1,400,000 men and made a shambles
of her northeastern departments. Of the 4,329 devastated communes, over
a thousand were completely destroyed. "Of some small communes,"
says William MacDonald, "it was almost literally true that not one stone
was left upon another." Over half a million homes, stores, and factories
were utterly demolished; mines, railroads, highways, power lines, and communications were wrecked; forests were denuded; and fields were filled
with shell holes, trenches, barbed wire, and unexploded shells.[3] The total
cost of reconstruction amounted to over 100 billion francs.[4]

Government. France in 1919 was a centralized republic with a President
elected for seven years by a joint session of Parliament and eligible for re-
election. Since he had to follow the advice of his ministers,[5] the President
wielded little power, the executive authority being exercised by the Premier. The legislature consisted of a Senate and a Chamber of Deputies.
The Senate had 300 members elected indirectly for nine years, one-third
every three years, by a departmental electoral college. The Chamber had
602 members in 1918 [6] elected directly for a four-year term in single-
member districts by all males over twenty-one. The Chamber initiated
money bills, but otherwise each house shared equal legislative authority.
When the Cabinet received an adverse vote in the Chamber,[7] it resigned.
The Chamber could be dissolved by vote of the Senate, but this expedient
was used only once. Since no party had a majority, each Premier had to

find support in a coalition and assign Cabinet posts to leaders of the component groups.

The French Party System. In 1919 there were ten political parties, ranging from Monarchists on the Right to Communists on the Left. Membership in the parties fluctuated a great deal because considerable independence was retained by the individual candidate, who often campaigned by himself and joined a party after taking his seat in the Chamber.

There were five Rightist parties. The *Action française* supported the Orleanist pretender, believed in a hereditary nobility and in the supremacy of the Church and the army. The Imperialists advocated the restoration of the Bonaparte dynasty. The *Action libérale populaire* (A.L.P.) had a clerical program; it wished to grant the Roman Catholic Church a privileged place in the French state and society. The A.L.P., however, supported the republican form of government and a liberal program of social reform. The Republican Federation was opposed to governmental regulation of business and therefore generally objected to social reforms. The Democratic-Republican Party was slightly anti-clerical and favored social legislation. The first three of these groups had only a handful of followers; most of the conservatives belonged to the last two parties.

To the right of the Center sat the Federation of the Left which advocated a conciliation with the Church and a three-year military service law. In the dead center was the Radical-Socialist Party (one of the larger groups), strongly anti-clerical. This party's title was a misnomer since it was neither radical nor Socialist. It did, however, promote social reforms by governmental regulation. To the left of the center were the Socialist-Republicans who favored the gradual and peaceful transformation of the Third Republic into a Socialist state. Their immediate program was to establish collective ownership of large-scale industries.

There were two Leftist parties, the Unified Socialists and the Communists. The Unified Socialists, affiliated with the Second International, wished to overthrow the bourgeois state. While not inclined to precipitate a proletarian revolution by force, they were unwilling to participate in any bourgeois ministry which would patch up the capitalistic regime. When the latter should crumble under the weight of its alleged injustices and inefficiency, the Socialists would be ready to step in and create a democratic, proletarian state. The French Communist Party, affiliated with the Third International in Moscow, advocated the violent overthrow of the bourgeois republic at the earliest favorable moment, the substitution of a temporary proletarian dictatorship, the abolition of all private property, and the eventual establishment of a classless society in a world federation of soviet republics. During the post-war period there was a tendency among these parties to unite into larger groups such as the Sacred

Union, National Bloc, National Union, and Popular Front whose appearances and dissolutions will be discussed below.

Local Government. For purposes of local government France was divided into ninety departments, each subdivided into arrondissements, cantons, and communes. The prefect, the executive in each department, was appointed by, and responsible to, the national government. Similarly a sub-prefect was appointed for the arrondissement, but the mayor of the commune was elected by the communal council. All these subdivisions, except the canton,[8] had elected councils to work with the appointed administrators.[9]

The Clemenceau Ministry. After the exultation of victory had subsided, the Clemenceau Ministry was subjected to fierce attacks. It was accused of truckling to Wilson's demands for leniency toward Germany. While some grumbled at the 200 billion franc war debt,[10] others accused the Cabinet members of war profiteering. Newspapers chafed at the continued censorship. The high cost of living, which bore heavily upon the worker and *rentier* class, was accentuated by the depreciation of the currency and high taxes. Unemployment faced the demobilized army, and soldiers and sailors began to mutiny and in various other ways to express their discontent. These disturbances caused politicians to regard the elections of November, 1919 with ominous forebodings.

Political Affairs

Clemenceau and the Sacred Union. From November, 1917 to January, 1920 France was governed by Georges Clemenceau and his Sacred Union Cabinet. Vigorous, aggressive action characterized Clemenceau's career. A bitter parliamentary and journalistic critic of moderate and conservative Cabinets, he eventually became known as the destroyer of ministries. A staunch republican, he opposed imperialism and clericalism, and was among those who defended Dreyfus. Because of his insistence on a more vigorous prosecution of the war, he was invited to form a ministry in the dark days of November, 1917. Clemenceau united the Right and the Left in a government of Sacred Union whose superior leadership achieved for France her desired victory — an event which gave Clemenceau the nickname of " Father of Victory."

The national and local elections were postponed during the war. Clemenceau refused to schedule elections until he had obtained the ratification of the peace treaties. In the meantime a new electoral law had been passed in May, 1919 which provided for proportional representation (*scrutin de liste*) in parliamentary elections. This move was designed to give fairer representation to minorities and encourage a national, rather than local, outlook on the part of deputies.[11] An amendment to permit woman suffrage was defeated during consideration of this bill, as was a similar proposal in 1922. France never extended the franchise to women, largely because the dominant parties feared that the majority of women would incline toward clericalism.

As November 16, 1919, the date of the elections, approached, only the Unified Socialists opposed the government. Alone among French parties, they had a disciplined organization and compelled loyalty to their program which, while demanding the socialization of industries, laid great stress on the injustice of the Versailles Treaty and advocated non-intervention in Russia. In general, however, France, like the United States, at that time experienced a Communist scare. Nearly all the parties of the Center and Right united under Clemenceau in a National Bloc to defend the treaty and combat Bolshevism. Upon these two issues the campaign was chiefly fought.[12]

The National Bloc won about 500 out of 626 seats. The Unified Socialists secured only 55 seats, or 46 less than they had in the preceding Chamber, although they polled 300,000 more votes than in 1914. This indicated that the new electoral law did not work to the advantage of the Socialists.

The National Bloc. In 1920 France had two presidential elections. Since Poincaré did not desire re-election, the National Assembly's choice lay between Paul Deschanel and Clemenceau. It was usual for a Premier to receive the presidency, but Clemenceau was loath to accept the rather empty honor. Prestige demanded, however, that he put himself forth as candidate, but Deschanel was elected (January 17, 1920).[13] Clemenceau at once resigned the premiership, being succeeded by Millerand.

A Progressive Republican, Deschanel had been a deputy since 1885 and President of the Chamber since 1912. Not long after his election to the presidency, he suffered a nervous breakdown and fell from the rear of a train. He resigned in September, 1920 and Millerand was chosen to succeed him. Alexandre Millerand was a Socialist who had been read out of the party for accepting a Cabinet post. By 1920 he was an archnationalist, demanding the last pound of flesh from defeated Germany as well as suppression of the Russian Communists. He would accept the presidency only on condition that he receive greater authority in matters of foreign policy than was customarily granted to the head of the state. By a vote of 695 to 97 the National Assembly acceded to his demands.[14]

Reconstruction. The most urgent problem facing the Sacred Union, and later the National Bloc, was the rebuilding of the devastated areas. Since Germany was very slow in making reparation payments, France had to borrow great sums from her former allies and by domestic bond flotations. Some delay ensued in adjusting claims and ascertaining the exact damages suffered by individuals. To facilitate the work of restoration, many householders and shopkeepers formed reconstruction cooperatives which negotiated with the government, purchased materials, and contracted for labor. By tireless energy and persistent effort, France's war wounds began to heal rapidly. In 1926 a prominent French economist wrote, " Her devastated regions are almost repaired, her mines are reopened, her fields are cultivated, her factories and plants are in full work." In seven short years 81 per cent of her houses, 91 per cent of her factories, and 93 per cent of her arable land were already restored.[15] More important than mere restoration, however, was the fact that out of the ashes of war arose a modernized France. With the latest and most efficient machinery, her new factories competed successfully with other industrialized nations. Tractors and reapers appeared on the salvaged farms. Reconstruction cooperatives led eventually to a wider acceptance of consumers' and farmers' cooperatives, to trade unions, and also to town planning and group housing.[16]

Recovery of Alsace-Lorraine. If, at the end of the War, Frenchmen grieved over the devastated regions, they rejoiced over the recovery of Alsace-Lorraine. Within a week and a half of the armistice, French troops reoccupied the provinces amid the universal rejoicing of the inhabitants; Parisians replaced the black shroud of mourning on the Statue of Strasbourg with garlands of flowers.

The annexation of peoples who have been separated from the mother country for almost half a century, however, created linguistic, political, religious, and economic problems. The linguistic difficulty was the first to appear, since 1,600,000 Alsace-Lorrainers spoke a German dialect and only 200,000 spoke French. German railroad officials, government functionaries, and school teachers were replaced with French men and women. The bewildered Alsatians and Lorrainers, unable to understand the officials and judges or read the posted regulations, soon began to protest. In Lorraine the railroad workers went on strike in the spring of 1919 and secured the appointment of a larger percentage of native officials. This was the first of many concessions made by France as she came to realize the need for preserving the loyalty of Alsace and Lorraine. Three hours of German instruction a week and religious education in German were permitted, while a teachers' strike in 1920 forced the government to appoint more German-speaking instructors.

The Government of Alsace-Lorraine. Alsace-Lorraine was also dissatisfied with the new local government. Accustomed to a large measure of home rule under Germany, the provinces were infuriated by the highly integrated and centralized administration now offered them. As a Lorraine businessman exclaimed: " It is incredible, the stupidity of this government! Not that I wish the Germans back, ach, non! But under this regime we are getting nowhere. We've got to do business, to live at peace with our neighbors. We cannot all be deputies and exist on eloquence in Paris." [17] Not until Millerand was appointed commissioner-general did a semblance of order appear out of chaos. With a locally elected council, Millerand proceeded to govern the provinces as a semi-autonomous region, and this system served not only as a convenient transition from German to French rule but also set in motion a movement in other parts of France for regional autonomy.

Religious Problems. The religious question also quickly appeared in Alsace-Lorraine. Seven-eighths of the population were Roman Catholic; under Germany they had a government-supported church, religious teaching in the schools, religious orders, and ambassadorial relations with the Papacy. In France, however, the situation had been reversed since 1870: the Church was no longer supported by the government; religious instruction was forbidden in the schools; most religious orders were banned; and diplomatic relations with the Pope were suspended. The reacquired provinces became alarmed when French anti-clericals demanded that French laws be immediately extended to Alsace-Lorraine. Millerand's administration, however, assured the Alsatians that the lay laws would not be enforced. Two French bishops were appointed to the sees of Strasbourg and Metz after agreement with the Pope. The French anti-clericals acquiesced and later even allowed the local governments in Alsace-Lorraine to pay the salaries of the clergy. The religious orders were permitted to give instruction in the schools. When, in 1921, France renewed diplomatic relations with the Papacy, apprehension concerning religious matters momentarily vanished.

Economic Readjustments. The complaint of the Lorraine businessman alluded to above reflected the economic maladjustment caused by the annexation. Germany no longer purchased much of Lorraine's pig iron or Alsatian textiles, and the French market for these commodities was far from a substitute. Besides, Lorraine needed the Ruhr type of coal for smelting her pig iron. No satisfactory solution of these problems was found until the conclusion of the Franco-German Commercial Treaty of 1927.[18]

The problem of currency exchange added to the bitterness of the inhabitants of the lost provinces. In 1918 France arranged to pay Alsatians and Lorrainers 1.25 francs for one German mark. This was better than par value, since the mark was depreciating more rapidly than the franc. But bank deposits were not so honored until 1919, and then only for native depositors. The delay cancelled the good feeling engendered by the liberal rate.

France and the Vatican. The religious problem in Alsace was closely connected with religious matters in the rest of France. The war had created a change of sentiment in favor of renewed relations with the

Vatican. Indeed the sufferings of war had revived the religious spirit; the priests had shown loyalty and valor in battle; and France needed the Church's influence more than ever to strengthen her diplomatic and im- perialist designs in the Near East. Furthermore, the National Bloc and the Vatican were both combatting Communism; Alsace and Lorraine tended to help the mother country become reconciled with the Holy See. In 1919 France unofficially consulted with the Pope on the appointment of the Bishops of Strasbourg and Metz; in 1920 France sent a representative to Rome for the canonization of Joan of Arc. In 1921 the Chamber and Senate approved the exchange of diplomatic representatives with the Vatican if the Pope would make France protector of Catholics in the East, persuade enemy peoples not to obstruct the peace terms, and give France the most-favored-nation treatment in the selection of bishops. France named Senator Charles Jonnart as Ambassador to the Holy See, and the Vatican sent Archbishop Bonaventura Cerretti as Nuncio to Paris.[19]

The rapprochement went further than an exchange of representatives. Three years of negotiation regarding the custodianship of Church property resulted in the Jonnart-Cerretti Accord (1924). The agreement provided that the French government retain custody of the great cathedrals as na- tional monuments, but the smaller edifices, such as local churches, were to be turned over to diocesan associations. In 1906 Pius X had opposed lay associations because they violated the rule of ecclesiastical discipline; but in 1924 Pius XI sanctioned the diocesan associations because they were submissive to the authority of the bishop.[20] No sooner had these arrange- ments been made, however, than the anti-clericals in the election campaign of 1924 began to beat their drums in ominous fashion.

Labor Problems. Two factors caused serious discontent among laboring classes between 1919 and 1924: the reactionary, anti-labor attitude of the National Bloc and the rising cost of living. In 1919 Clemenceau had tried to mollify labor with a law which provided for the eight-hour day and forty-eight-hour week without reduction of wages. This was to be applied by decree to suitable trades. Five million workers in thirty trades had come under the law's provisions by 1926.[21] But the National Bloc had come into power in 1919 on the crest of an anti-labor movement, and labor promptly responded with a series of strikes. In 1920 railroad workers went on strike in protest against the discharge of employees for union activity and government intervention on behalf of employers. Under the auspices of the *Confédération Générale du Travail* (C.G.T.), ship- ping, transport, public utility, mines, metal, and building unions called a sympathetic strike. At the end of three weeks the strike was called off because the government had arrested the leaders, and volunteers had acted as strike-breakers. The results were disastrous to labor: 22,000 railroad workers were dismissed, hundreds were imprisoned, the C.G.T. was dissolved by Parliament, membership of organized labor declined from 2,500,000 to 600,000, and finally in 1921 the extremist wing of the C.G.T. seceded and formed the rival organization of the C.G.T.U.[22]

Serious labor trouble again appeared in August, 1922 when the metal workers — who claimed they could not live on their dollar a day (12 francs)[23] — struck for higher wages in Le Havre. Dock workers, tramway and gas company employees, 22,000 in all, went on a twenty-four-hour sympathetic strike. The port of Le Havre was at a standstill. Troops were sent to break the strike, and in the street fighting which ensued three strikers were killed and fifty wounded. When the leaders were arrested and the two hostile confederations failed to cooperate, the strike ended. Many of the workers were tried on charges of rebellion.[24] In September, 1922 a strike broke out among seamen in protest against the government's withdrawal of the eight-hour day, but this too proved futile.

Elections of 1924. While the anti-Communist scare had subsided by 1924, labor's hatred for the National Bloc mounted. The parties of the Left, except the Communists, united to turn out the Poincaré ministry. The leading element in the Left Bloc were the Radical-Socialists led by Édouard Herriot. Encouraged by the British Labor Party's victory, Herriot advocated the following program: (1) guarantee of the right of collective bargaining; (2) substitution of an income tax for the consumers tax; (3) abolition of monopolies such as the sugar trust; (4) termination of the concessions made to the Church since the war; (5) reconciliation with Germany.[25] Poincaré had ordered the invasion of the Ruhr to obtain reparations by force.

The elections of May 11 resulted in a victory for the Left Bloc which won 296 seats, against the National Bloc's 274. The Radical-Socialists had 127 (largest of any party); the Unified Socialists 101; and the Communists 29, a gain of 16. Poincaré was forced to resign on June 1.

The Left Bloc and National Union. Immediately after the election a crisis arose between the new Parliament and President Millerand. The latter stood for nearly everything which the victorious parties opposed: reconciliation with the Papacy, a severity toward Germany, and the discipline of labor. Furthermore, as President, Millerand insisted on real power. The three principal parties of the Left Bloc passed resolutions refusing to form a ministry while Millerand remained in office. When Herriot rebuffed an offer of the premiership, Millerand appointed a stopgap Rightist cabinet to present his arguments for retaining office before Parliament. However, when the Chambers voted to delay consideration of his message, Millerand saw that the temporary cabinet must resign.

In the ensuing presidential election (June 13, 1924) the Rightists found some solace. The Left Bloc favored Painlevé, but the Rightists, joined with some recalcitrant Leftists, brought about the election of Gaston Doumergue, the first Protestant president of France. Herriot thereupon agreed to form a Cabinet.

Caillaux and the Amnesty Bill. Since 1918 France was divided over the treatment accorded certain men who had been accused of defeatism and pro-Germanism during the war. Joseph Caillaux, a Radical-Socialist and former premier, was the most important of these. Caillaux became convinced in 1917 that France ought to make a compromise peace. He therefore made contacts with prominent Germans who, he thought, felt the same way. When he began to suspect that the Germans were merely using him to sow disaffection at home Caillaux, as he claimed, dropped the negotiations. In January, 1918 Clemenceau ordered the arrest of Caillaux, who was brought to trial a year later before the Senate High Court on charges of treasonable relations and intelligence with the enemy. The defense based its arguments on "imprudent" rather than treasonable contacts.[26] The Court in April, 1920 declared Caillaux innocent of treason and intelligence but "guilty of commerce and correspondence with the enemy." He was sentenced to three years in prison, five years of exile from Paris, ten years of loss of civic rights, and payment of 50,000 francs (the cost of the trial). Caillaux was released on the ground that he had already served his prison term.

The Radical-Socialist Party, however, remained loyal to their fallen leader, accused the National Bloc of political persecution, and branded such trials deliberate miscarriages of justice. In the election campaign of 1924 the National Bloc warned the nation that the opposition would pardon Caillaux and other so-called "traitors." Their warnings were well-founded. In January, 1925 the Amnesty Law was passed which removed all penalties against Caillaux, Malvy (another condemned political leader), and the railroad strikers of 1920. Although the Senate would not vote to restore the strikers to their jobs, the government indicated they would try to obtain their re-employment. Within three months Caillaux was appointed Minister of Finance; Malvy had already been re-elected to the Chamber.[27]

Vatican Embassy Preserved. The Left Bloc was not so successful in carrying out its promise to abolish the French embassy at the Vatican. When the proposal was brought up in the Chamber, it met stout opposition from the Right and Center. Undismayed, the Left Bloc succeeded in suppressing the embassy in February, 1925 but compromised by allowing Alsace and Lorraine to send special representatives to the Vatican who were to continue to enjoy the benefits of the Concordat of 1801. Two months later Painlevé declared in forming a new ministry that the embassy would be retained " in order not to reopen an inopportune and harmful controversy." [28]

From that time on the Vatican curried favor with the French government in order to discourage suggestions about withdrawing the embassy. In December, 1926 the Pope signed a treaty respecting the religious honors due to French representatives in the East, and urged French Catholics to accept the republican form of government. In his New Year's message to the French President the Papal Nuncio praised France's Locarno Treaties. One week later the Pope put the monarchist paper, *Action française*, on the *Index* of forbidden books, and in 1929 not only branded its editors as heretics but threatened to excommunicate those who collaborated with them. Although this was done on doctrinal grounds, Pius XI knew it would please the French republicans.

Poincaré and the Franc. France had financed the war largely by borrowing. When it was seen in 1919 that reparation payments would not be forthcoming from Germany at once and that French revenue could not cover reconstruction costs and repayment of loans, the franc fell from 19 to 9 cents. With the invasion of the Ruhr in 1923 and the collapse of the mark, the franc declined to 3.6 cents. The Left Bloc ministries tried to stabilize the franc and balance the budget. More taxes and government economy were necessary, but powerful groups opposed both expedients. To avoid these pressures the Left ministries asked for decree powers. The Conservatives, however, refused to consent, fearing that the government would resort to a capital levy. Finally, when the franc dropped to 2 cents in July, 1926, Poincaré was asked to form a coalition ministry of Rightists and Leftists, including six former prime ministers, in order to stabilize the franc.

The new government of National Union, containing representatives of all parties except Socialists and Communists, was given decree powers which it immediately used to raise additional revenue of 9 billion francs by income and other taxes. It also passed a constitutional amendment providing for a Debt Redemption Fund from the tobacco monopoly, inheritance taxes, and the consolidation of the national debt. Economies were effected through administrative reorganization. Because of these measures and the confidence inspired by the veteran Poincaré, the franc rose to 4 cents, and the Bank of France had to step into the market to keep it from rising too fast and thereby disturbing recovery. On the advice of a committee of experts, stabilization was delayed until the depressing effects of deflation had vanished, and the price level had adjusted itself to the new value of the franc. Finally, in 1928, the franc was put on the gold standard and pegged by law, not at the pre-war rate, opposed by the experts, but at 3.93 cents. France again seemed prosperous, the budget showed a surplus, and Poincaré was hailed as the Savior of the Franc.[29]

Election of 1928. The renewed popularity of Poincaré brought a Rightist victory in 1928, in spite of the electoral law of 1927 which was supposed to favor the Left. The adoption of proportional representation in 1918 proved a disadvantage to the urban electorate since it gave the peasants an opportunity to nullify the labor majorities in the cities. Election of deputies by single-member districts seemed more democratic because it made the deputies more constituent-conscious and discouraged dictatorial power. Consequently the Electoral Law of 1927 provided for 612 single-member districts (*scrutin d'arrondissement*). If a candidate did not receive a majority in the first election, a run-off election was held.[30]

The elections of 1928 were the first conducted under the new law. Since Poincaré had all shades of opinion, except Socialists and Communists, in his Cabinet, he conducted the campaign in a liberal spirit, stressing his rescue of the franc and the Locarno Treaties. He attacked the Communists, however, for fomenting mutiny, accepting directions from a foreign power, and sabotaging parliamentary democracy.[31] The results showed a victory for Poincaré and the Rightists; the Leftist groups suffered losses. While the National Union as a whole gained 100 seats, the Radical-Socialists lost 17, the Socialists one, and the Communists 13. A new disturbing factor was the election of three Alsatian Autonomists.

Alsatian Autonomy. Alarmed in 1924 by the victory of the Left Bloc with its anti-clerical program, some extremists began to work for the autonomy of Alsace. Fifteen autonomist agitators were arrested and tried at Colmar in 1928. Seven others fled the country. It was this alleged persecution which brought about the election of three of the defendants, Ricklin, Rosse, and Dahlet, to the French Chamber. The Communists seemed to be deliberately abetting the discord between France and Alsace by voting for the Catholic Autonomists and furnishing them with legal defense. Five of the fifteen, including Ricklin and Rosse, were sentenced to one year in prison and five years exile. The autonomy movement declined rapidly, however, when Poincaré, himself a Lorrainer, assured the Alsatians of continued respect for their language, customs, and the religious concordat. When Hitler imposed a dictatorship on Germany in 1933, the Alsatian autonomy movement declined further.[32]

Social Insurance Act. Just before the elections of 1928 Parliament passed a comprehensive Social Insurance Law which went into effect in 1930. The labor federations had been advocating this legislation since the war. They had argued that the Alsatians and Lorrainers were allowed to continue the social insurance system inherited from Germany, and what was good for Germans and Alsatians was good for Frenchmen too. On the other hand, the industrialists of Alsace-Lorraine complained that they should be relieved of their contributions to social insurance, or else the system should be imposed on all French industries. The resulting law provided that: (1) all laborers with annual incomes of less than 18,000 francs pay 5 per cent and their employers 5 per cent; (2) the benefits included old-age pensions, invalidity pensions, medical and maternity care, and unemployment insurance; (3) sixty was to be the retirement age, and the pension would average 40 per cent of the annual wage; (4) agricultural workers and domestic servants were included.[33]

Strangely enough, the application of the social reform act led to bitter strikes, especially in Lille and Roubaix-Tourcoing. The workers demanded higher wages to help pay their contributions and meet the rising cost of living. The Minister of Labor, Pierre Laval, at last terminated the strike at Lille and finally even that at Roubaix-Tourcoing by compromise proposals.[34]

Elections of 1932. On the eve of the 1932 elections a bill was introduced by Georges Mandel, a political lieutenant of Clemenceau, providing that if the highest candidate in the first election received 40 per cent of the vote (instead of 50), there would not be a run-off. This measure was vigorously opposed by the Leftist parties, because it would prevent them from combining against Rightists in the second balloting, and was killed in the Senate. Laval was forced to resign and André Tardieu became premier.

The campaign began in April with the Radical-Socialists and Socialists in opposition. Poincaré had retired in 1929, and the Radical-Socialists had left the Cabinet, which thereafter tended toward the Right. Now the Leftists accused the government of serving big business, causing the depression, and spending too much money on armaments instead of fostering international reconciliation. Tardieu defended himself by pointing to the relief measures he had sponsored and by insisting that he had inherited the policies of Poincaré.

The elections in May brought a victory for the Left. Tardieu's Rightists lost 29 seats, while the Radical-Socialists gained 47, the Socialists 17, and the Communists 8. In June Tardieu resigned, and Herriot succeeded him. Four months later the senatorial elections increased by 5 the already large Leftist majority.

In May, 1932 President Doumer was assassinated by an insane Russian refugee, Paul Gorgulov. A joint-session of Parliament chose Albert Lebrun President by an overwhelming majority of 633 votes out of 826.

The Leftists and the Depression. By 1932 France was belatedly feeling the effects of the world-wide depression. Although employment was rising, the index of production declined from 140 in 1930 to 93 in July, 1932, commerce slumped 35 per cent between 1931 and 1932, and the unfavorable balance of trade rose to 10 billion francs. The depression in the United States reduced France's tourist trade, always an important factor in international exchange. The Treasury reserve fell from $80,-

000,000 to $2,800,000 and by the end of 1932 the governmental deficit reached $500,000,000.

Stern measures were required to meet the growing crisis. In addition to new taxes aggregating $56,000,000, the government pared $60,000,000 from national defense (a fatal mistake in the light of later events) and reduced salaries and pensions by 5 per cent. Herriot was also able to save $40,000,000 by refinancing bond issues at a lower rate of interest. In spite of these efforts to balance the budget, the government had to borrow $80,000,000 to meet current expenses.

In view of the crisis, France was in no mood to pay the December, 1932 installment of $19,000,000 on her American debt. Taxpayers were protesting against the increase in taxes, and civil servants were against salary reductions. Militarists thought that France should default since she had to reduce her defense appropriations. Herriot, having failed to persuade the United States to agree to a debt conference, insisted on making one more payment with the understanding that it would be the last until a conference were held. " I shall not be the man who will refuse to honor the signature of France." [35] The French Chamber, however, refused to approve the payment, and Herriot resigned in disgust, declining to form a new cabinet, or even participate in one.[36]

Every succeeding ministry struggled with the budget problem, making enemies both by enforcing economies and raising taxes. The revelation of several political scandals increased the clamor of the opposition, until democracy itself was threatened. The government-subsidized " Aeropostale," which monopolized air service to South America, was found to have falsified its balance sheets. A relative of the vice-president of the Chamber of Deputies was implicated. In October, 1933 a Socialist deputy revealed a tax evasion scandal involving senators, former ministers, publishers, industrialists, and bishops.[37]

The Stavisky Scandal nearly wrecked the Third Republic. Alexander Stavisky was a professional swindler who had escaped punishment for previous offenses through suspicious official neglect. When he disappeared from his Bayonne pawnshop in January, 1934 it was discovered that he had issued fraudulent bonds amounting to over 500,000,000 francs. The Minister of Colonies, prominent Radical-Socialists, and other leading politicians were implicated. When Stavisky was found dead, the police were accused of having murdered him to suppress evidence. Later Albert Prince, a magistrate involved in the Stavisky case, was killed under mysterious circumstances. These events intensified distrust of government officials. The parliamentary votes of confidence given to the Chautemps ministry only served to whip public fury into riotous outbreaks. Chautemps resigned in favor of another Radical-Socialist, Edouard Daladier. This change, however, proved quite unpopular and, when Daladier dismissed a prefect of Paris police, Jean Chiappe, serious anti-governmental riots occurred. A mob tried to storm the Chamber of Deputies on February 6, troops were called into the city, and in the ensuing disorders 18 were killed and 2300 injured. Daladier had to resign in his turn, and ex-President Doumergue, now over eighty years old, formed a coalition government. In 1935 those accused of complicity in the Stavisky scandal were brought to trial; eleven were acquitted and nine convicted.[38]

Constitutional Amendments. Premier Doumergue thought that France was ready for constitutional amendments which would strengthen the republican form of government. In September, 1934 he proposed to allow the Premier to dissolve the Chamber without the consent of the Senate, and forbid civil servants to strike against the government. The Leftist parties opposed these amendments because they would strengthen the executive branch of government and deprive civil servants of the rights of collective bargaining. When the Radical-Socialists resigned, Doumergue's Cabinet fell and the proposed amendments were forgotten.

Anti-Republican Societies. The success of Mussolini in Italy and Hitler in Germany and the scandals connected with the government of the Third Republic tended to bring into the open powerful French monarchist and Fascist organizations. The monarchist *Action française* and *Jeunesses patriotes* were involved in the riots of February 6. Before the disorders had ended, a Fascist group, the *Croix de Feu*, staged an orderly and disciplined parade as a protest against Parliamentary corruption.

The *Croix de feu*, led by Colonel de la Roque, became the chief Fascist threat to French democracy. It claimed a membership of 600,000, including many war veterans, and denounced democracy and Communism. Its program demanded a corporate state and industrial control by government experts. Later revelations showed that Tardieu and other officials had supplied De la Roque with government funds. Just as French parliamentary parties were numerous, so French Fascism was represented by many groups. In addition to the *Croix de feu*, Fascist organizations included the Francists, the Blue Shirts of Marcel Bucard, and the *Solidarité française*.[39]

The monarchists were equally active. Some joined the Fascist groups, others swelled the ranks of the *Action française*, the *Camelots du roi*, and the *Jeunesses patriotes*. In 1937, after armed societies were banned, a mysterious monarchist organization, the *Cagoulards* or Hooded Men, was uncovered. Some arms were found, and a few prominent generals, whom the police were not inclined to arrest, were implicated.[40]

In reply to the threats of monarchists and Fascists, the C.G.T. under the leadership of Léon Jouhaux called a one-day general strike (Feb. 12, 1934) which sobered their opponents considerably. Gaston Bergery, a Leftist leader, determined to organize a Common Front of Liberals, Socialists, and Communists to challenge the Fascists and monarchists. Under the leadership of Léon Blum, the Socialists in July, 1934 joined the Common Front "in the struggle against fascism and in defense of democratic liberties." The following October the Common Front won a by-election in Doumergue's home town.[41]

Clashes between the hostile groups were bound to occur. De la Roque threatened reprisals if the Leftists gained control of the government. When a law disbanding armed political societies was passed in December, 1935 the *Croix de feu* was transformed into a political organization called the French Social Party. With the approaching elections of 1936 the Rightists and Leftists ceased their campaigns of violence and relied on peaceful electioneering to gain their ends.

The Elections of 1936. When the Third International instructed its members to cooperate with liberal democratic groups everywhere against the threat of Fascism, the French Communists joined the Radical-Socialist and Socialist Parties to form the Popular Front. The Rightists, foreseeing Leftist coalitions in the run-off elections, tried in vain to substitute proportional representation for the single-member districts in parliamentary elections. With the failure of this maneuver both sides began a bitter campaign in March, 1936. The Popular Front accused the Rightists of Fascist tendencies and promised to nationalize the Bank of France, the munitions industries, and insurance companies. The Rightists denied that they were Fascists but insisted that the parliamentary regime should be modified to give the executive branch more power and longer tenure, as in the United States. Otherwise, they continued loyally to defend the status quo.

In the May elections the Popular Front secured 375 out of 618 seats. The Socialists with 145 had the largest representation, the Communists elected 71 deputies, and the Radical-Socialists 115. Léon Blum became Premier in June. His Cabinet, which the Communists refused to enter, contained several experts and, stranger still, three women. Blum declared that he would eschew revolutionary methods but led France toward a Socialist regime.[42]

The Blum Ministry. When the Blum Ministry took office, over a million workers, flushed with the Popular Front's victory, began a sit-down strike, demanding shorter hours, higher wages, and collective bargaining. By the Matignon Agreement which settled the strike and by a series of confirmatory laws Blum was able to obtain sweeping social and labor reforms: the forty-hour week, two-week annual vacations with pay, governmental guarantee of collective bargaining, compulsory arbitration of labor disputes, a public works program, credit insurance, debt decreases, and finally the nationalization of the munitions industries, the Bank of France, and the marketing of wheat. Labor's victory stimulated the trade union movement: the C.G.T. alone boosting its membership from two to five million.[43]

The path of the Popular Front was not smooth, however. The depression deepened; employers obstructed the government's program; and the menacing international situation created by the Spanish Civil War and by German and Italian aggression necessitated large expenditures for armaments. Faced with these difficulties, Blum tried to conciliate the vested interests by announcing a " pause " in his reforming zeal. In October, 1936 the franc was devalued from 6.6 to 4.6 cents, leaving 10 billion francs in the Tripartite Stabilization Fund. When the government went into the capital market for 5 billion francs in 1937, the loan was so greatly oversubscribed that confidence in the soundness of the French economy seemed restored.[44]

The darkening international situation in 1938 dictated many changes in economic policy. In April Blum asked for extraordinary decree powers to deal with the budget. When this was refused, he resigned, and Daladier formed a Cabinet whose policies tended gradually to undo the reforms of the Popular Front. In November, 1938 Daladier broke a general strike by the extraordinary device of calling all railroad and public service employees to the colors.

Foreign Policy. French foreign policy after 1918 could be summed up in one word — security.[44a] It was the French desire for security that led Clemenceau to impose disarmament and heavy reparations on Germany. When the United States failed to join the League, the National Bloc, under Millerand and Poincaré, relied for security on the military pacts with Belgium and the Little Entente and insisted on retaining a large army and navy.

Foreign affairs lurked in the background of many election campaigns and Cabinet crises, but seldom were they solely responsible for the overthrow of a Ministry. Two clear-cut instances in which a Cabinet fell over foreign affairs were the defeat of Briand in 1922 because of his conciliatory attitude toward Germany at the Cannes Conference and the resignation of Herriot in 1932 when the Chamber refused to authorize the semi-annual debt payment to America.

The Leftist governments of 1924, 1932, and 1936, under the leadership of Briand and Blum, were as determined on achieving security as their Rightist predecessors, but sought it by more conciliatory methods, such as the Locarno Agreement, the Kellogg-Briand Pact, and insistence on League action to curb aggressors. With the rise of Nazi militarism in Germany, France looked for security to its strong alliance with Great Britain and its friendship with Russia. Distrustful of force, the Leftist governments countered the aggressiveness of the dictators with a policy of appeasement. After imposing partial sanctions on Italy in 1935 as a

protest against the ruthless invasion of Ethiopia, France had to recognize
the Italian conquest. By its policy of non-intervention, she allowed the
Italian-sponsored Franco government to defeat the Loyalists in Spain
(1936–1939). No action was taken against Germany when, between
1935 and March, 1938, she rearmed, remilitarized the Rhineland in defiance of the Versailles Treaty, and absorbed Austria. By the Munich
Agreement of September, 1938 France even abandoned her ally, Czechoslovakia. Appeasement, however, did not bring peace. When Poland
was invaded on September 1, 1939 both France and England declared war
against Germany.[45]

Economic and Cultural Developments

The natural resources of France are very abundant. Coal mines —
scattered throughout France but particularly extensive in Lorraine, Artois,
the lower Loire Valley, and the Creuzot Basin — increased their production
from 25,000,000 metric tons in 1920 to 47,500,000 in 1938. In like manner,
the iron mines in Lorraine, Normandy, and Anjou tripled their output
from 12,000,000 metric tons in 1920 to 37,700,000 in 1937. There are
valuable deposits of bauxite in Provence, petroleum and potash in Alsace,
and tin, lead, zinc, and kaolin in Limousin. The swift streams of the
French Alps and Pyrenees provide ample hydroelectric power: installed
capacity rose from 750,000 h.p. in 1914 to 3,000,000 h.p. in 1928.

In spite of the destruction of war, France increased her forest area
from 24,000,000 acres in 1912 to 26,000,000 acres in 1935. The pines of
Gascony produce an abundance of turpentine and resin, and the chestnut
and walnut trees of the Cevennes and Alps produce both nuts and timber.

France, however, is primarily an agricultural country, with 41 per cent
of the land fit for plowing. Over half the population lives in the country
or in small towns and depends for a livelihood on agricultural activity.
The average holding of a French peasant is twenty-four acres. All the
crops suitable to a temperate climate are grown; wheat, wine, livestock,
and silk are the most important products. The following table indicates
the progress or decline in these agricultural products between 1920 and
1937:

Product	Unit of Measure	1920	1937
Wheat	Metric Tons	6,271,000	7,017,000
Wine	Gallons	1,310,000,000	1,030,000,000
Livestock	Head	29,000,000	37,100,000
Silk	Kilograms	9,200,000	641,000

Mechanized industry has not been introduced in France on so huge
a scale as in Germany and Great Britain. A large percentage of manufacturing has been carried on in small shops. Alsace, Artois, Paris, Lower

Seine, and Lyons are the most important industrial centers. The principal manufactures are iron and steel, chemical products, textiles (cotton, silk, linens, woolens, laces, and ribbons), automobiles, machinery, and refined beet sugar. In 1923 France exported 3,000,000 tons of manufactured goods; in the prosperous year of 1929, 5,350,000 tons; and as world trade became more restricted in 1938, only 2,700,000 tons.

Being centrally located in Europe, France has always considered foreign commerce a vital part of her business life. In general, imports consisted of foodstuffs and raw materials; and exports comprised manufactured goods, wines, fruits, and vegetables. In the post-war era most of her imports usually came from the United States and most of her exports went to Great Britain. In the same period there was generally an unfavorable balance in the visible items of trade. A table of exports and imports [46] for three different years indicates the changes which domestic and world conditions brought:

	1923	*1929*	*1938*
Exports (tons)	24,901,000	39,888,000	26,986,000
Imports (tons)	54,800,000	59,447,000	47,155,000
Balance of Trade (francs)	−2,254,000,000	−8,284,000,000	−15,396,000,000

This commerce was borne by vast and well-integrated systems of transportation. French navigable rivers (especially the Rhine, Seine, and Rhone) are connected by canals to form a network of over 6,000 miles of waterway. With the greater use of the automobile and truck, French highways have expanded from 24,000 miles in 1912 to 49,800 in 1933. In addition to 26,400 miles of railroads, 6,400 miles of airways have been put into service. In 1937 the Popular Front consolidated the railroads into the *Société nationale des chemins de fer* in which the government owned 51 per cent of the stock. The law provided that by 1982 the government would have complete ownership of the lines. In 1938 there were 2,000 miles of electrified railroads, and the Pétain government is undertaking further electrification. France's merchant marine has been greatly augmented until in 1938 she had 2,900,000 tons of shipping in contrast to 561,000 in 1915. Port facilities were also expanded. Le Havre and Cherbourg in the north, Bordeaux in the southwest, and Marseilles in the south were the principal ports, linked by various transportation facilities with Paris and Lyons, the leading railroad centers in the interior.

France's telegraph mileage has doubled since the First World War. The telephone mileage reached 123,000. Broadcasting stations were found in some of the larger French cities, and in 1930 about 1,500,000 French homes possessed radio sets.[47]

The economy of post-war France was deliberately modified by government policy. Since 1919 the tariff has aided industry, although agriculture suffered the effects of high rates. It was found that the protective tariff had a tendency to encourage unwise utilization of marginal lands, discourage improved methods, and make wheat-growing unstable because of the frequent changes in rates. The government also negotiated the International Steel Agreement of 1926 and the German Trade Treaty of 1927 which greatly aided the iron and steel industries.

Inflation of the currency, like tariffs, helped the government to regulate business. Industry and trade temporarily benefited from inflation, but the process had to be continued to perpetuate the so-called prosperity. When stabilization came in 1928, no harmful signs appeared, though it may have been partially responsible for the depression which set in after 1932. Agriculture was also benefited by the rising prices which accompanied inflation, but farmers had to pay more for their goods and found it less easy to obtain credit.

Credit difficulties for farmers, however, were overcome partially by state loans at low rates of interest. These stimulated farm ownership and modernization of equipment. A program of agricultural education was also sponsored by the government.

The state also stepped in to help and protect the laborer. We have already seen that in 1919 Parliament passed the Eight-Hour Law. In 1923 provision for a day of rest was added. A comprehensive Social Insurance Act was passed in 1928. Laws for collective bargaining, Saturday half-holiday, and vacations with pay did not come until the Blum Ministry of 1936. A survey of the state's economic activities will convince anyone that the principle of *laissez faire* was honored more in the breach than in the observance in France, the home of classical Physiocratic doctrines.[48]

Cultural Development: Literature. The war did not prevent the vigorous growth of French literature. The two decades 1919–1939 have produced as many masterpieces perhaps as any comparable period in French history.

Paul Claudel (1886–   ) is a typical poet of the post-war era. Converted early in life to Catholicism, he imbued much of his verse with mystical symbolism. " I am inspector of creation," he says, " I examine everything that exists; the steadfastness of the world is my beatitude." *La Messe de là-bas* (*The Mass from Afar*), *L'Ours de la lune* (*Moon Bear*), and the play *Otage* are representative of Claudel's post-war efforts.

Anatole France (1844–1924) continued to turn out remarkable novels after the war, notably *Le petit Pierre* (*Little Pierre*) and *La vie en fleur* (*The Bloom of Life*). Of more towering stature was Marcel Proust (1871–1922) whose *A la recherche du temps perdu* (*Remembrance of Things Past*), a formless, involved chronicle running to sixteen volumes, analyzes the decadent upper-class society of the pre-war era with the skill of a surgeon and the esthetic sensibility of the most refined of Frenchmen. Proust is perhaps the most important of twentieth-century novelists; certainly he is the most discussed. Difficult to read at a long stretch, he opens new vistas, probing into corners of the human soul where few had previously penetrated.

André Gide (1869–   ) has followed more conventional paths than Proust, but he has written two masterpieces, *Les Faux Monnayeurs* (*The Counterfeiters*) and *L'Immoraliste* (*The Immoralist*) — both analyses of moral decay — which will stand comparison with the best in French fiction. Jules Romains (1885–   ) has created in his seventeen volumes of *Les Hommes de bonne volonté* (*Men of Good Will*) a novel in which not one segment of society, as in Proust, but a cross section of it, is depicted. Numerous characters weave in and out of the story, developing in the aggregate perhaps the most complete picture of French life in the second half of the Third Republic that has yet been written. Roger Martin du Gard (1881–   ) was awarded the Nobel Prize in 1937 for his penetrating novel of family life, *Les Thibault*. André Malraux (1895–   ) is the foremost French Marxian novelist. His *Condition humaine* (*Man's Fate*) deals with the Chinese revolution; *Man's Hope* centers around the Spanish Civil War in which Malraux fought on the Loyalist side; and *Days of Wrath* describes the tortures of a Nazi concentration camp.

There were four great achievements in French historiography after the war. In a great cooperative work under the direction of Professor Ernest Lavisse, a number of France's well-known historians produced a ten-volume *Histoire de France contemporaine* in 1921. Between 1920 and 1926 another notable group of scholars under the leadership of Gabriel Hanotaux published the fifteen-volume *Histoire de la nation française*. Ferdinand Brunot, before his death in 1938, had brought nearly to completion his great *Histoire de la langue française* (*History of the French Language*), while Charles Langlois finished his famous four volumes of *La vie en France au moyen âge* (*French Life in the Middle Ages*) in 1928.[49]

Art. Post-war architecture in France has followed the international style of functional, spacious design — a conception not unlike the American skyscraper except that it emphasizes horizontal rather than vertical lines. One of the best-known members of this school is Le Corbusier, a native of Switzerland, but resident of France. He has tackled successfully the problems of modern urban housing, and at the same time has designed private dwellings, such as the *La Savoye* at Poissy-sur-Seine, which only a millionaire could afford. Le Corbusier's *Fondation Suisse* (*Swiss House*) of the *Cité Universitaire* (*University City*) in Paris appropriately adapts the Swiss lake-dweller motif to a student dormitory.[50] France contributed to the development of modern architecture and interior decoration by the beautifully designed pavilions of the Paris International Colonial and Overseas Exposition in 1931, the Paris International Exposition in 1937, and the Paris Exposition of Modern Decorative and Industrial Art in 1925.[51]

Modern architecture minimizes the use of sculptured decoration, yet sculpture has flourished in post-war France. Rodin died in 1917, but his influence persisted. Aristide Maillol (1861–   ) became the great master after 1918. Besides several war memorials, he executed the statue of the reclining goddess of *Fame* in honor of Cézanne, the painter.

France's leading painters of the post-war era were the post-impressionists Matisse and Picasso, and the cubist Braque. Henri Matisse (1869–   ) is famous for his clashing and contrasting colors, and the sharply outlined designs of his backgrounds and objects, as illustrated, for instance, in the *Femme à la violette* (*Woman with Violets*) and the *Odalisque au fauteuil* (*Odalisque Resting*). Pablo Picasso (1881–   ) refused to limit himself to any one style. In *La table* he tended toward the flat, geometric designs of cubism, while in his portrait of *Mme. Picasso* he returned to three-dimensional, realistic portraiture, almost Rembrandtesque in quality. Georges Braque (1882–   ) has been a cubist throughout his career; typical of his flat patterns are such works as *Nature morte à la mandoline* (*Still Life with Mandolin*).[52]

Early post-war French music was closely associated with the brilliant group called "The Six" — Milhaud, Honegger, Auric, Durey, Poulenc, and Germaine Tailleferre. Of these, three achieved outstanding renown. Darius Milhaud (1892–   ) has given unusually successful expression to the new dissonant idiom and developed many of its harmonic and polyphonic implications. He is known especially for the operas *Proteus* and *The Annunciation* and for many songs, piano pieces, and orchestral works. Francis Poulenc (1899–   ) has composed mostly piano music, chamber music, and songs — *Rapsodie nègre* and *Cocardes* being good examples of the last two types. Except for Ravel, Arthur Honegger (1892–   ) is perhaps the most popular of contemporary French composers. Written in the modernistic idiom of the Six, Honegger's two compositions, *Pacific 231* (descriptive of a railroad locomotive) and *Rugby* (descriptive of the English game), appear frequently on symphonic programs. His dramatic choral works, *Le roi David* and *Judith* are also performed.

Maurice Ravel (1875–1937) was probably the greatest French composer after Debussy. With less imagination than Debussy, he utilized the impressionistic innovations of his master to attain extraordinary orchestral effects. He could be witty, as in *Le Valse* (*The Waltz*), poetically descriptive as in the fragments from the ballet *Daphne et Chloë*, or boldly dramatic as in the extremely popular *Bolero*.[53]

Science. To think of French science in the twentieth century is to think, first of all, of the Curies. Marie Curie, co-discoverer of radium with her husband Pierre in 1900 and winner of the Nobel Prizes in both physics (1903) and chemistry (1911), conducted experiments in radioactivity until her death in 1934. Her work was ably continued by her daughter, Irene Joliot-Curie, who received the Nobel Prize in Chemistry in 1935 for her discovery of artificial radioactivity. The following year she was appointed Under-Secretary of State for Scientific Research by Léon Blum. Her husband, Frédéric Joliot, achieved renown for his investigations of gamma rays and for the discovery of a synthetic isotope of helium.

Another great French family of science were the De Broglies. Duke Maurice de Broglie, a member of the French Academy since 1934, showed how X rays split atoms into electrons of various categories. His younger brother, Prince Louis de Broglie, was awarded the Nobel Prize in Physics in 1929 for his contributions to the wave theory of mechanics.[54]

Education. Education in France has been free and compulsory since 1882 for all children between the ages of six and thirteen. This has led to a constantly reduced illiteracy. In 1911 there were 5,600,000 children in state-controlled primary schools. In 1925, even with the addition of Alsace and Lorraine, there were only 3,800,000 pupils. This was clear evidence of the tragedy of war and declining birth-rate.

The educational system was used to inculcate patriotism in French youth. The schools were highly centralized under the control of the *Conseil Supérieur* of fifty-two members, responsible to the Minister of Public Instruction. They prescribed the curricula, certified and promoted teachers, and selected the textbooks. Two-thirds of the hours of instruction in the elementary schools were devoted to nationalistic subjects such as Citizenship, French Language, French History, French Geography, French Songs, Military Exercises. In history, for example, the first grade studied forty heroes, only three of whom were foreigners. The teachers were perforce chauvinistic. If they deviated too far from the prescribed line of interpretation, they might be demoted. In like manner, the approved textbooks usually showed excessive national bias. The children were taught, for example, that Germany had been solely responsible for the war of 1914; the virtues of the French Revolution and accomplishments of the Third Republic were ceaselessly extolled. The textbooks, says Professor Hayes, " by their omissions . . . make it difficult for a French youth to be critical of French institutions or conduct, or to know of any services rendered to the world by modern foreign nations." Thus France, situated in the center of Europe, the hub of its multifarious avenues of trade and culture, was fostering in her youth an isolationism hardly conducive to the cosmopolitan role she had seemed destined to play.[55]

Overseas Empire

The French colonial empire in 1919 was 23 times as large as the mother country (4,600,000 square miles) and had about 1.7 times as many inhabitants (71,200,000). These possessions were scattered over the face of the globe. Among the larger and more valuable colonies were Tunis, Algeria,

Morocco, Equatorial Africa, Madagascar, Syria, and French Indo-China. France's mandated territories of Togoland, Cameroon, and Syria had a total area of 244,000 square miles and a population of 6,000,000.

The political significance of the empire has been largely that of bolstering national prestige and imbuing Frenchmen with confidence in their defensive strength and economic self-sufficiency. To be sure, there were advocates of a " Little France " like Clemenceau and Blum, who wished to repudiate the economic burdens of imperialism. French wheat farmers and wine growers disliked the competition they encountered from the colonies.[56] As a matter of fact, in 1920 Professor Gide went so far as to suggest that France transfer some colonies to the United States in lieu of debt payments.[57] But his was a lone voice. The French belief in their *mission civilisatrice* was as strong as the British assumption that it was the " white man's burden " to rule the benighted races of the earth. The Paris International Colonial and Overseas Exposition of 1931 helped to revive imperialist enthusiasm in the mother country. After 1933, it was necessary to emphasize to Frenchmen their imperial greatness in order to compensate for lost prestige in Europe.[58]

The French prided themselves on their colonial rule. They tried to civilize the natives by gradually Gallicizing them, but showed more understanding of local customs than the British did. Morocco, Tunis, and Indo-China were ruled through native princes by colonial administrators who kept firm hands on the controls of government. The work of Lyautey as Resident-General in Morocco was outstanding.[59]

Nevertheless Lyautey was compelled in 1926 to use force to put down a revolt led by a Moroccan chieftain, Abd-el-Krim. In Syria even more serious opposition to French rule arose. There Arab nationalists demanded independence and denounced France for her alleged favoritism toward Christians. High Commissioner Sarrail (1924–1925) resorted to force and terrorization to subdue the populace, but when a League of Nations report condemned such methods, France attempted to give Syria more self-government. However, High Commissioner de Martel in 1934 suspended the local Parliament when it refused to cooperate with him and returned to rule by decree.[60]

Without her colonies France could have played only a secondary role in world politics, and yet the colonial empire compelled her to modify her foreign policy. France formed an entente with England which finally became a military alliance partly to resist German demands for its lost colonies. To protect her Mediterranean Empire, France had to bow to Italy in both the Ethiopian and Spanish crises.

The colonies furnished much-needed man power for defense since France's population was not increasing appreciably. Of her peacetime army of 700,000, over 200,000 were colonials. Besides, the colonies furnished important naval bases such as Bizerta in Tunis, Oran in Algeria, Djibuti in French Somaliland, Dakar in West Africa, and Saigon in Indo-China. At the London Naval Conference of 1930 France's empire was the factor which prevented an agreement with Italy. France rejected Italy's demand for naval parity on the ground that her more extensive and scattered possessions required, proportionately, a much larger navy.

The economic significance of the colonies should not be overlooked. Not only did they furnish the mother country with needed raw materials such as rubber, cotton, ivory, timber, and minerals, but they supplemented France's food supply with wheat, rice, meat, sugar, wines, and fruits. In return, France exported to them machinery, automobiles, and clothing. Year by year this exchange of goods increased in value and volume. By 1934 France was sending 30.7 per cent of her exports to the colonies, in contrast to the pre-war figure of 12.8, and was receiving 27.6 per cent of her imports from colonial sources instead of 11.1 per cent in 1913. In spite of this trade, however, France's colonial empire remained a financial liability. Yet Frenchmen seemed convinced that, from the political and military points of view, the empire was essential to their welfare and well worth the expense it entailed.[61]

The Collapse of France

War soon brought momentous changes in France's political, social, and economic life. Abolition of Popular Front measures was not long delayed. The munitions industry was returned to the Schneider-Creusot management. With the need of increased production of war materials and the mobilization of 5 million men, the forty-hour week disappeared. Employers were allowed to use a fifty-hour schedule and 40 per cent of overtime pay was to be contributed by labor to the National Solidarity Fund devoted to the needs of evacuated families and dependents of soldiers. Because of Russia's cooperation with Germany Communist-controlled unions were harassed; in October, 1939 fifty unions were expelled from the Labor Bourse. In April, 1940 thirty-six Communist deputies were sentenced to five years' imprisonment, with the approval, incidentally, of the Socialist leader, Blum.

While Daladier raised the tax burden of the working class and abolished some of the governmental controls of business, he also compelled business to make sacrifices and undergo rigid wartime supervision. In October, 1939 a National Economic Bureau, headed by Daniel Serruys, was organized to control industry, trade, and consumption. This Bureau cut imports drastically and instituted strict supervision of all companies. Prices were fixed at their pre-war level to prevent profiteering, and a 100 per cent tax was imposed on profits above normal levels.[62]

The problem of financing the war was put into the capable hands of Paul Reynaud. He increased the tax rate in order to balance the ordinary budget, which in 1940 amounted to 349 billion francs. The separate war budget, which rose to 40 per cent of the ordinary budget, was financed by loans that were rapidly oversubscribed.

The most significant development of the war was the economic union of Great Britain and France. On November 16, 1939 the Allies signed agreements providing for far-reaching economic cooperation, a move that was described by Reynaud as " nothing less than an economic federation of Great Britain and France, with a customs union, a common currency, and the pooling of their vast economic resources." On February 16, 1940 a pact was signed which eliminated many of the trade barriers between the two countries. France was to buy more British coal and machinery; Great Britain was to purchase more French preserves, brandy, wines, and silks. A Franco-British Economic Coordinating Committee was created to direct the dual economy with Jean Monnet, a British subject of French parentage, as chairman. In this union France contributed her gold reserve and Great Britain her commercial and banking facilities. Thus the two powers were able to support their currencies, pool their purchases, finance their loans, and bid for the markets lost by Germany and the German-controlled states of Austria, Czechoslovakia, and Poland. More than that, they invited other nations to join their economic federation. As Daladier said on December 29, 1939: " This Franco-British union is open to all. . . . Europe should have a wider organization than that which has existed up to now." [63]

The failure of the Allies to go to the aid of Finland in her war with Russia not only shattered the neutrals' faith in Franco-British sincerity, but caused the downfall of the Daladier government (March 20, 1940). Reynaud succeeded without loss of time in forming a new Ministry which included Daladier as Minister of Defense.

When the *Blitzkrieg* began, however, France suffered greater disaster than Finland. On May 10 Germany simultaneously invaded Holland and Belgium. French and British troops threw defensive caution to the winds and emerged from their fortified lines to engage the foe. By the skillful use of air power, armored *Panzer* divisions, parachute troops, and " fifth columnists " behind enemy lines, the Germans forced Holland to surrender on May 14 and Belgium on May 28, broke through the French defenses at Sedan, and by relentless pressure and swift enveloping movements surrounded the Allied armies in Flanders. Heroic resistance by the British held up the Germans long enough at the Channel ports to permit the evacuation of about 250,000 men.

On May 19 Reynaud replaced General Gamelin with the veteran General Weygand, transferred Daladier to the Foreign Office, and named Marshal Pétain Vice-Premier. When Italy threatened to declare war, Daladier was dropped from the Cabinet, probably as a gesture of appeasement.

Causes of France's Disaster. These last-minute efforts were of no avail. Deep-seated ills, which for years had been propelling France toward disaster, could not be eradicated overnight. Thousands of officers disliked the republican regime and its left-wing politicians. They either had no heart for the war, or actually engaged in sabotage and other treasonable acts. Badly needed tanks were allowed to rust in railroad yards; unreliable regiments were placed at vital points like Sedan where the Germans easily broke through; anti-British sentiment was fostered among the French soldiers. Some commanders, including Gamelin, were criminally negligent in minimizing the need for mechanized equipment and putting their trust solely in the supposedly impregnable Maginot Line which, after the disaster, was called by wags the "Imaginary Line." Leftist governments helped to bring defeat by fostering pacifism and when at length they realized France's peril and discarded pacifism, it was too late to provide adequate equipment and build an air force to cope with Germany's mighty armies and *Luftwaffe.* Both Daladier and Reynaud failed to suppress the fifth columnists at the beginning of the war or speed up production of essential war materials. When the *Blitzkrieg* came, the Allies were hopelessly out-maneuvered and out-fought.[64]

Having forced the Allies to evacuate Flanders, the Germans on June 3 began a drive toward Paris from Normandy and Champagne. The poorly equipped and now demoralized French armies were no match for the swiftly moving invaders. On June 10 Weygand, exhorting his men to hold firm, cried, "This is the last quarter-hour!" Three days later the Germans entered Paris, which was undefended, and the government fled, first to Tours and then to Bordeaux. With the French armies and millions of civilians in panic flight along a jagged front, Reynaud sought desperately for outside aid. He begged the United States for "clouds of planes," although in reality France's fate was sealed. After a stormy Cabinet meeting, Reynaud, who wished to fight to the last and move the government to North Africa, was forced to resign in favor of Marshal Pétain, who opposed the continuation of the war. On June 17 Pétain asked for an armistice and honorable peace terms. The last quarter-hour was up. France was prostrate.[65]

Armistice Terms. Hitler forced the French on June 21 to sign an armistice in the same railway car in Compiègne Forest where Foch had imposed terms on the Germans twenty-two years before. Germany was to occupy all French territory north of a line running approximately from Geneva to Tours, thence southwards to the Spanish border. The French army, navy, and air force were to be demobilized and disarmed, except for those units determined by Germany to be necessary for the preservation of order at home and in the colonies. France was not to destroy military supplies, and Germany promised not to appropriate materials beyond the needs of the population in the occupied zone. France was to deliver those Germans residing on her soil who might be requested by the Nazis. An armistice with Italy, which entered the war on June 10, allowed the Italians to occupy a narrow strip of French Alpine territory, demilitarized a border area between Tripolitania and Tunisia as well as the coast of French Somaliland, and gave the Italians the use of the port of Djibuti and its railroad into Ethiopia.

Backward Glance. In the two decades, 1919–1939, France was the dominant power on the European continent. Excited by the hollow victory of 1918, she tried to keep her former adversary, Germany, impotent, so that her own supremacy would not be challenged. While France supported the League of Nations, in which French was one of the two official languages, she put her greatest trust in military alliances with the small democracies. For selfish reasons as well as from honest conviction, France therefore continued to foster democracy and nationalism on the Continent.

Not only was democracy upheld abroad, it was part of the French way of life. In the elections of 1924, 1932, and 1936 the victorious parties campaigned on platforms promising economic and political democracy. France became the haven for refugees from Fascist Italy, Germany, and Spain, and later from the conquered countries of Austria, Czechoslovakia, and Poland.

French democracy, however, had its powerful opponents. The capitalists of France, particularly the " 200 Families " who were said to control French industries, fiercely opposed, like their counterparts in England, the social reforms of the Leftist regimes. They were the prime movers in the appeasement of Hitler and Mussolini, symbolized in the shameless Munich Accord. Many of them, along with influential officers in the army and navy, yearned for a return of the monarchy or for a militaristic Fascist state. France's defeat in 1940 was partly due to the treachery of these two groups, and partly to the inefficiency, unpreparedness, and semi-paralysis of her parliamentary regime when faced by a powerful totalitarian adversary.

The French people essentially wanted peace, in spite of the occasionally belligerent attitude of their government. When Germany rearmed and remilitarized the Rhineland, France, instead of taking military action, negotiated an entente with Great Britain and eventually an alliance with Russia. Her failure to aid the Spanish Loyalists and appeasement of Germany lost her the support of the Central European countries as well as Russia. After Munich, France had no allies except Great Britain. The latter furnished a powerful navy, an intrepid air force, and a considerable army. But essentially the French had to bear the brunt of the German

attack.　The French army collapsed in 1940 before the bewildering innovations and amazing mechanized power of the German onslaughts in the
Battles of the Meuse, Flanders, and France.　With the signing of the armistice on June 22, French prestige declined to the lowest point since 1428.
Nor is France likely to recover her position in the family of nations for
many a year, regardless of who wins the present conflict.

REFERENCES

[1] For good discussions of the geography and ethnography of France see Gabriel Hanotaux, *Histoire de la nation française*, 15 vols., Paris: 1920, Vol. I by Jean Brunhes and Vol. II by Jean Brunhes and Pierre Deffontaines; and Ernest Lavisse, ed., *Histoire de France illustrée depuis les origines jusqu'à la Révolution*, 9 vols., Paris: 1911, Vol. I, Part I, by Vidal de la Blache, Part II by Bloch, and Vol. II, Part I, by Bayet, Pfister, and Kleinclausz.

[2] For the terms of the Versailles Treaty see the New York *Times*, June 10, 1919, p. 23, Articles 51–79.

[3] William MacDonald, *Reconstruction in France*, New York: Macmillan, 1922, pp. 23–38.

[4] William F. Ogburn and William Jaffé, *The Economic Development of Post-War France: A Survey of Production*, New York: Columbia Univ. Press, 1939, p. 66.

[5] In 1919 there were fourteen ministries: War, Foreign Affairs, Justice, Interior, Finance, Marine, Commerce (including industries, postal service, telegraph, and merchant marine), Public Works, Public Instruction, Colonies, Labor and Social Foresight, and Agricultural Reconstruction. Two temporary portfolios were for those of Industrial Reconstruction and Liberated Regions. The Premier (*Président du conseil*) usually headed one of the more important ministries.

[6] The number was increased by twenty-four when Alsace and Lorraine were annexed.

[7] Theoretically the Senate could force the Cabinet's resignation by an adverse vote, but actually it has succeeded in asserting this prerogative on only one occasion (1877).

[8] The canton is merely an election district and therefore has no regular governmental organization.

[9] For discussions of France's post-war government see Edward M. Sait, *Government and Politics of France*, Yonkers, N. Y.: World Book Co., 1921, and Frank M. Anderson, *Constitutions and Other Select Documents Illustrative of the History of France 1789–1907*, Minneapolis: H. W. Wilson, 1908, pp. 633–639.

[10] France had financed only 15 per cent of her war cost by taxation, Great Britain 50 per cent.

[11] For an explanation of the electoral law see *Review of Reviews*, November, 1919, LX: 535.

[12] On the election campaign see William MacDonald, "The Coming Election in France," *Nation*, August 30, 1919, CIX: 285–286; also *Nation*, November 22, 1919, CIX: 654:

[13] See Walter Littlefield, "Paul Deschanel as President of France," *Current History*, February, 1920, XI: 257–258.

[14] For the illness of Deschanel and the election of Millerand see "France under a New President," *Current History*, November, 1920, XIII: 263–267.

[15] Georges Lechartier, "The Program and Cost of Post-War Reconstruction in France," *Proceedings of the Academy of Political Science in the City of New York*, July, 1926, XII: 312–314.

[16] For modernization of French industrial plants see Ogburn and Jaffé, *op. cit.*, pp. 118–120; and MacDonald, *op. cit.*, pp. 122–140. For the cooperative movement in France see David Saposs, *The Labor Movement in Post-War France*, New York: Columbia Univ. Press, 1931, pp. 382–422; MacDonald, *op. cit.*, pp. 206–222, 332–337. On town planning see *ibid.*, pp. 257–274, 299–305.

[17] Quoted from Anne O'Hare McCormick, "Uneasiness of Redeemed Provinces," New York *Times*, July 2, 1922, Sec. III, p. 1.

[18] Ogburn and Jaffé, *op. cit.*, pp. 29–41, 547–548.

[19] Walter Littlefield, "Pope and France Resume Long-Broken Diplomatic Relations," New York *Times*, June 12, 1921, Sec. VII, p. 1.

[20] *Le Temps*, January 22, 1924, p. 3; January 23, 1924, p. 3.

[21] Saposs, *op. cit.*, p. 232.

[22] *Ibid.,* pp. 51–54, 60–61.

[23] New York *Times,* August 28, 1922, p. 2.

[24] New York *Times,* August 25 (p. 3), 26 (p. 2), 27 (p. 5), 28 (p. 2), 29 (p. 17), 30 (p. 17), December 3 (Sec. II, p. 4), 1922.

[25] For the election campaign of 1924 see John Bell, " The Coming Election Fight in France," *Fortnightly Review,* January, 1924, CXXI: 11–21; and Edouard Herriot, " What the Winners Want," *Living Age,* June 7, 1924, CCCXXI: 1083–1086.

[26] New York *Times,* February 21 (p. 3), March 10 (p. 17), 11 (p. 32), 1920.

[27] *Le Temps,* December 20 (p. 1), 1924; January 2–3 (p. 1), April 18 (pp. 1, 6), 1925.

[28] *Ibid.,* April 22, 1925, p. 6.

[29] For a discussion of the franc to 1928 see E. L. Dulles, *The French Franc 1914–1928,* New York: Macmillan, 1929, pp. 128, 151–158, 165–166, 416–461, 465–467, 477–478; and Paul Vaucher, *Post-War France,* London: Thornton Butterworth, 1934, pp. 87–95.

[30] See Carl Becker, " France Adopts Bill for Electoral Reform," *Current History,* September, 1929, XXVI: 966–968.

[31] H. G. Doyle, " Pre-Election Political Issues in France," *Current History,* May, 1928, XXVIII: 304–307.

[32] *Current History,* June, 1928, XXVIII: 491; July, 1928, XXVIII: 682.

[33] Saposs, *op. cit.,* pp. 267–279.

[34] Othon G. Guerlac, " Premier Tardieu's Record," *Current History,* September, 1930, XXXII: 1211; same in *Current History,* October, 1930, XXXIII: 131–132.

[35] For Herriot's speech see the New York *Times,* December 13, 1932, p. 17.

[36] For financial problems and the French default see Othon G. Guerlac, " The Perplexities of French Politics," *Current History,* January, 1933, XXXVII: 476–479.

[37] *Ibid.*

[38] *Current History,* XXXIX: 733–740; XL: 93–96, 224–228.

[39] On French fascism see Bertrand de Jouvenel, " France Stirred by ' Crosses of Fire,' " New York *Times,* September 29, 1925, Sec. VII, p. 10; also *ibid.,* February 11, 1934, Sec. IV, p. 1, Sec. I, p. 3; March 10, 1934, p. 7; March 12, 1934, pp. 1, 5; January 20, 1935, p. 6; February 13, 1935, p. 6; December 2, 1935, p. 1; October 27, 1937, p. 1.

[40] For monarchist organizations see New York *Times,* March 27, 1934, p. 11; September 29, 1935, Sec. VII, p. 10. On the Cagoulards, P. J. Philip, in *ibid.,* November 28, 1937, Sec. IV, p. 5.

[41] On the Common Front organizations see New York *Times,* February 12, 1934, p. 1; February 13, 1934, p. 1; March 27, 1934, p. 11; July 1, 1934, p. 3; July 16, 1934, p. 8; October 16, 1934, p. 27.

[42] For the election of 1936 see P. J. Philip, " Elections in France Promise Bitterness," New York *Times,* February 16, 1936, Sec. IV, p. 5; also *ibid.,* March 6, 1936, p. 14; April 26, 1936, Sec. VII, pp. 4, 20; May 4, 1936, p. 1; June 1, 1936, p. 10; June 5, 1936, p. 10.

[43] Norton Webb, " New Deal: French Style," *Current History,* June, 1937, XLVI: 45–48.

[44] *Ibid.*

[44a] Louis Aubert, " Security: Key to French Policy," *Foreign Affairs,* October, 1932, XI: 122–136.

[45] A good survey of French foreign policy since the First World War may be found in Vaucher, *Post-War France,* pp. 123–248.

[46] It would not be accurate to show comparisons of exports and imports in francs, since the franc fluctuated during the post-war period. Therefore the items are shown in tons.

[47] For statistical and other descriptive information on the economic development of France consult the *Annuaire statistique; Statesman's Year Book; International Year Books;* Paul Augé ed., *Larousse du XXᵉ siècle* (6 vols., Paris, 1930), III, 608 ff., Plates 8, 9, and 10; Hanotaux, *Histoire de la nation française,* II, chs. 26–36; Lavisse, *Histoire de France,* I, Part I, *passim;* Clough, *France, A History of National Econom-*

ics, ch. 9; and R. M. Haig, *The Public Finances of Post-War France*, New York: Columbia Univ. Press, 1929.

[48] For governmental intervention in the French economy see Ogburn and Jaffé, *op. cit.*, pp. 179–181, 299, 512–516, 548, 570–574; Saposs, *op. cit.*, Part II; Dulles, *op. cit.*

[49] For French literature since 1918 see Marcel Braunschvig, *La littérature française contemporaine de 1850 à nos jours*, Paris: Armand Colin, 1935, and André Rousseau, *Littérature du vingtième siècle*, Paris: Albin Michel, 1939, *passim.*

[50] A brief discussion of Le Corbusier may be found in *Harper's Encyclopedia of Art*, New York: Harper, 1937, I: 193.

[51] See "Exposition des arts décoratifs," *L'Illustration*, August 8, 1925, LXXXIII: Part II, 129–147.

[52] For French art since 1918 see Charles Terrasse, *French Painting in the XXth Century*, New York: Hyperion Press, 1939; Helen Gardner, *Art through the Ages*, New York: Harcourt, Brace, 1936, ch. 30; David M. Robb and J. J. Garrison, *Art in the Western World*, New York: Harper, 1935, chs. 15, 23, 32.

[53] For French music see Theodore M. Finney, *A History of Music*, New York: Harcourt, Brace, 1935, ch. 40; David Ewen, *Composers of Today*, New York: H. W. Wilson, 1934.

[54] See H. T. Pledge, *Science since 1500*, London: H. M. Stationery Office, 1939, ch. 17 ff., *passim.*

[55] C. J. H. Hayes, *France, A Nation of Patriots*, New York: Columbia Univ. Press, 1930, ch. 3.

[56] New York *Times*, December 18, 1938, Sec. VII, p. 17.

[57] *Ibid.*, June 5, 1920, p. 14.

[58] P. J. Philip, "France Looks to Her Empire," New York *Times*, December 18, 1938, Sec. VII, pp. 8–9, 17. See also *ibid.*, March 2, 1919, p. 4.

[59] E. W. Polson Newman, "French Methods in North Africa," *Fortnightly Review*, October, 1927, CXXVIII: 453–462. See also New York *Times*, December 18, 1938, Sec. VII, pp. 8–9.

[60] On French colonial policy see P. J. Philip, "France Looks to Her Empire," New York *Times*, December 18, 1938, Sec. VII, pp. 8, 9, 17; W. L. Middleton, "French Colonial Policy," *Contemporary Review*, August, 1934, CXLVI: 194–203; A. T. Polyzoides, "Syria's Revolt against France," *Current History*, July, 1922, XVI: 580–583; Emir Chekib Arslan, "Syrian Opposition to French Rule," *ibid.*, May, 1924, XX: 239–247; and "Why Krim Fights France," *Literary Digest*, June 6, 1925, LXXXV: 14–15.

[61] For the economic value of the French colonies see D. Gwynn, "France and Her Colonial Resources," *Contemporary Review*, September, 1923, CXXIV: 340–349; W. L. Middleton, "The French Colonial Conference," *Nineteenth Century*, May, 1935, CXVII: 605–612; and S. B. Clough, France, *A History of National Economics 1789–1939*, New York: Scribner, 1939, pp. 327–330.

[62] New York *Times*, September 15, 1939, p. 4.

[63] *Ibid.*, December 30, 1939, pp. 1, 3; February 1, 1940, p. 7; February 17, 1940, p. 3. For the cooperation of the British Labour Party and French Socialist Party see *ibid.*, February 23, 1940, p. 6.

[64] *Ibid.*, May 19, 1940, pp. 1, 36; June 6, 1940, p. 1. See also Heinz Pol, "Who Betrayed France?", *Nation*, July 6, 1940, CLI: 7–10, 27–30; and Pierre Lazareff, "The Fall of France," *Life*, August 26, 1940, IX: 68–75.

[65] New York *Times*, June 10, 1940, p. 1; June 11, 1940, pp. 1, 10; June 13, 1940, p. 2; June 14, 1940, p. 6; June 14, 1940, p. 5; June 15, 1940, p. 1; June 16, 1940, pp. 1, 22; June 17, 1940, p. 1; June 18, 1940, p. 1.

SELECTED BIBLIOGRAPHY

Billy, André, *La littérature française contemporaine*, Paris: Armand Colin, 1927. A good brief discussion of the more important writers of the last half-century.

Cornileau, R., *Du bloc national au front populaire*, Paris: Armand Colin, 1927. An up-to-date discussion of post-war politics.

Dulles, E. L., *The French Franc 1914–1928*, New York: Macmillan, 1929. A detailed study of the depreciation of French currency.

Garmy, René, *Histoire du mouvement syndical en France*, 2 vols., Paris: Bureau d'Éditions, 1934. Volume II discusses the subject in detail for the period since 1914.

Gide, Charles, ed., *Effects of the War upon French Economic Life*, Oxford: Humphrey Milford, 1923. A collection of five monographs describing French merchant marine, textile industries, finance, commerce, and labor at the end of the First World War.

Haig, R. M., *The Public Finances of Post-War France*, New York: Columbia Univ. Press, 1929. A thorough treatment of taxation, debts, currency, and expenditure in post-war France.

Hayes, C. J. H., *France, A Nation of Patriots*, New York: Columbia Univ. Press, 1930. A careful analysis of the institutions and methods used by France to inculcate nationalism in her citizens.

MacDonald, William, *Reconstruction in France*, New York: Macmillan, 1922. A thorough treatment of the problem and its solution up to 1922.

Maurois, André, *Tragedy of France*, New York: Harper, 1940. Brilliant analysis of the collapse of France.

Moulton, H. G. and Lewis, C., *The French Debt Problem*, New York: Macmillan, 1926.

Ogburn, William F. and Jaffé, William, *The Economic Development of Post-War France. A Survey of Production*, New York: Columbia Univ. Press, 1929. An excellent economic history of France for the first post-war decade.

Prévost, Jean, *Histoire de France depuis la guerre*, Paris: Editions Rieder, 1932. A very good general discussion of the period.

Saposs, David J., *The Labor Movement in Post-War France*, New York: Columbia Univ. Press, 1931. A thorough study of French labor problems and labor relations in the 'twenties.

Simon, André, *J'Accuse*, New York: Dial Press, 1941. An exposé of the venalities of French politics in the years preceding the Second World War.

Terrasse, Charles, *French Painting in the XXth Century*, New York: Hyperion Press, 1939. An adequate work on contemporary French painting.

Vaucher, Paul, *Post-War France*, London: Thornton Butterworth, 1934. A brief, but well-organized political, economic, and diplomatic history of France from 1919 to 1933.

CHAPTER VII

Belgium, Luxembourg, and the Netherlands

BELGIUM

" BELGIUM PLAYS A ROLE IN EUROPEAN AFFAIRS OUT OF ALL PROPORTION TO HER AREA AND POPULATION." — HENRI LAURENT

Geography. The Great Lowland Plain of Europe extends from Russia westward through north and central Germany and across north, central, and western France. Belgium with its area of 11,775 square miles lies athwart this great plain exactly at its narrowest segment, just south of the North Sea. The northwestern three-fifths of Belgium is low, flat or rolling country; the southeastern two-fifths gradually rises until at its southeastern border it develops into the Ardennes mountains. These also extend into Germany, Luxembourg, and France. Separating the Ardennes from the lowlands is the Meuse River which rises in France, flows northeastward through the Belgian cities of Namur and Liége and finally into the North Sea through the Netherlands. Farther to the northwest the Scheldt River enters from France, flows northeastward through Ghent and Antwerp, and thence through the Netherlands to the sea. The Belgians have an outlet to the sea at Antwerp, at the mouth of the Scheldt River, and at Zeebrugge along the North Sea coast. This has fostered a considerable merchant marine and furnished a convenient link to the great Belgian colony in the Congo.

Belgium's strategic location has made her the coveted object of powerful and ambitious neighbors. Situated along the narrowest part of the lowland plain, she also became a corridor for the invaders of France. During the Middle Ages, the English and French vied for the support of Flanders (western Belgium). The Dukes of Burgundy finally incorporated all of the " Lowlands " (including Holland) into a Burgundian state. This passed by inheritance first to the Austrian Hapsburgs and finally to Philip II of Spain. France in the seventeenth century tried to wrest the Lowlands from the menacing Spaniards. This effort failed, but France

---

This chapter by Lynn M. Case, Assistant Professor of European History, Louisiana State University, and John C. Engelsman, Assistant in History, Louisiana State University.

succeeded in having the Lowlands transferred to the less dangerous state of Austria in 1713. Not until 1793 did the French succeed in acquiring Belgium, which they later annexed to the empire. In 1814 Belgium was taken from France and given to the Netherlands, to which it belonged until, by the revolution of 1830, it became an independent state.

Great Britain, just across the Channel, always considered Belgium as a pistol pointed at her heart. Whoever controlled the trigger threatened the British Isles. After 1830, therefore, the British government insisted upon the neutralization of Belgium, and by the Treaty of London of 1839 obtained the promises of France, Prussia, Austria, the Netherlands, and Russia to observe the neutrality of the small kingdom. When Germany violated this promise in 1914, England used the occasion to declare war. After Belgian independence had been restored in 1918, the British allowed Belgium's neutral status to lapse and acquiesced in a Franco-Belgian Alliance. King Leopold III, however, reverted to a neutral status with the rise of Hitler. Unfortunately Germany again violated Belgium's neutrality in May, 1940, in order to outflank France's Maginot Line.

Ethnography. The 8,386,000 inhabitants of Belgium are divided into two distinct racial and linguistic groups. In the northern provinces of West Flanders, East Flanders, Antwerp, Limburg, and northern Brabant dwell about 4,000,000 Flemings of Teutonic origin who use dialects akin to Dutch. About a million of these people, particularly the business and professional classes, also speak French. In the remaining provinces the French-speaking Walloons, who have more Celtic blood, predominate. One of the chief problems of post-war Belgium was the conflict between these two groups.[1]

In addition to Flemings and Walloons, there is a small German minority. In the Belgian province of Luxembourg 31,400 German-speaking people reside; and when the Versailles Treaty in 1919 gave Belgium Eupen, Malmédy, and Moresnet, 64,000 more were added.

At War's End. By the end of November, 1918 the last German troops had left Belgian soil — a soil, however, which in West Flanders especially was blasted, muddy, bereft of trees, and strewn with the pulverized ruins of battle-scarred towns.

The natives, after the almost unendurable hardships and privations of war, went wild with joy as they welcomed the returning Belgian and Allied armies. Pathetically, though, an unusually large number of under-nourished and overwrought women and children fainted during the triumphal return to Brussels of their hero — King Albert. Soon afterwards, the Belgian martyr complex began to appear. Belgium expected to be loaded with attention and favors from the Allies, but instead their king had to beg concessions at the Peace Conference. The Belgians complained that financial help did not come immediately. They resented Wilson's

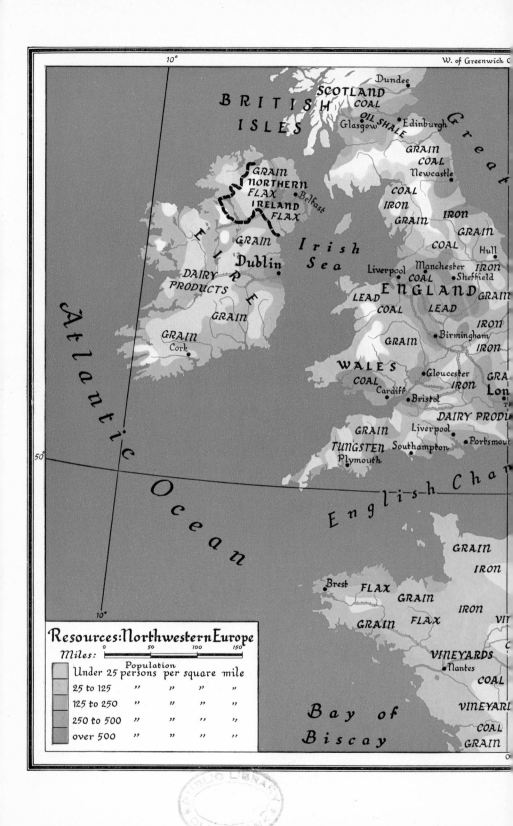

Dundee

B R I T I S H   SCOTLAND

I S L E S   COAL

OIL SHALE   •Edinburgh   Great

Glasgow

GRAIN
COAL

Newcastle

COAL
IRON

GRAIN   IRON

GRAIN

COAL   Hull

Irish

Sea   Liverpool   Manchester   IRON

COAL   •Sheffield

E N G L A N D   GRAIN

LEAD   LEAD

COAL

IRON

GRAIN   •Birmingham

IRON

GRAIN
NORTHERN
FLAX
IRELAND   •Belfast
FLAX

GRAIN

Dublin

E I R E

DAIRY
PRODUCTS

GRAIN

GRAIN
Cork

W A L E S

COAL   •Gloucester

Cardiff   IRON   GRA

Bristol   Lon

DAIRY PRODU

GRAIN   Liverpool

TUNGSTEN   Southampton   •Portsmout

Plymouth

A t l a n t i c   O c e a n

50°

E n g l i s h   C h a n

GRAIN

IRON

Brest   FLAX   GRAIN

IRON

GRAIN   FLAX   VI

GRAIN

10°

VINEYARDS
•Nantes

COAL

Resources: Northwestern Europe

Miles: 0   50   100   150

Population
Under 25 persons per square mile

	25 to 125 ,, ,, ,, ,,
	125 to 250 ,, ,, ,, ,,
	250 to 500 ,, ,, ,, ,,
	over 500 ,, ,, ,, ,,

B a y   o f

B i s c a y

VINEYARI

COAL

GRAIN

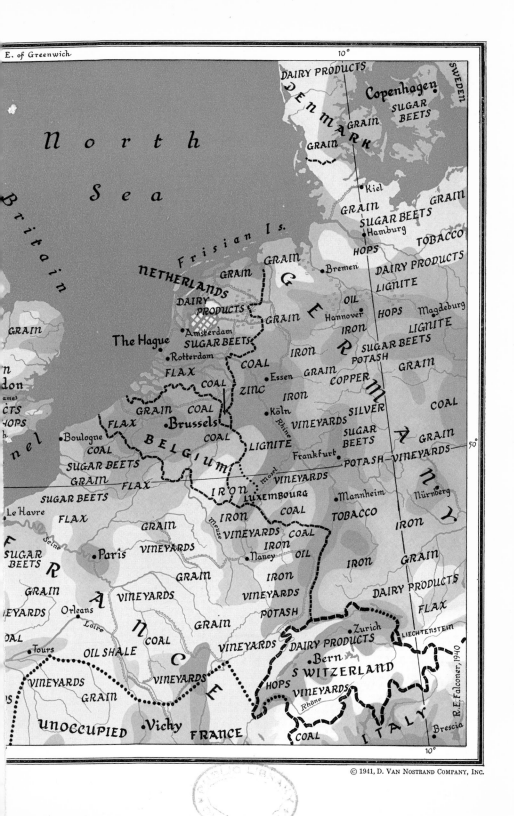

DAIRY PRODUCTS

SWEDEN

Copenhagen

D E N M A R K

SUGAR BEETS

GRAIN

GRAIN

N o r t h

S e a

•Kiel

B r i t a i n

GRAIN   GRAIN

SUGAR BEETS

•Hamburg

TOBACCO

F r i s i a n I s.

HOPS

DAIRY PRODUCTS

NETHERLANDS   GRAIN   GRAIN   •Bremen

G   LIGNITE

DAIRY

OIL

GRAIN   E   •Hannover   HOPS   Magdeburg

PRODUCTS

GRAIN   •Amsterdam   GRAIN   IRON   LIGNITE

GRAIN

The Hague SUGAR BEETS   R   SUGAR BEETS

n   •Rotterdam   IRON   POTASH   GRAIN

don   FLAX   COAL   IRON

ames   COAL   ZINC   •Essen GRAIN COPPER M

CTS   IRON

HOPS   GRAIN   COAL   •Köln   SILVER   COAL

h   FLAX   •Brussels   VINEYARDS   A

•Boulogne   B E L G I U M   COAL   SUGAR   GRAIN

COAL   LIGNITE   Frankfurt• BEETS   50°

SUGAR BEETS   IRON   POTASH–VINEYARDS   n

GRAIN   FLAX   VINEYARDS

SUGAR BEETS   IRON LUXEMBOURG •Mannheim   Nürnberg

Le Havre FLAX   IRON   COAL   TOBACCO   Y

F   GRAIN   VINEYARDS COAL   IRON

SUGAR   •Paris   VINEYARDS   IRON   OIL   IRON   GRAIN

BEETS   R   GRAIN   IRON

GRAIN   VINEYARDS   DAIRY PRODUCTS

EYARDS Orleans VINEYARDS   POTASH   FLAX

OAL   Loire   COAL   VINEYARDS   •Zurich LIECHTENSTEIN

•Tours OIL SHALE   DAIRY PRODUCTS

C   •Bern

VINEYARDS   VINEYARDS   S WITZERLAND

GRAIN   E   HOPS VINEYARDS

UNOCCUPIED   •Vichy FRANCE   Rhône   I T A L Y   •Brescia

COAL

failure to visit Brussels on his European tour. Finally the selection of Geneva in preference to Brussels as the seat of the League was interpreted as an affront.

Internal disunity also appeared. During the war the Germans had sown the seeds of discord between the Flemings and Walloons. Some now accused the former of consorting with the enemy, and several Flemish leaders were exiled. Factories were ruined or idle, 80,000 laborers were unemployed; and those who had jobs regarded their wages as inadequate. Bolshevism therefore began to find numerous adherents. Nevertheless, the people did not blame the government.[2]

Belgium emerged from the war with the same constitution she had in 1914. It provided for a limited, almost democratic, monarchy. The king had the power to initiate laws, dissolve Parliament under certain circumstances, and appoint the burgomasters of the communes. All other action by the king required the authority of responsible ministers. The Premier was the real executive; he appointed his eleven Cabinet colleagues, and formulated and carried out the policies of government as long as Parliament gave him support. The Parliament consisted of a Senate and a Chamber of Representatives. The 120 senators, who must be forty years of age and own considerable property, were elected for eight-year terms, one-half their number every four years, most of them by qualified voters over thirty, a few by the provincial councils. There were 186 representatives, one-half of whom were elected every two years by universal manhood suffrage (over twenty-five years of age) under a system of plural voting and proportional representation. A constitutional amendment required a two-thirds vote of a Parliament elected expressly on the constitutional issue involved. Considerable local self-government was allowed to the provinces and communes.[3]

Election of 1919. Before Belgium could undertake the gigantic task of reconstruction, it was necessary to inaugurate a new government. On the eve of the November, 1919 election certain electoral reforms were passed which provided for optional coalition lists in proportional representation, the use of the district rather than the province as the unit for the electoral lists, the introduction of universal manhood suffrage, and the reduction of the voting age from 25 to 21. In 1920 woman suffrage was granted for municipal elections, and a few years later a restricted number of women were permitted to vote even in parliamentary elections. As a result of the reforms the Socialists gained 27 seats in the Chamber in 1919, the Catholics lost 24, and the Liberals lost 12. The Socialists also gained in the Senate. The De la Croix Cabinet remained in office, since it was a coalition of the major parties.[4]

Reconstruction. Flanders was largely a shambles of burned houses, crumbled walls, twisted steel, half-destroyed cathedrals, gaping bridges, and razed forests. The city of Louvain looked like the ruins of Pompeii.[5] The reconstruction of the devastated areas cost Belgium $2,150,000,000.

At the Peace Conference Belgium was granted $2,640,000,000, or 8 per cent of the total reparations demanded from Germany, and was assured of priority in collections up to $500,000,000. Although she eventually received only about one-sixth of the reparations allotted to her, Belgium did obtain from Germany in the early post-war years much coal, livestock, farm and factory machinery, and rolling stock.[6]

With their own resources and with credits advanced on the promise of German reparation payments, the Belgians rebuilt their railroads in six months and by 1920, Cammaerts affirms, " had almost entirely restored their industrial and commercial equipment." Soil fertility had been recovered by 1922, and the livestock was almost back to pre-war figures. Housing lagged a little, but the towns were almost entirely rebuilt except Ypres, Dixmude, and Nieuport whose total destruction required a longer time for complete reconstruction.[7]

A world-wide controversy was evoked by the rebuilding of the Louvain Library. The American architect, Whitney Warren, insisted on retaining on the balustrade his original inscription: " Destroyed by German Fury; Restored by American Generosity." The rector of the university, Monsignor Ladeuze, ordered the inscription omitted. Against the protests of less charitable Belgians and in spite of a series of lawsuits by the architect, the liberal-minded rector had his way and the balustrade remained inscriptionless.

Eupen and Malmédy. Although Belgium had been the most favored of the victorious democracies at the Peace Conference, she fell victim to the more vicious promptings of nationalism as easily as any of her former enemies when she annexed Eupen and Malmédy. The Belgians agreed to a plebiscite in these regions only at the insistence of Woodrow Wilson, but they craftily thwarted a fair and secret vote. With a German population of over 50,000 only about 400 voted against Belgian sovereignty.[8] The representatives of the annexed regions in the Belgian Parliament continued, however, to protest against the injustice of the plebiscite, until in 1940 they were again returned to Germany by Hitler's victory over the Allies.

The Flemish Question. The chief political issue in Belgium after the war involved the satisfaction of Flemish demands. Stimulated by the Allied avowal of national self-determination and minority rights, the Flemings revived their conflict with the French-speaking Walloons. During the war the Germans had played upon this smoldering animosity by giving the two Belgian areas separate governments and converting the University of Ghent from a French to an exclusively Flemish institution. Although after the war the Flemings generally repudiated the German policy, they insisted on the use of Flemish in the schools, courts, administration, and army.

Some of these demands were satisfied by the law of 1921 which provided for the use only of Flemish by local officials in the Flemish regions, and of both Flemish and French by national officials. This angered the Walloons. " Let the Flemings," they said, " learn French, which is almost a universal European language." A law was passed in 1923 providing that Walloon and Flemish students at the University of Ghent take one-third of their courses in the other's language. In 1928, however, the bi-lingual practice was abandoned in the army, where the regiments were to speak the language of the region; and in 1930 bi-lingual instruction was abolished in the University of Ghent by making Flemish the official language. Finally in 1932, after further agitation and ministerial resignations, a comprehensive law was passed providing for: (1) the use of Flemish by administrative officials and teachers in Flemish-speaking regions; (2) the use of French in the Walloon regions; (3) the mandatory learning of the second language in high school; (4) Brussels, Eupen, and Malmédy were exempted from the provisions. There were still dissident and fanatically nationalist Flemings after 1932, but they were gradually absorbed into the Fascist groups.[9]

Stabilization of the Belgian Franc. At the end of 1921 Belgium's public debt almost equalled her total movable fortune (29,000,000,000 francs), and her annual deficit amounted to 4,500,000,000 francs. To remedy this situation a one per cent sales tax was imposed in 1921 which, together with partial payments of German reparations, tended to improve Belgium's financial status for a few years. In 1926, however, a serious crisis arose when the deficit of 1,000,000,000 francs caused fear in English banking circles that Belgium would be unable to float further international loans. Belgian francs were then thrown on the market, automatically precipitating a currency crisis and eventually causing the resignation of the Poullet Cabinet. Jaspar of the Catholic (conservative) Party formed a new Cabinet and gave Emile Francqui, as minister without portfolio, the job of undertaking stabilization. In order to obtain $100,000,000 from American, English, and other banks at even a high rate ($7\frac{3}{4}$ per cent) of interest, Belgium had to take stern measures toward stabilization. She was forced to turn over the railroad, telephone, and telegraph systems to private interests, compelling holders of government bonds to exchange them for securities in the private companies. Parliament also relegated most of its financial power to King Albert who, with the collaboration of Francqui, introduced new taxes, imposed rigid governmental economy, and stabilized the franc at 2.78 cents after it had fallen to 2.5 during the crisis. A new monetary unit, the belga, was established with a gold value of .2092 11 grams (current value about 14 cents), but this was used solely in international exchange.

The results of the stabilization of the preceding year were most gratifying. Commerce increased, bank deposits mounted, and stock market quotations rose rapidly. On the other hand, prices did not rise too much, and wages were not lowered. The country was quite satisfied with what might be called Belgium's first experiment with dictatorship.[10]

By 1934 Belgium, along with her neighbors, was sucked into the world depression. On March 16, 1935 the National Bank had lost 3,400,000,000 francs of its gold reserves. A bloc of continental countries, including Belgium and France, had tried to help each other to retain the gold standard, but on March 16 Belgium put gold dealings under government control and thereby went off gold. When France refused to make tariff concessions to Belgium in 1935, Theunis resigned; and the Van Zeeland coalition government of Catholics, Liberals, and Socialists depreciated the currency 28 per cent and inaugurated thoroughgoing reforms. In spite of the fact that Van Zeeland had been Vice-Governor of the National Bank, his plan provided for a government-controlled central rediscount and guarantee bank. He also advocated re-financing the government debt, work relief, higher wholesale prices, slightly higher retail prices and wages, friendly relations with Soviet Russia, and decree powers to the government for a year. The young king, Leopold III, who ascended the throne in 1934 at the death of his father, gave some evidence of dictatorial tendencies in getting the program accepted.[11]

The results of Van Zeeland's reforms were heartening. The budget of 1936 was nearly balanced; interest on the national debt was reduced from 7 to 4 per cent; and both exports and imports increased. In 1937, however, there was a recession in trade, accompanied by a long Cabinet crisis and the failure of a loan floated in England.

Labor Strife and Social Reforms. Labor disturbances were revived soon after the end of the First World War. The high cost of living in 1918 brought insistent demands for higher wages. The trade unions enjoyed a boom, and by means of numerous strikes gained some wage increases. The Socialist members of the Cabinet were instrumental in 1921 in passing a law providing for an eight-hour day. Further social legislation was passed in 1924 and 1925 providing for old-age pensions and death benefits for certain categories of wage earners and salaried employees. By amendments of 1926, 1929, and 1930 the Workmen's Compensation Act of 1903 was extended to include domestic servants and farm laborers. Advances in the cost of living after the decline of the franc, combined with wage deductions for social insurance contributions, led to the outbreak of a serious coal strike in 1930. As in 1921, this prompted the Socialist members of the government to push through Parliament additional labor legislation, such as the liberalization of pensions and compensations, and the provision of family allowances of about 40 cents per child to supplement wages. The severe depression of 1936 and the advent of the Van Zeeland

Ministry inaugurated a period of more sweeping reforms, including minimum wages of four francs an hour, the forty-hour week, six-day vacations with pay (1938), abolition of wage deductions, and a 10 per cent increase of unemployment insurance benefits.   The threat of war in 1939, however, by calling many laborers to the colors or to work on defense projects, resulted in the relaxation of many reform benefits.   Without losing their unemployment insurance, some men were given part-time work on defense projects.   Under certain circumstances the work day could be lengthened, and women and children were permitted to do night work.   Thus, as with all countries caught in the vortex of war, Belgium's peacetime reforms melted away under the heat of bloody conflict.[12]

Joys and Sorrows.   Belgium rejoiced at the marriage of the popular Prince Leopold and Princess Astrid of Sweden in November, 1926.   In 1930 she also marked the centenary of her independence by holding four expositions at Antwerp, Brussels, Liége, and Mons respectively.[13]   In the same year the marriage of Princess Marie José to Crown Prince Humbert of Italy seemed to augur closer relations between the two countries, and the birth of Prince Baudoin to Leopold and Astrid assured the succession to the throne.   On February 17, 1934, however, King Albert was killed while mountain-climbing near Namur.   When Queen Astrid met her death in a tragic automobile accident on August 29, 1935, Leopold, who had been driving at the time, was almost unconsolable in his grief.

Rexist Fascism.   The Fascist tendencies in Europe were bound eventually to affect Belgium.   Although the depression was not so distressing as in Italy and Germany, certain factors favored the rise of a Fascist movement. Belgian democracy and political parties suffered from the sluggishness and conservatism of old age.   Political corruption was allowed to creep in; the solution of serious problems met interminable delays; and enormous expenditures were authorized by Liberals, Catholics, and Socialists alike.   Increased Communist activity, accompanied by strikes and labor unrest, brought an alarm of impending revolution in the middle 'thirties.   Many youths were disgusted with the vacillations of the democratic state, and many older men wanted vigorous action to curb Communism.   Capitalizing on this unrest, young Léon Degrelle organized the Rexist Party to combat the status quo.   Although he greatly admired Mussolini and Hitler, Degrelle's program seemed moderate: he advocated extensive powers for the king, a corporative Parliament, abolition of the traditional political parties, but not a frontal attack on representative government.   In the election of 1936 the Rexists won 21 seats in the lower house and 12 in the Senate, polling 281,000 votes in the country as a whole.

In 1937 Degrelle challenged the old parties by running for Parliament in Brussels.   The challenge was accepted by Premier van Zeeland who became the government candidate for the vacancy.   Van Zeeland received

76 per cent of the vote. From that time on the Rexists declined, until in the election of 1939 they were reduced to only 4 seats in the Chamber.[14]

Economic Development. In the valleys of the Sambre and the Meuse, across central and eastern Belgium, are found large deposits of coal, iron, zinc, and lead, exploited on an increasing scale in the post-war years. The fertility of the soil is another important natural resource, and Belgium's agricultural production is an essential, albeit lesser, part of her economic activity. Potatoes, flax, wheat, and rye are the principal products of the north, while oats and sugar beets predominate in the south.

Belgium, however, is primarily an industrial country. Only one-sixth of her adults were engaged in agriculture (635,000) before the recent war and two-thirds were engaged in manufacturing (2,048,000). In northern and western Belgium, especially in the provinces of Flanders and the cities of Brussels and Antwerp, the manufacture of linens, woolens, and cotton predominates. The metallurgical industries, iron, steel, and zinc, are located in the valleys of the Sambre and Meuse, and construction shops are scattered all over central Belgium. Sugar refineries and distilleries are numerous in the southeast. Considerable progress was made in the steel industry between 1920 and 1936, but sugar and alcohol showed a decline in that period.

The commerce of Belgium was borne along her 1000 miles of navigable rivers and canals (particularly the Scheldt and Meuse rivers and the Albert Canal), 6400 miles of highways, and 6400 miles of railroads. The merchant marine totaled 105 ships, or 241,800 tons. Antwerp, at the mouth of the Scheldt, is the principal port. As the following table shows, Belgium's foreign trade has consistently shown an unfavorable balance: [15]

	1921	*1927*	*1938*
Imports	10,054,000,000 fr.	29,179,000,000 fr.	23,165,000,000 fr.
Exports	7,147,000,000 fr.	26,620,000,000 fr.	21,723,000,000 fr.
Balance of trade	—2,907,000,000 fr.	—3,559,000,000 fr.	—1,442,000,000 fr.

Belgium always had more trade and more favorable balances with France than with any other country.[16]

Overseas Empire. In the very heart of Africa, where the tropical jungles are most impenetrable, Belgium possesses a colony as large as the United States east of the Mississippi. The Belgian Congo and adjacent mandates of Ruanda and Urundi have an area of 920,000 square miles inhabited by 11,500,000 people or 3,000,000 more than the mother country. Ruanda and Urundi, part of former German East Africa, were received as mandates from the League of Nations by the Versailles Treaty and put under the government of the Belgian Congo.

The Belgian Congo is rich in natural resources and varied tropical products. Copper, tin, gold, and diamonds are extracted in great quantities;

large investments have been made in the last twenty years in the mining areas of this region. Likewise a great effort was made to clear more jungle land for cultivation. The principal products are rubber, ivory, cotton, palm-oil, coffee, and sugar. In addition to furnishing the mother country with needed raw materials and importing manufactured articles from Belgian factories, the Congo helped to reduce Belgium's adverse balance of trade. Between 1914 and 1936 the favorable trade balance of the colony had risen from $6,000,000 to $21,000,000. In view of this Belgium could well afford to make up the $1,760,000 colonial budget deficit of 1937.

When Hitler began to demand the return of German colonies and at the same time succeeded in remilitarizing the Rhineland, Belgium became worried about the safety of her colonies. Leopold carried on discussions with London, and finally Premier Spaak in December, 1937 declared that in any proposals for a redistribution of colonial areas Belgium would be willing to discuss the situation of Ruanda and Urundi.[16a] When the colony and mandates became separated from Brussels after Leopold's capitulation in 1940, they remained under the authority of the refugee government in France. Later, when that government was trapped in unoccupied France, Great Britain was able to retain the loyalty and cooperation of the Belgian Congo for the continuation of the war.

Foreign Policy. In 1919 Belgium abandoned her traditional neutrality and made a military agreement with France which provided for consultation between their general staffs and mutual aid in case of attack.[17] To enhance her security Belgium joined the League of Nations, and in 1925 signed the Locarno Treaties which promised her British, French, and Italian help in case Germany attacked her eastern frontier. In return Belgium promised to help Germany or France in case one was attacked by the other.

With a feeling of greater security, Belgium began to improve her international economic position. In 1921 a customs union was made with Luxembourg; a common tariff was enacted and the revenue was to be apportioned roughly in proportion to population. The proposal to extend the customs union to other countries divided Belgian opinion. The Flemings wanted to include the Netherlands, but the Walloons preferred France. After a long period of negotiation, a Belgian-Dutch commercial treaty was concluded in 1927 which did not create a customs union but provided for reciprocal commercial concessions. It also guaranteed to Belgium the construction of two new canals in the Netherlands to facilitate Antwerp's trade with the Rhine. Unfortunately the Dutch Parliament refused to ratify the agreement.[18]

In 1932 Belgium turned to France, but an agreement on France's rescinding of quota restrictions could not be reached.[19] Undaunted, Belgium again turned to the Netherlands, but without avail. The nearest approach to an agreement with the Netherlands came with the conclusion of the multilateral Oslo Agreement of 1937. Signed by Belgium, the Netherlands, Denmark, Norway, Sweden, and Finland, the agreement abolished all quota restrictions between the signatories and gave Belgium certain advantages in trading with these countries. Within a year, however, this experiment was discontinued because world conditions injected too many elements of uncertainty.[20]

War and rumors of war kept Europe in a state of perpetual alarm after 1930. When, in 1936, France failed to stop Germany's remilitarization of the Rhineland and the League of Nations proved incapable of saving Ethiopia, Leopold decided to drop the French alliance and return to the status of neutrality. While this pleased the anti-French Flemings, the Walloons showed such hostility that Spaak was forced to declare that Belgium was not returning to neutrality but to independence, that she would respect her signature (the French alliance) but did not want defensive alliances. This only made Belgium's position more confusing. Actually France, Great Britain, and Germany subsequently gave their small neighbor assurance of their respect for her neutrality.[21]

As Europe moved rapidly toward war, Leopold, fully aware that his country would be caught between the deadly rivalry of France and Germany, made energetic efforts to preserve peace. When Chamberlain and Halifax visited Rome in January, 1939 Leopold persuaded the rulers of the Netherlands, Denmark, Norway, and Sweden to issue an appeal to the four Great Powers for a European congress to settle permanently all matters in dispute. England and France unreservedly approved of the plan, but Germany and Italy withheld their assent, and therefore nothing came of it.[22]

Cultural Development: Literature. Just as France and Belgium were closely related economically, so were they intimately associated culturally. The best-known Belgian writer of the twentieth century, Maurice Maeterlinck (1862–   ), uses the French language. His early works are imbued with a fatalistic spirit, a belief that man is helpless to cope with his environment. His post-war works are more optimistic and cheerful. In his *Vie des fourmis* (*Life of the Ant*, 1930) and *Vie des thermites* (*Life of the Termite*, 1926) Maeterlinck produced not only valuable scientific treatises, but penetrating commentaries on the lives of men as well as insects. His *Avant le grand silence* (*Before the Great Silence*, 1936) brings his willing resignation to bear on the questions of life and death in veritable poetic prose. As one critic has remarked, " If his philosophy is not truly original, we must admire his harmonious and limpid style, the poetry which envelops with supreme charm the driest and most severe subject matter."

The greatest of contemporary Belgian historians was Henri Pirenne, who also used the French language. In seven volumes of his *Histoire de*

Belgique (1900–1932) he has traced with discriminating scholarship the history of his country from the earliest times to 1914.[23]

Art. The sculpture of George Minne (1866–   ) recalls the depressing fatalism of Maeterlinck, and yet, like his literary compatriot, he has shown signs of a more pleasant naturalism with less symbolic distortion in such post-war works as the *Bust of a Laughing Maiden* (1926). George Vantongerloo has devoted himself to abstract sculptural designs. In his *Construction* (1931) he produced a fourth-dimensional conception of both space and time by the arrangement and repetition of the geometrical, almost cubist, subject. In painting, René Magritte (1898–   ) has shown a spirit akin to Vantongerloo. In *Mental Calculus*, for example, he depicts a village, some houses of which take the forms of prisms and spheres in a half-surrealist, half-cubist motif.[24]

Music. Post-war Belgian music was divided into two distinct schools: Flemish and Walloon. The former has more serious and subdued characteristics, while the latter is recognized by its dramatic elements. Maurice Shoemaker belongs to the Synthesist branch of the Flemish school and is best known for his opera, *Das Christusbild* (*Picture of Christ*, 1933). Among the Walloons Léon Dubois (1859–   ) deserves special mention. Winner of the Grand Prix de Rome, he is known particularly for his operas, written in the Wagnerian tradition, and for his oratorio, *L'Avengle né* (*The One Born Blind*, 1922). A notable achievement in Belgian musical history was the establishment of the *Orchestre national de Belgique* on September 15, 1936.

Science. The best-known Belgian scientist of the post-war period is Dr. Jules Bordet. For his experiments and discoveries in toxicology he deserves to be called the Pasteur of Belgium. He was director of the Pasteur Institute at Brussels, professor of medicine at the University of Brussels, recipient of the Nobel Prize for Medicine (1919), and author of an important *Treatise on Immunity in Infectious Diseases* (1921).

Invasion and Collapse. After the Munich Agreement in September, 1938 Belgium shared with the rest of the world a great feeling of uneasiness. While Czechoslovakia was being swallowed up by Germany in 1939, Belgium had a serious domestic crisis. The Fleming, Dr. Adrian Maertens, condemned as pro-German during the First World War, was appointed to the Royal Academy of Medicine by the Socialist Premier, Spaak, as a gesture of reconciliation with his race. This action infuriated Walloon patriots. The Liberal Party deserted the Cabinet, and Spaak had to resign. Pierlot, appointed Premier, called for new elections in which Dr. Maertens was almost the sole issue. In the light of international dangers, King Leopold regarded this as a tempest in a teapot, and did not hesitate to express his disgust with Parliament and the political parties in a blistering public letter. When the votes were counted, the Catholics and Liberals were victorious; the Socialists, Rexists, and Nazis lost heavily. The Flemish Party managed to hold its own. Ultimately Dr. Maertens tendered his resignation from the Academy.[25]

Before the year was out Belgium had more serious matters to think about. The German invasion of Poland had an ominous ring, and steps were taken immediately to protect Belgium's neutrality and independence. Earlier in 1939 the Albert Canal had been opened, serving not only as a trade channel but a bulwark of defense on the northern and eastern frontiers; south of the Canal the scattered fortresses were now strengthened. After the outbreak of war the king took command of the army, received dictatorial powers, and decreed partial mobilization.

The economic effects of the war on Belgium can be best described in the words of Theunis on his visit to America: " Our country is the turntable of Europe, but the war has made it impossible to turn. Our entire economic system has been disrupted. Long established channels of trade are completely blocked." [26]

Worse was in store for Belgium. Her uneasiness mounted as she witnessed, one after another, Poland, Finland, Denmark, and Norway become victims of aggression. When German troops began to appear on her borders, complete mobilization was announced. However, even when every sign showed in the winter of 1939–1940 that Germany was preparing to invade Belgium, Leopold refused to hold staff conferences with the Allies.[27]

On May 10, 1940 the storm broke with all its fury. The Nazi legions struck savagely by land and air at both the Netherlands and Belgium. Only then did the Low Countries ask France and England for help. Belatedly the Allied soldiers emerged from behind their fortified lines. But before they arrived on the Belgian frontier they encountered roads choked with terrorized refugees, bombed and machine-gunned from the air. In the meantime the German armies, preceded by *Panzer* tank units, pushed steadily into the Low Countries. The Meuse was crossed at Maastricht; at several points bridges were not blown up to impede the invaders. Fort Eben Emael capitulated without much resistance. Such events were bound to create suspicions of fifth-column treachery. Through the Albert Canal, to Liége, Louvain, Brussels, through the Maginot Line at Sedan, around Flanders, to Boulogne, Calais – there seemed to be no way to stop the invaders. The Belgian, French, and British armies were caught in the Flanders pocket.

Leopold Capitulates. On May 28 Leopold surrendered to the enemy without consulting his allies. The French and British, unable to break out of the pocket and deserted on the left wing by the Belgians, fought a terrific rear-guard action by which they extricated about four-fifths of their troops but left behind enormous quantities of supplies, munitions, and equipment.

The captains and kings had departed, and for a time there settled over Belgium a brooding silence, like that of death.

At first the king was condemned by foreigners and fellow-countrymen alike. By the British and French he was accused of treachery for exposing their left wing and making necessary the costly evacuation of Dunkerque. By the Belgian Cabinet he was charged with an unconstitutional flouting of ministerial advice. Both Pierlot and Spaak denounced his decision and proceeded to recruit a new Belgian army on French soil and set up the Belgian government at Poitiers. Some units of the Belgian army refused to lay down their arms and either were taken prisoner or escaped at Dunkerque. The Belgian Congo threw in its lot with England. Some hostile elements in the Belgian Parliament even asserted that Leopold had always sympathized with the Nazis. They pointed to his threats to Socialists, his denunciatory letter of 1939, his German ancestry, and his German friends.

Time and circumstance, however, seemed to show Leopold in a better light. With the collapse of France, many realized that it would have been futile for Belgium to fight any longer. Perhaps Leopold recognized the futility of resistance in time to save the lives of hundreds of thousands of men. Little Belgium had again been used as the pawn of neighboring powers. As a matter of fact Leopold had not gone over to the side of the enemy, but considered himself a prisoner, like his soldiers, and remained immured in his Laeken Palace. Unlike his great father, however, he preferred to remain with his defeated soldiers rather than accompany his government into exile. The Belgians on the whole seemed to side with him, and even Pierlot's refugee government, unable to negotiate a reconciliation with Leopold through the auspices of the Vatican, managed to escape from Spain to England after the capitulation of France.[28]

The Belgian nation once more had to submit to German occupation and all the suffering imposed by the British blockade. Certain signs seemed to point to the transfer of the Flemish provinces to a new Dutch-Flemish state. The mines and metallurgical industries were reopened to serve the war needs of the conquerors, while the other industries, cut off from sources of raw material, were limping along at only 20 per cent of normal production. There were, therefore, in the summer of 1940, over a million unemployed in addition to a million returning refugees to be cared for in some manner. Many accepted the offer of work in Germany. The relief problem was accentuated by the scarcity of food. Normally 75 per cent of Belgium's wheat is imported, but now she had to rely on her own crops, which were not only scanty but would not have fed a fourth of her population had the harvest been good.[29] Starvation and sorrow seemed to be the unjust fate of this industrious and peace-loving people, whose chief crime seems to be that of living on Europe's main highway of destruction.

"*If Winter Comes. . . .*" Pirenne's voluminous history of his country tells a story of alternating periods of prosperity and misfortune. There were the tragedies of medieval wars, Alva's bloodletting, Louis XIV's conquests, Napoleon's dominations, and Germany's invasions; between them came the prosperous interludes of Burgundian commercial development, Austria's benevolent despotism, and national independence in the nineteenth century. The period from 1918 to 1939 was, on the whole, a happy respite. If in the winter of 1940–1941 the Belgian people were again brought under subjection to an invader, their king a captive in some secret retreat, their government a fugitive in a distant land, and their hearths haunted by the specter of famine, still may we not ask hopefully — " Can Spring be far behind? "

REFERENCES

1 A brief description of the geography and people of Belgium may be found in Frank Maclean's *Belgium*, New York: Dodge, c. 1914, pp. 5–13.

2 The conditions in Belgium immediately after the war are well described by Emile Cammaerts in " The Problems of Belgium," *Living Age*, May 21, 1919, CCCI: 713–715; and " Belgium since the Armistice," *Yale Review*, October, 1919, IX: 87–104. See also Isaiah Bowman, *The New World: Problems in Political Geography*, Yonkers, N. Y.: World Book Co., 1922, pp. 119–128.

3 The Belgian constitution is discussed in R. C. K. Ensor, *Belgium*, New York: Holt, n.d., ch. 7; and in Maclean, *op. cit.*, pp. 13–21.

4 New York *Times*, November 19, 1919, p. 8; November 20, 1919, p. 17.

5 " Pictures of War-Swept Belgium," *Literary Digest*, January 2, 1915, I: 20–21; " Belgium's Murdered Steel Industry," *ibid.*, June 7, 1919, LXI: 26–27; " Reparations," *World Peace Foundation Pamphlets*, Boston, 1922, V, No. 1, pp. 26–27.

6 " Reparations," *World Peace Foundation Pamphlets*, Boston, 1922, V, Nos. 1–3, *passim.*

7 The following two articles discuss the problems and progress of reconstruction: E. Cammaerts, " Belgian Recuperation," *Edinburgh Review*, January, 1922, CCXXXV: 108–121; and E. Cammaerts, " The Last Stage in the Reconstruction in Belgium," *Contemporary Review*, December, 1926, CXXX: 707–714.

8 " Has Belgium Annexed a Little Alsace-Lorraine? ", *Literary Digest*, April 9, 1921, 42–49.

9 For the Flemish movement see S. B. Clough, *History of the Flemish Movement in Belgium*, New York: R. R. Smith, 1930, especially chs. 7, 8, and 9; Louis Pierard, *Belgian Problems since the War*, New Haven: Yale Univ. Press, 1929, ch. 1; and Louis Pierard, " Belgium's Language Question: French vs. Flemish," *Foreign Affairs*, July, 1930, VIII: 641–651.

10 See " Belgium's Return to Solvency," *Literary Digest*, November 6, 1926, XCI: 10.

11 Henri Laurent, " Belgium under a New Leader," *Current History*, August, 1935, XLII: 481–487.

12 For detailed discussions of Belgian social reforms see " Belgian Experience with the Eight-Hour Day," *Survey*, October 15, 1923, LI: 90–91; " New Belgian Act on Family Allowances," *Monthly Labor Review*, December, 1930, XXXI: 1379–1381; " Revision of the Belgian Law on Insurance of Salaried Employees and of Wage Earners against Old Age and Premature Death," *ibid.*, pp. 1371–1378; " Revision on Belgian Workmen's Compensation Law," *ibid.*, pp. 1398–1399; " Changes in the Belgian Unemployment Insurance System," *ibid.*, November, 1934, XXXIX: 1113–1114; " Amendment of Belgian Law on Vacations with Pay," *ibid.*, January, 1939, XLVIII: 93; " Provisions of Belgian Labor Legislation of 1936," *ibid.*, September, 1936, XLIII: 616–618; " Increased Belgian Unemployment Insurance Benefits," *ibid.*, July, 1937, XLV: 111–112; " Reemployment Measures in Belgium," *ibid.*, January, 1940, L.: pp. 58–59.

13 On the Belgian centenary see " Le centenaire de l'indépendance belge " (" Centenary of Belgian Independence "), *L'Illustration*, July 5, 1930, LXXXVIII: Part II, 331–373, 382–383; H. Davignon, " Le centenaire de l'indépendance belge " (" The Centenary of Belgian Independence "), *Revue des deux mondes*, May 1, 1930, pp. 92–113; New York *Times*, July 21, 1930, p. 7.

14 For Degrelle and the Rexist movement see Harold Callender, " Fascism in Belgium," *Foreign Affairs*, April, 1937, XV: 554–563; Arved Arenstam, " Léon Degrelle, Belgium's *Enfant Terrible*," *Living Age*, August, 1936, CCCL: 505–509; and New York *Times*, April 12, 1937, p. 1.

15 The first column represents the franc before the worst depreciation and the last two after stabilization. Therefore the comparisons with 1920 cannot be determined exactly.

16 Statistics on all phases of Belgium's post-war economic life may be found in the *Statesman's Year-Book*, especially the years 1920, 1922, and 1938 for this study.

16a New York *Times*, March 23, 1937, p. 6; December 10, 1937, p. 7.

17 Belgium insisted that she would not act without a favorable vote of Parliament. See Emile Cammaerts, "International Situation of Belgium," *Contemporary Review*, May, 1921, CXIX: 625–632; and New York *Times*, September 1, 1920, p. 17; September 14, 1920, p. 17.

18 On the abortive Belgian-Dutch treaty see "Belgian-Dutch Treaty," *Review of Reviews*, July, 1927, LXXVI: 97; and E. Davis, "Belgium and Holland Isolated? ", *Harper's*, May, 1927, CLXXIV: 627–636.

19 Under these circumstances, Belgium's foreign minister, Hymans, declared, " any project for an economic union with France could not be realized and would be dangerous." New York *Times*, February 19, 1932, p. 7.

20 On the Oslo Agreement see *ibid.*, June 3, 1937, p. 5; and May 16, 1938, p. 9.

21 On Belgium's return to neutrality see New York *Times*, October 15, 1936, pp. 1, 5; October 29, 1936, p. 2; and C. L. Heymann, " Belgium, 1936; Her Neutrality Seems Close to a Risky Isolation," *Current History*, January, 1937, XLV: 66–70.

22 Jules Romains, " The Mystery of Leopold III," *Saturday Evening Post*, October 5, 1940, CCXIII: 20–21, 104, 106–107, 109.

23 For Maeterlinck see Marcel Braunschvig, *La littérature française contemporaine de 1850 à nos jours*, Paris: Armand Colin, 1935, pp. 291–292; and New York *Times*, December 21, 1930, Sec. IV, p. 4; and September 20, 1936, Sec. VI, p. 10. For a discussion of Pirenne see the *American Historical Review*, January, 1936, XLI: 403; and for a review of his work see *ibid.*, January, 1903, VIII: 380.

24 For Minne see C. R. Post, *A History of European and American Sculpture*, 2 vols., Cambridge, Mass.: Harvard Univ. Press, 1921, II: 194–195; C. H. Chase and C. R. Post, *History of Sculpture*, New York: Harper, 1925, pp. 473–474; and *Allgemeines Lexikon der Bildenden Küntsler von der Antike bis zur gegenwart* (33 vols., Leipzig: Seemann, 1930, XXIV: 579–580. For Vantongerloo see C. Gildion-Welcker, *Modern Plastic Art*, Zurich: Girsberger, 1937, pp. 115–117. A brief discussion of Magritte may be found in *Art in Our Time*, New York: Museum of Modern Art, 1939, No. 193.

25 On the election of 1939 see New York *Times*, March 7, 1939, pp. 1, 3; April 3, 1939, p. 1; April 4, 1940, p. 9.

26 *Ibid.*, October 22, 1939, p. 37.

27 Jules Romains, *loc. cit.*, pp. 109–110.

28 For the capitulation of Leopold III and the controversy it aroused see New York *Times*, May 28, 1940, pp. 1–2, 5; May 29, 1940, p. 4; June 28, 1940, p. 14; July 4, 1940, p. 4; August 11, 1940, p. 4.

29 *Ibid.*, Aug. 7, 1940, p. 1; Aug. 17, 1940, p. 4; *Time*, Sept. 2, 1940, XXXVI: p. 25.

SELECTED BIBLIOGRAPHY

Clough, S. B., *History of the Flemish Movement in Belgium*, New York: R. R. Smith, 1930. A detailed study of the Flemish problems in the periods before, during, and since the First World War.

Gibson, Hugh, *Belgium*, Garden City, N. Y.: Doubleday, Doran, 1939. More descriptive than historical.

Gooch, R. K., " The Government and Politics of Belgium and Holland," pp. 1043–1064, in J. T. Shotwell, ed., *Governments of Continental Europe*, New York: Macmillan, 1940. A very good survey of the background of Belgian politics, with a serviceable bibliography.

Pierard, Louis, *Belgian Problems since the War*, New Haven: Yale Univ. Press, 1929. A series of lectures on the Flemish question, labor problems, and the Socialist movement in Belgium.

LUXEMBOURG

Geography. The Grand Duchy of Luxembourg lies in west central Europe, a tiny land-locked island between the basins of the Meuse and Moselle rivers. It is formed by a portion of the Ardennes plateau in the north and an extension of the Lorraine plateau in the south. Practically the entire Grand Duchy is drained by the Moselle which, with the Sure and Our, forms its eastern frontier. The surface is, for the most part, rugged or mountainous and well forested.

Luxembourg has an area of 999 square miles or about three-quarters that of Rhode Island. North to south its greatest length is fifty-five miles, while it extends only thirty-four miles from east to west.

Historical Background. Its position and size have permitted Luxembourg to enjoy an independent existence based on the sufferance of its more powerful neighbors. Hemmed in by Germany on the northeast and east, by France on the south, and by Belgium on the west and northwest, it has been, through the centuries, the plaything of almost every successful invader of western Europe. After a period of Roman rule, when it was included in Belgica Prima, it became part of the Frankish Kingdom of Austrasia. Charlemagne, the Dukes of Burgundy, the Hapsburgs, Austria, Spain, France, and the Netherlands all in turn considered it a part of their dominions. In 1830, when Belgian independence was proclaimed, the government of the new kingdom claimed dominion over Luxembourg and held it until 1838, when it was divided into two parts, the eastern and smaller section being transferred to William I of the Netherlands who took the title of Grand Duke of Luxembourg and the western part to Belgium. In 1867, by the Treaty of London, independence was granted to the Grand Duchy under the nominal suzerainty of William III of the Netherlands. At the death of William in 1890, it reverted by salic law to the Walram branch of the House of Nassau which continued to rule until it was overwhelmed by Germany in May, 1940.

Ethnography. The population of Luxembourg is about 301,000 (1938 estimate), almost all of Germanic extraction, though Celtic and Roman elements may be traced. The vernacular is a Germanic dialect called " moselfrankisch," but French and German are the languages of officialdom and business. Ethnologically, the people of Luxembourg are probably closer to the Belgians than to any other European people.[1] In religion there is also a kinship with her western neighbor: except for 4000 Protestants [2] and about 3000 Jews all are Roman Catholic.

Luxembourg in 1918. From August, 1914 until the armistice of 1918, Luxembourg was in German hands; it emerged from the war with indeterminate status. Until the war it had been a constitutional monarchy ruled by Grand Duchess Marie-Adelaide, daughter of the Grand Duke Wilhelm of Nassau (died February, 1912). To allow a female to become heir-apparent to the throne it had been necessary for Parliament to pass a law in 1907 revoking the old family pact. Marie-Adelaide shared executive power with an appointed Ministry which depended on the confidence of the Chamber of Deputies of 48 elected for six years by direct vote. In addition, there was an Upper House or Council of 15 appointed for life by the ruler. It was felt by many that the Grand Duchess had been excessively pro-German during the war, and an active republican movement was in progress when the country was evacuated by Germany.

Domestic Politics. The customs union with Prussia and Germany, which had existed since 1842, expired on January 1, 1919. Luxembourg thereupon, because of its size, had to gravitate into the economic orbit of either France or Belgium. This feeling of economic dependence was linked to a movement for annexation to France. The struggle between " Autonomists " and " Annexationists " led to riots, a stillborn republic, and French intervention. On January 12, 1919 Marie-Adelaide abdicated, and the Chamber of Deputies, after a *coup d'état* by Premier Alweiss, chose her sister Charlotte Adelgonde as successor. The question of government and a customs union was submitted to a referendum on September 28. By a vote of 66,811 to 16,885, the people chose the monarchy, as it was then constituted. At the same time a customs union with France was voted.[3]

Constitutional Changes. In 1919 a Constituent Assembly redrafted a constitution which provided for increased democracy. Whereas sovereign power had formerly rested in the hands of the Grand Duchess, it was now to be vested in the nation, the ruler having only those powers granted her by the constitution or the laws of the land. Instead of limiting the franchise to male taxpayers over twenty-five, universal suffrage was decreed for those over twenty-one. Proportional representation was instituted.

There have been few constitutional changes since 1919. In 1924 five chambers were created, consisting of office workers, industrial workmen, traders and industrialists, agriculturists, and artisans, elected by all the voters of each class. The Deputies had to consider legislation which these chambers proposed and consult them before passing statutes affecting their group.

Government and Parties. In the government as it existed prior to the invasion of May, 1940 the Grand Duchess held the nominal executive power, with a ruler-appointed ministry responsible to the Lower House. Legislation was initiated by the Grand Duchess and a Chamber of Deputies of 55 who served for six years, half their number being elected every three years. The Council of State had only advisory powers. There were five leading parties: Catholics, Laborites, Radical-Liberals, Independents, and Democrats in the order of prominence. The heir-apparent (born January 5, 1921) was Prince Jean.

Customs Union. France in 1920 renounced the idea of a customs union; and in 1921 the small kingdom signed a convention with Belgium. The Luxembourg railroads were to be consolidated with those of Belgium under a single administration. With certain exceptions, customs were to be regulated by the Belgians, who were also to represent Luxembourg in certain foreign countries. The union was to last fifty years. A *" Conseil Supérieur "* or Board of Control of 5 members was created: 3 of them, including the President, were to be Belgians. This convention went into effect on May 1, 1922 and has continued to the present time.[4]

Economic Development: Minerals. Luxembourg is richly endowed with mineral resources. In addition to large iron workings in the south, there are deposits of lead, slate, copper, lime, dolomite, and quartzite. Only the iron has been extensively exploited; production in 1914 amounted to 1,827,-270 metric tons. The iron mines were largely in German hands until the end of the First World War. French and Belgian interests, for the most part, then replaced the Germans.[5] In 1938 there were seven steelworks and thirty-five blast furnaces in operation, with an output of 1,450,000 metric tons of iron ore, 1,551,000 tons of pig iron, and 1,437,000 tons of steel. Luxembourg thus played a significant part in the armament race of the 1930's.

Industry and Trade. Iron and steel production were Luxembourg's greatest industry and the largest source of her foreign trade. The only other manufacturing of importance were brickmaking, leather-working, and printing. Workers were protected by two kinds of compulsory insurance. Under a general law of 1925, later amended, provision was made for old-age and invalidity insurance on a contributory plan, with employer and employee each paying one-half the premium; the employer paid the entire premium on accident policies.

Agriculture. Although the soil of Luxembourg was not specially fertile, agriculture occupied about 32 per cent of the people. Potatoes and oats were the main crops, but beet root, rye, wheat, barley, and grapes were also grown. In 1938, 41,000 tons of oats were produced and 285,600 tons of potatoes. Farming was intensive, with 80 per cent of the small holdings worked by resident owners.[6]

Depression. Luxembourg's exports declined continuously in 1930 and 1931. To prevent unemployment in her chief industry, wages were reduced and miners were placed on an individual quota basis. From 1930 to 1934 the iron output dropped almost 50 per cent. In January, 1935 only twenty-one of the forty-seven blast furnaces were in operation. In line with Belgian policy, Luxembourg joined the Oslo powers in reciprocal tariff agreements which largely failed to alleviate the depression. In

1935 the little state lowered the gold content of her franc because of the devaluation of the belga. In 1936 a slow upturn began, due perhaps to the increased armament demands of her neighbors, and the year ended with a budget surplus. In 1937 thirty-five blast furnaces were in operation and there was again a budget surplus.

Ebb Tide. The militarization of Germany in the mid-'thirties occasioned great alarm in Luxembourg. With the seven Oslo powers, it reiterated its neutrality and desire for peace in 1937. When the Munich accord of 1938 was seen to be a mere stopgap in German expansion, continued efforts were made to preserve neutrality. Delegates were sent to the Oslo neutrality conference of August, 1939. Luxembourg affirmed that even if the steel mills should have to close, her neutrality would be maintained. When war came all belligerents renewed assurances that neutral rights would be respected if the other side did likewise. But with memories of 1914 and awareness of Hitler's string of broken promises, Luxembourg prepared for the worst. There was talk of mass evacuation of residents and of making the region an international hospital zone. A severe economic problem was created by the large budget deficit of 1940. When war broke out neutrality was maintained, though a large trade was carried on with Germany. It was said that Luxembourg acted as a funnel for illicit commerce in iron and tools between France and Germany.[7]

Fear of attack mounted when Germany massed troops on the Moselle and the construction of bridges across the river was observed. On May 10, while dive bombers and parachutists were heralding the beginning of a *Blitzkrieg* in the Low Countries, German forces marched into Luxembourg with no other impediment than a few hastily constructed anti-tank defenses set up as a symbol of resistance. Grand Duchess Charlotte, Prince Felix, and their six children fled to France. Their haven disappeared with the collapse of that country, and the Royal Family moved to Portugal. In July the House of Nassau migrated to the United States, the Grand Duchess herself arriving in October. Here they await the release of Europe from Nazi thralldom, an event which, they hope, will signalize the return of democracy to Luxembourg, under their guidance.

Luxembourg has been incorporated into the Reich's custom borders and reorganized according to German standards. Gustav Simon, Provincial Governor of Coblenz-Trier, is the Hitler-appointed Provincial Governor.

REFERENCES

[1] See Boulger, "Historic Claim of Belgium to Luxembourg," *Contemporary Review*, February, 1919, CXV: 165–170.

[2] Located mainly in the mining districts of southern Luxembourg.

[3] For details see Omond, "Belgium, Luxembourg, and Limburg," *Nineteenth Century and After*, March, 1919, LXXXV: 454–464.

[4] Renunciation of the customs union was the price France paid for the 1920 Franco-Belgian military alliance. See *Current History*, August, 1921, XIV: 869 and April, 1922, XVI: 170.

[5] The iron and steel industry was practically controlled by two French companies — Arbed (Acièries Réunies de Burbach, Eich-Dudelange), dominated by Eugène Schneider; Hadir (Hauts Fourneaux et Acièries de Differdange-Saint Ingbert-Rummelange), controlled by Theodore Laurent and a small French group.

[6] See *Le Grand-Duché de Luxembourg à l'exposition internationale de Paris*, Paris: 1937, p. 27.

[7] Frank C. Hanighen in "Selling to the Enemy," *Harper's*, March, 1940, 387–392, claims that Belgium and Luxembourg were used by French and German industrialists as "slots" through which to conduct illicit commerce in coke, iron, and tools. He quotes an *Iron Age* estimate that in December, 1939 some 20,000 tons of iron ore a day were sent to Athus, Belgium and from there shipped by a Belgium firm through Luxembourg to Germany.

SELECTED BIBLIOGRAPHY

Le Commissariat Général du Gouvernement Luxembourgeois, ed., *Le Grand-Duché de Luxembourg à l'exposition internationale de Paris*, Paris: 1937.

Putnam, Ruth, *Luxemburg and Her Neighbors*, New York: Putnam, 1919.

Schimberg, A. P., "Luxemburg," *Catholic World*, October, 1919, CX: 57–62.

Williams, M. O., "Grand Duchy of Luxembourg," *National Geographic Magazine*, November, 1924, XLVI: 500–528.

NETHERLANDS

" DEUS MARE, BATAVUS LITORA FECIT."
" GOD MADE THE SEA, THE BATAVI MADE THE SHORE."

Geography. On the northwestern coast of Europe, pushing back the waters of the North Sea, lies the Netherlands, or Holland as it is popularly and mistakenly called, for Holland rightly refers to but two of its eleven provinces.[1] This maritime kingdom, about half the size of West Virginia, is part of the great plain of northern and western Europe. Because of its location at the mouth of the Rhine, Maas (Meuse), and Scheldt rivers, it has been for centuries one of the foremost countries in Europe. Nowhere over 190 miles long, its maximum breadth is about 160 miles. Except for chains of low sand dunes along the coast and insignificant ridges, the only part of the country which has some elevation is in Limburg Province in the southeast.[2] Almost half of Holland lies below sea-level, necessitating those great protective dikes of dirt and stone for which the Dutch are famous.

Historical Background. The Netherlands is bounded by Germany on the east and Belgium on the south. Elsewhere it is surrounded by the North Sea into which the entire country is drained. Its strategic position and wealth have made this small nation one of the most coveted in Europe. It is natural, therefore, that wars should have played an important role in its history. Although it was not until A.D. 47 that the Frisians of the north were conquered, the armies of Rome occupied the country and held the southern part until almost the end of the empire. Subsequently the Franks secured control of the entire area. After Charlemagne, however, dynastic rivalry and Norse invasion brought renewed decentralization, and from the eleventh to the fifteenth centuries the Low Countries were subdivided into Marquisates, Duchies, and Counties. The Dukes of Burgundy reunited the provinces, to give way in turn to the Hapsburgs when the Emperor Maximilian I married a daughter of Charles the Bold. In 1556, at Charles V's abdication, Philip II was given the Netherlands along with Spain. His repressive policy, especially his religious persecution, alienated the Dutch and eighty years of war ended with the recognition of the independence of the seven provinces in the Treaty of Westphalia (1648). In spite of wars with both the French and the English, the seventeenth century was the golden age of Dutch history. The Netherlands became the leading commercial and maritime nation. Independence lasted until 1795. Then, after twenty years of Napoleonic domination, freedom was regained at Vienna (1815) and maintained until 1940.[3]

Ethnography. The peoples of the Netherlands are derived from both Gallo-Celtic and Germanic stock with the Rhine River roughly dividing these two races. Caesar found three main tribes in the region — the Belgae, Frisii, and Batavi. The majority of the present population is of Teutonic Batavian stock. In the extreme northern provinces are found most of the Frisians; in North Brabant and Limburg, the Flemings. The literary language is called *Hollandsch* or *Nederlandsch*, a Germanic tongue. The common spoken language differs considerably throughout the country, as almost every province has its distinct dialect. The Frisian dialect differs markedly from the others and might well be considered a separate language.⁴ Contrary to the practice of many European nations, the language of the state is also the court language.

Minorities. The Netherlands had no minority problem, as the number of foreigners was negligible. In 1938 there were over 150,000 Jews in a population of 8,728,000. The Germans numbered only about 50,000 but appear to have made a distinct contribution to the debacle of May, 1940 through their fifth-column activities.

1918. The Netherlands had not, as many thought, become wealthy because of her neutral position during four years of war. On the contrary, that struggle brought hardship and suffering to the entire land. Commerce, the lifeblood of the nation, was strangled. There was a fuel shortage, unemployment, and industrial stagnation.⁵ Continued fear of involvement in the war necessitated retention of large armed forces. By 1918 almost half the population of Amsterdam lived on charity and the national debt had been doubled. Yet the nation uncomplainingly assumed the burden of caring for hundreds of thousands of Belgian refugees.

Abortive Revolution. Naturally, war brought discontent and an increase in Socialist strength. In the elections of 1918 the Leftists showed a strength equal to that of the Conservatives. The coalition Ministry of Cort van der Linden fell and after much bickering the Catholic Ruys de Beerenbrouck formed a new Cabinet in what was generally regarded as a victory for the Conservatives.⁶ There was Socialist dissatisfaction upon which the labor leader, Troeslstra, sought to capitalize. He planned to overthrow the monarchy and establish a republic. Quick action by the loyalists and Dutch innate conservatism defeated his purpose. The government had received a scare, however, and was quick to attempt social reform in the next two years through such laws as the 45-hour work week and granting of woman suffrage.⁷

Political Framework. There has been little change in the structure of the Dutch government since the First World War. The House of Orange has ruled the Netherlands since independence was proclaimed in 1579. Queen Wilhelmina is Europe's longest reigning sovereign, having succeeded to the throne in 1890 and being crowned in 1898. The constitution of 1814, with its later amendments, forms the basis of the monarchy, which is hereditary only in a direct line.

Queen Wilhelmina has been a successful and beloved sovereign. Although austere and conservative, she has endeared herself to the Dutch by her directness, coupled with a thorough understanding of the country and its problems. The Court has shown moderation and omitted most of the customary trappings of royalty. Visits of foreign monarchs have been rare while the Queen rarely left the homeland, and has never seen her colonies. The monarch had both executive and legislative power.[8] There was a Cabinet and an appointive Council of State of fourteen, which the Queen consulted on legislative and many executive matters. The Cabinet was not theoretically a constitutional body but the Queen ordinarily appointed a Premier from the dominant group in the States-General who in turn suggested the personnel of the Ministry. The Cabinet was also responsible to Parliament and normally fell when it lost the support of that body.

The Parliament (States-General) was composed of two houses. The Upper House (*Erste Kamer*) with 50 members was chosen by the provincial legislatures for a six-year term — half retiring every three years. The Lower House (*Tweede Kamer*) had 100 deputies chosen for four years on the basis of proportional representation by direct vote of all those over 25 years of age. The Second Chamber, the Crown, or the Ministry initiated all legislation. In fact, the Upper House, though it had the power to reject, could not amend a bill. Parliament met at The Hague where the Court was located. The capital was at Amsterdam.

To regulate affairs of local importance, select the Upper House, and collect local taxes, each of the eleven provinces elected a unicameral legislature, by direct vote for four-year terms, which met twice a year. Provincial affairs were handled by a committee of 64 of these legislators called Deputed States.[9] In addition the approximately 1100 communes each elected local councils. The actions of all these governing bodies were subject to the approval of the Crown.

Domestic Politics: Parties. In the period since 1918 there has been a slight shift in party strength toward the Left but little change in the composition of the Cabinets. The main parties in the Second Chamber in 1918 were: the Catholics with 30 representatives; the Socialists with 22; the Anti-Revolutionists with 13; the Protestants (Christian Historical) with 7; the Liberal Union with 6; the Democrats with 5; the Old Liberals with 4; and 13 others. In the 1937 election they were distributed as follows: Catholics, 31; Social Democratic (Socialist), 23; Anti-Revolutionary, 17; Christian Historical, 8; Democrats, 6; Liberal Union, 4; National Socialist (Nazi), 4; Communist, 3; minor parties, 4. These parties were divided along religious rather than economic lines. Partly owing to proportional representation there was a multiplicity of groups (as many as 54 in 1933) in Parliament. Hence ministries were formed with difficulty and, more often than not, they were extra-parliamentary. However, this type of cabinet, coupled with the usual coalition of the Catholic and two Protestant parties (Anti-Revolutionary and Christian Historical), prevented frequent ministerial changes, so that in the forty-two years of Wilhelmina's reign there were but fourteen governments.[10]

Early Post-war Years. The Rightist Catholic-Calvinist Ministry of De Beerenbrouck remained in power from 1918 to 1925 with the exception of a brief interval in 1923 and 1924. Economically it was a difficult period. Retrenchment and attempted self-sufficiency were the order of the day in Germany, the natural outlet for 60 to 90 per cent of Dutch agricultural products. When a start had been made toward German recovery the French and Belgian occupation of the Ruhr in 1923 brought renewed depression. It was not until 1925 that prosperity returned to Dutch agriculture or industry.

In the political realm, although the coalition of the Right kept a three-fifths majority, frequent crises arose. The haven given the German Kaiser in 1918 provoked ill-feeling on the part of the Allies.[11] Holland and Belgium engaged in a boundary controversy. Partly as a result of an anti-Flemish reaction after the war, and partly because of the feeling that, since the neutrality provision of the Treaty of 1839 was to be abrogated so the old boundary provisions should be changed, Belgium demanded Limburg and part of Zeeland of Dutch Flanders. The people in the disputed area showed no desire for change, and the Dutch government refused to make any territorial concessions. Belgium, lacking the support of the Great Powers, could do nothing, and the crisis passed, only to be followed by years of negotiation over commercial rights on the Scheldt and elsewhere.[12]

Politics from 1922 to 1924 revolved around the country's financial position. Salaries and the normal functions of state were drastically reduced, while attempts were made to alleviate distress through agricultural subsidy and work relief projects such as the reclamation of the Zuider Zee. At the same time De Beerenbrouck advocated the retention of large armed forces and, in the Far Eastern colonies, a strong navy as a bulwark against Japan. The coalition split on this issue: 10 members of the Catholic Party voted with the Left to defeat the naval expansion bill of 1923. There followed months of political crisis; attempts to form a " Business Cabinet " failed and the old coalition was patched up. The new Finance Minister, Hendrik Colijn, enforced more drastic economies and in 1925 Holland had a balanced budget for the first time since the war.

Prosperity and Depression. In the election of 1925 the government bloc was reduced to a majority of four and the Ministry resigned. A Catholic-Calvinist coalition was continued by Colijn, the next Premier, but it split in November when, with the assistance of the Christian Historicals, the

Left passed a bill withdrawing the Dutch representative at the Vatican. After months of wrangling Dr. D. J. de Geer of the Christian Historical Party formed a ministry without regard to party groupings which remained in power until August, 1929. During that time conditions improved in spite of high German tariffs and Belgian competition, and this upturn continued until the middle of 1930. The depression which then struck the Netherlands brought chronic unemployment and unrelenting economic distress.

The coalition government of De Beerenbrouck continued in power until a revolt against his stringent economies brought a dissolution of the Chamber in 1933. In the new election the Anti-Revolutionary Party headed by Colijn showed increased strength, and he formed a Ministry on a program of deflation and continuance of the gold standard. Continued hard times (production, trade, and employment fell about one-third from 1929 to 1935), accentuated by the unstable monetary policy and self-sufficiency programs of most of Holland's customers, forced the Dutch government into greater control of agriculture and industry through subsidies and import quotas. Free trade was abandoned, and *ad valorem* duties were raised up to 20 per cent. Finally, after the pound, dollar, and franc had all left the gold standard, the guilder was forced to give way in September, 1936.[13] The result was a rise in trade, though unemployment did not abate. After a set-back in 1938 the upturn continued, though the government's advantage from it was largely offset by the need for increased defense appropriations in view of rising European tension. Continued unemployment brought discontent which was reflected in the rise of a Nazi party under Dr. Anton Mussert that polled 8 per cent of the vote in 1935. However, natural Dutch individualism reasserted itself and the Nazis received less than 4 per cent of the vote in 1937. In April, 1940 the National Socialist Party was assumed to have only about 50,000 members.[14]

In 1939 the Colijn Ministry fell when the Catholics refused to support a program of retrenchment and higher taxes.[15] Reorganization without the Catholics failed, and in August, 1939 De Geer formed a new coalition of Catholics, Christian Historicals, and, for the first time, Social Democrats. His policy was to continue defense and unemployment measures financed by borrowed money. This group stayed in power until events of May, 1940 brought an end to representative government.

Foreign Policy. The foreign policy of the Netherlands has always been based on two considerations — its size and trade. Hence the formula followed was: neutrality backed by a strong defensive force. The Dutch believed that their neutrality was preserved in 1914–1918 because of the mobilization of a strong army.[16] After the war there was a reversal of policy. The Netherlands joined the League of Nations, where it played an active role. The Queen's Scandinavian tour in 1922 seemed to presage closer relations with the neighboring small powers.

The failure of sanctions against Italy in 1935 in which the Dutch participated brought a loss of confidence in collective security and, in July, 1936, the Dutch returned to isolation and announced that they considered themselves free from collective League action. They refused to enter into further alliances or accept international guarantee of their frontiers, and concentrated instead on rebuilding their defenses. After Munich destroyed the balance of power, fear of Germany and Japan drove the Dutch closer to Britain. There was also greater collaboration with Belgium. The Netherlands participated in the conferences of the Oslo powers in 1938 and 1939. Before war broke out in 1939 and again in November, the Queen joined with King Leopold in appeals for peace and offers of their services in mediating the conflict. Following the plan of 1914, Holland maintained a strict neutrality, but mobilized its army.[17]

Economic Development. Most of the Netherlands' soil was reclaimed from the sea. This artificial area, comprising almost the eastern half of the country, is preserved by elaborate coastal and internal dikes and by a system of canals and pumps. It contains the best farm land, the principal cities, and the mouths of the great commercial rivers which have made the Netherlands the *entrepôt* for much of the trade of Europe. There are, altogether, some 5200 miles of waterways, which, built primarily for drainage, carried two-thirds of the nation's freight until 1940.

Natural Resources. Practically the only minerals found in the Netherlands are coal and salt, with veins in Limburg and at various points near the German border. Mining did not begin until the early twentieth century, but the production of coal was almost sufficient for home consumption. The government owned about half the mines. In 1918 Holland produced 3,399,000 metric tons of coal and 1,800,000 tons of lignite. By 1938 the production of coal rose to 13,488,000 tons, lignite declined to 171,000 tons; in that year the Netherlands produced 166,000 tons of salt, 456,000 tons of cement, and 299,000 tons of pig iron. In addition to these resources, there are peat swamps in Drenthe and Gelderland and about 500,000 acres of well-kept forest land.[18]

Agriculture. About 26 per cent of the country is under cultivation; divided among agriculture, horticulture, and animal husbandry. Farms are small (about 50 per cent are of less than twelve acres), and only about half as many people are employed in agriculture as in industry. About 25 per cent of the arable land lies in the beds of former lakes and marshes, called " polders," drained by continued pumping. The largest impoldering scheme, which began in 1924 and still continues, is the drainage of about three-quarters of the Zuider Zee. A new province of 523,000 acres is thereby to be created surrounding a fresh water lake called the Ijsselmeer

(Ysselmeer). The Zuider Zee was eliminated in 1932 by a twenty-mile dam, three hundred feet wide at the base, stretching from North Holland to Friesland. The first polder of 48,000 acres has been bearing crops, and the northeast polder of 100,000 acres is also practically complete. An interesting feature about the disposition of this new land is that the prospective owner may not borrow from the bank, or from anyone but his immediate family, in arranging for the purchase.[19]

The Dutch have not attempted to grow food crops in quantity for home consumption. Instead, they imported much of their cereals and fertilizers, and concentrated on commodities with a ready sale in world markets, such as dairy products, rye, sugar beets, and bulbs. During the 1930's, however, depression and fear of war brought a change. An attempt was then made to achieve greater self-sufficiency in vital necessities. The government fostered production through heavy subsidization. The marketing of most products was handled through cooperatives under government supervision.

Industry. With a population of well over 600 per square mile (exceeded in Europe only by Belgium), about 94 per cent of whom live in towns of over 2000 population, the Netherlands could not exist solely as an agricultural country. Much of its continued prosperity was therefore traceable to industry and trade.

Industry enjoyed a boom during the First World War. After the panic of 1921 it grew at an accelerated pace, until in 1940 industrial exports were more important than those of agriculture, horticulture, and animal husbandry combined. The leading manufactures were textiles, sugar, beer and ale, oleomargarine, radios, and cut diamonds. The workers were strongly unionized, and protected by one of the best social insurance systems in Europe. These comprised accident, invalidity, sickness, unemployment insurance and old-age pensions. The employer paid the premiums for the accident and invalidity insurance and pensions, but the contributions to the sickness insurance fund were shared equally by employer and employee. The unemployment fund was made up of union and governmental contributions. Special features included: accident insurance for farm workers, the pension age of 65, and sick benefits of 80 per cent of wages for a maximum period of six months.[20]

Foreign Trade. The Netherlands' unique location was the main reason why it became the third largest colonial and ship-building nation in the world, a great fishing center (it had 3,394 fishing vessels in 1937), and a leader in the carrying trade with a merchant marine (July, 1938) of 1482 vessels totaling 2,855,382 gross tons.

A large invisible income from shipping, banking, insurance, and foreign investments compensated for an unfavorable balance of trade in commodities.

The chief imports in the order of value (1937) were: tin ore, timber, wheat, and maize; the leading exports were tin ingots, wireless equipment, cotton piece goods, and butter. Germany, Belgium, the United Kingdom, and the United States were the Netherlands' best customers.

During the late 1920's there was a sharp upturn in trade. From 1929 to 1935 foreign commerce fell by two-thirds. This led to governmental control of exports and imports through the use of tariffs, quotas, and subsidies to bolster the sagging trade balance. After the devaluation of the guilder in 1936 foreign trade began to revive. This trend continued until war brought another curtailment.

Overseas Empire. In the Netherlands' golden age of the seventeenth century a colonial empire was built which, though later abbreviated through foreign conquest, still makes the mother country the third largest colonial power in the world. The relative size and status of the various colonies may be seen from the following:

Country	Area in sq. miles (approx.)	Population (estimated December, 1938)	Capital	Political Status
Netherlands	13,440	8,729,000	Amsterdam The Hague (seat of gov't)	Kingdom
Asia Netherland Indies (Java, Madura, Sumatra, Celebes, Borneo, New Guinea, Timor, Bali, etc.)	774,600	66,400,000	Batavia	Colony (since 1922 part of Netherlands)
America Curaçao (Curaçao, Aruba, Bonaire, Saba, St. Eustatius, & St. Martin)	403	95,000	Willemstad	Colony
Surinam (Dutch Guiana)	57,700	171,000	Paramaribo	Colony

As a part of the Kingdom of the Netherlands, the Netherlands Indies, inhabited by predominantly Mohammedan Malay stock, is subject to the legislation of the home government. The Crown appoints a Governor General to rule the area. He is assisted by an advisory council and a council of the heads of the home government departments. There is also a consultative body called the *Volksraad* (People's Council) which is partly appointed and partly elected by local councils in the more developed islands. The less developed or so-called " outposts," like Borneo and the Celebes, have been generally ruled by natives, supervised by governors under treaties or contracts. The mother country would never have attained its pre-eminent position without the colonies, while the colonies have greatly benefited from Dutch rule. They do not have dominion status, but the Dutch have not attempted to monopolize their trade or forced them to give special favors to the mother country. Since the debacle of May 10, 1940 the Indies have pursued a course quite independent of the mother country, and taken unto themselves what amounts to a dominion status. In the West Indies Curaçao is administered by a Governor and Privy Council appointed by the Queen and a Colonial Council partly elected and partly appointed by the Governor. The affairs of Surinam are directed by a Governor and Council appointed by the Queen, and a legislative body — the Colonial States — 10 of whose members are elected and 5 appointed by the Governor.

Political and Military Significance. The colonies have been one of the government's largest sources of income, though in the last half-century the gains have mainly accrued to individual investors. By slowly relinquishing its holdings in the colonies, the government lost a large annual income, while being forced at the same time to allocate increasing sums for protecting and developing the Empire. Rising colonial expenditures brought criticism and, upon occasion, caused the downfall of a Dutch Ministry. However, the government was determined to hold and protect the empire at any cost. Thus efforts were made to stamp out Communism in the colonies in 1926 and again in 1933; naval expenditure increased steadily after 1918. The possession of valuable territory in the East Indies has brought the Netherlands closer to Great Britain, for the latter could scarcely allow another and stronger power to encroach upon this vital region surrounding Singapore and blocking the trade route from England to Australia. The English fleet was, therefore, the Dutch first line of defense.

Economic Significance. Agriculture is the basic enterprise in the Indies, the chief export crops being sugar, rubber, coffee, and tea. Other important exports are spices; over 90 per cent of the world's quinine emanates from there. In recent years the production of tin and petroleum has assumed international significance. Free-trade was abandoned in 1934 as a result of the depression (for instance, sugar lost seven-eighths of its export value from 1929 to 1935). Import duties and quotas were then applied. The main imports are cotton goods, machines, and iron and steel products of which in 1937 Japan furnished 25 per cent, the Netherlands 19 per cent, and the United States 10 per cent. The leading exports are rubber, petroleum, and tin, 20 per cent of which in 1937 went to the Netherlands, 19 per cent to Singapore and 19 per cent to the United States. With its large population and tremendous resources, the Netherlands Indies are a rich prize upon which Japan has long cast a covetous eye. Should her present economic penetration there not be followed by political control, one can safely say that Japan will not allow any other nation than the Dutch to exercise suzerainty over the islands.[21] The Dutch West Indies are noted chiefly for oil refining and phosphate production at Curaçao and bauxite production at Surinam. Their position in the present world crisis is relatively secure because of the Monroe Doctrine.

Cultural Progress: Literature. The land of Erasmus, Grotius, and Spinoza can produce no names of equal caliber today. Yet in certain fields the quality of contemporary Dutch literary production will stand comparison with that of any other nation. This has been partly due to the renaissance which began in the 1880's, when the conventional romantic traditions were broken and a realistic spirit entered into Dutch literature. The fact that many Dutch authors are not well-known outside their native land is due in great part to the difficulty of conveying the literary excellence of their works into foreign languages.

Among modern Dutch poets Peter Boutens (1870–   ), translator of Æschylus, Sophocles, Sappho, and Homer, is outstanding for his unequaled technique. Boutens' original poetry, however, appeals to but a small group because of his introspective moods. Willem Kloos (died 1938) was probably the most gifted of the Dutch lyric poets of the post-war era. The sonnets composed in his youth show a higher level of acheivement than the work of his later years. Other notable poets are: P. N. van Eyck (1887–   ), author of *Herwaarts* (*Hither*); Hendrik Marsman (1899–   ), author of several volumes of verse, including *De Dood van Angele Degroux* (*The Death of Angele Degroux*); and Albert Verwey (1865–1937), who was also a notable literary historian.

The Dutch have made outstanding contributions to the modern novel. Louis Couperus (1863–1923), romanticist and realist, gave Dutch fiction a cosmopolitan and realistic sense which it lacked in the nineteenth century. Best-known among his works are probably *Oude Menschen: De Dingen de Vorbijgaan* (*Old People and the Things That Pass*) a family chronicle based on the consequences of crime, and *Boeken der Kleine Zielen* (*The Books of the Small Souls*) another family history which has been compared to Galsworthy's *Forsyte Saga*. Couperus' basic philosophy derived from the Greeks, the feeling that man is constantly pursued by an omnipotent destiny.

Anton F. Coolen (1897–   ) has produced an excellent saga of Dutch family life in *Kerstmis in den Kempen* (*Christmas in the Kempen*). Arthur van Schendel (1874–   ) is regarded by some as the prince of modern Dutch storytellers; one of his notable novels is *Het Fregatschip Johanna Maria* (*The Frigate Jane Marie*). Jo van Ammers-Küller has gained an international reputation with her novels, *The Rebel Generation* and *House of Joy*. The former is a family chronicle centering around the emancipation of women; the latter concerns a girl's desire to go on the stage. Other outstanding novelists are Simon Vestdijk (1870–   ), author of an autobiographical novel *Saint Sebastian* and of the popular *Het Vijfde Zegel* (*The Fifth Seal*), and Siegfried van Praag (1899–   ), famous for his biographical romances *Julie de L'Espinasse* and *Madame de Pompadour*, and a more recent work, *Minaares in Ongenade* (*Mistress in Disgrace*).

Music. The Dutch have left their mark on contemporary music. Willem Mengelberg and Willem van Hoogstraten both achieved international fame as conductors. Johann Wagenaar (1862–   ) is an eminent organist and composer of operas, such as *The Doge of Venice* and *Le Cid.* Willem Pijper (1894–   ) has written three symphonies, and sonatas for violin and for the cello. Dirk Schaefer (1874–1931) was an eminent composer of chamber music and piano pieces.

Architecture. A remarkable school of architecture has sprung up in the Netherlands, with Dr. H. P. Berlage, who built the Exchange in Amsterdam, and J. A. G. van der Steur, architect of the Peace Palace at The Hague, as its leaders.

Science. In science the country which has produced so many Nobel prize winners continued to make outstanding contributions in the post-war period through the work of such men as Dr. W. Einthoven on the diseases of the heart, Dr. Hugo de Vries on mutations, and Dr. P. Zeeman in magneto-optics.

Eclipse. May 10, 1940 may well be called the blackest day in three hundred years of Dutch history, for with that fateful dawn came invasion, demonstrating the futility of relying on guarantees of integrity from the Reich. Flooding by opening the dikes proved insufficient to overcome Germany's mechanized units, which were aided by dive bombers and fifth-columnists behind the lines. In four days the Battle of the Tulips was over, although parts of Zeeland continued to fight for some days longer. Queen Wilhelmina, Crown Princess Juliana, her husband, Prince Bernhard, and their two children fled to England. There the Queen still resides, while Juliana and her two children moved to Canada. The homeland is under the complete control of Germany, governed by the High Commissioner, Arthur Seyss-Inquart. Local government is still in the hands of the Dutch. Although the mother country is subjugated, the government of the Netherlands carries on the war, with the aid of the colonies and a portion of the fleet and army, from exile in England.[22]

The Dutch spent two thousand years in reclaiming their soil from the bottom of the sea, and fought for eighty bloody years to make their country independent. Such a spirit will not die, nor will such a country, doubtless, remain permanently subjugated.

REFERENCES

¹ In addition to the provinces of North and South Holland, containing about half the population, there are: Utrecht, Friesland, Overyssel, Groningen, Gelderland, Drenthe, North Brabant, Limburg, and Zeeland.

² The highest point of the North Ardennes reaches an elevation of 1,057 feet.

³ See W. H. Clafin and C. Dandliker, " Holland, Belgium, Switzerland," in Vol. XIII, *The History of Nations*, Henry Cabot Lodge, ed., New York: Collier, 1932.

⁴ Many Frisian and English words are the same, showing their common source.

⁵ Marjorie Bowen, *Holland*, London: Harrap, 1928, p. 17.

⁶ See Enno van Gelder, *Histoire des Pays-Bas*, Paris: 1936, pp. 181–182.

⁷ See K. van Hoek, " Wilhelmina Regina," *Atlantic Monthly*, October, 1938, CLXII: 474–482; and " European Neutrals and the Armistice," *Current History*, January, 1919, IX (Part 2): 70–75.

⁸ The Queen had power to dissolve the States-General, and measures were subject to her scrutiny before and after passage.

⁹ Six delegates were chosen from each province except Drenthe, which had four.

¹⁰ P. Geyl, " Holland in the Depression," *Contemporary Review*, April, 1934, CXLV: 411–420.

¹¹ For favorable comment see " Wilhelmina Regina," *loc. cit.*, 478; for the opposing view see " Does Holland Like Her Guest? ", *Outlook*, February 4, 1920, CXXIV: 185–186.

¹² Magazine comment leans strongly toward the Dutch point of view. See " Dutch-Belgian Boundary Controversy," *Review of Reviews*, August, 1922, LXVI: 218–219; or " Belgian Aims in Holland," *Nation*, April 5, 1919, CVIII: 533. For the Belgian view see Omond, " Belgium, Luxembourg, and Limburg," *Nineteenth Century and After*, March, 1919, LXXXV: 454–464.

¹³ For the economic crisis of the 1930's see " Holland and Its Clash of Interests," *Annals of the American Academy*, July, 1937, CXCII: 195–197.

¹⁴ Sweitzer, " Rebuke to Fascism," *Current History*, December 29, 1937, XCIII: 224; Wenner, " Dutch Cure for Fascism," *ibid.*, May 1938, XLVIII: 39–42.

¹⁵ Colijn was probably the greatest Dutch statesman since the last war. See Van Hoek, " Colijn of the Netherlands," *Living Age*, September 1, 1938, CCCLV: 45–49.

¹⁶ Germany later admitted that the strong Dutch army was a major factor in the decision not to risk invasion. See also Elmer Davis, " Belgium and Holland Isolated," *Harper's*, May, 1937, CLXXIV: 627–636.

¹⁷ For Dutch policy and defenses see Van Hamel, " Can the Netherlands Be Neutral? ", *Foreign Affairs*, January, 1938, XVI: 339–346.

¹⁸ Economic Intelligence Office, *An Economic Survey of the Netherlands*, Hague, n.d. (c. 1936).

¹⁹ Harris, " Land from the Sea," *Living Age*, May, 1939, CCCLVI: 274–276; and Kriusinga, " New Country Awaits Discovery. The Draining of the Zuider Zee," *National Geographic Magazine*, September, 1933, LXIV: 293–320.

²⁰ See also *Monthly Labor Review*, December, 1937, XLV: 1345–1354; *ibid.*, December, 1929, XXIX: 1293–1299; *ibid.*, August, 1938, XLVII: 313–321; *ibid.*, April, 1937, XLIV: 903–904.

²¹ See also bulletins of the Department of Economic Affairs of the Government of Netherlands Indies, Batavia, Java; or Seybold, " Colonies That Pay," *Review of Reviews*, July, 1936, XCIV: 51–54.

²² For the invasion of Holland see Eelco Nicolaas van Kleffens, *Juggernaut over Holland*, New York: Columbia Univ. Press, 1941.

SELECTED BIBLIOGRAPHY

Barnouw, A. J., *Holland under Queen Wilhelmina*, New York: Scribner, 1923. A good history.

——, *The Dutch: A Portrait Study of the People of Holland*, New York: Columbia

Univ. Press, 1940. A collection of delightful sketches on various aspects of Holland's life.

Department of Economic Affairs of the Netherlands Indies, *The Netherlands Indies,* Batavia, Java, N. I.: G. Kolff & Co., n.d. (c. 1938). A compendium of information.

Gooch, R. K., " The Government and Politics of Belgium and Holland," in Shotwell, J. T., ed., *Governments of Continental Europe,* New York: Macmillan, 1940, pp. 1043–1064. The best up-to-date analysis of Dutch politics.

Jitta, A. C. J., *Holland's Modern Renascence,* Hague: Nijhoff, 1930. A survey of Dutch commerce, industry, and agriculture in the last fifty years.

Kain, R. S., ed., *Europe: Versailles to Warsaw,* New York: Wilson, 1939, pp. 336–341. Extract of studies on recent foreign politics.

Germany

Introduction

Geography. Geography has played as large a part in determining the course of events and the character of social institutions in Germany as in any other country. The advantages of an insular position, so helpful to the British during the formative period of their national life, have never been enjoyed by the Germans. Traversed by numerous rivers and overland trade routes, Germany has always had the economic advantage of being located on or near the crossroads of Europe; but she has often had to pay the penalty for her central location by becoming a battle-ground in which non-Germans fought on her soil and her own people fought one another. The development of political unity, long delayed by rivalries among the German states and by interference from the outside, thus assumed a new and perhaps an exaggerated value in the minds of many Germans. The nationalism which the French had learned to take for granted, and the security from invasion which the people of Great Britain had always counted on, became practically synonymous in the German mind; but neither could be taken for granted. Nationalism had to be cultivated in Germany for the sake of the strength and the security it promised; and both nationalism and security were more talked about than among peoples by whom they had been earlier and more easily attained.

In a country with practically no geographic barriers to prevent invasion or check expansion, it was naturally assumed that national strength meant military strength. Walls of armed men must, for Germany, take the place of Italy's Alps, Spain's Pyrenees, and Britain's navy. This was especially true of her eastern boundary. The German-Polish boundary was always determined, in short, by the relative political and military strength of the two peoples, or by the readiness of their friends to support them.

Western Frontier. The western boundary was not much more stable. For a thousand years Franco-German relations revolved around the control of the Rhine, which France frequently tried to straddle, but which German

---

This chapter by Chester Verne Easum, Associate Professor of History, University of Wisconsin.

nationalists always regarded as a German stream. France controlled the right bank for only brief periods in the heyday of the First Republic and in the Napoleonic era, but she held the left bank from 1795 to 1815; while all of Lorraine had been under French control for more than a hundred years, and parts of Alsace for more than three hundred, when Germany recovered them by conquest in 1871.

Southern-Eastern Frontier. The boundary lines of southern and south-eastern Germany stood virtually unchanged in the century between the Peace of Vienna and the Peace of Versailles. Austria, including Bohemia, in which the German element constituted a favored minority, was a member of the Germanic Confederation from 1815 to 1867; and from 1879 onward Imperial Germany found an ally in Austria-Hungary, to which Austria and Bohemia, lately excluded from the German Confederation, belonged. The German-Czechoslovak boundaries of 1918 were virtually the same as those of 1914 between Germany and Bohemia.

The non-inclusion of Austria in the Second German Reich (created in 1871) was a result of her losing battle with Prussia for leadership of the German states. In that struggle Austria had been able sometimes to draw upon her non-German possessions and dependencies for men, money, and supplies, but she had been handicapped in the long run by the fact that her rival Prussia expanded northward and westward within Germany. In 1871 Prussia stood astride the Rhine and controlled the courses of the northward-flowing rivers and the whole southern shore of the Baltic (with ports at Stettin, at the mouth of the Oder, Danzig on the Vistula, and Königsberg and Memel farther east), while Austria (and Hungary) expanded southward and eastward, away from Germany.

Geographical Dilemma of Second Reich. After the unification of 1871 Germany became rapidly industrialized — a process in which the iron ore of Alsace-Lorraine, floated cheaply down the Rhine and smelted with the coking-coal of the Ruhr, played a prominent part. More railroads were built and state railway systems were coordinated to supplement the rivers and canals which had long been some of Europe's busiest inland waterways. As commerce increased and capital accumulated, the North Sea ports of Bremen and Hamburg gained a position in world trade comparable with that which they had held five centuries earlier in the Hanseatic League. With world trade, interest in colonies and sea power grew; Kiel and Wilhelmshaven were developed as naval bases. By 1914, with Germany still growing industrially, Pan-German expansionists were constantly calling attention to her alleged need of a larger working space. With territorial expansion on the continent blocked by the Franco-Russian alliance, and with only second- or third-rate colonial areas left open to her, Germany was compelled to face the prospect of contenting herself with commercial expansion only, or of resorting to the use of force. It is known now that Germany did not deliberately precipitate the First World War, although her aggressive struggle for what she called " a place in the sun " had done as much as anything to create an atmosphere of tension in which almost any international crisis was likely to provoke war. Once they found themselves at war, however, German leaders indubitably planned to demand, as fruits of victory, such territorial and other concessions as would materially improve the nation's economic position. Defeat, bringing with it economic disaster and loss of valuable resources, was therefore doubly bitter.[1]

Ethnography. The Germans are a comparatively homogeneous people, although certainly they are not all alike. There have always been physical, temperamental, and dialectical differences between the Low German of the north, the Middle German, and the High German of the south and of Austria. The Prussian has not generally mixed well with the Bavarian or Saxon, and their incompatibilities have not all been due to interstate rivalries; nor have the relations between Catholics (most numerous in the southwest and in the Rhineland) and Protestants (stronger in the north and northeast) always been entirely cordial. But sectional, racial, and religious differences have not, generally speaking, been more serious than in Italy, France, Great Britain, or the United States.

Minorities Problem. Yet Imperial Germany had its national minorities problems. In Alsace-Lorraine lived many people who, in 1914, were still French, preferred the French language (more for sentimental than for practical reasons), and would have welcomed a return to France. The German government of the province was efficient and economically beneficent, but tactless and generally unpopular. The Danes of northern Schleswig were, on the other hand, better handled and gave voice to less discontent; but they were not happy under German rule, and some Danish deputies were always ready to vote with the opposition in the Reichstag.

Problem of the Poles. The Poles were the most difficult to assimilate and least reconciled to German rule. In West Prussia and Posen the state and the Imperial government had tried to Germanize the Poles who lived there. A studied effort was also made to induce German settlers to move into these districts, and laws were passed to make land-owning easier for them than for Poles. In Upper Silesia the Poles served chiefly as laborers in mines and factories, and owned but little land; so they could not complain, as their brethren in Posen and West Prussia did, that the government was trying to dispossess them; but quarrels over language and schools tried the patience of both governors and governed.

Tolerance. Except in its treatment of national minorities, the Second Reich was traditionally tolerant. Freedom of religious belief was general, and the established churches, both Protestant and Catholic, were supported by special taxes or tithes collected by the government. Anti-

Semitism was not unknown, but it was unofficial and sporadic and neither violent nor widespread. Repressive legislation against both Catholics and Socialists was given a trial by Bismarck and later repealed or unenforced. *Effect of the Versailles Treaty.* By depriving Germany of the areas in which most of her alien population lived, the Treaty of Versailles practically solved her national minorities problems, although a considerable number of Poles and a few Danes were left within her borders. Dissident political groups, however, were more numerous than ever; and the framers of the Weimar constitution tried scrupulously by proportional representation to give all of them a voice in the government.

It remained for the National Socialists to focus attention, not for the first time in history but more sharply than before, upon what they called a " racial " minority — the Jews. The Jews constituted, anti-Semites said, an alien element which ought to be eliminated. All other minorities were to be *Gleichgeschaltet* — " coordinated," or lined up with the majority.

The Armistice and Peace Terms

The German Army in November, 1918. November, 1918, found the German people rapidly approaching complete exhaustion on both the military and the home fronts. Their armies occupied foreign soil in the Baltic states, Russian Poland, the Ukraine, Bessarabia, Rumania, France, and Belgium; but they had lost the war in the west. In the east and southeast the presence of a million armed men was necessary to enforce the harsh terms of the Treaties of Bucharest and Brest-Litovsk, and to insure the delivery of grain and oil of which Germany was in desperate need but which her overworked transportation system could not transport in sufficient quantities. Civilians and soldiers alike were underfed, and the army on the western front had, when the armistice was signed, lubricating oil and motor fuel for less than two weeks of fighting.

Its strategical position was equally precarious. More heavily dependent upon the railroads than the mechanized army of 1940, and finding the rough country of the Ardennes more of an obstacle, the Germans had to transport supplies chiefly through Liége or Metz. The trunk railway lines and the roads which paralleled them were equally vital as avenues of withdrawal. In early November the Liége line was threatened by the British advance through Belgium, while the Metz-Mezières line was cut by the French and Americans at Sedan. Still fighting a stout defensive action at the vital points, but unable either to maintain its position or to retreat rapidly enough to save itself, the German army was beaten and knew it.

Requests for an Armistice. Foreseeing precisely that situation but unable to prevent it, the German High Command had demanded in the last days of September that the Berlin government ask for an armistice. Chancellor Hertling hesitated to make the request, which he knew would be interpreted everywhere as a confession of defeat. Upon the insistence of von Hindenburg and Ludendorff, however, a new Chancellor, Prince Max von Baden, was appointed on October 3 who reluctantly appealed to President Wilson on the night of October 4 for an immediate armistice and a peace based on the Fourteen Points.

The request was not granted immediately. President Wilson had first to be assured that he was dealing with a government responsible to the German people; he would make no personal truce with the Kaiser, whom American and Allied propaganda had branded as an irresponsible war criminal. (The constitutional powers of the Reichstag were made somewhat more extensive in October.) Four successive notes from Wilson made it increasingly clear to the German leaders that their worst fears were to be realized. The army was not to be given an opportunity to withdraw without interference to a new position, where it might reorganize itself and then challenge its enemies to renew hostilities; the armistice terms meant capitulation, if not outright surrender. The French and British governments, moreover, had accepted the Fourteen Points as a basis of peace only with reservations as to reparations and the freedom of the seas that clearly presaged a punitive peace.

Although he had himself been the first to insist upon an armistice, Ludendorff proposed to break off the negotiations and fight on in the hope that the war-weariness of the Allies would induce them to offer better terms; but he was dismissed from his command. Von Hindenburg, who had at first agreed with his Quarter-Master General, decided that there was no alternative, and instructed Matthias Erzberger, head of the German Armistice Delegation, to secure such mitigation of the terms as he could — but in any case to sign.

Revolution in Germany. No other course was open to a leader conscious of his responsibilities. Before the actual signing of the armistice on November 11, revolutionary disorder had broken out, first (November 3) among the sailors at Kiel, then in Bavaria, and finally in Berlin. The home front had collapsed more suddenly and completely than the military. Further armed resistance, already hopeless, had been made impossible. Hoping for better peace terms without him, people who had never hated the Kaiser were ready to throw him overboard. William II, once revered by all Germans, had to abdicate on November 9 and seek sanctuary in Holland.

The leaders of the new provisional government, Scheidemann, Ebert, Mueller, and others, hoped that a bourgeois republic would be more generously treated at the peace conference than a government of any other character. They never dared to tell the people that the men who decided to ask for and accept the armistice had known only too well when they made that fateful decision that it meant surrender and only a victors' peace was in prospect. The army was not tricked into laying down its arms; and if the people were deceived as to the character of the peace terms they might expect, it was their own leaders, not President Wilson, who deceived them.[2]

The Establishment of the Republic. In the last six weeks of 1918 Germany was threatened with anarchy. To fill the political vacuum created by the collapse of the monarchy, a republic was proclaimed on November 9 by Philipp Scheidemann, the Social Democrat, to the crowd outside the Reichstag building as soon as he heard that the Kaiser had abdicated; but establishing a republic was much more difficult than merely proclaiming one. Many of the defenders of the existing social and economic order stood aloof from the new government, which they had not wished to see established and in which they had but little confidence, associating it with inglorious military defeat.

Moderation vs. Radicalism. At the other extreme, the left-wing Social Democrats or Spartacists, supplied with funds from Russia and led by Karl Liebknecht and Rosa Luxemburg, sought to lead the revolution along Bolshevik lines. The bourgeois character of the republic was determined only by the firmness of such Social Democratic leaders as Friedrich Ebert, emergency Chancellor under a provisional government of people's commissars, Gustav Noske who quickly organized a volunteer rifle corps for the suppression of rioters, Matthias Erzberger of the Catholic Center party, and the Jewish capitalist Walther Rathenau. By January 10, 1919, the worst revolts had been quelled, and Liebknecht and Rosa Luxemburg had met violent deaths at the hands of the police.

Meanwhile, fortunately, the public services were not interrupted, thanks to the efficiency and unshaken morale of the civil service. The government officials and employees were not enthusiastic republicans; theirs was a non-partisan and a non-political tradition; but they were Germans, and they continued to serve the Ebert government.

The Constituent Assembly. On February 6, 1919, a national assembly met in Weimar to draw up a new constitution. Before it met, two urgent questions had been answered: the government would be a federal republic, and the " revolution " would be moderate and political in character, undertaking no vast social changes.

Reaction to the Treaty of Versailles. The Versailles Treaty, drawn up without German participation, was submitted to a delegation headed by Count von Brockdorff-Rantzau on May 5. June 22 was the dead-line for its acceptance or rejection; and after canvassing all the alternatives and finding them even worse than the peace terms, the Weimar assembly, acting as a provisional national government, sent word at the last possible moment that it accepted the terms. The Treaty was signed on June 28, the fifth anniversary of the murders at Sarajevo.

Although their own history does not show them to have been consistently overgenerous in victory, most of the Germans have felt since 1919 that they were ungenerously treated in defeat. They were especially aggrieved by Articles 227, 228, and 231 of the Versailles Treaty. Article 227 charged the former emperor, William II, " with a supreme offense against international morality and the sanctity of treaties," but the Dutch government refused to extradite him for trial. In Article 228 the German government had to recognize " the right of the Allied and associated powers to bring before military tribunals persons accused of having committed acts in violation of the laws and customs of war." The accused were to be handed over to the Allies for trial. That provision was not enforced. Only a few rather perfunctory trials were held in German courts on charges preferred by the Allies; but even that was a humiliation hard for the republic to live down.

Article 231 contained the famous war guilt clause, designed to furnish a sort of legal and moral basis for the exaction of reparations. Because her troops had invaded alien territory and her naval forces had sunk merchant shipping, Germany must pay for some of the material damage. The Germans, interpreting it as an admission of undivided moral responsibility for the war itself, signed the Treaty only under outspoken protest against the war guilt clause, and never ceased to smart under its alleged injustice until Hitler denounced it in 1937. It might have been good policy for the powers to have agreed to the deletion of that clause when Germany joined the League of Nations in 1926, if not earlier; it was certainly good domestic politics for the National Socialists to denounce it.

The military and naval restrictions imposed by the Treaty rendered greater injury to Germany's pride than to her material interests. The army was limited to 100,000 men, long-term enlistments were made compulsory, the navy was reduced almost to nothing, and Germany was denied the right to maintain a military or naval air force, to re-fortify the Rhineland, or to maintain troops there. The Germans were not seriously threatened with invasion, but they smarted none the less under a sense of defenselessness and inferiority in armed strength, particularly after it became apparent that their neighbors were not going to disarm, and after France and Czechoslovakia fortified their German frontiers. The right to rearm unless others disarmed came to be looked upon by most Germans as an essential attribute of national sovereignty; without it they could never be free or equal to other nations. The supervision of commerce on the German rivers by international commissions, on which Germany was represented but which she could not control, was resented for the same reason.

Territorial Terms of Versailles Treaty. The territorial terms of the Treaty cut deep into the industrial resources of the country, as we have already pointed out in a previous chapter. The actual economic value to the German people of the overseas empire had never been established with any degree of precision; but the empire was lost; and there were many who felt the loss economically and others who felt it emotionally and turned a sympathetic ear to the charge that Germany had been " robbed " of her colonies and must, in self-respect, demand their return.

These territorial losses might have been partially compensated by the admission of Austria into the German federal republic. The union was desired and legally provided for by Germans and Austrians alike; but their former enemies compelled them to renounce it.

Germans Under Alien Rule. Millions of Germans found themselves in the unenviable position of national minorities under non-German governments. Some were in Alsace-Lorraine, others in the Saar, Moresnet, Eupen, and Malmédy. The Germans in North Schleswig, out-voted in a plebiscite, were not badly used by Denmark after the transfer. The Germans in Allenstein and Marienwerder voted for Germany and kept Poland from controlling the right bank of the lower Vistula.

On their eastern frontiers German nationalists found more about which to complain. The German cities of Memel and Danzig were severed from their fatherland. The Polish Corridor, which ran along the left bank of the Vistula through West Prussia, was deeply resented by Germany. In Posen and Upper Silesia, also awarded to Poland, lived a numerous German minority, who soon filled the records of the League of Nations and the Permanent Court of International Justice with their complaints against the Poles.

A small part of Upper Silesia was ceded to Czechoslovakia; but that was not the origin of the Sudeten German problem. The ancestors of most of the Sudeten Germans had lived in Bohemia for centuries. Their discontent was largely the result of the loss of special privileges granted by the Hapsburgs. Their cause was later championed by the German Nazis on nationalist and irredentist grounds.

To summarize: Germany was worn down by the war and materially and spiritually hurt by the punitive peace terms. That she would have been more generous to her defeated enemies if she had won the war is not indicated by the confidential correspondence of her leaders or by other treaties she had made. Self-commiseration, however, makes it easy for a person, or a people, to overlook inconvenient facts. It was natural for the Germans after the war to forget that much of their suffering resulted inevitably from an exhausting and unsuccessful war, and to blame everything upon the Treaty. The war was in the past; the Treaty they had always with them. So the government that recognized the defeat and signed the Treaty (called by unreconciled nationalists the *Diktat* or " dictated " peace of Versailles) carried a double handicap from the start. The Weimar republic went to bat, so to speak, with two strikes already called.[3]

Political Development: 1919–1940

The Weimar Constitution. The constitution drafted at Weimar was an ingenious instrument, ultra-modern in appearance and full of clever but complicated devices designed to make democracy work as Dr. Preuss, Professor of Political Science at the University of Berlin, its principal author, thought it should.

State lines were not wiped out but the new federal union was in many ways more highly centralized than the Hohenzollern empire had been. The states (called Länder) were still represented in a national council (Reichsrat), but its powers were much less extensive than those of the old federal council (Bundesrat). Like its prototype, the Bundesrat, the Reichsrat represented state governments, not people; but states were unequally represented in it, on a basis of one member for every 700,000 people, except that Prussia (whose population would have entitled her to two-thirds of the constituency) was to be limited to two-fifths of the total.

The legislative powers lost by the council of states were gained by the Reichstag, chosen by universal suffrage of persons over twenty years of age. Deputies (*Reichstagsabgeordneter*) were elected for terms of four years by a system of proportional representation intended to enable any party or group to elect one member for every sixty thousand votes it could muster. Acts of either Reichstag or Reichsrat had normally to be approved by the other, but the veto of the Reichsrat could be overridden by a two-thirds vote in the Reichstag. The national president (*Reichspräsident*) had no absolute veto, but by withholding his signature could compel the submission of a bill to a national referendum.

The Cabinet. Responsible leadership in both houses was expected of the Cabinet (*Reichsregierung*). The Chancellor (*Reichskanzler*), as chief of the Cabinet, was expected to be the active head of the government. Although nominally appointed by the President, it was assumed that he would be chosen by the majority party or parties in the Reichstag, and would name and control his own subordinates.

The President. The President, elected for seven years and eligible for re-election, was expected to be something of a figurehead, his powers being in general those usually left in the hands of a constitutional monarch. To be elected in the first balloting, the successful presidential candidate must poll a majority vote. If no candidate had a majority, a second election was to be held, in which new candidates might appear and old ones drop out, but in which a plurality would suffice. The first President, Ebert, was chosen by the Weimar assembly in 1919 and continued in office until his death in 1925.

Bill of Rights. Other interesting features of the Weimar constitution were Germany's first bill of rights, stressing the duties as well as immunities of the citizen, provision for the use of the initiative and referendum, a comparatively easy amendment process, and a provision that the states must administer and enforce federal law. The President could be impeached by the Reichstag, but a referendum might take the place of an impeachment trial. If vindicated by such a referendum, he was to be automatically declared re-elected for seven years, while the Reichstag which had impeached him was dissolved. There was a federal Supreme Court or court of last appeal at Leipzig, but it was not specifically empowered to set aside a federal law on grounds of unconstitutionality.

Defects of the Republic. If its constitution had been self-administering, and had worked as its authors intended, the Weimar republic might have survived indefinitely; but a constitution is not a government, and republican institutions are perpetuated only by popular conviction. There were not enough republicans in Germany, and even the best of her party leaders had had, in the Imperial Reichstag, more training in particularism and political obstructionism than in positive leadership or acceptance of responsibility.

The multiplicity of parties made a one-party administration impossible. Every cabinet had to serve several masters, gaining and holding office in the name of a coalition. The earliest cabinets were formed by the Majority Socialists or Social Democrats with Centrists and Democrats supporting and participating in them; later ones were usually composed of Centrists, members of the People's Party, and Social Democrats in varying proportions. Of all these, only the last-named were unreservedly committed to the republican form of government; the others merely accepted it, as Hjalmar Schacht and Gustav Stresemann did.

Cohesion within the Cabinet was often lacking. The constitution laid down the principle that all officials were " servants of the totality, not of any one party." Presumably then the individual Reichstag deputy should have voted on any measure only as an individual and as he saw fit. In practice, every party held its own preliminary meeting and instructed its members how to vote on every important question; hence the Reichstag never became a truly deliberative body. The vote being pre-determined, discussion was useless. Worse than that, members of coalition Cabinets were not only chosen but *instructed* by their party organizations; the Chancellor could not control them but was more often controlled by them. Political irresponsibility was the inevitable result, and Cabinet changes occurred with demoralizing frequency. Hitler's Cabinet of 1933 was the twenty-first since the drafting of the Weimar constitution in 1919.

GERMANY'S LOSSES

Schleswig-Holstein to Denmark, 1920

Memel to Lithuania, 1919
Free City of Danzig, 1920

E. PRUSSIA

Corridor to Poland, 1920 and Upper Silesia 1921

Eupen & Malmedy to Belgium, 1919

Saar to France, 1919

Czechoslovakia by Seizure, 1919

Alsace - Lorraine to France, 1919

The 2nd Reich, 1870-1918: ⌇
Versailles Excisions Dated.

U.S.S.R.

FINLAND

NORWAY

APRIL, 1940

Oslo

SWEDEN

Gulf of Bothnia

North Sea

GREAT BRITAIN

DENMARK
APRIL, 1940

Copenhagen

Baltic Sea

MEMEL
MARCH, 1939

GERMANY 1935

Berlin

DANZIG
SEPTEMBER, 1939

U. S. S. R.

Warsaw

CORRIDOR
SEPTEMBER
1939

GOVERNMENT
GENERAL
of
POLAND
SEPTEMBER
1939

The Hague
MAY, 1940

Brussels
MAY, 1940

BELGIUM
MAY, 1940

OCCUPIED

Paris

LUXEMBURG
MAY, 1940. Formally
Inducted Into Reich,
August, 1940

SAAR
reoccupied, 1935

SUDETENLAND
NOVEMBER, 1938

Prague

BOHEMIA - MORAVIA
MARCH, 1939

SLOVAKIA
AUGUST, 1939

HUNGARY

JUNE, 1940

LORRAINE
Annexed, Novem-
ber, 1940

FRANCE

Vienna

AUSTRIA
MARCH, 1938

SWITZERLAND

UNOCCUPIED

ITALY

YUGOSLAVIA

Rumania

SPAIN

ANDORRA

CORSICA
(France)

R.E. Falconer, 1940

The Growth of GERMANY 1935~1940

Boundaries, Oct. 1, 1940:
Acquisitions Shown Thus:

Miles: 0   100   200   300

Party Organization. Party membership meant more than mere support of the party at the polls. Members were enrolled and paid dues, thus providing the party with large sums of money, but this did not insure control of policies or choice of candidates by the rank and file. That was the work of the leaders and the salaried secretariat. The annual meeting (*Parteitag*) could only confirm policies already formulated, and the individual voter could only cast his ballot for a ready-made list of candidates. Since a candidate's chances of election depended upon the relative position of his name on the list, it was the party management, not the voter, that actually elected or defeated him.

There were many reasons for the failure of the republic, not the least of which was the weakness of the party system. Politicians seemed more interested in securing office than in serving the nation. Party discipline was well maintained, but cohesion among parties was not achieved and effective leadership was made difficult if not impossible.

Power of the Chancellor and President. With the Reichstag thus almost paralyzed by its own methods of procedure, and with ministries often merely tolerated rather than actively supported by it, the Chancellor and the President were more than once forced to fall back upon each other. The constitution empowered them, in a national emergency, to govern temporarily by presidential decree. These decrees were legally subject to subsequent approval or revision by the Reichstag, so that an appearance of constitutionality could be preserved, but every resort to government by decree meant a breakdown of the parliamentary process.[4] It also meant that the *Reichspräsident* assumed an importance never foreseen by the framers of the constitution. The "presidential" cabinets of 1931 to 1933 were less stable than parliamentary ones had been. Too much depended upon the advice given to the President by his confidential counselors, and upon his ability to understand that advice and weigh it against the recommendations of the Chancellor.

Opposition to Republicanism. Opposition to the republic was persistent and ubiquitous. Even while the constituent assembly was at work troops had to be called to suppress Socialist riots in Bavaria, the Ruhr, Magdeburg, Dresden, Leipzig, and Berlin. More serious Communist revolts occurred in the Ruhr early in 1920 and in Saxony in 1923.

At the same time political reactionaries and nationalists were also active. In February, 1920, government offices in Berlin were seized by some members of the so-called "National Union," headed by Wolfgang Kapp and supported by Captain Erhardt's "Marine Brigade" of volunteer fighters. The *Putsch* was broken by a general strike called by the unions at the request of the national government. Few of Kapp's followers were punished. It was already noticeable that the government troops were less ready to fire upon ardent patriots than upon Communists. The same relative leniency to those who attacked the republic in the name of patriotism was shown by the Stresemann government in the autumn of 1923 in its treatment of the leaders of the unsuccessful Munich Beer Hall *Putsch,* General von Ludendorff and Adolf Hitler. Hatred of the republic was also shown by the assassination in 1921 of Matthias Erzberger, head of the Armistice Delegation, and in 1922 of Walter Rathenau, the Minister who negotiated the Treaty of Rapallo with Russia.

Rise of Extremist Parties. Whether because it lacked political strength and self-confidence or because it was reluctant to use force against its own people, the republic (especially in its later years) was surprisingly tolerant of the many dissident groups who used their freedom of assembly and of utterance to criticize it adversely. The republic was in little danger of being overthrown by the Communists after 1923, but the National Socialist and Communist ranks filled up remarkably. In the Presidential election of 1925 the Communist candidate polled 1,871,815 votes. In the election of September, 1930, the Communist Party obtained 4,587,000 votes and in November, 1932, 5,980,240 votes. The success of National Socialism, as we shall see presently, was even more spectacular.

Always free to criticize one another and to compete for popular support, the parties began to fight in the streets and intimidate each other's supporters. Each had its organization of uniformed street-fighters: the Communists their *Rotefront,* the Social Democrats their *Reichsbanner,* the Nationalists the *Stahlhelm,* composed at first principally of war veterans, and the National Socialists their brown-shirted S.A. (*Sturmabteilungen,* attack sections or storm troopers) and their black-uniformed S.S. (*Schutzstaffeln,* " defense squads " or guards divisions). Such a phenomenon, like rule by decree, indicated the breakdown of popular government. Disarmed by their own belief in tolerance and freedom, hesitant and half-hearted in their use of force, the friends of social and political democracy were unable to defend it against opponents who were not handicapped by such inhibitions.

Parties and Politics. From 1920, when the first republican Reichstag was elected, until its dissolution in March, 1924, Germany had four Chancellors, Wirth, Cuno, Stresemann, and Marx. Stresemann became Foreign Minister in November, 1923, and remained in office until his death in October, 1929. He was probably the ablest statesman of the republican era. A bourgeois defender of capitalism, he was a true democrat. An ardent nationalist, he strove for conciliation with France and worked with Briand for true international cooperation within the framework of the League of Nations.

In 1925 the aged Field Marshal Paul von Hindenburg was elected President, and although he had been a servant of the Imperial regime, he took an oath to support the Weimar constitution and served as a non-partisan President. Hindenburg helped to conciliate some of the dissident factions in the government. The republican structure, however, was increasingly weakened after 1925 by lack of faith in the government and by the active hostility of powerful groups like the Junker landholders, great industrialists such as the steel magnates, Krupp, Thyssen, and Stinnes, rich bankers like Von Schroeder, the Hohenzollern family, and Dr. Hjalmar Schacht, President of the Reichsbank, who was the secret adviser of Hitler.

One coalition government succeeded another. The moderate parties held the balance of power in the Reichstag until Chancellor Heinrich Bruening was dismissed by President Hindenburg, whom he had just helped to re-elect, in May, 1932. These parties, however, wrangled with one another, thus giving the enemies of the republic plenty of " ammunition."

Communists and Nazis. The leading anti-republican parties gained strength rapidly after 1925. The Communists, led by Ernst Thaelmann, a mild and rather ineffectual person, drew their support chiefly from the discontented proletariat. The National Socialists appealed to the unemployed, whose numbers rose from 2,484,000 in the first quarter of 1929 to 6,128,000 in the first quarter of 1932, to the unhappy youth, the small entrepreneur and the white collar workers, all of whom found it increasingly difficult to eke out a livelihood as the depression continued.

The Nazi Leadership. The Nazis had a remarkable leader in the half-educated, fiery agitator, Adolf Hitler. Born in Austria in 1889, Hitler had imbibed the Pan-German doctrines which were current in his homeland in his youth. He served in the German army during the World War as a corporal, and afterwards was employed by the *Reichswehr* (the postwar German army) as a secret agent to report on political meetings in Bavaria. In this capacity he came into contact with Anton Drexler, who had organized a group of six compatriots which called itself the German Workers Party, a branch of a similar organization in Austria. Hitler joined the party as number seven and soon became its leader, while Drexler was ousted. Its name was changed to National Socialist German Workers Party, and its activities centered in Bavaria. In 1923 Hitler, in collaboration with General Ludendorff, led the ill-fated attempt to capture the municipal government of Munich. For this he was sentenced to Landsberg Prison, where he lingered for eight months, writing, with the help of Rudolf Hess, his flaming autobiography and blueprint of revolution, *Mein Kampf (My Battle)*. After Hitler's release from prison in 1924, his movement made swift headway, chiefly because he had persuaded the industrial magnate, Thyssen, that the Nazis would form a bulwark against the Communists and the trade unions. The friendship and subsidy of Thyssen paved the way for other financial contributions to the Nazi cause; considerable money came from foreign sources, such as Sir Henri

Deterding, the Anglo-Dutch oil tycoon, and even, it has been said, from Mussolini.

The National Socialists carried on effective election campaigns. With the help of Dr. Joseph Goebbels, a former Socialist, they organized masterful propaganda, utilizing the radio, the rostrum, and the press to full advantage. The two World War veterans, Captain Ernst Roehm and Lieutenant Hermann Goering, developed a loyal and disciplined corps of storm troopers. The Nazi method of political organization was similar to that of the Communists. They formed " cells " in factories, offices, and shops, marched in resplendent uniforms, engaged in street brawls with their opponents, and occasionally resorted to terrorism and assassination. Their program stressed the weaknesses of the republic, the necessity of removing the Jews from the economic and political life of Germany, the need for renouncing the Treaty of Versailles and fighting Bolshevism. They laid great emphasis on the Aryanization of Germany and the union of all Germans in Europe.

In Hitler, the self-appointed Messiah, the German people found a substitute for the Kaiser. The Fuehrer had an ingratiating manner, capable of charming vast crowds, electric and energetic. At heart Hitler was a Machiavellian, using all the arts of diplomacy to corral and enlist all sorts and varieties of men to his Swastika banners. He was particularly successful with the youth, whom he promised to lead to Utopia, once the decadent republic had been swept away. Hitler, however, worked within the framework of the Weimar constitution, and his perpetual boast was, " I shall take power by legal means," thus appealing to the basic German instinct for order and discipline.

The Accession of Hitler. In 1928 the National Socialist Party polled 800,000 votes and elected 12 deputies to the Reichstag. Two years later it returned 106 deputies. In April, 1932, when Hitler ran against Hindenburg for the presidency, he obtained 13,400,000 votes to the Field Marshal's 17,500,000. Nevertheless Hindenburg refused Hitler's demand of the Chancellorship. In the November, 1932, election the Nazis lost ground.

Bruening was succeeded as Chancellor by Franz von Papen, a prominent if bungling German secret agent in the United States during the World War. Von Papen could not obtain the confidence of the Reichstag and was dismissed by Von Hindenburg in favor of General von Schleicher. When the latter was, it is said, on the verge of executing a *coup d'état* and eliminating both Hindenburg and Hitler, the clique of Junkers, bankers and industrialists who dominated the aged President persuaded him to dismiss Von Schleicher and invite Hitler to assume the Chancellorship. On January 30, 1933, Hitler thus became the head of a Cabinet which included Nazis and Nationalists. The latter regarded Hitler as their tool, and were confident that they could force him to execute their demands, but they reckoned without the fact that the Fuehrer would let no scruples stand in his path.

In the election of March 5, 1933, the Nazi Party secured but 44 per cent of the vote, and it could form a majority in the Reichstag only in alliance with the Nationalists, who had polled 8 per cent. The Nazis then resorted to extra-parliamentary tactics to liquidate their opponents. After excluding the Communists and other opposition deputies by threat and strong-arm methods, Hitler obtained an Empowering Act from the Reichstag which enabled him to rule dictatorially, using his storm troopers and the Nazi secret police, the Gestapo, to silence, imprison or kill those who opposed the regime.

The Nazi Revolution. The National Socialist revolution has been described as a *Machtergreifung* (seizure of power, or *coup d'état*) and as the *Machtübernahme* (the taking over of power). Both descriptions are apt. At a blast from its trumpets — and the Nazis have made trumpet-blowing a part of their political system — the walls of the State set up at Weimar collapsed like those of Jericho. National Socialists had themselves done as much as anyone to weaken those walls; but their final success was due to the fact that in January, 1933, the edifice was already crumbling.

The Republic had scarcely had a fair trial, to be sure. Its handicaps were heavy, and fourteen years were, historically speaking, but a short proving period.[5] Yet there were patriots who could not dissociate the republic from the hardships and humiliations imposed upon Germany by the Versailles Treaty. In the relatively prosperous period of the middle 'twenties Germany seemed quite strong; but when she found herself engulfed by the depression, unemployment and distress destroyed people's faith in the government. Its social insurance program, although never generous, had been costly enough almost to provoke a taxpayers' revolt; while efforts of the Bruening Cabinet to institute economies estranged the employees of the state and those (landowners included) who looked to it for subsidies. The republican leaders, notably Stresemann and Bruening, had been to a certain extent successful in winning for Germany, by negotiation and conciliation, a position of equality among the nations and in freeing Germany from some of the more irksome provisions of the Peace Treaty; but their successes had not come quickly enough, and were not striking enough, to satisfy the more impatient and self-assertive German groups. And finally, the republic's failure to command respect and obedience at home led many who would not, in the abstract, have preferred a dictatorship to welcome the Hitler regime which, they hoped, would protect them against Bolshevism, domestic disorder, and potential foreign foes.

The Nazi Ideology. That the National Socialist program made a many-sided appeal is undeniable. Much of its propaganda was artfully based on German traditions. It glorified the state; so had Hegel. It stressed the obligation of the individual to serve the state; so had Frederick the Great, Kant, Fichte, and the Weimar constitution. It dignified labor, the daily service of the common man and woman, each in his own station; so had Martin Luther. Like Schopenhauer, it scorned as materialistic and nugatory the egocentric life spent in quest of self-satisfaction, and idealized devotion to something greater than the individual. It glorified the warrior, bravely launching into high adventure, scornful of comfort and safety; so had Wagner. It exalted, as Nietzsche did, the " superior " person or " leader," and exhorted all others to follow him gladly, finding their freedom in voluntary obedience. For ministerial responsibility to parliament and a politician's responsibility to his electorate National Socialism substituted the leader's recognition of his moral responsibility to the people, and made every official answerable to an immediate superior, as in a military hierarchy; this was substantially the conception of Frederick the Great. Finally the Nazis assured the German people that unity, courage, industry, and determination would make them invincible in everything they undertook.

The Appeal of Nazism. National Socialism appealed to the Germans' pride, recalling and magnifying the glories of their past, encouraging them to improve their minds and bodies by abstemious living, rigorous athletic training of their youth, and sterilization of the weak and unfit.

To the old, the Nazis offered security — of property to those who possessed it, pensions to those who did not; to the young, adventure. Its slogans were stimulating: " Germany, awake! " — " One people, one nation, one leader! "

It enabled the Germans to recover self-confidence by finding scapegoats for their failures and attributing their troubles to the malignance of other nations. Germany, Hitler told them, had not been beaten in the field but was betrayed by the revolution and by false promises of a decent peace. The Treaty of Versailles had been designed to prevent Germany's recovery, and the republic did not have the courage to throw off its chains.[6]

None but thoughtful persons inquired before the Nazi revolution what price they were to pay for the promised gains, and few were bold enough to ask such a question afterward. Soon the Germans knew, however, that although the cost was still undetermined it would be high. The appearance of unanimity created after the revolution by the one-party system — all other parties were outlawed — was achieved only by the systematic suppression of criticism and dissent. Where obedience was

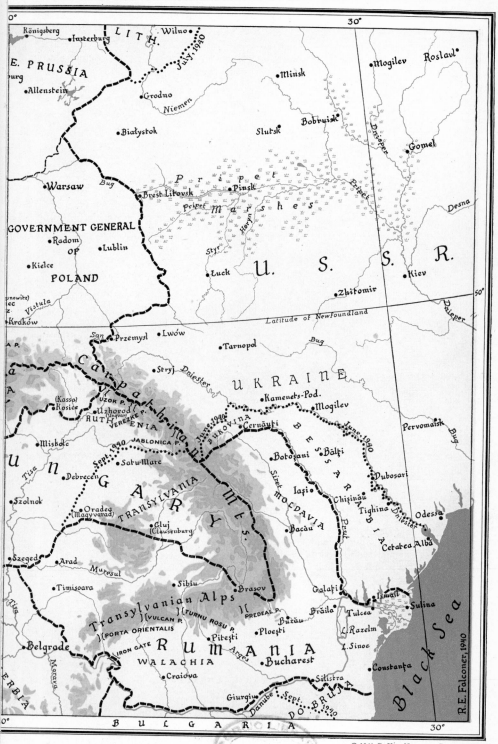

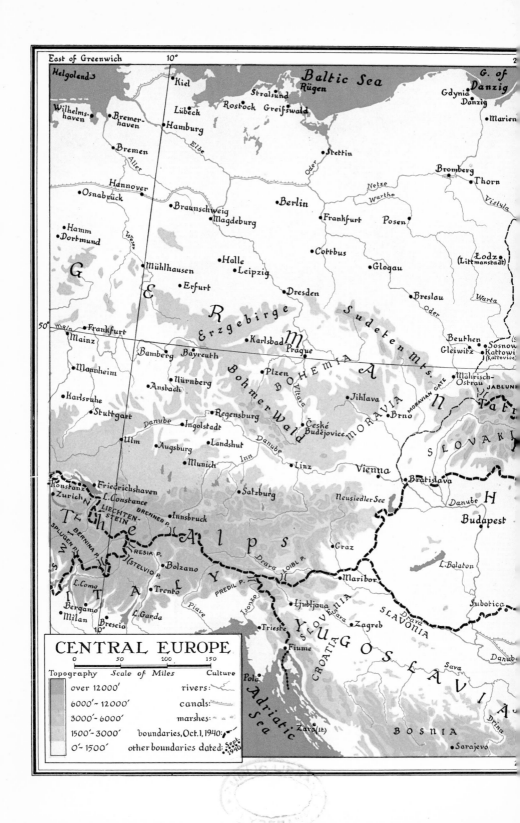

Helgoland ·ᛃ

Baltic Sea

G. of Danzig

Kiel

Stralsund   Rügen

Gdynia
Danzig

Wilhelms-haven

Lübeck
Bremer-haven

Rostock   Greifswald

·Marien

·Bremen

Hamburg

·Stettin

Bromberg
·Thorn

Elbe

Alles

Netze

Vistula

Hannover

Aller
Weser

Braunschweig

Berlin

Warthe

·Osnabrück

Magdeburg

Frankfurt

Posen

·Hamm
·Dortmund

G

·Halle

Cottbus

·Gloqau

Łodz
(Littmanstadt)

E

·Leipzig

·Erfurt

Dresden

·Breslau

Warta

Mühlhausen

Oder

50°
Frankfurt

R
Erzgebirge

Sudeten Mts.

Beuthen

·Mainz

Karlsbad

m
Prague

Gleiwitz
Sosnow
Kattowi
(Kattovice)

Bamberg   Bayreuth

·Mannheim

Plzen

B
O
H
E
M
I
A

A

Mährisch-Ostrau   JABLUNK

·Karlsruhe

Nürnberg
·Ansbach

Böhmer Wald

Vltava

Jihlava

n

Tatr
Fr

·Stuttgart

Regensburg

České
Budějovice

Brno

MORAVIA

MORAVIAN GATE

SLOVAKI

Danube

Ingolstadt

Danube

·Stuttgart

Ulm

Augsburg

Landshut

Inn

·Linz

Vienna

·Bratislava

H

·Munich

Konstanz
·Friedrichshaven

Zurich

L.Constance

Salzburg

Neusiedler See

Danube

Budapest

N

LIECHTEN-STEIN

BRENNER P.

·Innsbruck

T
h
e

A
l
p
s

Graz

L.Balaton

SPLUGEN P.

BERNINA P.

RESIA P.

STELVIO P.

Bolzano

Drava

LOIBL P.

Maribor

Subotica

·Trento

PREDIL P.

Isonzo

·Ljubljana

Piave

Drava

Sava

S
W
I
T

L.Como

I
T
A
L
Y

L.Garda

Save

·Zagreb

Danub

Bergamo
·Milan

Brescia

Piave

Triesre

Fiume

CROATIA

SLAVONIA

Y
U
G
O
S
L
A
V
I
A

Pola

Zara(It)

BOSNIA

Drina

CENTRAL EUROPE

| 0 | 50 | 100 | 150 |

Topography   *Scale of Miles*   Culture

over 12000'	rivers:
6000'–12000'	canals:
3000'–6000'	marshes:
1500'–3000'	boundaries, Oct. 1, 1940:
0'–1500'	other boundaries dated:

Adriatic
Sea

·Sarajevo

not prompt and voluntary, coercion was freely used. Not content with controlling or taking over the secular activities of the established churches, the Nazis denounced Christianity because of its international, inter-racial, and pacifist character, and because it recognized a " higher law " than that of their all-powerful state. Emphasis upon political conformity in the selection of teachers and students made the universities useful to the party in power, but resulted in a lowering of scholastic standards and the loss of independence. The non-German world as well as many Germans were horrified by the treatment of the Jews and by the calculated cruelty and terrorism of national policy.[7]

Foreign Policy. The foreign policy of both the republic and the Third Reich centered around the attempts to regain the territory and prestige lost by the war. The only real difference between the republic's aims and Hitler's, as publicly stated, was in method. The republic had to speak for a convalescent Germany; Hitler became the spokesman of a resurgent and aggressive nation. The republic had to use conciliatory methods because it was economically and militarily weak; the Third Reich was strong enough to risk defiance.

Foreign Policy of the Republic. There were several parts of the treaty which the spokesmen of the republic never pretended to accept, even though they were compelled to sign. Among these were the clauses relating to reparations, war guilt, war criminals, the Polish frontiers, and the loss of colonies.

Repudiating the charge that they had caused the war, the Germans naturally objected to being punished for having lost it; and they thought they had reason to believe that the primary purpose of the reparation claim was punitive. They therefore looked upon reparation not as a debt but an enemy claim, valid only if the enemy could collect. Convinced that France was determined to cripple them economically, the Germans defended themselves by paying as little as possible — and most of that with borrowed money. The injury done them was as much psychological as material, and their fight to evade payment was a matter of national policy as well as of economic necessity.

The thirteen years' dispute about reparations interfered with the economic recovery of Europe; but what probably mattered more to the world was that it shortened the truce between wars by giving the Germans a grievance which the National Socialists utilized for their own political advantage.[8]

Conciliation. Foreign Minister Stresemann was an ardent nationalist and patriot. But he was also a realist, convinced that Germany was in no condition to defy her foes and that she could recover only by adapting herself to the new order — at least until she was strong enough to change

it. He therefore followed a policy of conciliation, designed to restore economic relations between Germany and her former enemies. Hence his acceptance of the Dawes Plan and the Dawes loans.

Locarno Guarantees. Stresemann was also responsible for the Locarno agreements of October, 1925, in which the German-Belgian and German-French frontiers, as defined by the Treaty of Versailles, were guaranteed; Germany and France (also Germany and Belgium) agreed not to attack each other, or to resort to war, except to resist unprovoked attack or to carry out Article XVI of the League Covenant or a decision of the League, and to settle all questions by peaceful means. Great Britain and Italy were to guarantee the Locarno Pact by giving aid to any of the signatories in case the others violated it.

Locarno was the prelude to Germany's admission to the League of Nations in 1926. In 1928 Stresemann, for Germany, was one of the first to sign the Kellogg-Briand Pact.

Locarno also paved the way for the evacuation of the Rhineland by the Allied armies; Stresemann lived long enough to see that step practically completed. The negotiation of the Young Plan was his last public service.

Meanwhile the republic had maintained generally friendly relations with Russia. By the Treaty of Rapallo (1922) Germany became the first western power to recognize the Union of Socialist Soviet Republics, establish formal diplomatic relations, and resume trade with it. Just before Germany's entry into the League, a new " re-insurance " treaty with Russia was negotiated by Stresemann. Both militarists and industrialists saw possibilities of profitable cooperation with Russia, despite the mutual recriminations in which the two governments publicly indulged from 1933 to 1939.[9]

Revisionism. Stresemann's successors were also revisionists. In March, 1931, Dr. Curtius, Foreign Minister under Chancellor Bruening, proposed a customs union with Austria. Other continental European powers, however, regarded it as a step toward the absorption of Austria into Germany and a violation of the Treaty of St.-Germain and the Protocol of 1922 which laid down the conditions of an international loan to Austria. Their objection was sustained in September by an advisory opinion of the World Court. The " spirit of Locarno " died with the men who had met there.[10]

Chancellor Bruening, serving as his own Minister for Foreign Affairs after the withdrawal of Dr. Curtius, strove desperately for diplomatic triumphs abroad that would strengthen his government at home. Among his proposals were large-scale electrification projects for central Europe and the improvement of inland waterways, the immediate return of the Saar to Germany with compensation to France, and a settlement of the Polish Corridor question to give Germany an unimpeded overland route from East Prussia to West Prussia and in return guarantee Poland the

free use of the Vistula and the port of Danzig. But before Bruening could achieve concrete results he was dismissed by President von Hindenburg. The end of reparation payments and the recognition by Great Britain and France of Germany's theoretical right to rearm were not enough to pacify the militant German nationalists.

Revision by Unilateral Denunciation. The National Socialists had inveighed against the Treaty of Versailles since the founding of their party, and denounced the policy of fulfilment as one of degradation and that of conciliation as cringing. Ardent Pan-Germanists, they announced their intention to restore Germany to her rightful place among nations, and instead of negotiation substituted direct action or the *fait accompli.*

Nazi Germany was not at home in the League of Nations. The League Assembly was a parliamentary body, and the National Socialists had no use for old-style parliaments. The League professed adherence to collective security, which to the Nazis meant collective opposition to their plans for a resurgent Germany. The League Council worked by negotiation and often by compromise; the Nazis were not compromisers. Therefore Germany withdrew from the League in 1933.

Point by point thereafter, acting swiftly and at moments when the general diplomatic situation in other countries made effective opposition least probable, Adolf Hitler proceeded to free Germany from the provisions of the Treaty of Versailles. In 1935 rearmament and the resumption of conscription were announced; in 1936 German troops reoccupied the Rhineland and its re-fortification was begun, and the control of commerce on the German rivers was resumed. By 1935 both Memel and Danzig were dominated by Nazi parties and marked for eventual return to the Reich. On January 30, 1937, in his anniversary address to the Reichstag, the Chancellor announced that Germany no longer recognized that the war guilt clause of the Versailles Treaty had any validity.[11]

Expansion. The Nazi emphasis upon the organic and enduring unity of the nation (*das Volk*), and its filial relationship to the soil (*Boden*), implied that all Germans in Europe should be united. Those living outside the existing boundaries of the Reich should be brought within them if possible. Whether people or boundaries should be moved to accomplish that result would depend on circumstances; but as the Nazis did not, seemingly, take notice of obstacles to their plans, Germany's neighbors became understandably uneasy.

Austria. The annexation of Austria was logically the first step in bringing all the Germans of central Europe under the Nazi flag. Anschluss had been twice frustrated, at the end of the World War and in 1931. National Socialism at first attracted the Austrians less strongly than republican Germany. In spite of propaganda from across the border and German support of the Austrian Nazi party, the attempted *coup d'état* of July 25,

1934, seemed to accomplish nothing but the murder of Chancellor Dollfuss. But in 1938 the National Socialists had made considerable headway in Austria; Germany had cast off the shackles of Versailles; and Italy, which had moved an army to the Brenner Pass to defend Austria in 1934 and which Hitler had had to placate in July, 1936, by reaffirming his recognition of Austrian independence, was in 1938 Germany's Axis partner. Austria therefore fell into Hitler's lap in March, 1938.[12]

Czechoslovakia. The piecemeal seizure of Czechoslovakia in October, 1938, and March, 1939, was less easily defensible on grounds of kinship than that of Austria had been, although as much as possible was made of the alleged hardships suffered by the Sudeten Germans and of the appeals of the Czech Nazis for rescue. Economic and military reasons for the move were more substantial. Large-scale regional economic planning (*Grossraumwirtschaft*) demanded, from the German point of view, the inclusion of Bohemia and Moravia in the German economic sphere; while in any general European war Czechoslovakia, as an ally of any enemy, would be potentially dangerous to the Reich. Hence again the German troops marched in.

Poland. Until Germany was fully rearmed it was impolitic to push too hard its demands for a revision of the Polish frontier. But in an address to the Reichstag on April 28, 1939, Hitler denounced the non-aggression pact which he had made with the Polish dictator, Marshal Pilsudski, in 1934. By September 1, 1939, the Nazis virtually controlled the Free City of Danzig, an agreement with Russia had been reached that protected Germany's flank, and a look at the map showed how difficult it would be for Britain and France to send effective aid to Poland. Therefore German troops moved again.[13]

The swift conquest of Poland and the seizure of the Baltic states by Russia afforded Nazi Germany an opportunity to put into practice on a large scale some of its most ambitious plans for the resettlement of populations. Large numbers of Poles and Jews were dispossessed of their property in Danzig, West Prussia, Posen, and Upper Silesia, areas which were all reincorporated into Germany. Houses, lands, and businesses so acquired were turned over to eager migrants from Germany or used to indemnify Germans who were compelled to " emigrate " by agreement with Russia from Estonia, Latvia, Lithuania, and eastern Poland. Although many of the Baltic Germans had lived outside Germany for generations, they were still considered citizens of the Reich. At the same time, an agreement with Italy provided for the return to the Fatherland of German inhabitants of the Tyrol who should choose to move rather than accept complete Italianization.

World Revolution Marching On. Other conquests in 1939 and 1940 greatly extended Germany's *Lebensraum* or sphere of economic domination. After the conquest of Belgium and France, Eupen, Malmédy, and Moresnet were treated as if they had never ceased to belong to Germany, Alsace and Lorraine as if they would never again be given up. In all the occupied non-German countries some measure of self-government was granted, most in Denmark, which had not resisted invasion. In every case, however, the Germans dictated governmental policy and kept a watchful eye upon the harassed local officials. German control over what was being printed and broadcast was fairly complete. All the economic resources of the occupied areas had to be put at Germany's disposal if she chose to commandeer them. How much of the Nazi plan for the permanent reorganization of Europe was evident in the management of those parts of the continent under German control could only be surmised.

The Question of Colonies. Imperial Germany entered late, under the ostensibly reluctant leadership of Bismarck, into the general competition for overseas possessions. Aside from island trading posts and naval bases in the Pacific, her largest and most valuable colonies were German East and Southwest Africa, Togoland and Kamerun in equatorial west Africa. They were not ideally located. Much of southwest Africa was arid and, except for the highlands of German East Africa, the equatorial areas were unhealthful for Europeans. The German population in the colonies, soldiers and officials included, was less than 24,000 in 1914.[14]

In case of war, the colonies, wedged in among the British, French, Belgian, and Portuguese possessions, were in a dangerous position, but the German imperialists expected to eliminate some of the dangers. In 1898 and again in 1913, they had tried to persuade Great Britain to partition Portugal's African possessions, visualizing a German " Middle Africa " that would include all of the Congo Basin, then largely under French and Belgian control.[15]

Colonial ventures were not universally popular in pre-war Germany. The Social Democratic and Independent deputies in the Reichstag consistently opposed them on the ground that they meant increased appropriations, a larger navy, more power for the Kaiser, and greater risk of war. As a result of the parliamentary crisis of 1906, salutary reforms in the colonial administration were effected under a new Secretary, Dr. Dernburg. Although trading rights and concessions were profitable to some investors, the colonies were a burden to German taxpayers. Colonial expenditures between 1894 and 1913 were about 2 per cent of the total expense of government, while imports from the colonies were only 0.3 per cent and exports only 0.5 per cent of Germany's total foreign commerce.[16]

Yet there were an increasing number of people who thought that the colonies were worth keeping. Certainly, if returned to Germany, they might be made more profitable, and their resources would be more intensively exploited, a task for which the colonial administration (never abolished by the republic) was prepared. Yet the Nazi spokesmen said repeatedly that they would not fight for colonies, and it seems improbable that they would have done so. Talk about colonies had a " nuisance value," especially in dealing with the British, and may have been indulged in in the hope of softening the opposition Britain might otherwise offer to expansionist enterprises elsewhere.

Economic and Social Development: 1919–1940

Economic Development. The economic life of Germany from 1918 to 1939 may be briefly described as eleven years of recuperation from the effects of the war, followed by four years of depression and six of preparation for another war.

Recuperation was slow. There was great uncertainty as to the outcome of the various plebiscites, the amount of reparations, and the world's attitude toward the resumption of trade. Little foreign money was available. Inflation wiped out the assets of the lower and middle classes and tragically dislocated the German economy. The mark of the inflation period never " came back." The new *Rentenmark* that took its place had no basis but the resources of the country. Confidence in the currency would depend upon the solvency and financial integrity of the government. The comparative stability of the mark after 1924 was the result chiefly of the determination of both government and people never again to permit an inflation. Not everyone had been ruined by the inflation, however; only those who depended upon the purchasing power of a given amount of money. The government's own enormous internal debt was practically wiped out. Men who had bought real estate, or built homes or factories on borrowed capital, liquidated their loans easily.

With the restoration of confidence and some semblance of international good will, following the acceptance of the Dawes Plan in 1924 and the Locarno Pact of 1925, foreign capital poured into Germany to purchase national, municipal, and corporation bonds. The middle 'twenties were a period of rapid industrial expansion, and of cartels and " rationalization " to regulate competition by allocating raw materials and markets to cooperating industries and companies.

Depression. In 1929 the bubble burst. No more foreign loans were available, and creditors called for payment. Banks failed everywhere and in 1930 and 1931 cartels collapsed. The Hoover moratorium of 1931 recognized the seriousness of the German crisis but did not help to correct the conditions that caused it. A continued surplus of imports over exports increased the strain on Germany's credit and further complicated the foreign exchange problem.

Unemployment increased, and with it public expenditures for unemployment insurance, although the amounts paid to individuals were inadequate to meet even their subsistence needs. Agriculture suffered also, and the owners of large estates in the northeastern Germany, threatened or pretending to be threatened with bankruptcy, drew heavy subsidies (the *Osthilfe*) from the treasury. Government payrolls and pensions could not be reduced without stubborn political opposition.

Upon the heels of distress came disorder, and out of perplexity grew an instinctive desire to punish someone — first of all those who seemed to be prospering while others suffered. To the distressed, the perplexed, the vengeful, and the covetous, the National Socialist orators offered each his heart's desire; to everyone they promised what was just then most needed — work and security.

The Nazi Economy: Re-employment. The official Nazi program emphasized the right and duty of every man to work. When Hitler became Chancellor there were 6 million unemployed. Within a year and a half, the number had been cut in half; and by the end of three years practically all employable persons were off the relief rolls. The tremendous expansion of the war industries — the Nazis regarded another war as inevitable — absorbed a large part of the unemployed. Armament expenditures reached the staggering total of 31,100,000,000 marks (roughly about $7,750,000,-000) in the years 1933–1937.

That is not to say, however, that all those formerly unemployed were gainfully engaged in private industry. Many forms of activity might have been called invisible unemployment. But everyone was busy. The elimination of the Jews from commerce, industry, and the professions, opened many opportunities for employment to certified Aryans.

Regulation of Interest and Profits. The Nazi platform had also promised that " interest-slavery " would be abolished. Something was therefore done toward lowering interest rates on farm mortgages, and an " hereditary farmsteads law " was passed in order to create a new peasant (*Bauer*) land-owning class. The government also fixed minimum prices for agricultural products.

Under the Nazis business found itself more and more regulated by the government, while its profits were limited by law. Officials told the entrepreneur what wages he should pay, what hours and under what conditions his men should work, what contracts he might assume or reject, what materials would be allocated to him, where and at what price he might sell his products. Then he must share his profit with the government by paying taxes on it, contributing to the " winter relief " funds or other collections, taking his share of government loans, or (if working on a government contract) accepting payment partly in scrip or tax-anticipation warrants. Most businessmen were as busy as ever, but they wondered no doubt sometimes for whom they were working. In a sense, certainly, " interest-slavery " was broken, as the Nazis promised. No individual was free to enrich himself at the expense of others; all were controlled by the government which, in 1938, handled two-thirds of the national income.

Default on Foreign Debts. If the payment of interest and amortization on foreign debts could be called " interest-slavery," then that form of servitude was also ended. Despite all he had previously said about the sanctity of private debts, Dr. Schacht, as President of the Reichsbank and Nazi Minister for Economics, soon declared himself unable, in the face of unfavorable trade balances and the difficulty of procuring foreign exchange, to permit the transfer of funds for their payment.[17]

Self-sufficiency. The foreign exchange (*Devisen*) problem was serious not only because of " unfavorable " trade balances but because of the character of German purchases abroad. The largest sums were spent abroad, in order of magnitude, for (1) food, (2) propaganda, and (3) raw materials, such as iron ore, bauxite, oil, rubber, etc. Every effort was made to increase the production of food and restrict all imports except raw materials needed for war industries or as a war reserve.

Defense Economy. The new economic policy inaugurated in 1933 aimed (1) to make the country as nearly self-sufficient as possible and (2) to store up reserve stocks of food and raw materials to withstand a blockade in case of war. The first part of the program was called autarchy (*Autarkie*). The coordination of all phases of economic life with " defense " needs was called *Wehrwirtschaft* or a national defense economy.[18] In 1936 a Four-Year Plan was introduced, under the direction of Field Marshal Goering, for raw material self-sufficiency. It proposed to make Germany independent of foreign supplies of textiles and oil, and to reduce imports of base metals, iron ore, and rubber.

As steps toward autarchy wastage of materials was scrupulously reduced and scientists were encouraged to search for substitute (*ersatz*) materials, and remarkable though often expensive progress was made in that direction. Technological improvements and synthetic processes were devised with great speed, partly because the new government was willing to subsidize research liberally and place unlimited funds at the disposal of a new industry, and partly because it demanded them so imperiously.

The Labor Front. A " defense economy " that put the country's economic life on a war basis in peacetime meant a Spartan existence for the laboring masses. The new Labor Code, which became effective May 1, 1934, eliminated collective bargaining. Unions were abolished. Strikes and lockouts were made illegal, and it became almost impossible for a workman to leave one position in quest of another. Hours were lengthened and wages not much increased. The Labor Front, directed by Robert

Ley, helped to maintain the efficiency and morale of the workmen by providing more attractive working conditions, inexpensive vacation trips, educational and recreational opportunities, and stimulating the crafts-man's pride in his work. The Labor Front controlled working conditions, regulated the mobility of labor among industries and within geographical regions, formulated rules of business, and in fact, influenced every com-mercial transaction.

Foreign Trade. To conserve such cash balances as could be accumulated, the export and import business was put practically on a barter basis. German merchants were allowed to buy only in countries where the vendor would accept payment in goods. What they bought they either used at home or resold in the world market, sometimes in competition with similar goods from the same source. Their own goods they were ordered to sell where Germany could obtain needed imports. Merchants might be ordered (and subsidized if necessary) to buy or sell, regardless of loss or inconvenience, wherever the Nazi government dictated. In the first four years of the Nazi regime some progress was made in the direction of autarchy. Imports were reduced and exports increased: [19]

GERMAN FOREIGN TRADE
(in million marks)

	Exports	Imports	Balance
1932	5,739	4,667	+1,072
1933	4,871	4,200	+671
1934	4,167	4,440	−273
1935	4,270	4,159	+111
1936	4,768	4,218	+550

Cultural Life. Through the centuries, the Germans have revealed a genuine love of truth and beauty, and their contributions to the arts and sciences have won the admiration and gratitude of the world. Neither war nor the vicissitudes of peace could kill that love or put an end to those contributions. Cultural life under the republic was characterized by freedom, spontaneity, and cosmopolitanism; under the Third Reich by planned coordination and self-conscious nationalism.

Cultural Development. The republic was friendly to the arts. It was during the republican period that the Pergamon and German Museums were built in Berlin. With the approval of the government, court theaters of the old regime were maintained as people's theaters (*Volksbuehne*). Municipally supported symphony orchestras and opera companies gave concerts at moderate prices.

Literature. In the friendly, cosmopolitan atmosphere of the republic literature flourished. Gerhart Hauptmann (1862–   ) continued to turn out interesting dramas, although none to compare with such pre-war masterpieces as *The Weavers* or *The Sunken Bell.* Typical of the confused and lost post-war generation were the expressionistic plays of Ernst Toller (1893–1939), author of *Masses and Man* and *Draw the Fires*. The latter depicts the revolt of the sailors, " coolies of the Kaiser," against the Imperial regime as well as against the machine civilization to which they were chained. Georg Kaiser (1878–   ) in his play, *Gas*, analyzed the fundamental conflict in contemporary society between the omnipotence of the machine and the human beings who try to retain their natural instincts while forced to serve the machine.

The poetry of Stefan George (1868–1933) written after the war delineates the material decay of a generation that went through the holocaust but has strength and courage to create a new state (the title of one of his works) based on reality and imbued with high ideals. Rainer Maria Rilke (1875–1926), Czech by birth and Austrian by education, was more of a pure poet than George, and in essence a pantheist. His metaphysical verses are not destined to be widely read but he exemplified the more serene and mystical side of the German spirit, as typified in the lines: " Die and live again through change. Who shall say what brings the greater suffering? If the drink is bitter, turn thyself into wine. . . . And if the world forget thee, say to the unmoving earth, ' Thus do I move,' and to the flowing water, ' I flow with thee.' " [20]

The greatest German man of letters of our day is Thomas Mann (1875–   ). In his masterpiece, *The Magic Mountain* (1924), Mann discusses the chief intellectual problems of the age, the conflict of reason and emotion, of nationalism and internationalism, of altruism and selfishness. The characters of this novel, set in a Swiss sanatorium, form almost a microcosm of twentieth-century society. Heinrich Mann (1871–   ) is a less intellectual writer than his brother but perhaps a better portraitist. Of his numerous works, the historical novels are best known. Jacob Wassermann (1873–1934) wrote many romantic novels of which *The World's Illusion* is most familiar to American readers. To a younger generation belongs Erich Maria Remarque (1898–   ) who expressed the horrors of war and the disillusion of its aftermath in two immensely popular works, *All Quiet on the Western Front* and *The Road Back*. Lion Feuchtwanger (1884–   ) achieved renown for his novels of Jewish life, *Power, Josephus*, and *The Oppermanns*, while Emil Ludwig (1881–   ) is a fecund biographer, novelist, and playwright.

Journalism. In the happy days of the republic the press was free and unrestrained. Newspapers multiplied, and at least three were internationally famous — the *Frankfurter Zeitung*, the *Berliner Tageblatt*, and the *Vossische Zeitung*. The weekly illustrated magazine, *Der Berliner Illustrierte*, had a circulation of nearly 2 million. The publishers of all the papers just named were Jews, and Jews were active in intellectual and artistic fields.

Cinema and Music. German cinematic, musical, and theatrical productions set high standards of achievement. Berlin was one of the gayest capitals in the world in the 1920's. Actors and actresses like Werner Krauss, Fritz Kortner, Fritzi Massary, and Elizabeth Bergner played before receptive audiences. The theatrical productions of Max Reinhardt, Leopold Jessner, and Erwin Piscator attracted attention in all parts of the world; conductors like Otto Klemperer and Bruno Walter led brilliant symphonic performances.

In creative music Germany was not behind the other nations. Richard Strauss (1864–   ), the greatest German composer since Wagner and Liszt, was producing notable if not extraordinary works, including the ballet pantomime *Schlagobers* (*Whipped Cream*) and the opera *The Egyptian Helen.* Strauss' post-war compositions showed the same orchestral fertility as his earlier masterpieces, but the spark of originality had grown quite feeble. More in tune with the dizzy pace of contemporary life was the music of Paul Hindemith (1895–   ), regarded by some as Germany's leading modernist composer. Not as great an innovator as the Austrian Schönberg, Hindemith's most interesting works are written in dissonant counterpoint, that curious style which reflects the striving of the post-war generation for newer harmonies and stranger melodies. Kurt Weill (1900–   ) attracted much attention for his *Three Penny Opera* and a composition translating *Lindbergh's Flight* into radio music.

The radio, maintained by the Post Office out of the proceeds of a small tax on receiving sets, was free from commercial advertising and not yet given over to propaganda. The German cinema produced epochal works like *The Cabinet of Dr. Caligari*, Murnau's *Last Laugh,* and *Mädchen in Uniform.*

Art and Architecture. The most extreme development of expressionistic art occurred in post-war Germany in the work of George Grosz (1893–   ). His paintings and prints offer harsh commentaries on social life, conveyed in an extremely imaginative and often bizarre technique. Like Georg Kaiser, Grosz couched his satire in expressionistic terms, giving vent to his hatred and condemnation of the events he witnessed in that troubled, seething Germany of the 1920's in a style that baffled the layman. Käthe Kollwitz, the etcher and lithographer, put into her prints a similar consciousness of German *Weltschmerz* and a keen sympathy with the oppressed and underprivileged.

The Germans were among the leaders in the international style of post-war architecture. Walter Gropius (1883–   ) organized at Dessau his famous *Bauhaus* in 1926, a workshop designed to develop forms of architecture and interior decoration suitable to the machine age. The *Bauhaus* itself is an interesting example of the international style, with its vast windows filling the intervals between the steel sections, a structure that harmoniously combines the functional and the beautiful. Gropius also applied his genius for wedding these two ideals to various low-cost housing projects.

Art in the Third Reich. One of the first acts of the Nazi Ministry of Propaganda, headed by Goebbels, was the formation of a national Chamber of Culture whose members were to include all persons active in the musical world, the plastic and pictorial arts, the theater, literature, radio, the cinema, and the press. All were to be regulated.

The government had no thought of killing German culture; it meant only to canalize it, make it more Germanic, and use it for political purposes. In their own way, and by their own definitions, the Nazis encouraged artistic production. Prizes were offered in competitions of all sorts. Music was prodigally supported, especially the opera, the favorite of Hitler. Exhibitions of the "new German art" were set up under the most exalted sponsorship, and official comparisons contrasted it with the immoral decadence of what the republican period had produced. Comparisons drawn by other critics were generally less favorable to Nazi art.

The great German writers like Thomas Mann, Heinrich Mann, Erich Maria Remarque, Lion Feuchtwanger, and others, came to the United States, which indeed attracted the dispossessed creative souls of all of Europe. The symphony conductors Walter and Klemperer found posts in America, many of the actors and actresses went to England or the United States. The great German newspapers were bought for a pittance by the government from their Jewish owners and converted into Nazi organs.

Science. Pure science, like art, is non-political and cosmopolitan in character; and so is the scientist likely to be. Intellectualism is essentially individualistic, and scientific thought does not run naturally in nationalistic channels, although the scientist, as a citizen, may be a nationalist.

The disinterested scientist found the atmosphere of republican Germany more congenial than that of the Third Reich. An attitude of reverence for science and of respectful admiration of the scientist was traditional in pre-Nazi Germany. People believed in the potential omniscience and omnipotence of science as they believed in the benevolence of God; and the scientists were honored as its high priests. With the changing conditions that caused the collapse of the republic — a similar phenomenon appeared in other countries — unquestioning faith in science was weakened. Youth began, as Oswald Spengler had said, to "turn to the hammer instead of the pen, to the rudder instead of the brush, to politics instead of metaphysics." Older people questioned whether science was merely an ornamental feature of society or an instrument of social progress.

Thence it was but a step to the National Socialist view that the scientist must have a proper social attitude (the party claiming the exclusive right to declare what attitude was proper and to what use his discoveries should be put). The Nazi regime said it had no use for " abstract " science, not dedicated to the immediate amelioration of living conditions, or for a scientist indifferent to his obligations to his countrymen (as it defined those obligations).

If the scientist could meet Nazi standards as to race, political conformity, and other social attitudes, and was willing to devote his intellect and his energy to prescribed work, then the state could use him. The achievements of the nation's industries and public health services — and after September 1, 1939, of its war machine — furnished ample evidence that the new regime had succeeded in retaining the services of thousands of able scientists. The non-conformists and the racially impure, like Einstein, lost their positions or fled into exile. All Jewish and other non-Aryan savants were dismissed from their positions. Many came to the United States.

Education. The educational innovations of the Hitler regime closely paralleled those in the arts and sciences. In the republican era enrollment in the universities increased to twice that of 1913, with the result that hundreds of persons who received degrees could not find employment after 1929. After 1933 this trend was reversed. The number of students admitted to the universities was reduced, while the revival of industrial activity increased the demand for trained workers. By 1939 there was already a dearth of university-trained technicians in some fields.

During the lifetime of the republic education was comparatively free from governmental control and political propaganda. Intellectual enlightenment was recognized without question as the general objective of education, but its more immediate goals were only vaguely defined; the students were not indoctrinated with the idea that the republic was the best of all possible forms of government for Germany. Rather, by direct or indirect comparisons with happier days, teachers contributed more than a little to the unpopularity of the democratic system that maintained them.

National Socialism, after 1933, narrowed the purposes of education but defined them more clearly. Education, the Nazis said, must train the youth not for a secluded life of scholarship, divorced from farm, factory, and the market place, but for active citizenship. The most vital element in the new training was the inculcation of National Socialist ideology. Yet that was not enough. The virtues of non-totalitarian systems were denied, and their defects and failures were pointed out and exaggerated at every opportunity. New emphasis was placed on physical training and military sport, and on practical rather than purely academic instruction. Public school education was shortened by a year in order to gain time for labor service and military training.

The non-academic Nazi system of education was not entirely new. There had been a "youth movement" in Germany for more than a generation. During the republican period it had become especially popular, and upon this the Nazis could build. More complete coordination was soon evident, however, and such organizations as were not absorbed by the Hitler Youth and its affiliates were liquidated. Loss of control over the boys and girls of their congregations was one of the reasons for the resistance, generally passive, of the churches to the process of coordination (*Gleichschaltung*).

A striking feature of the Nazi system was the establishment of special schools for the training of political leaders. Less than a thousand students were admitted annually; these were selected on the basis of physical hardihood and courage, intelligence, and other qualities of leadership. Four years of training, each in a different region, were designed to develop these qualities and give the student a thorough knowledge of the land and its inhabitants, and of course thoroughly indoctrinate him with Nazi ideology.

In general, the experience of university professors was similar to that of other scientists. If they could qualify racially and ideologically, positions and opportunities were still open to them. Ostentatious patriotism and unquestioning loyalty to the Nazi regime were among the new requirements. For many who could not honestly accept the new ideology yet wished to retain their livelihoods, conformity constituted protective coloration.

Conclusion

The Germans are a persistent and ingenious people with a special genius for organization and an exceptional capacity for determined and united action when well and boldly led. Those qualities, combined with their outstanding technological achievements in nearly all fields, have enabled them to make the most of their rather limited natural resources. Having acquired most of their land by fighting for it and their wealth by working for it, they have learned to look upon war and work as indispensable means of self-preservation and advancement. Power politics failed in 1914 either to get them what they wanted or keep them out of war. The limited successes of the republic, which adopted a conciliatory policy in its international relations, were not sufficient to keep them, when brutal and impulsive men took over their government, from turning back to power politics (*Machtpolitik*), and plunging nearly all of Europe into a Second World War.

REFERENCES

1 The influence of geography upon political and economic life was developed into a science, Geopolitics, by a school of German writers headed by Karl Haushofer, Professor of Geography in the University of Munich and now head of the *Volksbund für das Deutschthum im Ausland*. The Swedish geographer Kjellen and the German Ratzel were precursors of this school. Contemporaries or followers of Herr Haushofer are his son Albrecht, Professor of Geography in the University of Berlin, and Kurt Vowinkel. The periodical *Geopolitik* is one of their organs. (See also A. Whitney Griswold, " Paving the Way for Hitler," *Atlantic*, March, 1941, pp. 314–322 and the bibliographical article by Joseph S. Roucek in *The Educational Forum*, May, 1940, p. 469, notes 12 to 16.)

The territory or *Lebensraum* occupied by a people should, according to the " geopoliticians," furnish that people a living. If it cannot do so, then neighboring peoples should mutually adapt their economies so that they will supplement one another and enable all to earn a living. This economy based on a large area is called *Grossraumwirtschaft*. Geopolitics furnishes a convenient theoretical justification for Germany's coordination of the economies of southeastern Europe with hers. The size of the " great economic area " is determined only by the practical exigencies of the moment. Economic cooperation with Germany has generally meant eventual German political control.

2 For details on the events preceding the armistice the following books and articles are recommended: Matthias Erzberger, *Erlebnisse im Weltkrieg*, Stuttgart: Deutsche Verlags Anstalt, 1920, especially pp. 274 ff.; Erich Ludendorff, *Ludendorff's Own Story*, New York: Harper, 1920, especially II, pp. 380–386, 423; R. H. Lutz, *Fall of the German Empire*, Palo Alto, Cal.: Stanford Univ. Press, 1932, especially II, pp. 381–499, and *Causes of the German Collapse*, Palo Alto, Cal.: Stanford Univ. Press, 1934; Arthur Rosenberg, *The Birth of the German Republic*, New York: Oxford Univ. Press, 1931, especially pp. 237, 240; Charles Seymour, *American Diplomacy during the World War*, Baltimore: Johns Hopkins Press, 1934, pp. 300–315; and Veit Valentin, " Vorgeschichte des Waffenstillstandes," *Historische Zeitschrift*, Vol. 134, pp. 57–64. The findings of the Reichstag committee of investigation are best studied in its published report, *Die Ursachen des Zusammenbruchs im Jahre 1918*, 12 vols., Berlin: Deutsche Verlagsgesellschaft für Politik und Geschichte, 1928–1929.

These sources do not substantiate either the " stab in the back " thesis or the more commonly accepted statement that the Allies and the United States assumed a contractual obligation to give Germany a peace based on the Fourteen Points, although the latter is less clearly disproven than the former.

3 See also James T. Shotwell, *What Germany Forgot*, New York: Macmillan, 1940.

4 A partisan but useful account of German political history in 1918 and 1919 is found in Arthur Rosenberg's *The Birth of the German Republic*. For the text of the Weimar constitution see H. L. McBain and L. Rogers, *The New Constitutions of Europe*, New York: Doubleday, 1923. For discussions of it see R. Brunet, *The New German Constitution*, New York: Knopf, 1922; Elmer Luehr, *The New German Republic*, New York: Minton, Balch, 1929; Harold Quigley and H. T. Clark, *Republican Germany*, New York: Dodd, Mead, 1928; and James K. Pollock, Jr., " The German Party System," *American Political Science Review*, XXIII: 859–891. A general history of the republican period is found in H. G. Daniels, *The Rise of the German Republic*, London: Nisbet, 1927.

5 It was fourteen years after the declaration of American independence that the United States government began to function under its present constitution. It took the Third French Republic four years to draft a republican constitution, eight to elect its first republican President, and fourteen to declare permanent that form of government.

6 Read the autobiographical portions of *Mein Kampf*, Boston: Houghton Mifflin, 1933, especially the story of Hitler's youth.

⁷ Unbiased works on National Socialism are few; it is a subject rarely discussed dispassionately. Edgar A. Mowrer's *Germany Puts the Clock Back*, New York: Morrow, 1932, was one of the first book accounts in English. Its title indicates the trend of its argument. Calvin B. Hoover's *Germany Enters the Third Reich*, New York: Macmillan, 1933, H. Powys Greenwood's *German Revolution*, London: Routledge, 1934, and R. T. Clark's *Fall of the German Republic*, New York: Macmillan, 1935, are good examples of honest efforts in the years 1933 to 1935 to understand and explain the Nazi revolution. Professor Stephen H. Roberts, writing in 1937 *The House That Hitler Built*, New York: Harper, 1938, was more successful. Frederick L. Schuman's *The Nazi Dictatorship*, New York: Knopf, 1935, and Stephen Rauschenbush's *March of Fascism*, New Haven: Yale Univ. Press, 1939, are antipathetic to Hitlerism. Hermann Rauschning's *Revolution of Nihilism*, New York: Alliance, 1939, and *The Voice of Destruction*, New York: Putnam, 1940, are written by a disgruntled former National Socialist leader in Danzig. Pastor Martin Niemöller's autobiographical *From U-boat to Pulpit*, London: Hodge, 1936, and the collection of his sermons, *Here Stand I*, Chicago: Willett, Clark, 1938, are of special interest, although they do not give a complete survey of the church problem.

⁸ See Hjalmar Schacht, *The End of Reparations*, New York: Cape and Smith, 1931.

⁹ See Herbert Rosinski, *The German Army*, New York: Harcourt, Brace, 1940. Rosinski is a former German army officer.

¹⁰ The opinion was rendered by a vote of eight to seven. Although the judges were serving on the Court as individual jurists, not as diplomats, their opinions in this case generally reflected or confirmed the political positions already taken by the governments of their countries. Mr. Kellogg of the United States and Sir Cecil Hurst of Great Britain were among those who delivered a joint dissenting opinion.

¹¹ See Waldo E. Stephens, *Revisions of the Treaty of Versailles*, New York: Columbia Univ. Press, 1939.

¹² The German-Italian "Axis" agreement was made on October 25, 1936.

¹³ For arguments that Hitler was ready in September, 1939, to precipitate a general war and therefore disregarded Anglo-French pleas for conciliation with Poland see Otto Tolischus, *They Wanted War*, New York: Reynal and Hitchcock, 1940.

¹⁴ Statistics taken from the *Statistische Jahrbuch für das Deutsche Reich* by Grover Clark for his *Balance Sheets of Imperialism*, New York: Columbia Univ. Press, 1936, p. 34.

¹⁵ See Mary E. Townsend, *The Rise and Fall of Germany's Colonial Empire*, New York: Macmillan, 1930, pp. 323 and 344.

¹⁶ Grover Clark, *op. cit.*, pp. 43 and 67.

¹⁷ The Dawes loan bonds were some of the last to go. New interest-bearing dollar bonds were issued subsequent to default, in some cases, in payment of past-due interest on the original issues; but in order to collect his interest on one of them after September 1, 1939, the holder had to certify that he was not a citizen of a country at war with Germany.

¹⁸ The word "defense" (*Wehr*) was on everyone's tongue in Germany in those days. The new national army was called the *Wehrmacht* only, or defense force, and all sorts of rules were called "defense" regulations.

¹⁹ Figures are taken from *Germany: The Last Four Years*, by "Germanicus," Boston: Houghton Mifflin, 1937, p. 58.

²⁰ Quoted by Félix Bertaux, *A Panorama of German Literature*, New York: Whittlesey House, 1935, p. 108.

SELECTED BIBLIOGRAPHY

Ball, Margaret M., *The Anschluss Movement, 1918–1936*, Palo Alto, Cal.: Stanford Univ. Press, 1938. A careful study.

Brady, Robert A., *The Spirit and Structure of German Fascism*, New York: Viking, 1937.

Bruntz, George G., *Allied Propaganda and the Collapse of the German Empire in 1918*, Palo Alto, Cal.: Stanford Univ. Press, 1939. One of the most intelligent attempts yet made to estimate the value of Allied propaganda.

Buell, Raymond Leslie, *Poland: Key to Europe*, New York: Knopf, 1939. By a distinguished student of international relations.

Childs, Harwood L., *The Nazi Primer, Official Handbook for Schooling the Hitler Youth*, New York: Harper, 1938.

Clark, Grover, *A Place in the Sun*, New York: Macmillan, 1936. See also the same author's *Balance Sheets of Imperialism*. Mr. Clark is skeptical of the economic value of colonies.

Dawes, Charles G., *A Journal of Reparations*, New York: Macmillan, 1929.

Falkenhayn, Eric G. A. S. von, *The German General Headquarters Staff and Its Decisions, 1914–1918*, New York: Dodd, Mead, 1920. Less revealing than R. H. Lutz's *Fall of the German Empire*, but useful.

Feder, Gottfried, *Hitler's Official Programme and Its Fundamental Ideas*, London: Allen & Unwin, 1934. By one of the principal Nazi ideologists.

Grzesinski, Albert C., *Inside Germany*, New York: Dutton, 1939. Covers the republican as well as the Nazi period.

Keynes, John Maynard, *The Economic Consequences of the Peace*, New York: Harcourt, Brace, 1920. Keynes was one of the first to challenge the reparation demands on economic grounds.

Royal Institute of International Affairs, *Germany's Claim to Colonies*, New York: Oxford Univ. Press, 1939. A pre-war study.

——, *Raw Materials and Colonies*, New York: Oxford Univ. Press, 1936.

Schnee, Heinrich von, *Die deutschen Kolonien vor, in, und nach dem Weltkrieg*, Leipzig: Quelle & Meyer, 1935. Volume LVII of the series *Wissenschaft und Bildung*, by a former colonial official.

Waller, Willard, *War in the Twentieth Century*, New York: Dryden Press, 1940. See especially the chapters by Walter Consuelo Langsam on Versailles and Vernon Kirkpatrick on National Socialist Germany.

Wolff, Theodor, *Through Two Decades*, London: Heinemann, 1936. By the former editor of the *Berliner Tageblatt*.

CHAPTER IX

Austria

" AS ONE BETWEEN TWO MASSING POWERS I LIVE
WHOM NEUTRALITY CANNOT SAVE
NOR OCCUPATION CHEER."
— C. DAY LEWIS

Geography. Pre-war Austria was part of the Dual Monarchy, an extensive empire, comprising 240,000 square miles (the third largest state in Europe) and more than 51 million persons of several nationalities. The Austrian half of the monarchy embraced 116,000 square miles inhabited by 28 million people.

Austria-Hungary was geographically compact, rich in natural resources, and largely self-contained. It comprised most of the territory within the mountain arch that encloses the south of Central Europe, formed by the line of the Alps-Sudeten-Carpathians. Austria-Hungary controlled 400 miles of the Adriatic shore, 700 miles of the Danube, and had a 1,000-mile frontier with Germany.

Imperial Austria was the focal point of two great historical highways: the East-West route along the Danube, and the Amber route connecting the Baltic Sea with the Danube and the Adriatic. The Danube is in reality a corridor linking central with southeastern Europe, and Europe with Russia and the Near East. Historically, the Hapsburg monarchy had long been the defensive outpost of central Europe against the Ottoman Turkish thrust. The geographic significance of pre-war Austria is revealed in the names of the trains that ran through Vienna: " Paris-Budapest-Bucharest-Istanbul (Orient Express)," " Vienna-Trieste-Rome," " Vienna-Warsaw."

Post-war Austria. Defeated Austria, already separated from her former non-Austrian provinces by the natural dismemberment of the empire, was reduced by the Treaty of St.-Germain (1919) to an area of 32,369 square miles, with a population that numbered 6,760,000 in 1934, nearly 2,000,000 of them living in Vienna. Austria emerged from the war with 26.5 per cent of her former territory and 23 per cent of her population. She was now a land-locked state, extending 230 miles along the Danube, and with weak natural frontiers separating her from Italy, Switzerland, Germany, Czechoslovakia, Hungary, and Yugoslavia.

The Austrian half of the Hapsburg Empire had been highly industrialized, and Vienna was the clearinghouse for goods shipped from eastern Europe and the Near East to the west. Vienna was also the financial,

This chapter by Huntley Dupre, Professor of History, University of Kentucky.

banking, and railroad center not only for the empire, but for southeastern Europe as well. The Viennese banks largely controlled the great industrial undertakings in the empire.

Post-war Austria was largely agricultural, having lost virtually all of its resources for industry, and its principal factories to Czechoslovakia. Vienna became the capital of a small sovereign state. Austria was left with a surplus of scenic beauty, in her Alps, Vienna, and the Tyrol, but with much of the poorest and the most mountainous lands of the old monarchy; only 24 per cent of her soil was arable.

Unlike most of the new states, Austria was homogeneous, with negligible national minorities. These included 98,000 Czechs and Slovaks, 43,-000 Slovenes, 44,700 Serbo-Croats, and 25,000 Magyars. The Klagenfurt Basin, with a minority of Slovenes, was voted into Austria by plebiscite in 1920, under provisions of the Treaty of St.-Germain. The efforts of the 140,000 Austrians in Voralberg in 1918 and 1919 to unite with Switzerland were frustrated by Switzerland. The Burgenland transfer occasioned some controversy with Hungary.

The Austro-Hungarian Empire. To understand post-war Austria, as well as the unsolved nationality and social problems of the Danubian peoples, it is imperative to review Austrian history.

The Hapsburg Monarchy had the opportunity in the nineteenth century of incorporating into a political and economic unit the several nationalities over which it ruled. After the Dual Compromise (*Ausgleich*) with the Hungarian landed Magnates in 1867, however, the centrifugal forces of the Austro-Hungarian Empire steadily increased at the expense of the centripetal forces. The catastrophe of the First World War gave the final impulse to a process of dissolution already well advanced. The outmoded statesmanship of the Hapsburgs, the aggressive policy of expansion at the expense of the South Slavs, and the reactionary views of the Magyar aristocracy that were constantly seeking the independence of Hungary and obstructing every progressive movement within the empire, combined to prevent the establishment of a state within which the various nationalities could live freely and prosper in a customs-free union.

The Ancient Hapsburg Monarchy. Austria had a colorful history. An outpost (*Ostmark*) of the Holy Roman Empire, it was separated from Bavaria in 976, when the history of Austria proper may be said to have commenced. Rudolph of Hapsburg, who became Emperor of the Holy Roman Empire in 1273, possessed himself of the duchy, and thereafter until 1918 the Hapsburgs ruled the Austrian lands. From 1438 to 1740 the Austrian Hapsburgs virtually without exception, were elected emperors of the loosely federated Holy Roman Empire. Austria became the great defender of Christian Europe against the Ottoman Turks. In 1526, after the deaths of the kings of Hungary and Bohemia in battle with the Turks, the nobles of these two kingdoms elected Ferdinand of Hapsburg as their king. Three years later the Turks actually besieged Vienna.

The Austrian and Spanish Hapsburgs were the valiant defenders of the Catholic faith during the Protestant Reformation, the Catholic Counter Reformation, and the Religious Wars. The Thirty Years' War was precipitated in Bohemia by patriotic Czech nobles revolting against Hapsburg absolutism, and the victorious Hapsburgs, aided by the Jesuits, almost succeeded in completely Austrianizing the Czechs during the next two hundred years. Hungary was reunited to the Crown in 1699. The War of the Spanish Succession (1702–1713) added the Spanish Netherlands, Naples, Sicily, and Milan to the Hapsburg Empire.

The wars against Napoleon exhausted Austria, but left her with the Italian states, and made her the champion of conservatism against nationalism and democracy. Metternich tried to seal Austria, which retained hegemony over the 38 German states, against every breath of liberalism and modernism. This postponed the national unification of the Germanies, a task that Austria was both unfitted for and opposed to. The Emperors, until the end, considered the state as their own personal patrimony.

The Dual Constitution. The Hungarians won their independence in 1848, but the Emperor crushed them with the aid of Croat and Russian troops. Francis Joseph ascended the throne in 1848 at the age of eighteen, and ruled for sixty-eight years, dying in 1916, never having forgotten that he was a child of the revolution and always regarding the people as a revolutionary mob. In 1859 Austria lost Lombardy to Italy. In 1864 Austria and Prussia fought Denmark over Schleswig-Holstein and then quarreled over the spoils, setting the stage for Prussia's Seven Weeks' war (1866) on Austria, which finally excluded Austria from the German Confederation and made possible Prussia's unification of Germany (1871).

In the crisis of defeat Austria was compelled to effect the *Ausgleich* with Hungary. The two peoples, German and Magyar, divided the empire between them under a common ruler, and with three joint departments of government.

In 1910, 35.58 per cent of the population in Austria was German and 60.65 per cent Slavic. In the seventeen Austrian provinces or crown lands dwelt 9,950,000 Germans, 6,436,000 Czechs-Moravians-Slovaks, 4,968,000 Poles, 3,519,000 Ruthenians, 1,253,000 Slovenians, 788,000 Serbo-Croats, 768,000 Italians, and 275,000 Rumanians. There were altogether 7,300,000 South-Slavs in Austria-Hungary and 3,300,000 in Serbia and Montenegro.

Despite some attempts at political and social reforms and the institution of universal suffrage in 1907, the unity of the state was more and more threatened by the nationalist agitation of the oppressed minorities. By annexing Bosnia and Herzegovina in 1908 Austria antagonized the Slavs within and without the empire, including Russia, the champion of Pan-

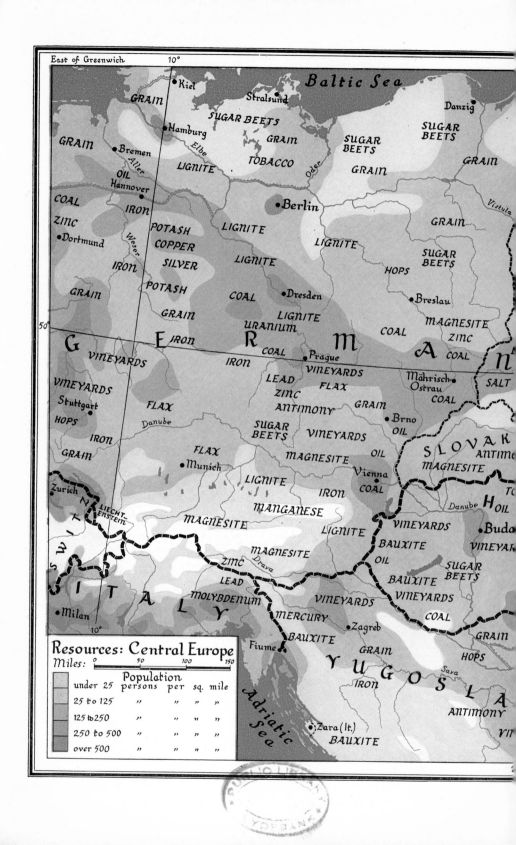

Baltic Sea

• Kiel

Stralsund

GRAIN

Danzig •

SUGAR BEETS

• Hamburg

GRAIN

SUGAR BEETS

SUGAR BEETS

GRAIN

Bremen •

GRAIN

Elbe

TOBACCO

GRAIN

GRAIN

LIGNITE

Oder

OIL

Hannover •

COAL

IRON

• Berlin

GRAIN

ZINC

POTASH

LIGNITE

• Dortmund

COPPER

LIGNITE

LIGNITE

SUGAR BEETS

SILVER

HOPS

IRON

POTASH

COAL

• Dresden

• Breslau

GRAIN

GRAIN

LIGNITE

MAGNESITE

IRON

URANIUM

COAL

ZINC

G

VINEYARDS

E IRON

COAL

R

m

A

COAL

n

IRON

• Prague

VINEYARDS

Mährisch-
Ostrau •

SALT

VINEYARDS

LEAD

FLAX

COAL

Stuttgart •

ZINC

HOPS

FLAX

ANTIMONY

GRAIN

• Brno

SLOVAK

Danube

SUGAR BEETS

OIL

ANTIM

IRON

VINEYARDS

OIL

MAGNESITE

GRAIN

FLAX

MAGNESITE

OIL

T

• Munich

Vienna •

Zurich •

LIGNITE

COAL

Danube

H OIL

LIECHT-
ENSTEIN

MANGANESE

IRON

LIGNITE

• Buda

S W **T**

MAGNESITE

VINEYARDS

MAGNESITE

BAUXITE

VINEYAR

Drava

OIL

SUGAR BEETS

ZINC

LEAD

BAUXITE

I T **A** L **Y**

MOLYBDENUM

VINEYARDS

VINEYARDS

• Milan

MERCURY

COAL

10°

BAUXITE

• Zagreb

GRAIN

Fiume •

Y

GRAIN

HOPS

Adriatic
Sea

U

G

O

S

L

A

IRON

Sava

• Zara (It.)

ANTIMONY

BAUXITE

VI

Resources: Central Europe

Miles: 0   50   100   150

	Population
under 25	persons per sq. mile
25 to 125	,, ,, ,, ,,
125 to 250	,, ,, ,, ,,
250 to 500	,, ,, ,, ,,
over 500	,, ,, ,, ,,

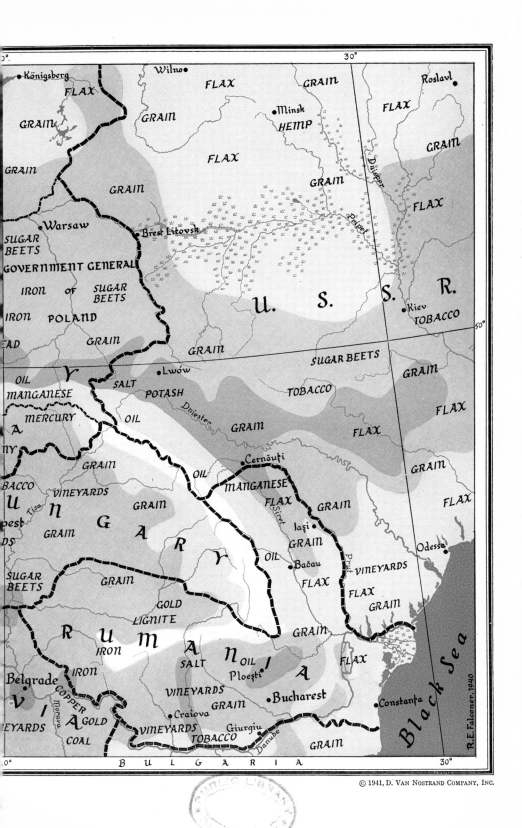

Slavism in the Balkans. At the same time Germany was compelled to support the irresponsible foreign policy of her Hapsburg partner in the Triple Alliance.

Francis Joseph held full executive power and had an absolute veto over legislation. He chose the ministers, usually from the subservient bureaucracy and aristocracy. The Chancellor was responsible solely to the Emperor. After 1907 the Reichsrat became an unruly impotent arena of racial quarrels. In 1907 it had 264 German and 246 non-German members.

After 1907 Austria-Hungary became a debtor nation, importing part of its food supply, and borrowing abroad to pay for its imports. In 1913 the unfavorable trade balance reached 449,000,000 crowns. This was largely due to the insistence of the Magyars after 1895 on high protective tariffs and on the restriction of agricultural production, which reduced the food supply at home, raised prices and rents, and contributed to the growing misery of the masses.

World War. Austria's reckless foreign policy was a central factor in the road to war on which the European powers were traveling at increasing speed after Austrian troops occupied Bosnia and Herzegovina in 1878. As the World War progressed Austria's military contributions to the Central Powers diminished, owing to divided counsels, the breakdown in the supply system, increasing food shortage, the desertion of Czechs and other nationals, to the rising national movements, the collapse of the parliamentary system, the incompetence of the aged Emperor, and intransigence of the Magyars.

The Chancellor, Count Stuergh, prorogued the Reichsrat early in the war, and for two years governed arbitrarily. Stuergh was assassinated on October 21, 1916; Francis Joseph died on November 21, and his grand-nephew Charles came to the throne. From January until May, 1917 Charles extended fruitless feelers for peace. The first war Parliament met in May, 1917. From July, 1918 the German parties in the Reichsrat consulted together regularly, and committed themselves to a peace based on Wilson's Fourteen Points. Communist efforts at revolt, then and later, were unsuccessful, although some Soldiers' and Workmen's Councils were established as early as January, 1918.

The Dissolution of the Dual Monarchy. Charles issued his famous manifesto on October 16, 1918 proclaiming the federalization of Austria, but left the Hungarian crown lands undisturbed. This belated pronouncement only confirmed the natural dissolution of the empire. The Poles, Czechs, and South-Slavs seceded on October 15, 18, and 19 respectively. Hungary declared her sovereign independence on October 22. The Emperor appointed Dr. Lammasch as Chancellor on the following day, and the latter released all civil servants from their oath of allegiance to the monarchy. Both in Austria and in the secession states the political revolution was bloodless, largely because of the loyal and efficient assumption of the national services by the Hapsburg civil servants.

The Emperor accepted Lammasch's resignation on November 11 and abdicated. The Provisional National Assembly immediately took over the government and appointed a Provisional Council, representing the three German parties, the Social Democrats, Christian Socialists, and Pan-Germans. The Provisional Assembly resolved on November 12 that " German-Austria is a democratic Republic. German-Austria is a constituent part of the German Republic."

The Provisional Assembly finished its work on February 6, 1919, and popular elections were held for the Constituent Assembly. In the campaign the Social Democrats and the Pan-Germans vigorously championed Anschluss with Germany, while the Christian Socialists opposed it. The Social Democrats polled 1,210,000 votes and secured 72 seats, the Christian Socialists 1,039,300 votes and 69 seats, and the Pan-Germans 593,000 votes and 26 seats. The Socialist Karl Seitz was elected President of the Assembly, which met for the first time on March 4, and announced that union with Germany would be effected by a treaty to be ratified by the parliaments of both countries. The Weimar Assembly had already committed itself to the union. The Austrian Constituent Assembly on April 3 passed the Hapsburg Exclusion Act.

Aftermath of War. The condition of the Austrians in 1918 and 1919 was frightful. Because of the Allied blockade, food rations were reduced to nearly one-fourth the peacetime amounts. The Inter-Allied Commission soon took control of the fuel supply, and Hoover's American Relief Administration the food supply. Allied credit of $100,000,000 was granted to Austria in the first two years after the war to prevent starvation, but even so, of 186,000 Vienna school children examined, less than 4 per cent had sufficient nourishment. In May, 1919 there were 185,000 unemployed in Austria.

The Constituent Assembly adopted the new constitution on October 1, 1920. On September 6, 1919 the Treaty of St.-Germain had been presented to the Assembly. Article 88 read: " The independence of Austria is inalienable otherwise than with the consent of the Council of the League of Nations." The Constituent Assembly signed the Treaty under formal protest, and thus repealed its former action for union with Germany. Article 80 of the Treaty of Versailles compelled Germany to respect the independence of Austria.

The Federal Republic. The Austrian Constitution of 1920 provided for a Federal republic, with a bicameral Federal Assembly, and a Ministry responsible to the popularly elected Nationalrat or Lower House. The Bundesrat formed an advisory Upper House representing the nine provinces. The members of the Nationalrat were elected by universal male suffrage under proportional representation for four-year terms. This body chose the Ministry, but not from its own members, although the ministers could participate in parliamentary debate. The two houses, meeting together as the Federal Assembly, elected the President of the republic for a four-year term. In 1929 the President became popularly elected. A Supreme Court with powers of review was established. The provincial diets were unicameral. Each elected a *Landeshauptmann*, who executed the mandates of the federal government. In the first election held under this constitution (1920) the Christian Socialists polled 1,198,780 votes and secured 82 seats, the Social Democrats, 1,037,638 votes and 62 seats, and the Pan-Germans 332,613 votes and 20 seats. Dr. Michael Hainisch was elected President.

The Social Democrats were moderate, gradualist Socialists, largely concentrated in Vienna and in other industrial centers. They had supported the war, although in 1917 a younger group began to oppose the government and the war. The Social Democrats had able leadership in Victor Adler, Karl Renner, Karl Seitz, and Otto Bauer. The Christian Socialists, founded in the 1880's by Karl Lueger, recruited their adherents chiefly among the peasants and lower middle class; they were anti-Semitic and anti-capitalistic, and feared and detested the urban Socialists. The outstanding leader among the Clericals was Monsignor Ignatz Seipel, a Jesuit, former Professor of Moral Theology, Minister of Social Welfare in the government of Emperor Charles, and a supple, astute statesman.

Financial Storm and Stress. In the first nine years after the war Austria struggled with five major financial problems (1) an adverse foreign trade balance; (2) unemployment; (3) currency disorganization; (4) unbalanced budgets; and (5) shortage of operating capital.

The war brought inflation. On July 23, 1914 there were 2,130,000,000 crowns in circulation, with a 74.6 per cent gold coverage. On October 26, 1918 there were 33,529,000,000 crowns in circulation, with only a 1.0 per cent gold coverage. In the first three years after the war governmental revenues failed to cover one-half the expenditures, owing to imperative social burdens, particularly the need of feeding large masses of people. The capital of Austrian banks rose from 800,000,000 crowns in 1918 to 84,000,000,000 in 1923. Meanwhile Austrian currency declined rapidly. On August 25, 1922 the crown reached 83,600 to the dollar, and 16,940 paper crowns equaled one gold crown.

In February, 1922 Great Britain, France, Italy, and Czechoslovakia made large loans to Austria. In the summer Chancellor Seipel visited the foreign ministers of Czechoslovakia, Germany, and Italy, and on September 6 appeared before the Council of the League of Nations to appeal for help. On October 4, 1922 the three Geneva Protocols were signed, organizing financial aid to Austria, under a Commissioner-General and a Committee of the Guaranteeing Governments, Great Britain, France, Italy, and Czecho-slovakia. The loans were to run until 1943, fiscal reforms were to be instituted, and the budget balanced. Protocol I provided that the political independence and territorial integrity of Austria were to be respected, and Austria was not to compromise its independence.

The treasury ceased printing money on November 18, 1922 and the crown was stabilized. The League of Nations sent Dr. A. R. Zimmerman as Commissioner-General of Austrian finances. January 2, 1923 the new Austrian Bank began operations. A League loan of 650,000,000 gold crowns ($130,000,000) was floated in 1923, but in 1924 there was a severe crisis due to overspeculation, and at the end of the year a new monetary unit, the schilling, was created, equal to 10,000 crowns, and with a fixed gold value. The budget was balanced for the first time in 1925.

Parties and Ministries. With the parliamentary elections of 1920 the Christian Socialists became the leading party, the Social Democrats forming the chief opposition. In the next eighteen years there were eleven Cabinets all representing a coalition of bourgeois parties, usually under a Christian Socialist Chancellor. The succession of Chancellors follows: Mayr (1920), Schober (a Pan-German, 1921), Seipel (1922), Ramek (1924), Seipel (1926), Streeruwitz (1929), Schober (1929), Vaugoin, Emter, and Buresch (1930 to 1932), Dollfuss (1932), and Schuschnigg (1934 to 1938). The last parliamentary government, the Coalition headed by Dollfuss, was established on May 30, 1932. It was opposed to Nazification of Austria and to Anschluss with Germany. Dollfuss had a bare majority of one.

The Anschluss Movement. Despite treaty prohibitions, agitation for Anschluss went on steadily in Austria and Germany until 1926. In 1920 Anschluss meetings were held in Vienna and throughout Austria by the National Democratic League and the National Democratic Party. The *Deutsche Arbeitsgemeinschaft* (German Workers' League) was organized on June 5, 1920 under the inspiration of Dr. Dinghofer to champion Anschluss. In 1921 the League held large demonstrations in Innsbruck and Salzburg. A plebiscite held in the Tyrol on April 24, 1921 resulted in a 98.6 per cent majority for Anschluss. In a plebiscite in Salzburg on May 29, 1921 95,000 out of 102,000 voters assented to union with Germany. The *Oesterreicheisch-deutsch Arbeitsgemeinschaft* (German-Austrian Workers' League) was founded on April 29, 1925 by Professor Richard Wettstein to promote Anschluss.

In March, 1924 the German Chancellor Marx and Foreign Minister Stresemann visited Austria. A convention of July 29, 1925 abolished visas between the two countries. A German People's League (*Volksbund*) was organized in Vienna in June, 1925 favoring economic union with Germany. The Social Democrats strongly advocated Anschluss in 1925, but the Christian Socialists opposed the movement. From the signing of the Locarno

Pact in November, 1925 until the death of Stresemann on October 5, 1929 the German government held aloof from the Anschluss movement although popular demonstrations continued. On October 2, 1927 75,000 Pan-Germans held an Anschluss demonstration in Vienna on the occasion of Hindenburg's eightieth birthday. Similar outbursts occurred on July 19 and 20, 1928, when the *Deutscher Sängerbund* came to Vienna for the Schubert Festival, although Seipel's government remained uninterested. The rejection of Dr. Curtiers' German-Austrian Customs Union in 1931 by the Treaty Powers was a hard blow for the Anschluss advocates.

National Socialism in Austria. The National Socialist movement originated in pre-war Austria. In 1909 Dr. Walter Riehl and Rudolph Jung organized the United German Workers' Federation which became the German Social Workers' Party in 1910, adopted a program in 1913, and changed its name to *Deutsch-Sozialistische Arbeiter Partei* (German Socialist Workers' Party) in 1916. In May, 1918 its name was again changed to *Deutsche National-sozialistische Arbeiter Partei* (German National Socialist Workers' Party), and the Swastika became its emblem. In 1918 a Sudeten branch was formed. Hitler, born in Austria, had been Pan-German, anti-Hapsburg, and pro-Prussian.

The first important interstate convention of the National Socialists was held on December 13, 1919, and the German DNSAP was founded on February 24, 1920 by Anton Drexler. Close relations were maintained between the German and Austrian groups until after the abortive Beer Hall *Putsch* in 1923. Article I of the German Nazi program called for the union of all Germans on the basis of self-determination.

In addition to the Nazis Austria had an indigenous Fascist movement led by Ernst Ruediger. Prince von Starhemberg, who organized a private *Heimwehr* army of 100,000, was Minister of Interior in the Cabinet of Vaugoin in 1930, and lived on excellent terms with Mussolini.

The Dollfuss Dictatorship. Engelbert Dollfuss called " Millimetternick," because of his height (he was barely five feet) became Chancellor in May, 1932. Dollfuss had distinguished himself as a soldier during the war, became a doctor of laws, and organized the Provincial Chamber of Agriculture in Lower Austria. A devout Catholic, he was the protégé of Monsignor Seipel. As Chancellor, Dollfuss secured the aid of Mussolini in the struggle against the Nazis. Opposition developed steadily in Parliament to Dollfuss' economic and political reforms, to the loan of $42,000,000 under the Lausanne Protocol, and to his anti-Nazi crusade.

Because of the deadlock in Parliament, President Miklas invested Dollfuss with emergency powers on March 4, 1933. The parliamentary officers resigned, and Parliament was dissolved. On March 6, the day after the German plebiscite sanctioning the Hitler regime, the Austrian Nazis met in Vienna and demanded the resignation of Dollfuss' government.

Miklas refused the Chancellor's offer to resign, and Dollfuss proceeded to establish a dictatorship with the support of the Christian Socialists, the Peasant Party, and the Fascist *Heimwehr*. The Social Democrats and the Nazis remained in vociferous opposition.

Dollfuss dissolved the Socialist militia, the *Schützbund*, on March 30, and outlawed the Communist Party on May 26. On May 13 Dr. Frank, the Bavarian Minister of Justice, spoke to 5000 Nazis in a Vienna suburb. The government ordered him to leave Austria, and Dollfuss forbade the display of all private uniforms, flags, symbols, and emblems. On June 12th the Minister of Security Emil Fey ordered all Brown Houses (Nazi head-quarters) closed and some Nazis were arrested. Members of the army and civil servants were forbidden to belong to the National Socialists.

In June, however, Nazi terrorism was renewed and on June 19 the government dissolved the armed Nazi groups who thereafter carried on their activities secretly. The Fatherland Front was established as a government-sponsored party and on September 11 Dollfuss announced that Austria would be a Christian state built on *ständische* (corporate) foundations, with authoritarian leadership. On September 21 he reorganized the government, taking over five portfolios himself. Major Emil Fey became Vice-Chancellor, and Kurt von Schuschnigg Minister of Justice.

Civil War. Dollfuss was determined to crush his two chief enemies, the Nazis and the Socialists. When Nazi terrorism broke out afresh in January, 1934 he protested to Germany and appealed to the League of Nations.

The Socialists were a tougher problem. Dollfuss had already terminated the grants voted by Parliament to the municipal government of Vienna. He now dissolved the City Council, arrested the Mayor Karl Seitz when the latter resisted, and appointed a Federal Commissioner. On the night of February 11, 1934 Dollfuss' militia raided the Schützbund's head-quarters in Linz and demanded the confiscation of its ammunition. There was a skirmish, and fighting spread to Vienna. This was the signal for a general strike, which, however, was not complete, partly owing to the fact that the government imprisoned many of the Socialist leaders. But the Socialists answered the call to arms. They barricaded themselves in the lovely municipal apartments. Major Fey sent a huge army against them, and the Socialists were bombarded until they ran out of ammunition and had to surrender. The civil war lasted three days in Vienna, and several days longer in the provinces. Thousands were killed and wounded; many fine dwellings were reduced to rubble.

Thereupon the Social Democratic Party was dissolved and the trade unions made illegal. The industrial workers never forgave the Fascists for this crime, and carried on their activities *sub rosa*. By destroying the Social Democratic Party Dollfuss alienated a large element which probably would have gladly supported the government in its fight upon the Nazis.

Only a few days before the Anschluss did Schuschnigg, Dollfuss' successor, become reconciled with the trade unionists, and then it was too late to stem the Brown (Nazi) flood.

Nazi agitation declined temporarily after the blood bath of February. On February 17 France, Italy, and Great Britain issued a joint declaration supporting Austria's independence and territorial integrity.

The Authoritarian Corporate State. On May 1, 1934 Dollfuss proclaimed the new authoritarian Constitution which had been approved on April 30 by a hastily summoned rump Nationalrat. The new political system not only received the blessings of the Church but owed a great deal to Catholic ideology and Italian precedent. The constitution provided for five councils: a Federal Chamber, Council of State, Council of Culture, Economic Council, and Council of Provinces. Legislation was to be submitted by the government to the last four Councils before being presented to the Federal Chamber, which could approve or disapprove, but not discuss or amend bills. The burgomasters of the towns were to elect the Federal President for a seven-year term from a list of three candidates proposed by the Federal Chamber. The president was to choose the Chancellor, who would not be responsible to the Federal Chamber. He would also appoint the provincial governors. The constitution was to go into effect whenever it became convenient, and in the meantime the government assumed all legislative power. This constitution had not yet come into effect in March, 1938 when Germany occupied Austria. In the meantime Austria was governed by decree.

The Nazi Putsch. Renewed Nazi bombings and riots began in May, 1934 and were climaxed by the *Putsch* of July 25 when a Nazi band seized the Chancellery and assassinated Dollfuss. Prompt action by the Austrian police thwarted the plot. Mussolini sent four divisions to the Austrian frontiers and declared his intention of preserving Austria's independence.

The Schuschnigg Dictatorship. Kurt von Schuschnigg succeeded Dollfuss as Chancellor. The son and grandson of high army officers, he was practicing law in Innsbruck when he fell under the friendly eye of the astute Seipel. Entering parliament at twenty-nine, he became Minister of Justice at thirty-four, and added the portfolio of Education the next year. Schuschnigg was a devout Catholic, something of a mystic, sincere and upright, but deficient in his judgment of men and somewhat naïve. Schuschnigg had organized the Catholic youth as well as a private clerical army. He continued the dictatorship of Dollfuss, with Starhemberg as Vice Chancellor and head of the Fatherland Front. In May, 1935 the Austrian army was incorporated into the Fatherland Front, and in October, Major Fey was dismissed, leaving his rival Starhemberg to vie for supreme power with Schuschnigg.

The friends of the Hapsburgs, who never renounced their rights to the throne, were gaining ground in 1935; even Schuschnigg was reputed to be a monarchist at heart. By June, 1935, 700 villages had conferred honorary citizenship upon the pretender, Otto, and 200 societies had made him honorary president. On July 10, 1935 the Federal Chamber approved a bill repealing the Hapsburg Exclusion Act of April 3, 1919 and empowering the government to restore " suitable parts " of the confiscated Hapsburg property.

Schuschnigg denounced the military clauses of the Treaty of St.-Germain on April 1, 1936 and decreed universal conscription. Finally in May, Starhemberg was eased out of the Cabinet, leaving Schuschnigg as virtual dictator. Baar-Baarenfels of the *Heimwehr* was made Vice Chancellor and deputy Leader of the Fatherland Front, which became the sole legal party in Austria. In spite of Schuschnigg's efforts to popularize his regime, the government met with stout opposition, particularly from the Social Democrats who were driven underground after the civil war of 1934, and from the Nazis, who, financed by Germany, became more belligerent. In July, 1936 Schuschnigg managed to secure an agreement with Germany by which Hitler promised to respect the independence of Austria and not interfere in her domestic affairs on condition that Ministers friendly to the Nazis be added to the Cabinet.

Foreign Relations. Austria after 1918 gradually regularized her relations with her neighbors. She was admitted to the League of Nations in 1920, and in December, 1921 Chancellor Schober signed the political and economic Treaty of Lana with Czechoslovakia. In 1924 commercial treaties were made with France, Germany, and Czechoslovakia, and within a year Austria had concluded agreements with twenty-three states. On the heels of the abortive Customs Union with Germany in 1931, André Tardieu presented in February, 1932 a plan for an international police force. Nothing came of this and Mussolini countered in 1933 with a plan for bilateral treaties. In May, 1934 Italy and Austria signed political and economic protocols at Rome which facilitated reciprocal commercial relations. Mussolini sponsored Dollfuss' Fascist state and, it is said, partly instigated the attack on the Socialists of February, 1934. In the Ethiopian War Austria remained loyal to Italy and declined to participate in sanctions.

Economic Development. About one-third of Austria's population after the war derived its living from industry, one-third from agriculture and forestry, and one-eighth from commerce. There was a large number of unemployed. By 1925 Austrian agricultural production had fallen below the level of 1915, and her industrial output was probably not above 80 per cent of the pre-war total. Austria had to import wheat from Hungary and coal from Czechoslovakia. She produced enough potatoes for domestic consumption, but only 34 per cent of her wheat, 80 per cent of her rye, and

50 per cent of her meat. Sufficient hydroelectric power was developed to provide exports to Germany.

Austria had an unfavorable balance of trade of 1,106,000,000 schillings in 1920, 2,805,000,000 in 1926, and 301,700,000 in 1935. In 1925, 38.8 per cent of her exports went to other Danubian states, whence came 44.1 per cent of Austrian imports. In 1937 when German economic pressure became operative, Austrian exports to the Reich amounted to 180,000,000 schillings and imports 233,000,000 schillings. In the same year exports to her four Danubian neighbors, totaled 333,000,000 schillings and imports 393,000,000 schillings.

Traffic on the Danube declined greatly after the war. Vienna derived some income from bank services for the Danubian countries, and the tourist traffic brought much needed foreign exchange — 647,000 visitors came in 1923 and 946,000 in the first ten months of 1924 — but these did not materially reduce Austria's unfavorable trade and financial balances.

The peasants of Austria owned 89.1 per cent of the cultivable land, but the forests belonged to the great landowners, to the state, or to local governments. The peasants were well organized in producers' and consumers' cooperatives, and credit societies were numerous. Owing to Socialist influence in the government, an eight-hour day and the forty-eight-hour week in industry were established by law in December, 1919. Later, unemployment insurance was added. Austria was left, however, with a top-heavy bureaucracy and with a superfluity of professional men. Generally speaking, the living standards of the working class improved after the war as compared to Imperial days, although that of the middle class had declined. But unemployment left a heavy toll of misery: there were 225,000 idle in the first quarter of 1929 and 362,000 three years later.

Financial Crisis. After a few years of prosperity in the middle 'twenties hard times returned to Austria in 1929. It was necessary for the powers to loan her $62,000,000 in 1930, to be used for public works, railroads, and as aids to agriculture. The federal budget from 1927 carried a deficit of over 100,000,000 schillings. When Austria's largest bank, the Kreditanstalt, failed in May, 1931 the government decided to guarantee a large part of its liabilities. The Bank of England extended a temporary credit of 150,-000,000 schillings, and the Bank for International Settlements also provided a loan. On July 15, 1932, by the Lausanne Protocol, a maximum loan of 300,000,000 schillings was granted by the signatory powers.

Socialist Government in Vienna. Vienna went overwhelmingly Social Democrat after the war. In the March, 1919 elections the Socialists won 100 out of 165 seats in the City Council. Part of the province of Lower Austria, the municipality's powers were limited by the Provincial Diet. On January 1, 1922 Vienna became a separate province and thereafter contributed 70 per cent of the Austrian government's income.

Under the spur of socialist leadership, the Municipal government of Vienna launched a great housing program in 1923, at first as an emergency measure to meet the housing crisis, and then as a permanent social policy directed by Hugo Breitner, Anton Weber, and Professor Julius Tandler. Housing was regarded as a public utility and as a social service comparable to schools and parks. The housing program was financed principally from a dwelling construction tax, with the deficit drawn from general revenues. Rents were low and were based on the cost of administration and upkeep only. So well was Vienna governed that in 1923 it had a surplus of 42,-000,000 gold crowns in the treasury.

By the end of 1933 over 58,000 dwellings, mostly huge apartment buildings, had been erected at a cost of $155,000,000 harboring 250,000 persons, or one-eighth of the city's population. The largest unit was the Karl Marx Hof, with 1382 apartments, containing 5000 people. Many buildings had mothers' clinics, wading pools, theaters, and gardens, and some had community laundries and kitchens. The city also loaned money to cooperative associations to build suburban garden homes.

The municipality acquired control of the bus and trolley lines, the water and lighting systems, and established a municipal brewery, bakery, ice plant, and crematorium. These far-reaching innovations irked the rest of the country, and the Social Democrats whose strength resided chiefly in Vienna recruited, in self-protection, the *Schützbund*, which numbered 90,000 trained men in 1931.

Cultural Life. Austrian *Gemütlichkeit* was shattered by the war and its aftermath. Vienna, the capital of a great empire, became a shadow of its former self. The Imperial palaces were turned into museums: where caparisoned footmen formerly trod, now the proletariat gazed in wonder. The gayety of the Viennese was dimmed by their poverty and hardships; their love of music and dancing, their coffee house and café life, were not as lustrous as of yore. Few Viennese could afford expensive entertainment. Tourists, however, flocked to Vienna in great numbers until the world depression. The dance halls, the theaters, and cafés resounded to the tread of gay Americans, Britons, Germans, and others. The luster of Vienna was dimmed, but not extinguished. It was only after the Nazi occupation of Austria that the city's laughter became inaudible, the tourists ceased to come, and the once-brilliant capital was reduced to the insignificant status of a provincial city.

Literature and Music. Under the republic the creative arts flourished. Talented musicians composed famous works and writers of genius created plays, novels, and poems whose fame spread beyond the borders of Austria. The leading post-war Austrian composer was Arnold Schönberg (1874–   ), who introduced a new system of melody construction which divides the scale into twelve tones, none of which is more important than the other. The absence of tonality which results is known as *atonality*. Typical of Schönberg's atonal works are the dramatic pieces, *Die glück-liche Hand* (*The Lucky Hand*) and *Pierrot Lunaire*, and various composi-tions for piano and orchestra. Schönberg called his music " expression-istic " and like expressionistic painting and drama, it is difficult to understand. Nevertheless Schönberg created a school, of whom the most important were Alban Berg (1885–1935), author of the successful opera *Wozzeck* (1922), Anton Webern (1893–   ), composer of many songs and instrumental compositions, and Egon Wellesz (1885–   ) who has written several operas on Greek subjects and much chamber music. Ernest Krenek (1900–   ), born in Vienna of Czech parents, is a disciple of Hindemith. Krenek achieved international fame with his jazz opera *Jonny spielt auf* (*Johnny Strikes Up*).

Until recent years the great annual festival at Salzburg formed a su-preme attraction for music lovers from all parts of the world. With the Anschluss this event has lost its international importance.

Literature. Perhaps the most illustrious name in post-war Austrian litera-ture is that of Arthur Schnitzler (1862–1931). The novels and plays of Schnitzler represent the very spirit of an Austria which has endured untold suffering but which refuses to believe that life is not worth living. Most of Schnitzler's work centers around the pursuit of woman by man; it is brilliant, sophisticated comedy predicated on the philosophy that " No matter how great or how grave our actions seem, we do nothing on this earth which is not play. We are forever playing, and the wise man is he who realizes that it is all a game." A doctor by profession, Schnitzler's analysis of human character was to some extent influenced by Freud. Best known, perhaps, of Schnitzler's later works are *Fräulein Elsie* (1924), *Casanova's Return* (1918), and *Flight into Darkness* (1931).

Hugo von Hofmannsthal (1874–1929) was the last great Austrian poet. The lyrics and dramas of Hofmannsthal hearken to the pre-war world of symbolism and neo-romanticism. When the Austrian revolution came, he remained in his ivory tower. The leader of expressionist writers in Austria was Franz Werfel (1890–   ), poet, playwright and novelist, best known in the United States for his novel, *The Forty Days of Musa Dagh*. Stefan Zweig (1881–   ) is a pleasing biographer and literary critic, best known perhaps for his *Marie Antoinette* and *Erasmus*, while Arnold Zweig (1887–   ) is famous for his novels, *The Case of Sergeant Grischa* and *Education at Verdun*.

Science. Vienna after the war was a great medical center, the clinics of the University of Vienna attracting students from all over the world. Sig-mund Freud (1856–1940) created a system of psychology based on psy-choanalysis which has had an incalculable influence. Although criticized for its lack of scientific validity, Freudianism has offered the troubled generation which emerged from the war new keys to the understanding of human behavior. It is a commentary on the fate that overtook Austria after the Anschluss that Freud had to be ransomed from the Nazis at a huge sum; he went to England, where he died.

Collapse of Austria. The Austro-German agreement of July, 1936 was but an armistice. Mussolini became cool toward Austria in 1937, as the Rome-Berlin axis acquired substance. The monarchist movement acquired increasing popularity, and although Schuschnigg seemed to favor such a solution of the Austrian problem, he did nothing about it, knowing that the succession states abhorred the Hapsburgs, and the Allied Powers frowned upon them. Nor could Schuschnigg force himself to enlist the aid of the workers and the Social Democrats against the Nazi peril until it was too late.

As Nazi propaganda in Austria was threatening to precipitate civil war, Schuschnigg was forced to submit to a humiliating and brutal interview with Hitler at Berchtesgaden on February 12, 1938, where apparently an ultimatum was handed to him. On February 16 Schuschnigg reorganized his Cabinet according to Hitler's demands, giving the three strategic posts of Justice, Foreign Affairs, and the Interior to Nazis. When the new Minister of the Interior, Dr. Arthur Seyss-Inquart, returned from a visit to Hitler on Feburary 18, Nazis were permitted to join the Fatherland Front and a general political amnesty was decreed.

Yet Schuschnigg had one trump card to play before succumbing to German demands for Anschluss. He announced a plebiscite on March 9 for Sunday, the 13th, at which all persons over twenty-four were to vote on the question of whether Austria was to be independent or not. This move infuriated Hitler who threatened on March 11 to order an attack on Austria unless the plebiscite was called off. Rather than cause bloodshed Schuschnigg, after a pathetic farewell broadcast, resigned on March 12 and was succeeded by the traitorous Seyss-Inquart. It has been estimated that perhaps 65 per cent of the Austrians would have supported Schuschnigg in preference to forcible union with Nazi Germany. On Seyss-Inquart's "invitation," German troops, followed by Hitler, made a triumphal entry into Austria. President Miklas resigned on March 13. Schuschnigg had an opportunity to escape but preferred to stay and be interned by the Germans.

Seyss-Inquart became Governor of Austria, which was renamed Ostmark. Italy acquiesced to the Anschluss and the other powers would or could do nothing. The Austrian Catholic Church put up some resistance. The Jews were mercilessly tortured by enraged Nazis; their property was confiscated; thousands were killed or sent to concentration camps. Austria was rapidly absorbed into the Third Reich and on April 10 the usual Hitlerian plebiscite was held throughout Greater Germany to sanction the

rape of Austria. Less than one per cent of the voters dared to give a negative answer. Germany confiscated the 240,000,000 schillings of the Austrian National Bank. Unemployment declined at once as Austrians were
placed in Germany's war industries. But the tax burden was soon 50 per
cent higher than under the Austrian republic.

Joseph Buerckel was named Procurator for the Liquidation of Austria
and Reich Commissar for the Reunion of Austria with Germany. He had
seven *Gaus*, or districts, in his jurisdiction. In April, 1940 the Nazi leader
in each district took the title *Gauleiter* and Procurator, combining party
and state functions. Each is directly responsible to Hitler. Buerckel was
chosen *Gauleiter* and Procurator for Vienna.

The political arrangements of the Danubian states are undergoing radical change as Germany spreads its wings, but the fundamental nationality
and social problems of the Danubian peoples remain unsolved. The Austrian Nazis were bitterly disillusioned after the Anschluss. They expected
Austria to retain its independence under a Nazi regime. Instead the
Germans took control of the government, coordinated Austrian industry
and agriculture to suit their own purposes and reduced the once proud
nation to the status of a province in the great German Empire.

SELECTED BIBLIOGRAPHY

Ball, M. Margaret, *Post-War German-Austrian Relations: The Anschluss Movement*, Palo Alto, Cal.: Stanford Univ. Press, 1937. A scholarly, comprehensive and detailed treatment.

Bertaux, Félix, *A Panorama of Literature*, New York: Whittlesey House, 1935.

Fodor, M. W., *South of Hitler*, Boston: Houghton Mifflin, 1937. Vivid sketches of personalities and movements by the Vienna correspondent of the Manchester *Guardian*, himself a liberal Magyar.

Fuchs, Martin, *Showdown in Vienna*, New York: Putnam, 1939. A loosely organized but lively account of the last days of the republic by a former personal aide of Schuschnigg, himself a Legitimist.

Gedye, G. E. R., *Betrayal in Central Europe*, New York: Scribner, 1939. Perhaps the best book on the last years of Austrian independence.

Graham, M. W., *New Governments of Central Europe*, New York: Holt, 1926. Excellent historical summary of the Hapsburg monarchy and the establishment of the republic, with a description of the new constitution and the political parties.

Hardy, C. O., *The Housing Program of the City of Vienna*. An objective treatment, well illustrated.

Jaszi, Oscar, *The Dissolution of the Habsburg Monarchy*, Chicago: Univ. of Chicago Press, 1929. Brilliant historical and sociological analysis of the Hapsburg monarchy.

Layton, W. T. and Rist, Charles, *The Economic Situation of Austria*, Geneva: League of Nations Reports, 1925. An indispensable, comprehensive document by the official investigators appointed by the League of Nations.

Lengyel, Emil, *The Danube*, New York: Random House, 1939. A readable account of the historical role of the Danube River with emphasis on post-war Austria. Lengyel was the Vienna correspondent of the New York *Times*.

Macartney, C. A., *The Social Revolution in Austria*, Cambridge: Cambridge Univ. Press, 1926. Scholarly analysis of social democracy and its limitations and mistakes in the Austrian republic.

Pasvolsky, Leo, *Economic Nationalism of the Danubian States*, New York: Macmillan, 1928. Indispensable study of the economic aspects of life and politics in the Danube Basin.

Redlich, Joseph, *Austrian War Government*, New Haven: Yale Univ. Press, 1929. A definitive study by Austria's greatest modern historian.

Royal Institute of International Affairs, *South-Eastern Europe*, Oxford: Oxford Univ. Press, 1939. A competent collaborative study dealing with political, economic, and social problems.

Schuschnigg, Kurt von, *My Austria*, New York: Knopf, 1938. The philosophical, poignant autobiography of the last Chancellor of Austria. It reveals both Schuschnigg's strength and weakness as the head of a state.

Steed, Henry Wickham, *The Hapsburg Monarchy*, London: Constable, 4th ed., 1919. An excellent description of the monarchy by the long-time correspondent of the London *Times*. The chapter on the Jews needs to be read with caution.

CHAPTER X

Switzerland

" LET THOSE WHO DESPISE THE CAPACITY OF THE SWISS, TELL US BY WHAT WONDERFUL POLICY, OR BY WHAT HAPPY CONCILIATION OF INTERESTS, IT IS BROUGHT TO PASS, THAT IN A BODY MADE UP OF DIFFERENT COMMUNITIES AND DIFFERENT RELIGIONS, THERE SHOULD BE NO CIVIL COMMOTIONS, THOUGH THE PEOPLE ARE SO WARLIKE, THAT TO NOMINATE AND RAISE AN ARMY IS THE SAME."

— DR. JOHNSON

Historic Origins. Switzerland is a tiny country that has been a testing ground for those profound problems in human relations which stem from differences in language and religion. The Swiss have gradually resolved these in an enlightening and pragmatic fashion.

Independence and democracy began for the Swiss in 1291 when the freemen of the three forest cantons of Uri, Schwyz, and Unterwalden bound themselves into an " Everlasting League." This was a loose confederation of practically sovereign communities. By 1513 it had thirteen members. Until the end of the eighteenth century Switzerland was a preponderately Germanic country. On the eve of the French Revolution, six of the cantons were direct democracies, four were aristocracies and three oligarchies.

In 1798 and 1803 the French revolutionaries and Napoleon gave the Swiss their first written constitutions. The reactionary federal constitution of 1814–1815 which restored the old aristocratic and oligarchic cantonal governments fostered dissatisfaction among the people and in 1830 popular pressure resulted in the peaceful transformation of these illiberal governments into liberal democracies. Out of the brief civil war of 1847 came the democratic constitution of 1848, which, with some partial revisions and a total revision in 1874, remains the fundamental law of the Swiss republic.

The Country. Switzerland has an area of 15,944 square miles, or one-half that of Maine, inhabited by about 4,200,000 people. It is composed of twenty-two cantons (three of which have half-cantons) and 3087 communes.

The scenic grandeur of Switzerland is proverbial. The country is profusely dotted with snow-capped peaks. The lofty Alps, with fifty peaks of 15,000 feet or more, cover 61 per cent of Switzerland's total area; the rugged Jura mountains, rising to altitudes of 4500–5200 feet comprise 12 per cent, and the Midlands 27 per cent. The Rhine, Danube,

This chapter by Huntley Dupre, Professor of History, University of Kentucky.

Rhone, and Po rivers all rise in Switzerland or receive affluents rising there. Nearly three-fourths of Switzerland serves as a watershed for the deep-channeled Rhine. Forty per cent of Switzerland's frontiers are contiguous with Italy, 30 per cent with France, and 30 per cent with Greater Germany.

One-fourth of Swiss territory is unfit for cultivation. Geneva and Berne each have over 100,000 people, Basle over 150,000 and Zurich 313,-000. Berne and Zurich are the largest cantons, with populations of 609,249 and 619,044 respectively; the half-canton of Appenzell Interior with 13,-988 inhabitants is the smallest. Switzerland is divided into small physiographic units which preserve a large measure of local autonomy and account for the federal system of government. All of the cantons and cities are highly individualistic and retain colorful regional customs.

In addition to guarantees of the surrounding European states and its own strong natural defenses, Switzerland's greatest security lies in its possession of the strategic transalpine routes and passes which no neighboring power would want to see in the hands of a possible enemy.

Switzerland has long been the refuge of exiled scholars and scientists and malcontents from other countries. Geneva is the meeting place of more international meetings than any other city in the world. It is also the home of such international organizations as the Postal Union, International Red Cross, the Y.W.C.A. and Y.M.C.A., and the moribund League of Nations.

A Tri-lingual State. Switzerland has two major religions and three major and one minor language. Religious differences have been the cause of prolonged discord, and constitute the greatest competitive loyalties within the country. Fortunately linguistic and religious affiliations criss-cross, thus tending to reduce the friction caused by each. By the Constitution of 1848 the three main languages of Switzerland — German, French, and Italian — are the national languages of the Union. Owing to excellent language instruction in the schools, most of the Swiss have a mother tongue, and a second and third (not " foreign ") language.

The distribution on the basis of mother tongues was given by the census of 1930 as follows: German, 2,924,314 (71.9 per cent); French 831,100 (20.4 per cent); Italian, 242,034 (6.0 per cent); Romanche, 44,204 (1.1 per cent). German is the only official language in fourteen cantons, French in three, and Italian in one. In the Italian and German cantons the official language is the mother tongue of over 90 per cent of the population. In some cantons there are two official languages, and in the Grisons German, Italian, and Romanche are all official languages. In the four mixed cantons the distribution varies greatly.

Religious Pluralism. The 1930 census showed that 57 per cent of the population (2,230,536) adhered to the Protestant faith and 41 per cent (1,666,-

317) to the Catholic. Protestants outnumber the Catholics in twelve cantons, of which nine are German- and three French-speaking cantons. The Catholics outnumber the Protestants in ten, including seven German, two French, and one Italian cantons. There are strong religious minorities, particularly Catholic, in many cantons. The Catholics are organized politically and are generally pillars of conservatism. Religious tolerance has developed slowly, and is guaranteed by the Constitution of 1848 and the revision of 1874. The First World War caused great tension between German- and French-speaking citizens, but persistent efforts were made to alleviate the crisis. The New Helvetic Society, founded in 1914, did much to bridge the gap. The famous address, " Our Swiss Standpoint," distinguishing between neighbors and brothers, delivered by the poet Carl Spitteler before the New Helvetic Society in Zurich on December 14, 1914 did more than everything else perhaps to restore Swiss unity. The famous Wettstein Motion passed in the Council of States on June 17, 1915 was designed to restore and promote federal unity. Switzerland emerged from the war with greater solidarity than ever. The rise of the totalitarian states on her borders has strengthened the desire for continued unity and independence.

The Swiss State. The large amount of cantonal and local autonomy enjoyed by the Swiss has contributed greatly to their ability to live alongside each other in mutual toleration, despite differences of language and religion.

Switzerland attained political democracy earlier than any other European peoples, and her democratic institutions are the " products of a long period of peaceful evolution, tested by experience, justified by results." [1] Switzerland has a bicameral legislature, each branch of which has equal legislative powers. The Council of States consists of 2 members from every canton, while the National Council is popularly elected, its members being chosen for four-year terms by proportional representation by all men over twenty. The two houses, meeting together as the Federal Assembly, elect the Federal Tribunal and the 7 members of the Federal Council which forms the executive branch of the government. Each councillor heads an administrative federal department. The members of the Council do not sit in the legislature. The chairman, called the President of the Swiss Confederation, changes annually. The President for 1940 was Dr. Marcel Pilet-Golaz, the youngest member of the Federal Council, representative from the small canton of Vaud. Switzerland is remarkably free of governmental corruption and the spoils system is nonexistent. [2]

The initiative and referendum are prominent features of Swiss democracy, the former serving as an instrument of progress, the latter as a conservative brake. The referendum originated in the 1830's and the initiative was first introduced in Vaud in 1845. The federal referendum was adopted in 1874, the initiative followed in 1891, and in 1921 the optional referendum on treaties was introduced.

Switzerland has long had universal, compulsory military service. Infantry training of 153 days is provided. The service is called the "Recruit School," and until recently the examinations for entry were decidedly scholastic in character. There are only a small number of professional officers, and from 1871 to 1914 the army was without a commander-in-chief. During the First World War the Swiss army was kept wholly or partially mobilized for over fifty months, at a total cost of more than a billion francs. In this emergency the Federal Assembly reluctantly granted the Federal Council almost dictatorial powers.

Local Democracy. The Swiss pay more attention to cantonal and municipal government than to federal government. Political parties develop around local issues, and are organized on a cantonal basis. Loyal to the federal union, the Swiss insist on freedom for the canton. Each canton has its self-drafted constitution. Where representative democracy prevails, these provide for a unicameral legislature, called a Great Council. Executive power is vested in a Council of State. Five small cantons still practice direct democracy. The annual meetings of the citizens in these regions, usually held in April or May in a great meadow adjacent to the cantonal capital, are effective demonstrations of the simplest form of political democracy, rich, colorful and dramatic. Some municipalities still hold town meetings. More citizens usually participate in these assemblies than in federal elections, although, for example, the elections for the National Council in 1919 attracted 80.4 per cent of the qualified voters and the capital levy referendum of 1922 brought out 85.3 per cent of the electorate to the polls.

Political Parties. The Radicals (or Independent Democrats) dominated Swiss politics in the last half of the nineteenth century, with the Catholic Conservatives in opposition. The Radicals advocated a strong federation and liberal, democratic institutions. Today the Radicals favor state intervention for the protection of society against the abuses of industrialism, although their present program lacks definiteness. The Catholic Conservatives, who have steadily opposed a strong federation, believe in private property but are anti-capitalistic and anti-socialistic. The Social Democratic is the strongest of the remaining parties. Since 1919, however, no single party has commanded a majority in the National Council. The composition of the council after the elections of October 29, 1939 was as follows: Radicals, 50; Social Democrats, 45; Catholic Conservatives, 44; Peasant Party, 21; Liberal Conservatives, 6; Independents, 9; others, 12. The Council of States had 18 Catholic Conservatives, 15 Radicals, 3 members of the Peasant Party, 3 Social Democrats, and 2 Liberal Conservatives.

The program of the Social Democrats represents a combination of political liberalism and Marxian economics. They advocate economic planning, achieved by a democratic, anti-Fascist, and anti-capitalistic labor front. In recent years they have pursued a distinctly nationalist policy, attracting many civil servants, public officers, and Protestant clergymen to their ranks. The Social Democrats have a strong organization and are closely affiliated with the powerful trade unions. The party sponsors a great variety of educational, sports, musical, dramatic, and youth societies, and conducts summer courses to train party workers. Some of the other parties sponsor similar activities. The Communists polled less than 1.5 per cent of the total vote in 1928; two-thirds of its strength was derived from Zurich. The Peasant Party represents agrarian interests and is strongly opposed to the Social Democrats. In fact, virtually all parties regard the Social Democrats as their chief opponents.

The Civil Service. The Swiss civil service is very competent. In 1920 there were 74,398 federal employees, of whom 39,410 were in the state railway services. In the same year the cantons and municipalities employed 77,715 civil servants, of whom 35.6 per cent were schoolteachers. The federal and local services account for 8.3 per cent of the total gainfully employed. By 1929 nearly 90 per cent of the civil servants were members of labor unions. Many sit in the cantonal legislatures or in the National Council. In the Grand Council of Basle-Stadt, for instance, 44 out of 130 members were federal or local civil servants. The Public Officials Act of June 30, 1927 regulates the state services and provides for sickness, accident, and death benefits for government employees. Article 23 of the Federal Law forbids them to strike.

The Situation in 1918. At the close of the First World War there was considerable suffering, owing to the shortage of coal and food, the stoppage of the tourist traffic, and the rise in prices. The workers presented an eleven point program to the Federal Council in July, 1918 and when these were not met launched strikes in Zurich and Berne that led to a general strike on November 11, in the course of which bloody clashes between strikers and troops occurred. In Zurich some civil servants participated in the fracas. The government issued an ultimatum that quickly terminated the strike but this brief labor revolt helped to speed the introduction of proportional representation and the forty-eight-hour week in 1919.

Subventions are granted to the cantons totaling one-sixth of all federal expenditures. The cantons receive the entire net profit from the alcohol monopoly, the management of which is in federal hands. One-tenth of this income must be used for combatting alcoholism. An effort in 1929 to license the widespread home production of distilled liquors from fruits, roots, berries, and herbs was defeated by referendum, but in the following year ingenious legislation was approved by which the government buys all such liquor produced for sale. The Social Democrats have proposed several important measures since the war which were subsequently turned down by the voters, including a direct federal tax (1918), a capital levy bill (1922) and a referendum on the *initiative de crise*, a far-reaching proposal for economic and financial reconstruction (1935).

Debt and Defense. In 1938 the national debt, rising steadily because of defense expenditures necessitated by the external crisis, reached 1,529,000,-000 francs. In 1939 the army was reorganized and the military training age reduced to nineteen. On November 1, 1939 the Swiss army consisted of 480,000 actives and 100,000 trained reserves. A constitutional amendment was passed on June 4, 1939 permitting additional taxes for national defense and public works totaling 330,000,000 francs, of which approximately 171,000,000 francs were allocated for defense.

Herr Gustloff, the leader of the German Nazis, was assassinated on February 4, 1936, and on February 18 the Federal Council prohibited all German Nazi organizations.

Foreign Policy. The Great Powers, by an Act of November 20, 1815, made the neutrality of Switzerland an essential part of the international law of Europe. The Swiss Diet had already adhered to this principle on May 27, 1815. In May, 1848 the Swiss reaffirmed this policy. After the First World War, the National Council and the Council of States voted to join the League of Nations. The people affirmed this move on May 16, 1920. Article 435 of the Treaty of Versailles and Article 21 of the Covenant of the League emphasized the neutrality of Switzerland, which was to be exempt from participating in military sanctions.

There was some inconsistency between League membership and traditional Swiss neutrality, particularly as long as the defeated powers were outside the League. Switzerland therefore welcomed the entry of Austria in 1920 and Germany in 1926, and greatly deplored the subsequent withdrawals of Germany and Italy. Switzerland opposed League efforts to enforce peace through collective action. Indeed, as Professor Rappard points out, neutrality and collective security are, for Switzerland, mutually exclusive. He describes the present Swiss policy vividly: " For Switzerland, to resort to a . . . modern metaphor, neutrality is the parachute which she will not abandon until international flying becomes safer." [3] On May 14, 1938 the Council of the League of Nations, complying with a Swiss request, exempted Switzerland from participating in economic sanctions. Since Hitler's invasion of Poland in September, 1939 and subsequent German conquests, Switzerland has naturally felt uneasy concerning her safety.

The Swiss Economy. The economy of Switzerland is greatly dependent upon the world at large. With its multitudinous scenic attractions Switzerland draws the heaviest and most profitable tourist trade in Europe; 43,000

Swiss are normally employed in the hotel industry whose gross receipts normally exceed $50,000,000 a year. The depression has had a catastrophic effect on this lucrative business, which has fallen from 500,000,000 to less than 200,000,000 francs, and public subventions are necessary to keep many resorts open.

Foreign trade statistics further demonstrate Switzerland's dependence on the outside world. Before the depression, Switzerland ranked third among European nations in per capita foreign trade. Since then it has risen to first place. In 1929 the total Swiss foreign trade was $917,000,000 or $224 per capita; in 1934 this figure had fallen to $432,000,000, or $105 per capita. Switzerland imports food, textiles, coal, iron, and chemicals, and exports chiefly cotton and silk manufactures, clocks, and dairy products. Switzerland has been a high tariff country since 1884.

In 1930 21.7 per cent of the population was engaged in agriculture, 44.6 per cent in industry, 9.8 per cent in the building trades, 4.8 per cent in hotel services, 5.3 per cent in the professions and civil services, and 2.2 per cent in hospitals and schools.

Industry. Industry is conducted largely in small plants, using highly skilled workers. A considerable proportion of Swiss handicrafts are still produced in the home, and there are some complaints of " sweating," low wages, and child labor in home industries.

Between 1913 and 1928 the real wages of skilled workers rose by about 27 per cent, and of unskilled workers by 25 per cent. The price index in 1924 was 100, in 1922 it had soared to 222, but declined to 126 in 1935. The federal debt soared from an index figure of 100 in 1919 to 319 in 1935. Since the depression the federal government has intervened extensively in business through subsidies to certain industries, has stimulated purchasing power through public works, and protected domestic producers by means of import quotas.

Agriculture. Nearly one-fourth of the land is unproductive, and one-half is in pasture and forest. Livestock and dairying account for three-fourths of the total agricultural production. Small holdings and intensive cultivation are the rule. The " great farmers," who own above seventy-five acres, possess altogether but 3 per cent of the total farm acreage; the " middle farmers," with holdings between twelve and seventy-five acres, control 37 per cent, and the " small farmers," who till less than twelve acres, account for 60 per cent. As already noted, the farmers are organized in the Peasant Party, whose affiliate, the Peasants' Union, issues valuable agricultural reports that are widely distributed. The farmers are strongly represented in numerous consumers' and producers' cooperative societies. The Swiss Union of Consumers' Societies is a federation of 500 organizations with 360,000 members divided among 1800 locals in 900 communes. These cooperatives have an annual turnover of 330,000,000 francs.

The Catholic Concordia Societies include 88 organizations with 8000 members and 180 depots. There are some independent cooperatives. The Dairy Cooperatives, federated in 1907, have 3500 members.

Wealth and Savings. Switzerland has the highest per capita wealth in the world, although it is not a land of great resources, and most people live simply and frugally. In 1918 there were 2,817,795 savings-bank deposit books in Switzerland, which meant that 72.9 per cent of the population had savings accounts.

Education. The Swiss are among the most literate of peoples. This is evident not only in the caliber of the public schools and in the great respect for education, but in the multitude of voluntary educational and cultural activities. There are six universities and one federal institution of higher learning, the Polytechnicum of Zurich. The Graduate Institute for International Studies in Geneva opened its doors in 1927 with a distinguished international faculty.

The caliber of Swiss teachers is unusually fine and the profession is endowed with great prestige. Sixty per cent of the teachers in the primary schools and 85 per cent in the secondary schools are men. There are no prejudices against married women, and in the rural parts of Berne canton 600 out of 2800 teachers are married couples. Continuation schools, adult education, and People's Universities are widespread in Switzerland. The most successful People's University is located in Zurich. Many cities have People's Houses or communal centers equipped with libraries and with facilities for lectures, dramas, and concerts.

Cultural Activities. There are numerous workers' theaters in the towns, and dramatic presentations form a part of nearly every organization's program. Performances are frequently given in the open air. The most interesting, perhaps, of Swiss dramatic festivals is that sponsored by the Wine-Growers of Vevey every twenty or twenty-five years. The last one was held in 1927. This magnificent spectacle is a " medley of poetry, of music, and of color. It is a hymn to labor and to peace." [4] Selzach, a village of 1200 in the Catholic canton of Solothurn, stages a devout and moving Passion Play.

The number of sports, nature, bicycle, hiking, and shooting societies are legion, although the Swiss are not addicted to competitive sports, and not a single stadium can be found in the country.

Singing societies and other musical groups are common. All Social Democratic locals have musical societies. National singing festivals are held every three or four years. One hundred and fifty singing societies participated in the Lausanne festival in 1928, with 12,610 singers in competition. An organized effort is made to collect and preserve folk songs and dialects. Eight volumes of the *Schweizerische Idiotikon,* a great dialect dictionary, have already appeared.

With one paper per 9,908 persons, Switzerland has probably the greatest newspaper " density " in the world, although the average circulation is low. Of the approximately 1000 publications, 350 are devoted to politics. Four dailies have an international reputation: the *Bern Bund*, the *Neue Zürcher Zeitung*, the *Gazette de Lausanne*, and *Journal de Genève*. The Social Democratic *Rote Revue* and the Radical monthly, *Politische Rundschau*, exert powerful influences on the intelligentsia.

Social Life. Swiss family life is noted for its stability and integrity, yet the divorce rate is second only to that of the United States. In 1924 Switzerland had one divorce for every 11.3 marriages, the greatest incidence appearing among the poorer classes and being largely due to economic causes.

The Protestant Blue Cross League and the Swiss League of Catholic Abstainers advocate temperance but not prohibition. The New Helvetic Society is a national forum for the discussion of political questions. It publishes valuable studies by outstanding scholars and political leaders, including the yearbook, *Die Schweisz*, and holds two or three assemblies annually. Switzerland has six libraries with from 270,000 to 650,000 volumes.

Swiss Literature. The Swiss have made important contributions to recent historiography, a field in which they excel. Eduard Fueter is among the greatest of living historians; Alfred Stern has written the outstanding political history of Europe from 1815 to 1870; Eduard His is the author of the best history of Swiss public law. Carl Spitteler (1845–1924), winner of the Nobel Prize in 1924, is Switzerland's outstanding post-war literary figure. Romain Rolland has called him the greatest German epic poet since Goethe. Francesco Chiesa is an important poet, writing in Italian.

Art. Barthélemy Nenn (1815–1893) was a great Swiss painter, and his pupil Ferdinand Hodler (1853–1918) is probably the most impressive artist Switzerland has produced. The country is rich in carvers of wood, stone, and metal. Some of these do exquisite work.

Summary

The Swiss lead simple, democratic, creative lives in their narrow valleys. They have learned to harmonize their deep linguistic, religious, and political differences. As one authority has remarked: " The Swiss are fond of likening their country to a rambling old châlet of twenty-two rooms, all strikingly peculiar but all under the same broad and sheltering roof." [5] Their political experiments and cultural activities have flourished because of the enduring peace that has been vouchsafed them amidst turbulent and belligerent neighbors.

James Bryce regarded Switzerland as the most democratic of nations, its citizens showing, on the average, a higher political intelligence and keener interest in public affairs than in other countries. Bryce concluded: "But after all, the most interesting lesson it [Switzerland] teaches is how traditions and institutions, taken together, may develop in the average man, to an extent never reached before, the qualities that make a good citizen — shrewdness, moderation, common sense and a sense of duty to the community. It is because this has come to pass in Switzerland that democracy is there more truly democratic than in any other country." [6]

REFERENCES

1 Robert C. Brooks, *Civic Training in Switzerland*, Chicago: Univ. of Chicago Press, 1930, p. xvii.

2 See E. D. Simon, *The Small Democracies*, London: Gollancz, 1938.

3 William E. Rappard, *The Government of Switzerland*, New York: Van Nostrand, 1936, p. 144.

4 Brooks, *op. cit.*, p. 389.

5 *Ibid.*, p. 302.

6 James Bryce, *Modern Democracies*, New York: Macmillan, 1921, Vol. II, p. 449. Sir Ernest D. Simon, a modern student of democracy, comes to the same conclusion.

SELECTED BIBLIOGRAPHY

Brooks, Robert C., *Civic Training in Switzerland*, Chicago: Univ. of Chicago Press, 1930. An extremely comprehensive introduction to Swiss institutions and culture, readable and sympathetic.

Friedrich, C. J. and Cole, Taylor, *Responsible Bureaucracy: A Study of the Swiss Civil Service*, Cambridge: Harvard Univ. Press, 1932. Indispensable for an understanding of the Swiss civil service.

Oechsli, Wilhelm, *History of Switzerland, 1499–1914*, Cambridge: Cambridge Univ. Press, 1922. An authoritative work by a distinguished scholar who was Professor of History at the University of Zurich.

Rappard, William E., *The Government of Switzerland*, New York: Van Nostrand, 1936. This scholarly analysis is by the distinguished Swiss political scientist.

Shotwell, J. T., ed., *Governments of Continental Europe*, New York: Macmillan, 1940. The chapters on "The Political System of Switzerland," by Arnold J. Zurcher, are excellent.

Simon, E. D., *The Small Democracies*, London: Gollancz, 1939.

Chapter XI

Czechoslovakia

WHERE IS MY HOME? WHERE IS MY HOME?
'MONG MEADOWS, STREAMS ARE CREEPING,
IN THE FORESTS RUSTLING WINDS ARE MURMURING.
EVERYWHERE BLOOM SPRING AND FLOWERS,
IN THIS PARADISE OF OURS,
LAND OF BEAUTY, OH, DEAR FATHERLAND,
THOU'RT. MY HOME, BEAUTEOUS LAND,
THOU'RT MY HOME, BEAUTEOUS LAND.

— *Czechoslovak* National Anthem

From Versailles to Munich

Geography. Czechoslovakia occupied a peculiar position on the map of Europe. With an area about that of Illinois, it was a landlocked island, 600 miles long and 45 to 174 miles wide, situated on the great watershed between the Black, Baltic, and North seas, resembling in shape a long wedge with the thick end to the west and the thin to the east. If — to change the metaphor — Czechoslovakia were a fish its head would be Bohemia, inhabited largely by Czechs, with Germans predominating along the western Sudeten border; its body would consist of the provinces of Moravia and Silesia, largely inhabited by Czechs, and Slovakia, peopled by Slovaks. The tail would consist of Carpathian Ruthenia.

This thin strip of territory was sliced in 1918 from the old Austro-Hungarian monarchy. To the disadvantage caused by the inordinate length of the state was added the fact that Czechoslovakia had no direct access to the sea and was therefore at the mercy of the port authorities of Hamburg, Bremen, Gdynia, and Trieste. In some degree this difficulty was counterbalanced by the internationalization of the Danube and the facilities allowed the Czechoslovaks in the harbors of Stettin and other Baltic and Adriatic ports.

Situated in the very heart of Europe, Czechoslovakia saw the collision of races, cultures, and ideas. Here passed part of the northern frontiers of the Roman Empire; migrating tribes of Gauls, Germans, and Slavs passed over this area. Here the incursions of Turks and Tartars were held up, and here in the sixteenth century the Eastern and Western Churches came into conflict. On this soil broke out the struggle between southern Catholicism and northern Protestantism, a struggle for which the Czech people paid heavily. Even the climate of Czechoslovakia repre-

---

This chapter by Joseph S. Roucek, Associate Professor of Political Science and Sociology, Hofstra College.

sents a transition from west to east. Along the German border, in the Sudeten or Ore mountains, there were industrial and mining towns; but as one moved eastward, through Slovakia and into Ruthenia, one had a sense of passing into agrarian, feudal Russia.

The territory of Czechoslovakia has always been an outstanding commercial and military route between eastern and western Europe.[1] Through this region passed the Amber Route which from time immemorial linked the Baltic with the Adriatic. Hence it was only natural that Czechoslovakia should have been historically exposed to tremendous pressure. Its frontiers shifted frequently, and it lost its independence to the Austrians and Germans when they established domination over the Danubian basin.[2]

Ethnography. As waves of people moved over this part of Europe, Czechoslovakia became the home of an intermixture of national and racial groups tossed about by the ebb and flow of conquest. The Sudeten Germans of Bohemia, the Poles of Silesia, the Hungarians of Slovakia, and the smattering of Jews and Gypsies formed the " minority peoples " of 34.5 per cent in the new state, while the Czechs formed 51 per cent (with the Slovaks, 65.6 per cent) of the total population of 13,612,000 (1921). To these minorities were added 3,123,500 Germans who lived within the boundaries of historical Bohemian provinces and in Slovakia, Spish, and Ruthenia. Czechoslovakia also harbored 745,430 Hungarians, who for the most part were interspersed with Slovaks in the border districts of Slovakia and Carpathian Ruthenia, 461,890 Ruthenians living in Carpathian Ruthenia and eastern Slovakia, 180,850 Jews, and 75,850 Poles in the Teschen district of Silesia. There were 76.3 per cent Roman Catholics, 7.3 per cent Protestants, 3.9 per cent Greek Catholics, 3.9 per cent adhered to the Czechoslovak Church, 0.5 per cent to the Eastern Orthodox Church, and 2.6 per cent were Jews. With the formation of the new state, there was a strong drift away from Rome, resulting in the establishment of the Czechoslovak Church.

Creation of Czechoslovakia. The frontiers of Czechoslovakia were recognized by the peace treaties and the Conference of Ambassadors (July 28, 1920). To the so-called " historic lands of Bohemia, Moravia, and Silesia " were added Slovakia and Carpathian Ruthenia, former parts of Hungary. Czechoslovakia also received the German district of Hluchin (285 square kilometers) and Austrian Valtiche and Vitorez. Ruthenia was incorporated in the republic as an autonomous territory, a union resulting from the agitation of American Ruthenians who desired to save their compatriots from the ruthless Magyars. Altogether, Czechoslovakia occupied 54,196 square miles.

Historical Basis of the State. Czechoslovakia was not a new nation when it constituted itself a state on October 28, 1918. A Czechoslovak declaration of independence had been proclaimed in Washington on October 18,

1918 by the Czechoslovak National Council, recognized by the Allies as a *de facto* belligerent government, and headed by Thomas G. Masaryk as Prime Minister, Milan R. Stefanik as Minister of National Defense, and Edward Beneš as Minister of Foreign Affairs.[3]

The roots of this state went back to the fifth century. Sometime in the fifth century the Czechs and Slovaks settled in the regions they still occupy. The invasion of Europe by the Magyars (903–907), a Turanian race, divided the Czechoslovaks from the southern (Yugo) Slavs. Slovakia was cut off from the Czechs for more than ten centuries and hence developed its peculiar type of culture under Hungarian domination.

The Czechs meanwhile had developed their own state in Bohemia, which attained great prominence under the Luxembourg dynasty. When the Black Prince of England defeated blind John of Bohemia in 1346, he was proud to adopt John's crest as his own — the three feathers and the motto *Ich Dien* (I serve) still used by the Duke of Windsor. John's son, Charles IV (1346–1378), made Prague the political and cultural capital of Central Europe.[4] In time the kings of Bohemia controlled lands as far as the Baltic and ranked first among the seven electors of the Holy Roman Empire.

Three Centuries of Subjugation. The fourteenth century saw the beginnings of the Czech struggle against German aggression. German colonists had found their way across the Sudeten mountains and became town-builders, architects, craftsmen, and merchants. Violent Czech revulsion against Germanism was fused with the Protestant movement of John Hus who became the champion of the Czech people.

The Hussite Wars did not, however, check the increasing strength of the Germans, and the position of the Czechs was further weakened in 1526 when Ferdinand of Hapsburg was elected King of Bohemia. The Czech aristocracy grew increasingly alarmed at the danger of Germanization, and this culminated in the rebellion of 1618. The Czechs renounced their allegiance to the Hapsburg Emperor and declared their national independence. But, badly supported by their Protestant allies, the Czechs were, after two years, defeated at the battle of the White Mountain. Terrible reprisals followed. The Czech people were left without leaders, and the Czech language was spoken only by the hewers of wood and drawers of water.

During the next three centuries the Germans thoroughly subordinated the Czechs. But the memory of a distinct national existence lingered, and its preservation was no doubt aided by the fact that the division between upper and lower classes largely coincided with the division between German and Czech.

The national revival began at the end of the eighteenth century, when a Czech middle class slowly emerged. The Czech language was now intensely developed and studied. In the 1830's the foundations of modern Czech literature were laid, stressing the antithesis between German and Slav. After 1848 the Czech leaders pressed for a reorganization of the Hapsburg monarchy on a federal basis. But the ruling Austrians refused to grant many concessions. The spread of education helped, however, to create a Czech official class, and every extension of the franchise brought the Czechs into new positions.

The Slovaks were not so well prepared, however, for their liberation as the Czechs. Under the Magyar regime the 2 million Slovaks had no more than 276 elementary schools, not a single secondary school, and only three political journals.

The First World War. The Czechs and Slovaks were liberated by the influence of Thomas Garrigue Masaryk and a handful of conspirators, who grasped the opportunity of the First World War to awaken interest in Czech independence. They journeyed through Europe and America, proclaiming not only that the Czechoslovaks had a right to independence but that it was essential to the much needed reconstruction of Europe.

Masaryk. Son of a coachman, Masaryk [5] represented both tribal wings of the republic he helped to create: his father was Slovak, his mother Moravian. By marriage to an American and later contacts with the United States he was exposed to the democratic philosophy which came to dominate his thought.[6] Masaryk was elected deputy to the Austrian Reichsrat in 1891 and quickly became known as one of the ablest political leaders of Bohemia, the head of a small party who called themselves the "realists." When war came, Masaryk fled to Switzerland and began to work for the liberation of his people. England aided him almost from the first. Masaryk roved busily through Europe, Asia, and America, rallying Czechs everywhere. With the help of France he formed Czech legions from prisoners captured by the Allies. Soon these were fighting against the Central Powers. When Russia collapsed a Czech army was in Russia. Ultimately this army trekked to Siberia to combat the Bolsheviks.[7]

Masaryk ably exploited the feats of the Czech legions. On May 20, 1918 Secretary Lansing issued a proclamation expressing American sympathy with Czechoslovak and Yugoslav aspirations for independence. Austria sued for peace, expressing willingness to federalize its empire. But Masaryk checkmated this move, and immediately issued a proclamation of Czechoslovak independence which met with an enthusiastic reception. With Allied victory, independence was won.

The Legal Foundations of the Czechoslovak State. The Czech National Council seized power in Prague on October 28, 1918 on the basis of the Washington declaration of independence and the temporary Czech government formed in Paris on October 14 and recognized by the Allies. Delegates of all the Slovak parties assembled on October 30, 1918 to organ-

ize a Slovak National Council which affirmed the right of self-determination, denied authority to the Hungarian government " to speak and act in
the name of the Czechoslovak nation living within the limits of Hungary,"
and declared that " the Slovaks form linguistically and historically a part
of the Czechoslovak nation."

The representatives of the new state — one group representing the
extra-legal administration at Prague and the other the Provisional Government at Paris — met at Geneva, ratified all the military and diplomatic
actions of the National Council, and formulated a program for the first
Revolutionary Assembly. This assembly convened on November 14,
1918 in Prague, deposed the Hapsburgs, proclaimed a republic, elected
Masaryk as President by acclamation, set up a Cabinet with Kramář as
Premier, Beneš as Foreign Minister, and Rašín as Finance Minister, and
enacted a provisional constitution.

The Constitutional Democracy. The temporary constitution of November, 1918 created a democratic republic and abolished the privileges
of birth and class. The definitive constitution, ratified by the National
Assembly on February 29, 1920, was to be the only document of its kind
in Central Europe which survived for two decades. Partly modeled on the
American constitution, it was redolent of Jeffersonian ideals of democracy
and government by the consent of the governed, but contained a strong
dash of nationalism and Socialism.[8]

The constitution created a centralized, not federative state. Only
Carpathian Ruthenia was guaranteed extensive autonomy. Legislative
power was vested in a bicameral Parliament: a House of Deputies whose
members were elected for a term of six years, and a Senate elected for
eight. The President was chosen by both houses, sitting in joint session,
for a term of seven years. The constitution permitted only two terms
but the first President, Masaryk, was allowed to hold office for seventeen
years.

In the elections each party decided on its candidates and also on the
order in which they were listed. Thus the parties directed the deputies'
votes; in fact, deputies were expelled from the party if they failed to vote
according to the caucus. As a result, parliamentary discussions soon declined in importance. Decisions were made in advance by party leaders
meeting in their secretariats or parliamentary clubs. The real legislative
work was done in committees of delegates from the parties which formed
the government.

The dominance of political parties led to the gradual diminution of the
powers of the Senate. As the parties controlled the votes of their members,
the lower house became the decisive arena of the legislature. The ministers
were exclusively recruited from this body.

The Cabinet, appointed by the President, was responsible to the

Chamber of Deputies. A permanent committee — two-thirds of its members chosen from the lower house and one-third from the upper — was to take the place of the National Assembly during its vacations. The presidential powers were subordinated to those of the Assembly, but Masaryk exercised moral influence which transcended the influence of the President as implied in the constitution.

Constitutional amendments required a three-fifths majority of each chamber. In addition, a constitutional court was expressly entitled to proclaim invalid enactments found to conflict with the constitution. However, no law was ever invalidated. Furthermore, in contrast to the experience of neighboring states, the Czechoslovak constitution was not even amended.

The constitution guaranteed racial and religious rights, and in general incorporated the provisions of the international treaties for the protection of minorities.[9]

The Czechoslovak Party System.[10]   There were always more than a dozen parties in Parliament, owing to the system of proportional representation and to the tendency of central European parties to form along racial, class, and ideological lines. The system of coalitions, however, worked better than the multitude of parties would indicate, and the complexion of Prague governments was always more or less uniform. Parliament gradually became more conservative after the initial burst of reforming zeal.

In general, five main parties dominated national politics. The largest was the Agrarian Party, of which nearly half the membership was Slovak. Originally representing the huge class of landowning peasants created after the war as a result of beneficent land reforms, it later became the spokesman of the growing agricultural industries, of state monopolies and banks, of semi-national industries like armaments, and of huge cartels in all fields.

The National Democratic Party led by Dr. Karel Kramář represented industrialists, bankers, and property owners. One of its members, Dr. Alois Rašín, was the first Minister of Finance. As representative of the urban classes, the party suffered from dissension in its ranks created by conflicting interests of employers and employees, manufacturers and consumers, industrialists and artisans.

The Populist (Catholic) Party represented the Center in the Czechoslovak Parliament. During the war its leaders were pro-Austrian, but shortly before the formation of the Czechoslovak state the party changed its attitude and became a firm supporter of the Masaryk government. It appealed to the Catholic agriculturists and workers, promoting its ideas vigorously by means of the press and gymnastic and agricultural organizations. Its perennial leader was Monsignor Jan Šrámek.

The Slovak Politicians. There was also a Slovak Populist Party, vociferous advocate of Catholicism, conservatism, and Slovak autonomy. It expressed the resentment of the less educated but easily led Slovak masses against the attempts of Prague to secularize the republic and replace the Hungarian administrators, teachers, and priests by Protestant and free-thinking Czechs. The Czechs were extremely nationalistic and hardened by nearly a century of struggle for independence, but nationalism and liberty were vague concepts to the Slovaks and Ruthenes, whom their former Hungarian rulers had encouraged neither to educate themselves nor to grow to political maturity. The Slovak Populists were led by Father Andrea Hlinka (1864–1938). He summarized their program as follows in an address in America in 1926:

" All that we wish to secure is the political independence guaranteed by the provisions of the 1918 Pittsburgh Agreement. We are trying to defend our language, religion and national customs, which are not Czech but distinctly our own, from the same treatment they received from the Hungarians and Germans."

Actually, the Pittsburgh Agreement,[11] a document signed by representatives of American Czech and Slovak societies on June 30, 1918, was carried out with the exception of the creation of a parliament for Slovakia. While the Czechs held that the Slovak Administrative Council amounted to a parliament, Father Hlinka pointed out that it did not have legislative power.

Czechoslovakia's linguistic and cultural cleavage was much like that of Belgium, with the Slovaks forming a " Flemish " problem. Conflict between Czechs and Slovaks became acute from 1927 to 1929, but Hlinka's cause received a setback with the conviction of Dr. Vojtěch Tuka, one of his assistants, of high treason. After Munich, Father Tiso took over the leadership of the Slovak Clericals, who showed their preference for " Slovak " rather than " Czechoslovak " patriotism and for Hitler rather than Beneš in March, 1939. At no time did Hlinka's party represent more than one-third of Slovakia's electorate, the rest of the votes going chiefly to the Czechoslovak Agrarians and Social Democrats. Dr. Milan Hodža, the Agrarian Prime Minister and Dr. Ivan Dérer, the Social Democratic Minister of Justice, were both Slovaks.

The Leftist Parties. The Left wing consisted of the Czechoslovak National Socialist Party (unrelated to the Nazis) and the Czechoslovak and German Social Democratic Parties. The National Socialist Party was founded in 1896 as a reaction against the Czech Social Democrats by patriotic petit bourgeois and proletarians. It differed from the Social Democrats in its social composition and the importance it attached to nationalism. A kind of unofficial leadership of the party was assumed by Beneš. The Czech Social Democrats formed the strongest party in the early years of the republic. Its Left wing joined the Third International at the end of 1920 and the organization never regained its strength. The Social Democrats adapted the Marxist program to the need of the Czechoslovak people. They were able to effect the passage of bills creating an eight-hour day, old-age insurance, and other social reforms. The Communist Party, in spite of the large number of votes it polled, was torn by unending dissensions, leading to frequent dismissal of leaders; it was also generally bewildered by the changing foreign policies of Moscow, to whom it looked for leadership.

Composition of Parliament. Czechoslovak politics are illuminated by the following table showing the composition of the four parliaments:

Czechoslovak Parties	April 1920	Nov. 1925	Oct. 1929	May 1935
Agrarian	40	46	46	45
Social Democratic	74	29	39	38
Progressive Socialist	3			
National Socialist	24	28	32	28
National Democratic	19	13	15	17
National Union			3	
Trades and Crafts	6	13	12	17
Czech Catholic	21	31	25	22
Slovak Catholic	12	23	19	22
Fascist				6
	199	183	191	195
Other Parties				
Communist		41	30	30
Sudeten Germans				44
German Social Democrats	31	17	21	11
German Agrarian	13	24	16	5
German Christian Socialist	9	13	14	6
German Nationalist	12	10	7	
German National Socialists	5	7	8	
German Democratic	2			
German Trades			3	
Hungarian National	1		4	
Hungarian Christian Socialist	5	4	5	9
Hungarian-German Social Democratic	4			
Independent		1	1	
	281	300	300	300

Minority Parties. Not all the deputies joined their separate minority parties. Some were affiliated with the larger Czechoslovak political groups — Social Democratic or Communist. In general the various nationalities of the republic were fairly represented in the House of Deputies, as seen in the following table:

	1920	1925	1929	1935	Proportion of Population	Deputies
Czechoslovaks	199	207	208	206	68.66%	66.9%
Germans	73	75	73	72	24.00	22.3
Hungarians	9	10	8	10	3.33	4.8
Ruthenians		6	6	8	2.67	3.8
Poles		2	3	2	0.67	0.6
Jews			2	2	0.67	1.3
	281	300	300	300	100.00	99.7

The Germans had an Agrarian Party, a Christian Socialist Party and a Small Traders' Party. While these gradually abandoned their negative attitude towards the republic, the German Nationalist and German National Socialist parties maintained an irreconcilable Pan-German and anti-Semitic policy. Both of the latter groups were absorbed by Henlein's Sudeten Party in 1935.

Only two Magyar parties were strong enough to elect deputies: the Christian Socialist and National parties. The three Polish factions united in the 1929 elections and joined the Czechoslovak Social Democratic Party. Ruthenians were obliged to support the national parties in order to attain the required electoral figure. The National Christian Party, which cooperated with the Czech Populists, was led by Augustin Vološjn, who became, for a brief period, the Premier of Ruthenia after its secession from Czechoslovakia.

In spite of basic national, religious, social, and economic differences, the Czech parliamentary system functioned successfully and gave the republic one of the most stable governments in Europe.

Advent of Beneš to the Presidency. On December 14, 1935 Masaryk, aged 85, resigned his office and was succeeded by his Foreign Minister, Dr. Edward Beneš. Of all the creators of the Czech state, Beneš was, next to Masaryk, the most popular. As Foreign Minister he had served the republic well, being a staunch adherent of the League of Nations, the architect of the Little Entente, and the foremost spokesman of the small nations in international councils.

Son of Czech peasants, Beneš studied in several European universities, including Paris and Dijon, a fact that explains his pro-French and anti-German sympathies.[12] In 1914 he met Masaryk and became his closest collaborator. While the latter went abroad to organize revolution, Beneš at first remained behind. It was his duty to keep open the lines of communication between Prague and Masaryk in Switzerland. When he began to be suspected, Beneš escaped to Switzerland. His task was to make the Allies conscious of his fatherland, and in this he did an eminent job. It was Beneš who sat on Balfour's doorstep, tirelessly hunted Clemenceau, pestered Lord Robert Cecil, and beleaguered Lord Derby until he won from each formal recognition of Czechoslovak's right to independence. Beneš, Masaryk, and General Štefanik also created the Czech army which fought with the Allies.

Foreign Policy. Like every satiated state, Czechoslovakia wanted to live at peace with her neighbors. Hence Prague's foreign policy consisted, in brief, of Western orientation — reliance but not absolute dependence on France and sincere support of the League of Nations and all efforts directed toward collective security. As an answer to Hungarian irredentism, the Little Entente of Czechoslovakia, Rumania, and Yugoslavia was formed. From these main lines the foreign policy of Czechoslovakia did not waver until the debacle of Munich (September, 1938). An alliance was also concluded with Russia, complementing the France-Czechoslovak pact, guaranteeing military protection of her borders in the event of invasion.

Economic Development. Czechoslovakia was relatively rich in agricultural and mineral resources. With the exception of platinum, the country had practically every useful mineral, including coal, iron, copper, silver, lead, and gold. An important source of radium ore as well as of finished radium is found in Joachimsthal. The excellent China clay of northwest Bohemia gave rise to a famous porcelain industry. Naphtha, obtained in Moravia and Slovakia, was used mainly for the production of heavy lubricant oils.

The Czechoslovak economy maintained more or less equilibrium between agriculture and industry. To a certain extent, industrial output exceeded agricultural production, especially in the western part of the republic; in the east, in Slovakia and particularly Ruthenia, agriculture predominated.

Industries. Of Austro-Hungarian industries Czechoslovakia inherited all the porcelain factories, 92 per cent of the sugar industry, 92 per cent of the glass, 87 per cent of the barley, 75 per cent of the cotton, and 46 per cent of the alcohol output. Of the minerals, Czechoslovakia received three-fourths of the coal, two-thirds of the graphite beds, almost all the silver mines, and the chief gold mines. The capacity of Czechoslovak industries was greatly in excess of domestic needs, so that the country exported huge amounts of commodities; its favorable balance of trade in 1937 reached $35,000,000. Prague exported sugar, Brunn textiles, Moravská Ostrava steel, Bratislava dynamite and high explosives, and Pilsen beer, heavy machinery, locomotives, and rail equipment. At Zlín was located the mammoth shoe factory of the Bata family. Glass-making had been a famous industry in Bohemia since the sixteenth century. The Czech textile trade was highly developed and Czech musical instruments and laces were known all over the world.

Unemployment. The advent of the world depression cut sharply into Czech foreign trade, resulting in a phenomenal growth of unemployment. With but 50,000 unemployed in the first quarter of 1929, Czechoslovakia had more than twelve times that number (626,000) three years later. Except for France and Belgium, which also felt the depression rather late, this was the most spectacular growth of unemployment in that short period in the world.[13]

The struggle against unemployment included valiant efforts to regain or discover new foreign markets, the financing of a large number of public works, and tax concessions for private building and repair activities. The larger cities organized Labor Corps of unemployed young men who worked on parks, sporting grounds, and other non-competitive undertakings.

Nine-tenths of the 718,000 industrial establishments employed from one to five persons each, while some 2 per cent employed more than twenty. Of the income-producing wealth of the country, possibly two-thirds belonged to the companies employing less than twenty persons. Practically all workmen belonged to unions, and " work committees " of employees were recognized by law. There were labor courts, and the work week was limited to forty-eight hours. Worker and employer contributed in equal amounts to a health-insurance fund; in addition there were various provisions for accident and old-age insurance.

Agriculture. The importance of agriculture was apparent from the fact that the country's farms, apart from buildings and inventory, represented more than one-third of the national wealth, and provided occupation for nearly 40 per cent of the population. The great landowners were expropriated by the 1919 Land Reform Law which made it illegal for one person to own more than 350 acres of arable land, or more than 625 acres in all. The original owners were reimbursed on the basis of the average land values of 1913–1915.

The Land Reform had its repercussions in the internal and foreign policies. Since the Czech nobility was practically wiped out or exiled in 1620–1621 and the new aristocracy was German or Hungarian, the representatives of these minorities charged that the plan was designed to dispossess them, and sent frequent complaints to the League of Nations. Another complaint was that German applicants were intentionally overlooked in making allotments. This might have been true, the difficulty being that the Germans were concentrated in mountainous districts along the German frontier, where the arable land was limited and where there were few large estates to be divided.

Numerous industries in Czechoslovakia were linked up with an extensive network of agricultural cooperative societies which embraced one-third of all landowners. More than 33 per cent of the country was in forests which were partly coniferous and partly deciduous and formed the basis of a large lumber industry.

Since foreign trade was the most important item in Czechoslovakia's balance of payments, special attention was devoted to the adjustment of commercial relations with foreign states. Czechoslovakia purchased considerable quantities of raw material from abroad and paid for them with the export of finished goods or natural products.

Czechoslovakia created a currency of her own in 1919. By 1925 the deflation crisis had been largely overcome and the government began to stabilize the budget and retire the national debt. A prominent feature of Czech finances were the items for productive investments, mainly on road construction (the Road Fund), railway extension, waterways (the Waterway Fund), electrification of the rural districts, river regulation and land reclamation. In 1925 there was a budget surplus and a year later state undertakings were placed on a purely commercial footing, definite limits being assigned to administrative expenditures, so that it was possible to simplify and stabilize the state budget.

Cultural Development: Literature. The cultural development of post-war Czechoslovakia has been indissolubly connected with the creation in the previous century of a literary language and the popularization of Czech history.

With its rich background, Czechoslovak literature started on a new life in 1918. Numerous authors of the pre-war school were still popular with the masses, but a flock of young writers appeared, eager to express their war experiences or integrate Czech literature with the latest world trends. The outstanding representative of the "old school" was the historical novelist Alois Jirásek (1851–1930). Jirásek lost his popularity after the war but regained it after the tragedy of Munich. The novels of Karel V. Rais (1859–1926) and Josef Holeček (1853–1929) depicted the quiet lives of their native heaths. Tremendous influence on the growth of Czech literature was exerted by the criticism of Masaryk, a sort of dignified "Menckenism."

The post-war generation, said Karl Čapek, "produced its most beautiful work in the sphere of the lyric, which manifestly is to be regarded, together with music, as the purest medium of expression of the Czech spirit." [14] The greatest poet of this epoch was the mystical Otoka Březina (1868–1929).

The Czech writer best known abroad was Karl Čapek (1890–1938). A cosmopolitan spirit, he tried to counteract the excessive nationalism of his people by using fantastic, Utopian themes, beginning with his novel *Krakatt.* Čapek achieved international renown as a dramatist. His *R.U.R.,* a protest against the growing mechanization of spiritual life, added the word "robot" to our vocabulary. *The Insect Comedy,* the joint work of Karl and his brother Josef (1887–1927), describes the folly of the idle rich, of wars, of the materialistic middle class, and of Socialist demagogy. Karl's *Makropoulos Secret* is a satire on inordinate longing for longevity.[15] After the Čapeks, probably the best known of Czech authors abroad is Francis Kozik, whose *The Great Debureau* won the 1939 All-Nations Prize Contest.

Slovak literature is of comparatively recent origin, owing to the late development of a native literary language. Světozar Hurban-Vajanský (1847–1916) was one of the most influential of Slovak poets and prose writers. Curiously enough, he opposed the Czechs and regarded Russia as the future liberator of his people. The greatest Slovak poet and intellectual leader was Pavel Országh (1849–1921), better known under his pseudonym, Hviezdoslav.[16]

Music. The Czech excel perhaps, as Čapek, said, in music above all other arts. Antonín Dvořák and Bedřich Smetana have enriched the world with music that is distinctly Czech in spirit yet international in appeal. Of the post-war generation Leo Janáček (1854–1928) was perhaps the outstanding composer, a man of stormy temperament, delicate and restless, who applied himself to popular motives. The violin school of Otakar Ševčík produced famous artists – Jan Kubelík, Jaroslav Kocina, and František Ondříček.

Art. Max Švabinsky's portraits and etchings have been popular in the United States. Jóža Úprka won fame as a painter of Slovak peasant life. The name of Alfons Mucha is known in America for a series of monumental pictures, " The Slavonic Epochs," glorifying Slav history. An elemental talent, great power, and stylistic discipline featured the sculpture of Jan Stursa.

Education. Education was free for all citizens from kindergarten to university, and scholarships provided for poor but gifted students. Adult education received tremendous impetus with the setting up of educational committees in every community to conduct lectures and adult courses and operate libraries under supervision of the Masaryk Institute of Adult Education.[17] As a result of such efforts, illiteracy was lower in Czechoslovakia (7.5 per cent in 1921 and 3.25 per cent in 1930) than in any country in central and eastern Europe.

During the post-war years, considerable international attention was granted to Sokol Congresses, scheduled every six years. The Czech Sokol was founded in 1862, the name, meaning falcon, being the traditional symbol of folk heroes. During the years of Hapsburg dominance, Sokol groups served to keep Czech nationalism alive. When the war broke out members filtered into Allied armies, formed Sokol legions and fought their old masters. One out of every 20 persons in Czechoslovakia belonged to a Sokol, welded together by means of adult education and gymnastic training. Their flashing uniforms — red shirts, grey jackets slung from their left shoulders, and little round caps with falcon feathers — never failed to rouse national enthusiasm.

The Sokols were but one of numerous educational activities in the country. In line with Masaryk's unceasing emphasis on universal education as the basis of democracy, the republic made available secondary and higher education to the Slovaks, where before 1918 they were practically non-existent. Special schools were also established for minorities. Thus 96.2 per cent of German, 94 per cent of Hungarian, and 92.5 per cent of Polish children received instruction in their native tongues. German Polytechnical schools in Prague and Brno were supported by the state — as were all minority schools. Two new universities, Masaryk University at Brno and Comenius University at Bratislava, were established.

Under German Domination

Shadow of Nazism. The surprise of the 1935 elections was the strength of Henlein's Sudeten Party. The roots of the Henlein movement can be traced to the defeat of Germany and Austria in 1918. German discontent was constant, partly justifiable and partly unreasonable. When the new state was formed Masaryk actually crushed the Kramář Party which represented extremist anti-German elements.

The German minority was from the beginning treated more generously in Czechoslovakia than in any other country. Their complaints, however, arose chiefly from economic causes. The Germans had subscribed heavily to Austrian war loans, which were liquidated by the Czech state at 75 per cent. Believing that the new state would not survive, the Germans speculated heavily on the German mark; they were wiped out by the inflation of 1923.

Since Hitler offered the Czech Germans a possibility of regaining their dominant status, Nazism appealed to many of them.[18] The economic crisis after 1929 gave a powerful impetus to the movement, for the German districts of North Bohemia, once the workshop of the Hapsburg Empire, were extremely hard hit. The Sudetenland became an industrial graveyard, owing to Germany's drive for self-sufficiency (autarchy). Furthermore, a larger proportion of Germans were engaged in industrial occupations than Czechs. The Germans claimed they were discriminated against in administrative positions and private industry, that government funds went more copiously to the Czech areas than to German regions. These complaints were true. But the uncooperative attitude of the Germans towards the republic in its early years was partly responsible for the situation.

The elections of May, 1935 gave the Henleinists 44 seats out of 72 German mandates. German Centrists (Catholics) and Agrarians joined with Henlein in the general celebration that followed the annexation of Austria in March, 1938. Yet, before Munich, the Henleinists did not monopolize the politics of the German-speaking areas. In addition to the 55 Henleinists in the Prague Parliament, there were 11 German Social Democrats and 5 German Communists.

The Henleinists made astonishing gains in the municipal elections of May, 1938, held under the shadow of Austrian Anschluss and the threat of invasion. The Henleinists now demanded legal status for the German minority, autonomy for Sudetenland, and Prague's renunciation of its alliance with Russia.

Hitler's Fifth Column. The diplomatic aspects of Munich are dealt with in other chapters of this book. Suffice it to say that, as we now know, Hitler had decided in May, 1938 to dispose of the Czechoslovak problem in his own way. Thus, while professing allegiance to his country, Henlein was taking orders from Hitler, whose demands grew bolder as the spring and summer of 1938 progressed. The more concessions granted by Beneš, under pressure from London and Paris, the more blatant the Sudeten Nazis became. German newspapers and radio broadcasts described, in ever-accelerating intensity, imaginary tortures of Germans in Czechoslovakia. Lord Runciman was sent to mediate the crisis, but his real purpose, as we learn from Sir Nevile Henderson's memoirs, was to convince the Czechs that they ought to yield.[19] Indeed, Runciman spent most of his time at the chateau of the German Prince Hohenlohe. Meanwhile clashes between Sudetens and Czechs multiplied.

After Hitler's hysterical address at the annual Nazi Party meeting at Nuremberg, Chamberlain flew to see the Fuehrer at Berchtesgaden (September 15). The crisis was not settled, however, until Germany had dispatched a large army to the Czech frontiers, and Mussolini, appearing in an unusual role as peacemaker, persuaded Hitler to agree to a four-power conference at Munich on September 30. At this momentous gathering, attended by Hitler, Mussolini, Daladier, and Chamberlain, it was decided to yield the Sudetenland to Germany.[20] The Czechs were not even consulted. Since the sixth century the Sudeten mountains had served as a barrier against the eastward push of the Teutonic tribes. Now it fell to Germany without a struggle. The state of Czechoslovakia was rendered defenseless and the German *Drang nach Osten* (push to the east) became a reality, as predicted by the insolent jingle which the Nazis had plastered on Czech frontier barriers,

> "Edward, save up your pence,
> For Adolf soon will be over the fence."

The "Second" Republic of Czechoslovakia. Under the Munich Pact, the territory seized from Czechoslovakia was about the size of Belgium. The international commission, " composed of Germany, the United Kingdom, France, Italy, and Czechoslovakia," was really a cardboard organization created to satisfy public opinion in France and Britain; Germany's delegates simply dictated their demands. Furthermore, during October, 1938, Poland sent an ultimatum to Prague and its troops occupied Teschen and Bohumin in Silesia. During November portions of Slovakia and Carpathian Ruthenia were allotted to Hungary. Altogether, under the terms of Munich, Czechoslovakia lost roughly one-third of its previous area, retaining 36,180 square miles; its population was reduced from 14,729,000 to 9,807,000 inhabitants.[21]

On the Way to the " Protectorate." Since the presence of President Beneš in Prague was considered a source of irritation to Hitler, the Czech leader resigned his post on October 5, and on the 22nd departed for London. The day before, a new cabinet was formed under General Syrový, with Dr. František Chvalkovský, a Germanophile Agrarian leader, as Minister of Foreign Affairs.

When Parliament convened on November 29, anti-Jewish measures were introduced. On November 30, Dr. Emil Hácha, an unimaginative President of the Supreme Court, was elected President. Syrovy was succeeded by Rudolf Beran, a shrewd Agrarian leader, who was granted dictatorial powers on December 14 by a Parliament controlled by the National Unity Party which had absorbed the dissolved Agrarian Party, the Czechoslovak National Socialist Party, the Czechoslovak Small Traders' Party, the Clericals, and the National League. Further Nazi influence was also seen in the government order abolishing the Communist Party.

Little more than a week after Munich, Hlinka's Slovaks demanded autonomy. Czechoslovakia was therefore reconstituted as a federal union of Czechs, Slovaks, and Carpatho-Ukrainians, with central departments of national defense, foreign affairs, and finance; in addition to the legislative bodies for the provinces of Bohemia-Moravia, Slovakia, and Carpathian Ukrainia, there was to be a joint legislative parliament (but it was never realized). The Slovak Diet (limited to the Slovak People's Party) of 63 members was elected on December 18, 1938, under Premier Tiso. A similar Fascist pattern appeared in Carpathian Ruthenia where only the People's Party was allowed to exist.

Although the Prague government went a long way to meet Nazi demands, Berlin's ultimatums became more insistent. The 400,000 Germans left in the new Czechoslovakia were entrusted with " a special mission," and the Vienna radio station incessantly incited the Slovaks to secede.[22] The Nazis endeavored to create the impression that Czechoslovakia was collapsing from within and that they were needed to protect the victims of Czech " brutalities " and of " plundering Hussite mobs." On March 12 the Prague government decided to intervene in Bratislava against the Slovak extremists by deposing Tiso, the Catholic Premier, and appointing Karel Sidor, the heir to the patriotic tradition of Father Hlinka, as Premier.

The March Crisis. Berlin was obviously displeased with the bloodless liquidation of what it had hoped would be a revolt. On March 13 the discharged Slovak Premier was summoned to Berlin and confronted with an ultimatum asking him to proclaim the independence of Slovakia. They also ordered Hácha to convoke the Slovak Provincial Parliament in order to make decisions concerning the future status of Slovakia. The Parliament refused on March 14 to vote the separation from the Czechs.[23] When the Nazis threatened invasion the Slovak Parliament capitulated and proclaimed the independence of its country.

Independent Slovakia. The creation of a separate Slovak state separated the Ruthenians from the Czechs, and the provincial government at Chust had to proclaim its independence also. " Never has a people declared itself ' free ' so reluctantly as did the half million Ruthenes of this tiny province." [24] Premier Vološín thanked the Czechs " for their twenty years of support which helped us to strengthen our national consciousness and cultural progress." After 24 hours of independence, Hungarian troops invaded the territory and on March 16 Premier Teleki announced the incorporation of Ruthenia in Hungary.

German Occupation of Czechia. Meanwhile Hácha had followed Tiso to Berlin on March 14, " on his own volition, in the hope of sparing his country the horrors of invasion and of securing by his abasement at least a measure of generous treatment " — as we learn from Sir Nevile Henderson's *Failure of a Mission*, although the French *Yellow Book* reveals that the German occupation of Prague was not, as the British Ambassador suggests, an unanticipated shock. Hácha was terrorized into placing " the destiny of the Czech people and lands trustfully in the hands of the Führer," " in the interests of pacification." German troops had occupied two Czech cities even before Hácha's arrival in Berlin. By skillfully manipulating the train service, Hitler's train reached Prague next morning before Hácha's, and on March 15 the transformation of Bohemia and Moravia into a German Protectorate was announced to the Czechs from the upper windows of the Hradschin Palace, the ancient residence of Bohemia's kings and Czechoslovakia's Presidents. In familiar Nazi fashion trucks carried away more than $100,000,000 in gold and currency, the Gestapo began rounding up " undesirables " from carefully prepared lists, and concentration camps appeared in Bohemia.

The Protectorate. Hitler then undertook to " protect " Slovakia also and signed a treaty with Tiso at Vienna on March 18, 1939 legalizing German military occupation of the country. Special political status was reserved for the small German minority of about 100,000 and a German Under-

Secretary of State was created. In August, 1939 the development of the Polish-German crisis brought an announcement that "owing to the existing situation" German forces had taken military possession of the state and as a reward the Teschen region ceded to Poland the preceding October was incorporated into Slovakia.

The fiction of the independence of Bohemia-Moravia and Slovakia has been kept up. The Czech President has his own Cabinet, appointed with the Protector's "approval." The Protector's office, a vast and complex apparatus with 16 divisions, became, in fact, the exclusive source of legislative and administrative power of the Protectorate. Konrad Henlein was appointed head of the civil administration and his former aid, K. H. Frank, State Secretary and Chief of Police. The extension of German laws for the defense of the Reich to the entire protectorate made Nazi legislation supreme. A policy of de-nationalization was put into effect by moving the Czech workers to the Reich and sending their children to German schools; the property of the Czechs and Jews who fled abroad was given to Germans. Germans from the Baltic states were resettled around Prague, breaking up Czech compact settlements.

Slovakia's fictitious independence was expressed in a new Slovak constitution of July, 1939. It described the country as a Christian National Republic and permits the existence of only one party, Hlinka's former separatists. Every citizen must belong to one of the five "corporations" (agriculture, industry, finance, liberal professions, and public service). The State council replaced the Senate and is composed of the representatives of the corporations, the delegates of Hlinka's People's Party and nationality groups, the members of the Cabinet, and the delegates sent by Parliament. The President is elected by Parliament for seven years, with powers resembling the rulers of the authoritarian states. In Bohemia-Moravia, 99.25 per cent of all Czechs joined the National Union Party, but attempts were made by the Nazis to break up the Union by supporting small groups of Czech anti-Semite Fascists.[25] The National Union aimed to preserve the spirit of Czech nationalism, to deepen the sense of solidarity among the different social classes, and to educate the masses to an understanding of their country's present situation. Opposed to Socialism, it favored a corporative state.

Czechoslovak Revolutionaries Abroad. Beneš immediately set about to organize a world-wide movement for the liberation of his homeland. Following the outbreak of war between Great Britain and Germany in 1939, Beneš declared from London that the Czech people were at war with Germany and set up a provisional Czechoslovak government. On October 7, 1939 he announced an agreement with the French government "authorizing us to reconstitute the Czechoslovak army in France." On November 17, 1939 the Czechoslovak National Committee was formed in Paris, with

Beneš at its head. On December 20 the British government, through Lord Halifax, the Foreign Minister, announced the recognition of the Committee as " qualified to represent the Czechoslovak peoples." After the collapse of France in June, 1940 the Committee was transferred to London and the Czechoslovak army was evacuated from France to England. On July 21, 1940 London recognized the Provisional Czechoslovak government with Beneš as President, Monsignor Jan Šramek as Prime Minister, and Jan Masaryk, son of the first President, as Foreign Minister.

A number of outstanding Czechoslovak leaders who have succeeded in escaping the Nazis are striving to preserve their civilization abroad. At home, forbidden all political rights and expression, with all meetings and lectures banned, newspapers closely censored, the Czechs have turned again to their ancient heroes. Ruled by the Nazis, they are not subdued.[26] Like the unwise conqueror in Machiavelli's *Prince* the Germans are " obliged to stand knife in hand, never able to depend on his subjects because they, owing to continually fresh injuries, are not able to depend on him."

REFERENCES

1 Emanuel Moravec, *The Military Importance of Czechoslovakia in Europe.* Prague: Orbis, 1938, is a valuable analysis of the geographic basis of Europe's history.

2 Ferdinand of Hapsburg was elected King of Bohemia and Hungary in 1526. In this Confederation Slovakia was once again united with the Bohemian Kingdom which was now the focus and main element of the front against the Turks. This election put the Czech crown into possession of the Hapsburg house until 1918.

3 The Czechoslovak Declaration of Independence of October 18, 1918 is often confused with the Declaration of Common Aims of the Independent Mid-European Nations, signed at the Independence Hall, Philadelphia, on October 26, 1918, possibly because the pictures showing Dr. Masaryk reading the latter proclamation have been wildly circulated in the United States. See Jaroslav Mrázek, *Woodrow Wilson a Americké Uznání čs. národní rady za vládu de facto* (*Woodrow Wilson and the American Recognition of the Czechoslovak National Council as the Government de facto*), Prague: the author, 1933.

4 The Charles University of Prague, founded in 1348, was a Czech institution, established by a Bohemian (Czech) king, Charles IV. With the absorption of the remnant of Bohemia-Moravia by Germany in 1939, the German Protector proclaimed this University a German institution on the theory that it was founded by Charles IV in his capacity as Holy Roman Emperor, although the University was chartered in 1348, and Charles became Holy Roman Emperor only seven years later, that is, in 1355.

5 See Joseph S. Roucek, "Thomas Garrigue Masaryk as Politician and Statesman," *Social Science*, October, 1931, VI: 272–278; and "Eighty-Fifth Birthday of President Masaryk," *ibid.*, April, 1935, X: 201–202; and "Masaryk as Sociologist," *Sociology and Social Research*, May–June, 1938, XXII: 412–420.

6 Masaryk's philosophy is the most systematically presented in his *The Making of a State*, New York: Stokes, 1927.

7 For the latest and best account of the Czech exploits in Siberia, see R. E. Dupuy, *Perish by the Sword*, Harrisburg, Pa.: Military Service Publishing Company, 1939.

8 The text can be found in: *International Conciliation*, October, 1922, No. 179.

9 A useful short summary of the accomplishments of Czechoslovakia's democracy is: Brackett Lewis, *Facts about Democracy in Czechoslovakia*, Prague: American Institute in Czechoslovakia, 1938. For more details about the problem of minorities, see J. S. Roucek, *The Working of the Minorities System under the League of Nations*, Prague: Orbis, 1928.

10 The best analyses are Charles Hoch, *The Political Parties in Czechoslovakia*, Prague: Orbis, 1936; S. Grant Duff, *Europe and the Czechs*, New York: Penguin Books, 1938, pp. 98–117.

11 For the best pro-Czech analysis of the Pittsburgh Agreement by a Slovak political leader, see Ivan Dérer, *The Unity of the Czechs and Slovaks. Has the Pittsburgh Declaration Been Carried Out?* Prague: Orbis, 1938.

12 For Beneš' career and ideology, see Edward Hitchcock, *He Built a Temple for Peace*, New York: Harper, 1940; J. S. Roucek, "Edward Beneš," *Social Science*, April, 1935, X: 200; and "Edward Beneš as a Sociologist," *Sociology and Social Research*, September–October, 1938, XXIII: 18–24.

13 See G. D. H. Cole, *A Guide through World Chaos*, New York: Knopf, 1934, p. 262.

14 *Czechoslovakia*, Prague: Orbis, n.d., "With an Introduction by Karel Čapek," p. 48; *Contemporary Czechoslovak Literature*, a reprint from *Books Abroad*, Autumn, 1937, XI: 1–36, is the best source in English on Czechoslovakian literature.

15 See J. S. Roucek, "Requiescat Karel Čapek," *Books Abroad*, Spring, 1939, XIII: 171–172.

16 For a good background of Slovak literature, see *An Anthology of Czechoslovak Literature*, selected and translated by Paul Selver, London: Kegan Paul, 1929.

[17] J. S. Roucek, "Adult Education in Czechoslovakia," *School and Society,* January 2, 1932, XXXV: 19–21, and January 25, 1936, XLIII: 125–127.

[18] See J. S. Roucek, "The Case for Czechoslovakia," *World Affairs Interpreter,* October, 1938, IX: 235–243; and "Czechoslovakia — The Watchdog of Europe's Peace," *Social Science,* October, 1938, XIII: 277–283.

[19] See Nevile Henderson, *The Failure of a Mission,* New York: Putnam, 1940.

[20] Martin Gellhorn, *A Stricken Field,* New York: Deull, Sloan and Pearce, 1940, is a moving story of Prague during the Munich crisis.

[21] Based on J. S. Roucek, "The 'Second' Republic of Czecho-Slovakia," *The Journal of Geography,* March, 1939, XLVIII: 89–98; and "Europe after Munich," *Social Science,* January, 1939, XIV: 17–22.

[22] Josef Hanč, "Czechs and Slovaks since Munich," *Foreign Affairs,* October, 1939, XVIII: 102–115, is a very good summary of this period.

[23] For the most complete story of the separation of Slovakia from Czechoslovakia, see V. S. Hurban, "Slovakia, Springboard to the East," in New York *Times,* February 11, 1940.

[24] Hanč, *op. cit.,* p. 105.

[25] Early in the summer of 1939 even General Gajda entered the National Union with his National Fascist Party.

[26] See Bernard Batt, "The Czech Struggle against Nazism," Pamphlet No. 4 published by the American Friends of Czechoslovakia, New York.

SELECTED BIBLIOGRAPHY

Beneš, Edward, *My War Memoirs,* Boston: Houghton Mifflin, 1928. A readable account of Beneš' techniques and of his political philosophy.
——, *Democracy Today and Tomorrow,* New York: Macmillan, 1939. A review of Beneš' experiment in democratic statesmanship and his hopes for the future of democracy.
Bloss, Esther, *Labor Legislation in Czechoslovakia,* New York: Columbia Univ. Press, 1938. A factual description.
Borovička, J., *Ten Years of Czechoslovak Politics,* Prague: Orbis, 1929. A very readable, more or less official account of Czechoslovakia's post-war politics.
Bowman, Isaiah, *The New World,* Yonkers, N. Y.: World Book Co., 1928. Chapter 14 is a good account of Czechoslovakia's geographical-political problems.
Čapek, Karel, ed., *President Masaryk Tells His Story,* New York: 1935. Probably the best introduction to Masaryk's personality and philosophy.
Crabitès, P., *Beneš, Statesman of Central Europe.* New York: Coward-McCann, 1936. Written by a man who had never seen Beneš; deals primarily with international politics.
Duff, S. Grant, *Europe and the Czechs,* New York: Penguin Books, 1938. A readable survey of the events leading to Munich.
George, G. J., *They Betrayed Czechoslovakia,* New York: Penguin Books, 1938. The story of the betrayal by a Czech.
Kerner, R. J., ed., *Czechoslovakia, A Record of Two Decades.* Chapter IX, "Czechoslovakia and Her Minorities," pp. 171–192 by J. S. Roucek. Berkeley, Cal.: Univ. of California Press, 1940. The whole work is the best encyclopedic introduction to various aspects of Czechoslovakia.
Krofta, Kamil, *A Short History of Czechoslovakia,* New York: Macmillan, 1934. By an outstanding Czech historian, a former Foreign Minister.
Masaryk, T. G., *The Making of a State,* New York: Stokes, 1927. Indispensable for an understanding of Masaryk's ideology.
Nosek, Vladimir, *The Spirit of Bohemia,* New York: Brentano, 1927. A general review of Czech history, literature, and art.
Opočenský, Joseph, *The Collapse of the Austro-Hungarian Monarchy and the Rise of the Czechoslovak State,* Prague: Orbis, 1928. A good factual account from the official Czechoslovak standpoint.

Pergler, Charles, *America in the Struggle for Czechoslovak Independence*, Philadelphia: Dorrance, 1926. A summary of American policy toward the Czechs during the First World War.

Seton-Watson, R. W., ed., *Slovakia, Then and Now: A Political Survey*, London: Allen and Unwin, 1931. A series of pro-Czech articles edited by an Englishman.

Wiskemann, Elizabeth, *Czechs and Germans*, New York: Oxford Univ. Press, 1938. Fair to both sides.

Chapter XII

Spain and Portugal

" SUCH BE THE SONS OF SPAIN, AND STRANGE HER FATE!
THEY FIGHT FOR FREEDOM WHO WERE NEVER FREE,
A KINGLESS PEOPLE FOR A NERVELESS STATE;
HER VASSALS COMBAT WHEN THEIR CHIEFTAINS FLEE,
TRUE TO THE VERIEST SLAVES OF TREACHERY:
FOND OF A LAND WHICH GAVE THEM NOUGHT BUT LIFE,
PRIDE POINTS THE PATH THAT LEADS TO LIBERTY;
BACK TO THE STRUGGLE, BAFFLED IN THE STRIFE,
WAR, WAR IS STILL THE CRY, ' WAR EVEN TO THE KNIFE.' "
— BYRON: *Childe Harold's Pilgrimage*

Spain

Geography. From a strictly geographical viewpoint Spain and Portugal constitute a peninsula jutting from another peninsula (Europe). The " peninsularity " of Spain and Portugal with respect to Europe matches the " insularity " of Great Britain. Although Spain and the rest of Europe are connected by a neck of land almost 300 miles wide, intercommunications are obstructed by the Pyrenees mountains which stretch from the Bay of Biscay to the Mediterranean. This barrier, which attains a maximum height of 11,000 feet (almost double that of our Appalachians), has but few natural passageways, the most famous being the pass of Roncevalles. The Spanish peninsula is approachable from the east by way of the island steppingstones of the Balearics. From the days of the ancient Greeks to Mussolini's recent seizure of Majorca, the Balearic Islands have served well those who sought to dominate the peninsula from the Mediterranean. The southern approach is by way of the peninsula of Moroccan Tangier and the Strait of Gibraltar. Spain's accessibility is, however, more apparent than real. He who approaches from the north by land finds few passes; he who approaches the Mediterranean coast finds few good harbors (the outstanding exception being Barcelona). Most of the great seaports are on the Atlantic, a fact that helps to account for Spain's imperial expansion into the Americas and for Portugal's close relations with England.

The Spanish peninsula comprises an area of approximately 190,000 square miles or about the size of California. It is 500 miles across the peninsula from Lisbon east to Valencia and an equal distance from Gibraltar north to Santander. Central Spain is of about the same latitude as San

This chapter by Loren C. MacKinney, Professor of History, University of North Carolina.

Francisco, but except for the northern regions, the climate is subtropical, due to the prevailing winds and ocean currents from the south. Thus the fertile eastern and southern coastal areas produce rice, olives, grapes, oranges, and other tropical fruits. In general, the Iberian peninsula manifests contrasts more marked than those found in other European countries. There are 2500 miles of seacoast, combined with an average elevation above sea level approximating that of Switzerland; torrential rains overflow the steep river valleys, but there are also regions of intense drought. The peninsula has coastal sections which produce a wealth of tropical fruits, but also arid central plateaus on which sheep flourish only by a migratory existence. There are highly civilized and prosperous urban centers, as well as hinterlands of primitive peasant folk living much as did their medieval ancestors.

The central expanse of arid land dominates the geography of Spain. The Castilian plateau, 2000 feet or more above sea level in the central portions, is separated from the fertile outer portion of the peninsula by a rim of mountains. It is also traversed from east to west by two ranges (the Guadarrama and the Morena), and elsewhere by lesser ranges. About 60 per cent of the total area of the Iberian peninsula is non-agricultural; these regions, however, contain rich deposits of minerals. Most of the agricultural sections have so little, or such irregular rainfall, that irrigation is necessary.

The coastal rim is composed of several important agricultural or commercial regions. To the south, the basin of the Guadalquivir River has from ancient times supported a prosperous agricultural and commercial population. Along the western coast is Portugal and its northern neighbor, Galicia. Here are harbors and small but fertile valleys; one of them, near Oporto, has a unique soil and climate that produces the peculiarly flavored grapes from which port wine is made. The Asturian coast, along the Bay of Biscay, and the Basque provinces have more mineral and commercial than agricultural resources. Finally, along the Mediterranean coast lies the Catalonian plain with its industrial cities. Of all the sectional units bordering Spain's central plateau, only Portugal has maintained an independent political existence. Castile remains the mistress of the remainder of the peninsula, dominating the surrounding regions from her central plateau, like a medieval baron from a lofty castle.

Ethnography. Racially the Iberian peninsula has a fundamental homogeneity. The people are more purely Mediterranean than those of any other European country. There is little variation from the dark, short, wiry longheads, who are believed to have been dominant since the days of the cave men of Altamira and their successors, the Iberians, who gave their name to the peninsula. Tall, blue-eyed Spaniards, possibly descendants of the early Celtic or Visigothic conquerors, are rather rare. Most interesting of the Spanish minorities, though quite small in numbers (less than 1,000,000), are the Basques of the western Pyrenees. They still maintain a strongly marked identity, most noticeable in their language, native dress, and intense separatism. In the last-mentioned characteristic they are surpassed only by the Catalans, whose separatism is due more to economic and political than to racial factors. The Catalans, quite as much as the Portuguese, would seem to be destined by geography, race, and economy for independent national existence. They constitute a Spanish problem comparable to that of Ireland in the British Empire.

Spain in 1918. Spain,[1] like many neutral nations, profited greatly from the First World War. Having maintained her neutrality successfully, she emerged in 1918 not only unravaged by warfare but strengthened in almost every way. None of the warring powers had been alienated. The government had, perhaps deliberately, permitted German submarines to use Spanish ports, and dealt leniently with German saboteurs. At the same time the Barcelona and Bilbao industrialists had sold war materials to the Allies in increasing quantities. Meanwhile King Alfonso played the role of a humanitarian neutral, and Spanish diplomats served as intermediaries between the warring powers.

Catalonia and other industrial regions were enriched by wartime profits. From 1914 to 1918 the income of typical manufacturing enterprises in Barcelona almost doubled each year. An unfavorable national trade balance of about 250,000,000 pesetas in 1913 was converted into a favorable balance of well over 500,000,000 pesetas in 1917. Meanwhile the national debt was cut in half. While the commercial metropolis of Barcelona, the industrial region of Bilbao, and other favored cities were enjoying prosperity, agricultural Spain was left comparatively untouched. As a consequence, in the post-war period Spain was divided, so to speak, into two nations: the old agricultural and feudal Spain and the new Spain of industrial wealth and proletarianism. The one was monarchical, clerical and conservative, the other seethed with radical agitation and movements for social justice. By 1918 Spain was drifting toward the economic, social, political, and ideological disunity which came to a bloody climax twenty years later.

Domestic Politics. Spain's internal history from 1918 to 1938 has been dominated by changes as momentous as those in Germany, though the drift of events was in opposite directions. Within these two decades Germany rose from defeat, civil war, and despair to unity and victorious self-confidence, whereas Spain drifted from a position of prosperity, international prestige and relative political stability to the anarchy of civil war and foreign intervention.

We turn now to a survey of the decaying constitutional monarchy of Alfonso XIII, the military dictatorship of Primo de Rivera. the republic

SOUTHWESTERN EUROPE

Scale of Miles
0   50   100   150

Topography
over 12000'
6000'-12000'
3000'-6000'
1500'-3000'
0'-1500'

Culture
rivers:
canals:
marshes:
boundaries, Oct. 1, 1940:
French boundary dated 1940

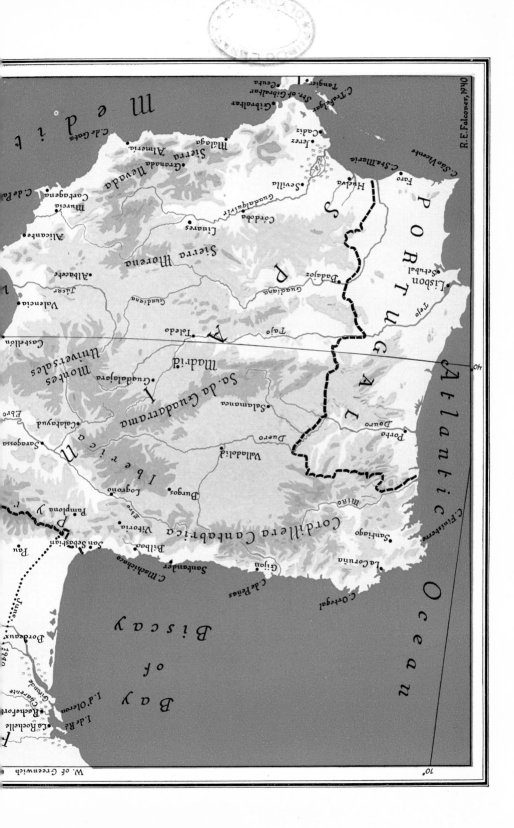

of 1931, and the totalitarian dictatorship of Francisco Franco. In this survey we shall see that Spain's vicissitudes parallel the cycle through which many lesser European nations have passed in recent years; namely, from constitutional monarchy to post-war republicanism, and thence to dictatorship of an increasingly totalitarian form.

Alfonso's Government. The weakness of Alfonso's constitutional regime was revealed in 1917 when a serious effort was made to overthrow the monarchy. In the larger industrial centers, Catalonia in particular, Anarchist and Syndicalist leaders organized general strikes and fomented revolution. Thanks to the loyalty of the soldiery, the revolt was crushed, and the monarchy continued its precarious existence, with four ministerial changes in the year 1917 alone.

From 1918 to 1923, Alfonso's regime disintegrated rapidly, for no combination of liberal or conservative ministers could survive either the intrigues of the army *juntas* or the pettiness of the parliamentary politicians. The year 1920 was relatively peaceful, but in 1921 two long-standing problems assumed such critical proportions that the monarchy was shaken to its foundations.

The less serious problem was that of Catalan autonomy. Catalonia had emerged from the First World War more prosperous than before, and also more discontented. During the pre-war period (1912–1914) the four Catalan provinces had secured virtual self-government and the Catalan politicians lost no opportunity to agitate for additional rights. President Wilson's advocacy of self-determination inspired them to demand complete autonomy shortly after the armistice, and later on, the visit of General Joffre to Barcelona was the occasion for violent demonstrations against the Madrid government. Like the British in their handling of the Irish question, the Spanish government postponed the issue with vague suggestions of home rule for all the separatist regions of the peninsula. Matters drifted on until the Riffian revolt of 1921, when the Catalans took advantage of the governmental crisis to press their demands. For two years thereafter it seemed likely that they might secede unless virtual independence was granted. With the establishment of the Rivera dictatorship in 1923, the movement was crushed, only to rise again with the republican regime of 1931.[2]

The Riffian Revolt. Far more serious for the prestige of the monarchy was the defeat of the Spanish army at Annual, Morocco in 1921. After years of vain efforts at extending Spanish control in Morocco, General Silvestre, with the approval if not the urging of the king, decided to take drastic action against the wild Riffian tribesmen and their bold leader, Abd-el-Krim. Advancing far into Riffian territory, General Silvestre rashly occupied an indefensible position where he lost not only his own life but practically his entire force of more than 8000 men.

The Aftermath. In the parliamentary investigation that followed, the political leaders saw to it that the brunt of the blame fell on the king and the military leaders. Alfonso's enemies referred to the battle as "the criminal action of the tyrant king," and the novelist Blasco Ibáñez treated the episode with biting sarcasm in his *Alfonso XIII Unmasked.* Since the scandal reflected on the entire regime, the republicans exploited the situation to the fullest. The hostile temper of public opinion had been indicated earlier in the year by the assassination of a conservative premier (Dato). Now the Syndicalist and Anarchist leaders instituted a reign of terror which continued for two years, raging with particular violence in Barcelona. The murder of a Roman Catholic cardinal indicated the resentment of the revolutionists against the clergy as well as the king. As we have seen, Catalan separatism was also involved. By the middle of the year 1923 Spain seemed on the verge of anarchy.

The Rivera Dictatorship. The situation was saved for the monarchy by military dictatorship. At the suggestion of a group of army men Alfonso agreed that General Primo de Rivera should take active direction of the government. Accordingly, on September 13, just before the scheduled presentation of the parliamentary report on the Moroccan disaster, General Rivera proclaimed martial law.

Two years later Alfonso justified his action as follows: "What else could we do? . . . While at Barcelona they assassinated in broad daylight, and while our social and economic life was on its way to disintegration, parliament was occupied with wretched questions concerning the parishes, or with the satisfaction of its grudges. Things could not continue thus. General Primo did what you know. He told me that he could solve the situation in three months and return to legality within the period prescribed by the constitution. This was not my opinion. I believed that three months would not be enough."[3]

In reality, however, the causes for the *coup d'état* were more complex. As in most post-war countries, Spain's old political, social, and economic balance of power had been completely upset by the rising burgher, peasant, and proletarian classes. The result was a revolutionary movement in which the proletarian radicals sought to overthrow not only the king and the army, but all conservative vested interests, such as the clergy, the landed nobility, and the wealthy capitalists. The king and his conservative supporters resorted to dictatorship in order to save their way of life. For them, at least, the Rivera regime was a great success, and the general public, disgusted with the violence of the Barcelona radicals and the incompetence of the Madrid politicians, was not averse to a strong governing hand.

Rivera's Government. The dictatorship did not lapse within the constitutional period of three months. It lasted for six years, from 1923 to 1929, and during this period Spain had peace and a considerable degree of prosperity. With Rivera in power, economic conditions improved. To be sure, there was a strict censorship, and all competitive political activities, including elections, were abolished. But this was represented as the suspension of a badly muddled parliamentary system pending necessary readjustments. Meanwhile executive and legislative authority was vested in the dictator and his advisory council, called the Directorate, consisting of military men, each of whom exercised civil and military control over a section of Spain. Rivera, however, was the real ruler, and all decisions were promulgated by his decree. Later the Directorate was replaced by a Council of Ministers, composed largely of officials of the Patriotic Union, a permanent party modeled after Mussolini's " Black Shirts."

Rivera's Accomplishments. The first fruits of the dictatorship were surprisingly favorable. According to a summary in the London *Times*, " Efficiency and order succeeded wasteful futility, graft, and violence. The murderous conflict between employers and workers in Barcelona, which cost hundreds of lives, was ended. Government departments learned to do their business; great schemes of public works were carried out and there was a wave of unaccustomed prosperity. The terrible drain of blood in Morocco was stopped by a brilliant and decisive campaign." [4]

This analysis gives a reasonably fair picture of the early years of the dictatorship, when Rivera's administration, like a new broom, swept clean. The Moroccan crisis was ended in unbelievably successful fashion, thanks to good fortune, vigorous efficiency, and an effective attack on the Riffs by the French forces in their portion of Morocco. At any rate the Riffs were defeated, forced to surrender, and thus Spanish military prestige was restored.

Political Measures. The Catalan problem was settled in an arbitrary way. The autonomous administration and language that the four provinces had enjoyed for years were abolished and all resistance was crushed by the rigid application of martial law. The same methods of repression were applied everywhere, and with general success, against opponents of the new regime. Agents of the dictator fought Anarchists and other revolutionary bands with their own weapons of terror. Outspoken radicals, among them several professors, were dismissed from office.

Social Reforms. Similarly effective methods were used in eliminating corrupt public officials. The government also proved its efficiency in constructive social reform. An extensive public works program relieved unemployment and weakened the efforts of radical agitators among the proletariat. A law providing for joint committees of workers and employers in various lines of production served as a step toward the solution of labor problems. Municipal housing projects were encouraged by government-supported loans, and the public works program made marked progress in the erection of school buildings, among them the University City at Madrid.

Economic Measures. Rivera's handling of economic affairs showed efficiency. Early in 1924, by dictatorial decree he established a Council of National Economy which was able to claim a number of achievements. Hydroelectric power began to revolutionize the appearance of the Spanish countryside, even though the peasantry still clung to their primitive modes of existence. Modern auto highways were built, railways extended and modernized. Ports were equipped with up-to-date dock facilities, telephone systems were expanded and automatic exchanges introduced. Experiments in scientific farming and irrigation gave promise of real progress in agriculture. Industry was speeded up to such a degree that manufacturers became fearful of overproduction and the government was forced to set up a regulatory commission. In finance, likewise, the hand of totalitarianism was evident. Monopolies, taxes, tariffs, and international loans were rigidly controlled. By 1927, for the first time in decades, the governmental budget was at least nominally balanced and the national currency comparatively stable. It is probable, however, that the financial situation was made to appear more favorable than it actually was.

Decline of the Rivera Government. From 1928 onward, the record sheet of the Rivera government is increasingly unfavorable. There were minor irritations such as censorship of private correspondence, tapping of telephone wires, and the like, which hurt the government's popularity without increasing its prestige. The very moderateness of the regime signified underlying weaknesses. Only Communists, Syndicalists, and Anarchists were treated harshly. Other political offenders suffered light penalties, which were often remitted. The lenient treatment of a group of rebellious army men in 1926 encouraged radical propaganda and subversive activity. Within three years the government was overthrown by the action of its own paid officials in the universities and the army.

The dictator's first serious setback arose over a question of the extension of academic privileges to certain Catholic colleges. He disregarded the protests of the University of Madrid and the National Federation of Universities, whereupon the Student Union staged a strike. The dictator promptly imprisoned the President of the Madrid Student Union and ordered the suspension of all offending students, at which their fellows, among them Rivera's own nephew, paraded the streets and burned the dictator in effigy. Soon the professors began to join the movement for academic freedom. As it became evident that the cause was too popular to crush, Rivera capitulated. But the students, reveling in their newfound power, continued the fight in an all-university strike (January, 1930) to force the release of their student President and several professors. All of this had an important part in the fall of the Rivera regime.

Resignation of Rivera. As in 1923, however, the *coup de grâce* to a tottering regime was delivered by the army. In 1929 the same army corps that had been punished so mildly in 1926 mutinied. The revolt was easily put down by the use of airplanes, but in the trials of the culprits the king and the general public sided with the army, and Rivera's effort at exemplary discipline suffered defeat. Not long thereafter, when the king openly opposed Rivera's plan for a new constitution, the dictator called on the army leaders to support him and force the king to submit or abdicate. They refused, and the general, reading the handwriting on the wall, resigned (1930) and went into exile in France, where he died shortly. Thus the king and army that had set up a military dictatorship in 1923 overthrew it in 1930. To be sure, the king called another general, Berenguer, to form a new government which was to observe the old constitution, but in reality this was merely a front, behind which the king hoped to regain control. The new regime lasted less than a year and was marked by mounting discontent.

General Disorder. Meanwhile, thanks to the restoration of constitutionalism, the republican revolutionaries were able to carry on effective propaganda. So active in the cause were the university men that it was called " the professors' republic." The first blood shed for the cause, however, was that of students. The University of Madrid, particularly the medical school, became a veritable republican fortress from which student radicals issued to combat monarchist and Catholic youth organizations.

Meanwhile, in the large cities proletarian labor organizations were staging general strikes and acts of violence. More strikes occurred in the year 1930 than in any previous year, although this record (514) was surpassed in 1931 with 704. Finally the government attempted a rigorous policy of repression when republican-inspired mutinies broke out in two garrisons. At the king's insistence that " blood must be spilled," the ringleaders were executed. Such eleventh-hour severity militated against the government. The culprits were hailed as martyrs. Soon twelve revolutionary leaders set up a provisional republican government. The arrest of six of them merely added fuel to the flames. A manifesto appeared summoning all professional men and workers, and especially young men, to support the republic.

The Berenguer ministry eventually succumbed, and its successor, headed by Admiral Aznar, reverted to a policy of such extreme leniency that imprisoned republican leaders found it possible to direct their subversive campaign from prison. At the trial of sixty republican conspirators, the defense was allowed full freedom to present its case with dramatic effectiveness. Eighteen men who received sentences were escorted from the courtroom in triumph, and the government decided to commute the sentences. Even this final gesture of governmental leniency was answered by riots on the part of the students and their proletarian allies.

Abdication of Alfonso. Such was the situation early in April, 1931, when elections were held, the first free elections in eight years, resulting in heavy republican majorities in the industrial cities. The monarchy was doomed. On receipt of the returns the republican leaders called on all governmental officials to submit to the will of the nation, and King Alfonso, after a last effort to save the monarchy, agreed to abdicate. On April 14, in a farewell message to a group of his officials, he announced that he was going into exile in order to prevent bloodshed, but that he renounced none of his traditional rights. An auto spirited him to Cartagena where a cruiser waited to carry him to France. The rest of the royal family, after a trying night during which a mob threatened to invade the palace, followed him to France by rail. Thus passed the Bourbon dynasty.[5]

The Republic of 1931. Immediately after taking over the government, the republican leaders in Madrid proclaimed Alcalá Zamora as President and declared a national holiday. Soon trouble developed in Catalonia where a separate republic had been proclaimed, thus threatening the unity of the nation. A break was avoided when the Catalans abandoned their idea of a " Confederation of Iberian Republics " and agreed to the restoration of their old autonomous " Generalitat." Thus Spain made the immediate transition from monarchy to republic with no bloodshed and little excitement, but during the following month the "immaculate " republic, the brain child of professordom, received its baptism of violence. On Sunday, May 10, 1931, a group of Madrid monarchists, inspired by the inflammatory press releases of a conservative newspaper in support of the exiled king and the Catholic religion, struck a taxi driver who had shouted " Long live the Republic! " Before long the assailants were besieged in their monarchist club by an angry mob. Later the offices of the offending newspaper were raided, and on the following day several Catholic edifices were burned. The violence spread, and for two days churchmen and church buildings were attacked in many cities throughout southern Spain. The fury subsided, leaving conservative folk frightened and resentful. The new government's response to the situation was to pass several anti-clerical measures.

The New Constitution. Meanwhile in many northern cities, the Anarchists and Syndicalists, in order to force the selection of a more radical ministry, incited general strikes. At San Sebastian six rioters were killed. Throughout the rest of the year the government had conflicts with extreme revolutionists. With increasing forcefulness, police, regular troops, artillery, and airplanes were employed to quell disorders. Meanwhile the Constitutional Convention was drawing up a republican constitution. The membership of the convention was predominantly Leftist, with the various professions represented as follows: 123 lawyers, 65 professors, 41 doctors, and 24 workmen. It is noteworthy that the lawyers now outnumbered the professors in the national councils. By December a constitution of strongly socialistic tendencies had been adopted. It provided for a President, a Premier and council of ministers, and a unicameral legislature (Cortes) to which the premier and ministry were directly responsible. On December 11, 1931, President-elect Alcalá Zamora was formally driven to his palace, 40,000 copies of the constitution were dropped from airplanes, and Spain celebrated another national holiday.

Spanish history since the founding of the republic can be roughly divided into four two-year periods, two of which were dominated by the Leftists and two by the Rightists. Two years of rule by the Left (December, 1931 to November, 1933) were followed by two years under Centrist and Rightist leaders (November, 1933 to February, 1936); after an interim of a few months under the Leftist " Popular Front," came civil war (July, 1936 to January, 1939), followed by a period of Fascist reconstruction.

The Azaña Government. Leftist rule, with Alcalá Zamora as President and Manuel Azaña as Premier, was a chaotic period of trial and error for the young republic. A number of constructive reforms were launched but none of them were worked out completely in time to be effective.[6] The Clerical problem was handled with much the same rigorousness as in France; church and state were separated, religious equality was proclaimed, the property of Clerical orders was confiscated, the Jesuit order abolished, and Clerical influence in education reduced to the vanishing point. Most of this legislation, however, was invalidated by the fall of the Leftist government in 1933. Greater progress was made in military reform. The top-heavy aristocratic officerdom was greatly reduced by a drastic pension system, and short-term universal military training was introduced. Unfortunately many of the pensioned officers devoted themselves to intrigue against the republic. The most needed and promising of reforms was the agrarian law which provided for the abolition of ancient feudal dues and the expropriation of all uncultivated land and all estates of exiled monarchists. To these were added the confiscated church properties. Unfortunately, as with most of their reforms, the republican politicians studied and discussed the problem with such deliberation that by the time the law was completed the nation was ready to vote out the Leftist government.

The Azaña government displayed far more decisiveness in dealing with its political opponents. Syndicalist rebels in Catalonia and Bilbao, monarchists in Madrid, discontented republicans in Seville, peasants at Casas Viejas, and even radical students of the University of Madrid were suppressed with such severity that the opposition began to revile " the government of mud, blood, and tears." Restrictions on the press and a more rigid law of Public Order added to a discontent which was finally registered in the November, 1933 elections. Out of 473 seats in the Cortes, the Leftists retained only 99. The balance of power swung to the Center (167 seats) and Right (207) parties.

The Conservative Republic. It soon became apparent, however, that the nation had exchanged Leftist tyranny for the lethargy and petty feuds of the politicians of the Center and Right. The period of their control from November, 1933 to February, 1936 saw no constructive reforms, and the government degenerated into a succession of falling ministries. The agrarian problem became steadily worse, and when the Supreme Court ruled against an important Catalan land law, the Madrid government found that it had stirred up the old question of regional autonomy. Encouraged by Basque resistance to the tax policy of the central government, the Catalan deputies walked out of the Cortes. Eventually the Barcelona radicals, proclaiming themselves the sole defenders of true Spanish republicanism, precipitated a revolt. It was quickly suppressed, and as a result Catalonia lost her autonomy and became once more " a colony of Madrid." Later, during the brief " Popular Front " in 1936, Catalonia's age-old privileges were recovered, only to be abolished by Franco two years later.

Meanwhile the ineffectiveness of the Madrid government was accentuated by widespread disturbances, one of which took on the characteristics of civil war. As is common to radical revolts in Spain, the Asturian trouble began with a general strike, at Oviedo (October, 1934). It developed into a small-scale civil war as about 6000 well-armed rebels, many of them miners, attacked the government forces in the city. After a week of ferocious street fighting, in which some 1300 were killed, the government troops regained control of the devastated remains of one of Spain's outstanding cities.

The Popular Front. In the ensuing year (1935) ineffective proposals were made for revising the constitution and balancing the budget, accompanied by increasing political disorder. In January, 1936 the government called for the election of a new Cortes. Under the able leadership of Azaña, a Leftist coalition, called the " Popular Front," won a sweeping victory, and with it a working majority of 256 seats (more than double the former strength of the Left).

With the accession of Premier Azaña and the " Popular Front," it became evident that radicalism was in the ascendancy. Unfortunately, many of the victorious leaders, including those returning from burdensome exile, were inclined to vengeful violence. There were widespread murders and riots, and acts of wanton destruction against churches throughout Spain. It has been estimated that within four months there were over 300 strikes (a third of them general strikes) and 170 churches were burned. Peasant outbreaks occurred as the new government failed to speed the distribution of lands long promised by republican politicians. Less apparent, but more sinister, was the plotting of the desperate leaders of the conservative military, Clerical, and monarchist factions. Inspired by Mussolini and Hitler, certain Fascist groups were known to be planning a *coup*. Governmental repression was answered with terrorism, and soon political murders, perpetrated after the fashion of American gunmen, were occurring in broad daylight in Madrid and other large cities.

Civil War. The inevitable break came on July 17, 1936 with the revolt of General Franco and his Moroccan regiments. On the following day, apparently by preconceived plan, the generals at various military centers in the peninsula joined the revolution. To check them, the local republican leaders called general strikes and summoned the workers to arms. In Madrid and Barcelona, where the Rebels were quickly overpowered, the Loyalists took cruel vengeance, not only on prisoners but also on churches. The central government, however, was strangely ineffective. Azaña, who might have become a great war leader, had recently been elected President, and stood firmly for constitutional procedure. Lacking a strong Premier, the " Popular Front " disintegrated, with the Communists in most regions taking the lead in local defense.

Franco's Superiority. Meanwhile General Franco had landed in Spain and soon the Rebels had possession of most of the south. They also controlled a stretch of the northwestern coast, and General Mola established himself at Burgos. The war raged for over two and a half years, with Franco slowly gaining control of central and eastern Spain. His victory was due chiefly to outside aid; he was given constant and effective assistance by Germany and Italy, while the Loyalists were either hampered or received intermittent aid by the wavering democratic powers. From the outbreak of the war, if not before, Hitler, Mussolini, and also Salazar, ruler of Portugal, supplied Franco with war materials, and later with fighting men. The Loyalists obtained considerable material from France and Russia, but not until Franco had built up a tremendous superiority in equipment. Even after the European nations made a non-intervention agreement, Franco continued to receive effective outside aid. It is estimated that at the outset he operated at a disadvantage of 1 to 4 in airplanes. After two months of so-called " non-intervention," he had a superiority of 12 to 1 in planes and 20 to 1 in tanks. During the fall of 1936, while scattered bands of inexperienced Loyalist militiamen were struggling to keep the enemy from Madrid, the United States and England put an embargo on arms to Spain lest they aid the cause of world Communism. France and Russia were not fearful of Communism but were slow in acting. As a result the Loyalist cause appeared to be hopeless.

Course of the War. By November, 1936, however, there came a turn in the tide. Russia began to " observe " non-intervention in the same manner as Italy and Germany: that is, by direct military aid. It was probably the arrival of Russian planes and foreign volunteers early in November that saved Madrid from Franco's Moors. Meanwhile the Loyalist government became more effective, with a coalition which included, for the first time in Spanish history, Anarchists cooperating with Socialists and Communists. In mid-November Franco's sagging cause received diplomatic recognition from his allies, Italy and Germany. Even so, the quick victory expected by the Rebels was not forthcoming. Although Madrid was threatened, and Loyalist communications between Valencia and Barcelona were harassed by sea and from the recently acquired Italian air bases in Majorca, the Fascist forces made little progress. Furthermore, the defenders of Madrid were heartened by an unexpected victory over the vaunted Italians at Guadalajara. Thanks to the bombing efficiency of Russian planes and the fighting spirit of two international brigades (composed of Italian and German exiles along with Americans and other anti-Fascists) the enemy was thrown back with heavy losses. With the Madrid front deadlocked, the Fascists concentrated their attacks elsewhere. After capturing the important Basque port of Bilbao (June 19, 1937), Rebel forces drove steadily eastward to the north and south of Madrid. Madrid held out against constant bombing and shelling, but eventually Valencia was captured and Barcelona isolated. On October 22, 1937 the Rebels captured Gijón, wiping out Loyalist resistance along the Biscayan coast. On April 15, 1938 the Rebels severed Catalonia from the rest of republican Spain.

Through the dreary months of 1938, Franco's German and Italian allies poured supplies and men into Fascist Spain while American, British, and French statesmen dawdled over the various aspects of neutrality and non-intervention. Eventually Russia ceased to render effective aid to the Loyalists. Madrid, harder and harder pressed, suffered hunger, disease, and also republican terrorism, inspired by fear of the Fascist " fifth column." Barcelona, under Communist and separatist leadership, both physically and spiritually isolated from Madrid, stoutly resisted the horrors of modern air bombing. The end came during the winter of 1938–1939, with Loyalist officials fleeing for safety and refugees streaming northward to France. Franco's triumphant entry into Barcelona (January 26, 1939) signalized the end of the war.

Fascism Triumphant. The Spanish republic fell, overwhelmed by an alliance of Spanish Clericals, military men, great landowners and wealthy industrialists, which was supported lavishly with men and munitions by Mussolini and to a lesser extent by Hitler. The disorganized radicalism of the Popular Front, together with the hesitancy of the democracies in Europe and America in coming to the aid of the Loyalists, helped to nullify the courageous defense of the republic. Fighting against overwhelming odds, the Loyalists showed the world a magnificent example of valor and tenacity.

As for Franco, the fortunes of victory had catapulted him from the command of a comparatively unpopular military faction into the leadership of a nation of 25 million people.

The Franco Government. Franco's powers and his Fascist state evolved amid the exigencies of war. Early in the conflict a military Directorate was formed. With the deaths of the more prominent generals such as Sanjurjo (one of the original conspirators against the republic) Franco assumed a more dictatorial role. Early in 1937 he merged his somewhat disunited following into a closely knit party, the *Falange Española Tradicionalista,* and abolished all other political organizations. The aims of the Falangistas, and therefore of the new Fascist state, were embodied in a twenty-six point constitution, which summoned all individuals to bow to the nation's collective will. The nation (it was asserted) must develop a strong army and navy, and a " spiritual axis " with Spanish America; banks and public utilities must be nationalized, and church and state " coordinated " but without impairing the dignity of the state. In carrying out these ideals, Franco's leadership was supreme. He appointed a council to supervise industry, labor, and agriculture. In January, 1938 the military Directorate gave way to a Ministry, of which Franco was President and also Minister of War. So far, the dictatorship could be viewed as a revival, in a more brutal fashion, of the Rivera regime. In August, 1939, however, Franco proclaimed himself absolute dictator with the power of naming a National Council of 75 persons, and appointing his successor.

The Era of Reconstruction. The evolution of Franco's personal authority makes it clear that the Spanish revolution of 1936–1939 was in large measure part of the world totalitarian revolution. The ground was cleared for the building of a new state, for the civil war destroyed much of old Spain. Death had taken about 5 per cent of her population: over 700,000 in battle, and over 300,000 in executions, air raids, and other ways. In Barcelona and Madrid thousands of buildings were made unusable by artillery and air bombardment. Everywhere roads, bridges, and railroads were destroyed, business life and agriculture badly disorganized. There were also complicated problems of reorganizing man power; almost a million men were in Fascist uniform, about 600,000 Loyalists were in captivity and, what was more disturbing to the Franco regime, at least half the nation had republican sympathies.

The dictator's handling of the situation was typically Fascist. There were strict emergency measures; martial law in certain regions, rationing of food, the use of prisoners for reconstruction work, and special courts to try Communists and republicans.[7] In order to speed rehabilitation, the government prescribed fifteen days a year of labor without pay for all citizens. Of the Fascist military forces, over half were demobilized, leaving about 300,000 men under arms in September, 1939. Strikes were outlawed, the press and communications censored and consumption of gasoline rationed.

Economic Progress. Just how much Franco has accomplished since the end of the war it is impossible to state, for information is scanty and highly colored. Internally Spain seems to be slowly recuperating. It will doubtless take years for the nation to attain the economic prosperity it enjoyed during the early years of the Rivera regime. Never during the twentieth century had Spanish industrial and agricultural production been so great, governmental deficits so low, and expenditures on public works so high as at that time.[8] During the 1930's Spain's material resources were employed with increasing inefficiency. Never had there been such loss of man power in strikes as during the republican regime [9] and such useless destruction of life and property as during the civil war. It is certain that the Fascist regime will bring some improvement; it may be that Franco, like Salazar in Portugal, will strike a medium somewhere between the inefficiency of competitive capitalism and the inhuman regimentation of forced labor.

Foreign Policy. In foreign policy, as in domestic affairs, Spain has drifted into rough waters; from the prosperous neutral of 1914–1918 it has become a militant Fascist state. During Rivera's dictatorship Spain withdrew from the League of Nations and crushed the Riffs in Morocco. Franco's indebtedness for German and Italian aid in establishing his regime made him, as some said, a tool of the Rome-Berlin axis. In August, 1940 Spain signed a mutual assistance pact with Portugal. In spite of the fact that Portugal still retains her ancient commercial ties with England, it seems apparent that Fascist Portugal is being drawn more closely to Spain.

The drift of events suggests the possibility of Spain's recovering Gibraltar, should Germany defeat Britain, and with it the control of the western entrance to the Mediterranean. Such a change, at the expense of Great Britain, is in line with recent Spanish claims to extensive regions of the African Atlantic coast south of Morocco.[10] In similarly aggressive fashion Franco looks far to the westward where he sees another usurper, the United States, whose supposedly imperialistic ambitions in Central and South America he would check by the creation of an Iberian Hispanic-American axis.[11]

Cultural Progress: Literature.[12] The literary history of twentieth-century Spain is dominated by two disasters, the Spanish-American War which brought to full bloom the " generation of 1898," and the civil war of 1936 which destroyed or exiled the existing generation of free and independent writers. From 1898 to 1936, Spanish writers were greatly concerned with the social, economic, and political problems of their native land. Most of them were radical reformers who crusaded against corrupt politics, Cleri-

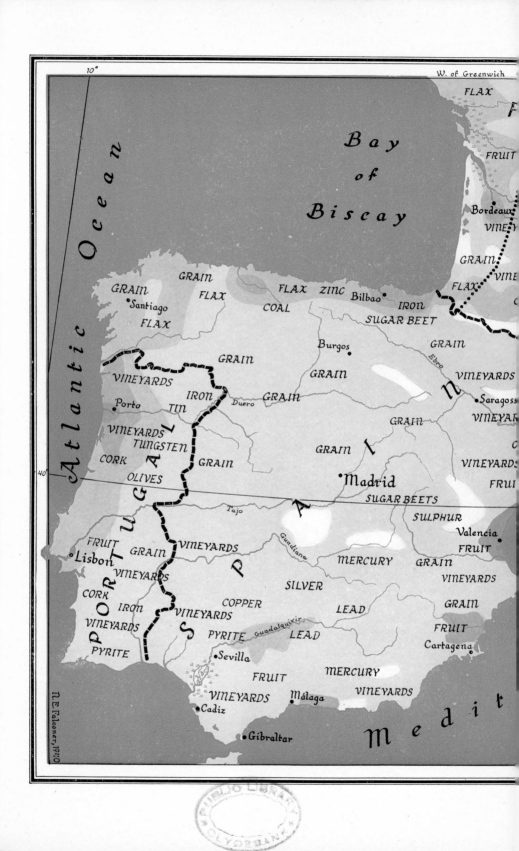

Atlantic Ocean

Bay of Biscay

FLAX

FRUIT

Bordeaux

VINE

GRAIN

VINE

FLAX

GRAIN

GRAIN

FLAX

Santiago

FLAX

FLAX ZINC Bilbao

COAL

IRON

SUGAR BEET

Burgos

GRAIN

GRAIN

GRAIN

VINEYARDS

Saragoss

VINEYARDS

Porto

IRON

TIN

Duero

GRAIN

GRAIN

GRAIN

VINEYARDS

TUNGSTEN

CORK

GRAIN

Madrid

VINEYARDS

OLIVES

SUGAR BEETS

FRUI

Tajo

SULPHUR

Valencia

VINEYARDS

FRUIT

MERCURY

GRAIN

FRUIT

Lisbon

GRAIN

VINEYARDS

Guadiana

SILVER

VINEYARDS

CORK

COPPER

LEAD

GRAIN

IRON

VINEYARDS

PYRITE

Guadalquivir

LEAD

FRUIT

VINEYARDS

Cartagena

PYRITE

Sevilla

MERCURY

FRUIT

VINEYARDS

VINEYARDS

Málaga

Cadiz

Gibraltar

Mediter

Ebro

PORTUGAL

SPAIN

VINEYARDS

40°

R.E.Falconer, 1910

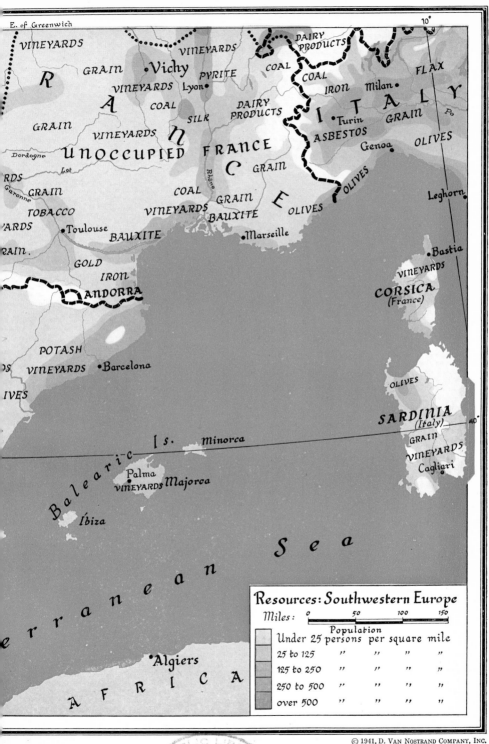

E. of Greenwich

VINEYARDS

GRAIN •Vichy PYRITE
VINEYARDS Lyon•
COAL

GRAIN
VINEYARDS

Dordogne
UNOCCUPIED FRANCE

Lot

RDS
GRAIN
Garonne

TOBACCO
•Toulouse BAUXITE

ARDS
•Marseille

RAIN.

GOLD
IRON

ANDORRA

POTASH

VINEYARDS •Barcelona

IVES

Is. Minorca
Balearic

Palma
Majorca
VINEYARDS

Íbiza

VINEYARDS

DAIRY
PRODUCTS
COAL COAL
IRON Milan• FLAX
SILK DAIRY
PRODUCTS
Turin GRAIN
ASBESTOS
Genoa OLIVES
GRAIN OLIVES
COAL GRAIN
VINEYARDS BAUXITE OLIVES
OLIVES
Leghorn•

•Bastia

VINEYARDS

CORSICA
(France)

OLIVES

SARDINIA
(Italy) 40°

GRAIN

VINEYARDS
Cagliari•

Po

e
a
n
S e a

r r a n
e
•Algiers

A F R I C A

Resources: Southwestern Europe

Miles: 0   50   100   150

	Population			
	Under 25 persons per square mile			
	25 to 125	,,	,,	,,	,,
	125 to 250	,,	,,	,,	,,
	250 to 500	,,	,,	,,	,,
	over 500	,,	,,	,,	,,

© 1941, D. VAN NOSTRAND COMPANY, INC.

calism and the caste system, and the rhetorical romanticism of the nine-teenth century.[13] Thus, among the prose writers, we find men such as Mi-guel Unamuno (1864–1936), a sturdy Basque novelist, poet, and essayist who criticized the monarchical regime of Alfonso XIII, was sent into exile by Rivera, and finally died under the Franco regime. Although of a more academic temperament, José Ortega Gasset (1883–   ), Professor of Phi-losophy at Madrid, mercilessly exposed the social and economic evils of his nation in works such as *Invertebrate Spain*. Spain's passion for self-criticism was carried on with a more refined touch by the popular essayist, José Martínez Ruiz (1874–   ) who is known as " Azorín."

Among the more erudite men of letters were many supporters of the republic, such as the eminent essayist, ambassador, and Minister of Educa-tion, Salvador de Madariaga (1886–   ); the philologist and historian Menéndez Pidal; and the legalist Fernando de los Ríos who directed the ministries of education and justice and served as ambassador to the United States.[14]

Contemporary Spanish drama has turned its back on the past in un-mistakable fashion in the works of Jacinto Benavente (1866–   ), Nobel Prize winner of 1922, author of *Saturday Night*, *The Passion Flower*, and *Bonds of Interest*, plays written with genial humor and social conscious-ness. The racy comedies of Serafín (1871–   ) and Joaquín Quintero (1873–   ) are brilliant genre pictures of Andalusian life. Of their nu-merous dramas, *A Hundred Years Old* and *The Lady from Alfaqueque* are perhaps best known in the United States.

The Spanish novel has made vigorous strides in the twentieth century. Some of the novelists did not yield completely to the modern spirit. Among these can be found Ricardo León, who criticized the spirit of the generation of 1898 and exalted the religious idealism of old Spain,[15] and Gabriel Miró and Ramón María de Valle-Inclán, who impress the reader with their literary artistry rather than revolutionary fervor.

One of the most famous of reformist novelists was Blasco Ibáñez (1867–1928), author of *The Four Horsemen of the Apocalypse*, *Blood and Sand*, and other popular works. Ibáñez was an interesting combination of stylist and iconoclast. In the early part of his career he wrote tales of regional life, flavored with anti-clericalism and republican sentiment. *The Four Horsemen*, a World War story, gave him an international reputation and thenceforth, according to some critics, he tended to commercialize his talent in the writing of spectacular works. However this may be, during the last decade of his life he displayed an increasing revolutionary zeal, turning his vigorous pen to the task of unmasking Alfonso XIII.

Among other revolutionary novelists Pío Baroja (1872–   ) has the widest following abroad. His works, such as the trilogy, *Memoirs of a Man of Action*, were influenced by Dickens, Dostoievsky, and Nietzsche.

Ramón Pérez de Ayala (1881–   ), in spite of his Jesuit education, satirized the clerical educational system in the novel, *A.M.D.G.* Ayala became one of the intellectual fathers of the republic. Ramón Sender (1901–   ) is a fiery revolutionist out of whose personal experiences have come powerful novels like *Seven Red Sundays* and *Counter-Attack in Spain.*

The Arts. Twentieth-century Spain has been by no means as productive in the plastic arts as in literature. Ignacio Zuloaga (1881–   ) and Sorolla y Bastido (1886–1903), though not to be compared with Goya or El Greco, have painted native scenes with a harsh realism that is typically Spanish. Zuloaga has achieved fame as a portrait painter, Sorolla as a painter of brilliant sea-scapes. Pablo Picasso (1881–   ) and Salvador Dali (1904–   ), though Spanish born, came under the influence of the French. Picasso is, with Braque, the leader of the Cubist movement, that school of painters which values form for its own sake and disregards or slights meaning and content. Dali is perhaps the most forceful of Surrealist painters. He depicts illogical and impossible facts in a style that is grotesquely appealing. The creations of Dali are masterpieces of spectacular realism set in a fantastically unreal atmosphere.

Music. Manuel de Falla (1876–   ) is the outstanding contemporary Spanish composer. His music gaily assimilates Spanish folk tunes with complicated modern orchestral techniques, as in the oft-played ballet, *The Three-Cornered Hat*, and the opera *La Vida Breve.*

With the advent of the Franco regime, Spain's cultural life was tragically disrupted. Some pro-Loyalist writers like Unamuno and the lyric poet García Lorca, met death at the hands of the Rebels. Others took up arms for the republic. When the Fascists triumphed nearly all of Spain's intellectual leaders fled the wrath of Franco. Many of them found warm welcome in Mexico, the United States, and South America, fertilizing, along with the exiled Germans, Italians, Austrians, and other emigrés, the cultural life of the New World. In this, as in other respects, the loss of Europe is the gain of other continents.

Portugal

Political Chaos. Portugal's role in the twentieth century is as unenviable as that of many a small nation caught in the whirl of conflicting political movements. In domestic affairs, Portugal has traveled the same troubled path as Spain, though without the devastating influences of foreign intervention and a prolonged civil war. As in Spain, the monarchy was overthrown (in 1910) but without extreme violence. This was followed by a republican regime which, for almost two decades (from 1910 to 1928), manifested little stability or efficiency. The state was afflicted with both corrupt politicians and a revolutionary military force. Twice during the period (in 1915 and 1918), rebellious members of the navy bombarded Lisbon. Premier after premier and ministry after ministry were overthrown. In the course of a political struggle in 1921 the premier was murdered. Finally, in 1926, the republic gave way to a military dictatorship, which brought the state to the verge of bankruptcy and a communistic revolution within two years.

Dictatorship of Salazar. The situation was saved by Dr. Oliveira Salazar, formerly a professor of economics at the University of Coimbra, who became Premier and Minister of Finance in 1928. Under his government Portugal found political stability and economic regeneration. Within a year he had balanced the budget (a condition unrealized since 1914), reduced both the national debt and the interest rate, and proven his ability to give the nation an efficient and not too autocratic government. The Salazar dictatorship has followed Italian lines, its basis being the party of National Union which supports Roman Catholicism and modified totalitarianism.

The Corporate State. The economic aspect of Salazar's regime has taken the form of a planned economy in which each producing unit is encouraged to regulate itself in the interest of the commonwealth; at the same time the government is ready to coerce recalcitrants and coordinate the whole system. Corporate units have been established in agriculture, industry, and finance. For instance, the government controls the wine trade by means of a federation of growers and a guild of exporters. By similarly effective regulation the raising of wheat, which Portugal had not produced in sufficient quantity, was increased to the point where it was found necessary to restrict the crop. Salazar lays great emphasis on self-discipline and cooperation for the welfare of the nation.

Foreign Policy. As already noted, Portugal is torn between the conflicting interests of her friends, England and Italy. For centuries Portugal has been closely bound to England by economic, diplomatic, and military ties.[16] At the beginning of the First World War she supported England, and from 1916 on Portuguese soldiers stood shoulder to shoulder with the Allies on the western front. On the other hand, Portugal in recent years has been drawn strongly toward Italy, by reason of her Fascist type of government and by the fact that both nations aided Franco in the Spanish civil war. It is an open question which will prove the stronger, Portugal's ideological unity with Italy, or her long-standing ties with England. Whatever the outcome, it is apparent that the influence of Italian Fascism in both Spain and Portugal, along with their common adherence to Roman Catholicism, has created a closely knit group of Fascist powers in the western Mediterranean which will play an increasingly important role in European affairs.

REFERENCES

[1] Unless otherwise specified we shall use the term " Spain " with reference to the Castilian and Catalonian portions of the peninsula, and exclusive of Portugal. Important trends in Portuguese history that differ from those in other parts of the peninsula will be noted.

[2] See below, p. 293.

[3] See J. Tharaud, *Rendez-vous Espagnols*, Paris: Plon, 1925, p. 24.

[4] Quoted from J. Brandt, *Toward the New Spain*, Chicago: Univ. of Chicago Press, 1933, p. 370. The " Times " analysis follows the same optimistic interpretation as that of the official government summary of the accomplishments of the regime. See W. Langsam, *Documents and Readings*, p. 605. For an unfavorable account, see F. Manuel, *The Politics of Modern Spain*, ch. 3.

[5] It has been remarked that " Alfonso was a good king as kings go, and as good kings go, he went, without bloodshed." It is noteworthy that, except for the lack of extreme violence in the case of Spain, the passing of Alfonso's monarchy was quite similar to that of Louis XVI of France.

[6] See W. Langsam, *Documents and Readings*, p. 607 ff. for examples of the reform program; viz., extracts from the republican constitution, the religious legislation, the educational program, and the Catalan Statute of Autonomy.

[7] Out of a series of recorded trials, about a third of those accused were condemned to death and executed.

[8] In 1926–1927, according to the Encyclopaedia Britannica, production in typical fields of industry and agriculture attained the following amounts (in metric tons): iron and steel, 1,100,000; copper 48,000; zinc 16,000; mercury 2,000; wheat 3,942,000; barley 2,008,000; grapes 4,612,000; wine 28,325,000; olives 2,517,000. Spain most closely approximated this high point during the abnormally prosperous period of the First World War. Between that favored period and the regime of Rivera came the postwar depression. Similarly unfavorable trends marked the late years of Rivera's dictatorship, and the republic. See above, note 4, for conflicting ideas concerning the success of the Rivera regime.

[9] In 1930 there were 368 strikes (with 247,000 workers involved); in 1931, 610 (236,000 workers); in 1932, 435 (269,000 workers); in 1933, 1046 (843,000 workers), etc. See F. Manuel, *The Politics of Modern Spain*, p. 128.

[10] Spain already possesses Ifni, Cape Juby Territory, Rio de Oro, Fernando Po, Annobon, Elobey, Corisco, and Rio Muni, in this region; also the Canary Isles in the Atlantic Ocean.

[11] In event of an Axis victory, Franco might dream of repossessing the New World colonies that once belonged to Spain. During the reign of Philip II, it will be noted, Spain's colonial empire included Portugal and her possessions in the Far East. He gave his name to the Philippine Islands.

[12] Without in any way shifting responsibility, I wish to thank my friend, Professor N. B. Adams, of the Department of Spanish of the University of North Carolina, for helpful criticisms on various points in this chapter, and especially on Spanish culture.

[13] The revolutionary spirit is, however, inconspicuous in Spanish poetry, which has a delicacy and refinement of feeling and expression that tends to dominate all other characteristics. There are, however, noteworthy exceptions, such as the Communist poet, Rafael Alberti, and his wife.

[14] In the last-mentioned capacity, he delivered an address that is a noteworthy analysis of educational conditions in Spain and the republican program of reform. See W. Langsam, *Documents and Readings*, p. 621 ff.; E. Peers, *The Spanish Tragedy*, p. 48 ff., gives an interesting and sympathetic account of the many intellectuals who served the republic in official capacities. In contrast, F. Manuel, *The Politics of Modern Spain*, pp. 121, 182, berates the intellectuals as turncoats, describing Fernando de los Ríos in ironical terms (p. 85).

[15] In Portugal the tendency to revert to the ideals of the past has been similarly emphasized, notably by the novelists, Antheri de Figueiredo, Manoel Ribeiro, and

Acquilino Ribeiro; by the essayists, Ramalho Ortigão and Eça da Queirez; and by the poet, Guerra Junqueiro.

16 Portugal has found a market for most of her port wine in England. She has also been dependent on Great Britain for the security of her communications with the remaining colonies of her once great overseas empire; notably the Azores and Madeira Islands, and Angola and Mozambique in Africa. Portugal still has strong ties with Brazil which was once a colony.

SELECTED BIBLIOGRAPHY: SPAIN

General Works

Brandt, J. A., *Toward the New Spain*, Chicago: Univ. of Chicago Press, 1932. A favorable survey of the development of republicanism in Spain from the republic of 1873 to that of 1931; especially good on the earlier phases.

Gannes, H. and Repared, T., *Spain in Revolt*, New York: Knopf, 2nd ed., 1937. A detailed, but hastily written and highly colored account of the entire period of the republic; valuable for its emphasis on labor problems and its exposition of the proletarian viewpoint.

Gasset, J. Ortega y, *Invertebrate Spain*, New York: Norton, 1937. Selected essays from the works of the noted republican liberal.

Kain, R. S., *Europe: Versailles to Warsaw*, New York: Wilson, 1939, Vol. XIII, No. 4 of *The Reference Shelf*, contains (pp. 214–231) an excellent survey of Spain and Portugal since 1938; particularly good on Franco's rebuilding of Spain.

Langsam, W. C., *Documents and Readings in the History of Europe since 1918*, Philadelphia: Lippincott, 1939. Chapter 8, dealing with Spain, contains well-chosen extracts.

Madariaga, Salvador de, *Spain*, New York: Scribner, 1930. An historical survey with emphasis on the contemporary period, by one of Spain's most brilliant scholars.

Manuel, F. E., *The Politics of Modern Spain*, New York: McGraw-Hill, 1938. A well-documented, Leftist interpretation of the entire period of the republic and the decline of the monarchy; valuable for its portrayal of the clash of social and economic interests.

Padelford, N. J., *International Law and Diplomacy in the Spanish Civil Strife*, New York: Macmillan, 1939. A thorough, scholarly account; especially valuable on the problems of neutrality and non-intervention.

Peers, E. A., *The Spanish Tragedy, 1930–1936*, New York: Oxford Univ. Press, 1936. A rather brief but thoroughly objective, chronological account by an English professor who knows Spain and its people intimately; the emphasis is on political narrative.

——, ed., *Spain: A Companion to Spanish Studies*, London: Methuen, 1938. An historical survey of various aspects of Spanish civilization with special emphasis on the contemporary period; especially useful for literature and the fine arts.

Robles, Gil, *Spain in Chains*, New York: American Press, 1937. A bitter condemnation of the Leftist republic, and a plea for an authoritarian, nationalist regime, by a prominent republican Rightist who joined the Rebels.

Smith, R. M., *The Day of the Liberals in Spain*, Philadelphia: Univ. of Pennsylvania Press, 1938. Contains a scholarly account of the republican constitution of 1931.

Villalba, A. M. Mendizábal, *The Martyrdom of Spain; The Origins of Civil War*, New York: Scribner, 1938. Developments in Spain from 1923 to the end of the republic, as seen by a liberal Spanish professor, who condemns both the Rightists and Leftists for Spain's woes.

Young, G. Y., *The New Spain*, London: Methuen, 1933. A spirited analysis of the monarchical regime, and the early months of the republic of 1931, by a former English diplomat who was favorably impressed by the Rivera dictatorship.

Civil War

Acier, Marcel, *From Spanish Trenches*, New York: Modern Age, 1937.
Bates, Ralph, *Lean Men*, New York: Macmillan, 1935, *The Olive Field*, New York: Dutton, 1936, and *Sirocco*, New York: Random House, 1939.
Bernanos, George, *A Diary of My Times*, New York: Macmillan, 1938.
Bessie, Alvah, *Men in Battle*, New York: Scribner, 1939.
Borkenau, F., *The Spanish Cockpit*, London: Faber, 1937.
Cardozo, H., *The March of a Nation*, New York: McBride, 1937.
Johnstone, Nancy, *Hotel in Spain*, New York: Longmans, Green, 1938.
Knoblaugh, H., *Correspondent in Spain*, London: Sheed and Ward, 1937.
Langdon-Davies, John, *Behind the Spanish Barricades*, New York: McBride, 1936.
Lunn, A., *Spanish Rehearsal*, London: Sheed and Ward, 1937.
Matthews, Herbert, *Two Wars and More to Come*, New York: Carrick, 1938.
Merin, P., *Spain between Death and Birth*, New York: Dodge, 1938.
Morrow, F., *Revolution and Counter Revolution in Spain*, New York: Pioneer, 1938.
Moss, G., *The Siege of the Alcazar*, New York: Knopf, 1937.
Paul, Eliot, *The Life and Death of a Spanish Town*, New York: Random House, 1937.
Rolfe, E., *The Lincoln Battalion*, New York: Random House, 1939.
Ruiz Vilaplana, A., *Burgos Justice*, New York: Knopf, 1938.
Sender, Ramón, *Seven Red Sundays*, New York: Liveright, 1936, and *Counter-Attack in Spain*, Boston: Houghton Mifflin, 1937.
Sheean, Vincent, *Not Peace but a Sword*, Garden City, N. Y.: Doubleday, Doran, 1939.
Sommerfield, John, *Volunteer in Spain*, New York: Knopf, 1937.
Strong, A., *Spain in Arms*, New York: Holt, 1937.
Timmermans, R., *Heroes of the Alcazar*, New York: Scribner, 1937.
Watson, K., *Single to Spain*, New York: Dutton, 1937.

PORTUGAL

Braganca-Cunha, V. de, *Revolutionary Portugal, 1910–1936*, London: Clarke, 1937, A solid, popularly written work.
Cotta, F., *Economic Planning in Corporative Portugal*, London: King, 1937. A scholarly account, favorable to the Salazar regime.
Derrick, M., *The Portugal of Salazar*, London: Sands, 1938. A rather popular discussion of Salazar and the structure of his government.
Salazar, Oliveira, *Doctrine and Action: The Internal and Foreign Policy of the New Portugal, 1928–1939*, London: Faber, 1939. Salazar's own statement of the principles of his regime and their expression in the political, economic, military, and diplomatic life of Portugal.
West, S., *The New Corporative State of Portugal*, Lisbon: The SPN Books, 1937. An inaugural lecture at Kings College, London, by a Professor of Portuguese. A valuable brief survey.

Chapter XIII

Italy

"BETWEEN 1935 AND 1940, WE SHALL FIND OURSELVES AT A POINT WHICH I SHOULD CALL A CRUCIAL POINT IN EUROPEAN HISTORY — WE SHALL BE IN A POSITION TO MAKE OUR VOICE FELT, AND TO SEE AT LAST OUR RIGHTS RECOGNIZED." — MUSSOLINI in May, 1927

Geography. The Kingdom of Italy covers an area of 120,956 square miles. This includes the territory of the peninsula proper, Sardinia, Sicily, and minor islands but not the African empire. The boot-shaped peninsula is 760 miles long and juts out into the Mediterranean for about 600 miles, almost dividing the sea into two parts. This part of the country is about 100 miles wide, and nowhere over 150 miles. There are numerous bays and gulfs but the eastern coast has few good harbors. The Apennines cross the northern part of the peninsula obliquely, then run nearly parallel with the coast. The rivers are mostly mountain torrents, and the Po and Tiber have more historical than commercial importance. Some 10 per cent of Italian soil is unproductive. While the southern region is mainly mountainous a substantial portion of Italy's wheat crop is raised in Sicily and the Apulian Tableland.

Background of Italian History. Though Italy is a homogeneous geographical unit, her political unity dates only from 1871. Subject to foreign influences for centuries, and broken up into a congeries of small states, the peninsula was divided into three main regions. The Germanic influence had been strong in the north, the richest part of the country. The nineteenth century found this section ready to adapt itself to the industrial revolution; the bulk of Italian industry is concentrated there. The north is progressive and comparatively wealthy. Before unification the central part of the peninsula, the Papal States, acted as a barrier between north and south. The southern third, the former Kingdom of the Two Sicilies, bore the imprint of Greek, Arab, and Norman cultures. Closer to Africa than to the rest of Europe in respect to climate and natural products of the soil, long misgoverned, highly illiterate, devoid of industry, it had sunk to a low estate and was looked down upon by the progressive north. Italy thus suffered from deep-rooted regionalism — parochialism would perhaps be a better word. The movement for unification, if it had deep historical roots, did not reach far into the masses of the people, many of whom spoke dialects so divergent that the Piedmontese or the Venetian could only

---

This chapter by René Albrecht-Carrié, with added sections on agriculture, industry, foreign trade, and the drive for autarchy, by Anthony Netboy.

communicate with difficulty with the Sicilian or the Calabrese. The movement for unification was idealistic and literary, supported chiefly by the small bourgeoisie, and only the devotion and the craft of a handful of leaders carried it into successful execution. Political unification did not solve regional problems, however, and the Italian state had to navigate with trimmed sails between a north contemptuous of a backward and corrupt south which it felt it was subsidizing, and a south which considered itself exploited while seeking in political activity a short cut to preferment and access to the benefits which the national exchequer alone could confer. The destruction of the temporal power of the Pope was an added source of complications. In short, Italian history from 1870 to 1914 was marked by slow, if steady, progress along economic lines; continuation of the real — as against the merely political — unification. The political and parliamentary record, however, was not inspiring or free from corruption. This easygoing system was perhaps the best suited to existing conditions but the war and its immediate aftermath subjected it to a severe strain.

Italy in the First World War. It is a common belief in Italy that the country, having won the war, lost the peace, partly as the result of intrigues on the part of her allies, partly because of the ineptitude of her own representatives. This belief antedates the advent of the Mussolini regime but has been sedulously cultivated by it. In order to understand post-war Italian history this belief must be examined in some detail.

In 1914 Italy was allied with Germany and Austria-Hungary in the Triple Alliance. On the general plea that the Central Powers were the aggressors whereas the Triple Alliance was a defensive pact, Italy remained neutral. She then proceeded to negotiate with her nominal allies, seeking to obtain the cession of the Italian-speaking territories of Austria-Hungary in exchange for a promise of continued neutrality. Negotiations having proved unsuccessful, Italy turned to the Entente, from whom she secured the promise of sufficient rewards to induce her to join their side. The agreement was embodied in the Treaty of London of April 26, 1915 and on May 24 Italy declared war on Austria-Hungary.[1]

At the Peace Conference. Italy would probably have received the promised booty had not the war developed in unexpected ways. The entry of the United States into the war tended to give the conflict the aspect of an ideological crusade with emphasis on national self-determination and democratic liberties. As a result Italy was placed in a position apart from her allies. A corollary of the emphasis on self-determination was the repudiation of secret treaties — easy enough where Russia was concerned but not so with the Treaty of London which promised Italy, among other things, the northern half of Dalmatia. The American peace program recommended (Wilson's Ninth Point) that the Italian frontiers should be drawn " along clearly recognizable lines of nationality." Inasmuch as the Treaty of London would have incorporated into Italy compact groups of alien populations there were clearly the makings of a difficult situation. If, on the one hand, Italy subscribed to the Wilsonian program she was in danger of losing a substantial part of her expected spoils. If she insisted on her pound of flesh, in the form of strict adherence to the written engagements of her allies, she ran the risk of isolation.

Events turned out even worse for Italy than this unpromising beginning augured. Partly because she was weaker, partly because she concentrated too narrowly on the purely national aspects of the war — *la nostra guerra* (" our war ") — Italy found herself at the Peace Conference in the guise of a poor relation. The United States, Great Britain, and France were naturally more interested in the German problem, especially since Austria-Hungary had disintegrated into its component parts. When Italian problems were finally discussed, Wilson assumed an intransigent attitude. He was willing to give Italy the Brenner frontier (her present boundary with Germany) but in the east would not deviate from the line which had been drawn by his experts.[2] The Italians handled their case poorly. The two chief delegates, Orlando and Sonnino, favored divergent tactics. The result was that they made a plea for the Treaty of London line, justifying their claims on ethnic, strategic, or historic reasons as seemed to suit their case best. In addition they put in a claim on ethnic grounds for the city of Fiume.[3] The Italians' psychological misunderstanding of Wilson and the Americans was only matched by Wilson's unprecedented move when, on April 23, 1919, he issued a public statement on the Italian dispute. Even those Italians who were most favorably inclined to the Wilsonian program could not stomach this action, which only played into the hands of the more intransigent nationalistic parties. The chief Italian delegates withdrew from the Conference, but their bluff was called and they returned empty-handed and in a weakened bargaining position.

Changing Ministries. Their failure was largely instrumental in the overthrow of Orlando's ministry in June, 1919. Nitti, his successor, could make no headway against Wilson's determined opposition and it was not until 1920, after Wilson and the Democratic Party had been repudiated in the American elections, that the Treaty of Rapallo, negotiated directly between Italy and Yugoslavia, provided a temporary settlement of the Fiume issue. In the meantime, the poet d'Annunzio in September, 1919 had seized the city of Fiume where he set up an independent regime, going so far as to declare war upon Italy. He was finally ejected at the end of 1920. The Free State of Fiume set up by the Rapallo Treaty was annexed to Italy in 1924.

The Colonial Question. The colonial question, which was of relatively minor importance in 1919, became one of the keystones of later Italian foreign policy. The Treaty of London of 1915 was extremely vague on this subject. It promised Italy full sovereignty over the Dodecanese islands which she had occupied " temporarily " since the war with Turkey in 1912. In Africa she was promised " compensations " in the form of " frontier rectifications " of her existing possessions in the event that her allies enlarged their own territory. In Asia Minor she was to receive a " just share " in " the region of Adalia "; in 1917 her claims in that area were enlarged to comprise the southern half of Anatolia, including Smyrna.[4] But the German possessions and the non-Turkish portions of the Ottoman Empire were distributed as mandates to the British and French Empires while the Greeks were sent to Smyrna.

All this was done without consulting the Italians, and strangely enough they acquiesced, merely entering in the record a statement that they were entitled to compensations. Accordingly, a committee of Britain, France, and Italy was set up in May, 1919 to examine the Italian claims. The Italians could secure neither Jibuti, which they sought from the French, nor a mandate for Togoland which they suggested as an alternative. They accepted the British promise of the cession of Jubaland and of frontier rectifications between Libya and Egypt. From France Italy received some minor rectifications of the western frontier of Libya, but the treaty of September 12, 1919, whereby this was effected, specified that it only partly satisfied the provisions of the Treaty of London, which was thereby kept alive.

Italian Territorial Gains. As a result of the war, Italy had secured *Italia Irredenta* and, in fact, rather more than that. The Brenner frontier which she had obtained on the plea of strategic necessity reversed the irredentist problem, for it gave her 250,000 German Austrians who certainly had no wish to become Italians. On her eastern border, the line of the Treaty of London which she had likewise secured (also on strategic grounds) placed within her borders some 750,000 Slovenes and Croats who would have preferred union with their kinsmen in Yugoslavia. Italy's claim to Dalmatia had no ethnic foundation despite the acknowledged influence of Rome and Venice in that region. Her colonial acquisitions were of little significance. It is true that Italy did not secure all that was promised her in the Treaty of London, but the unforeseen disappearance of Austria-Hungary made her in some respects the nation in Europe that benefited most from the war. Yet it is almost no exaggeration to say that this, the greatest advantage of all, has never been mentioned in Italy; even the signing of the Treaty of St.-Germain was allowed to pass almost unnoticed.

Italian Resentment. It was not so much that Italy did not gain all that she expected but the manner in which this came about that rankled the Italians. In 1919 Italy was the weakest among the victorious powers and this was brought home to her in a manner that caused deep resentment. Italy's influence had derived in great part from her position between two fairly balanced groups of powers. A member of the Triple Alliance, with simultaneous commitments to the Entente, Italy had been in a good position to temporize and sell her services to the highest bidder. But in 1919 the balance had been destroyed and Italy had little to offer. The Allies showed little understanding of this situation; they could not be expected to side with Italy and enforce the terms of the Treaty of London against the will of America, on whom they were all highly dependent, but they might have evolved a compromise by offering her compensations elsewhere. An Italian mandate in Africa or Asia would have had psychological significance far out of proportion to its physical value. Thus arose the myth of the " mutilated " or " lost " victory.

Post-War Discontent. Italy's losses in men and wealth were less than those of Great Britain or France, but being a poor country she suffered proportionately more than her allies. The economic pressure — and the powerful attraction of the Bolshevik revolution on the working classes of Europe — made for social discontent. The soldiers returning home to seek jobs and struggle with the rising cost of living felt restless and disappointed. The first reaction, in the elections of 1919, was a large increase in the Socialist Party representation in Parliament and the emergence of the Catholic *Partito Popolare* (Popular Party). Between them these two parties controlled half the votes in the Chamber of Deputies. There was need for strong government, not necessarily repressive, but resolute and knowing its own mind. The tradition of the Italian Parliament did not offer much ground for hope.

Giolitti Ministry. On June 19, 1919 the Orlando ministry was overthrown and was succeeded by the Nitti ministry. Nitti, veteran liberal, was adept at the game of political intrigue. He sought to steer a middle course, avoiding definite decisions, and managed to retain office until succeeded by Giolitti (June 9, 1920). Eighty years old, Giolitti was the very incarnation of the Italian parliamentary system. Whether in or out of office, he had dominated the political scene for decades. Strongly opposed to Italy's participation in the war, his influence had suffered a setback. Giolitti believed that mankind in general and Italy in particular could only progress by gradual stages. His record and his age did not make him the man from whom one could expect in 1920 startling innovations. In fact, he refused to take too seriously the unrest produced by the war and when in September, 1920 labor agitation reached a point where the factories were occupied by the workers, he was not alarmed but took the sensible view that the fever would work itself out. This in fact happened, for the workers soon found that it was easier to occupy the factories than to run them. The episode, however, had important repercussions. It sharpened the quarrel between the two wings of the Socialist Party and an actual split followed at the beginning of 1921.

Giolitti, who had avoided antagonizing the powerful Socialists in Parliament, thought the time was ripe to rid himself of this embarrassing opposition. He therefore dissolved the Chamber and in the elections gave support to the newly formed Fascist Party. This was good old-fashioned electoral tactics. To be sure, the Fascists were rather prone to use direct action against their enemies, but Giolitti believed that they would gradually be tamed by participating in the parliamentary system. This could have happened only if the system had continued to function instead of disintegrating further and if the Fascists had had a different philosophy. The Fascists secured only 35 seats in the new Parliament, but Giolitti was overthrown in June and succeeded (July 5, 1921) by Bonomi. The Socialists had lost some of their strength in Parliament and the opposition to them had stiffened since the occupation of the factories — an event that thoroughly frightened the propertied classes. Without strong leadership in a chamber that could not produce a stable majority, Parliament became a spectacle of impotence. The weak government of Bonomi gave way in February, 1922 to the weaker ministry of Facta.[5] The Fascists became bolder. Becoming alarmed at Fascist progress, the Socialist trade unions resorted to their last weapon, the general strike. But the strike was a failure and further undermined the Socialist movement.

The March on Rome. A situation had arisen which could not long endure. The middle classes had been thoroughly alarmed by the radical groups, who in turn had shown themselves incapable of establishing power. The country was weary of political strife and murderous violence. Under these circumstances, the Fascists made preparations to seize the government and their cohorts began to converge on Rome. Facta offered his resignation on October 27, 1922 and the next day the government decided to proclaim a state of siege, but the king, uncertain of the army's attitude, refused to sign the proclamation. On October 29, therefore, he invited Benito Mussolini, leader of the Fascists, who was watching developments from Milan, to form a new government.

Mussolini at the Helm. On his first appearance before Parliament as Prime Minister on November 16, 1922, Mussolini said:

" I make this appearance as a purely formal act of courtesy. . . . I decided against pushing my victory too far. I could have exploited it to the end. I could have made this hall, dark and grey, a bivouac for my squads."

That such words could be spoken to the deputies is a measure of the decline of their influence, and one may be tempted to wonder why they were not dismissed without further ado. But when the Fascists came to power in 1922 they did not have an elaborately worked out social and economic program. Born out of discontent with the confusion and uncertainty that existed after the war, Fascist ideology was fashioned largely by circumstances. (Mussolini has indeed acknowledged the inconsistencies of Fascism and even boasted about it.) This flexibility has been more of a help than a hindrance to the Fascist state for it has made it possible to cast off inconvenient ideas or personalities according to the dictates of expediency. With the passage of time there is a tendency to become prisoner of the enacted record, but Mussolini has remained the dominant influence.

Mussolini's Career. Born in 1883 of poor parents,[6] Mussolini soon displayed signs of a strong personality. The poverty and the injustices which he saw around him could only produce rebellion in a young man of spirit, a reaction which would find its normal channel of expression in Socialist agitation. Taking the simplest, in fact almost the only, way out of his milieu, he obtained a normal school diploma in 1901 in preparation for a teaching career. He was in Switzerland from 1902 to 1904, supporting himself as best he could, taking part in Socialist agitation, arrested in Lausanne, expelled from Berne, all the while completing his education, reading widely, and acquiring the use of foreign languages.

By 1910, having served his term in the army, taught school, taken part in labor agitation, he was ready to assume the editorship of the weekly *La lotta di classe* (*The Class Struggle*) published in his native province of Forlì. Mussolini's socialism was of the militant variety. His outspoken opposition to the Tripolitan war earned him a prison term. In 1912 he became a member of the executive committee of the Socialist Party and editor of the *Avanti*, the party newspaper. At the beginning of the war he was an isolationist, but a realization of the revolutionary possibilities of the conflict and the feeling that Italy must not be a mere spectator turned him into an interventionist. He resigned the editorship of the *Avanti*, was expelled from the party, and founded his own newspaper, *Il popolo d'Italia*, where he conducted, with his wonted gusto, a violent pro-Allied campaign.

Drafted in 1915, he was wounded in 1917 and returned to newspaper work. The chaos of the years 1918–1919 led him not to discouraged apathy, but to the conviction that the situation ought to be taken in hand by whatever means necessary.

Organization of the Fasci. On March 23, 1919, with a handful of adherents, Mussolini founded the *fasci di combattimento* in Milan. Branches were organized throughout Italy, but the Milan *fascio* gradually assumed the leadership. The Fascist program, in so far as such a thing existed, may be described as a blend of Socialism and nationalism; it was violently opposed to Communism, and set about to counter violence with violence. In the uncertain atmosphere of the time the Fascists attracted a motley following, of young people for the most part: university students and ex-soldiers, idealistic youths imbued with patriotic fervor, *petit bourgeois* frightened by Socialist and Communist agitation, and a numerous rabble always ready to fish in troubled waters. One may wonder how Mussolini,

long the exponent of Socialism, could suddenly become the leader of reactionary forces. But the distinction was not so clear-cut as may seem;
much of the Socialist program was retained by the Fascists and the war
provided the nationalistic impetus. It should also be remembered that
Mussolini is a man of action rather than of thought. Ideas have had considerable influence on him, but only as stimuli to action, not as ultimate objects of contemplation. The possible inconsistency of numerous and
quickly apprehended if imperfectly digested ideas collected during the
process of self-education never hampered his will power.[7]

Progress of Fascism. Fascism did not sweep the country. In the elections
of 1919 Mussolini, running as an independent in Milan, was defeated and
not a single Fascist was sent to Parliament. In May, 1920 the Fascists numbered 30,000. In February, 1921 after the occupation of the factories,
they were 100,000 and in the elections of that year managed to obtain
35 seats in the Chamber. More and more they stood out as the enemies of
Communism and of the labor unions. The Fascists raided the headquarters of their opponents and destroyed their newspapers. By 1922, with the
government reduced to impotence, Mussolini's adherents had secured the
support of powerful elements among the propertied classes, and power fell
into their hands essentially because the squabbling parliamentary groups
seemed incapable of making it function. As a keen student of this phenomenon observes: " The Fascist revolution was not a revolution but only
the potentiality of one. A government had been seized, but the State had
yet to be conquered." [8]

The Conquest of the State. In appearance a new ministry had been formed
which would govern according to time-honored precedent. Even the
membership of the Cabinet was not exclusively Fascist, though the Fascists
naturally held the key posts. Since there would have been little point in
leaving the government at the mercy of the adverse vote of the Chamber,
it was granted wide discretionary powers. Parliament was allowed to continue on condition that it abdicate, for the moment at least, and Mussolini
set about to conquer the state, a task that was essentially accomplished
within six years.

In 1923 a new electoral law was enacted designed to insure a permanent Fascist majority. On the plea that the diversity of parties had caused
the breakdown of government, the party which received the largest vote
(provided this was at least 50 per cent of the total) would elect two-thirds
of the deputies. There was little doubt that the Fascists would receive a
large vote in the elections held on May 6, 1924, for if their own numerical
strength was not large, they had the support of the Rightist groups, and the
prospect of the restoration of orderly government had a strong appeal for
that large non-political mass which exists in every nation. Just what support the Fascists would have commanded in a free election will never be

known, for by the use of threats, cajolery, lack of secrecy in the balloting, and kindred devices,[9] they received 5,000,000 votes against 2,250,000 for the opposition parties. The government now had at its disposal an amenable parliamentary majority.

Murder of Matteotti. But the heat and bitterness of the election found an echo in Parliament, where the Socialist Matteotti launched a bitter attack upon the government on May 30, 1924. A few days later he was murdered. The sensation rocked the country: murder as an instrument of government was taken more seriously than accidental killings in street brawls. The opposition left Parliament and men like Salandra, Orlando, and Giolitti withdrew their support from Mussolini. High-ranking Fascists were implicated, and for a time the fate of the regime was at stake. But in the end the episode served to strengthen Mussolini's hold on the party and the country. The opposition had been deprived of one of its best leaders, and once it had withdrawn seemed content to sit in solitary splendor. At the same time, Mussolini, by his willingness to assume responsibility for the deeds of the party, was able to demand of it greater discipline and personal loyalty, and to assert control over its more lawless elements. Despite his glorification of violence, Mussolini has always regarded it merely as a tool for a purpose.

Organization of the Fascist State: Il Duce. Parliament having been tamed, the task remained of coordinating the other organs of the state. Just as Parliament was allowed to continue, so were the Crown and the constitution retained. The laws of December 24, 1925 and January 31, 1926 gave the Italian system its Fascist shape. On the plea that Parliament had encroached upon the prerogatives of the Crown, the Prime Minister is now responsible to the king alone; he can no longer be displaced by an adverse parliamentary vote. The Ministers are appointed and removed by the king upon his recommendation. He alone may hold several ministerial posts. The supremacy of the Prime Minister is a distinctive feature of the Fascist system in contrast to parliamentary practice. Ministerial posts have been frequently reshuffled. This " changing of the guard," designed to give administrators a wide variety of experience, is doubtless an element of vitality of the regime so long as it is kept free of corruption. At the same time it leads to palace intrigues and emphasizes the dependence of all on the will of the Duce (the leader).[10]

The Grand Council. The Head of the Government is President of the Grand Council (*Gran Consiglio*) of the Fascist Party. Originating in 1923, the Council was elevated to a state institution by the law of December 9, 1928, amended on December 14, 1929. The Council " coordinates and integrates all the activities of the regime issued from the revolution of October, 1922." [11] Its secretary is the secretary of the Fascist Party. The Council *must* be *consulted* on all constitutional questions, but otherwise its meetings are called at the discretion of the Head of the Government, who also controls its agenda. The Council names the Prime Minister, which means in effect that the issue of leadership is to be threshed out within the inner circle of the party.

The Council also draws up the lists of candidates in elections. The electoral law of 1928, superseding that of 1923, provided that out of a list of 1000 names, 400 would be selected by the Grand Council. These would then be submitted to the electorate with a Yes or No alternative, a 50 per cent vote deciding the election. In the elections of 1929 the Fascist list received 8,517,838 favorable against 135,773 negative votes; the record was improved in 1934 when the corresponding figures were 10,043,000 and 15,-265. In 1938 the Chamber of Deputies was abolished, its place being taken by a new Chamber of Fasci and Corporations.

The Grand Council is the real seat of power, the connecting link between the party and the state, or rather the organ in which the two are merged. In a sense it amounts to a third chamber, the only one in which genuine debate and discussion could take place. The Senate was retained in its old form, having never been a source of serious opposition. It was also easy to fill it with Fascist sympathizers as vacancies arose. However this system may have differed from the pre-war parliamentary setup, a veneer of legality was preserved.

Conversion of the Civil Service. One of the first moves of the Mussolini regime was to convert the civil service to Fascism. A royal decree of December 30, 1923 reorganized the bureaucracy. It was not, of course, possible to install tried adherents of the party in all posts at one stroke, but the power of dismissal for incompatibility with the general political aims of the government (law of 1925) sufficed to induce in civil servants if not enthusiastic approval at least passive acquiescence to Fascism. Moreover, membership in the party became a requirement of new appointees. Control of local government was likewise secured by the abolition of elected provincial and municipal bodies. This increased centralization had beneficial effects — for a time at least — in a country suffering from regionalism to the extent that Italy did.

The Fascist Pyramid. Ultimately, the Fascist system has to depend on force, as what state does not. In Italy the display, if not the use, of force is very much in evidence in the abundance and variety of uniforms worn by civil officials and military men alike. To establish the regime on a secure foundation, it was necessary for the Fascists not only to control the central organs of the state, but the very life of the nation. This was effected in a variety of ways. In the administrative system the Fascist party is supreme. Only party members may hold office. Membership is a badge of loyalty to the regime. In the early days, the movement attracted individuals of varying dependability, but later recruits were sifted carefully and some of the original members were weeded out through successive purges. Through the constitutional position of the Grand Council, the party in effect became an organ of state. Its authority was centralized in Il Duce who is at the head of a pyramid embracing the Directorate and the National Council, the Federal Secretaries and Directorates, and the local *fasci*. The party also supplies the state militia (Voluntary Militia for National Security), or Black Shirts, numbering some 450,000, or roughly one-fourth of its membership.[12]

The Syndicates. Fascism aimed at reorganizing every aspect of national life. Labor, in so far as it was organized before the Fascist era, was represented by the Socialists and the *Popolari*. In the early days, while the Fascists were fighting the trade unions, they began to organize their own labor unions. Soon these were the only ones in existence. In 1926 a Charter of Labor was promulgated which set up the present syndical organization of Italy. This law granted official recognition to syndicates of employers or employees (trade associations and unions) which have power to make contracts. Strikes and lockouts were forbidden; labor differences have to be settled directly or arbitrated between employers and employees. The labor contracts, moreover, are binding on all persons within the occupational or territorial jurisdiction of the syndicates. This system, firmly centralized in the hands of the state which must approve of the syndical officers, makes it possible to readjust wages with ease and to spread employment; it has given labor a certain protection but has proved quite satisfactory to the employers.

The Corporations. The syndicates are not concerned with matters of economic policy, which fall to the corporations. A Ministry of Corporations was created in 1926 but the National Council of Corporations was not inaugurated until 1930, and the corporations themselves did not come into existence before 1934. There were ultimately twenty-two corporations through which the state regulates the entire economic life of the nation. Thus, in theory at least, this activity, instead of being allowed to find its own equilibrium, could be coordinated by a central planning board. This was in part the Fascist answer to the problems created by the limitations of capitalist economy; it also aimed at creating the utmost productivity. The Fascist regime endeavored to develop the physical resources of the country, with a view to increasing Italy's wealth and making it independent of the outside world. Considerable progress was made along many lines; the exploitation of mineral resources was intensified; most successful perhaps has been the development of water power.[13] Fascism, glorifying the peasant, has encouraged land reclamation and improved methods of cultivation. The regime boasted of the newly founded communities in the reclaimed Pontine marshes, and of the " battle of wheat " designed to make Italy self-sustaining in this staple.[14] The program for self-sufficiency (autarchy) received an added impetus from the application of sanctions by the powers during the Ethiopian War. Italy, however, of all major countries, is least in a position to attain this goal.

Agriculture. Unlike Hungary, Rumania, and the Ukraine, Italy has no rich tracts of black alluvial soils. Numerous swamps were drained under the government's reclamation plan, and the people were taught to improve the soil. At the present time, the northern region is the most intensely and efficiently cultivated part of the country; modern methods of farming are being introduced among central and southern farmers, while, at the same time, the government continues its policy of dividing landholdings into small farmer-owner units in order to further its program of nationwide "intensive farming." According to the 1937 statistics, 48.2 per cent of Italy's working population was engaged in agriculture. Owing, however, to the shortage of land, her most vital crop — wheat — was not produced in sufficient quantities. In fact, despite the drive for autarchy in agriculture, there was still a deficit of 15 per cent in the production of foodstuffs. To meet this condition, the government had, during the past decade, made great strides towards converting the Italian farmers to intensive rather than extensive methods of cultivation. The chief crops are wheat, oats, beans, potatoes, and semi-tropical fruits. Stock raising and dairying are also important.

By 1938, approximately 11,682,935 acres of swamp- and grasslands had been integrally reclaimed or were in the process of being reclaimed. New rural centers had been built, such as Littoria, Sabaudia, Pontinia, Aprilia, and Pomezia, and 60,000 persons had been established in modern farm units on the newly reclaimed soil. Elaborate land reclamation projects were also conducted in the colonies, notably in Libya and Italian East Africa.

Almost one-quarter of the total area of Italy is forest; however, due to the shortage of land, Italy is dependent upon foreign markets for its lumber. With the development of Ethiopia, it was expected that this deficiency would be somewhat overcome. Subsoil deposits have always been regarded as a negligible factor in the economic resources of the nation, but a program of intense government research greatly increased the output of old mines and quarries.

Industry. Without petroleum, iron, and coal, Italian industry is severely handicapped. (More than 95 per cent of Italy's coal is imported.) While the north is by far the greatest industrial region, large industries have been recently introduced in the vicinity of Rome and Naples. The ironworks at Terni, the chemical factories near Naples, the railroad shops near Foggia, and numerous other industrial activities are now absorbing a great part of central and southern Italy's excess labor. But it is important to remember that Italian industry depends on imported raw materials, thereby causing a drain on the financial resources of the nation. Despite the increased mineral output in recent years, Italy's imports of metals has risen as industrial activities — particularly armaments and airplane manufactures — have increased.

Foreign Trade. Italian imports are normally about a billion dollars a year, exports about $750,000,000. Italy imports 25 to 35 per cent of its wheat, mostly hard wheat for macaroni, but exports rice. Olive oil is exported sparingly, citrus fruits in very large quantities. Leather gloves, straw hats, and embroidered silk shawls constitute important exports, while machinery, cotton, and jute are imported. Italy's large foreign trade deficits are, in peacetime, partially offset by tourist traffic and remittances by Italians dwelling overseas (10 million Italians live abroad, mostly in the Americas). Germany was Italy's principal customer; then followed, at a great distance, the United States, Britain, and Switzerland.

The Drive for Autarchy. According to the Fascists, "self-sufficiency means the uninterrupted mobilization of all the country's energies and resources, overlooked and neglected in the past and all capable of being embodied immediately or at least within the space of a very few years, in the cycle of economic production. . . . This creation of wealth will have a beneficial effect on Italy's foreign trade. . . . It is merely a matter of shifting the bases of trade in such a manner as to permit complete Italian autonomy in policy, an autonomy which could not be realized without a corresponding economic autonomy. This coordination of efforts will undoubtedly lead eventually to new mutual interests between Italy and the other nations." [15]

In line with this reasoning, the Supreme Autarchy Commission promoted a campaign based on the following program: (1) a nationwide increase in acreage by means of reclamation and tilling of lands previously unused; (2) an increase in yield through the introduction of modern scientific methods; (3) exploitation of industries hitherto not developed or abandoned because the product was unprofitable, or inferior to foreign production; (4) production of substitutes when raw materials are lacking. Special impetus was given to the mining industry: the government endeavored to exploit low-yield ores in order to conserve foreign exchange as well as to keep mines functioning in case of emergency. Efforts were also made to develop synthetic rubber, fibers, cellulose, and textiles.

Education. In order to remold the very soul of the nation it was necessary to inculcate the appropriate beliefs into the younger generation. Italian youth passing in succession through the Fascist Wolf Cubs (ages 6 to 8), the *Balilla* (8 to 14), and the *Avanguardisti* (14 to 18), is carefully coached in the creed of *Credere, Obedire, Combattere* (to believe, to obey, to fight).[16] The school system became a medium for inculcating Fascist doctrines. School teachers must be party members; schoolbooks are prepared or approved by the state. Conflict with the Church was avoided by making religious education part of the curriculum. The peculiar blend of democracy (in the social rather than political sense) and authoritarianism that went into the making of Fascism was not at odds with Catholic views. But here, as in the Lateran Treaty of 1929 (discussed in the next chapter), the Church surrendered primacy to the state. As Giuseppe Prezzolini has said: " Only through Fascist policy was the Church able to show its numbers and its moral force. It is a lay and political movement which has enabled Catholicism to exercise its function in Italy; not Catholicism's own forces." [17]

In 1932 members of the teaching profession were required to take an oath of allegiance to the party. Those who objected lost their positions. In 1938 anti-Semitic laws were enacted. In view of the infinitesimal number of Jews in the country, the effect of the racial laws on the life of the nation was negligible save in the universities, where Italy has lost some of her greatest scholars and scientists. The press, too, is rigidly controlled; indeed it too has become an organ of state.

Cultural Development. The variety of uncoordinated ideas out of which Fascist doctrine has been woven makes it impossible to speak of a Fascist art or literature as such. Nevertheless certain tendencies have been emphasized in the Fascist era. An effort was made to revive the glories of Rome — the Rome of the Caesars rather than that of the Popes — in order to strengthen national unity and overcome the inferiority complex from which modern Italy has suffered. In a country with so rich a cultural heritage there was naturally no dearth of material for such an endeavor. The unearthing and preservation of the relics of ancient Rome have been pursued with a vigor tainted with artistic ruthlessness.

It is characteristic of dictatorial regimes to indulge in grandiose public works. Fascist Italy witnessed an ambitious building program which gave splendid opportunities for the exercise of native architectural talent. The new buildings have been inspired to a considerable extent by the modern trend toward utilitarian simplicity rather than by slavish imitation of classical models. There is a tendency to eschew the more extreme forms which have been popular in northern countries.

There was no great burst of creative endeavor in the plastic arts in Italy after the war. Futurism, an Italian creation, dated from about 1909. Futurism, an iconoclastic movement, had roots in politics, in social conditions, and in the impact of mechanical development upon modern life; it extolled the ' esthetic ' qualities of the machine in contrast to older standards. With other recent artistic movements it had in common a tendency to make up in loudness of assertion what it lacked in consistency of ideas. As a distinct movement it was short-lived though not without influence. It is too early to discern the effects of Fascism on the cultural life of the country. To some extent the arts can be removed from politics. If an official state doctrine offers little inspiration to thought, there has been considerable freedom of discussion among the loyal *élite*.

Literature. There was a Futurist movement in poetry, led by F. T. Marinetti (1878–   ), author of *Mafarka the Futurist* and *King Bombance*. Marinetti became an adherent of Fascism, as did the fiery Gabriele d'Annunzio (1863–1938), Italy's greatest poet and novelist in his heyday. Although a national hero after his capture of Fiume, d'Annunzio was denied a spectacular role in Fascist Italy. The decadent tendency of his art made him a figure out of the past rather than a symbol of the regenerated Italy of Mussolini's day. Italy's greatest contemporary philosopher, Benedetto Croce (1866–   ) also seemed out of harmony with the Fascist era. But the magnitude of his reputation made it possible for him to pursue his labors relatively undisturbed, after some early unpleasant incidents. Croce has continued to issue important historical and philosophical treatises down to the present day, and he symbolizes the loftiest ideals of the Italian spirit.

The most prominent names in literature belong for the most part to an earlier generation. Luigi Pirandello (1867–1936) was the most famous of Italian playwrights. Except in a superficial way, his work did not reflect Italian culture but the culture of post-war Europe with its ideological confusion and troubled soul. His dramas, such as *Right You Are If You Think You Are* and *Six Characters in Search of an Author*, expound the theme that universal truth is unknowable to man; that, in short, right you are if you think you are. This thesis, elaborated with infinite patience and dramatic skill, serves as the basis of Pirandello's most effective plays. Grazia Deledda (1872–   ), a Sardinian, was awarded the Nobel Prize in 1926 for the romantic novels and stories of her native isle.

Guglielmo Ferrero (1872–   ) is the best known of contemporary Italian historians. His *Greatness and Decline of Rome* (1907–1909) emphasized parallels with modern Italian development and served Mussolini's purpose of awakening the Italian people to their great heritage. *The Story of Christ* (1921) by Giovanni Papini (1881–   ) is the most popular work of a man who wrote a famous autobiography and remarkable critical essays. One of the leading Italian critics is G. A. Borgese (1882–   ) now an exile in the United States.

Music. The renaissance of Italian music which was well advanced by 1914 continued after the war. Opera was no longer an overwhelming interest and leading composers turned to instrumental music.

The outstanding contemporary Italian composers have followed more conservative lines of development than their northern brethren. Ottorino Respighi (1879–   ) attained an international reputation for two symphonic poems, *The Fountains of Rome* and *The Pines of Rome*. The important works of Francesco Malipiero (1882–   ) include modernist pieces for the stage and orchestra. Ildebrando Pizetti (1880–   ) has combined in his instrumental music classic forms with the modern idiom, while his pupil Mario Castelnuovo-Tedesco (1895–   ) in a similar manner has tried to harmonize old vocal forms with the modern idiom. Alfredo Casella (1883–   ) has written a great deal of orchestral and piano music, some of it intensely national, in a free harmonic vein. With Malipiero, Casella stands among the advance guard of Italian composers.

Giacomo Puccini (1858–1924), the greatest Italian operatic composer after Verdi, survived the war by six years. His last works, *Gianni Schicchi* (1918) and *Turandot* (first performance, 1926), reveal no perceptible falling off in his genius. Pietro Mascagni (1863–   ), composer of *Cavalleria rusticana*, and Italo Montemezzi (1875–   ), whose fame rests on *The Love of Three Kings,* have produced no works since the war to rank with these masterpieces. The last opera, *Nerone,* of Arrigo Boito (1842–1918) was performed posthumously in 1924 in Milan. The La Scala Opera of this city was one of the premier operatic organizations of the world.

Foreign Policy. The nationalistic basis of Fascism has naturally manifested itself in Italy's relations with the outside world. When the Fascists came to power, their first task was to re-establish internal order. Hence they pursued, in general, a moderate foreign policy, although the outside world watched Italy with certain misgivings.

Fiume. In January, 1924 the Free State of Fiume was annexed to Italy while Yugoslavia secured Porto Baros and harbor facilities in Fiume. A Pact of Friendship and Collaboration between the two nations went into effect at the same time.

The Corfu Incident. The Giolitti government recognized the independence of Albania, retaining only the islet of Saseno at the entrance of the Bay of Valona. In November, 1921 the powers (Great Britain, France, Italy, and Japan) signed a declaration affirming Italy's special interests in Albania, whose boundaries were established by the Conference of Ambassadors. The determination of the Albanian-Greek boundary was entrusted to an international commission. While pursuing its labors, General Tellini, head of the commission, and three of his Italian colleagues, were murdered on August 27, 1923 in the neighborhood of Janina. Mussolini's reaction was immediate: despite a submissive Greek reply to his sharp ultimatum, the Italians occupied Corfu after having bombarded it. The Greeks turned to the League of Nations and also agreed in advance to accept the decision of the Conference of Ambassadors. This body accepted a proposal which emanated informally from the Council of the League: the Italians consented to evacuate Corfu upon payment of 50,000,000 lire. This first test of the League as peacemaker did not augur well for its future, as the case was settled essentially among the Great Powers who yielded to Italian threats.

Asia Minor and Africa. In accordance with her post-war policy of retrenchment, Italy began to withdraw from Asia Minor in 1921, and a year later came to terms with Nationalist Turkey. In August, 1923 the Treaty of Lausanne gave formal recognition to the new Turkey. Italy finally secured title to the Dodecanese islands and Rhodes in addition to the islet of Castelrosso. These Italian gains, although not unexpected, contributed to Turkey's suspicion of Italy's motives even though a pact was signed between the two countries in 1928.

The promised colonial cessions of 1919 were slow in materializing. France, we have seen, had agreed in 1919 to rectifications of the western frontier of Libya. The agreement was ratified by the French Parliament in 1922, Italy insisting again that the question of adequate compensations under Article 13 of the Treaty of London of 1915 remain open. The eastern frontier with Egypt was finally established by a treaty with that country in December, 1925, and the cession of Jubaland, which had been held in abeyance by the British attempt to link the issue with that of the Dodecanese, was finally effected by a treaty of June, 1924.

Laying the Basis for Expansion. The next decade may be described as a period during which the Fascist Party, having firmly established its hold upon the country, used its increased power to extend Italian influence in international councils and lay the foundations for imperialist expansion.

This period has often been described, with a measure of accuracy, as that of French domination of the continent. Such a situation was not to Italy's liking. Italy sought to extricate herself from the position of a poor relation by reverting to the time-honored tradition of the balance of power. At first she sought to extend her power among the Balkan and Danubian states.

Balkan Alliances and Pacts. After the liquidation of the Corfu incident, Italian relations with the Greeks improved, and in 1928 Italy signed a pact with them. Italo-Yugoslav relations remained difficult for the most part. The Belgrade government might have been more accommodating, had it not been for the strong anti-Italian bias of the Slovenes and Croats. The convention relative to Fiume, Zara, and Dalmatia, drawn up in 1925, was not ratified in Belgrade until 1928, and that during the absence of the Croat deputies. Even so, this was the signal for anti-Italian riots. Albania was an added source of friction. Ahmed Zogu, conspiring in Belgrade, seized power in Albania in 1925, but the following year Italy managed to establish a virtual protectorate over the country. Relations were not improved by the assistance which Italy was suspected of giving to the Macedonian Revolutionary Organization whose activities exacerbated Yugoslav-Bulgarian relations.[18] In April, 1927 Italy signed a Treaty of

Amity and Arbitration with Hungary. Yugoslavia, fearful of encirclement, ratified in November, 1927 a Treaty of Alliance with France. Within a few days Italy and Albania announced a military alliance.[19]

Franco-Italian Relations. Friction with France, manifesting itself in rivalry in central and southeasten Europe, was kept alive by various causes. There was an understandable antipathy between the two contrasting regimes, especially as the Fascists made no secret of their contempt for " decadent " democratic institutions and the " rotten body of liberty." France, traditionally a haven for political refugees and by far the strongest foreign intellectual influence in Italy, became the headquarters of anti-Fascist agitation and plotting. Naval rivalry, especially in the Mediterranean, Italy's *mare nostrum* (our sea), proved a difficult question. At the Washington Conference of 1921, France was induced to accept parity with Italy in capital ships, but made it clear that this had no relation to other categories, yet in subsequent discussions Italy persistently endeavored to extend the precedent. The result was much unpleasant bickering. There was some relaxation of tension between Italy and France in 1928 but the improvement was short-lived. A recrudescence of the naval dispute prompted Mussolini to make a series of bellicose anti-French speeches in 1930. " Words are very fine things; but rifles, machine guns, warships, aeroplanes, and cannon are still finer things," said Mussolini. " They are finer, Blackshirts, because right unaccompanied by might is an empty word. Fascist Italy, powerfully armed, will offer her two simple alternatives: a precious friendship or an adamantine hostility."

German-Italian Relations. Germany and Italy were at odds over the Austrian Tyrol. The Fascist regime has pursued a policy of repression and denationalization in that region, but despite this fact a Treaty of Conciliation and Arbitration was signed in December, 1926 between Italy and Germany. In general Italy, failing to displace French influence in central Europe, turned increasingly to revisionism. Yet in 1931 the issue of a German-Austrian customs union found Italy in opposition to Germany.

Mussolini's reaction to the advent of the Hitler regime was the proposal of a Four Power Pact between Great Britain, France, Germany, and Italy, predicated on a frank recognition of the fact that the four powers would assume responsibility for the maintenance of peace in Europe. Russia was to be excluded. This was the very antithesis of the ideas represented by the League of Nations and was open to obvious and serious criticisms. However, considering the ineffectiveness of the League and the possibility of bringing Germany into orderly cooperation with the other powers, Mussolini's proposal revealed qualities of statesmanship. Whether the scheme would have served to preserve the peace or accelerate German expansion must remain a matter for speculation. In any case the plan, though enacted, had run into such a storm of protest and had been so emasculated in an attempt to allay these protests, that it lost all significance.

Italo-Austrian Relations. After the bloody suppression of the Austrian Socialists in February, 1934 the Dollfuss government became thoroughly dependent on Italy for its existence. In the face of German aggressiveness, Italy increased her hold upon Austria and Hungary when the Rome Protocols were signed in March. Undaunted, Nazi agitation in Austria went on apace and on July 25, 1934 Chancellor Dollfuss was murdered. When the plot to seize the government miscarried, the Austrian Nazis were promptly repudiated by Germany; the appearance of Italian troops on the Brenner being a strong incitement toward this gesture.

Both Italy and Hungary were implicated in the assassination of King Alexander of Yugoslavia in October, 1934 having given shelter, if not encouragement, to Croat terrorist organizations. But the danger of international complications was avoided when Hungary was induced to accept a mild censure at the hands of the League while, by common consent, Italy was ignored.

The Franco-Italian Agreement of 1935. The accession to power of the Nazis in Germany caused the other powers to take stock of their position. The revival of Germany was potentially as threatening to Italy as to France, hence it furnished a good occasion for these countries to mend their quarrel. Laval went to Rome and on January 7, 1935 a Franco-Italian agreement was announced. Cooperation in maintaining the independence of Austria was an obvious common interest. As a settlement of her longstanding claims under the Treaty of London, Italy received a strip of desert along the southeastern border of Libya, a small corner of French Somaliland, and 2500 shares in the Jibuti-Addis Ababa railway. The disputed status of Italians in Tunisia was also clarified. Italy was satisfied with such small concessions because of an agreement concerning Ethiopia contained in Laval's secret letter of *désistement*, interpreted by himself to mean economic disinterestedness on the part of France in favor of Italy, but in Italy to mean an unrestricted free hand.

Dispute with Ethiopia. This attempted liquidation of the Franco-Italian dispute laid the foundation of a new and more bitter controversy. For Mussolini had made up his mind to seize Ethiopia, the only remaining part of Africa not controlled by the European powers. Unhampered by fine scruples of legality and encouraged by the precedent of Manchukuo, he was willing to undertake the risks of this adventure.[20] Failing to goad Abyssinia into aggressive action, Mussolini used a boundary dispute with Italian Somaliland as a pretext for aggression. On December 5, 1934 occurred the Walwal incident [21] and Italy proceeded with her military preparations.

Mussolini demanded reparation from Ethiopia but refused to arbitrate. The subject of Ethiopia does not seem to have been mentioned at the Stresa conference of April, 1935, called in response to Germany's re-establishment of conscription. The so-called Stresa front proved a frail edifice which the Anglo-German Naval Treaty of June did not help to bolster.

Conquest of Ethiopia. The Italian invasion of Ethiopia began on October 3, 1935 and, after Italy had been declared guilty of aggression by the League, limited sanctions were imposed in November. Britain and France were determined not to push sanctions to the point of war, and Laval in particular used delaying tactics which earned his country little gratitude in Italy. The net effect of sanctions was to solidify Italian opinion behind Mussolini's campaign without effectively hampering his military efforts, which came to a successful conclusion in May, 1936.

The Rome-Berlin Axis and the Spanish War. Taking advantage of the rift in the Stresa front, Germany remilitarized the Rhineland in March, 1936. The two dictators found themselves drawn to each other, not so much by mutual sympathy, as by a realization of the advantages that each found he could reap from the actions of the other. This collaboration became increasingly close after the Austro-German agreement of July, concluded with Mussolini's blessing.

In July also, broke out the Spanish Civil War. On the plea that they could not tolerate the existence of a " Red " government in Spain, Italy and Germany intervened actively in that country and gave General Franco sufficient help to destroy the Republic.

Taking advantage of the general confusion, Hitler proceeded at last to annex Austria in March, 1938. There was little left for Mussolini but to acquiesce as gracefully as he could in the overthrow of the cardinal principle of Italian foreign policy.

The British government considered that the appearance of German troops on the Brenner would be an opportune time to detach Italy from the Axis. In April an Anglo-Italian agreement was concluded, which was predicated, however, on a quick termination of the Spanish war. This calculation proved wrong and Italy, deeply committed in Spain, had no choice but to aid Franco until he achieved victory, even if that meant continued estrangement from Britain.

The Munich crisis in September, 1938 was another German triumph. Italy did not want war and Mussolini indeed exerted himself to preserve peace, albeit on Germany's terms. In November an anti-French campaign was launched with a cry for Tunisia, Corsica, and Nice, and on December 17 the Laval-Mussolini agreement was formally repudiated.[22]

Events of 1939–1940. On March 15, 1939 the Germans appeared in Prague; Mussolini again approved. Shortly afterward Il Duce bestowed another crown, that of Albania, upon King Victor Emmanuel. When a new crisis

" arose " in the summer over German relations with Poland, Mussolini again sought to preserve the peace on Germany's terms. But the " long armistice " came to an end and the Second World War broke out. Italy remained neutral, declaring herself in a state of non-belligerency and later pre-belligerency. Finally on June 10, 1940, when France was virtually defeated, Italy joined her ally. Just before the signing of the Franco-Italian armistice her armies opened their campaign and advanced a few miles within French territory. A Franco-Italian armistice was concluded on June 24, 1940.

Where does Italy stand today? Down to 1935 she followed a moderate policy of which she retained full control. She then proceeded to unleash certain forces which have in turn controlled her actions. The war to date has been a series of German successes, but it is not finished. In the event of German failure, unlikely as that seems at the moment, it would be very difficult, though perhaps not altogether impossible, for Italy to extricate herself. In the opposite case, the prospect will be open to her of vast acquisitions. But however alluring these may be, the balance in Europe would again be destroyed, and if she found Franco-British dominance burdensome she may have occasion to test how much more effective German control can be. German expansion has dealt a severe blow to her influence in central Europe, and for some time she has merely been following in the wake of Germany; she might easily find herself reduced to the status of Germany's first protectorate. Her plea would be that it is British and French policy which have driven her into this position. There is no denying the short-sightedness of these powers in failing to understand an essentially psychological grievance. The argument is sometimes presented that Europe is going through the birth-pangs of a new order, a painful process involving the inevitable destruction of the old. Perhaps. Whether a brave new world is being made out of the destruction of painstakingly acquired physical and moral values time alone can tell. So far, of the destruction alone we can be certain. In the causing of it, as well as in the creation of the new order, whatever it is to be, no one will deny Italy an appropriate share.

REFERENCES

[1] Italy did not declare war on Germany until a year later.

[2] This line, which came to be known as the " American" or " Wilson" line, ran roughly along the middle of Istria. It represented a compromise between ethnic and strategic considerations.

[3] According to the census of 1910, the city proper had 22,488 Italians and 13,351 Slavs. If the suburb of Sušak, physically but not legally a part of Fiume, were included, the corresponding figures would be 23,988 and 24,351. The surrounding country is solidly Slav.

[4] This agreement of St. Jean de Maurienne was never ratified by Russia, a fact which Great Britain and France later claimed rendered it invalid.

[5] For sketches of some of the leading Italian personalities of the time, see Carlo Sforza, *Makers of Modern Europe*, Indianapolis: Bobbs-Merrill, 1930.

[6] Much has been written about Mussolini, most of it exaggerated praise or denigration. A deliberate attempt has been made in Italy to create a myth and to suppress evidence relating to the earlier part of his career. What may be termed an " official" biography is that by Signora Sarfatti.

[7] It is interesting to recall the estimate of Mussolini made by one of the men whose ideas have exerted a decisive influence on him. In 1912 Sorel wrote: " Our Mussolini is not an ordinary Socialist. Believe me, you will one day perhaps see him at the head of a sacred battalion, saluting the flag of Italy with his sword. He is an Italian of the fifteenth century, a *condottiere*. No one yet knows it; but he is the only man of energy capable of repairing the weakness of the Government."

[8] Herman Finer, *Mussolini's Italy*, New York: Holt, 1935, p. 313.

[9] It is well to remember that the manipulation of elections in Italy had not been unfamiliar to the former liberal regimes.

[10] Fascists who seemed to show too great an aptitude for leadership have been pushed into the background. The cases of Rossoni, Balbo, and Grandi are good illustrations.

[11] The membership of the Grand Council consists of: (1) permanent members, its President Mussolini, and the Quadrumvirs of the March on Rome, Bianchi, Balbo, de Bono, de Vecchi (only the last two now surviving); (2) *ex officio* members, the presidents of the Senate and Chamber, certain ministers, and some others; (3) a group of three-year appointees chosen by the Head of the Government.

[12] The militia is voluntarily recruited and unpaid. Out of it are drawn such special groups as the Railway Militia, the Militia of Ports, etc., which are paid, full-time occupations.

[13] For figures on the economic development of Italy see the excellent work of Louis R. Franck, *Les Étapes de l'économie fasciste italienne*, Paris: La Librairie économique et sociale, 1939.

[14] The production of wheat increased from an annual average of 60,700,000 quintals for the period 1926–1930 to 72,760,000 quintals in 1931–1935. The gain is due to a greater yield rather than to an increase in acreage, and Italy is still dependent on imports for her average annual consumption of 80,000,000 quintals. For contrasting views of the program of land reclamation, see Giuseppe Tassinari, *Ten Years of Integral Land Reclamation under the Mussolini Act*, Faenza: Lega, 1939, and Gaetano Salvemini, " Can Italy Live at Home? ", *Foreign Affairs*, January, 1936.

[15] *Italy Today*, New York: Italian Library of Information.

[16] Membership in these organizations is voluntary but social pressures and the accruing advantages are strong inducements to join. About 50 per cent of the population in the age groups involved are members.

[17] Giuseppe Prezzolini, *La cultura italiana*, Milan: " Corbaccio," 1930, pp. 129–130.

[18] In 1928 Italy refused to join Great Britain and France in urging Bulgaria to suppress the Comitadji.

[19] It was denied in Italy that the two events had any connection. Other friendship treaties were signed by Italy with Czechoslovakia in 1924, with Spain in 1926. In

1927 Italy recognized Rumania's annexation of Bessarabia, mainly to counteract the effect of similar French action.

[20] The Anglo-Franco-Italian tripartite agreement of 1906 guaranteeing the integrity of Ethiopia was still in force. In 1923 Ethiopia had become, with Italy's support, a member of the League. An Italo-British attempt at laying out spheres of influence in 1925 had been blocked by French and Ethiopian intervention at Geneva. Finally, in 1928 a Treaty of Conciliation and Arbitration had been signed between Italy and Ethiopia.

[21] Walwal was said to be sixty miles outside of Italian Somaliland, but the district had been occupied by the Italians since 1930, though without Ethiopian assent.

[22] See Vera Micheles Dean, "Italy's African Claims against France," *Foreign Policy Reports*, June 1, 1939; René Albrecht-Carrié, "The Present Significance of the Treaty of London of 1915," *Political Science Quarterly*, September, 1939, LIV; Robert Gale Woolbert, "Italy's Role in the European Conflict," *Foreign Policy Reports*, May 1, 1940.

SELECTED BIBLIOGRAPHY

Albrecht-Carrié, René, *Italy at the Paris Peace Conference*, New York: Columbia Univ. Press, 1938. A documented study of Italy's role in the peace negotiations.

Borgese, G. A., *Goliath, The March of Fascism*, New York: Viking, 1938. This book by one of Italy's distinguished exiles constitutes a general introduction to the historical and literary background of Fascism.

Currey, Muriel, *Italian Foreign Policy, 1918–1932*, London: Nicholson and Watson, 1932. A strongly colored interpretation by a British sympathizer.

Field, George Lowell, *The Syndical and Corporative Institutions of Italian Fascism*, New York: Columbia Univ. Press, 1938.

Finer, Herman, *Mussolini's Italy*, New York: Holt, 1935. An excellent study of Fascism as a system of government and its effects on various phases of Italian life.

Rosenstock-Franck, Louis, *L'Économie corporative fasciste en doctrine et en fait*, Paris: Librairie universitaire J. Gamber, 1934.

——, *Les Étapes de l'économie fasciste italienne*, Paris: La Librairie sociale et économique, 1939. This and the preceding work contain a wealth of information on the economic condition of Italy under Fascism.

Macartney, M. H. H. and Cremona, Paul, *Italy's Foreign and Colonial Policy, 1914–1937*, New York: Oxford Univ. Press, 1938. This is an essentially impartial, though not unsympathetic, study.

Megaro, Gaudens, *Mussolini in the Making*, Boston: Houghton Mifflin, 1938. An exhaustive and thoroughly documented study of Mussolini's career until he became one of the Socialist leaders.

Monroe, Elizabeth, *The Mediterranean in Politics*, London: Oxford Univ. Press, 1938. A competent survey of the position of Great Britain, France, and Italy in the Mediterranean, examining in turn the problems which confront each of these powers.

Mussolini, Benito, *Fascism: Doctrine and Institutions*, Rome: "Ardita," 1935. This is the English translation of the article written by Mussolini in the *Enciclopedia italiana*. Its main interest derives from its authorship.

Prezzolini, Giuseppe, *La cultura italiana*, Milan: "Corbaccio," 1930. An able survey of the various phases of Italian cultural life by a critic who has taken an active part in the literary activity of the country.

Salvemini, Gaetano, *The Fascist Dictatorship in Italy*, New York: Holt, 1927. A severe, but carefully documented, indictment of the idea that Fascism saved Italy from Bolshevism in 1922 and re-established the reign of law in the country, by a distinguished historian and a former member of the Italian Parliament.

Sarfatti, Margherita G., *The Life of Benito Mussolini*, New York: Stokes, 1925. An
" official " biography and of interest as such in showing how the Mussolini myth
has been created; should be compared with Megaro's work.
Schneider, Herbert W., *The Fascist Government of Italy*, New York: Van Nostrand,
1936. A sketchy but convenient introduction to the subject; contains a useful
bibliography.

CHAPTER XIV

The Papacy in Post-War Europe

The Pontificate of Benedict XV, 1914–1922

The two decades since the end of the First World War have been a peculiarly trying epoch for the Roman Catholic Church. It has been a period of both gains and losses in political power and prestige along the various fronts of the Church's far-flung activities. But for a definitive judgment as to ultimate gain or loss we shall have to wait. Meanwhile we must content ourselves with a bare chronicle of political and diplomatic activity, slighting questions of a purely doctrinal or ecclesiastical nature unless they have discernible political repercussions. The universality of the Church and the multiple and comprehensive interrelation of its dogma and activities may make such a distinction seem arbitrary, but it is hoped that the attempt is at least justifiable.

Benedict XV: War and Peace. When the war broke out in 1914 Pius X was in his eightieth year. Its coming was a severe blow to him, and he is reported to have refused to bless Austrian arms, saying: " I bless only peace." Pius died on August 20, 1914,[1] and was succeeded by Giacomo della Chiesa who took the name of Benedict XV. His was the difficult task of guiding the Papacy through the stormy years of the war — a war which saw millions of the faithful pitted against one another, each side calling for the Pope's support and sharply suspicious of his neutrality.

When Italy joined the Allies in the spring of 1915, arrangements were made by the Italian government to permit free communication between the hierarchy in Germany and Austria. Benedict endeavored scrupulously not to take sides, and perhaps the best proof of his neutrality is the fact that his appeal for peace of August 1, 1917, addressed to all belligerents, setting forth principles of justice, moral right, diminution of armaments, and arbitration of international disputes, was rejected by the warring governments, although the plea found considerable popular support in all countries. Neither side was willing to talk of " peace without victory " at that stage of hostilities.[2] The papal proposal was particularly unpleasant to the Italian government and Baron Sonnino, the Foreign Minister, went so far as to declare in Parliament that the peace move was inspired by the Central Powers. The maintenance of neutrality was not easy, for the Holy See was a part of the city of Rome. In neutral minds, however, the Papacy gained prestige from a courageous and difficult, if futile, stand.

This chapter by S. Harrison Thomson, Professor of History, University of Colorado.

Post-War Reaction. With the coming of peace a revulsion against war made itself felt among all classes in every state in Europe. In Catholic countries the Papacy helped in the gigantic task of reconstruction. But in some countries it naturally lost ground as the regimes it had supported crumbled and new governments antagonistic to the Church took their place.

Italy. In 1870 Pope Pius IX refused to recognize the rights of the newly formed Italian state in Rome, and in protest became a voluntary prisoner in the Vatican. His recommendation to Italian Catholics of abstention from political life (announced in 1868) became a virtual prohibition in 1885. But Benedict XV began, during the war, to encourage the participation of Catholics in Italian politics. In November, 1919 he expressly withdrew the 1868 decree — *Non expedit* — and Catholicism once more became a political force in Italy. Don Luigi Sturzo, a Sicilian priest of rare magnetism and political ability, formed the Italian Popular Party (*Partito Popolare Italiano*) on January 20, 1919. It secured 98 seats in the 1919–1920 Parliament, becoming the second largest party in the nation. Sturzo's movement made the strongest appeal to the peasant and laboring classes. Some bloody clashes occurred between the Popular Party and the Fascists. The *popolari* were accused of espousing Bolshevism, but, all the evidence indicates that the charge was fantastic. The coming of the Fascist regime doomed the Popular Party, which was liquidated along with other non-Fascist political groups.

France. With the restoration of Alsace and Lorraine, strongly Catholic provinces, the French government wanted to replace the German bishops of Metz and Strasbourg with French prelates. This request was granted by the Pope. Soon afterward diplomatic representatives were exchanged between France and the Vatican. Normal diplomatic relations, broken off in 1905, were resumed in May, 1921. It is significant that this move provoked lively discussion in the Italian press, and a realistic settlement of the so-called "Roman Question" was widely demanded. The anomaly of Italy's non-recognition of the juridical actuality of the Papacy, which other great powers saw fit to recognize, was not lost on the Italian public.

The Action Française. The French political party Action Française had a predominantly Catholic membership. It grew in numbers and influence in the early post-war years, but its extreme nationalism was not regarded favorably by the Papacy.

Germany. The position of the Catholic Church in Germany immediately after the war was, if anything, less comfortable than it had been in Imperial days. With complete separation of church and state, and confessional and educational freedom assured under the Weimar constitution, the Church in Germany began to regain in some measure the confidence of the masses. Berlin and the Vatican exchanged diplomatic representatives in

1920, and negotiations were begun for a concordat. The German representation in the College of Cardinals was restored to its pre-war proportions by the elevation to the cardinalate of two archbishops, Faulhaber and Schulte. Thus the end of Benedict's pontificate found relations between the Reich and the Papacy restored and its German religious, educational, and social missions in a flourishing state.[3]

Austria-Hungary and the Succession States. War between Italy, the seat of the Papacy, and Austria, the traditional bulwark of the faith, was probably the greatest source of embarrassment to Benedict XV in the years of the conflict. Emperor Charles' response to Benedict's peace proposal of August 1, 1917 was the most sympathetic of all the replies that were received. The last thing the Papacy would have desired, disruption of the Hapsburg Empire, came to pass in October and November, 1918. The task of papal diplomacy in the Danube Basin thereafter became immensely more difficult, for over a territory which had previously been under one government devoted to the Vatican, six governments now ruled, and the loyalty of none of them was ever assured. Political upsets might make papal policies unpopular overnight.

Austria. The republic of Austria was predominantly Catholic in population, but anti-clericalism and Socialism were vocal. Some " incidents " occurred before normal diplomatic relations were re-established early in 1920. On January 24, 1921 the Pope made an appeal to the Allied Powers to consider Austria's dire need and lend her a helping hand. No immediate tangible result followed, but Benedict had at least made an honest and eloquent effort.[4]

Hungary. Though Catholicism was not so strong in Hungary as in Austria, the Church was sufficiently powerful to be the object of confiscatory legislation and sporadic persecution under the communistic regime of Béla Kun in 1919. When the conservative reaction set in, however, the Papacy's prestige was re-established. Diplomatic representatives were exchanged (July–October, 1920). The Papacy obviously favored the restoration of Charles, but was careful to avoid overt support of his 1921 *Putsch.* All anti-Catholic elements in the Danubian region were on the alert to prevent the restoration of the Hapsburgs and were correspondingly relieved when the *Putsch* failed. For some time thereafter relations between republican and nationalistic parties and the Papacy became cool.

Czechoslovakia. The republic of Czechoslovakia was the scene of the most consistent and determined opposition to papal political aims. The Czechs identified the Church with the oppressive Hapsburgs. The Czech population was predominantly Roman Catholic, but the Czech Protestant groups (Hussite, Lutheran and Reformed), were articulate, respected by the people, and well organized. In Slovakia the Catholics, led by Monsignor Hlinka, were more faithful to the Church than in Bohemia and Moravia, but Hlinka failed to read correctly the signs of the times: reaction was not yet in order. At the first census, taken in 1921, a surprisingly large percentage of the population denied connection with any confessional or denominational group. A million persons, among them some hundreds of Catholic priests, joined the newly formed Czechoslovak Church which was Catholic in form but national in temper. The relations of the Prague government with the Papacy were strained. The Pope went so far as to accept the separation of church and state (September 11, 1920), but on other matters that seemed to the Czechoslovak government equally important, no concessions were offered. Beneš went to Rome in February, 1921, but an agreement on problems of secularization of Church property, permission for the clergy to marry, nomination of bishops by the government and similar questions, could not be reached. This uncertain situation was destined to endure for seven more years.[5]

Great Britain and Ireland. The Roman Catholic population in England, Wales, and Scotland numbers well over 2 million; in all British lands, almost 15 million. There has never been a concerted effort — nor is it likely — to unite English Roman Catholics into a political party as in France and Germany. There were four cardinals in the whole British Empire, one from Ireland, one from French Canada, and two from England. Of these, one, Cardinal Gasquet, was uninterruptedly at the Vatican, so that all English Catholics were represented by a single cardinal. This scanty representation was freely criticized in Catholic circles in England and throughout British lands. During the war the English government tried to maintain friendly relations with the Vatican, and in June, 1918 the Prince of Wales paid an official visit to the Pope; mutual diplomatic representatives were maintained through the war. The presence of a delicate Irish problem may be assumed to have played some part in English diplomacy. An unfriendly Papacy would naturally have been unwilling to urge the Catholic Irish to support the British war effort or abstain from political agitation against England. It was therefore incumbent upon both Downing Street and the Vatican to stay on good terms.

Poland. The Polish people, oppressed by Protestant Prussia and by Orthodox Czarist Russia, had remained faithful to Roman Catholicism for centuries. The restoration of the Polish state was thus a source of gratification to the Papacy. In the troubled years from 1918 to 1921, Benedict took a paternal interest in Poland, and the papal nuncio, Monsignor Achille Ratti, gained the respect and gratitude of the Polish people. Two Polish prelates were raised to the cardinalate, and Poland took her place in the family of Catholic states.

Russia and the Baltic States. The collapse of the Czarist autocracy presented an opportunity to the Papacy. The Baltic states, though largely Lutheran, except for Lithuania, were glad to be rid of the Romanoffs.

They early received papal recognition of their independence, and the establishment of diplomatic relations with the Vatican was an additional bond. While the Romanoffs were on the throne the Eastern Orthodox Church, bitter and unrelenting enemy of the Roman Church, was the only licit confession in Russia. After the 1917 revolutions, when church and state were separated, the Roman Church was on a parity with the Orthodox Church. The Vatican abhorred Bolshevism, but also realized that its very opposition to Orthodoxy gave Roman Catholicism a great opportunity. The Bolshevist leaders invited the Roman Church to send missionaries to compete with and undermine the Orthodox Church, yet were preparing at the same time a far-reaching atheistic campaign.[6]

Benedict XV in Retrospect. The pontificate of Benedict XV covered the incredibly trying years of the First World War and the peacemaking. Events were too tumultuous for any pope, however sagacious, to be able to initiate successfully any policies. The best that the Papacy could expect was to keep abreast of the rapid and dynamic changes, to steer a middle course, avoiding commitments or political alignments which might prove ephemeral, and limit its activities to the broader and less debatable aims of the Catholic faith. Though attacked from many quarters, Benedict may be regarded as having kept the Papacy on a high level of supranationalism in politics in a time of rabid nationalism. This in itself was no mean achievement. The advice and sagacity of Cardinal Gasparri (1852–1934), Papal Secretary of State, was of enormous help to Benedict.

The Pontificate of Pius XI, 1922–1939

Benedict died on January 22, 1922 and Cardinal Achille Ratti, Archbishop of Milan, was chosen his successor on February 6, 1922. Scholar, linguist, Prefect of the Vatican Library and papal nuncio in Poland, he had been a cardinal only seven months when elected to the chair of St. Peter. His long pontificate of seventeen years was to be almost as trying as that of his predecessor. The post-war turmoil and the crescendo of tension leading to an even more ghastly catastrophe made his task extremely ungrateful. Great political changes were imminent in Europe. The Allies had ostensibly won the war, but the final result was exhaustion for nearly all the belligerents. Everywhere weakened, democracy gave way in some countries to an authoritarian state. The effects of inflation and economic collapse were sure to be reflected in the attitude of peoples accustomed to regard the Church as enamored of the old order, as conservative and even reactionary. How would the new pope adapt himself to these vital changes?[7] We shall trace the main lines of papal policy in the principal countries of Europe in order to understand the pressure of circumstance under which the Papacy had to work.

Italy. Eight months after the accession of Pius XI, the Fascist legions marched on Rome. The " Roman Question " — that is, the dispute over the political and juridical relationship of the Pope to the Italian state — now became more important than ever. The Popular Party led by Don Sturzo held views quite antithetical to those of the Fascists. Pius' position was delicate. Pius felt that he must eventually bless the Fascist regime, on the grounds that it was the only one which could stem the rising tide of Communism. Mussolini professed his loyalty to the Church, insisted upon religious education in the schools, favored government participation in Catholic festivals, and made other conciliatory gestures. Pius, in turn, in an encyclical (*Ubi arcano*, December 23, 1922) said: " Italy will never have anything to fear from the Holy See." The Fascist state and the Papacy were drawing together. The Popular Party had to be sacrificed. In the spring of 1923 pressure from the Vatican caused a split among the *popolari* and on June 9, 1923 Sturzo resigned and soon went to London as an exile. There is no doubt that the Vatican sanctioned the destruction of the *popolari*. Whether Pius was deceived by Mussolini's promises to respect Catholic religious and educational aims is not so easy to answer. In 1926 the Balilla was founded to indoctrinate Italian youth with Fascist ideals, and Pius was obliged to disband the Catholic youth groups (January 24, 1927). The Vatican had lost another major engagement.

Catholic Action in Italy. Pius had founded the Catholic Action (*Azione cattolica*) in October, 1923 as an inclusive organization of Catholic youth and laity, to encourage their participation in the social and religious program of the Church. The Fascists, distrustful of the Action, charged it with carrying on subversive political activity, and many violent attacks on the Action took place. Little attention was paid to Pius' frequent and forthright protests, and indeed the Pope continued to encourage the Action in every possible way. Both sides were adamant and public opinion in Italy began to demand an understanding and solution of the " Roman Question."

The Vatican Treaties. After pourparlers for over a year, the Lateran Treaty was signed on February 11, 1929 by Cardinal Gasparri and Benito Mussolini. The Vatican City was recognized as a sovereign temporal state, with territory of about 100 acres including Castel Gandolfo, the summer home of the popes. Italy promised to pay the Vatican 750 million lire in cash and one billion lire in 5 per cent Italian state negotiable bonds — a total of about 92 million dollars — " as a final settlement of its financial relations with Italy resulting from the events of 1870." Finally, a concordat made the Catholic faith the state religion.

The Italian dignitaries who signed the Treaty had hardly left the Vatican, however, before Pius had occasion to complain of flagrant violations of the concordat, particularly with regard to Fascist control of education.

Tension between the Quirinal and the Vatican continued for years. The membership of the Catholic Action showed a sharp increase, but Fascism became more aggressive and a crisis was reached late in 1931. In the meantime it was commonly said that persistent government pressure, direct and indirect, had succeeded in Italianizing the Catholic Action, while both in Italy and abroad it was freely remarked that the Pope had become a Fascist. Nevertheless a new understanding was reached in February, 1932; since then the Papacy has seemed more complacent toward the Fascist state. The Pope was bitterly criticized by Roman Catholics everywhere for his quiet acquiescence in the conquest of Ethiopia. During the last years of his pontificate Pius was deeply interested in social and educational questions in Italy, apparently accepting the Fascist thesis that to the state belonged control of Italian politics.[8]

France. The relations of the Papacy with France were relatively peaceful for three years after the reconciliation of 1921. In 1924 the anti-clerical government of Edouard Herriot threatened to recall the French ambassador to the Vatican, seriously considered the laicization of parochial schools, particularly in Catholic Alsace-Lorraine, and planned more rigid control of religious congregations. A furore of opposition from the Right brought about the fall of the Herriot ministry (which had only a narrow majority to begin with). The next ministry, Briand-Painlevé, returned to a policy of friendly cooperation with the Church.

As a gesture of conciliation the ban upon Charles Maurras, one of the prominent leaders of the Action Française, held secret since 1914, was published in 1926. The Archbishop of Bordeaux published a letter (August 25, 1926) in which he accused the leaders of the Action of " atheism, agnosticism, anti-Christianism, anti-Catholicism, amoralism." The indignant protests of Maurras were of no avail. Pope Pius, as we noted in a previous chapter, put the party journal, *Action Française*, on the Index. Papal disapproval naturally brought an exodus of sincere Catholics from the party. One of the most influential French cardinals, the Jesuit Billot, had been quite sympathetic with the aims and activities of the Action, and in protest resigned his cardinalate on September 13, 1927.

In the next decade a steady tendency was discerned on the part of the Papacy in favor of democratic and liberal movements in France. But many devout Catholics did not hesitate to point out that in Spain absolutism found its most powerful support in the Church.[9]

Germany. At the time of his elevation to the Holy See, Pius was not popular in Germany because of his activity as nuncio in Poland. It was some time before public opinion, carefully nurtured by the papal nuncio in Berlin, Monsignor Pacelli, was able to counteract the earlier antagonism. The relations between the Weimar republic and the Holy See had not been regularized under Benedict, and this was the arduous task to which papal diplomacy devoted itself in the decade 1922–1933. The constitution of the republic had not entirely suppressed the ancient states (*Länder*), so that separate concordats had to be negotiated with the various constituent governments, as well as with the Reich as a whole. The Papacy endeavored to reach an agreement with the Reich first, but this turned out to be impossible, and Bavaria was the first state in the Reich to sign a concordat (March 19, 1924), giving the Catholic Church preferred status as to education and control of its own congregations, though the state demanded that all instructors should be German citizens and be adequately trained either in a German university or a papal seminary. The Papacy was allowed to express its choice in the nomination of bishops, but promised to avoid naming any prelate to whom there might be objections on political grounds. In the face of some Protestant opposition, a concordat was concluded between the state of Prussia and the Vatican on June 14, 1929. As Prussia was predominantly Protestant it was not to be expected that the Papacy would obtain the preferential status accorded in the Bavarian concordat. The Catholic clergy were given no place in public education — Pius objected to this exclusion — but on the whole it was a workable agreement, and past misunderstandings as to the nomination of bishops were obviated. These were followed by an agreement with Anhalt (January 4, 1932) and a concordat with Baden (October 12, 1932), the former being less, the latter more favorable to Catholic interests than the Prussian treaty.

National Socialism and the Papacy. Soon after coming to power Hitler sent Vice-Chancellor Franz von Papen, a Catholic, to the Vatican to negotiate a concordat for the Reich which was signed on July 20, 1933. The Roman Catholics were assured confessional freedom, communication between the Vatican and the German bishops, secrecy of the confessional, inviolability of the property of religious institutions, and freedom of religious instruction in Catholic schools. But the state could veto episcopal appointments for " political " reasons. Almost all of the thirty-odd provisions have been repeatedly violated by the Nazi government, though in many cases it flatly denied such violation. The words " political," " purely religious," " loyal," are interpreted so broadly by the government as to leave Catholics no leeway at all. The Center Party had dissolved itself on July 5, 1933 and it is surprising that the Concordat was signed two weeks later. Nazi leaders made no secret of their desire to eliminate the Church from political life. Some of the Pope's advisers counselled against ratification. But Pius, albeit with grave misgivings, did ratify the Concordat (September 10, 1933). Within a few months Nazi leaders and the press began to attack it.

The Concordat has been inoperative since the early months of 1934. The faint hope of some Catholics that they might influence National Socialism in a Christian direction was soon shown to be illusory. The feelers put out by the Pope in 1935 and 1936 concerning a union of the church and state in a common war on Bolshevism failed to soften the determination of the Nazi leaders to tolerate no rivals. In the succeeding years pressure on the Church steadily tightened: Catholic papers were suppressed, Catholic laity were forcibly weaned from the Church, Catholic youth were forced into the Hitler youth movement, Catholic education was suppressed, the clergy imprisoned, and monks and nuns tried on charges of immorality. Christianity, Catholic or Protestant, is an anachronism that cannot be allowed to obstruct the progress of the Reich. Catholicism, in its turn, if true to its traditions, cannot compromise. Thus the issue is clear. As matters stand today, the Church cannot win this battle. What the future holds may well be another question.[10]

Spain. During the pontificate of Pius XI Spain loomed large in the foreign affairs of the Papacy. For centuries Spain had been one of the bulwarks of Catholicism in Europe, and no other confession was allowed legal existence. Education was completely in the hands of the clergy, though 40 per cent of the population was illiterate. Although estimates may vary as to the exact wealth of the Church in Spain, it was out of proportion to the social benefits accruing to the country. The Church was therefore in a bad bargaining position when demands were insistently made that education and social controls be taken out of clerical hands. Primo de Rivera, however, a devout Catholic, resisted this pressure and arranged for King Alfonso and the Queen to visit the Pope. The first visit of a Spanish monarch to the Vatican in several generations, it caused a storm of protest among Spanish anti-clericals.

The Church and the Spanish Revolution. Economic conditions deteriorated markedly in Spain in the late 'twenties. The anti-clericals blamed the Church, and with some justification. Pius made some efforts to improve clerical education and morals, but native inertia was incorrigible. The writing on the wall was clear. The Spanish Church faced a day of reckoning. De Rivera's retirement and Alfonso's dethronement (April 13, 1931), imperiled the status of the Church.

Without consulting the Vatican, the republican government, headed by Zamora, in the course of the next few months disestablished the Church, dissolved the monastic and religious orders, confiscated their property, expelled the Jesuits, and removed clerics from the public school system. All this was done with enthusiasm and expedition. The hierarchy must have been amazed to learn that large numbers of their flock had apparently no longer any love for Mother Church. Pius instructed the clergy to accept the republic as a *fait accompli,* but he protested against the extreme measures in a strongly worded encyclical, *Dilectissima nobis,* and excommunicated the heads of the government (June 3, 1933). In 1935 a reaction began to set in and the Catholic party elected 120 deputies to the Cortes

(Parliament). This revival incensed the liberals and demonstrations against the Church and the orders broke out early in 1936, presaging the bitter civil war that engulfed Spain in July.

From the beginning of the war the Papacy expressed its antipathy to the Loyalists, and in 1938 came out openly for General Franco. The Papacy thus found itself allied with Nazi Germany and Fascist Italy who had openly supported the insurgent (Nationalist) government. Catholic opinion in France, England, and the Americas was almost entirely favorable to the Rebels, but in non-Catholic circles the Papacy lost considerable respect through this alliance.[11]

Austria. The sad economic plight of Austria made the task of the Catholic Church extremely perplexing. Vienna was strongly Socialist and anticlerical. But a Catholic priest, Monsignor Ignaz Seipel, was able, by supreme political sagacity, to govern Austria from 1922 until his death in 1932 either as Chancellor (1922–1929), as member of the ministry, or from behind the scenes. His aim was to form a bloc of Roman Catholic states in central and southeastern Europe, probably headed by a Hapsburg prince in accordance with known papal wishes. While Seipel was in power, the Vatican was intimately associated with Austrian foreign policy through the papal nuncio, Monsignor Sibilia.

The Social Democrats, predominant in the industrial capital, Vienna, were outvoted by the dominantly Catholic population of the rest of Austria. These two groups, Catholics (Christian Socialists) on the one side and Social Democrats on the other, were at bitter odds on internal policies and the matter of Hapsburg restoration, but they found themselves in agreement on the question of Anschluss. It is significant that two outside powers were also opposed to Austria's absorption into Germany: Fascist Italy (out of jealousy) and the Vatican (because a strong Reich would mean a weak German Church).

Dollfuss, von Starhemberg and Schuschnigg, the rulers of Austria from 1932 to 1938, were all devout Catholics, and the struggle of the Catholic Christian Socialists against the Social Democrats continued. On July 5, 1933 a concordat between the government of Chancellor Dollfuss and the papal nuncio, Cardinal Pacelli, was signed at Rome. By this document the juridical position of the Church was confirmed; the Church was given complete freedom in its administration, secular and monastic, save that the state reserved the right to make objections on " political " grounds to a nominee to a bishopric. The Church was permitted freely to acquire and administer new properties, and the state promised to maintain its financial support of the Church. The favorable position of the Catholic clergy in the Austrian educational system was in general confirmed. In 1936 Italy effected a rapprochement with Germany and papal support of the movement against Anschluss suddenly disappeared. After the Anschluss in March, 1938 the Church in Austria was severely persecuted, as in Germany. Even Cardinal Innitzer was subjected to violence.[12]

The Succession States. Papal relations with the succession states can be said to have undergone no significant changes during the pontificate of Pius XI. The Concordat of 1935 with Jugoslavia was not ratified because of the strong opposition of the national (Greek Orthodox) church. With Czechoslovakia only a "modus vivendi" could be arranged (February 2, 1928). The state was unwilling to forget its fundamental aversion to the Church which had for centuries supported the Hapsburgs. Elsewhere in central and southeastern Europe little alteration took place in the Church's status.

Soviet Russia. In the early years of his pontificate Pius had evidently hoped that the new regime in Russia would make it possible to heal the breach between the eastern and the western branches of the Church, but the growth of the anti-religious movement dispelled this illusion. Having made several futile gestures of friendship toward Chicherine, the Russian Foreign Minister, Pius concluded that there was no point to further overtures. He tried to induce the nations of western Europe (May, 1932) to refuse to recognize Soviet Russia unless freedom of religion were guaranteed, but again his plans were frustrated. Missionaries were sent to Russia with food during the famines of the 1920's, but the Soviet authorities charged the priests with unlawful propaganda and many were imprisoned. The Pope was able to free some of them through diplomatic pressure, but others languished in prison, and a few are known to have been executed. The repeated condemnation of Bolshevism by Pius XI and his successor Pius XII gives little hope that Catholicism will rise in Russia in the near future.[13]

Great Britain. Official relations between the Papacy and Great Britain were friendly during the pontificate of Pius XI. King George V and Queen Mary paid an official visit to the Vatican in May, 1923 and several important British statesmen have visited the Pope since that time. The claim is made that the Roman Catholic Church is steadily gaining in numbers in Great Britain, and a vigorous intellectual revival among English Catholics has taken place. But it would be a serious error to conclude that this intellectual and spiritual renaissance has significant effect upon British political life. English Catholics have been, throughout the centuries, too consciously English to allow the Pope any measure of political influence in Great Britain, or, for that matter, in the British Empire.

Baltic States. In the Baltic states the Catholic Church has not, in recent centuries, had a large following, nor any considerable political influence. A concordat (negotiations for which had been begun in 1920 under Benedict XV), generous in its provisions toward the Church, was signed with Latvia on May 30, 1922. The other Baltic states had already established

friendly diplomatic relations with the Holy See, but their Catholic populations were so small as not to create the need for a detailed and formal
concordat.[14]

Summary

The seventeen-year pontificate of Pius XI (died February 10, 1939)
was a period of extraordinary stress even for a Papacy long accustomed to trials and tribulations. A definitive judgment of the wisdom and
effectiveness of its diplomatic policies is as yet hardly possible, for the
world is still struggling with the currents of thought and emotion with
which the Church had to deal in those crucial decades. Several things,
however, are reasonably certain. Papal policy was determined by Pius XI
himself. A scholarly, well-informed and strong-minded pontiff, Pius was
influenced by few of his advisers. Responsibility for mistakes must then
rest upon his shoulders. Papal diplomacy in at least five cases has been
sharply criticized by Catholic as well as non-Catholic observers: the suppression of the Italian Popular Party at the behest of the Fascist government; the outspoken approval of the Italian conquest of Ethiopia; the support of Franco's revolution in Spain, made possible only by Fascist and Nazi
intervention; the support of reactionary governments in Austria, and the
awkward handling of the Action Française in France. On the other
hand, even in these cases, all the facts may not yet be known, and there is
an indisputable record of the Catholic Church's heroism in Nazi Austria,
Germany, and Russia, for which Pius must be given due credit.

Pius XII (Cardinal Eugenio Pacelli) began his pontificate under circumstances even more difficult than those which faced Pius XI. He has
thus far given evidence of courage and devotion to Catholic ideals. With
Italy at war, it is quite understandable that his position imposed silence on
many subjects concerning which he would like to speak out. Yet on
Easter Day, 1941, Pius came out boldly for a universal and just peace, for
merciful treatment of prisoners and civilians in occupied areas, and for
restraint in the use of homicidal weapons. In a world where talk of war
and slaughter was omnipresent, this was a courageous and refreshing plea,
showing that the Church was still a powerful force for peace.

REFERENCES

1 Josef Schmidlin, *Papstgeschichte der neuesten Zeit,* Munich: Kösel und Pustet, 1935, III: 169–177.

2 Schmidlin, *op. cit.,* III: 210–218. There seems to be no evidence that Benedict at any time made any diplomatic move to secure personal representation at the Peace Conference. Cf. Schmidlin, *op. cit.,* III: 312. The uncertainty of the Papacy's position in Italy may be gauged by the offer from the King of Spain and his government (May 28, 1915) to give the Pope refuge in Spain for the duration of the war. E. Devoghel, *La Question romaine,* Paris: Bloud et Gay, 1929, pp. 17–21.

3 Schmidlin, *op. cit.,* III: 277–284; von Lama, *op. cit.,* pp. 78–95, 201–210.

4 Schmidlin, *op. cit.,* III: 284–286; von Lama, *op. cit.,* pp. 94–103.

5 F. J. Vondracek, *Foreign Policy of Czechoslovakia,* New York: Columbia Univ. Press, 1937, pp. 93–97; Mila Liscová, *The Religious Situation in Czechoslovakia,* Prague: Orbis, 1925, pp. 36–60; Schmidlin, *op. cit.,* III: 286–290.

6 Schmidlin, *op. cit.,* III: 304–310; William Teeling, *Pope Pius XI and World Affairs,* New York: Stokes, 1937, pp. 64–76.

7 Teeling, *op. cit.,* 106–117; Devoghel, *op. cit.,* 33–39; Schmidlin, *op. cit.,* IV: 18–36.

8 Wilfrid Parsons, *The Pope and Italy,* New York: America Press, 1929, contains a translation of the three-fold treaty, and the semi-official account of the ceremony of the signing of the Concordat from the *Osservatore Romano* of February 11–12, 1929; Humphrey Johnson, *The Papacy and the Kingdom of Italy,* Boston: Small, Maynard, 1927, pp. 77–174, traces the beginnings of conciliation; Geo London, *De Pie IX à Pie XI,* Paris: Editions des Portiques, 1929, traces the steps leading up to the Concordat; Schmidlin, *op. cit.,* IV: 37–115.

9 Loisy, *op. cit.,* pp. 109–231; Maurras and Daudet, "*L'Action Française*" *et le Vatican,* Paris: Flammarion, 1927, the entire book a collection of reprints of articles, letters, and manifestoes having to do with the suppression of the *Action;* Schmidlin, *op. cit.,* IV: 115–122; Seldes, *op. cit.,* pp. 294–297; P. T. Moon, *The Labor Problem and the Social Catholic Movement in France,* New York: Macmillan, 1921, pp. 316–365.

10 Schmidlin, *op. cit.,* IV: 156–167; Teeling, *op. cit.,* 215–223; Nathaniel Micklem, *National Socialism and the Roman Catholic Church,* London: Oxford Univ. Press, 1939, is a detailed study of the acts and pronouncements of the parties to the struggle from 1933 to 1939; see also Michael Power, *Religion in the Reich,* London: Longmans, 1939; Waldemar Gurian, *Hitler and the Christians,* New York: Sheed and Ward, 1936, pp. 119–156.

11 E. A. Peers, *Spain, the Church and the Orders,* London: Eyre and Spottiswood, 1939, pp. 98–198, a fervid apology for the work of the Church in Spain; Joseph McCabe, *The Papacy in Politics To-day,* London: Watts, 1937, pp. 1–31, based on much personal observation, but too bitter in some places to give the reader confidence, though the facts are indeed acceptable.

12 McCabe, *op. cit.,* pp. 83–95; Seldes, *op. cit.,* pp. 342–346; Schmidlin, *op. cit.,* IV, 125–129.

13 Teeling, *op. cit.,* pp. 265–275; Pierre Batiffol, *Catholicisme et Papauté,* Paris: Lecoffre, 1925, pp. 53–90; McCabe, *op. cit.,* pp. 155–161; Schmidlin, *op. cit.,* IV: 175–179.

14 Schmidlin, *op. cit.,* IV: 134–139, 179–184.

SELECTED BIBLIOGRAPHY

Acta apostolicae sedis, Rome and Vatican City, Vol. I, 1909, published to date. This is the official organ of the Holy See, and contains all official documents without comment.

Bauer, C., "Papacy," *Encyclopaedia of the Social Sciences,* XI: 559–568.

Bernhard, Joseph, *The Vatican as a World Power,* New York: Longmans, Green, 1938. A penetrating interpretation covering the entire history of the Papacy.

Carroll, M. J., "The Catholic View of Peace," ch. 32, pp. 647–662, in Brown, F. J., Hodges, Charles, and Roucek, J. S., *Contemporary World Politics*, New York: Wiley, 2nd ed., 1940. An able summary of the Catholic outlook on world affairs.

Eckhardt, C. C., *The Papacy and World Affairs*, Chicago: Univ. of Chicago Press, 1937.

Fernsworth, Lawrence, "The Vatican in World Politics," *Virginia Quarterly Review*, Autumn, 1940, XVI: 485–498. A journalistic but quite valuable account.

Hart, C. A., ed., *Philosophy of the State*, Washington, D. C.: Proceedings of the American Catholic Philosophical Association, 1939. Discussion of the various problems confronting the world today by the leading American thinkers.

Loewenstein, Prince Hubertus zu, *A Catholic Looks at Fascism*, New York: Modern Age, 1940. Priests, politics, and the future of religion.

Magner, James A., "The Catholic Church in Modern Europe," *Catholic Historical Review*, April, 1937, XXIII: 1–16.

Maritain, Jacques, *Scholasticism and Politics*, New York: Macmillan, 1940. Nine essays by a Catholic philosopher, based on a series of lectures delivered at the University of Chicago on religious and philosophical questions and on the Catholic position in world affairs.

Ryan, J. A. and Boland, F. J., *Catholic Principles of Politics*, New York: Macmillan, 1940. A new, enlarged and up-to-date edition of *The State and the Church*.

Seldes, George, *The Vatican: Yesterday, Today, Tomorrow*, New York: Harper, 1934. The history and inner workings of the Vatican, tracing its influence on the spiritual and political life of the world.

Teeling, William, *Pope Pius XI and World Affairs*, New York: Stokes, 1937.

The Pope Speaks, New York: Harcourt, Brace, 1940. The papers of Pius XII, with a biography by Charles Rankin.

CHAPTER XV

Hungary

". . . I HAVE THE BOLDNESS TO SAY, THAT HUNGARY WELL DESERVES YOUR SYMPATHY, THAT HUNGARY HAS A CLAIM TO PROTECTION, BECAUSE IT HAS A CLAIM TO JUSTICE . . ."

— SPEECH OF LOUIS KOSSUTH IN WASHINGTON, D. C. JANUARY 5, 1852

Between Two Wars

Geography. Hungary lies along the Middle Danube Basin, a region which has served as the gathering place of many peoples. Surrounded by the unbroken chains of the Carpathians, the Danube Basin for a length of 950 miles encircled historical Hungary. In the south, the Danube and the Drave, as well as the Bay of Fiume with the adjacent Adriatic coastline, completed what was called by the great French geographer, Reclus, the most perfect natural boundary line found anywhere in Europe. The Treaty of Trianon assigned to Hungary only the central portion of this territory, and detached the whole area of the northern and eastern Carpathians, between the Drave and Save rivers, as well as the Adriatic coast, including Fiume.

The very heart of post-war Hungary is called the Great Plain (Alföld), lying 250 feet above sea level, and watered by the Danube and Tisza rivers with their numerous tributaries, all flowing from the Carpathians. One of the chief agricultural regions of Europe, the region is particularly adapted to grain farming, cattle raising, horse breeding, fruit and vegetable growing.

West of the Danube lies Transdanubia including Lake Balaton, a hilly section with varied agricultural land and some forests, about 250 square miles, with a length of 50 miles and a maximum width of 10 miles. Lake Balaton is 420 feet above sea level, its banks flanked by watering places, and the hills around covered with fine vineyards. West of Lake Balaton is the Bakony forest, an upland which, however, never reaches 2000 feet. The extreme northwest of Transdanubia is called the Little Hungarian Plain (Kis Alföld), an excellent agricultural region, which partly belongs to Slovakia.

The northern Tisza valley consists of low rolling hills, which are dotted with orchards and vineyards, the home of the famous Tokaj wine. South of this region is the wild grassland, the Hortobágy, the home of large herds of horses, cattle, sheep, and swine.

This chapter by Tibor Kerekes, Chairman, Department of History, The Graduate School, Georgetown University.

Having lost by the Treaty of Trianon its principal mineral resources and industrial plants to Czechoslovakia and Rumania, Hungary became chiefly an agricultural country, dependent on her western neighbors, Germany and Italy, for the importation of raw materials and industrial products, as well as for markets for her agricultural surplus. This economic dependence explains Hungary's friendship with the dictatorships, regardless of the general dislike for dictatorial rule in Hungary.

The return of Ruthenia (Carpatho-Russia) in 1939 added valuable and much needed forest regions to Hungary. With it were also recovered the only opal mines in Europe in the Kassa (Kosice) district. The return of Northern Transylvania (August 30, 1940) secured some mineral resources such as coal, salt, silver, and nickel, with extensive forest and farming areas.[1] By the reacquisition of these provinces Hungary once more extended her frontier to the crest of the Carpathians in the north and east.[2]

The Historic Foundations of Hungary. The Kingdom of Hungary, which was divided into five parts by the Treaty of Trianon, was one of the oldest of European states; in 1896 it celebrated the thousandth anniversary of its existence.[3]

A branch of the Finno-Ugrian ethnic family, the Hungarians, one of the last of the Asiatic migrating peoples, appeared in 896 on the slopes of the Carpathian mountains and descended upon the plains of the great Danube and Tisza rivers. In this country, which had been a Roman colony, there dwelt in the ninth century a number of ethnic groups, without political unity. In the east and northeast lived the Bulgars. The marshy region and the plains between the Danube and Tisza were for the most part uninhabited. In Pannonia (Transdanubia) dwelt scattered groups of Slovenes and further south Croatians; Avars were settled on the right bank of the Danube, while Slovaks occupied a small region around the city of Nyitra. It is definitely established that neither Ruthenian, Serb, nor German settlements were in existence at the time of the Hungarian conquest. If there were some remains of Romanized people in that region contemporary documents fail to mention it. The Hungarians, politically organized under the leadership of Prince Árpád, and inspired by the desire to establish a permanent home, soon conquered these sporadic tribes and absorbed the various racial elements. By the early tenth century the Hungarians obtained dominion over a geographically compact region, particularly suitable for agriculture and cattle breeding, and well protected on all sides by the Danube and Drave rivers, and the ring of the Carpathians.

King Stephen, who founded the Hungarian Kingdom in the year 1000, made Christianity the religion of the Magyars. The Hungarians never tire of emphasizing that the English Magna Charta is only seven years older

than Hungary's Golden Bull, signed in 1222 by Andreas II. The peak of
Hungary's medieval power came with King Louis the Great (1342–1384);
his dominions reached from the Black Sea to the Baltic and south to the
Mediterranean.

Ethnography. When the Hungarians entered the Danube Basin in 896,
they found only scattered remnants of Bulgars, Avars, Slovenes, some
Slovaks in the northwest, and a larger and better-organized group of
Croats in the southwest. The Hungarians either absorbed these racial
groups, or, as in the case of the Slovaks, left them in their Carpathian
mountain recesses. Only the Croats, also conquered by the Hungarians,
received autonomy and a large measure of political independence, which
they retained until the end of the First World War.

From the available historical evidence we may conclude that the early
period of the Hungarian Kingdom was void of racial problems. Hungary
represented a single national state.

A change began with the Tartar invasion in the thirteenth century.
Entering from the east through the passes of the Carpathians, the Tartars
devastated the greater part of Hungary in 1244, decimating the population
or taking them into slavery. After this disaster began the slow infiltration
of the Slovaks into the northern mountainous region (Slovakia) and the
Rumanians into Transylvania. During the thirteenth century the Ruthenians from Poland began to enter the territory known as Sub-Carpathia or
Ruthenia. These arrivals replenished the working population and the
Hungarian landlords were only too glad to offer them homes in order to
repopulate the deserted territory. Thus by the end of the fourteenth
century the Carpathian lands were inhabited by the Slovaks and Ruthenians
in the north, and the Rumanians in Transylvania. This immigration, which
continued into the fifteenth century, was not numerous enough to change
the ethnic character of the country; the Hungarian stock remained in the
majority. Proof of this fact is found in the national register, drawn up in
the reign of the great Hungarian king, Matthias Corvinus (1440–1490),
when the population of Hungary numbered 5 million, of which 80 per
cent were Hungarians.

The Turks defeated the Hungarians at Mohács in 1526, occupied Buda,
the capital, and the Lowlands — the most populous part of Hungary —
and held it until 1686. The remainder of the country was divided into
two parts: the west and north accepted Hapsburg rule to escape Turkish
occupation; Transylvania became an independent principality ruled by
Hungarian princes. When, finally, the Turks were expelled at the end
of the seventeenth century and Hungary was reunited under the Hapsburg
emperor, Leopold I (1657–1705), the census showed the reduction of the
population to some two and a half million, of whom only 50 per cent were
Hungarians.

Bent upon the rehabilitation of the territory devastated by the Turks, the Hapsburgs embarked upon a policy of colonization. Large numbers of German, Serbian, and Rumanian colonists were settled, principally in central and southern Hungary (Bácska, Bánát, and Slavonia). The census taken under Joseph II in 1787 revealed that the population had risen to 8 million, but of these only 39 per cent were Hungarians; the rest belonged to alien races. These recent immigrants naturally showed no attachment to the historical Hungarian state. Furthermore, the Hapsburgs made German the language of the Imperial administration. This danger to the territorial integrity of the kingdom, and to the use of the Hungarian language within it, brought forth a strong nationalist movement with its confessed purpose the restoration of independent Hungary. The uprising of the Hungarians under the leadership of Louis Kossuth in 1848–1849 was suppressed by Francis Joseph only with the help of Russian arms and by inciting some of the nationalities against the Magyars. Thus the first serious racial problem and the beginning of antagonism among the various minorities in Hungary dates back to the middle of the nineteenth century.

The Modern Aspects of Hungary's Minorities Problem. The collapse of the Hungarian uprising in 1849 was followed by a period of rigid oppression, during which Austria's policy of centralization was forcefully carried out. German became the language of administration and even of the schools. The nationalities soon realized that their opposition to Hungary did not receive the expected reward from the Hapsburgs. The Hungarians, on the other hand, discouraged and frightened, accepted the views of Francis Deák, who favored an understanding with the Hapsburgs and tolerant treatment of the racial minorities. Francis Joseph was also convinced that the best interest of the Crown required a compromise and recognition of Hungary's historic rights and territorial integrity. The consequence was the Compromise (*Ausgleich*) of 1867, which established the Dual Monarchy. The Hungarian nationalities were not included in this agreement although the Nationalities Law of 1868 attempted to solve the minorities problem. This law declared that " in virtue of the political unity of the Nation, to which all citizens of the country belong, irrespective of their nationality " Magyar is the language of the state. In the county assemblies and local courts, in their denominational schools and churches, the minorities could, however, use their native language. Even in state-supported schools, " wherever citizens of any nationality were living together in considerable numbers they must be given opportunity to receive instruction in their own mother tongue up to the point when higher education begins."

Unfortunately this liberal measure was never fully applied, principally because the Serbian and Rumanian minorities claimed that it did not provide absolute equality, fulfil their demand for territorial autonomy, or provide for a federated state. Many Hungarians, on the other hand, feared that the use of the non-Magyar languages would lead some of the minorities, particularly the Rumanians and Serbians, into the cultural and thence political orbit of countries adjacent to Hungary, and ultimately disrupt the Hungarian Kingdom.

The general international situation in the late nineteenth century also contributed to the failure of the Law of 1868. The Pan-Slav movement, fostered by Russia, produced intensive agitation for Greater Serbia and Greater Rumania, and this in turn convinced the Hungarian political leaders that a multiplicity of languages would militate against the unity of the state. The Law of 1879 therefore prescribed the knowledge of Hungarian for every teacher, and the Law of 1883 made the Magyar language and literature compulsory subjects in secondary schools. While these laws, too, were never strictly enforced, and the denominational schools continued to use the language of the minority groups, the irritation they created further alienated the nationalities and turned them against the Hungarian state.[4]

With the Compromise of 1867 Hungary, for the first time since 1526, became master of her own destiny. The result was an unprecedented political, cultural, and economic revival. The independent Hungarian Parliament initiated a great number of economic and social reforms. The national finances were put on a sound basis. Feverish building activity produced many new towns, roads, bridges, and railway lines, and transformed Budapest into a beautiful modern city. But below the surface there was much dissatisfaction. The extreme nationalists resented the attitude of the various nationalities, who refused to be assimilated; the political liberals criticized the franchise which gave the vote only to some 6 per cent of the population; and the landless peasantry, which comprised by far the greater portion of the population, clamored for land reform. All these questions were seriously studied in the years preceding the First World War, and it is reasonable to assure that their solution would have been worked out had that catastrophe not completely interrupted the internal development not only of Hungary but of Europe.

Hungary and the First World War. The assassination of Crown Prince Francis Ferdinand brought in its wake general tension among the nations of Europe. Hungary, through Prime Minister Stephen Tisza, counseled caution. In a special memorandum presented on July 8 to the Emperor, Tisza declared himself " after most scrupulous consideration to be unable to share the responsibility for an attack on Serbia." And when the growing evidence unmistakably had shown the complicity of the Serbian government, Tisza consented at the joint Cabinet meeting on July 14 to the sending of an ultimatum, and in case of its non-fulfilment to a war on Serbia, if the Austro-Hungarian Empire would openly declare against annexation of Serbian territory. This attitude of the Hungarian Prime Minister became known only after the revolution of 1918, when the Austrian Socialists published the secret minutes of the Cabinet meeting of July 14, 1914.

The war was not unpopular in Hungary. Even the nationalities, with perhaps the exception of the Serbians, supported it. The valor of the Hungarians was highly praised by ally and foe alike. But as years passed and the demand on Hungarian man power became more exacting, dissatisfaction became evident. After the death of Francis Joseph in November, 1916, confidence in Austro-Hungarian leadership was seriously shaken. The new king, Charles IV, readily accepted the advice of those who believed that a separate treaty with the Allies would not only restore peace but save the monarchy. Perhaps the entry of the United States into the conflict and the Fourteen Points of President Wilson convinced the Hungarians more than anything else of the futility of the war. Military reverses, return of large numbers of soldiers from Russia after the Treaty of Brest-Litovsk with anti-militaristic and communistic ideas, the growing economic hardships and privations caused by the blockade, the increasing restlessness of the nationalities whom the Allies promised complete independence, and finally the capitulation of Bulgaria (September 29, 1918), brought the downfall of the Austro-Hungarian government.

The Bitterness of Defeat. Rioting broke out in Budapest on October 30, 1918. The next day Count Tisza was assassinated and the pacifist, pro-French Count Michael Károlyi was appointed Prime Minister. Events followed in rapid succession. On November 1 the Austro-Hungarian Armistice Delegation met with General Diaz in Padua to arrange an armistice, which was concluded on November 3. For reasons not sufficiently clear Károlyi led, on November 6, another armistice delegation to Belgrade, where he met with General Franchet d'Esperey. The armistice signed here on November 13 placed the frontiers of Hungary deep inside historical territory, and Hungarian troops had to withdraw behind this line. In the meantime Károlyi's Minister of War, Linder, recklessly disbanded the troops which were pouring back from the fronts, while Serbia, Rumania, and newly recognized Czechoslovakia quickly sent armies into Hungary to protect their nationalities.

Meanwhile Károlyi tried to appease his radical-liberal supporters by declaring the transformation of Hungary into a democratic republic, with himself as President. To the great disappointment of the Hungarian republicans, the other democracies showed no sympathy or understanding of the Hungarian republic. Well meant but hastily applied reforms of the old nationalities problem received no attention by the racial groups, the Slovaks joined the Czechs, the Croats united with the Serbs, and the Rumanians of Transylvania with their brothers in Rumania. The more conservative elements withdrew their support from Károlyi, who in turn decided upon an exclusive socialistic government on March 20, 1919. But not even this concession could appease the Communists, who under the direction of Moscow decided to take matters in their own hands. Yielding to pressure, Károlyi resigned his presidency " into the hands of the proletariat," [5] and Béla Kun, an emissary of Lenin, proclaimed the Bolshevik republic on March 21. A period of ruthless bloodshed and destruction characterized the Bolshevik reign and led to its collapse by the Rumanian occupation of Budapest on August 3, 1919.

Meanwhile a counterrevolutionary government was established in Szeged. This government came under the leadership of Admiral Horthy who succeeded in negotiating an agreement with the Allied Powers; the Rumanians were persuaded to withdraw. The entry of the national Hungarian army with Admiral Horthy at its head into Budapest on November 16 marked the end of the revolutionary period.

Horthy's Regime. The Hungarians wished to have no more republican experiments. Consequently, the first act of the new regime was " Law I of 1920 " which restored the status quo by annulling the measures of the Károlyi and Kun governments. Hungary once more became a constitutional monarchy. Because of the opposition of the Allies and the succession states to the Hapsburgs, the throne was declared vacant, and Parliament elected Admiral Horthy Regent on March 1, 1920. As head of the state the Regent represents the king and exercises most of the royal rights. He appoints high-ranking officials, the judges and army officers. He convokes, adjourns, or dissolves Parliament. He sanctions laws enacted by Parliament and has the right to return to Parliament for reconsideration any act already accepted by them.

Political Machinery. The Legislative Assembly consists of two houses: the House of Commons and the Upper House. The members of the House of Commons are elected by males over twenty-three who have completed the fourth grade of primary school. Women voters must be thirty years old and have completed the sixth grade; if they have an independent income, or are married and have children, only the completion of the fourth grade is necessary. All college graduates, regardless of age, have the right to vote. The secret ballot is used in the cities and towns, the open ballot in the villages.

Members of the Upper House are partly elected and partly appointed. The Cabinet is chosen by the Regent in accordance with the political situation in Parliament, particularly in the Lower House. The local and district governments are under the jurisdiction of the Cabinet, but every head of the county is appointed by the Regent.

Magnates vs. Gentry. From a realistic standpoint the Hungarian political regime is quite unique. " Unlike other Central European states, post-war

Hungary has at no time enjoyed more than nominally democratic institutions. Her political system, based on a restricted franchise and — until recently — on the open ballot except in the case of the cities, resembles in many ways that of Great Britain in the eighteenth and early nineteenth centuries, and reflects a semi-feudal social structure which has only recently begun to show signs of crumbling." [6] In fact, until 1933, when the various National Socialist groups made their appearance, Hungarian politics was dominated by the magnates, or great landed proprietors and their opponents the numerous gentry, small landowners and bureaucracy. Political reform was left virtually in abeyance between 1867 and 1918; almost the only point at issue between these two groups was Hungary's relations with Austria; thus the Liberal Party (and especially the extreme Rightists, representing the magnates and higher Catholic clergy) favored the link with Austria as a safeguard of Hungary's independence; the Party of Independence regarded the union with Vienna as dangerous. Both parties favored the unitary Hungarian state.

Post-War Hungarian Politics. Hungary has retained the historical title of "kingdom," although there is no king and no dynasty; the head of the state, Admiral Horthy, is called "Regent." This ruler, furthermore, is an admiral, but there is no navy; he acts as Regent pending the return of the Hapsburgs, to whose representative, the late Emperor Charles, he refused to yield.

Horthy's powers are undefined. He can be, if he desires, a dictator. In fact, in 1933 the Regent's powers were increased by conferring on him the rights enjoyed by the king in dissolving and adjourning Parliament. A law passed in July, 1937 augmented his powers. Hungary's post-war ministries, however, responsible to the partly elected and partly appointed Parliament, have functioned in accordance with orthodox parliamentary procedures.

Count Bethlen's Administration and the Magnates. Between 1919 and 1932 Hungary was ruled by three aristocratic Prime Ministers — Count Teleki (July, 1920 — April, 1921), Count Bethlen (April, 1921 — August, 1931), and Count Gyula Károlyi (August, 1931 — September, 1932). The first post-war elections (January, 1920), held in accordance with the franchise act drafted by Károlyi's socialistic government in 1919, returned a number of smallholders and peasants to Parliament. The new government annulled all the measures of its two republican predecessors; furthermore, Count Bethlen re-established the open ballot at the elections of 1922, with the result that the number of peasant and proletarian deputies was reduced almost to the vanishing point. Consequently, although elsewhere in central Europe agrarian reforms were introduced, changing the social structure of their respective countries, only a comparatively moderate measure was pushed through the Hungarian Constituent Assembly by Szabó's Small Holders' Party in December, 1920.

Hungary in the eyes of western democracies remained a feudal country; maldistribution of land is its chief problem. In 1934 there were 1,228 large estates, comprising 29.5 per cent of available land; 10,000 middle-class estates embracing 18.3 per cent of the country; and 840,000 smallholders, owning 52.2 per cent of the national acreage. Of the latter, 450,000 were without sufficient land to support their families. In addition, there were 700,000 landless peasants. Altogether the agrarian proletariat numbered 3 million out of a total agricultural population of 4.5 million.

In Bethlen's administration the political division between magnates and gentry had evaporated, since the constitutional relationship with Austria-Hungary had disappeared and the problem of a Hapsburg restoration was settled by the failure of the ex-Emperor Charles' attempts to regain the throne in March and October, 1921. Bethlen was able to unite almost all the propertied interests into a Party of National Unity; furthermore, in 1921, the Small Holders' Party joined his bloc in return for land reform. The opposition was of minor significance. From the right came the criticism of the Legitimists, organized mainly in secret societies, led by Counts József Károlyi, Johann and Aladár Zichy, and the Markgrave Sigray; Left wing opposition was reduced to impotence by Bethlen's conclusion of a pact with the Social Democrats in 1931 which gave them a certain amount of free speech and permission to join such trade unions as had not already been dissolved.

Bethlen strove for revision of the Trianon Treaty, and gained Italy's friendship in 1927. His Cabinet fell in 1931 as a result of the impact of the world economic crisis on Hungary's economy and the uncovering of a number of financial and political scandals.

The Gömbös Government, 1932–1936. With the passing of Bethlen, the government bloc began to fall apart. In 1931 a new party of Independent Small Holders and agricultural laborers, directed by Eckhardt and Gáal, began to press for moderate agrarian and electoral reforms; in 1932 a Hungarian Swastika Party appeared. At the same time the National Union Party began to be dominated by the gentry and middle-class elements, forcing the magnates to form the Legitimist Christian Social Party in 1933.

Bethlen's successor, Count Gyula Károlyi, was in power for only about a year. He was succeeded by General Gömbös, the representative of the gentry and anti-Legitimists. Gömbös' early attempts at dictatorial rule gained him the nickname of "Gömbölini," although he was the only man who ever rose from the lower ranks of the army to supreme military power. His Cabinet was the first since 1867 without a member of the nobility. Leader of the Hungarian Fascists, Gömbös was supported by several hundred thousand Magyar youth, organized into the Awakened Hungary Society which became the moving spirit of the army.

The struggle between Gömbös and former Premier Bethlen ended in March, 1935 with a victory for the former. Parliament was dissolved and a pro-German and pro-Italian Cabinet was formed. In the ensuing general elections the National Unity Party won more than two-thirds of the parliamentary seats.

Darányi's Government, 1936–1938. With the death of Gömbös in October, 1936, Darányi, his former colleague, assumed the helm. The Hungarian National Socialist movements now took the spotlight. While Gömbös was able to unite the various Hungarian Nazis within his party, a number of independent Nazi organizations now arose, characterized by their great variety of leadership and programs, and promoted by Count Alexander Festetics, Dr. Ferenc Reiniss, and Major Ferenc Szálasi. While Dr. Reiniss made the greatest headway among state officials, Count Festetics, like Major Szálasi, organized the landless and unemployed peasantry. The Nazis also found a ready response among the anti-Semitic middle classes, the unemployed intellectuals, and in the army. The government did not know which way to turn — whether to follow the traditions of parliamentary feudalism or to combat the revolutionary forces by some amelioration of social conditions. Compromise measures were adopted; sometimes the Fascist leaders were jailed; moderate agrarian and electoral reforms were passed; and Jewish participation in professional and commercial undertakings was restricted. At the same time, radicalism was checked by the granting of more constitutional powers to the Regent and the Upper House.

Imrédy's Government, 1938–1939. The absorption of Austria by the Reich in March, 1938 gave a further impetus to Hungarian Nazi propaganda. Darányi was replaced in May, 1938 by Dr. Imrédy, a former President of the Hungarian National Bank. Imrédy's government accelerated land and social reforms, introduced compulsory labor service and increased armaments expenditures, and took strong steps against subversive activities. New Jewish restrictions were passed. Oddly enough Imrédy was forced to resign in February, 1939 because of the discovery that he had some Jewish blood.

Teleki's Government. He was succeeded by the Minister of Education, Count Teleki, an aristocrat and a friend of Count Bethlen. Teleki modified Imrédy's anti-Semitic and agrarian measures. But the government had to make concessions to the German minority, which was allowed to organize a *Volksbund* along Nazi lines. A section of Slovakia was transferred to Hungary by the German-Italian award of November 7, 1938. Notwithstanding Hungary's annexation of Ruthenia and her establishment of a common frontier with Poland, the dissolution of Czechoslovakia in March, 1939 made it obvious that Budapest had lost the power to oppose Berlin's wishes. The second anti-Jewish law was passed on May 3, 1939 and the Hungarian Jews feared that it might be a prelude to even more drastic restrictions. The measure went into operation on October 1, 1939 and ranked second only to the German Nuremberg Laws in severity. On June 24, 1940 all six Nazi groups in the Hungarian Parliament, with an aggregate representation of 60 members, decided to amalgamate into a parliamentary bloc. But the increase from 6 to 43 of Nazi representatives in Parliament in June, 1939 was not so significant as the figures indicated, since these were the first elections in which the secret ballot was used. In fact, the most important result of the election, in which all parties had a chance to campaign openly, was that the great majority of Hungarians rallied to the support of the government party, in spite of outside pressure and internal unrest, exploited to the full by the Nazi leaders.

Foreign Policy. By the Treaty of Trianon, Hungary lost 75 per cent of her territory and 60 per cent of her population. Slovakia in the north was taken by Czechoslovakia, Transylvania in the east by Rumania, Croatia and other areas in the south by Yugoslavia, and Burgenland in the west by Austria. While all these regions were inhabited by predominantly non-Magyar populations, considerable Hungarian minorities were included (1,480,-000 in Rumania, 500,000 in Yugoslavia, and 700,000 in Czechoslovakia).

Hungary has never ceased agitating for revision.[7] This became a national creed after the war. Magyar children were told that their "brothers" were under "temporary" alien rule beyond the frontiers. "Nem, nem, soha" (No, No, Never) was the battle cry of the entire nation. The three principal beneficiaries of the Trianon Treaty, Czechoslovakia, Rumania, and Yugoslavia, responded by forming the Little Entente in an effort to paralyze Magyar irredentist agitation. Mussolini built his "Il Duce Line" of diplomatic fortifications by exploiting Magyar bitterness. In reward for her "irreconcilability," Hungary obtained a large part of Slovakia in September, 1938, and at the second partition in March, 1939 received the province of Sub-Carpathian Ruthenia; in September, 1940 northern Transylvania was awarded to Hungary by the Vienna agreement between Germany and Italy.[8]

Economic Development. Hungary is principally an agricultural country. More than 90 per cent of her total area is under cultivation. Of her population more than half derives its living from the soil. The 1930 census showed that, of this agricultural population, 48 per cent represented the earning population and 52 per cent were dependent on them. Of the agricultural earning population 26.3 per cent were independent landowners, tenants, or laborers paid in kind, 27.2 per cent were assisting family members, 10.7 per cent farm servants on annual salary, 35.6 per cent farm hands and day laborers, and 0.2 per cent farm functionaries. Almost half the national income is derived from farming.

The principal crop is wheat, of which Hungary is Europe's largest exporter next to Russia. Other grain products are rye, barley, oats, and corn. Potatoes are grown mostly by smallholders in sandy soil, while sugar-beet is grown on the large estates. These crops comprise about 82 per cent of all agricultural production, the rest consists of tobacco, flax, hemp, and vegetables.

One of Hungary's important exports is wine, grown on the Tokaj hills, in Badacsony and Somlyó along the Balaton, and in Eger. The total yearly wine production is between 2 and 3 million hectoliters.

The seeming backwardness of land reform is not due to an undemocratic spirit but rather to the peculiar climatic conditions of Hungary. The arid summer in the wheat-growing regions requires dry-farming methods, with its characteristic deep ploughing and uniform cultivation of wide stretches. This method needs the extensive use of machinery and systematic organization, which naturally would not be available to small landowners. Land reform must carefully guard against lowering the national income, which depends chiefly on agriculture. This was the principal consideration in all measures inaugurated since the First World War.

The extensive pasture lands and the Hungarian's innate love of horses and cattle has produced a high level of animal husbandry. The state created model studs as far back as the eighteenth century. Breeding has been constantly improved. These studs furnished, in the post-war period, most of the needs of the Polish cavalry. The ordinary cattle are big, white long-horned animals, descendants of those left in Hungary by the Longobards. For dairy purposes the Simmenthal breed is most extensively used.

Post-war Hungary was almost completely deprived of mineral resources, except for some iron ore and low-grade coal. Nevertheless, a substantial manufacturing industry has been developed. There are flour mills, sugar factories, alcohol distilleries, and breweries; the iron, steel, and metal industries, machine workshops, and electrical plants supply most of the home demand and provide exports for the Near East and even for western Europe. This is due to the intensive utilization of the available natural resources and to improved methods of manufacture. There are more than 3500 factories, employing over 275,000 persons.

Cultural Development: Literature. Hungarian literature after the war " sought a new conception of the world which should be healthy, energetic, and modern." The novel superseded lyric poetry as the most popular medium of expression. The esthetes, or proponents of art for art's sake, were outnumbered by those who strove to give utilitarian meaning to their work.

Kálmán Mikszáth (1849–1922), author of witty and charming tales of village life, lived to see the turmoil of the post-war period. Sigismund Moricz, preoccupied with the lives of the brutish peasants and corrupt petty tradesmen, was typical of the new realistic school of novelists. At the opposite pole were the idealistic novels of Géza Gárdonyi (died 1923). Also typical of the post-war Hungarian novel were Kosztolányi's romance *Nero the Decadent* and Babits' epic in prose and verse, *Son of Death*.

There was an efflorescence of Hungarian drama, which strove to create new and lasting values, both poetic and philosophical. The plays of Ferencz Herczeg (1863–   ), Ferencz Molnár (1878–   ), Louis Biró, and Melchior Lengyel were performed successfully in the theaters of many countries.[9] The dramas of Molnár are in the romantic tradition of sophisticated comedy, written in a style that is essentially cosmopolitan, although the sentiment may be peculiarly Hungarian. The four men mentioned above were only a few of the numerous playwrights who made the Hungarian drama an outstanding art form, and whose works succeeded in transmuting the refined Hungarian spirit in whatever language they were performed. The Budapest theaters were the glory of that jovial capital until the Germans spread their tentacles over Hungary.

There were many periodicals in Hungary and a harvest of critical and scholarly works. The object of the Hungarians was to maintain a higher cultural level than surrounding peoples.

In the lost provinces of Transylvania and Slovakia ardent Hungarian nationalism was kept alive by writers using the mother tongue.

Music. The homeland of Liszt has produced several composers of international significance in the last generation. Ernst von Dohnányi (1877–   ), director of the Budapest Conservatory, has written pianoforte, chamber, and orchestral music that is performed fairly often. Zoltán Kodály (1882–   ) has incorporated the rich Magyar folk music in his many beautiful compositions. Bela Bartók (1881–   ) is the greatest of Hungarian folk-song enthusiasts. A pleasing composer in his own right, he has published, in twelve volumes, collections of 2700 Hungarian and 3500 Magyar-Rumanian folk songs.[10]

Of much greater international fame is Franz Lehár (1870–   ) whose scintillating operettas, *The Merry Widow*, *The Count of Luxemburg*, *Gipsy Love*, and others, have enjoyed a vogue on two continents. Lehár's music, like Molnár's comedies, captures the rhapsodic sentimentality, the sensuous and romantic charm of Magyar life.

Education. One of the most serious of Hungarian problems was an overproduction of intelligentsia. As a consequence, the *numerus clausus*, restricting Jewish enrollment in the universities and higher schools to 5 per cent, was introduced in the early 'twenties. The Jews, incidentally, dominated the cultural and commercial life of Hungary until anti-Semitic restrictions were enforced. In recent times the rural educational system has steadily developed, and special efforts have been made to improve the training of elementary and secondary school teachers.[11]

Hungary and the Second World War

In 1939 the Budapest government undertook simultaneously to align itself with the Rome-Berlin axis, crush the Nazi movement in Hungary, and carry out intensive reforms intended to nullify the effective Nazi propaganda. The acquisition of large territories from Czechoslovakia and Rumania was not an unmixed blessing, since it meant absolute dependence for Hungary on her German masters.

After its brief experience with Bolshevism in 1919, Hungary has managed to maintain the same form of government, at least within a parliamentary framework, and to keep the feudal class in power. Under the unchanging regency of Admiral Horthy, this kingdom without a king has enjoyed greater stability than neighboring countries. The bloodless recovery of Transylvania (the homeland of Count Teleki, Hungarian Premier until his suicide in March, 1941) obviously implied a *quid pro quo*. In 1938–1940 the Axis partners were establishing a new order only in their own interests. Whether Hungary will continue to reap benefits will depend not so much on her own policy but on the ability of the Axis partners to reorganize the continent of Europe.

REFERENCES

1 Until September, 1940 historic Transylvania proper was the eastern part of Greater Transylvania, the northwestern third of Rumania. Of the approximately 2,370,000 people turned over to Hungary with the ceded portions of Transylvania, Hungarians classify 48 per cent as Hungarian and 43 per cent as Rumanian; Rumanian estimates based on the 1930 census classify 52 per cent as Rumanian and 39 per cent as Hungarian.

2 There has been a lively historical controversy whether the Hungarians were in possession of Transylvania and the Bánát long before the Rumanians. There is no proof that the former Hungarian territory was inhabited by the Rumanians before the thirteenth century. See Oscar Jászi, *The Dissolution of the Habsburg Monarchy*, Chicago: Univ. of Chicago Press, 1929, p. 306, note 5; J. S. Roucek, *Contemporary Roumania and Her Problems*, Palo Alto, Cal.: Stanford Univ. Press, 1932, p. 4. Economically the returned territory contained both assets and liabilities to Hungary. In wheat and cereals it is barely self-sufficient. The great reserve of Transylvanian natural gas remained in Rumania, leaving Maros-Vasarhely (Tirgue-Muresului), an important town far in Hungary, without fuel or light. Also the coal, gold, and iron foundries were left in Rumania. Hungary, on the other hand, obtained most of the silver mines, timberlands, and cattle. The Hungarian part of Transylvania does not represent a considerable industrial competitor to the mother country, for its only vital industries are timber and leather.

3 See Josef Diner, *La Hongrie*, Paris: Librairie des Sciences Politiques, 1927, a survey of Hungarian history. Ferenc Eckhart, *A Short History of the Hungarian People*, London: Grant Richards, 1931, is perhaps the best introduction to Hungarian history in a western language; Louis Eisenmann, *La Hongrie Contemporaine, 1867–1918*, Paris: Delagrave, 1921, is the best account of Hungary's political history after the compromise of 1867: Jenö Horváth, *Modern Hungary, 1660–1920*, Budapest: Külügyi Társaság, 1922, is an authoritative account, with useful bibliography, but a nationalistic approach; Paul Teleki, *The Evolution of Hungary and Its Place in European Politics*, New York: Macmillan, 1923, is a moderate pro-Magyar account.

4 André de Hevesy, *Nationalities in Hungary*, London: Unwin, 1919, is a general criticism of the government's pre-war policy; Ernest Ludwig, *Le sort des minorités en Hongrie et en Tchécoslovaquie*, Budapest: Presse des Associations Scientifiques Hongroises, 1922, is a defense of Hungarian treatment of its minorities; C. J. C. Street, *Hungary and Democracy*, London: Fisher Unwin, 1923, discusses the Hungarian oppression of its nationalities. R. W. Seton-Watson's numerous publications before and during the First World War were influential in their consistent attacks on Hungary's nationalist policy.

5 Michael Károlyi, *Fighting the World*, New York: Boni, 1925, is a surprisingly moderate account of his activities.

6 Royal Institute of International Affairs, *Southeastern Europe*, New York: Oxford Univ. Press, 1939, p. 62.

7 Cf.: J. S. Roucek, "Danubian and Balkan Europe," ch. 15, in F. J. Brown, Charles Hodges and J. S. Roucek, *Contemporary World Politics*, New York: John Wiley, second edition, 1940, p. 332; Albert Apponyi and others, *Justice for Hungary*, London: Longmans, 1928, is an eloquent plea for revision; L. K. Birinyi, *The Tragedy of Hungary*, Cleveland, O.: Author, 1924, denounces the mutilation of Hungary; László Buday, *Dismembered Hungary*, London: Grant Richards, 1923, is a statistical survey of Hungary during and after the First World War; Harold Temperley, "How the Hungarian Frontiers Were Drawn," *Foreign Affairs*, April, 1928, is an important study refuting some Hungarian claims.

8 Cf. P. E. Mosely, "Transylvania Partitioned," *Foreign Affairs*, October, 1940, XIX: 237–244.

9 Cf.: *Hungaria*, London: Ivor Nicholson & Watson, 1936; *Hungary Yesterday and To-Day*, London: Grant Richards, 1936, chs. 12, 13, 14, 15; John Brophy, *Ilonka Speaks of Hungary*, London: Hutchinson, 1936, chs. 18, 19, 20.

¹⁰ *Ibid.;* Károly Viski, *Hungarian Dances,* London: Simpkin Marshall, 1937, is a colorful and scholarly introduction to Hungary's peasant art, music, and dances.

¹¹ Joseph Szentkirályi, "Hungary," *The Phi Delta Kappan,* November, 1939, XXII: 87–91, is the latest, although somewhat "official" survey, of Hungarian education.

SELECTED BIBLIOGRAPHY

Almond, Nina and Lutz, R. H., *The Treaty of Trianon,* Palo Alto, Cal.: Stanford Univ. Press, 1935. A careful review of the history and provisions of the Treaty.

Apponyi, Albert, and others, *Justice for Hungary,* London: Longmans, 1928. An eloquent plea for revision.

Eckhart, Ferenc, *A Short History of the Hungarian People,* London: Grant Richards, 1931. Factual and brief.

Horváth, Jeno, *Modern Hungary,* Budapest: Pfeifer, 1928. An excellent review of Hungary's international position from 1815 to 1918.

Jaszi, Oscar, *Revolution and Counter-Revolution in Hungary,* London: King, 1924. An important account of the three Hungarian revolutions of 1918–1919, by one of Károlyi's ministers, now Professor at Oberlin College.

Macartney, C. A., *Hungary and Her Successors,* New York: Oxford Univ. Press, 1937. One of the most dependable studies of this controversial field.

Papers and Documents Relating to the Foreign Relations of Hungary. Collected and edited by Francis Deák and Dezsö Ujváry, New York: Columbia Univ. Press, 1940. Revelations of the negotiations in 1920 in which France wooed Hungary as a permanent and strong friend.

Pribichevich, Stoyan, *World without End,* New York: Reynal and Hitchcock, 1939. Excellent chapters on Hungary's problems.

Teleki, Paul, *The Evolution of Hungary and Its Place in European Politics,* New York: Macmillan, 1923. By the late Premier of Hungary, an authority on geography; factual and convincing; with an extensive bibliography.

Tormay, Cécile, *An Outlaw's Diary,* London: P. Allan, 1924, 2 vols. A vivid and sensational picture of Hungary during the Károlyi and Béla Kun regimes.

Wiskemann, Elizabeth, *Prologue to War,* New York: Oxford Univ. Press, 1940. A lucid and dependable account of the Reich's penetration of the Danubian countries.

Wolfe, Henry C., *The German Octopus,* Garden City, N. Y.: Doubleday, Doran, 1938, ch. 17, is an excellent journalistic introduction to Hungary's general problems.

CHAPTER XVI

The Balkans

"XI. RUMANIA, SERBIA, AND MONTENEGRO SHOULD BE EVACUATED; OCCUPIED TERRITORIES RE-
STORED; SERBIA ACCORDED FREE AND SECURE ACCESS TO THE SEA; AND THE RELATIONS OF THE
SEVERAL BALKAN STATES TO ONE ANOTHER DETERMINED BY FRIENDLY COUNSEL ALONG HISTORICALLY
ESTABLISHED LINES OF ALLEGIANCE AND NATIONALITY; AND INTERNATIONAL GUARANTEES OF THE
POLITICAL AND ECONOMIC INDEPENDENCE AND TERRITORIAL INTEGRITY OF THE SEVERAL BALKAN
STATES SHOULD BE ENTERED INTO." — FROM WILSON'S FOURTEEN POINTS

For convenience we shall consider here as the Balkans that area occupied by the states of Albania, Bulgaria, Greece, Rumania, and Yugoslavia
as constituted after the First World War. The geography of this region
presents a strange anomaly. While almost universally described as a connecting link between East and West, the Balkan peninsula itself is totally
unconnected, "neither compact nor self-contained." [1]

Geography. The routes from Belgrade to Salonika and from Belgrade to
Istanbul have served since ancient times for the transit of invaders and
traders. The Danube River binds central and southeastern Europe both
economically and geographically. The narrow straits of the Dardanelles
and the Bosphorus separate Europe from Asia and the islands of the Aegean
are but a giant's steppingstones from continent to continent.

On the west the Balkans are bounded by the Adriatic; on the east the
Dniester River separates Rumania from the plains of Russia. The Black
Sea, by opening the Balkans to Russia and Turkey increases, rather than
reduces, the problems of those who live on its western shores.

Natural Resources. Great differences in climate prevail between various
parts of the peninsula. Large fertile areas are limited in number, with Rumania and Bulgaria the most favored. In this particular, Greece, Albania,
and much of Yugoslavia are sadly handicapped.

The geography of the peninsula has produced its intricate racial pattern, and the three factors of geography, racial complexity, and intervention by the powers, have made the Balkans the powder keg of Europe.[2]

Racial Composition. A thousand years ago the principal nationalities now
represented in the Balkans today were already settled there, although
they were not the original inhabitants nor was theirs the original culture
of the area. In the Minoan Age, Greece and the Aegean islands had pro-

---

This chapter by Elmer Louis Kayser, Dean of University Students, Professor of
European History, George Washington University.

duced a rich civilization, contemporaneous with that of imperial Egypt and Mesopotamia. The Balkan peninsula had known the glories of the Periclean Age and of the Hellenistic Period. Balkania was part of the provincial structure of the Roman Empire. Through the Balkans, in days of Roman decline, had passed Goths, Vandals, and Huns. Traces of these peoples are today found in the history rather than the ethnography of the area. Although the modern Greeks take pride in an asserted cultural tie with the ancient Hellenes and the Rumanians cling tenaciously to an alleged Roman origin, it is the late-comers who have fixed the present racial character of the peninsula. To this there is one outstanding exception; the Albanians, not without some reason, claim descent from the ancient Thracians and Illyrians, although later conquered by other peoples.

Before the coming of the Slavs into the Balkans, Rome had already been divided into the Eastern and Western Empires, and after the death of the Emperor Theodosius in 395 the two parts were never united. The Eastern and Western Churches were finally severed at the end of the eleventh century. Croats and Slovenes gave allegiance to the Roman pontiff while Rumanians, Greeks, Serbs, and Bulgars looked for guidance to the Metropolitan in Constantinople. As heirs to the Eastern Empire, the Sultans became the overlords of the eastern Balkan peoples, while Croats and Slovenes found their masters in the Hapsburgs. Thus, to the divisive influence of Balkan geography were added diverse religious and political traditions.

Toward the end of the fifth century, the movement of Slavs into the Balkan peninsula was well under way. A relatively small group, the Slovenes, who had settled in the northwestern part of the peninsula, was to fix the racial character of the South Slav state, Yugoslavia. Another and larger group at the same time pushed into the lower Danube valley and gradually spread through the greater part of the region.

Of the post-World War Balkan states, only one, Yugoslavia, bore a name really descriptive of its racial character. The others, though predominantly Slav, bore non-Slav names. Bulgaria was originally settled by the Bulgars, a Mongolian tribe, who conquered the area in the seventh century only to be absorbed later by the numerically superior Slavs. Rumania perpetuated the Rumanian claim to descent from the legions which conquered Dacia in the reign of Trajan. Rome withdrew her legions, but traces of her language remained. The name Greece is justified in part by the language of her people, but here again there are mixed racial elements among whom the Slav predominates.

Post-War Minorities. That political lines should coincide with ethnic and geographical ones is hardly to be expected in Europe. It is certainly not the case in the Balkans. For example, Macedonia has been aptly described as " a political problem rather than a geographical entity." [3] Bulgarians, Yugoslavs, and Greeks have claimed Macedonia and sought to impress

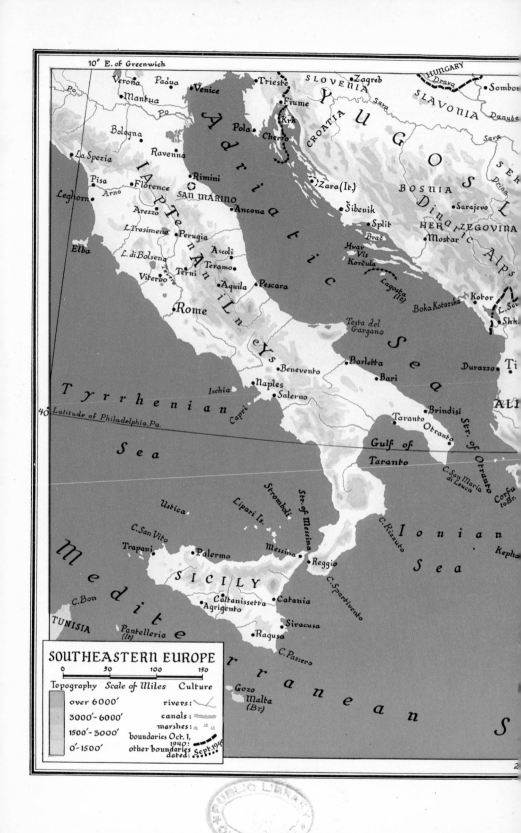

10° E. of Greenwich

Po

Verona Padua Venice
Mantua
Po

SLOVENIA Zagreb HUNGARY
Trieste Drava Sombor
Fiume SLAVONIA
Krk Danube
Pola CROATIA Sava
Cherso Sava

Bologna
La Spezia Ravenna
Pisa Florence Rimini
Leghorn Arno SAN MARINO
Elba Arezzo Ancona
L.Trasimeno Perugia
L. diBolsena Ascoli
Viterbo Teramo
Terni
Rome Aquila Pescara

A d r i a t i c

Zara(It.)

BOSNIA Dinaric
Sarajevo Drina
Šibenik HERZEGOVINA
Split Mostar
Brač
Hvar Alps
Vis
Korčula
Lagosta
(It.) *S e a*
Boka Kotorska Kotor
L.Scu
Shk

Testa del
Gargano
Benevento Barletta Durazzo Ti
Bari ALI
Naples
Ischia Salerno
Capri Brindisi
Taranto Otranto
T y r r h e n i a n
40 Latitude of Philadelphia, Pa.
Gulf of
S e a Taranto
C. San Maria
di Leuca
Corfu
to Br.

Stromboli
Ustica Lipari Is. Str. of Messina
C. San Vito Messina *I o n i a n*
Trapani Palermo C. Rizzuto Kepha
Reggio
C.Bon SICILY C. Spartivento *S e a*
Caltanissetta Catania
Agrigento
TUNISIA Siracusa
Pantelleria Ragusa
(It.) C. Pasiero

M e d i t e r
Gozo
Malta
(Br.) *r a n e a n* *S*

SOUTHEASTERN EUROPE

0   50   100   150

Topography *Scale of Miles* Culture

over 6000' rivers:
3000'–6000' canals:
1500'–3000' marshes:
0'–1500' boundaries Oct. 1,
1940:
other boundaries
dated:

their cultural pattern on its people. Some 600,000 Bulgaro-Macedonians lived in Yugoslavia and more than 80,000 in Greece.

Rumania and Yugoslavia had German minorities of about 750,000 and 500,000, respectively, dwelling for the most part in areas formerly incorporated within the Austro-Hungarian Empire. Rumania also had over 1.4 million and Yugoslavia nearly half a million Hungarians. In Bessarabia and Northern Bukovina, incorporated into Rumania, there were more than half a million Ukrainians. In Greece, Bulgaria, and Yugoslavia, Jews formed an infinitesimal part of the population, but Rumania had a Jewish minority of 4 per cent. In Bessarabia and the Dobrudja, Rumania inherited about 300,000 Bulgarians.

These, it must be remembered, represented only the major minorities in an area where, due to the frequent shifting of boundaries, particularly within the present century, minorities seemed to be the rule rather than the exception.

Territorial Status after the War. The territorial status of the Balkans was fixed by the Treaty of London (May 30, 1913) between the Balkan nations and Turkey, the Treaty of Bucharest (August 10, 1913) between the Balkan states and Bulgaria, and various World War treaties.

The status of Albania was fixed in 1913. Bulgaria, on the losing side in the First World War, failed to get back South Dobrudja and Macedonia which she had lost in 1913, and in addition had to yield to Greece the land between the Kavalla and Maritsa rivers, her corridor to the Aegean. Rumania was tremendously increased in size by the addition of the former Hungarian territories, Transylvania, and part of the Banat, Bukovina (previously held by Austria), and Bessarabia (belonging to Russia).

Yugoslavia consisted of Serbia, Montenegro, Bosnia-Herzegovina, Croatia, Slavonia, part of the Banat, the Voyvodina, lands in Slovenia and Dalmatia, and a section of Macedonia.

Rumania

During the post-war period (1919–1939) Rumania was the most prominent Balkan state, due in large measure to her size and resources. She had been accorded exceedingly favorable treatment by her victorious allies: her territory was doubled and Germany was forced to repudiate the Treaty of Bucharest.

Political Structure. Before the First World War, Rumania was ostensibly a parliamentary state with two major parties alternately in control. The Conservative Party, representing the land-owning group, had a German orientation. The Liberal Party was strongly pro-French and drew its strength from the professional, business, and financial classes. The outcome of the war discredited the Conservatives and gave the Liberals, the party led by the Bratianus, increased prestige, on the basis of which they dominated the government almost without a break from 1922 to 1928 and four years again from 1933 to 1937.

The major opponent of the Liberals after 1926 was the National Peasant Party, composed principally of the older National Party of Transylvania, led by Maniu, and the former Peasant Party. The Liberal and National Peasant Parties generally agreed on foreign policies, but disagreed on domestic affairs.

Post-War Political History. The post-war political history of Rumania falls roughly into two periods with 1933 as the dividing line. During the first period economic questions dominated internal politics. During the second period Rumania's national life was greatly affected by problems arising from, or stimulated by National Socialism, either in its German form or in Rumanian versions.

Rumania's three major minorities emphasized and intensified her political problems. The Hungarians, forming 7.9 per cent of the total population and concentrated chiefly in Transylvania, maintained constant agitation for return to Hungary. The Germans, comprising 4.1 per cent of the population, were readily susceptible to Nazi propaganda. As for the Jews, Rumanian anti-Semitism was of long standing.

The Bratianus. Modern Rumania practically took form under King Carol I (who ruled from 1866 to 1914) and the Bratianu family, leaders of the Liberal Party. Ion C. Bratianu the elder (died 1891) organized the Liberal Party, which under his sons (Ion, Vintila and Tinu), became an organ of the vested interests. Reforming zeal had to be sought elsewhere.

During the greater part of the decade following the First World War Ion Bratianu (1864–1927) was in power. Of the result of elections Bratianu had no fear: the government could always come through. Peasant groups, overcoming from time to time their characteristic inertia and reluctance to enter politics, offered constant protests against the Liberals' forced industrialization of the country and sought free elections which would accurately register the popular will. Under Ion Bratianu the Liberal Party put through a new constitution in 1923. Theoretically, the constitution of 1866 was a liberal document as judged by the best western European pattern of the time. Actually it gave the ruler totally unchecked power. The constitution of 1923 guaranteed civil liberties and forbade suspension of the constitution. In view of King Ferdinand's poor health the Premier had a provisional regency council appointed so as to circumvent Crown Prince Carol in case of his father's demise.

The fears of Ion Bratianu that Carol might not find him indispensable never materialized. Carol renounced the throne in 1925 and went to live in Paris with his Jewish mistress, Magda (or Elena) Lupescu. Giving way before economic pressure, Bratianu resigned in March, 1926 to be succeeded by the war hero, General Averescu. The political zeal of Averescu and of Octavian Goga, his Transylvanian ally and Minister of the Interior, and the failing health of the king alarmed Bratianu and suggested to him that it would be wise to resume control of the government. Averescu's fall in June, 1927 was followed by an election overwhelmingly favorable to Bratianu. When Ferdinand died in July, 1927, Carol's son Michael became king with a regency composed of his uncle, Prince Nicholas, the Patriarch and the President of the Senate. Before the year ended Ion Bratianu was dead.

With the less competent Vintila Bratianu, who succeeded his brother as head of the government, the great days of that political dynasty came to an end. Vintila was forced out in a wave of agrarian discontent (November 3, 1928). He died two years later.

The Return of Carol. The premiership of Iuliu Maniu, head of the National Peasant Party, indicated a marked change in Rumanian politics. Maniu was pledged to agrarian reform and opposition to all infringements on the civil rights guaranteed by the constitution of 1923. The new government's beginnings were wholly favorable. The election held to determine the strength of Maniu's ministry was honestly conducted and highly satisfactory in its results. Constitutional guarantees seemed to mean something. Even the Jews were protected. Unfortunately, bureaucracies rarely fall with the governments that create them. Maniu had to face sabotage within the civil service, and bitter criticism when he called for increased taxation to underwrite new governmental activities. The world economic situation began to make the Premier's position untenable, and in order to thwart his opponents, he decided on the recall of Carol who re-entered Bucharest in June, 1930, deposed his son and recovered the crown.

Maniu found that the king had a mind of his own, at least as far as reconciliation with his estranged wife Helen went, that the influence of his mistress Magda Lupescu had not terminated, that the monarch was an astute politician, and that in spite of a change in rulers, the economic crisis still continued. On October 6, 1930 Maniu was forced to resign in favor of Mironescu, who shortly gave way to Professor Nicholas Iorga, a distinguished historian.

Iorga. A former tutor of the king, Iorga had no substantial political following. In the election of June, 1931 his bloc polled 48 per cent of the votes. Under the election law of 1926, this constituted a majority, since the party polling 40 per cent of the vote received at least half the seats in the House of Deputies and a share of the remainder proportionate to its popular vote. This law, along with the government's control of the choice of candidates, made parliamentary government a farce and ministerial responsibility impossible.

As the personal rule of the king got under way rapid shifts in cabinets became a common political device. Pitting parties and politicians against each other Carol virtually destroyed his opposition. Iorga was succeeded by Voida-Voevod of the National Peasant Party, the latter by Maniu in 1932. Voida-Voevod was reappointed in 1933 only to be supplanted by Ion Duca, a Liberal. All cabinets were formed merely by royal command, the requisite parliamentary majority seemingly could always be arranged.

The Rise of the Iron Guard. With the assassination of Premier Duca by the Iron Guard in December, 1933, the second period of post-war Rumanian political history began. From this time onward, Fascism dominated the scene. In the previous period the dynamic element had been the desire of the peasants, despite their natural dislike for politics, to have a voice in the government more nearly proportionate to their numbers. Between 1933 and 1940 politics was a struggle for power between King Carol and the Iron Guardists, who were supported by Germany.

With the Nazi triumph in Germany Rumanian Fascism became more conspicuous, although its tenets had long been advocated by various native groups. The Christian Defense League had existed before the First World War and the Iron Guard had been heard of long before the assassination of Premier Duca thrust it on the center of the political stage.

Codreanu. The founder of " The League of the Archangel Michael," later known as the Iron Guard, was Corneliu Zelea Codreanu. His anti-Semitic activities first brought him into prominence in 1923, when he shot the gendarmes who were attempting to arrest him. Popular acclaim led to his acquittal. Soon thereafter the League was formed with the swastika as its emblem. In 1930, the name Iron Guard was adopted. The organization expanded rapidly, appealing especially to dispossessed aristocrats, disgruntled young intellectuals, and to numerous souls who ascribed their poverty to the prosperity of the Jews. In addition to its anti-Semitism, the Iron Guard was active in pointing out corruption and inefficiency in the civil service and in agitating for agrarian reform.

The government dissolved the Iron Guard on the eve of the 1933 elections, an act for which Duca paid with his life. The banned Guardists thereupon became the nucleus of the All-for-the-Fatherland Party. In 1935, the trend toward Fascism was strengthened by the formation of the National Christian Party out of the union of the National Agrarians, led by the Transylvanian Octavian Goga, and the Christian Defense League, led by Professor Cuza.

Carol's Personal Rule. The growth of Fascism was not the only problem with which George Tatarescu, Duca's successor, had to cope. His royal master was becoming more agile in both international and internal politics. By Carol's order, his brother, Prince Nicholas, was excluded from the succession, stripped of his honors, and ordered to leave the country. In the election of December 21, 1937 Tatarescu received only 38.5 per cent of the vote, less than the statutory 40 per cent. Realizing that this was a personal censure, Carol appointed a Cabinet dominated by the National Christian Party. The Iron Guard was ignored. Their response was a series of pogroms, accompanied by blatant violations of minority rights. The king was forced to recognize the popular hostility and on February 10, 1938 appointed a Cabinet of National Union, headed by the Patriarch, Dr. Miron Cristea, and consisting largely of former ministers. When Cristea died a year later he was succeeded by Calinescu. The king now governed by decree.

The New Constitution. On February 24, 1938 Carol's new constitution was submitted to a plebiscite, in which less than 1 per cent of the voters failed to register " yes." Superficially, at least, the constitution of 1938 did not change the governmental structure. There was a Cabinet, but it was not responsible to the legislature. Parliament was still bicameral. Members of the lower house had to be proportionately selected from those engaged in the professions, manual labor, agriculture, business or industry. The Senate consisted of hereditary and ex-officio members, nominated by the king and elected by " the constituted bodies of the Senate." The king could declare war, make peace, conclude treaties, veto acts of Parliament, and rule by decree in the absence of Parliament. By a decree of April 14, 1938 all political parties were dissolved and succeeded by a single party, the Front of National Rebirth. Carol had become the Fuehrer as well as king.

The Iron Guard and the National Peasant Party refrained from voting in the plebiscite on the constitution. The minimum age (thirty years) prevented many of the younger Iron Guardists from voting, and Codreanu's mixed Polish and Hungarian origin disqualified him for the Cabinet. Accused of complicity in a murder plot, Codreanu and several Iron Guard leaders were arrested in April, 1938. On November 30, while being transferred from one place of confinement to another, Codreanu and his associates were shot while attempting to escape, the government announced. In less than a decade Carol had acquired absolute power, thanks to the support of the church and the army, and his own political dexterity.

Rumanian Economy. Rumania was a predominantly agricultural country, industry employing less than one million of the nation's 19.5 million inhabitants. Her marked industrial development since 1935 had been due largely to the rearmament program. Rumanian farms for the most part were tiny; draft animals were scarce and modern agricultural techniques virtually unknown. The major crops were wheat and maize. Timber was exported in decreasing amounts, owing to governmental control of cutting. The high prices paid by the state monopoly induced the farmers to raise enough tobacco to meet home demands. Oil production, Rumania's major industry, was largely in the hands of foreign companies. While responsible for only

4 per cent of the national income, it accounted for 40 per cent of Rumania's exports. In spite of the fact that the output of oil was constantly decreasing, it occupied a dominant role in the external relations of Rumania.

Yugoslavia

Yugoslavia was the second largest Balkan country in area and population. This state owed its creation not so much to the peacemakers at Paris as to the desire of kindred South Slav peoples to form a unified state. Serbs, Croats and Slovenes constituted more than four-fifths of the total population. The three largest minorities were, in the order of size, German, Hungarian, and Albanian. Racial divisions within the Yugoslav group were complicated by religious and economic differences. The Serbs were Greek Orthodox, the Croats and the Slovenes Roman Catholic.

Origins of Modern Yugoslavia. Yugoslavia was formed from territories previously embraced within the Austro-Hungarian Empire, in addition to Montenegro and Serbia. The Serbs had had an empire as far back as the fourteenth century; there was a kingdom of Croatia in the tenth century; and Montenegro obtained its freedom from the Turks in the fourteenth century.

The impending collapse of the Dual Monarchy had led to the establishment of a National Council of Croats and Slovenes in October, 1918 in association with delegates from Bosnia-Herzegovina. Shortly after the collapse of the Dual Monarchy, the Serbian government agreed to set up a temporary Yugoslav-Serb organization. The Regency of the new state was accepted by Prince Alexander of Serbia. The deposition of King Nicholas by the Montenegrins and their union with Serbia completed the Yugoslav state, which for reasons of national policy was first called the Kingdom of the Serbs, Croats, and Slovenes.

Constitution of 1921. Out of the Constituent Assembly of 1920 came the Constitution of 1921, modeled, like the Rumanian Constitution, on that of Belgium. Laws passed by the unicameral legislature, the Skuptchina, were not subject to the Crown's veto. Deputies elected on a basis of proportional representation served for four years. The auspices for this constitution (it lasted until 1929) were not favorable to begin with. More than half the population was illiterate, particularism was rampant and there was no tradition of democratic participation in the government.

The Croat Problem. The confusion of Yugoslavia's first decade was not due entirely to political inexperience. The Croats were an obstreperous element from the beginning. Indeed, they had never given their consent to the constitution. Having enjoyed some sort of autonomy under the Dual Monarchy, they resented the minority role to which they were assigned in the new state. The party organization of Yugoslavia reflected the basic Serb-Croat conflict. The Radical Party was the most powerful Yugoslav party until the death of its great leader, Nicholas Pashitch (1845–1926). Organized in 1881 on radical principles, it gradually moved toward the right and became the organ of Serbian nationalism. In his sixty years of public service Pashitch helped to guide Serbia through the Balkan and First World Wars with spectacular territorial gains. Though he had signed the Corfu Declaration in 1917, laying the basis for the Serb-Yugoslav union, Pashitch until the end of his life worked for a strongly centralized state.

In this he was opposed by the leader of the Croat Peasant Party, Styepan Raditch (1871–1928). Raditch consistently opposed the acquiescence of the Croats in the government and sought friends for them abroad. He favored Germany and Russia, and condemned France. On June 20, 1928, in the course of a debate in the Skuptchina on the ratification of the Nettuno convention with Italy, which he claimed worked against Croat interests, Raditch and two of his colleagues were shot to death. The Croat deputies immediately seceded from Parliament and threatened to establish their own administration at Zagreb. On January 6, 1929, with constitutional government in collapse, King Alexander undertook to rule by decree, ascribing the failure of parliamentary government to " blind party passions."

The Personal Rule of Alexander. With General Pera Zhivkovitch as his Premier, Alexander began to revamp the state. Civil liberties were abridged, the judicial system was overhauled, and the civil service reorganized in the interests of greater efficiency and economy. The army was purged of those suspected of disloyalty to the state and all societies and parties were disbanded. In place of the provincial system, the state was divided into nine *banovinas*, each governed by a Ban named by the king. On October 3, 1929 the name of the state was changed to Yugoslavia to indicate its homogeneity.

A new constitution was proclaimed on September 3, 1931 by the king, who reserved the right to suspend it " whenever the public interest is generally menaced." While the languages of the three major nationalities became official, only one nationality was recognized by law. The king became the commander-in-chief of the armed forces, appointed and dismissed ministers and civil officials, promulgated laws, passed on constitutional amendments, and safeguarded the unity of the state.

A bicameral legislature was introduced. Senators were nominated by the king, deputies were elected for a four-year term on the basis of universal suffrage by open ballot. The nine *banovinas* were divided into administrative districts which in turn were sub-divided into communes. All laws enacted in the *banovina* councils had to receive the sanction of the Council of State, the highest administrative body in the kingdom.

Along with the constitution went the electoral law of September 12, 1931. This measure outlawed all but the government party by providing that every electoral list must be approved by twenty electors in each of the three hundred odd districts and the party leader must be endorsed by sixty voters. Unfortunately, the political situation was not stabilized thereby. Discontent became increasingly vocal. Dr. Matchek, the Croat spokesman and successor of Raditch, was imprisoned on a charge of trying to upset the government.

Assassination of Alexander. On October 9, 1934 King Alexander and the French Foreign Minister Barthou were assassinated by a Macedonian revolutionary at Marseilles. The youthful Peter II, then but eleven years old, was proclaimed king under a Regency consisting of Prince Paul, a Serb, Dr. Stankovitch, and a Croat, Dr. Perovitch.

The Regency. The elections of May, 1935 brought into power the Yugoslav Radical Union with Dr. Stoyadinovitch, its leader, as head of the government. This bloc was composed of the Serb Radical Party, the Catholic Slovenes led by Father Koroshetz, and the Bosnian Moslems. Successive elections kept this government in power until February, 1939. The Union was pledged to maintain the Karageorgevitch dynasty [4] and, in general, the Constitution of 1931, making such concessions to decentralization as political expediency demanded. The principal opposition came from Matchek's United Opposition formed in October, 1937 by a union of the Croat Peasant Party, the Independent Croat Democrats, the Yugoslav Democrats, and the Agrarian Party. Its platform called for a restoration of civil liberties, Croat autonomy, and agrarian reform. The domestic policy of Stoyadinovitch was closely associated with his foreign policy. In general, the Premier veered toward the Rome-Berlin Axis, chiefly because of Yugoslavia's economic ties with Germany and Italy. Yugoslavia's trade with Germany more than tripled between 1932 and 1938. Italy's good offices were employed in easing Yugoslavia's relations with Hungary and Bulgaria.

The Concordat. In this curious domestic and foreign policy, the Concordat with the Vatican played a bewildering role. Signed July 25, 1935, it was not brought up for ratification by the Skuptchina until two years later. Then the storm broke. Since the Orthodox population outnumbered the Roman Catholic only by a six to five ratio, it was not unreasonable that the legal position of the Catholic Church should have been regularized by the Concordat. The Orthodox Church excommunicated all those who voted for ratification, the Radical Party expelled all who did not. The Concordat bill was finally passed on July 23, 1937 but six months later the government announced that it would not be carried out. If the government had hoped in one sweep to placate both Italy and the Roman Catholic Croats, it had won a Pyrrhic victory, and then surrendered even that.

In February, 1939 Dr. Stoyadinovitch resigned in a revival of the Serb-Croat conflict, the Croats as ever, demanding political equality and the decentralization of Yugoslavia into a federated state. Later five enraged Croat ministers gave up their portfolios. With the growing confusion in European politics it was more important than ever that Yugoslavia be united internally. But no solution of the Serb-Croat question seemed possible as long as Stoyadinovitch and Matchek were the negotiators.

The new Premier, Cvetkovitch, promised to give Croat demands his early attention and asked for legislative permission to extend local autonomy and decentralize the government. In April conversations between the government and the Croat leaders brought an agreement on an autonomous Croatia, the absorption of Czechoslovakia by Germany in March having given Matchek a potent argument. On August 24, 1939 Matchek became Vice-Premier. Two days later Croatia was granted autonomy, with a Parliament of its own. The Yugoslav Parliament was dissolved and a general election was called. Only the approach of a European war induced the Croats and Serbs to bury their differences. That it brought a permanent settlement was doubtful.

The Economy of Yugoslavia. About 80 per cent of the Yugoslav population depended on agriculture and forestry. Since it was far less expensive to ship produce up the Danube than by rail across to the Adriatic, the agricultural products of Yugoslavia found their way principally into the markets of central Europe. The two chief crops were maize and wheat. A large volume of timber, pigs and cattle, both live and slaughtered, were also exported.

" Yugoslavia is much more important as a producer of minerals than any other country in South-Eastern Europe." [5] Copper was the most valuable mineral, with lead and zinc next in importance. Yugoslavia produced about one-tenth of the world's supply of bauxite. As contrasted with great mineral producing countries, however, her output was relatively negligible, the total annual production being worth about one milliard dinars (less than 20 million dollars).

Greece

Greece was the third largest Balkan state in area and population.

Embarking on a war of independence in 1821, Greece had had a longer independence than any of her neighbors except Montenegro. Greece's entry in the First World War, was due to her great statesman, the Cretan, Eleutherious Venizelos (1864–1936), who dominated national politics for almost two generations. Schooled in the struggles of the Cretans for union with Greece, Venizelos' was the hand which guided his country through the Balkan Wars and First World War. Because of his pro-Germanism

King Constantine was deposed by the Allies. Greece received considerable dividends after the war: a large part of Thrace, Adrianople, and trusteeship over Smyrna. Venizelos was defeated in elections of November, 1920 and Constantine was restored to the throne. The sudden revival of aggressive nationalism in Turkey forced Greece to yield Smyrna and Eastern Thrace. At the close of the First World War Greece was ruled by King Alexander, second son of Constantine. Alexander died in 1920. Constantine recovered the throne but on his unlucky head fell much of the blame for the Greek debacle in Asia Minor and again he was forced into exile. His son, George II, succeeded, but in the following year (1923) he too was expelled.

The Republic. On March 25, 1924 Greece was formally declared a republic with Admiral Paul Konduriotis as provisional President. There now developed a basic cleavage in Greek politics between republicans and anti-republicans. The test in party orientation was largely a matter of its attitude toward Venizelos. The early leader of the royalist groups was Demitrius Gunaris, leader of the Populist Party. Gunaris and several royalist colleagues in the Ministry were shot amidst the general rage at the destruction of Smyrna. After Gunaris' death, the anti-republicans consisted of the Populists, the National Democrats led by General Kondylis, and General Metaxas' Party of Free Opinion. This alignment was opposed by the Liberals of Venizelos and two smaller parties, the Conservative Republicans and the Progressive Liberals.

The years 1924 to 1928 were marked by frequent political shifts, with accumulating discredit to the state. It was not until the end of 1928 that the new constitution, more than four years in the making, was proclaimed. Civil liberty was guaranteed, and manhood suffrage provided for, a bicameral legislature was established, and control over the national exchequer was placed in the hands of the lower house. Without a liberal tradition of government, however, the Greek constitution was destined to have little effect.

Return of Venizelos. Venizelos remained in the background during the years of confusion. In 1928 desire for change no less than the generally unsound economic condition of the country, brought the veteran statesman a healthy electoral majority and again he became Premier. Venizelos could not, however, check the progressive disintegration of parliamentary government. There were abortive attempts, such as that of General Pangalos, to seize power. Party alignments broke down. In 1932, Venizelos was forced to resign, the one bright spot in the four years of his administration being his conduct of foreign affairs, culminating in a treaty with Greece's ancient enemy, Turkey. In a few months, however, Venizelos was back in office, Premier for the eighth time. Within two months his Cabinet fell. Implicated in the military plot against the government of

General Plastiras, he retired to Paris, that haven of disillusioned statesmen and broken politicians, where he died in 1936.

The Restoration of the Monarchy. In March, 1935 discontented elements in the army staged an insurrection in the hope of checking the gradual elimination of republicans by the Tsaldaris government. General Kondylis, Minister of War, joined by General Metaxas as temporary Minister without Portfolio, crushed the revolt and began a systematic purge of republicans. In October, 1935 the constitutionally minded Premier, Tsaldaris, was forced out. Kondylis became Regent and Premier. The National Assembly voted to substitute the Constitution of 1911 for that of 1928, and to restore the monarchy. On the basis of a plebiscite showing 97 per cent in his favor, King George returned to Athens and tried to rule as a constitutional, non-partisan monarch.

The Regime of Metaxas. As one after another of the elder statesmen died, the problem of government became acute. In the spring and summer of 1936 disorders began to develop throughout Greece. The king called one of the few remaining experienced politicians to form a cabinet, General Jean Metaxas (1871–1941), trained in the military academies of Evelpides and Berlin, Chief of Staff in 1911, who had been exiled by the Allies, but had returned in 1920 and had immediately become politically active. Ostensibly to meet the dangers of a general strike, Metaxas executed a *coup d'état* on August 4, 1936 and announced that he would not yield power until he had " achieved a complete reëstablishment of Greek society." On December 17, 1936 he proclaimed that Greece would be transformed into a corporative state.

The Economy of Greece. Fifty-five per cent of Greek soil was unproductive. Her large population was constantly growing. In 1922 it was increased through the transfer of more than a million Greeks from Asia Minor. Immigration to the United States was held down by quota. Greece had no minerals and was the only Balkan state that imported basic foods in large amounts. Yet her standard of living was high, and one-third of the population lived in urban communities. This anomalous situation may be explained by: (1) Grecian crops, particularly tobacco and currants, had great market value. (2) The large merchant marine brought considerable revenue. (3) As Greece became more industrialized, she profited increasingly by the high business and technical capacity of her people, prime requisites in a modern world.

Bulgaria

Bulgaria was the only Balkan state which agitated for revision of World War treaties. Reversals in the Second Balkan War and in the First World War had complicated her relations with neighboring states and led her into different foreign alignments. Whatever stability post-war Bulgaria enjoyed was due in large measure to the intelligence of King Boris III, who succeeded his father Ferdinand on October 3, 1918.

Stamboulisky. In the next four years the Agrarian League, headed by Stamboulisky, was the dominant party. Stamboulisky's unrelenting favors to the peasants, however, brought the strong opposition of the army and professional classes, while his policy of rapprochement with Yugoslavia enraged the Internal Macedonian Revolutionary Organization (I.M.R.O.).

The I.M.R.O. Founded in 1893 to promote the cause of independence from Turkey, the I.M.R.O. continued to maintain its headquarters in Bulgaria and from there carried on intrigues in Greece, Yugoslavia, and elsewhere. Mihailoff, its leader, encouraged terroristic methods, and political assassination became their specialty. A combination of intellectuals, army officers and the I.M.R.O., seeing that constitutional means could not overthrow the peasant Premier, staged a *coup d'état*, killing Stamboulisky in 1923 and inaugurating a reign of terror.

For a period of eleven years Bulgaria was ruled by coalition governments, whose only consistent policy was an unwillingness or inability to curb the activities of the I.M.R.O. Along with the general conviction of some clear-sighted Bulgarians that the I.M.R.O. would have to be suppressed grew the belief that only a *coup d'état* involving seizure of the state could suppress this invisible government. The feat was engineered on May 19, 1934 by Colonels Damian Veltcheff and Kimon Gheorghieff. The first was the organizer of the Military League, the second the leader of the civilian Zveno. Each of these groups agitated for a government strong enough to exercise its will without obstruction from secret organizations or political parties. With the country in the hands of the Veltcheff-Gheorghieff coalition, dominated by the army, Boris could only acquiese in the situation. The I.M.R.O. was dissolved and Ivan Mihailoff fled.

The Return to Civil Control. Boris, however, slowly recovered control, and on January 22, 1935 the two colonels were forced out of the government. General Zlateff, their successor, went along the same road on April 18, 1935. A year later the Military League was dissolved.

The new civil government was headed first by Tosheff who was succeeded on November 23, 1935 by Kiosseivanoff. Just when it seemed that the baneful influence of the army was being put under control, however, another danger arose in the accelerated activity of the National and Social Movement. This group, organized by Professor Tsankoff, Stamboulisky's successor as Prime Minister, advocated a totalitarian government with Boris as leader. Although the king had been in touch with Hitler and Mussolini, he astutely realized that in a Fascist state he would be the Victor Emmanuel, not the Duce. On October 10, 1936 the headquarters of the National and Social Movement were closed and for a time its activities were at an end.   Any revisionist agitation, however, was apt to revive the movement.

An electoral law of October 21, 1937 fixed the membership of the Sobranye at 160 elected by adult males and married women and widows. Political parties were prohibited.

The Economy of Bulgaria.   Although four-fifths of her people depended upon agriculture, only about two-fifths of the land was arable.   Bulgaria had improved the situation by reducing grain production and substituting such crops as tobacco.   In terms of national income, more was realized from handicrafts than from industry.   National economic life was in a large degree under state control through the Minister of Industry, the activities of the State banks, and the buying operations of the Cereals Board.

Albania

The smallest and newest of the modern Balkan states, Albania's hectic career of independent existence lasted from July 29, 1913 to April 14, 1939.   In the first eight years Albania was recognized by the powers as a sovereign principality after revolting from Turkey, was ruled by William of Wied for half a year, was occupied alternately by the Allied and Central Powers during the First World War, then by Italy who was later evicted. Albania was admitted to the League of Nations, and in November, 1921 was again recognized by the powers as an independent state.

Lack of railroads and educational institutions indicated the backwardness of the country.   Turkey's baleful influence could not be readily effaced, and Albania made but little cultural and economic progress.

The Rise of Zog.   For 1920 to 1924 the state was under the control of a Council of Regency.   During this period, there came to the fore Ahmed Bey Zogu (born 1895), who during the First World War had become prominent enough to be interned in Vienna because of his interest in Albanian independence.   After the war, Zog fought both Italians and Yugoslavs, and brought about recognition of Albania's independence by the Peace Conference.   After he had been Minister of the Interior and Prime Minister, Zog was driven out, only to return and overthrow Fan Noli who led the movement against him.   Zog became President on January 31, 1925 and assumed the crown on September 1, 1928.

Zog attempted reforms on a large scale, seeking to remove the marks of Turkish rule and make Albania a European state.   By the law of December 1, 1928 Albania was described as a constitutional monarchy with a unicameral legislature whose 58 members served for four years.   The king as well as the Parliament could initiate laws.   Behind an intricate constitutional façade, Zog was all powerful.   Education was made free and compulsory, and freedom of assembly and the press assured, except when the public peace was jeopardized.

End of Albanian Independence. Although restless under Italy's influence, Zog could do little to improve Albania's situation. Yugoslavia, who had aided Albania financially in 1924 and 1925, was no longer in a position to lend assistance. In 1925, by convention with Italy, the National Bank of Albania was established and the Society for the Economic Development of Albania (SVEA) organized, both under Italian supervision. The Treaty of Tirana (1927) provided for mutual support and collaboration, to the extent of giving Italy the right of intervention whenever Albania requested. In the following year a Treaty of Defensive Alliance with Italy was signed. King Zog's efforts to demonstrate his independence were met by Italian naval demonstrations. The events of April, 1939, when Zog became a fugitive and Albania a part of the kingdom of Victor Emmanuel, were but the logical conclusion of Italian aggression.

Cultural Development of the Balkans

Education. The hectic events of the twenty years between the two World Wars described on the preceding pages had made a marked impression on those responsible for public instruction in the Balkans. After political liberalism of a sort had been given lip service and failed, attention was directed to that which should have preceded any liberal experiment — education of the masses.

Sons of the peasants, ambitious but undisciplined, managed through privation to reach the universities. There they received a classical education and perhaps went on to prepare for a profession. Unfortunately while graduating out of their own social class, they frequently could not earn a livelihood. The professions of law and medicine were overcrowded, yet the demand for scientifically trained agriculturalists, metallurgists, and engineers could not be filled. From the disgruntled, impoverished lawyers and physicians and unemployed intelligentsia were recruited the supporters of extremist political movements.

Educational Reform. There was great need not only for practical education but for a revision of the general educational system in the Balkan countries. Yugoslav education, as Stoyan Pribichevich remarks, was a waste of time as preparation for living in a modern world.[6] The great Professor Iorga called for the abandonment of the Rumanian system of education where the discipline of the barracks of the Second French Empire was superimposed on German pedagogical regulation.[7] Even in Greece a Minister of Education demanded less classical education and more professional training in agriculture and pisciculture.[8] The head of the Balkan Institute in Belgrade summed up the situation admirably when he

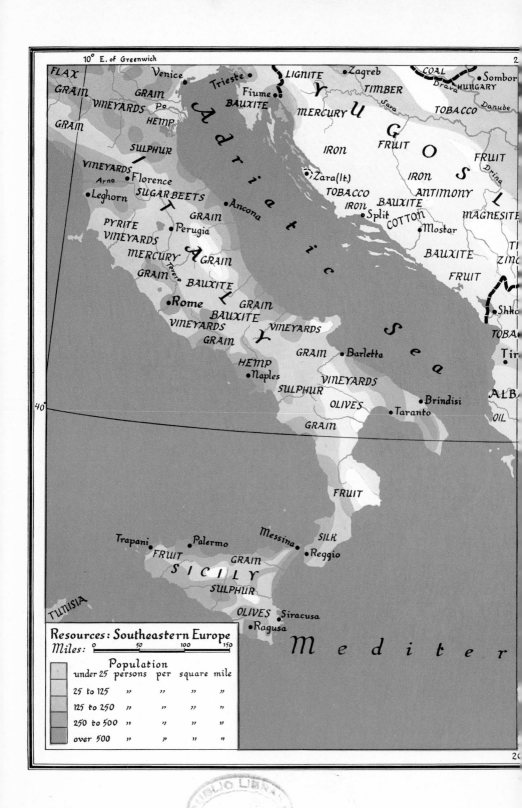

FLAX

GRAIN

GRAIN

VINEYARDS Po

HEMP

GRAIN

Venice

Trieste

Fiume

LIGNITE

Zagreb

COAL

Sombor

HUNGARY

Drava

TIMBER

Danube

TOBACCO

BAUXITE

MERCURY

SULPHUR

VINEYARDS

Arno Florence

Leghorn

SUGAR BEETS

PYRITE

VINEYARDS

MERCURY

GRAIN

GRAIN

Perugia

GRAIN

BAUXITE

Rome

BAUXITE

VINEYARDS

GRAIN

Ancona

GRAIN

VINEYARDS

GRAIN

HEMP

Naples

SULPHUR

OLIVES

GRAIN

Zara(It.)

TOBACCO

IRON

Split

IRON

FRUIT

IRON

ANTIMONY

BAUXITE

COTTON

Mostar

BAUXITE

FRUIT

Shko

TOBA

Tir

VINEYARDS

Barletta

VINEYARDS

Brindisi

Taranto

MAGNESITE

ZINC

ALB

OIL

FRUIT

Trapani

Palermo

FRUIT

SICILY

GRAIN

SULPHUR

OLIVES

Ragusa

Messina

Reggio

SILK

Siracusa

TUNISIA

Adriatic

Sea

Mediter

40

Resources: Southeastern Europe

Miles: 0   50   100   150

Population

under 25 persons per square mile

25 to 125   ,,   ,,   ,,   ,,

125 to 250 ,,   ,,   ,,   ,,

250 to 500 ,,   ,,   ,,   ,,

over 500   ,,   ,,   ,,   ,,

said: " The future inhabitant of the Balkans will have to be taught that it is possible to read Tolstoy and Bernard Shaw, to listen to serious music on the wireless or to be interested in the theatre and yet spend his days tilling the soil." [9]

With three universities in Yugoslavia, four in Rumania, one in Bulgaria, and two in Greece, along with various specialized institutions, there was a sufficient number of schools to serve as a basis for the educational renaissance. Some progress had indeed been made. For example, the new University of Salonika attempted to give practical instruction rather than produce more lawyers and physicians.[10] The *numerus clausus* was employed in some cases in order to spread the benefits of higher education among all national groups. Reforms were not confined to the higher institutions. Illiteracy was met by a general extension of elementary education and the development of secondary schools.

Literary Progress. In the creative arts some significant developments took place in the Balkans between the two World Wars. In both letters and art, the Balkanites have too often tended to imitate foreign models, themes, and tendencies, particularly those of France, rather than exploit native subject matter and literary traditions.

Rumania. Like other parts of southeastern Europe, Rumania has been slow in producing a rich prose literature. The plays of Caragiale, the novels of Zamfirescu, and the short stories of Bratescu-Voinesti — to select but a few — are representative of a new and robust literature. Among the essayists Dobrogeanu Gherea (1855–1920), the author of *Studii critice*, and among the historians Nicholas Iorga (1871–1940),[11] are representative of the more serious scholars whose work, begun long before, extended into the post-war period and compelled general recognition.

Bulgaria. In Bulgaria, Ioan Vasoff (1850–1922) bridged the earlier and later periods. His output was enormous — novels (*Under the Yoke* is perhaps the best known), stories, poems, dramas, most of them nationalist in sentiment. The lay sermons of Michailovsky (died 1927) sought vigorously to revive a spiritual life among the Bulgarian people. More recently there arose a gifted school of younger lyric poets deeply influenced by western European models.

Greece. In Greece the period from 1910 to 1928 has been described as " the age of the conquest of literature by the living language." Particularly rich in short stories and novels, the less serious literature of the Greeks has become noticeably more western and Byzantine. In the fields of scholarship, particularly literary criticism, philology, political and social sciences, much creditable work had been done.

Fine Arts. Certainly the most creative contemporary Balkan artist is Ivan Mestrovitch (1883–   ), a native of Vrpolje in Slavonia, the son of Croatian peasants. His sculpture, remarkably free from foreign influence, betrays a Byzantine sense of design, along with compelling boldness and peculiar sensitiveness. Mestrovitch helped to create a nationalist art movement in his native land which included Racki the painter, Rosanditch and Panitch the sculptors, and Pletchnik the architect.

Balkan names will not be lacking when the history of the culture of the period is finally written. Iorga is among the great national historians, and Mestrovitch among the eminent sculptors of all time. Such geniuses would no doubt have continued to appear without radical educational reorganization in the Balkan countries. But it is upon a well-trained and enlightened citizenry rather than on the occasional genius that social progress depends. Before the next period of great political change it is to be hoped that the educational leavening of the post-war period will have had time and opportunity to become effective in this backward part of the world.

Foreign Affairs

Before Hitler. After 1918, it was evident that those Balkan states which had fought beside the Allies had, in common with France, a desire to maintain the status quo. It was also obvious that Italy's unfulfilled ambitions, based on the secret Treaty of London (1915), complicated her relations with Yugoslavia and Albania.

Mutual fear of Hapsburg restoration and revisionist ambitions united Czechoslovakia, Rumania, and Yugoslavia in the Little Entente of 1920 and 1921. By the Treaty of Rapallo (1920) Italy and Yugoslavia composed many of their difficulties. The Balkans were further stabilized when, after the Treaty of Lausanne (1923), Turkey became a status quo power. The general determination to prevent an Austrian Anschluss began to take form so definitely that Balkan alarm on that score materially decreased.

The resurgence of Fascist Italy with its aggressive imperialism destroyed any sense of security that might have existed in the Balkans. In spite of solemn assurances of friendship, Italy's moves in Albania in 1926 and 1927 and her increasingly friendly relations with Bulgaria gave Yugoslavia ample cause for apprehension. As the tension between Italy and France increased, naturally the relations of their Balkan satellites became more strained.

The economic crisis, bringing a proposal for an Austro-German Customs Union (1931), revived the old fears of Anschluss. When, in lieu of a Customs Union, Italy began to work for a Danubian Union between Austria and Hungary (1933 and 1934), Balkan alarm increased. The triumph of National Socialism in Germany (January, 1933) and the collapse of the World Economic Conference (1933) aroused new fears.

After Hitler. The Little Entente immediately reacted to the Nazi menace by implementing their alliance. In September, 1933 Greece and Turkey signed a treaty guaranteeing each other's frontiers.

Meanwhile, efforts were made to create a Balkan Federation. Bulgaria refused to renounce her revisionism, but finally on February 9, 1934 a Balkan Pact of Understanding was signed by Greece, Turkey, Rumania and Yugoslavia, and was designed to preserve the status quo against possible disturbances by Bulgaria, Hungary, or Albania. A permanent council was organized. Each signatory joined in a mutual guarantee of frontiers and promised to enter into no commitments with other Balkan states without consultation. Secret protocols provided for mutual assistance to the victims in case of aggression.[12]

1934–1938. Temporarily a common fear of Germany brought Italy and France together and led to a guarantee of Austrian independence (1934). Undoubtedly Italy's economic cooperation and military support at the time of Dollfuss' assassination prolonged Austria's independence. While the tragic death of Alexander of Yugoslavia at Marseilles (October, 1934) complicated efforts at an understanding in the Balkans between Italy and France, a pact was signed in January, 1935 to which Great Britain agreed. Before the benefits of this arrangement could be appraised, however, Germany started to rearm on a gigantic scale. Anxious to retain her prestige, France entered into a Mutual Assistance Pact with the Soviet Union (May, 1935). When the Rome-Berlin Axis was formed in October, 1936, the majority of the Balkan states began to modify their positions in order to provide, if necessary, for greater freedom of action. Significantly enough, Bulgaria and Yugoslavia signed a Treaty of Friendship (January, 1937), and eighteen months later, Bulgaria and the four signatories to the Balkan Pact signed a Treaty of Non-Aggression (July 31, 1938). Of grave concern to her Balkan neighbors was Yugoslavia's rapprochement with Italy (March, 1937).

The last months of 1937 brought increasing evidences of disintegration of the European order. Italy adhered to the Anti-Comintern Pact of Germany and Japan, and a month later resigned from the League. The long-drawn-out discussions between Hungary and the Little Entente states were abruptly ended.

The New War. The dramatic events of the year 1938 destroyed the Little Entente and the importance of its western contacts, and in so doing gave greater significance to the Balkan Entente. The Italian occupation of Albania (April, 1939) brought to the Balkans a realization of the menace of the new European order. Fears of revisionism grew apace. Pledges of assistance were extended by England and France to Greece and Rumania. As German armies invaded Poland and shortly afterwards Russo-German collaboration began, no one could say that the new war would not in time ignite the Balkans.

It might be well here briefly to recapitulate by individual states the general trend of foreign relations during the period between two World Wars.

Rumania. Rumania was at first led by her fears of revisionism into the Little Entente and an alliance with France. As a status quo state, she willingly entered the Balkan League. After Munich, Rumania naturally sought whatever guarantees her Western friends could offer, yet, at the same time, internal Fascist forces and self-interest made her yield to the economic demands of the Reich.[13]

In 1940, Rumania lost approximately 41,300 square miles, or 36 per cent of her territory. Russia occupied (July, 1940) Bessarabia and Bukovina along Rumania's north central frontier. Somewhat less extensive was Rumania's loss to Hungary, who took a little less than half of Transylvania (September, 1940). At the same time Rumania ceded the southern part of the Dobruja region to Bulgaria. Of the 19.5 million subjects over whom King Carol ruled in August, 1940, his son Michael, who succeeded Carol on his abdication in September, inherited approximately 13 million, for Rumania had lost more than six and a half million people (equal to the population of Texas), as shown in the following table:

SUMMARY OF CHANGES IN RUMANIA BY OCTOBER 1, 1940

	Square Miles	Approximate Population
To U.S.S.R.	21,000	3,760,000
To Hungary	17,400	2,370,000
To Bulgaria	2,880	406,000
Still Rumanian	72,600	13,225,000

At the beginning of October, Hitler's armies entered Rumania, obviously a logical consequence of its dismemberment and presaging continuation of Germany's traditional — but recently interrupted — policy of *Drang Nach Osten* (Push to the East). These steps were explained at that time as a German desire to consolidate sources of supply in the Balkan-Black Sea area and to organize a position from which the British hold upon the eastern Mediterranean might be threatened.

Yugoslavia. Yugoslavia feared an Austro-German Anschluss or Hapsburg restoration. Accordingly, she joined the Little Entente — like Rumania — and cultivated friendly relations with France. After Hitler's coming into power, Yugoslavia turned toward the Rome-Berlin Axis, largely because of improved trade relations with Germany and diplomatic assistance from Italy.

Greece. Greece undoubtedly preferred an alliance with England and France to partnership with Germany and Italy, as her acceptance of the

Franco-British pledge of assistance (April 13, 1939) indicated. As a status quo state, she was a member of the Balkan League. Her dictatorial government, however, made her spiritually akin to the Axis Powers. The Greek problem was: Is acquiescence or resistance to aggression the best way to preserve national integrity?

Bulgaria. In addition to war association and revisionist aspirations, Bulgaria had added reason to favor Germany; her economic recovery was intimately associated with increased trade with Germany. Moreover, the powerful National and Social Movement was a Bulgarian counterpart to German National Socialism.

Albania. Because of the failure of all other sources of assistance, Albania after 1925 was forced into the Italian orbit. Economic conventions, treaties of mutual support and defensive alliance foreshadowed the occupation of Albania by Italy in April, 1939.[14]

Conclusion. To account for Balkan instability in both foreign and domestic affairs should not be difficult. In the peninsula, Rome and Byzantium, Catholic and Orthodox communicants, Hapsburgs and Turks have clashed through the centuries. Despoiled by all, it was dominated by none. Accessible to central Europe, the peninsula was divided geographically into isolated fragments.

After their emergence as national states, the Balkan countries experimented with liberal governments with disastrous results. The principle of self-determination, which fostered the territorial growth of most Balkan states, also strengthened the opposition and intransigence of minorities. Economically, the Balkans were poor and backward states. The great majority depended upon the soil for their livelihood but little fertile land was available and that was parceled out parsimoniously among a numerous population. Because nature in general was not prodigal, and where she was generous men had been tardy in utilizing her gifts, the Balkan peoples had not used their energy to promote material well-being. Rather than exploit nature, they had exploited each other, and their stronger neighbors took advantage of their confusion by exploiting them.

REFERENCES

¹ Royal Institute of International Affairs, *South-Eastern Europe*, New York: Oxford Univ. Press, 1939, p. 3.

² Cf. Griffith Taylor, "Cultural Aspects of Romania, Yugoslavia and Hungary," *Canadian Geographic Journal*, Vol. XX, No. 1, pp. 22–39.

³ Joseph S. Roucek, *The Politics of the Balkans*, New York: McGraw-Hill, 1939, pp. 138–9.

⁴ This dynasty was founded by Karageorge (1766?–1817) who in 1804 became the leader of the Serbian rebels against the Turks. His murder in 1817 was largely effected by the leader of the Serbian revolutionaries, Milosh Obrenovitch (1780–1860). This act inaugurated a perpetual feud between the Karageorgivitch and Obrenovitch dynasties.

⁵ Royal Institute of International Affairs, *South-Eastern Europe*, London: Oxford Univ. Press, 1939, p. 142.

⁶ Stoyan Pribichevich, *World without End*, New York: Reynal and Hitchcock, 1940, p. 313.

⁷ Joseph S. Roucek, *Contemporary Roumania*, Palo Alto, Cal.: Stanford Univ. Press, 1932, p. 373.

⁸ Rom Landau, *Search for Tomorrow*, London: Nicholson and Watson, 1938, p. 369.

⁹ *Ibid.*, pp. 369–370.

¹⁰ Robert J. Kerner, *Social Science in the Balkans and Turkey*, Berkeley, Cal.: Univ. of California Press, 1930, p. 101.

¹¹ Iorga was born in 1871. After studying in Paris, Berlin, and Leipzig, he became professor of universal history in the University of Bucharest. Two of his works are translated into English: *The Byzantine Empire* and *A History of Roumania*. Iorga was killed in an Iron Guard "Purge" November 28, 1940. Cf. J. S. Roucek, "Postwar Roumanian Literature," *Books Abroad*, January, 1932, VI: 11–13. Suggestive information, although based purely on "official" material, can be found in R. P. D. S. Taylor, ed., *Handbook of Central and East Europe, 1937*, Zurich: Central European Times Publishing Co., 1937.

¹² For a full discussion and documents, see R. J. Kerner and H. N. Howard, *The Balkan Conferences and the Balkan Entente 1930–1935*, Berkeley, Cal.: Univ. of California Press, 1936.

¹³ See *Geographic News Bulletin*, Washington: National Geographic Society, October 7, 1940, Vol. 19, Bulletin No. 3.

¹⁴ Cf. F. J. Brown, Charles Hodges, J. S. Roucek, *Contemporary World Politics*, New York: Wiley, 1940, ch. 15, "Danubian and Balkan Europe," pp. 326–355.

SELECTED BIBLIOGRAPHY

Clark, Charles M., *United Roumania*, New York: Dodd, Mead, 1932. An informative book, popular in style; includes an historical survey, data on varied phases of Rumanian life, and a selected bibliography.

International Reference Library, *Politics and Political Parties in Roumania*, London: Arthur Barron, 1936. A useful compendium of political information, including a who's who.

Jaszi, Oskar, *Dissolution of the Habsburg Monarchy*, Chicago: Univ. of Chicago Press, 1929. Highly authoritative and readable; one of the best histories of the Dual Monarchy's last phase; contains a selected bibliography.

Kerner, R. J. and Howard, H. N., *The Balkan Conferences and the Balkan Entente 1930–1935*, Berkeley, Cal.: Univ. of California Press, 1936. A general sketch of the historical backgrounds of the movement for Balkan unity, with a detailed and highly authoritative treatment of the special period, containing English translations of the more important documents and a full bibliography.

Landau, Rom, *Search for Tomorrow*, London: Nicholson and Watson, 1938. Primarily a search for basic spiritual factors in the life of the Near East, valuable because of the interviews with many of the important Balkan figures.

Miller, William, *Greece*, New York: Scribner, 1928. A brief survey of the first century of modern Greece, followed by a full account of the decade after the First World War, with an interesting and dependable survey of contemporary Greek life.

Mitrany, David, *The Effect of the War in Southeastern Europe*, New Haven: Yale Univ. Press, 1936. A valuable study of the political and economic effects of the First World War on the Balkan area.

——, *The Land and the Peasant in Rumania*, London: Oxford Univ. Press, 1930. An important work dealing with the agrarian problem in its historical aspects and describing in detail the reforms of 1917 to 1921 and their social and political results.

Pribichevich, Stoyan, *World without End*, New York: Reynal and Hitchcock, 1940. A readable and useful account of Balkan types and characters.

Roucek, Joseph S., *The Politics of the Balkans*, New York: McGraw-Hill, 1939. A dependable study of recent political history and Balkan governments, with suggestive chapters on foreign affairs.

——, *Contemporary Roumania and Her Problems*, Palo Alto, Cal.: Stanford Univ. Press, 1932. A short historical sketch followed by a full discussion of political and economic problems, with a good bibliography.

The Royal Institute of International Affairs, *South-Eastern Europe*, London: Oxford Univ. Press, 1939. A useful work dealing with the international relations, politics, and economics of Hungary, Turkey, and the Balkan states during the post-war period.

Schevill, Ferdinand and Gewehr, Wesley M., *History of the Balkan Peninsula*, New York: Harcourt, Brace, 1933. A well-rounded and extremely readable general history of the area.

Swire, Josiah, *Albania*, London: Williams and Norgate, 1929. A general survey with a detailed account of the period since independence, based largely on English and French materials.

Taylor, Griffith, "Cultural Aspects of Romania, Yugoslavia and Hungary," *Canadian Geographic Journal*, January, 1940, XX: 22–39. A general summary in its relation to the geography of the area.

Chapter XVII

Turkey and the Near East

"THE MAIN POINT WAS THAT THE TURKISH NATION SHOULD BE FREE TO LEAD A WORTHY AND GLORIOUS EXISTENCE. SUCH A CONDITION COULD ONLY BE ATTAINED BY COMPLETE INDEPENDENCE. VITAL AS CONSIDERATIONS OF WEALTH AND PROSPERITY MIGHT BE TO A NATION, IF IT IS DEPRIVED OF ITS INDEPENDENCE IT NO LONGER DESERVES TO BE REGARDED OTHERWISE THAN AS A SLAVE IN THE EYES OF CIVILIZED HUMANITY."
— SPEECH OF LATE PRESIDENT ATATÜRK, OCTOBER, 1927

Geography and Ethnography

Geography. The Turkish republic and the Near East occupy a key position at the crossroads of three continents — Europe, Asia, and Africa. Its geographical significance lies in that primary fact, as well as in the natural richness of the area. In addition to Turkey, the Near East consists of Iraq, Syria, Palestine, Transjordania, Saudi Arabia, and Egypt. Altogether these diversified lands total about 2,000,000 square miles, or two-thirds that of the United States. The Turkish republic has an area of about 294,416 square miles, about 10,000 of which are in Europe. The Kingdom of Iraq possesses 140,000 square miles, along the course of the Tigris-Euphrates river system, stretching from the Persian Gulf to the southern frontiers of Turkey. Syria has an area of 57,900 square miles, Transjordania 34,740, and Palestine only 10,429 square miles. Saudi Arabia, built around the nucleus of the former kingdoms of the Nejd and the Hejaz, reaches a total of about 1,000,000 square miles; Egypt about 383,000 square miles.

There are many vital geographic spots in the Near East. First among these is Constantinople (Istanbul) and the Straits, control of which has almost always brought dominating influence in the Near East as a whole. To the north of Istanbul lies the Balkan Peninsula, the shortest land route between Europe and Asia. On the east and west are the Black and Aegean seas. To the south is the Anatolian Plateau, the classic homeland of the Turkish people, and Mesopotamia, Land of the Two Rivers, a portion of the Arabic homelands. Along the eastern Mediterranean coasts are Syria and Palestine, territories of immense strategic significance. In many ways, for instance, the ports of Haifa, Tripoli, and Alexandretta are the gates to Mesopotamia, Persia, and the East. Palestine, in particular, occupies a key position in the eastern Mediterranean. It flanks the Suez Canal, domi-

---

This chapter by Harry N. Howard, Professor of History, Miami University, Oxford, Ohio.

nates British Imperial communications with India and the Far East, and is an air base of great importance. The port of Haifa is the terminus of the Iraq oil pipe line as well as a significant naval base for the British Mediterranean fleet. Across the Isthmus of Suez, in North Africa, is Egypt, cradle of an ancient civilization, an organic and historic part of the Near East.

A glance at a map of Eurasia and Africa, with these geographical factors in mind, reveals the essential reasons why the Near East has been in the forefront of human history — from preliterary days to our own. In historical perspective the Near East has been the meeting place of three continents. In this general region western civilization took form and substance. Here was the cradle of three great world religions — Judaism, Christianity, and Islam.[1] Here center today many of the great problems with which statesmen and peoples must grapple.

Ethnography. The great Near Eastern highway is literally strewn with the wrecks of peoples and nations. Turkey has a population of 16,000,000, of which 86 per cent is Turkish. There are more than a million Kurds and 100,000 Greeks and Arabs respectively living within the borders of Turkey. The state of Iraq harbors about 3,670,000 people, practically all of them Arabs; Syria has 3,630,000 people, the vast majority of whom are Arabs. The population of Palestine is 1,418,618, including 402,000 Jews, the rest Arabs. Transjordania, separated from Palestine in 1922, has an estimated population of 300,000 Arabs. The 16,000,000 people of Egypt are of mixed origin ethnically, but Arabic and Moslem in culture. If one adds to this melange the 4,500,000 Arabs of Saudi Arabia the population of the Near East totals almost 50,000,000. In general, the Near East is a region of peoples who have been divided by the barriers of culture and religion, though from time to time they were united into great empires, Egyptian, Assyrian, Persian, Helenistic, Roman, Sarasenic, and Ottoman Empires.

The Near East after the War

Partition of the Ottoman Empire. Following the First World War the Ottoman Empire was partitioned along the lines of the secret agreements which the Allies had arranged in 1915–1918, though Imperial Russia, as a result of the Bolshevik revolution, was no longer a party to those bargains.[2] Moreover, in addition to the Balfour Declaration of November 2, 1917, providing for a Jewish National Home in Palestine, an Anglo-French Declaration of November 7, 1918 had pledged " the establishment of indigenous governments and administrations in Syria and Mesopotamia, now liberated by the Allies, and in the territories the liberation of which they are engaged in securing, and recognizing these as soon as they are actually established." By the San Remo agreement of April, 1920, however, the mandates of Iraq and Palestine were assigned to Great Britain, while that for Syria, including the Lebanon, was assigned to France. It was not until December 23, 1920 that France and Great Britain defined the boundaries of Syria and Palestine.[3]

The Near East found no peace until the disastrous Greco-Turkish struggle came to a conclusion in the Turkish victory at Smyrna in September, 1922. As a result, the Turks returned to Europe — to Constantinople and Eastern Thrace. But the Straits were to be " internationalized " under the League of Nations. The capitulatory regime, initiated in 1535–1536, was to be abolished forever. Some 1,000,000 Greek inhabitants of Turkey were to be exchanged for 400,000 Turkish residents of Greece. While Turkey gave up all claims to the Hejaz, Palestine, Mesopotamia, Syria, the Dodecanese Islands, Cyprus, and Egypt, she retained sovereignty over the real homelands of the Turks — Smyrna (Izmir), Turkish Armenia, Cilicia, Anatolia, Adalia, Istanbul, Gallipoli, and Eastern Thrace.

The treaties of Sèvres and especially Lausanne laid the foundations for the independence of the other Near Eastern nations. The Arabs in Iraq achieved independence in 1932, and the Egyptians, really under British rule since 1882, in 1936. King Ibn Saud of the Nejd conquered the Hejaz in 1924, and founded the Kingdom of Saudi Arabia. But Palestine and Syria, for obvious reasons, continued as mandates.

The Temper of the People. In the old days religion constituted the determining cultural factor among the Near Eastern peoples; in the post-war era nationalism increasingly became the dominant note. This was noted above all in the Turkish Republic. Gradually nationalism spread among the Arabs — though the expressions of that sentiment took different forms in different Arabic lands.[4] In Iraq and Saudi Arabia, for instance, the people were gradually united behind their kings, Faisal and Ibn Saud, though the latter, owing to his Wahabite ancestry, placed more stress on the religious element than did Faisal and his successors in Iraq. In Syria, the Arabs, Christians (with the exception of Catholics) and Moslems, seemed essentially opposed to the French mandate. The Jewish-Arab conflict has been the tragic theme of Palestine history since 1918.

Political Heritage. The political heritage of Turkey and the Near East, whether in the negative or positive aspects, came from the late Ottoman Empire, based on the theocratic concepts of medieval Islam. Too much stress, however, should not be placed on the " backwardness " of the Near East as a heritage of the Ottoman Empire and the Moslem religion, since that backwardness may be traced to an agricultural economy and the shift in trade routes in the late fifteenth and early sixteenth centuries. Nevertheless it may be said that the theocratic system hampered adjustments to changes of time and circumstances. It required the dissolution of the Ottoman Empire to pave the way for modernization as well as nationalism of the Near East. Indeed, the Turks " lost an empire " only to become a sat-

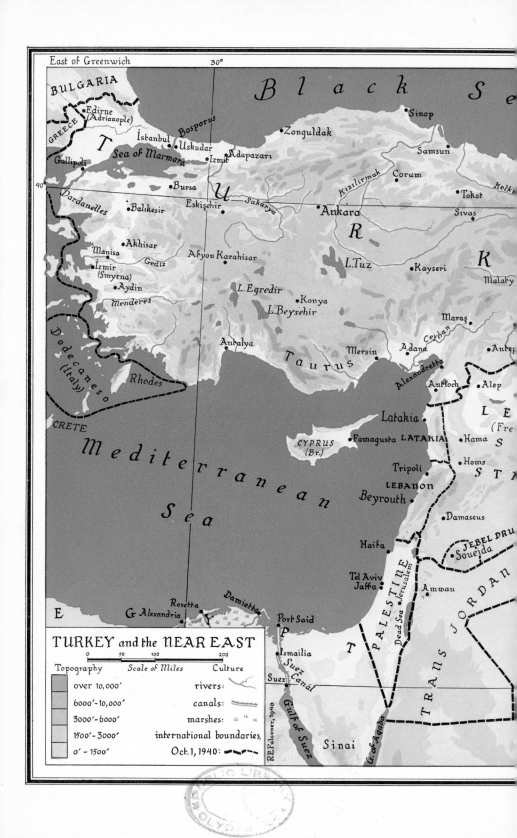

TURKEY and the NEAR EAST

Topography   Scale of Miles   Culture
| | | | | |
0   50   100   200

over 10,000'   rivers:
6000'–10,000'   canals:
3000'–6000'   marshes:
1500'–3000'   international boundaries,
0'–1500'   Oct.1, 1940:

R.F.Falconer, 1940

isfied national community for the first time in their long and troubled history.

Turkey

The Regeneration of the Turks. The Turkish Republic, after eleven years of almost constant warfare (1911 to 1922), arose from the wreckage of the Ottoman Empire to build a modern nation.

Kemal Ataturk. In general, the story of Turkish regeneration centers about the personality of Kemal Ataturk (Mustapha Kemal Pasha), the first President of the republic. Born in Salonica in 1881, the son of a customs official, Ataturk was trained as a soldier. He showed a pronounced aptitude for leadership, and, though sympathetic with the ideals of the Young Turk Movement of 1908–1909, was never really a member of that group. Neither did he favor Turkey's entry into the war on the side of the Germans, though he performed a brilliant service for his country in the victory at Anafarta in the Dardanelles campaign. It was Kemal who led the struggle against the hated Treaty of Sèvres. Determined to organize the Anatolian peasants for resistance against the Greeks and the Allies, Kemal called meetings at Erzerum and Sivas in July and September, 1919 in which the basic principles of Turkish nationalism were laid down. On April 23, 1920 the newly organized Grand National Assembly of Turkey, in its first session at Ankara — destined to be the new capital of the country — elected Ataturk President and commander-in-chief of the army. It also decided to frame a fundamental law, and adopt the Turkish National Pact, which had been accepted by the Parliament at Istanbul in January, 1920.

The Turkish declaration of independence, proclaimed the unity of the peoples of Anatolia and Thrace and guaranteed minority rights to the few non-Turkish elements in those ancient lands. Turkey was to " enjoy complete independence " and " liberty." There were to be no external restrictions on the political or economic independence of the nation. Commercial freedom in the Straits was to be permitted, but Istanbul and the strategic waterway itself were to be under Turkish sovereignty.

Establishment of the Republic. While the Sultan still asserted his authority at Istanbul, under the protection of British troops who landed there in March, 1920, the political and constitutional developments which concern us here took place at Ankara. The Greco-Turkish War did not end until the fall of 1922 and the convening of the Lausanne Conference. Only on the eve of that conference was the Sultan's government abolished by the Grand National Assembly at Ankara. Meanwhile, on January 21, 1921 the Assembly passed the Fundamental Law on Organization which became the basic law of Turkey until its modification in 1924. Under this measure the Assembly declared itself to be " the true and only representative of the nation, and exercises, in the name of the nation, the sovereign rights."

It was not until October 29, 1923 that Turkey formally became a republic. As the Turkish chieftain declared in 1927: " It was necessary to proceed by stages, to prepare the feeling and the spirit of the nation and to try to reach our aim by degrees, profiting meanwhile by our experience. . . . But we never disclosed the views we held." [5] Ataturk, of course, became President, and was to guide the destinies of the nation until his death on November 10, 1938. " By any test a genius," it would be difficult to conceive of the development of Turkey without his strong hand and liberating dictatorship.

Constitution of 1924. On April 20, 1924 a new constitution, which with some modifications has remained as the basic law, was adopted. It consists of one hundred and five articles, the first of which declares that " The Turkish state is a republic." Sovereignty belongs to the nation, but the Assembly " exercises the sovereignty of the people." Through the President and a Council of Ministers, it also wields executive power. Members are chosen for four-year terms by citizens twenty-two years of age or over. The President is given wide powers. He appoints the Premier and Cabinet from among the members of the Assembly. The judiciary are declared to be " independent and safe from any interference, and are subject only to the law." The constitution lays down a broad program of social reconstruction. Moreover, it contains a bill of rights declaring that all Turks " are endowed at birth with liberty " and are " all equal before the law." Among the " natural rights " of citizens are: " inviolability of person, right or freedom of conscience, thought, speech, press, travel, contract, labor, property and possession, assembly, association or incorporation. . . ." " The press is free within the limits of the law; it is not subject to any control or censorship previous to publication." Teaching is " free, under the supervision and control of the state and within the scope of the law." Article 88 declares that " with regard to citizenship, all the inhabitants of Turkey are, without distinction of religion or race, called Turks." Final articles provide for local government, state officials, finance, and amendment. Amendment is effected by a two-thirds vote of the Assembly. Of particular significance have been the Amendment of 1928 removing religious matters from the constitution and that of 1935 incorporating the program of the People's Party into the constitution.

The People's Party. The People's Party came into being in December, 1922. Though Turkey is neither totalitarian, Fascist, nor Communist, it is a one-party state. The party statutes and program were laid down in 1923. Like political groups in other authoritarian countries, the party is well-organized, highly centralized, and severely disciplined. Its statutes stipulated that " the supreme permanent chief of the party is Kemal Ataturk (i.e., the President of the Republic, today Ismet Inonu). Its headquarters are at Ankara." The statutes forbid " any deviation toward the right or left " among members, who must be eighteen years of age, of spotless character, and must not have been opposed to the national struggle or the ideals of the new Turkey. The party organs consist of a Supreme Presidency, a Council of the Supreme Presidency, a Grand Congress and a General Directing Committee, Provincial Directing Committees and Congresses and sub-organizations reaching into the smallest villages, the Parliamentary Group of the Party, and the Council of the Party. All members are bound to obey without reservation or restriction decisions arrived at by the Council of the Supreme Presidency. Every four years a Grand Congress is held in which the program of the next quadrennium is laid down.

The party programs of 1931, 1935, and 1939 are especially significant in that they formulated the basic lines of national policy,[6] though this was substantially true of the earlier gatherings as well. Among other things, Turkey is declared to be a " nationalist, populist, statist (*étatiste*), secular and revolutionary (reform) republic." The 1935 program called for the application of broad principles in education and suggested planned economy. The 1939 program provided no fundamental alteration in basic Turkish policies.

Social Reforms. From the very beginning, republican Turkey has been moving in the direction of secularism, nationalism, and industrialism. Turkey has made the transition from medieval Islam to modern nationalism, from medieval agrarianism to modern industrialism and machine technology, more rapidly and systematically than other nations of the Near East.

The process of secularization was especially significant. The Caliphate and the Ministry of Cults and Evkaf were abolished on March 3, 1924, the religious courts a month later. On September 8, 1925 the *tekkes* of the dervish orders were abolished and the orders outlawed. At the same time (August, 1925) the fez and veil were eliminated, and men and women were ordered to dress like western Europeans. The international calendar was introduced on December 26, 1925.

Judicial and Religious Reforms. More significant than these changes was the introduction of western European codes of law. The Islamic *Sheriat* was no longer to be the basis of Turkish law. On February 17, 1926 the Swiss Civil Code was adopted; on March 1 the Italian Penal Code and on May 29 the German Commercial Code. Essentially the legal reforms went into effect in October, 1926, and thus " orthodox Mohammedan Private Law, after a sway of more than thirteen hundred years over the realms of orthodox Islam, ceased to be Law in that Turkish realm which for nearly as many centuries had been its greatest and most powerful supporter."[7] The last vestiges of Islam as a state religion were eliminated when all reference to religion was stricken from the constitution by an amendment of

April 9, 1928. In May, 1935 Sunday rather than Friday became the day of rest, and all members of the clergy — Christian, Jewish, and Moslem — were forbidden to wear clerical garb except in the performance of their specific duties.

Naturally these changes outraged conservative religious and other elements. Some were alarmed at the concentration of authority in the hands of a man like Ataturk, and withdrew from the People's Party in January, 1925 to organize the Progressive Party. A revolt broke out among the Kurds in 1925 and a severe Law for the Maintenance of Public Order was passed in March, 1925. It was abolished only four years later. In July, 1926 a plot against Ataturk's life was uncovered at Izmir. In 1930 Ataturk himself recognized the general discontent and encouraged his friend, Fethi Okyar, to organize the Liberal Party, but the move failed to materialize, owing partly to disturbances in the country.

Educational Reforms. In the realm of educational and cultural reform, the republic of Turkey took a major step on March 3, 1924 when it closed the theological schools and enacted a Law of Uniform Education. A new Ministry of Education was set up. On November 1, 1928 the old Perso-Arabic alphabet was abolished and a Latin alphabet adopted. Today there is a well-developed structure leading from elementary and secondary to trade, professional and technical schools, and colleges and universities.[8] The University of Istanbul, completely reorganized in 1933, brought to its faculties a number of scholars driven from Nazi Germany. Especially important for adult education was the organization by the People's Party throughout the country of the *Halkevleri*, or People's Houses.

Economic Changes. Among the fundamental aspects of the Turkish reforms were the economic and industrial changes. Though Turkey may remain agrarian, machine techniques seem destined to prevail in agriculture as in industry. Characteristically these changes are being initiated under a system of planned economy, or Five-Year Plan. A high tariff structure was established in 1929, but it was not until July 14, 1934 that a planned economy was introduced. Since state intervention was a prerequisite to industrialization, state capitalism became the order of the day. The aim was " to make Turkey . . . an economically independent and integrally organized unit." Essential phases of the plan were to find within Turkey a market for raw materials and to assure the Anatolian peasant the necessary manufactured products, as well as lay the foundations for national defense.

Costs of Planning. The original plan called for an estimated expenditure of $32,600,000 financed through a series of State Banks. Distinct advances have been made in the sugar and textile industries. An $8,000,000 loan from Soviet Russia aided in the importation of textile machinery. Participation of English capital in the Karabuk Iron and Steel Works was significant. Moreover on May 27, 1938 an Anglo-Turkish Credit Agreement was signed involving a loan of $80,000,000 for the construction of new ports, harbor improvements, mineral exploitation, industrial enterprises and rearmament.[9] The great coal mines at Zonguldak on the Black Sea have been under Turkish direction. A great public works program was undertaken. Ankara was rebuilt at a cost of $100,000,000. About 7000 kilometers of railway are under state operation; more than $225,000,000 has been spent on railways during the republican era, and there are now about 30,000 kilometers of relatively good roads.

Social Problems. Industrialization and the introduction of modern technology have brought in their wake a host of social problems. First among these has been the labor problem. The last census indicated that out of a population of 16,000,000 about one-fourth live in towns and cities. About 4,500,000 are engaged in agriculture, 300,000 in industry and 260,000 in commerce. Not until June 8, 1936 was a modern Labor Law passed, covering such items as compulsory labor contracts, an eight-hour day and minimum wage scales, labor of women and children, sanitation and safety, compulsory arbitration of labor disputes, prohibition of strikes and lockouts, and social insurance. In 1935 women were elected to membership in the National Assembly. Indeed women gradually took their places in all walks of life. It should be noted, too, that in 1935 family names were required to be taken, and thus another Islamic custom was discarded. Early in the republic a Ministry of Public Hygiene and Social Welfare was established, and in 1936 a School of Hygiene was set up in Ankara. Equally significant steps have been taken in prison reform. Of particular importance is the Turkish Penal Colony on the Island of Imrali, in the Sea of Marmara.

President Inonu. Few could question Turkey's leadership in the westernization of the Near East. That leadership was not relinquished when the reins of power fell into the hands of President Ismet Inonu on November 11, 1938. The new President was an able soldier whose qualities were demonstrated in the Balkan Wars, the First World War, and the Greco-Turkish War. He proved an exceptional diplomat as chief of the Turkish Delegation at the Lausanne Conference in 1922–1923. Inonu was the first and almost the perennial Premier of the Republic. Indeed Ataturk, Inonu and Fevzi Cakmak, the Chief of the General Staff, were the triumvirate who guided the destinies of the republic. Inonu revealed his philosophy a few years ago when he remarked:

" Our revolution . . . is not the continuation or the consummation of the intermittent attempts at reform of Ottoman social life. . . . We have not bound ourselves to narrow and dogmatic conceptions in order to elevate the Turkish nation. The first and unending duty is never to turn back for any reason from paths once trod. . . . The second duty of the revolution is to travel in a positive, dynamic and constructive direction. It is necessary to teach the great masses of the people the pure and cultural order of the revolution and to meet the material expenses required for this. The greatest malady we have to combat is ignorance; and the highest road we are to follow is the road of positive knowledge. . . . It is positive science which assures and continually increases the constructive and creative power of the human mind. . . . Just as the goal of the Turkish revolution is the struggle for national liberty, so the assurance of the economic needs of the masses is another primary duty. When the Turkish revolution is looked upon as a continuous movement, one will see to it that it will never stop."

Iraq and Saudi Arabia

Iraq. In nationalization and westernization the Turks have merely been the leaders in the Near East — offering examples, sometimes reluctantly accepted by their more conservative neighbors. The case of Iraq is interesting. Assigned to Great Britain, with the exception of Mosul (until 1925), at San Remo in 1920, the British established the Emir Faisal on the throne in 1921, following a 96 per cent favorable plebiscite, and after the French had driven him from Syria. Though a mandatory relationship was not really regularized by the League of Nations until September, 1924, Anglo-Iraq relations were established on the basis of a treaty of alliance in October, 1922. In accordance with the terms of the mandate, Iraq was to become increasingly independent. The constitution of 1924 provided for a constitutional monarchy, responsible government and a bicameral legislature, with a nominated Senate of 20 members and a Lower House of 150 elected members. A British High Commissioner, however, held supreme power. Nevertheless, on December 14, 1927 Great Britain recognized Iraq's independence, and on June 30, 1930 the alliance was renewed. The British promised to support Iraq's entry into the League of Nations, which took place in 1932.

Iraq's first king, Faisal, who believed in a liberal, constitutional monarchy constructed along western lines, died in 1930 and was succeeded by his son, Ghasi, who was killed in an automobile crash in 1939. The throne is now occupied by Faisal II, born in May, 1935. Economic difficulties, plus the removal of the guiding hand of Faisal I, have brought political troubles to the new state. A *coup d'état* by Hikmet Sulaiman and the Chief of Staff Bakir Sidki in 1936 removed the Progressive Party of General Said Pasha and the Nationalist Party of Yasin Pasha from the political stage. But in August, 1938 Bakir Sidki was assassinated and Hikmet Sulaiman resigned. In December, 1938 Said Pasha became Premier, formulating progressive, nationalist and Pan-Arab program.

Attempts have been made to restore Iraq's ancient fertility through the development of modern irrigation schemes. Economically the Mosul oil fields are especially important. Gradual, but vital changes in the moderniz-ation of education have been made in recent years, though conservative tribal and religious elements have opposed these changes.[10]

Saudi Arabia. Saudi Arabia, or Saudiye, covers the interior of the Arabian Peninsula and the Kingdom of the Hejaz along the shores of the Red Sea. Its capital is Riyadh, in the Nejd. The Holy Places of Islam, Mecca and Medina, fall under the sovereignty of Saudi Arabia. This vast realm, with a population of about 4,500,000 Arabs, which came formally into ex-istence in 1932 with the union of the Hejaz and the Nejd, is the personal creation of King Ibn Saud, who was born in 1880 at Riyadh, his present capital. The country in general, and the Nejd in particular, is the seat of the puritanical and warlike Wahabite Moslem sect. Saudi Arabia is still in a backward condition; there are some automobiles and poor roads, and the technical equipment for a small army, including some tanks and air-craft. The Hejaz Railway connects Damascus with Medina, but the Hejaz section is not yet in use.

Ibn Saud is perhaps the most powerful personality in Islam today. While his attempts to modernize Saudi Arabia, owing to Wahabite con-servatism, have been confined to the army and the adoption of automobiles, he has, nevertheless, strengthened the central power and promoted a degree of security and order hitherto unknown in that wild region. Ibn Saud ap-parently aspires to the Caliphate and his ultimate political aims appear to center about Pan-Arabism.

Syria, Palestine, and Egypt

Syria. Culturally Syria was probably the most advanced of Arabic com-munities. Like Palestine, it remained a mandated country. Emir Faisal, son of King Hussein of the Hejaz, who had done so much to insure Arabic cooperation with the Allies in the Near East, was proclaimed King by a Syrian Congress in 1920, but the French authorities forced Faisal to leave the country. Placed under French mandate, Syria underwent periodic and repeated reorganizations and finally was divided into four parts: (1) the republic of Lebanon, with Beirut as the capital, August 31, 1920; (2) the state of Syria, with Damascus as the capital (including the districts of Damascus, Aleppo, Hama, Homs, Hauran, Dair az Zur, and Alexandretta), January 1, 1925; (3) the government of Latakia, May 14, 1930; and (4) the government of the Jebel Druse, April 5, 1921.[11]

France has had serious difficulties in Syria since the establishment of the mandate, as exemplified in the Damascus revolt of 1925 and the rebellion of the Jebel Druse in 1925–1927. Arab nationalists were especially outspoken in Syria, its birthplace in the nineteenth century. The Lebanon, with its

Christian Catholic majority, has been not unfavorable to the French mandate. After a number of efforts at conciliation and attempts to solve the problems of Syrian unity and independence, a Franco-Syrian Treaty was signed on September 8, 1936 which promised Syrian independence within three years. The Pact, however, was never ratified by France.

Many Syrians were incensed when they lost control of the district of Alexandretta (Hatay), France having reached an agreement with Turkey (1939) making that district (about 40 per cent of the population was Turkish) autonomous and then incorporating it into the Turkish Republic. Syrian independence was postponed indefinitely by the war. What effect the defeat of France will have on the Syrian mandate remained to be seen, though it was clear that a German-Italian victory would end all hopes of genuine independence.

The Puzzle of Palestine. Palestine is a small and relatively poor country guarding the Suez Canal. The Jews were determined to build a National Home (Dr. Chaim Weizmann, President of the Zionist Organization, told the Peace Conference on February 27, 1919 that their aim was " to build up gradually a nationality which would be as Jewish as the French nation was French and the British nation British "), while the Arabs feared for their economic as well as political independence. All around Palestine the Arabs saw their kinsmen achieve total or partial independence — in Iraq, Saudi Arabia, Syria, and Egypt. They felt that the Jews stood in their way in Palestine, a country which had been Arabic and Moslem for 1300 years. A recent writer has graphically summarized the basic conflict: [12]

" In the midst of their startling successes, some Zionists — not always well informed — have come to regard the Palestinian Arabs and their problems as of only secondary importance and Palestine as exclusively the country of the " manifest destiny " of the Jewish people. Some Jewish and non-Jewish observers, fascinated by the hsitorical appeal of the land and by the desire for a large-scale solution of the " Jewish problem," have not always taken into full account two factors inherent in the situation: the limited absorptive capacity of the country, which is very small, with only few fertile districts and no important natural resources, and the existence of a relatively very large Arab population, which since the beginning of the World War has become strongly conscious of its national aspirations."

Although they constitute less than one-third the population, the Jews, in view of their western techniques and culture, have played the leading role in every phase of Palestinian life. The result has been serious strife between Arabs and Jews. A long series of outbreaks, costing many lives, brought a Royal Commission of Inquiry to investigate the situation in 1936. Its report of July 7, 1937 [13] recommended a division of the country into a Jewish state, an Arab state and a small enclave, under a British mandate, including both Jerusalem and Bethlehem, and connected by a corri-

dor with the sea.   Since both Arabs and Jews opposed the scheme, it was
soon abandoned.   With the war of 1939, a kind of tactical and tacit truce
was called, while Great Britain moved to conciliate both parties, particularly the Arabs.

Progress of Palestine.   Meanwhile, Palestine had made enormous progress
since 1918.   Jewish investments in industry and agriculture reached about
£ 30,000,000.   The Jews laid out some 230 agricultural settlements and
drained the swamps of North Palestine.   Numerous industries were
founded and the city of Tel-Aviv, with a population of about 150,000, was
constructed.   A modernized Hebrew language was adopted and a complete educational system, including a new university, was set up.

The Problem of Egypt.   Egypt's major problem in the post-war years
was to achieve independence from Great Britain, which had made Egypt
a protectorate in December, 1914.   Theoretically Great Britain ended the
protectorate on February 18, 1922, but reserved the right to guard Egypt
with its vital Suez Canal, protect foreign interests and minorities in Egypt,
and control the Anglo-Egyptian Sudan.   A strong nationalist movement
struggled for full independence of the country, but no genuinely amicable
settlement was reached until August 26, 1936, when a treaty of alliance
between Egypt and Great Britain was signed, recognizing Egyptian independence.   Great Britain undertook to withdraw its troops, except a garrison of 10,000 soldiers and 400 aircraft in the Suez Canal region; Alexandria and Port Said became British naval bases.   Moreover, in case of war,
Great Britain was to have the right to move troops across Egypt.   The
Treaty involved a mutual defense pledge, though Egypt was not bound to
fight unless attacked.

Government.   The Egyptian constitution of 1923 provided for a Lower
House of 150 members, chosen by general franchise for a period of five
years, and an Upper House of 100 members, sixty of whom are nominated
by the king.   The government is responsible to the Lower House.   The
Turco-Albanian Mohammed Ali Dynasty rules Egypt, the present king
being Farouk I, who succeeded King Fuad in 1936.

In general Egypt has pursued a policy of gradual modernization without injuring the sensibilities of conservative Moslems.   The abolition of
the hated capitulatory regime in May, 1937 signalized Egypt's increasing
freedom from western control.[14]

Foreign Policy: The Near East and the Western World

The foreign policy of the Near Eastern peoples is based on the fact
that the region is an inter-continental highway possessed of great natural
resources.   Turkish policy, in the years after 1918, centered fundamentally
about the question of the Straits.   From 1920 until the eve of the Second

World War, the Turkish republic had a close friendship, though not an actual alliance, with the Soviet Union. In July, 1932 Turkey entered the League of Nations, as did the Kingdom of Iraq. After 1930 Turkish foreign policy was designed to assure her own security and independence through friendship and cooperation with her Balkan neighbors. That policy was supplemented by the so-called " Near Eastern Pact " of July 8, 1937 among Turkey, Iraq, Iran, and Afghanistan — a consultative and non-aggression pact to which, it was hoped, Saudi Arabia and Egypt, not to mention Syria when it became independent, would eventually adhere. Moreover, on July 20, 1936, at the Conference of Montreux, Turkey succeeded in obtaining a new Convention of the Straits, in substitution for the Lausanne Straits Convention, which gave her substantial sovereignty over this strategic waterway.[15]

Turkish Alliances. As the war clouds began to gather, the Turkish Republic moved in the direction of France and Great Britain. Relations with Great Britain had slowly but steadily improved since 1923 until the closest possible understanding obtained, though by 1936 Franco-Turkish relations were troubled by the dispute over the Alexandretta (Hatay) district of Syria. Turkey desired the territory primarily because of fears that Italy might seek a foothold in Asia Minor once France's mandatory authority over Syria was removed.[16] The Sanjak of Alexandretta became an independent province, known as the Hatay Republic, by the terms of the Franco-Turkish Treaty of June, 1938, and a year later was incorporated in the Turkish Republic when France and Turkey signed a mutual assistance pact. As the war began Turkey became a non-belligerent ally of France and Great Britain through the Treaty of Alliance of October 19, 1939.[17] Though not pledged to fight against the Soviet Union, it was felt that Turkey might prove a powerful ally should Germany move through the Balkan peninsula, Italy fish in the troubled waters of the eastern Mediterranean, or Soviet Russia resume her march toward Istanbul and the Straits.

The Allied Position. The western allies, indeed, appeared to occupy a powerful position in the Near East during the early phases of the war. A large army, variously estimated at from 150,000 to 500,000, was assembled under General Maxime Weygand. Allied military, air and naval forces were to defend the Suez Canal and Constantinople and the Straits, the two strategic keys to the Near East. Moreover, they might deprive both Germany and Italy of the oil resources of the Near East, remembering that Lord Curzon once remarked that the Allies of 1914–1918 had floated to victory on a sea of oil. These forces might draw Turkey at last into the war, and organize the Near Eastern and Balkan regions for resistance to Nazi-Fascist aggression. The Near East, it should be remembered, is also part of the bulwark protecting India.

The defeat of France in June, 1940 radically altered the strategic

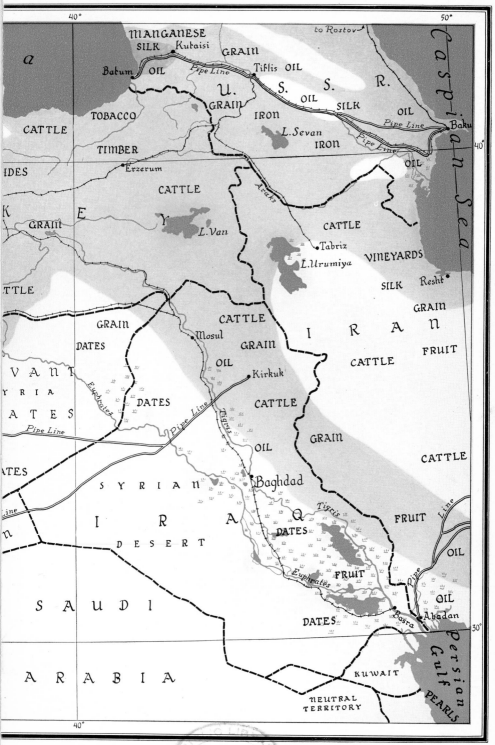

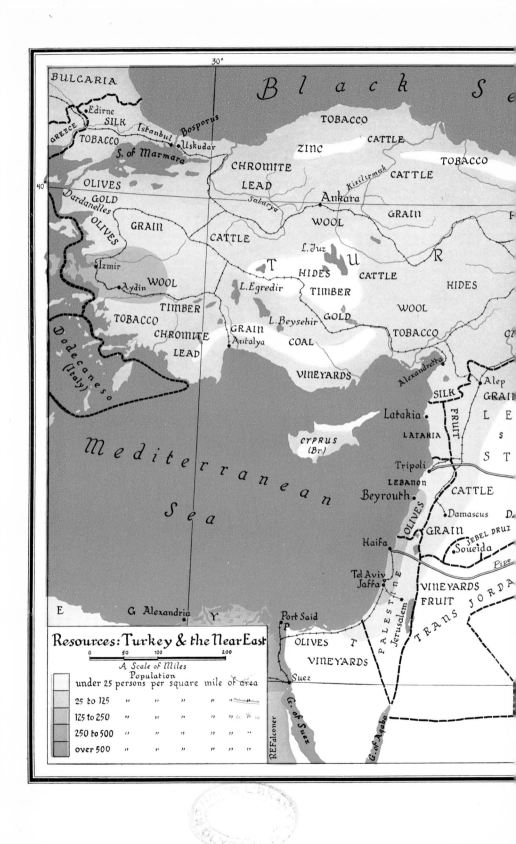

BULCARIA

Black Sea

GREECE

•Edirne
SILK
TOBACCO
Istanbul
Bosporus
•Uskudar
S. of Marmara

TOBACCO

CATTLE

ZINC

TOBACCO

CHROMITE
LEAD

OLIVES

GOLD
Dardanelles

OLIVES

GRAIN

CATTLE

Sakarya

Kizilirmak

Ankara

WOOL

GRAIN

CATTLE

TOBACCO

•Izmir

WOOL

•Aydin

TIMBER

TOBACCO

CHROMITE

LEAD

T

L. Juz

HIDES

L. Egredir

TIMBER

CATTLE

U

GRAIN
•Antalya

L. Beysehir

GOLD

COAL

WOOL

R

HIDES

TOBACCO

VINEYARDS

Dodecaneso (Italy)

Mediterranean

Sea

Alexandretta

SILK

Alep
GRAI

FRUIT

Latakia•

LATAKIA

L
E

CYPRUS
(Br)

Tripoli•

LEBANON

Beyrouth•

CATTLE

•Damascus

OLIVES

GRAIN

JEBEL DRUZ
•Soueida

Pipe

Haifa•

Tel Aviv
Jaffa•

VINEYARDS

FRUIT

JORDA

TRANS

PALESTINE

Jerusalem•

E

G Alexandria

Y

Port Said
•P

OLIVES

T

VINEYARDS

Suez•

G. of Suez

G. of Aqaba

D.

S
T

REFalconer

Resources: Turkey & the Near East

0   50   100   200

A Scale of Miles

Population
under 25 persons per square mile of area

25 to 125   „   „   „   „

125 to 250   „   „   „   „   „ „ „

250 to 500   „   „   „   „   „ „

over 500   „   „   „   „   „ „ „

situation of the Near East. Not only was France out of the battle, but Italy had entered the lists against Great Britain, while Turkey, despite her obvious interests, found it impossible to take a clear stand unless there were strong indications of success. But Great Britain was still the ally of both Egypt and Iraq and held Palestine as a mandate. Moreover, it seemed clear that if the French hold over Syria were loosened, Great Britain and Turkey might take over that territory to prevent its falling into Italian hands. The fate of Great Britain, however, would determine the fate of the peoples of the Near East.

The Economic Foundations of the Near East

The Turkish Economy. The Near East is endowed with great and varied agricultural and mineral wealth. As a whole, it is an agrarian region, a fact which, in part, explains its rather slow tempo of development. Turkey produces wheat, maize, millet, rye, oats, and various vegetables and fruits. Turkish olives, raisins, figs, dates, and tobacco are known the world over. More than 80 per cent of the people live on the farm. Turkey contains important deposits of coal, chrome, boracite, emery, lead, copper, mercury, arsenic, antimony, zinc, sulfur, silver, and iron. Oil has recently been discovered in the vilayet of Siirt, north of the Tigris River, though its importance is yet to be judged. The Zonguldak coal fields, on the Black Sea, are the largest in the Near East.

Economy of the Eastern Countries. As we move more deeply into Asia, we note significant differences in landscape, climate, and products of the soil. There are not so many high mountains, though a large part of Turkey is a plateau. Syria produces mostly tobacco, wheat, fruits, wine, silk, cotton, barley, corn, olives, grapes, and citrus fruits. Ports under French mandatory control command ancient trade routes between the Levant and the Middle East, and between Turkey and Egypt. While transit trade is still important, it does not consist of silks, spices, pearls, and camphor from India, as in the Middle Ages, but — until the war interfered — of Iraq oil for both France and Italy, livestock from Iraq and Turkey for Palestine, and raw wool from Turkey for the United States. Syria, Palestine, and the Lebanon are not especially fertile since much of the land is poorly watered. The products of Palestine are similar to those of Syria. Iraq, on the other hand, possesses a potentially rich soil, which brings forth wheat, barley, rice, millet, tobacco, and dates. The great mineral resource of Iraq consists of the Mosul oil fields, known since Biblical times, for which Great Britain and Turkey struggled in the early years after the First World War. The controversy was not settled until January, 1926. While the Mosul oil fields are operated by the Royal Dutch Shell and Standard Oil groups, the only company at present producing considerable amounts of oil in Iraq is the Iraq Petroleum Company, working in the Kirkuk fields. Most of Iraq's oil exports, which totaled more than 4,000,000 tons in 1938, were sent by pipe line across the desert, half of it to Haifa and half to Tripoli. About three-fourths of the shipments went to France. Today the refinery at Haifa is capable of turning out about 2,000,000 tons a year.

The Arabian Economy. Saudi Arabia is chiefly desert country, and in general, not very fertile. Nevertheless it also produces substantial amounts of oil; more than 500,000 tons in 1939. Production is under the control of the California Arabian Standard Oil Company, an American corporation. Oil exploration is also undertaken by Petroleum Concessions, Ltd., jointly controlled by the Anglo-Iranian, the Royal Dutch Shell, and French and American interests. This company is prospecting in Transjordania, Syria, Qatar, Trucial Oman, and Cyprus.[18]

The Egyptian Economy. Egypt is blessed with mineral resources, while among her agricultural products are cereals, sugar cane, cotton, tobacco, and fruits. There is a variety of minerals — phosphates, ochres, sulfate of magnesia, building stones, gypsum, salt, gold, alum, copper, beryl, granite, and sulfur. Petroleum has been found recently and Egypt's output of oil has increased considerably, reaching about 700,000 tons in 1939. A British corporation, the Anglo-Egyptian Oilfields, Ltd., is in charge of production.

Summary of Near Eastern Problems

The Near East has always played a vital role in world history and politics. From the most ancient to the most recent days, the so-called " Eastern Question " has troubled the chancelleries and the minds of European statesmen.

The First World War and its aftermath prepared the groundwork for a veritable revolution in the Near East. In that era the Ottoman Empire, with its foundations in medieval Islam, passed into history and there emerged from its ruins the Turkish Republic, the independent kingdoms of Iraq, Saudi Arabia, and Egypt, the French mandate in Syria, and the British mandate in Palestine. The region as a whole, and especially Turkey, passed through the processes of nationalism and secularization, while modern technology began to make its appearance. These changes have necessitated a readjustment in the relationships between the Near Eastern peoples and those of Europe and the world. The era of independence had come, an era in which the peoples of the Near East insisted on taking their rightful place in the family of nations. As Nazi, Fascist, and Soviet aggression moved toward domination of the Near East, it was obvious that those forces could provide no genuine or lasting solution of the manifold problems of the region. The Near Eastern peoples would thrive best only if they preserved their independence in some kind of association with their neighbors.

REFERENCES

[1] For a brief and timely survey of the Near East see Philip W. Ireland, "The Near East and the European War," *Foreign Policy Reports*, March 15, 1940, XVI, No. 1: 1–16.

[2] See Harry N. Howard, *The Partition of Turkey, 1913–1923: A Study in Diplomatic History*, Norman: Univ. of Oklahoma Press, 1931, ch. 6, for details.

[3] See Royal Institute of International Affairs, *Great Britain and Palestine, 1915–1939*, London: Oxford Univ. Press, 1939, pp. 12–14.

[4] One of the best works in English on the Arabs is George Antonius, *The Arab Awakening*, Philadelphia: Lippincott, 1939.

[5] See especially Mustapha Kemal Pasha, *A Speech Delivered by Ghazi Mustapha Kemal, President of the Turkish Republic, October 1927*, Leipzig: Koehler, 1929.

[6] See The Republican Party of the People, *Program Accepted by the Fourth Grand Congress of the Party*, Ankara, Turkey: Programme du Parti Républicain du Peuple, *Texte adopté par le Vème Grand Congrès du Parti* (May, 1939), Ankara, October 12, 1939.

[7] Count Léon Ostrorog, *The Angora Reform*, London: Oxford Univ. Press, 1927, p. 90.

[8] Donald E. Webster, *The Turkey of Ataturk*, Philadelphia: American Academy of Political and Social Science, 1939, ch. 15; Harry N. Howard, "Education in Turkey," *The Phi Delta Kappan*, November, 1939, XXII, No. 3: 79 ff.

[9] See Sait Emin Ozbek, *La Sümer Bank et l'industrialisation de la Turquie sous la République*, Lyon, 1938.

[10] The best general work on Iraq is Philip W. Ireland, *Iraq: A Study in Political Development*, New York: Macmillan, 1938.

[11] Syria had a population of 1,696,638 and an area of 49,100 square miles; the Lebanon a population of 592,812 and an area of 3600 square miles; Latakia a population of 286,920 and an area of 2800 square miles; and the Jebel Druse a population of 51,780 and an area of 2400 square miles.

[12] Hans Kohn, *Revolutions and Dictatorships*, Cambridge: Harvard Univ. Press, 1939, p. 321.

[13] Palestine Royal Commission, *Report*, July, 1937, Cmd. 5479. See also the excellent study, *Great Britain and Palestine*, The Royal Institute of International Affairs, 1915–1939.

[14] See Royaume d'Egypte, *Traité d'alliance entre Sa Majesté le Roi d'Egypte et Sa Majesté dans le Royaume-Uni*, Londres, le 26 Août 1936, Cairo, 1936; *Actes Signés à Montreux le 8 mai 1937*, Lausanne, 1937.

[15] *Actes de la Conférence de Montreux concernant le régime des Détroits. 22 juin–20 juillet 1936. Compte Rendu des Séances Plénières et Procès-Verbal des Débats du Comité Technique*, Paris, 1936; Turkey No. 1, 1936. *Convention Regarding the Regime of the Straits with Correspondence Relating thereto. Montreux, July 20, 1936*, Cmd. 5249.

[16] For the Turkish documentary evidence see: *La question d'Alexandrette et d'Antioche*, I, II, III, IV, Ankara, 1936.

[17] The text is in Treaty Series No. 4 (1940). *Treaty of Mutual Assistance between His Majesty in respect of the United Kingdom, the President of the French Republic and the President of the Turkish Republic*. (With Special Agreement and Subsidiary Agreements.) Ankara, October 19, 1939. (Ratifications deposited at Ankara, November 16, 1939.) Cmd. 6165.

[18] There is a brief summary of the oil situation in "World Resources in Petroleum," *The Bulletin of International News*, June 29, 1940, XXVII, No. 13: 769–776.

SELECTED BIBLIOGRAPHY

Allen, Henry G., *The Turkish Transformation*, Chicago: Univ. of Chicago Press, 1935.

Armstrong, H. C., *Gray Wolf — Mustafa Kemal. An Intimate Study of a Dictator*, New York: Minton, Balch, 1933. A frank and in many ways a good biography of Mustapha Kemal. Should be read, however, in comparison with other studies of the late Turkish leader. See also H. C. Armstrong, *Lord of Arabia — Ibn Saud. An Intimate Study of a King*. Penguin Books, n.d.

Ataturk, Kemal, *A Speech Delivered by Ghazi Mustapha Kemal, President of the Turkish Republic, October 1927*, Leipzig: Koehler, 1929. This is the famous " six day " speech, indispensable for any student who wants to study the making of modern Turkey.

Cumming, Henry H., *Franco-British Rivalry in the Post-War Near East*, New York: Oxford Univ. Press, 1938. A good summary of the subject.

Foster, Henry A., *The Making of Modern Iraq. A Product of World Forces*, Norman: Univ. of Oklahoma Press, 1935. A good summary of the evolution of the new Iraq kingdom.

de Haas, Jacob, *Palestine — The Last Two Thousand Years*, New York: Macmillan, 1934. A general historical manual on Palestine, which loses much of its objectivity in its discussions of the post-war era.

Howard, Harry N., *The Partition of Turkey: A Diplomatic History, 1913–1923*, Norman: Univ. of Oklahoma Press, 1931. A study of the downfall of the Ottoman Empire and the foundations of the Turkish republic.

Kohn, Hans, *A History of Nationalism in the East*, New York: Harcourt, Brace, 1929. An excellent general account of Near Eastern nationalism.

——, *Western Civilization in the Near East*, New York: Columbia Univ. Press, 1936. General survey of the processes of westernization.

Luke, Sir H. C., *The Making of Modern Turkey*, London: Macmillan, 1936.

Parker, John and Smith, Charles, *Modern Turkey*, London: Routledge, 1940. A well-balanced, popular account of the development of modern Turkey based on some firsthand investigation.

Schonfeld, Hugh J., *The Suez Canal*, New York: Penguin Books, 1940.

Shotwell, James T. and Déak, Francis, *Turkey at the Straits. A Short History*, New York: Macmillan, 1940. An excellent brief summary of the problem of " Constantinople and the Straits."

Toynbee, Arnold J., *The Western Question in Greece and Turkey*, London: Constable, 1922. Excellent for the period 1919–1922.

—— and Kirkwood, Kenneth P., *Turkey*, New York: Scribner, 1927. Excellent for the post-war development of Turkey, with historical background.

Turkey No. 1 (1923), *The Lausanne Conference on Near Eastern Affairs, 1922–23*, Cmd. 1814. Indispensable documentary source for study of the post-World War Near East.

Webster, Donald E., *The Turkey of Ataturk: Social Process in the Turkish Reformation*, Philadelphia: The American Academy of Political and Social Science, 1939.

Wilson, Sir Arnold T., *The Suez Canal: Its Past, Present, and Future*, London: Oxford Univ. Press, 1933. A good account, somewhat polemical.

Zaki Ali, *Islam in the World*, Lahore, India: Shaikh Muhammad Ashraf, 1938. By a liberal Moslem, with good chapters on the Near East.

CHAPTER XVIII

The Union of Soviet Socialist Republics (Russia)

IT IS PLEASANTER AND MORE USEFUL TO CARRY ON THE "EXPERIMENT OF THE REVOLUTION"
THAN TO WRITE ABOUT IT. — LENIN, *The State and the Revolution*

Geography. The Union of the Soviet Socialist Republics or the U.S.S.R., as the former Russian Empire has been officially known since 1922, occupies a vast area of some 8,000,000 square miles, or approximately one-sixth of the land surface of the globe. The distance from Russia's western frontier in Europe to her eastern border on the Bering Sea is about 10,000 miles, while almost 3000 miles separate the extreme northern and southern points of her territory. Unlike western Europe, the immense Russian plain is unbroken by any important natural obstacles. The customary subdivision into European and Asiatic Russia, therefore, cannot be justified on topographical grounds. The Pamir tableland and the high ranges of the Caucasus and Shaian mountains are situated on the outskirts of the Soviet empire, and the Ural mountains, which are traditionally considered the boundary between Europe and Asia, are merely glorified hills of about 1500 feet elevation.

Climate. The climate ranges from the bitter cold of the Arctic Circle, through the balmy sunshine of the Caucasus and the Crimea, to the scorching heat of the Turkestan, and vegetation from the bleak tundra in the north to the luxuriant orange groves and cotton plantations of the south. The major portion of European Russia is situated in the temperate zone, where climatic conditions do not differ essentially from those of central Europe, although they become more rigorous as one proceeds eastward.

Geographical factors favorable to the formation of a highly centralized form of government have influenced the historical development of Russia, and have given her policies a distinctly continental character. Russia's shore line is quite insignificant in comparison with the size of her territory; her longest sea frontier, that on the Arctic Ocean, has no political or economic significance except near the Finnish border, where the port of Murmansk is kept open to navigation by the Gulf Stream throughout the year. The northern Pacific coast is separated from the industrial and

This chapter by Michael T. Florinsky, Lecturer in Economics, Faculty of Political Science, Columbia University.

commercial centers of Russia by the sparsely populated vastness of Siberia. The only link between the Far East and European Russia, the Trans-Siberian railroad, was not completed until the end of the nineteenth century. The Caspian is a closed sea and the outlets from both the Baltic and the Black seas are controlled by foreign powers. Russia, moreover, did not acquire the shores of the Baltic until 1721, and those of the Black Sea until the last quarter of the eighteenth century. Most of her Baltic provinces were lost at the end of the First World War but she recovered practically all of them in 1940. The natural resources of Russia, still largely unexploited, are very extensive and it is believed that the U.S.S.R. is self-sufficient in all industrial raw materials except rubber and a few minerals.

Strategic Location. Although by far the largest portion of Russian territory lies east of the Urals, the Soviet Union is primarily a European power. Siberia is, in a sense, a colonial area whose development is still in its initial stage. Russian interest in the Far East has been, and still remains, relatively unimportant, and her interference in the affairs of that part of the world, are sporadic and usually not very successful. European developments are of more immediate concern to the Moscow government.

Russia's European frontier, as it emerged from the turmoil of the war in 1918, was very different from that of 1914. The European states bordering on the Soviet Union at the end of the First World War were Finland, Estonia, Latvia, Poland, and Rumania. The first four of these countries (and Lithuania which had no common frontier with the U.S.S.R.) had formerly been parts of the Russian Empire. The Russo-Rumanian frontier was moved eastward in 1918 as a result of the annexation of Bessarabia by Rumania.

In 1939–1940 the Soviet European frontier was again drastically revised. The partition of Poland in September, 1939 re-established the German-Russian border and brought the Soviet Union in direct contact with Hungary. The Russo-Finnish War led to the annexation by the Soviets in March, 1940 of the Karelian isthmus, with the port of Viborg and substantial territories on the western and northern shores of Lake Ladoga, as well as the lease to Russia of the peninsula of Hanko. The annexation of Bessarabia and northern Bukovina, ceded by Rumania at the end of June, 1940, was followed two months later by the incorporation into the Soviet Union of Latvia, Estonia, and Lithuania. Thus by August, 1940 the U.S.S.R. had regained her sovereignty over most of the territories that were severed from the Czarist Empire. The new frontier brought Russia once more in immediate contact with Germany, gave her ice-free ports on the Baltic, and strengthened her position as a great European power, a position she had occupied for over two centuries.

German influence, largely because of the geographical proximity of the two countries and their many historical ties, has always been strong in both the political and the economic life of Russia. The political rapprochement between the Russian Empire and France and the creation of the Triple Entente, which led Russia to participate in the war of 1914 on the side of the Allies, appear in retrospect as a deviation from the general historical trends of the country. The Moscow-Berlin agreement of August, 1939 reasserted the traditional cooperation between Russia and Germany and, indeed, made possible the revision of the western frontier of the Soviet Union, as was candidly admitted by Molotov, Chairman of the Council of People's Commissars and Commissar for Foreign Affairs, in his speech before the Supreme Soviet on August 1, 1940. The interest of Moscow in the Black Sea and in the straits of the Dardanelles makes the Soviets an active factor in the Near East.

Population. Strange as it may appear, the actual size of the population of the Soviet Union was uncertain until quite recently. A census taken in 1937 and acclaimed at the time by the Soviet press as a remarkable achievement was abruptly cancelled on the ground that it violated the fundamentals of census taking. The second Five-Year Plan estimated the population in 1937 at 180.7 million. The preliminary official returns of a new census recorded on January 17, 1939 put the population on that date at 170.5 million. This discrepancy between this figure and the equally official figure of 1937 has not been explained. Of the 170.5 million, 81.7 million were males and 88.8 million females.

Urbanization. The progress of city life is indicated by the increase of the urban population from 26.3 million or 17.9 per cent in 1926, to 55.9 million or 32.8 per cent in 1939. The rural population declined from 120.7 million or 82.1 per cent in 1926, to 114.6 million or 67.2 per cent in 1939. The territorial expansion of 1939–1940 netted the Soviets some 23 million inhabitants, the total population on August 1, 1940, having been officially given as 193 million.

Ethnography. According to a study made by the Russian Academy of Science the population of Russia comprises not less than 169 ethnic groups. Of the 49 " nationalities " listed in the preliminary returns of the census of 1939, by far the most important were the Slavs. The three branches of the Russian people constituted 78.1 per cent of the total population (Great Russians, 58.4 per cent; Ukrainians, 16.6 per cent; White Russians, 3.1 per cent). Other ethnic groups accounting for more than one per cent of the entire population were as follows: Uzbeks, 2.9 per cent; Tartars, 2.5 per cent; Kazakhs, 1.8 per cent; Jews, 1.8 per cent; Azerbaidzhanians, 1.3 per cent; Georgians, 1.3 per cent; Armenians, 1.3 per cent.

The number of languages spoken by the peoples of the U.S.S.R. is almost as large as the number of ethnic groups; the use of local languages is encouraged by the Soviets, who take pride in having completely revised the policy of Russification followed by the Imperial government. Some of the local languages, however, are those of very primitive people and have no literature and even no alphabet. The wisdom of using these languages in the schools even after an alphabet has been devised is open to serious doubt, and it would seem that not a few of them have, at least as cultural mediums, a purely theoretical existence.

Although the vast majority of the Russian population belonged, in the past, to the Greek Orthodox Church, almost every other religion was represented in the Czarist Empire. Article 124 of the Soviet Constitution of 1936 guarantees freedom of both religious worship and anti-religious propaganda. The Communist government, however, discourages the former and encourages the latter. No information is available on the present religious affiliations of the peoples of the U.S.S.R., but religious observances are considered incompatible with honest support of the Communist state.

The Two Revolutions of 1917.[1] The First World War wrought a more drastic change in the political, social and economic structure of the Russian Empire than in that of any other country. The Romanov dynasty, which had ruled Russia since 1613, and the regime of limited constitutional monarchy,[2] were swept away in the revolution of March, 1917 and succeeded by a Provisional government headed, first, by the liberal Prince Lvov and, later, by the moderate Socialist Alexander Kerensky. The March revolution was a spontaneous popular movement which had grown out of the century-old protest against the inept and oppressive rule of the monarchy, a protest that developed into an open revolt under the impact of wartime conditions, including a general breakdown of the machinery of government, disorganization of supplies, the terrible losses and shocking military reverses suffered by the army, the discredit cast upon the regime by the infamous influence exercised in court and government circles by the adventurer, Gregory Rasputin, a general desire for peace, and a lack of comprehension of the aims of the war.

The Provisional Government. The Provisional government unwisely tried to rally the country around a program of " war to a victorious end " and a Constituent Assembly elected by direct secret ballot on the basis of universal suffrage. But the army was tired of fighting, democratic tradition had no roots in Russia, and the state of economic and social chaos that followed the March revolution doomed in advance all attempts at an orderly administration. The Provisional government at once found itself in conflict with the Soviet (Council) of Workers' and Soldiers' Deputies which had been organized in Petrograd simultaneously with the Provisional government itself. Similar Soviets sprang up all over the country. The Bolshevik leaders, who had had no immediate part in the overthrow of the monarchy, soon assumed control of the revolutionary movement of which the Soviets became the center.

The Bolshevik Revolution. Lenin returned to Petrograd from Switzerland in April, 1917 and his slogans " immediate end of the war," " all land to the peasants," and " plunder what has been plundered," or the abolition of all private property, met with an immediate response from the masses. The disorganization of the army, which was already well-advanced before the revolution, and the peasant movement directed against the owners of large estates, were probably the two chief forces that brought about the fall first of the monarchy and then of the Provisional government. When after a short struggle the Kerensky government was overthrown on November 7 (October 25, old Russian calendar) by an armed insurrection staged by the Bolsheviks, a newly formed Council of People's Commissars, headed by Lenin, assumed control of Russia.

Civil War. The Constituent Assembly duly met in January, 1918 but was immediately dissolved, an event that passed almost unnoticed. The provisions of the extremely harsh Treaty of Brest-Litovsk between Russia and the Central Powers, signed on March 3, 1918, were annulled by the terms of the armistice imposed upon Germany by the Allies. A number of border territories in the north and west, as already noted, severed their connection with Russia after the war. The independent Ukraine, supported by Germany, collapsed soon after the defeat of the Central Powers. Russia, in a state of complete turmoil, was rapidly drifting toward civil war. These chaotic conditions led to the temporary occupation in 1918–1920 of various sections of the country by the anti-Bolshevik " White " armies and foreign troops. All the institutions of the old regime were swept away in the revolution and the entire political, social, and economic framework had to be rebuilt from the ground.

Four Stages of Soviet History. The process of disintegration that started in 1917 continued to gain momentum in the early years of Soviet rule. This stage was followed by a gigantic effort at reconstruction on a new ideological and economic basis, a vast undertaking from which emerged, in the words of Stalin, " an entirely novel Socialist state, unprecedented in history."

First Period. It is customary and helpful to distinguish in the historical evolution of the U.S.S.R. four distinct periods. The first or introductory period, lasting from the seizure of power by the Bolsheviks in November, 1917 until the middle of 1918, was characterized by the endeavor of the Moscow government to consolidate its position at whatever cost. The Treaty of Brest-Litovsk officially ended Russia's participation in the war while on the " domestic front " her main efforts were directed toward breaking down the resistance of " class enemies " — that is, toward the elimination of the former proprietary groups — without, however, embarking on a sweeping nationalization of either industry or agriculture. Banking, foreign trade, and some separate branches of industry were taken over by the state. The decrees of these early days were not so much practical legislative measures as, to use Trotsky's felicitous expression, the enunciation of a party doctrine " in the language of power."

Second Period. The character of the second period, from the middle of 1918 to the spring of 1921, which is known as War Communism, was determined largely by civil war and foreign intervention. White armies, organized by anti-Bolshevik Russians in the south, in the north, in the former Baltic provinces, and in Siberia, received the full support of the Allies. Foreign intervention brought French or British troops to Odessa, the Crimea, and the Caucasus. The British had an expeditionary force in Archangel, while in Siberia the Allied soldiers rubbed shoulders with the Americans, the Japanese, the Czechs. A war with Poland broke out and the Allied blockade effectively cut Russia off from the rest of the world. Partly under the pressure of an extreme military emergency and partly for ideological considerations the Bolshevik government issued a series of extreme Communist measures, some of which, however, were never applied in full. All industry was ordered nationalized, agriculture was made subject to stringent government control, labor was conscripted and plans were made for the substitution of state-organized barter for the monetary economy.

Rigid centralization, requisitions of foodstuffs, and super-inflation were among the principal characteristics of this period. It was generally believed at the time both in Russia and abroad that the co-existence of capitalism and Communism could not last. This theory, however, proved erroneous. The White armies collapsed one after another, Allied troops were withdrawn, the blockade was lifted, and the war with Poland brought to an end. The unbearable hardships imposed by War Communism provoked a strong hostile reaction, especially among the peasants and in the armed forces, and led to a number of violent rebellions against the Communist rule.

Third Period. The abandonment of War Communism in the spring of 1921 ushered in the New Economic Policy or the period of economic restoration, that is, a return to pre-war economic levels, after industrial production had fallen to a mere fraction of what it had been in 1914. Relations with western Europe became normal with the *de jure* recognition of the Soviet government by Germany in 1922 and by Great Britain, Italy, and France in 1924. The stringent economic policies of War Communism were dropped, the currency was stabilized, and the farmers were again permitted to dispose of the produce of their land.[3] A limited degree of economic freedom was restored, especially in the field of distribution. It was officially stated that by 1926–1927 the pre-war economic level of production had been regained.

Fourth Period. About 1927 there began a new period in the history of the Soviet Union, a period of Socialist reconstruction on the basis of planned economy and cooperation with the capitalist world, with the establishment of the classless Communist society as its ultimate aim. This period is not yet completed. The Soviet-German agreement of August, 1939, which revolutionized Communist theory and radically changed Soviet foreign relations, has had no effect on the domestic policies of the Moscow government.

Communist Doctrine and the Leaders. A reference, however brief, to the vagaries of Communist theory may contribute to an understanding of the evolution of Soviet policies. Until 1924 the idea was generally accepted in Communist circles that a Socialist revolution, in order to be successful, must take place simultaneously in at least several advanced industrial countries. This doctrine was much in evidence in the pronouncements of the Soviet leaders under War Communism, when it was confidently expected that world revolution was imminent. The failure of the international revolution to develop led Stalin to revise his views on the subject and to enunciate at the end of 1924 the theory of "socialism in a single country," according to which a country possessed of a large population and vast natural resources — such as the Soviet Union — was perfectly capable of building up a complete socialist system within its own borders. This, however, could not be regarded as a "final victory," for in the hostile capitalist environment lay the threatened danger of intervention. To this new doctrine, which was one of the chief points of disagreement between Stalin and Trotsky, Stalin attached the greatest importance. According to his own statements it provided the necessary theoretical background for the launching of the first and subsequent Five-Year Plans which, in turn, necessitated close cooperation with the capitalist nations.

Role of the State. The second theoretical point of importance in the present discussion is the doctrine of the "withering away" of the state. It is a basic principle of Marxism and Communism that the class struggle is the great moving force behind the evolution of human institutions, and that the state is always a dictatorship of the ruling class, which under capitalism is, of course, the bourgeoisie. The ultimate object of Communism is the building up of a classless society, to be attained after a successful revolution and the transition stage of a dictatorship of the proletariat. The proletarian state of the transition period must, in the words of Lenin,[4] "begin at once to wither away and cannot fail to wither away." The Communist society of the future will have no classes and therefore will not be a state. Lenin incautiously indicated two essential elements in the mysterious process of the "withering away": the abolition of the standing army, which is to be replaced by a popular militia, and the disappearance of the bureaucracy. It is claimed by the Soviet leaders that in the U.S.S.R. classes have been eliminated and that the Communist society is in the making. Yet the army, the police, and the bureaucracy are larger and more powerful than ever and there is no indication of the " withering away " of the state as Lenin foresaw it. Stalin attempted to remedy this anomalous situation by amending Lenin's theory of the state in his address to the eighteenth congress of the Communist Party on March 10, 1939. According to his thesis the retention and, indeed, the immeasurable strengthening of the state under Communism, a development that is irreconcilable with the doctrine of Lenin, is due to the capitalist environment; so long as this environment persists the state will be retained by the Soviet Communist society. It will " wither away " when the Communist revolution has triumphed in other countries. Stalin's two revisions of the fundamental ideas of Communism have been acclaimed as revelations by the Soviet press. They undoubtedly have the advantage and charm of extreme simplicity, but it is unfortunate, from the Marxian point of view, that they violate the basic principles of Marxian analysis.

The Leaders. These theoretical quibbles are significant in view of the character, training and previous experience of the men who, by an extraordinary concurrence of circumstances, found themselves in 1917 in control of the former Russian Empire. Surprisingly few of the names or, more frequently, pseudonyms of Russian revolutionary leaders were known to the general public. All of them were professional revolutionaries, who had spent most of their lives in exile, either abroad or in Siberia, hunted by the police, engrossed in doctrinaire squabbles, cut off from direct contact with Russian life, devoid of experience in business or statecraft.

Lenin (Vladimir Ulianov) was a fanatical revolutionary, uncompromising and ruthless in the achievement of his ultimate object, yet subtle and endowed with a real flair for practical policies that would favor his designs. He was ably seconded by Leon Trotsky (Bronstein), master of Marxian dialectics, creator of the Red Army, and the fiery leader of the masses in the early years of the revolution. The death in 1924 of Lenin, whose authority in Moscow had been supreme, brought Trotsky face to face with his old antagonist Stalin, a man little known at the time outside party circles. The clash between the two led to Trotsky's exile, first to central Asia and in 1929 abroad. Joseph Stalin (Dzhugashvilli), son of a Georgian cobbler, received a meager schooling in an obscure theological seminary in the Caucasus. Stalin does not have the political acumen of Lenin, or the effervescent brilliance of Trotsky, but he commands in a superlative degree those peculiar abilities that make a perfect party " boss." His firm control of the machinery of the Communist Party, whose Secretary General he has been since the days of Lenin, makes Stalin what he is today — the dictator of the former Empire of the Czars.

U.S.S.R. in EUROPE

Scale of Miles | 0 100 200 300 400 500

POPULATION DENSITY

Under 26 persons per square mile
26 to 64 " " " "
64 to 128 " " " "
128 to 256 " " " "
256 to 512 " " " "

© 1941, D. Van Nostrand Company, Inc.

The Communist Party. The Communist Party is the pillar of the Soviet system. Its origins go back to 1898 when nine now forgotten revolutionaries met in Minsk, Russia, and organized the Russian Social Democratic Labor Party. At its second congress in London in 1903, the party split over a minor question of organization into two factions: the Bolsheviks, literally " majority " group, and the Mensheviks, or " minority." Eventually the breach between the two factions widened; the Bolsheviks, led by Lenin, usually pursuing the more radical policies. The Bolshevik faction had never had a wide following (its membership early in 1917 was officially given as 23,600) and its advent to power in November, 1917 was as much a surprise to most of its leaders as to the outside world. In 1918 the Bolsheviks took the name of the Russian Communist Party, which was again changed to the All-Union Communist Party of the Bolsheviks in 1925. The All-Union Communist Party is officially a section of the Third (Communist) International, a world alliance of Communist parties, established in Moscow in 1919.

The original program of the Social-Democratic Party adopted in 1903 was concerned chiefly with the overthrow of the Imperial regime. In 1919 this program was superseded by the one now in force, a program embodying the views of Marx and Lenin on the impending doom of the capitalist and imperialistic system, and outlining policies by which the Soviet Union can expedite world revolution. This program is, however, no longer considered adequate and the eighteenth congress of the party (1939) appointed a commission under the chairmanship of Stalin to draft a new program which will be submitted to the next congress.

Although its program has been changed only once, the charter of the party, which determines its inner organization, has been revised several times, the most important amendments having been introduced in 1922, 1925, 1934, and 1939. " The Party," according to the 1939 version of the charter, " is the leading nucleus of all organizations of toilers, both social and state, and ensures the successful construction of communist society." The party organization is comprised of an extensive network of territorial agencies integrated on the basis of what is euphemistically called " democratic centralization," that is, rigid control from above.

Party Agencies. The foundation of the pyramid of party agencies is provided by the " primary party organs " (formerly called " cells ") which are established in every enterprise, farm, office, etc., having at least three party members. The number of " primary party organs " in March, 1939 was officially given as 113,060. On the " primary party organs " is superimposed a complex structure of higher party organs that runs parallel to that of the administrative subdivisions of the U.S.S.R. The supreme authority in the party is, in theory, the All-Union Congress which is scheduled to meet every three years, a rule loosely observed in practice:

the sixteenth congress met in 1930, the seventeenth in 1934, the eighteenth in 1939. The large membership of the congresses (about 2000) and the short duration of their sessions prevent them from exercising any effective control, and they invariably vote unanimously on the resolutions submitted by the leaders. The congress, which elects a central committee of some seventy members with an equal number of alternates, in theory exercises the functions of the congress when it is not in session, but in practice meets only at long intervals. The actual direction of party activities remains in the hands of three agencies appointed by the central committee: the Secretariat headed by Stalin, the Political Bureau, and the Organization Bureau. The functions of these two bureaus, which are said to consist of ten members each, are not clearly defined.

Allied Organizations. In theory the party is run on the principle of " intraparty democracy," which means complete equality of all members and their right to participate freely in framing policies. In practice, however, no departure from the " general line " laid down by Stalin is tolerated. Admission to the party is on the ground of " personal merit " and the former stringent requirements have been greatly eased by the 1939 amendment to the charter. A noteworthy innovation is the provision that prospective members need not understand the party program, they must merely " accept " it. The normal road to membership in the party is through the *Komsomol* or Alliance of Communist Youth. The party consists of candidates, or members on probation, and full members, all bound by strict discipline and compelled to carry out the decisions of the leaders. The membership is highly restricted. According to official, although somewhat controversial figures, the high point in party membership was reached in 1934 when members and candidates totaled 2.8 million. On March 1, 1939 there were 1,588,900 members and 888,000 candidates, or a total of 2,477,700: that is, something like 1.5 per cent of the entire population was enrolled in the party.

Purges. Party members are from time to time subjected to an examination as to their ideological orthodoxy, devotion to Communism, and personal conduct.[5] Such examinations, followed by mass purges, took place in 1921, 1926, 1927, 1933. The monster purge that followed the murder in December, 1934 of Kirov, one of Stalin's closest friends, lasted from 1935 to 1939 and, unlike previous purges, was accompanied by sensational trials and the execution of a number of Bolshevik leaders. Between 1934 and March, 1939 466,000 members, or almost 25 per cent of the total membership in 1934, and 516,000, or well over 50 per cent of the candidates of that year, were expelled from the party. According to Stalin, expulsion from the party is to a member a " question of life or death." Mass purges were abolished by the 1939 Amendment to the Charter, but the weeding out of individual undeserving members has been retained. The purpose of

Stalin's drastic action would seem to be the rejuvenation of the party and the elimination of the " old Bolsheviks," until recently a privileged group. This object has been largely achieved. At the 1939 congress 50 per cent of the full-fledged delegates were 35 years of age or younger, while another 32 per cent were in the age group 36–40. The distribution of membership is suggested by the fact that out of 1,574 delegates to the eighteenth congress 659 were party officials, 283 belonged to the army, navy, or the police, 230 were in industry, 162 were state and trade unions officials, while only 63 were farmers. The remaining delegates represented the transportation industries, the arts and sciences, and the Komsomol. All delegates are invariably in agreement with Stalin.

Until 1936 the Communist Party had no official standing in Soviet law. While Articles 126 and 141 of the constitution of that year acknowledged its leading position, the document added nothing to the party's already unchallengeable supremacy.

The Constitutional Framework: Constitution of 1918. It was only by slow and painful stages that the present Soviet state emerged from the utter chaos and confusion that prevailed in Russia in 1917–1920. The Soviets (Councils) of Workers' and Soldiers' Deputies which, as has already been pointed out, sprang up all over the country in 1917 were purely revolutionary organizations and had no basis in law. In 1918 the first Soviet constitution sanctioned in large measure the form of government that had come into existence more or less spontaneously. It established the Russian Socialist Federated Soviet Republic (RSFSR) whose somewhat uncertain boundaries embraced a territory much smaller than that of the future Soviet Union, as important sections of the country were at that time still in the hands of anti-Bolshevik forces. In December, 1922 the first Congress of the Soviets created the Union of Soviet Socialist Republics, or the U.S.S.R., which originally consisted of four constituent republics: the RSFSR, Ukraine, White Russia, and Transcaucasia.

The constitution of 1918 was superseded by the constitution of 1924 which, like its predecessor, was imbued with the spirit of proletarian dictatorship. The administrative framework consisted of a pyramid of Soviets with gradually widening jurisdiction, while the foundation of the structure was provided by the village Soviets, on which were superimposed the Soviets of the larger administrative subdivisions, with the All-Union Congress of the Soviets — the supreme organ of the Union — at the top. The Council of the People's Commissars elected by the congress was its chief executive organ. The franchise was limited; the urban population was given a much larger representation than were the inhabitants of rural areas; elections were indirect, that is the deputies of the higher Soviets were elected by those of the lower Soviets; and balloting was not secret, but by a show of hands.

Later Constitutions.   The clearly restrictive character of the constitution
of 1924 was no longer considered suitable by 1935, when, according to
Soviet leaders, classes in the U.S.S.R. were about to disappear; nor did it
add to the prestige of the Moscow government among democratic nations whose good graces the Bolsheviks had been courting, especially after
the Soviet Union joined the League of Nations in 1934.   Moreover the
Communist Party was so firmly in control of Russia that the constitutional
and administrative machinery really mattered little.   The decision to
endow the country with a new constitutional charter was announced in
February, 1935 and the draft of the new constitution, issued in June, 1936
was, after an unprecedented publicity campaign, unanimously adopted by
the eighth congress of the Soviets on December 5, 1936, a date which became a public holiday.

Under the new constitution the Soviet Union continued as a federal
state but from 1922 to 1936 the number of constituent republics had increased to eleven, a change achieved not by any expansion of territory
but through the breaking up of the larger administrative units.   The following enumeration of the constituent republics listed in the original constitution of 1936 and the population figures recorded by the 1939 census
may help to make clear the structure of the Union and the relative importance of its component elements: the RSFSR, 109.3 million; Ukraine,
31 million; White Russia, 5.6 million; Azerbaidzhan, 3.2 million; Georgia,
3.5 million; Armenia, 1.3 million; Turkman, 1.3 million; Uzbek, 6.3 million;
Tadzhik, 1.5 million; Kazakh, 6.1 million; Kirghiz, 1.5 million.   Five constituent republics were added to the Union in 1940 through annexation
of new territories: the Karelian-Finnish in March, and the Moldavian (the
Rumanian-speaking part of Bessarabia), the Latvian, the Lithuanian, and
the Estonian, in August.

Centralization.   In theory all constituent republics enjoy equal rights, including the right to secede, but in practice the RSFSR dominates the
Union and any incipient movement toward independence has invariably
been suppressed as counterrevolutionary.   The powers of the constituent
republics, moreover, are strictly limited by those of the federal government.   The federal government exercises exclusive control over foreign
relations, national defense and the police, budget, money, credit, insurance,
transport, communications, the judiciary, and the preparation of civil and
criminal codes.   It administers the monopoly of foreign trade and formu-
lates the economic plan, which embraces practically all the activities of the
nation.   The federal government also " determines the basic principles "
for the exploitation of national resources, for education and public health,
and for labor legislation.   It is specifically provided that the constitutions
of the constituent republics must fully conform with the principles of the
federal constitution.   The constitution provides for the further subdivision

of the constituent (or " union ") republics into smaller territorial units. On October 1, 1938 the 11 constituent republics consisted of 22 autonomous Soviet Socialist republics (17 of them were included in the RSFSR), 74 territories and provinces, 9 autonomous provinces, 30 regions, 3,464 counties, and 808 cities and towns. The inner boundaries are being continuously shifted and the number of subdivisions has greatly increased since 1938.

The Supreme Soviet. The highest organ of the Union, the Supreme Soviet of the U.S.S.R., consists of two chambers: the Council (Soviet) of the Union elected on the basis of one deputy for every 300,000 of the population, and the Council (Soviet) of Nationalities, to which each constituent republic sends 25 deputies, each autonomous republic 11 deputies, each autonomous province 9 deputies, and each national region one deputy. The Supreme Soviet, sitting as a body, elects its Presidium of some 40 members, which exercises important functions, especially when the Supreme Soviet is not in session, and the Council of People's Commissars of the U.S.S.R., the chief executive organ of the Union. The number of the People's Commissars of the U.S.S.R., that is the heads of federal departments or People's Commissariats of the U.S.S.R., has been greatly increased since 1936, the whole administrative machinery having been rebuilt on the basis of greater specialization. The Supreme Soviet is elected for a term of four years and must meet at least twice a year, but the sessions held in 1938–1940 were invariably very short and the proceedings largely perfunctory.

Local Government. The constituent republics and the autonomous republics duplicate the government of the Union, except that their respective powers are much more restricted. Under the constitutions of these republics, adopted in 1937, each has a unicameral Supreme Soviet and a Council of People's Commissars. The smaller subdivisions — territories, provinces, autonomous provinces, regions, counties, cities, and rural localities — are administered by Soviets elected for two years.

   In contrast with its predecessors, the federal constitution of 1936 embodies the principle of the separation of powers. Legislative powers are exercised by the Supreme Soviet, executive powers by the Council of People's Commissars, and judicial powers by elected courts and legal officers (Law on the Judiciary, 1938). The constitution of 1936, moreover, introduced universal franchise for all citizens over 18 years of age, equal and direct suffrage and the secret ballot. The U.S.S.R. is thus equipped with all the technical perquisites of a western constitutional democracy.

The Political Regime in Action: Dictatorship of the Proletariat. Notwithstanding these constitutional changes the Soviet regime is usually and rightly described as a dictatorship. Stalin has claimed on various occasions that the U.S.S.R. is both a dictatorship of the proletariat and the most democratic country in the world. Obviously the term democracy means something different in Moscow from what it means in the western world. The political system of the Soviet Union rests on three pillars: the supremacy of the Communist Party, which is the only party in the U.S.S.R., the mechanics of Soviet elections, and the wide discretionary penal powers vested in the secret police and in the courts.

Role of the Communist Party. The legal basis for the supremacy of the Communist Party is supplied by Articles 126 and 141 of the constitution which provide, respectively, that the agencies of the Communist Party are " the leading nucleus of all organizations . . . both social and state," and that they are entitled to nominate candidates for the elective assemblies. The significance of these provisions will appear from an examination of the machinery of elections. Three elections were held in the Soviet Union in 1937–1939: the election to the Supreme Soviet of the U.S.S.R. in December, 1937, the election to the Supreme Soviet of the constituent and autonomous republics in June, 1938, and the election to the local Soviets in December, 1939. All followed the same pattern. Each election district had only one candidate endorsed by a " bloc of party and non-party people " or by a " bloc of party and non-party Stalinites." The nomination of candidates was by a show of hands, the names being suggested by the local agency of the party. No registration was required, the list of voters being prepared by the local Soviets; election day was a national holiday, and everyone was urged to vote. In the 1937 election 91 million voters, out of a total of 93 million, went to the polls; in 1939 92.8 million out of 93.5 million. The percentage of votes cast for the sole candidate varied from 96 to 100. Of the 569 delegates of the Council of the Union, 81 per cent were members or candidates of the party, and of the 574 members of the Council of Nationalities 71 per cent had party affiliations. The local elections of 1939 resulted in the choosing of some 1,281,000 delegates to 68,190 Soviets of various types. Although only 34.4 per cent of the members of local Soviets had party affiliations, the balance of the delegates, in the local as well as higher assemblies, was made up of people euphemistically described as " non-party Bolsheviks " or "non-party Stalinites." Naturally every Soviet assembly, from the highest to the lowest, invariably votes unanimously in favor of policies and measures submitted by the leaders.

The Secret Police. The dreaded GPU or secret police, since 1934 under the People's Commissariat of the Interior, enjoys extrajudicial powers and the right of life and death over Soviet citizens. The number of its victims is unknown, but it controls a vast network of concentration camps that dot the bleak wilderness of Russia's arctic region. The untiring activities of the police are ably seconded by the Soviet courts, with a penal code containing a formidable array of provisions for the protection of the regime. Noteworthy among them are the provisions dealing with crimes against

U. S.

A.

Arctic

Novaya Zemlya

Europe

Archangelsk

Caspian Sea

Aral Sea

Sinkiang

Mongolia

POPULATION

Under 2 persons per square mile

2 to 26 persons per square mile

Scale of Miles

0 100 200 300 400 500   1000

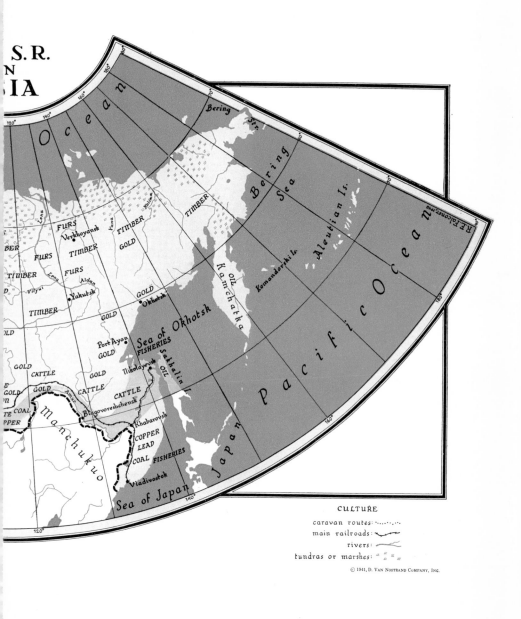

S.R.

N

IA

O c e a n

Ocean

Bering

Str.

B e r i n g

S e a

Aleutian Is.

R.E.Falconer

120°

140°

160°

180°

180°

160°

Lena

FURS

Verkhoyansk

TIMBER

TIMBER

GOLD

TIMBER

Kolyma

Komandorski Is.

P a c i f i c   O c e a n

FURS

TIMBER

Lena

FURS

Aldan

Vilyui

Yakutsk

Oil

Kamchatka

BER

TIMBER

GOLD

TIMBER

LD

GOLD

GOLD

Okhotsk

Sea of Okhotsk

OLD

Port Ayan
GOLD

FISHERIES

GOLD

CATTLE

GOLD

CATTLE

Nikolayevsk

Oil

Sakhalin I.

GOLD

CATTLE

CATTLE

Amur

COAL

Blagoveshchensk

PPER

M a n c h u k u o

Khabarovsk

COPPER
LEAD

COAL   FISHERIES

Vladivostok

Sea of Japan

180°

160°

140°

140°

120°

J a p a n

CULTURE

caravan routes: ⋯⋯⋯
main railroads: ⌒⌒
rivers: ⌒
tundras or marshes: ≋ ≋

© 1941, D. VAN NOSTRAND COMPANY, INC.

the "administrative order" which make punishable "any activity that weakens the power and authority of the state" even if it is not an infringement of the law (Article 59 [5], edition 1937). This and similar provisions of the code offer unlimited latitude to the Communist courts and, together with the discretionary powers of the police, effectively nullify the inviolability of person and domicile guaranteed by the Soviet constitution.

Under the one-party state, democratic trappings do not conceal but rather emphasize the dictatorial character of the Soviet rule. The essence of political democracy, as it is understood in this country and in western Europe, is the existence of a free and vigorous opposition as a necessary element in the conduct of government. Such opposition is incompatible with both the theory and practice of the Soviet state.

Planned Economy.[6] Drastic as are the changes that have occurred in the political organization of Russia since 1918, they appear almost trifling when compared with the truly revolutionary transformation of her economic system. Class society and its corollary, "the exploitation of man by man," are, in Marxian theory, the inevitable products of the economic inequality resulting from private ownership of the means of production. The Soviet government, therefore, has abolished private enterprise in the field of banking, industry and commerce and has reduced it to a minimum in that of agriculture. Market competition and the mechanism of prices which, under capitalism, regulate (not, of course, without considerable friction) supply and demand and the flow of capital and labor, do not exist in a Socialist society. Here the state is the sole producer and distributor of practically all commodities. The elimination of private competition that bulwark of the capitalist order created a vacuum that has been filled by the introduction of planned economy, seemingly the only possible alternative. It is claimed, moreover, that economic planning is one of the greatest advantages of Socialism since it removes the " anarchy of production " inherent in the competitive system and does away with the accompanying evils or recurrent overproduction, depressions, and unemployment. A comprehensive economic plan, therefore, is the basic feature of the Socialist order and its adoption is dictated by practical exigencies as well as by ideological considerations.

The First Five-Year Plan. Spasmodic attempts at economic planning during the period of War Communism were given up in the spring of 1921. In February of that year, however, the government created the State Planning Commission or Gosplan, a committee of the Council of People's Commissars, which although frequently remodeled since still remains the central planning agency. In April, 1921 a special committee was appointed, on the initiative of Lenin, to prepare a plan for the electrification of Russia. In 1925 were issued the first " control figures," or a program of economic development for 1925–1926; planning on a large scale began only with the inauguration on October 1, 1928 of the first Five-Year Plan. By that time, according to the official view, the Soviet Union had regained the pre-war economic level in both industry and agriculture, and the Communist Party had definitely accepted Stalin's doctrine of " socialism in a single country ": that is, it had assumed that it would be possible to build a complete Socialist order in Russia irrespective of what happened in the outside world.

The mechanics of the preparation of the plan are extremely complex. Its basic principles are laid down by the Soviet government and the Communist Party, they are then embodied in a concrete program by the Gosplan and a vast system of subordinate planning agencies. These can be broadly divided into two groups: those organized according to the territorial or horizontal principle, and those organized according to the functional or vertical principle. Every government department, industrial enterprise, and farm is consulted regarding the planned assignment it will eventually receive, and it is practically compulsory for each to cooperate in the preparation of a counter-plan which invariably calls for more exacting quotas. The chief function of the planning agencies is the coordination of statistical material, the preparation of planned assignments, and checking the actual performance.

Second and Third Five-Year Plans. The first Five-Year Plan was declared completed by January 1, 1933 — that is, in four years and three months — the second Five-Year Plan by January 1, 1938. The third Five-Year Plan has been theoretically in operation since that date but in August, 1940 the full text was not yet available and the only information regarding its contents was to be found in the summary reports of the Soviet leaders. Each of the three Five-Year Plans presents a program of economic, social, and cultural development. It lays down the objectives to be achieved not only in industrial and agricultural production, but also in education, public health, social insurance, the printing and circulation of books and newspapers, and so on. There are special provisions dealing with labor conditions, cost of production, quality of goods, per capita consumption, wages and hours, productivity of labor. The general aims of Soviet planning, as defined in Article 11 of the constitution, are the increase of public wealth, the improvement of the material and cultural standards of the working people, and the strengthening of the Soviet Union and its capacity for defense. More concretely, the practical economic objectives of planned economy have thus far been the advancement of industrialization with special emphasis on heavy industries, collectivization of farming, and the reduction of costs through increase in the productivity of labor. Each of the Five-Year Plans, moreover, is regarded as a definite stage on the road to the classless communist society.

Difficulties of Appraisal. An objective appraisal of Soviet planning is made extremely difficult by the inadequacy of the available statistics which, although numerous, are conflicting, incomplete, and indeed bewildering. Planned assignments and figures of performance are given sometimes in the "unchangeable prices of 1926–1927," sometimes in current prices, and in the absence of an index of prices the two sets of figures are not comparable. Official sources only too frequently contradict one another. Nevertheless a closer study of the planning procedure leads to the conclusion that the plan, contrary to the widely accepted opinion, is not a blueprint, but rather a drive for the achievement of certain objectives and that it is more a slogan than a carefully analyzed program of action.

Modifications of the Plans. The Five-Year Plans have been continuously modified by yearly plans and plans for even shorter periods and the revision is at times so thorough as to amount to a complete abandonment of the original program. The drastic alterations that have been made in the three plans may be traced to three principal sources: (1) changes in the policies of the government and the Communist Party, of which the most striking example is the redrafting of the collectivization program under the first Five-Year Plan; (2) the state of the world market which, instead of the planned expansion, brought about a huge decline of Soviet exports under the first Five-Year Plan, an unforeseen development that led to the exclusion of provisions dealing with foreign trade from the second and third Five-Year Plans; [7] (3) the frequent failure of Soviet enterprises to fulfill their assignments, especially to reduce costs, eliminate waste and defective production, and increase the productivity of labor.

The inefficiency of Soviet planning is strongly suggested by acclaim that greets overfulfillment of the quotas, for if the component elements of the plan were properly coordinated overfulfillment would be no less disruptive than underfulfillment, which is so bitterly denounced. It must have come as a great shock to many foreign admirers of Soviet planned economy to read in Stalin's report of March 10, 1939 that many of the assignments of the second Five-Year Plan were "fantasy, if not worse."

Cost of Industrialization. The huge program of industrialization has been very costly. Capital investments under the three Five-Year Plans amount to something like 350 billion rubles, or 70 billion dollars at Moscow's official rate of exchange. Soviet revenue increased between 1931 and 1940 from 19 billion rubles to 184 billion rubles. The chief source of revenue is the turnover tax which provided 61 per cent of the total revenue in 1931, 79 per cent in 1937, and 59 per cent (109 billion rubles) in 1940. The turnover tax is a general sales tax; its rates are very high and often reach 60 per cent, 70 per cent or even 90 per cent *of the sales price.* The rates are particularly high on articles of general consumption and in 1937 (the last year for which information is available) two-thirds of the yield of the tax was collected on foodstuffs. This form of indirect taxation imposes particularly heavy sacrifices on the poorer section of the population, for the margin between the lower and higher incomes is still not unimportant.

Soviet planning may claim to its credit the industrialization and collectivization of Russia on a gigantic scale and in record time — if these developments are considered desirable. The process, however, has been extremely painful and costly. Planning has raised intricate problems of economics, especially in the realm of prices. In spite of the government's heroic measures the productivity of labor continues to be low and the cost of production correspondingly high. The quality of production is still poor as compared to western countries, and there is a chronic shortage of consumers' goods. The Soviet experiment has proved so far that the socialist economic order can exist, but it still remains to be proved that it is more equitable and efficient than an economy based on private enterprise and initiative and the profit motive.

The New Society. The constitution of 1936 outlines the basic principles of the society that has grown up in Russia since 1918. Land, natural resources, industrial enterprises, and housing facilities in cities and towns have been nationalized (Article 6); but " the right of personal property of citizens in their income from work and their savings, in their dwelling houses [in rural districts] and auxiliary husbandry, in household articles and utensils, and in articles of personal use and comfort, as well as the right of inheritance of the personal property of citizens is protected by the law " (Article 10). " Work in the U.S.S.R. is a duty and a matter of honor for every able-bodied citizen on the principle: ' He who does not work, shall not eat.' In the U.S.S.R. the principle of Socialism is realized: ' From each according to his ability, to each according to his work ' " (Article 12). This all-important provision sanctions the piece-wage system, which is an essential feature of Soviet planned economy and the chief incentive in the drive for higher productivity of labor. The constitution also guarantees to all citizens " the right to work " safeguarded by " the socialist organization of national economy "; " the right to rest " provided by the seven-hour day (abandoned in June, 1940 when the six-day forty-eight-hour week was introduced), annual vacation with pay, and recreation facilities; " the right to material security," that is, disability insurance and old-age pensions; " the right to education " or compulsory universal elementary education, and opportunities for free higher education with government support of students. The latter articles bear a striking resemblance to the corresponding provisions of the program of the German National Socialist Party, Mussolini's Charter of Labor and other basic documents of the Fascist regimes.

Agriculture. In spite of the rapid progress of urbanization and industrialization, the Soviet Union still remains a primarily agricultural country, the rural population in 1939 representing 67.2 per cent of the total. But the structure and organization of the farming community has been completely altered. The large estates of the nobility and the Church were swept away in the first revolution of 1917. Since 1918 small peasant farming has likewise undergone a complete transformation. The short-lived experiment in rigid state control under War Communism was succeeded by a period of relative economic freedom. The Communist program of collectivization of farming, while never completely abandoned, has been kept in abeyance. Even the first Five-Year Plan provided that collective and state farms were to increase merely from 2.7 per cent of the total area under crops in 1928 to 17.5 per cent in 1932. In 1928–1929, however, the Communist Party changed its mind and embarked on a drastic program of collectivization, accompanied by a ruthless " liquidation of the *kulaks* (more prosperous peasants) as a class," and the deportation of some 4 or 5 million of these unfortunates to the camps of the GPU. By the end of 1932, 78 per cent of the total area under cultivation was in the hands of the collective and state farms, and in 1938 collectivization was practically completed. In January, 1939 the collective farmers and their families numbered 75.6 million, or 44.6 per cent of the total population, while the number of individual farmers had shrunk to 3.0 million, or 1.8 per cent.

Collective Farming. The so-called " socialist sector " in agriculture comprises two elements: the state farms (*sovkhoz*) and the collective farms (*kolkhoz*).[8] The *sovkhozi* are large state owned and state managed agricultural enterprises. They have not been a success and much of their acreage since 1936 has been turned over to the collective farms.

The collective farms of the *artel* type, which dominate Soviet agriculture, are in theory voluntary cooperative organizations whose members are the collective farmers. The land is " public socialist property " but the legal right to its use belongs to the farm in perpetuity. All agricultural land, buildings used for communal purposes, machines and the more important implements, draft animals and stocks of seeds, are the " public socialist property." Members of the farm, however, retain under individual control their homesteads with an adjoining plot varying in size from one-quarter to one hectare, small implements and some livestock. The collectivized section of the farm is cultivated jointly by the members, who are organized into brigades under an appointed brigadier. All types of farm work are classified in terms of " labor days," an abstract unit which takes into account the elements of physical exertion, skill, and the " social usefulness " of the work. The evaluation of a day's work in terms of " labor days " usually varies from half of a " labor day " to two " labor days." The net proceeds of the farm are distributed according to the number of " labor days " credited to each farmer at the end of the year. There is an elaborate system of premiums for the brigadiers and for the rank and file if they fulfil or exceed the planned assignments, and a formidable array of punishments for those who fail. No farmer is permitted to refuse the work to which he is assigned. The administration of the farm is elected, but the chief executive officer, the director, who need not be a member of the farm, invariably has the backing of the local agency of the Communist Party. In theory the collective farms pay no rent, but they are under obligation to surrender to the state a considerable proportion of their harvest at nominal prices. Receipts from this source constitute one of the largest items of Soviet revenue.

Important features of Soviet agriculture are the Machine Tractor Stations (MTS) which own practically all tractors and combines and supervise the work of the collective farms. In 1938 there were 438,000 tractors and 153,000 combines; practically none were available a few years earlier.

Obstacles to Collective Farming. The attitude of the peasants toward compulsory collectivization was disclosed by the wholesale slaughter of their domestic animals during the drive of 1928–1930. Recent government decrees (April 19, 1938; May 27, 1939; April 7, 1940) denounce the gross abuse of power by farm directors and local officials, and the stubborn tendency of the collective farmers to neglect the collectivized portion of the farm and concentrate on their homestead allotments, the size of which have been expanded in contravention of the law. Russian peasants have always been the stepchildren of an unkind fate; whether their economic and general status has been improved under the Soviet rule remains uncertain.

Industrial Labor. Hired labor comes next in importance to the collective farmers. According to the preliminary returns of the 1939 census, the number of hired workers, both industrial and rural, and their families was 54.6 million, or 32.2 per cent of the entire population. The number of industrial workers and employees in 1938 was officially given as 28 million. The position of labor and labor organizations in the U.S.S.R. is determined by the theory that the Soviet Union is a state of workers and that therefore the interests of labor and of the state are identical.

The disappearance of unemployment in which the Moscow government rightly takes pride occurred more or less by accident. The first Five-Year Plan called for an increase in industrial workers from 11.3 million to 15.8 million. By 1932 this figure reached 22.8 million. The untiring efforts of the government had been directed to the improvement of labor discipline and efficiency. Unemployment insurance was abolished in 1930, wages were put on a strictly piece-rate basis, obligatory " norms " of performance have been steadily increased, and there is an uninterrupted flow of often repetitious decrees designed to encourage labor to higher exertion, make workers stay on their jobs, and punish laggards.[9] The trade unions have a large membership, and since 1933 have administered social insurance, the appropriations for which were greatly increased. The chief task of the trade unions, however, is the enforcement of labor discipline and the promotion of efficiency. For all practical purposes they are just another government agency. The average monthly wage of an industrial worker in 1938 was officially given as 289 rubles, but the decree of November 1, 1937 raised the minimum monthly wage in industry and transport employment to 110 rubles. The absence of an index of the cost of living makes these figures largely meaningless and the trend of real wages under planned economy remains a matter of conjecture. It is reasonably clear, however, that the standard of living of industrial labor remains low.

The Bureaucracy. Lenin proclaimed that one of the chief characteristics of the future Socialist society would be the disappearance of bureaucracy. It is somewhat of a shock to find, therefore, in the 1939 census that the number of employees and their families was 29.7 million, or 17.5 per cent of the entire population. There is approximately one official for every three collective farmers and every two workers. This huge bureaucracy is the new privileged class of the Soviet Union. Under the guidance of the Communist Party, it controls every aspect of national life. In the exercise of its functions the bureaucracy is spurred by the inducement of power and financial rewards. The upper limit of salaries, according to the decree of August 29, 1938, is 2000 rubles per month (except when higher remunerations are granted by the Council of People's Commissars) and officials, especially party officials, have ample opportunities to obtain various favors such as better lodgings, which are at a premium. The press and authoritative Soviet pronouncements continually denounce the procrastination, inefficiency, corruption, and stupidity of the bureaucracy. Nevertheless, while some office-holders are "purged" others take their places in increasing numbers.

The abolition of the "exploitation of man by man" in the Marxian sense — that is, the elimination of private employers — has been achieved in the U.S.S.R. But unfortunately a state, even a socialist state that is supposed to "wither away," must be administered by human beings, and so far there is nothing in the Soviet experiment or in other historical experience to indicate that a privileged bureaucracy does its job better than do private employers.

Schools. Russia has traditionally enjoyed the unenviable reputation of being an illiterate country. This reputation was largely deserved although in the absence of adequate data not even the approximate percentage of literacy on the eve of the revolution can be determined, frequent statements to the contrary notwithstanding. It should be kept in mind, moreover, that a law adopted by the Imperial Parliament in May, 1908 provided for the gradual introduction of universal primary education. The reform, had it been carried out according to schedule, should have been completed in 1922.

The Soviet government has made an earnest effort to promote the advancement of literacy and technical education. In 1938–1939 the number of students reached the imposing figure of 21.3 million in primary schools, 12.1 million in secondary schools, and 601,000 in higher schools. According to the census of 1939 the literacy in the country was 81.2 per cent, the older age groups providing the larger proportion of illiterates. The number of men and women who had gone through the primary and secondary schools was, in 1939, 77.7 per 1000 of the population, and those who had received higher education 6.4 per 1000. The endeavor made by the government to advance literacy and technical knowledge is commendable but the results thus far obtained cannot be considered striking.

Literature. In the realm of arts the Soviet revolution has failed so far to produce any work of real importance. The chief " proletarian " author of the U.S.S.R. is still the late Maxim Gorki (1863–1936) who spent most of the latter part of his life in Italy. His literary fame was achieved under the Imperial regime during which he wrote the majority of his books. Some of the other Soviet authors, for instance Alexis Tolstoi and Vsevolod Ivanov, were like Gorki recognized members of the craft before 1917. Among the younger generation the most promising is, perhaps, M. A. Sholokhov, author of *And Quiet Flows the Don.* The work of these writers, however, if not devoid of literary merit, cannot be regarded in a class with the great classics of Russian literature. The only exception is, perhaps, the remarkable although much disputed little volume of poems, *The Twelve,* by another survivor of the old regime, Alexander Blok (1880–1921). Written in 1918 *The Twelve,* which does not lend itself to interpretation in English, has captured something of the fervor and deep tragedy of the early revolutionary days and is likely to remain an important contribution to Russian literature.

Other Arts. Little need be said about the other arts. Composers such as Prokofiev, already known under the old regime, and the much younger Shestakovich show talent and imagination but one would not call their work great. The French novelist André Gide, previous to his conflict with the Moscow government, remarked of an exhibition of Soviet paintings he visited in Russia in 1936 that it would be more charitable to say nothing about it, a verdict confirmed by most foreign critics when the pictures were sent on a tour abroad. It is only fair to observe that Russia has never produced important painters, just as she never had a great national architecture. The Soviets have added nothing to the country's reputation in this respect. The traditional high standards of the Russian theater and ballet have been more or less maintained but have certainly not been improved upon. The Soviet moving pictures, in spite of often inferior photography, have won

Russian Accretions: 1939-1940

International Boundaries: ~~~

The Territorial Gains Are
Identified on the Map by Date.

Miles: 0 100 200 300

R.E.Falconer

some praise abroad perhaps not so much because of their intrinsic artistic value, as because they afford a welcome relief from the appalling vulgarity of Hollywood.

Freedom of Thought. The sterility of the Soviet revolution in the cultural field may, perhaps, be explained by the relatively short time the Communist regime has been in power; by the death, persecution, and flight abroad of a great many leaders in art and science; by the hardships of everyday life which absorb all the energies of the citizens; and, last but not least, by the stifling influence of the Communist regime. The " party line " — rigid, yet unpredictable, capricious, and shifting — must be closely followed in every field of intellectual endeavor. No deviation from it is tolerated. Not a fresh thought, not a critical opinion is permitted to penetrate a Soviet classroom or to appear in the hopelessly dull and dreary pages of Soviet newspapers and magazines which read like government department reports. The expression of love and admiration for Stalin, obligatory for all Soviet citizens, has grown into a monstrous ritual and each of the leader's pronouncements, however crude, commonplace, and unenlightening, must be treated as a revelation. The requirement of unwavering conformity with Communist doctrine reduced to the humble intellectual level of Russia's dictator is not conducive to freedom of thought and expression without which art and science cannot perform their function in society. The suffocating intellectual atmosphere of the Soviet Union is probably the real reason why the magnificent flight of revolutionary inspiration expressed by Blok in the magic of his verse has not been duplicated since and has given place to distressing mediocrity.

The U.S.S.R. and the World. A realization of the dual nature of the Soviet state affords a guiding thread through the entanglements of Moscow's foreign policy. The U.S.S.R., heir to the historic tradition of Imperial Russia, is, on the one hand, a great national and, in recent years, a strongly nationalistic power; on the other, she is the standard-bearer of revolutionary Communism and the mainstay of the Third (Communist) International whose object is the struggle, if necessary by armed force, for world revolution. During the early period the revolutionary element clearly had the upper hand in Soviet foreign policy. It was the failure of the international revolution and the acceptance of Stalin's doctrine " socialism in a single country " that brought to the fore the national element. The Soviet Union endeavored to cooperate with the capitalist powers and in 1934 joined the League of Nations which she had always denounced as a capitalist conspiracy. The Third International obediently revised its program in 1928 and proclaimed that the defense of the U.S.S.R. against capitalist aggression was the primary duty of the international proletariat.

The German-Soviet agreement of August 23, 1939, and the subsequent developments in eastern Europe would seem to have been inspired by a peculiar combination of the two chief ingredients of Soviet foreign policy: aggressive and crude nationalism and no less aggressive and crude revolutionary Communism. The Soviet-German agreement was the determining factor in unleashing the war of 1939. It is an old Communist theory that revolutions grow out of wars and, of course, nothing better serves the cause of revolution than the mutual extermination of capitalist powers. The recovery by the Soviet Union in 1939–1940 of most of the territories lost in 1918 is both flattering to Russian nationalism and pleasing to the Communists since it means the spreading of the Soviet system, although it is not easy to reconcile the view of Marx and Lenin with the unpalatable fact that the latest " conversions " to Communism have been achieved not through proletarian revolutions, but at the point or under the protection of German bayonets and with the connivance of Adolf Hitler.

The Soviet Experiment. The western expansion of the Soviet Union and the calamitous conditions in Europe have given a new significance to the Soviet experiment. The chaotic state of the world is often ascribed to the inherent weakness and imperfections of the capitalist regime, and Communist Russia, the only great power at peace in Europe, appears to many as the sole promise of a better future. There must be a large number of people in the countries which in 1939–1940 had their first thorough experience of the harsh realities of the Soviet rule — that is, in eastern Poland, the annexed portion of Finland, Bessarabia, Latvia, Estonia, and Lithuania — who do not share this optimistic view. But their voice is not heard. The inequities of the capitalist regime are near at hand, familiar, and widely advertised. The Soviet Union is distant, vast, and mysterious. The barrier of language, insurmountable for most foreigners, combined with sociological dogmatism, has facilitated the spreading of misinformation. Critical factual accounts of Soviet conditions are only too often discarded as prejudiced, partial, and biased. There is a seemingly unshakable belief among the so-called radical circles in every country that the proletarian revolution cannot be wrong, that the rule of the " working class " *must* lead to a more equitable political and social organization. The facile optimism that has permeated most of the historical schemes and made the process of human development appear to be a necessary evolution from lower to higher forms of civilization naturally gravitates toward the Communist slogan of the " abolition of the exploitation of man by man." It is only too often overlooked that though revolutionary destruction is relatively easy, the re-building of a tolerable human society is slow, painful, and terribly costly in terms of both wealth and human suffering.

REFERENCES

[1] Cf. M. T. Florinsky, *The End of the Russian Empire*, New Haven: Yale Univ. Press, 1931; Count V. N. Kokovtsov, *Out of My Past*, Palo Alto, Cal.: Stanford Univ. Press, 1935; Sir Bernard Pares, *The Fall of the Russian Monarchy*, New York: Knopf, 1939.

[2] After the reforms of 1905–1906 the legislative powers of the Czar were exercised jointly with a two-chamber Parliament which, however, was elected on the basis of a very restricted franchise and had no control over the executive branch of the government.

[3] Cf. Maurice Dobb, *Russian Economic Development since the Revolution*, New York: Dutton, 1928.

[4] Vladimir I. Lenin, *The State and the Revolution*.

[5] Cf. Paul Scheffer, "From Lenin to Stalin," *Foreign Affairs*, April, 1938; Joseph Barnes, "The Great Bolshevik Cleansing," *Foreign Affairs*, April, 1939.

[6] Cf. W. H. Chamberlin, *The Soviet Planned Economic Order*, Boston: World Peace Foundation, 1931; G. T. Grinke, *The Five Year Plan*, New York: International Publishers, 1930; L. E. Hubbard, *Soviet Money and Finance*, London: Macmillan, 1936; L. E. Hubbard, *Soviet Trade and Distribution*, London: Macmillan, 1938.

[7] The state monopoly of foreign trade introduced in 1918 has been retained ever since. The highest point attained by Soviet exports was 1,036 million rubles in 1931. The foreign trade of the U.S.S.R. was affected by the depression in a manner not different from that observed in capitalist countries. The monopoly of foreign trade, nevertheless, has several advantages from the government's point of view: it eliminates the possibility of competition from better and cheaper imported goods; allows the importation only of such commodities as are considered socially desirable; and makes possible the shifting of purchases from country to country to meet the exigencies of the economic and political situation.

[8] Cf. W. Ladejinsky, "Collectivization of Agriculture in the Soviet Union," *Political Science Quarterly*, March-June, 1934; W. Ladejinsky, "Soviet State Farms," *Political Science Quarterly*, March-June, 1938; L. Volin, "Agrarian Collectivism in the Soviet Union," *Journal of Political Economy*, October-December, 1937; L. Volin, "Agrarian Individualism in the Soviet Union," *Agricultural History*, January-April, 1938; L. E. Hubbard, *The Economics of Soviet Agriculture*, London: Macmillan, 1939.

[9] In the summer of 1940 the Soviet government took drastic action to increase production. The labor day was lengthened without increase in wages. No workers or employees were permitted to change their place of employment or resign, except in case of ill-health or old age. A mass conscription of young workers was introduced at the end of the year. Free instruction in the upper grades of the high schools and in colleges and universities specifically provided for by the constitution of 1936 was abolished. Cf. Michael T. Florinsky, "Stalin's New Deal for Labor," *Political Science Quarterly*, March, 1941.

SELECTED BIBLIOGRAPHY

Central committee of the Communist Party of the Soviet Union, *History of the Communist Party of the Soviet Union*, New York: International Publishers, 1939. Latest official history of the party.

Chamberlin, W. H., *Soviet Russia*, Boston: Little, Brown, 1931. A sympathetic discussion by the former Moscow correspondent of the *Christian Science Monitor*.

——, *Russia's Iron Age*, Boston: Little, Brown, 1934. A critical account by the same author.

Citrine, Sir Walter, *I Search for Truth in Russia*, New York: Dutton, 1937. Account of a visit to the Soviet Union by the President of the International Federation of Trade Unions.

Florinsky, M. T., *World Revolution and the U.S.S.R.*, New York: Macmillan, 1933. A study of the evolution of Communist theory and its repercussions.

——, *Toward an Understanding of the U.S.S.R.*, New York: Macmillan, 1939. Revised version in James T. Shotwell, ed., *The Governments of Continental Europe*, New York: Macmillan, 1940.

Land of Socialism Today and Tomorrow, Moscow: Foreign Languages Publishing House, 1939. Reports and speeches of the eighteenth congress of the Communist Party of the Soviet Union, March 10–21, 1939.

Lenin, V. I., *The State and the Revolution*, London: British Socialist Party, 1919. Lenin's celebrated discussion of the evolution of the state.

Littlepage, J. D. and Bess, Demaree, *In Search of Soviet Gold*, New York: Harcourt, Brace, 1938. The enlightening account of an American engineer who spent ten years in the Soviet Union.

Souvarine, Boris, *Stalin, A Critical Survey of Bolshevism*, New York: Alliance, 1939. An admirable account of the growth of the Bolshevik movement.

Strong, Anne L., *The New Soviet Constitution*, New York: Holt, 1937. A good translation of the constitution of 1936 and a useful but uncritical account of earlier constitutional developments.

Tracy, M. E., *Our Country, Our People, and Theirs*, New York: Macmillan, 1938. A useful parallel discussion of institutions and conditions in the United States, Italy, Germany, and the Soviet Union.

Trotsky, Leon, *The Revolution Betrayed*, New York: Doubleday, Doran, 1937. A bitter indictment of Stalin's rule.

Webb, Sidney and Beatrice, *Soviet Communism: A New Civilization?*, New York: Scribner, 1936. An account of conditions in the Soviet Union before the adoption of the constitution of 1936.

Wolfe, Henry C., *The Imperial Soviets*, New York: Doubleday, Doran, 1940. A good journalistic account of Soviet foreign policy.

CHAPTER XIX

Poland

POLAND'S GLORY IS NOT VANISHED
WHILE HER SONS REMAIN.
AND HER FLAG THAT ONCE WAS BANISHED
SHALL RETURN AGAIN.

POLAND'S SONS AGAIN WILL MUSTER
AND DRIVE OUT THE FOE
WILL BRING BACK HER ANCIENT LUSTRE
BRING HER JOY FOR WOE.

— Verses from the *Polish* NATIONAL ANTHEM
English version of EDWIN MARKHAM

The Pole has been a constant factor in European history for the past 1100 years, even when he was a man without a country. He has been the anvil upon which other nations have beaten their plowshares into swords.[1] Much of his past is a monotonous record of bickerings and petty internal struggles, and of losing battles with neighboring foes. Poland is always being partitioned, whether by its own rulers or by outside coalitions; its boundaries are forever changing; it is constantly a victim.

However, hardship, injustice, and despair have not made the Pole cynical, hopeless, or callous. They have made him seek self-expression through the intangible avenues of music, the arts, and religion. They have made him visionary and perhaps unpractical. Nevertheless, that the forces which have beaten his body have tempered his spirit, can be seen by his rapid advance whenever he has been untrammeled.

The Location of Poland. At first, Poland was a motley assortment of Slavic tribes dwelling on the eastern frontier of Germany in the ninth century.[2] Those Slavic peoples who were not absorbed or annihilated by the advancing Germans were organized in the early tenth century into a thriving and rapidly expanding state under shrewd and capable leadership. From then until now, the boundaries of Poland have shifted as the sands of the seashore.

Poland was situated at the crossroads of trade, between eastern and western Europe, an advantageous position in times of peace, when culture develops from various directions and riches similarly increase; but fatal

---

This chapter by Oscar G. Darlington, Associate Professor of History, Hofstra College.

during wars when it becomes, like Belgium, an arena for neighboring armies. Such a position has enabled Poland to be strong only when Germany and Russia were weak. Otherwise, Poland when permitted any separate identity, has been a buffer state.

The question might well arise why a people as vigorous, patriotic, and intelligent as the Poles should not have capitalized on this central position, to spread in both directions, as they did in their earlier history, and as Germany is doing at present. The answer is in part to be found in the age-old, internal conflict; in part it is geographical. Except for the Carpathian mountains which lie along its southern limit, and a few miles of streams and marshland, Poland had virtually no natural boundaries. Especially was this true on the east and west, where dwelt its most hostile neighbors. The frontier between Poland and Russia was, from a geographical point of view, almost everywhere artificial; except for the marshes of Pinsk, virtually without rivers, mountains or even hills, so that there could be truth in the story of peasants who got the Soviet guards drunk every night and moved the frontier posts out gradually until they had put their village inside Poland.

Boundaries in 1919. To make matters worse, the Treaty of Versailles left the outlines of resurrected Poland as hazy as if it were appropriate that a re-embodied spirit should have a dim borderland.[3] Many of its boundaries were left for plebiscites or war to decide.

The Polish Corridor. The ill-fated " corridor " has caused more trouble than perhaps any small strip of land in modern Europe.[4] Almost all experts agreed that Poland needed an outlet on the Baltic. Moreover, a narrow neck of territory, Pomorze, or Pomerania, peopled mainly by Poles, ran from Poland to the Baltic; but east and west of this were lands which historically have been indisputably Prussian. With Prussians to right and left, the tenure of the Corridor by Poland was doomed to unceasing controversy and ultimate loss.[5]

Poland's Physical Features. Poland emerged from its post-war struggles with the Bolsheviks, and from various plebiscites and squabbles which finally defined its borders, the sixth largest country in Europe in area; in 1939 it also ranked sixth in population. The territory comprised physical features as varied as its people, with lake country, rivers, marshes, mountains, wide timber areas, extensive farm lands and even a bit of seashore extending 87 miles along the Baltic.

In climate, Poland was again at the crossroads between east and west with changeable, moody weather and moderate temperatures throughout the year in the coastal and western section; and in the east ferocious winters.

Minority Groups. Some of the most difficult problems of Poland arose from its various minority groups.[6] Not only did they form a large fraction of the population, but each minority had lawful guarantee of civic and political rights. Moreover, Poland was pledged by treaty to assure them instruction in their own language and their due share of public money for social and religious ends. These provisions of the treaty with the Allies were incorporated in the Polish constitution.

The Poles, themselves harassed and oppressed minorities for a century and a half, should have realized how indestructible a racial minority can be, and that large numbers of unassimilable peoples are sources of weakness to any state. Moreover, the ancient Polish monarchy had tried for centuries to assimilate Cossacks, Germans, Lithuanians, and Ruthenians,[7] even in an age when the masses were without a voice, and the aristocracy of the various units were aware of the advantages of Polish connections. Thus it must have been national enthusiasm and ambition that inspired Polish leaders to extend their borders by force and annex great units of non-Polish peoples with basic differences in language, religion, and cultural background.[8]

The White Russians. The Russo-Polish Treaty of Riga (1921) gave Poland, roughly speaking, the boundary of 1793, and about 1,500,000 White Russians, which meant that three-fourths of the population of the three eastern provinces, Norvogródek, Wilno, and Polesie were not Poles. Though the White Russians formed one of the least disturbing minorities, their low economic and cultural status was a drag upon the Polish state, especially because of the treaty responsibilities before mentioned. Likewise, the acquisition of White Russia helped to spell Poland's doom in 1939, when Russia took the opportunity to re-patriate her own people.

The Jewish Minority. Three other outstanding minorities were the Ukrainians, Germans, and Jews. The Jews constituted [9] one of the major problems of Poland, since they comprised one-tenth of the population (3,500,000 out of approximately 35,000,000), entrenched for centuries in vital places. Medieval Poland encouraged the Jews to trade and engage in industry. Polish nobles were too proud to carry on business; Polish peasants too unenlightened; and all good Christians too pious to disobey ecclesiastical restrictions upon the use of money.

Dominance of the Jews. Unlike France and England, Poland had developed no native middle class; thus the Jews and Germans came to form that class in Poland. They built and populated the towns and cities, brought culture and wealth through their wide international connections and formed a stratum of society as far above the swarming, primitive peasants as it was below the élite. Consequently, Jews, persecuted elsewhere in medieval Europe, found a haven in Poland which, at one time, harbored around 80 per cent of the race.

Anti-Semitism. The nineteenth and twentieth centuries witnessed a revulsion against the Jew's supremacy. With the development of nationalism, the Pole felt increasingly competent and impatient to conduct his own affairs, and opposed the Jewish monopoly of trades, industries and professions. Undoubtedly, the one-tenth Jewish minority exercised upon the nine-tenth majority an influence out of proportion to its numbers. Jews operated over half the commercial enterprises of Poland, owned half the mills, virtually monopolized the retail trade, dominated the professions of law and medicine, and so completely controlled the handicrafts that 87 per cent of the haberdashers were Jewish, 85 per cent of the shoemakers, 97 per cent of the capmakers, 78 per cent of the goldsmiths, to say nothing of furriers, tanners, glove-makers, hairdressers, and bakers, occupations in which they formed a controlling element.[10] Most of the Jews lived in towns and cities, where their percentage of the population ranged from over a fourth of Warsaw and Cracow to 90 per cent in such eastern towns as Pinsk. The reaction against the Jews swung so far that the effort to solve the problem of this troublesome minority by forced emigration and wholesale attempts at annihilation, rebounded against the young nation which did not have enough qualified Poles to fill professional and commercial posts.[11]

The German Minority. The German minority [12] was not so numerous as it was influential. The Germans, of whom there were nearly a million, were scattered over the country (as were the Jews). There were, of course, areas where the Germans [13] tended to concentrate, especially in industrial and mining centers such as Polish Silesia; the city of Lódz, though located in the section previously belonging to Russia, was mainly German and Jewish. Lódz alone contained about one-fifth of all the Germans in Poland. However, these did not have any Nazi connections and were, if anything, hostile to the Hitler regime, as were many of the German settlements. Since a goodly proportion of the Germans were large property owners, and exempt from the agrarian reforms, they added to the economic burdens of the state, while forming at the same time a constant element of danger in the event of any national crisis.

The Ukrainian Minority. The Ukrainian minority [14] numbered about 3,500,000. The Ukrainians, however, were not scattered, but lived near the eastern border, and desired autonomy, as did most of the numerous submerged racial units in middle Europe.

The characteristics and sympathies of these Ukrainians were Russian rather than Polish. In culture, language, and religion, they belonged to the east rather than to the west. Mainly illiterate and hostile to Polish domination, they could only multiply the problems of a poor and unstable country. But for four centuries before its dissolution, Poland had included this section of the Ukraine. Hence, despite the obstacles set by the hostile intrigues of Germany, Russia, or the Ukrainians themselves, by armed opposition, or by the League of Nations, Poland stubbornly demanded the Polish Ukraine and held out doggedly until she got it.

Poland proceeded to treat the Ukrainians as Prussia had previously dealt with the Poles, with identical results: indignant resistance, steady opposition to Polish fifth-column tactics, and persistent agitation for autonomy.

The minorities added appreciably to the burdens of the new Polish State. Together the minorities by 1939 constituted about a third of the entire population. However, Poland's natural rate of increase, second in the world after Japan, would eventually have reduced this percentage. The race to out-populate the minorities was indeed encouraged by the government despite an already chronic problem of overpopulation. The parents of six living sons could have the president of the republic as godfather to the seventh, and he would give them a savings account. In 1939, these godchildren numbered 2500.

Political Problems after the World War. The problems thus far discussed could be solved only by a well-organized government, which resurrected Poland lacked. For 123 years the country had had no national existence. In 1795, it had been divided between Austria, Prussia, and Russia, and these widely differing nations subjected the Poles to oppression and suppression of all national traditions, culture, and spirit. Moreover, each section met an entirely different type of oppressive administration and resisted it in every possible way with constant evasion, and major and infinite minor insurrections.

Austrian Poland. For about fifty years after the last partition Austrian Poland was despoiled and impoverished, and oppressed politically, economically, and culturally; class was set against class and faction against faction; Polish customs, language, and institutions were suppressed. In the latter half of the nineteenth century, however, the Poles were permitted self-government and their culture was allowed to develop freely. The Austrian Poles alone had opportunities to maintain their language and traditions, and develop capable scholars, scientists, and politicians.

Though not a free or separate country, Austrian Poland from 1867 knew the problems of representative government and coped with them intelligently through its parliamentary assembly and increasing participation in the Austrian government. Here the Polish faction, even though it was dominated by the wealthy landowners without regard for the welfare of the people, grew to be an important element in the Dual Monarchy, provided some of Austria's most capable statesmen, and often exercised a determining influence on her financial and foreign policy.[15] Gradually, with the abolishment of serfdom, the social strata of Austrian Poland became equalized by the rise of the peasantry and consequent decay of the landed gentry. The scaffolding was prepared for truly democratic government with strong Socialistic leanings.

Prussian Poland. Russian and Prussian Poland did not fare so well. In the latter, German settlers were encouraged and assisted by the government, and a concerted, but mainly futile effort was made to Prussianize this area by evicting the Poles from the land. It was the Polish Roman Catholic Church, probably more than any other power, that, despite partitions, oppression, and misfortunes, kept alive Polish traditions, language, and spirit. However, Prussian Poland in 1918 was entirely unready for self-government. The Prussian Poles had had almost no political experience.

Russian Poland. The racial kinship of the Poles and Russians might well have provided a basis of understanding and compromise, but the stubborn individualism of the Pole and his loyalty to the vision of a free Poland, his religion and an innate predilection for strife, together with the intolerance and arrogance of Czarist Russia made a friendly administration of Russian Poland impossible. The area was governed despotically by men regarded as unfit for administrative duty in Czarist Russia itself. They tried to reduce the Poles to the status of helots, destroying the homes and property of the landed gentry wherever possible, systematically attempting to undermine the hold of the Roman Catholic Church, and striving to eradicate Polish initiative and cultural traditions, so that those who wanted to be more than beasts of burden had to emigrate. This policy produced a spirit of sullen anarchy but did not succeed in obliterating the Poles' persistent love of country and liberty, nor did it extinguish Polish culture.

Poland's Post-War Struggles. The welding of these conflicting racial elements into anything like a nation would have been a fairly superhuman undertaking even for a passive, peace-loving race. With the temperamental, headstrong, ambitious Poles it seemed impossible. The vague, undetermined boundaries, especially in the east, the unfairness of the various plebiscites, the determination of the Polish leaders to incorporate in the new state all the land Poland had ever possessed, kept the country at war for several years and almost caused the destruction of Poland at its rebirth.

Destruction of War. By the time the various border disputes had been settled and Pilsudski had made terms with Bolshevik Russia in 1921, a large part of the country was in ruins. Over 11,000,000 acres of agricultural land and nearly 15,000,000 acres of forest were devastated by the wars of 1914–1921.[16] Millions of farm buildings and animals were lost.

There was naturally an almost total eclipse of industry, due to the destruction of factory buildings and mining equipment, as well as huge thefts by invading armies of machinery, raw materials, and stocks of manufactured goods. Invading belligerents carried away 4,661 million cubic feet of timber, thousands of electrical motors and other machinery, and before leaving the country blew up 7500 bridges and destroyed nearly a thousand railway stations.[17]

Poland's problem was obviously not one of mere reconstruction, as was that of France or Belgium with their stable governments and long, continuous development. The Poles, without a currency, legal system, and political unity and composed largely of people with no political experience, had to create a mechanism of government and build stable social institutions. The first task was that of coordinating social and racial differences due to a century of triplicate allegiances.

The National Temper. The national attitude toward the newly constituted government was a unique mixture of optimism and distrust. Over a century of opposition to oppressive rule made readjustment to the new situation difficult, and the lifelong distrust of government never entirely melted away from many of the older Poles, whose lives had been formed under foreign domination. The Germans and Russians had almost made the Pole believe that he lacked capacity for self-government, as evidenced by the plebiscites in the frontier districts of Marienwerder and Allenstein in East Prussia. There, though the population was predominantly Polish, the region voted to remain under Germany, largely through lack of confidence in the new state.

The new regime clearly had to win over its constituents. At first there was a tendency for the populace to blame the government for their hardships and not until a new generation had arisen was government accepted as a matter of fact.

Pilsudski and Paderewski. Polish politics centered around personalities rather than principles, and Poland was piloted through an epoch of inevitable chaos by two men of invincible patriotism, Joseph Pilsudski and Ignace Paderewski, who belong in a class with the founders of the United States. "The vision of a strong and independent Poland has been the lodestar of my existence," said Paderewski, and these words were equally true of Pilsudski. Different in many respects, these men were alike in their complete devotion to Poland, though by a strange twist of fate neither was born in a part of Poland that was set free.

Pilsudski [18] was a realist, Paderewski [19] an idealist. Both had unlimited capacity for work, sacrifice, and defeat. Pilsudski's experiences in Russian and German prisons had made him a man of iron. Paderewski was a more spiritual character who could win world sympathy for the cause of Polish independence. Pilsudski led Poland's armies to victory and brought a semblance of order out of pandemonium in the new state. Only Pilsudski and Paderewski among Polish leaders seemingly could rise above factions, political aims, and self-interest. Pilsudski and Paderewski were as the body and soul of Poland. Pilsudski the "body" died in 1935, four years before the destruction of all he had accomplished; Paderewski the "soul" lived on, fighting, as ever, for the liberation of his countrymen, a symbol of the indestructible spirit of Poland.

Reconstituted Poland found itself with two governments, the Polish National Committee in Paris, headed by Roman Dmowski, a conservative, and supported by Paderewski; and the Regency Council at Warsaw headed by Pilsudski, a former Socialist. The Allies recognized the Dmowski government and admitted it to the Peace Conference, while simultaneously, the Warsaw government held elections to choose delegates who should meet before the spring of 1919 and frame a constitution.

Thus Poland was threatened with dissension which would seriously have weakened her position at the Peace Conference, but for the diplomacy of Paderewski who journeyed to Poland and brought the two governments together by a compromise. Pilsudski became President and Paderewski, Premier; Dmowski and Paderewski were to represent Poland at the Peace Conference. It was clear, however, that beneath all political bickering there was but one basis of alignment — for or against Pilsudski.

Pilsudski's Career. Joseph Pilsudski was a Lithuanian noble who hated Russian absolutism. In his stormy pre-war career he was expelled from medical school for revolutionary activity, implicated in a plot to murder the Czar, and sentenced to Siberia, whence he escaped. He edited a revolutionary journal which for seven years evaded the Russian police.

After war broke out Pilsudski organized a group of 300 enthusiasts in Cracow and set off, with Austria's blessing, to conquer Russia. Like Garibaldi fifty years earlier, Pilsudski soon saw his regiment expanded to a legion, and in time it became, with the approval of the Central Powers, an army fighting against the Czar. When Russia crumbled in 1917, and Poland was ignored in the Treaty of Brest-Litovsk, Pilsudski was imprisoned at Magdeburg for objecting to Germany's sacrifice of Polish rights. From prison he came to head the Regency Council at Warsaw.

Domestic Politics. This brief summary of Pilsudski's life up to 1919 throws light on the domestic politics of Poland. Pilsudski now disavowed Socialism; his reply to a radical sums up his position: "We were both on the same train, but I got off at Polish Independence Station and you went on." However, the Right feared him, especially when in 1919 he formed a Left government to prevent Poland, he said, from going Bolshevik.

The Right put through a constitution modeled upon that of the Third French Republic, with a national assembly consisting of two chambers, the Senate and the Seym. Power was lodged in the Seym. Suffrage was universal for those over twenty-one. The President, elected by the assembly for a term of seven years, was little more than a figurehead.

As commander-in-chief of the army Pilsudski was probably the determining factor in political affairs. The masses trusted him, and the Legions who had followed him into battle adored him. In fact, most of the political leaders throughout Poland's brief independence were drawn from the 300 men whom he organized into a legion in Cracow.

Parliamentary Dissension. It was to the infinite credit of Pilsudski and his followers, that they allowed parliamentary government with its bickerings, petty parties, and personal jealousies to continue, hoping that in time the nation would learn how to make democracy work. The prevalent illiteracy of the Pole made true democracy impossible. To most of the early delegates to the Seym sectional, racial, or personal interests were dearer than the commonwealth. They lacked national vision as completely as the pre-partition Diet, and formed tiny political parties which squabbled over superficialities while basic problems waited to be solved.

The result was political chaos. From 1921 to 1926 Poland had no less than eighty political parties; this short era also produced fourteen different Cabinets.[20] No wonder Pilsudski became disgusted and likened the Seym to " a locomotive drawing a pin " and said the debates were so boresome that flies dropped dead from the ceiling.

The Coup d'État of May, 1926. A crisis developed in May, 1926 when the Seym attempted to wrest control of the army from Pilsudski and give it to the politicians. The great man knew that this would be fatal. The Seym could be inefficient but not the army, for in the last analysis it was Poland's only guarantee of freedom. Moreover, the army was staunchly loyal to Pilsudski, its creator. Consequently Pilsudski came out of his political retirement and marched on the capitol. After three days of street fighting the government was defeated.

Then the true caliber of the patriot came out. A man of moderate patience might have set up a dictatorship, a self-seeking autocrat would have ruthlessly quenched the light of liberty. Instead, Pilsudski let the nation express its approval of his deed by electing him President, then refused the office and took only that of Inspector General of the Army. The powers of the President were somewhat increased, but the outstanding result of the *coup* was the formation of a non-party bloc in the Seym which won the election of 1928. In the 1930 election the issue was clearly for or against Pilsudski, and this time the government was not above employing illegal methods, so that parliamentary government became virtually a form without substance. Even so, Pilsudski did not tamper with the machinery of democratic rule.

Dictatorship of Pilsudski. Through the next five years Pilsudski emerged in every crisis as Poland's strong man, the benevolent dictator, now holding one office, now another, determining who shall be elected, using or threatening to use force, but always trying to help his country rise above petty feuds and learn to rule itself. Shortly before his death in 1935 Poland was given a new constitution which strengthened the power of the executive. The attempt to eliminate Poland's parliamentary inefficiency fatally revived that other bane of her existence, government by a clique. After 1926 the clique changed but little. Moscicki, a non-political university professor, was sponsored by Pilsudski for the presidency, and in 1932 he was re-elected, to serve until 1940.

After Pilsudski's death Poland was ruled by a group of his colonels headed by Joseph Beck and Smygly-Ridz, who tried to maintain the Marshal's system without any one personality dominant. The last few years of free Poland witnessed a growing political consciousness among the peasants and the increasing power of the Peasant Party. Eventually, the rise of a free, literate generation, might have produced an electorate equipped to participate in genuine democratic government.

Poland's Foreign Policy from 1919 to 1932. Three factors influenced Poland's foreign policy: geography, her immediate neighbors, and economic needs. It has been said that Poland was a buffer state between two mighty and unscrupulous powers, that she was unprotected by natural frontiers, with the narrow " corridor " the only avenue to the sea. It has been further shown that Poland manifested almost unvaryingly a stubborn and pugnacious attitude not only toward her neighbors but toward those countries which helped to re-establish her freedom. It is self-evident that no country as weak and honeycombed by internal dissension as Poland could long survive without strong allies, and that those allies could not be the greedy neighbors, Russia and Germany, who had once partitioned her, and whom she continued to defy and antagonize. If she sided with either, she was in danger of being swallowed; if she resisted both, she might be partitioned. Poland's wisest course was to seek the friendship of nations which wanted to prevent the growth of Germany and Russia, or could profit by having a prosperous Poland form a buffer state between them.

From 1933–1939. Until 1932 Poland looked for security to the League of Nations. When that body proved impotent, and France indifferent, Poland had to conciliate hostile neighbors. Of course, Germany resented her existence and openly vowed to subjugate Poland, until the wisdom and diplomacy of Pilsudski in 1934 arranged a ten-year non-aggression pact with Hitler. A similar pact had been signed with Russia in 1932. The great Marshal feared Communism more than Nazism. After Pilsudski's death, the Nazi menace drove Poland to form mutual assistance pacts with France and England, thus antognizing Hitler and tending to nullify the pact of 1934. In these shifts of foreign policy — from reliance upon the League of Nations to a non-aggression pact with Germany and later to guarantees of her frontier by France and England — Poland was consistently seeking security, with what results the autumn of 1939 tragically demonstrated.

Poland was invaded by the Germans on September 1, 1939. The Poles fought valorously but their inadequate mechanical equipment, their lack of air power, treacherous fifth-column tactics led to quick defeat. The Polish armies were overwhelmed after six weeks.

Economic Development: Natural Resources. Poland's natural resources [21] were highly varied. The coal fields of Upper Silesia ranked third in European production. The oil fields near Boryslaw produced 500,000 tons yearly and gave Poland the largest refinery in Europe. Poland was the second largest zinc producer in the world!

In contrast to Germany, Poland produced all her oil, coal, and iron, three essentials of industry. Moreover, salt came from near Cracow, basalt from Volkynia, potassium from Kalisz, timber from the Carpathians and the eastern provinces, 20 per cent of Poland being forest land. All of these products came from the mountainous southern rim of Poland. The greater part of the country was fertile, easily worked farm land.

Transportation. Transportation was scarcely a problem, owing to Poland's extensive river and canal system and the lack of geographical barriers. The Vistula River with its tributaries, the San, Pelica, and Bug, all rise in the mining and industrial sections and make transportation to Warsaw and the sea a downhill matter. Railroad and highway traffic also profited by the easy northward slope over the gently rolling plain that comprised most of Poland. Flood seasons were destructive of bridges but helpful to the lumbermen. In the southwest the Dniester carried Polish goods to the Black Sea where, by a trade agreement with Rumania, Poland had docks and boats.

Agriculture. Poland was a predominantly agricultural country, over 60 per cent of its people having been peasants, and only 19 per cent engaged in mining and industry. Poland literally belonged to the peasants. Two-thirds of all land under cultivation (43,244,250 acres in 1938) was in small holdings of less than 37 acres. The peasant is Europe's stabilizing force.[22] For centuries he has lived and labored in the same way, having learned, ages ago, not to expect too much from any government, that the best government is that which protects his property rights and lets him alone.

Agrarian Reforms. The Polish peasant was reported to have the lowest standard of living in Europe by those who measure life in terms of electric lights, radios, silk stockings, and doctor's bills, but his outdoor life taught him to value God above gadgets, religion above physical comforts, a few acres of land above the welfare of a distant Warsaw regime. He saw little meaning in the government, and no meaning in taxes until the government put into practice four popular agrarian policies: (1) The Land Reform Law of 1920 which, by 1939, had broken up large landed estates into 700,-000 independent holdings; (2) the consolidation of scattered strips of land into single blocs easier to work and improve; (3) the draining or irrigation of 3,212,430 acres of wasteland; (4) government provision of excellent chemical fertilizer at cost, from a large state-owned plant.[23] The last was due entirely to Poland's President, Moscicki, the chemist who invented the process and who in 1927 built at Moscice a state plant of 50 buildings, covering 1500 acres which could produce 200 carloads of fertilizer daily, a scientific achievement of world importance, and a great factor in Poland's increased agricultural output. This discovery not only freed Poland from the necessity of importing nitrogen products, but permitted her actually to export about half of her fertilizer output to Germany, Finland, and other European countries.

Poland's crops were varied. In rye and potatoes she was the second largest producer in Europe. Poland was self-sufficient in food production.

Industry. Poland was not an industrial country and had merely laid foundations for technological progress. Although possessed of valuable natural resources, the nation lacked capital, equipment, and technicians. The government believed that an industrialized Poland would absorb the excess population [24] and strengthen the country in a military sense. It aimed at supplying native industries with raw materials and Polish markets with manufactures, hoping to achieve self-sufficiency both in peacetime and war. Since all of Poland's industrial centers were in vulnerable locations along her borders, a Central Industrial Region was created, as far in the interior as possible, though events proved that no section of the country was safe from air attack.

The Rise of Gdynia. The construction of the Baltic port, Gdynia, represented Poland's attempt to gain full economic independence. Between 1924 and 1935 Gdynia, a tiny fishing village of 300 people, grew to be the largest port on the Baltic with a population of 150,000. Gdynia rose with the speed of an early American " boom town," until by 1938 it was doing more business than Danzig. The development of Gdynia was evidence of the growing importance of Poland, but it was a large factor in arousing the jealousy and hostility of her neighbors.

Foreign Trade. Poland's foreign trade had a vital influence on her internal affairs, for only as she sold goods abroad could the impoverished state procure foreign loans to finance the construction of roads, bridges, railroads, canals, and other public works. Her principal customers were Great Britain, Germany, and the United States to whom she sold mainly agricultural products, chemical fertilizer, timber, and coal. By 1938 Poland had begun to export locomotives and railway rolling stock.

Cultural Development. It seems apparent that the world of politics and economics is not the sphere in which the Poles have won secure distinction. Even in the days of her greatest glory, Poland was constantly at war with herself and with her neighbors. She has contributed some of the greatest individuals to whom humanity pays homage, but her social classes have always been at variance with each other and with the state. Poland has usually coveted her neighbor's lands and treated her minorities neither benevolently nor wisely.

On the whole a remarkable degree of order was achieved during Poland's brief existence, considering the circumstances here set forth; but it

must be conceded that the glory of the Pole is not in government but in
the arts and sciences.

Joseph Conrad (1857–1924) and Madame Curie (1867–1934) typify
the modern Polish literary and scientific spirit respectively. Though Conrad wrote in the language of his adopted country, his works are as much
Polish as English. Conrad knew almost no English until he was twenty-
one and had to learn it to qualify as a British seaman. Madame Curie accomplished her great work not in her native Poland but in France. Ignace
Paderewski (1860–1941) typifies not only the Polish patriot but the Polish
artist. Sensitive and spiritual, the virtuosity of Paderewski has given de-
light to two generations of concert-goers.

Education. At the birth of the new nation the educational problem was
enormous. Illiteracy was almost universal. There was an empty exchequer, a lack of proper school buildings, and a dearth of qualified teachers. Yet this did not dismay the state, as facts and figures show.

All possible educational agencies were put to work with almost unbelievable energy. The army became an educational institution for its illiterate soldiers. The churches, social organizations, Boy Scouts, Girl Scouts,
and Y.M.C.A. helped to combat widespread illiteracy. A movement to
establish public libraries was inaugurated. Private schools were encouraged, training schools for teachers were founded. There were kinder-
gartens, special classes for backward pupils, vocational schools, agricultural schools, state and private colleges, and universities. Buildings came
into being miraculously, the result of Polish energy and courage, and inspired by new-found freedom. Within a decade schools had increased 500
per cent. By 1932, the school system was reorganized on democratic
lines.

The Fourth Partition. As in the eighteenth century Poland was partitioned in October 1939 by her powerful neighbors into three sections: the
western part went to Germany, the eastern to Russia, and the south-central
portion became a Government General under German military domination, but outside the German customs and currency borders. Thus, over
half of Poland is now controlled by Germany, with the provinces of Posen
and Pomorze annexed outright. Germany received about 18,000,000 people, Russia 14,000,000, and Lithuania 500,000 when Vilna was restored to
its mother country.

Twenty years after the Polish National Committee headed by Dmowski
had established headquarters there, Paris again sheltered a Polish government. In 1919 there was a Poland without a government; in 1939 there
was a government without a country. When the Nazi war machine conquered France in less time than it had taken to subdue Poland, the government in exile moved to England.

Meantime, fragments of the Polish army found their way to Norway,

France, and England. It was estimated that about 75 per cent of Poland's aviators escaped to neutral countries, and though Polish planes were interned by the neutrals, the fliers formed a Polish air unit in France of nearly 6000 men. Many became aces of the R.A.F. during the summer and autumn of 1940.

Poland Today. Poland held out for six weeks against the ruthless, smashing attack of the Nazi invaders.[25] That bald fact, in the light of subsequent Nazi conquests, proclaims the caliber of the Pole. It is consistent with his patriotic past, his indestructible spirit which survived when there was no country named Poland, no flag, and no organizing center. If the nation denominated Poland between 1919 and 1939 had been in truth only twenty years old, if there had not endured a distinct, imperishable Polish spirit, the battle of Warsaw would not have been among the great battles of the world. Though disaster long blotted its name from the list of countries, and now has done so again, nothing is more characteristic of Poland than a certain basic persistence that argues foundations made not of sand but of soul.

REFERENCES

[1] Quoted from a lecture by Professor Francis J. Tschan of Pennsylvania State College.

[2] Perhaps the outstanding writer on the background of Poland is Dr. Roman Dyboski, the author of *Poland*, London: Benn, 1933; of the article " Poland " in the fourteenth edition of the *Encyclopaedia Britannica;* and of a collection of interesting lectures *Poland, Old and New*, New York: Oxford, 1926.

[3] The Peace Conference gave Poland territory in which the population was " indisputably Polish." Thus two-thirds of Poland's " frontier " was hazy, and this situation directly led to a war with Russia, a successful *coup d'état* against Lithuania to get Vilna, an unsuccessful one in Upper Silesia when Korfanty attempted to repeat the Vilna coup, three troublesome plebiscites in Allenstein, Marienwerder, and Silesia, strained relations with Czechoslovakia and Rumania over the possession of eastern Galicia, and desperate wirepulling at Paris. For a detailed treatment see Stefan Karski, *Poland Past and Present*, New York: Putnam, 1933, pp. 138–160.

[4] Germany's claims are stated by Sir Robert Donald, *The Polish Corridor and the Consequences*, London: Butterworth, 1929, and Poland's position is well presented by Casimir Smogorzewski, *Poland's Access to the Sea*, London: Allen and Unwin, 1934; see also Richard Hartshorne, " The Polish Corridor," *The Journal of Geography*, May, 1937, XXXVII: 161–176.

[5] In view of Hitler's recent solution of the problem it is interesting to re-read Frank Simonds, *Can Europe Keep the Peace?*, New York: Harper, 1932, ch. 7, "The Polish Corridor."

[6] An authoritative treatment of Polish racial minorities is found in *La Pologne et le Problème des Minorities*, J. Paprocki, ed., Warsaw: Institut pour l'Étude des Questions Minoritaires, 1935.

[7] Roman Dyboski, *Poland*, p. 155.

[8] *Ibid.*, p. 157.

[9] See A. G. Duker, *The Situation of the Jew in Poland*, American Jewish Congress, 1936, and S. Segal, *New Poland and the Jews*, New York: Furman, 1938.

[10] Other facts and interesting tables are in *Poland Today*, Warsaw: Ibi Illustrated Information Bulletins, 1939.

[11] Anti-Semitism and the economic boycott of Jewish tradesmen are well described by Raymond Buell, *Poland: Key to Europe*, New York: Knopf, 1939, pp. 292–319.

[12] For the Polish view of the German minority, as well as of other minorities, in Poland, see S. J. Paprocki, *Minority Affairs and Poland*, Warsaw: Nationality Research Institute, 1935.

[13] Until 1930, when a Polish-German minority treaty provided for equal treatment of minorities, Germany had no treaty obligation to its Polish minority although Poland was compelled by the League of Nations to extend favorable rights to its German citizens.

[14] For Poland's point of view toward the Ukrainians see M. Felinski, *The Ukrainians in Poland*, London, 1931. The Ukrainian position is contained in V. J. Kushnir, *Polish Atrocities in the West Ukraine*, Jersey City: United Ukrainian Organizations of the United States, 1931.

[15] See Dyboski, *Poland*, p. 62, for a discussion of Polish contributions to Austrian culture and government.

[16] For a vivid, firsthand description of Poland's devastation in 1920 read W. J. Rose, *Poland*, London: Penguin Books, 1939, pp. 109–124.

[17] Buell, p. 82, citing Górecki, *Poland and Her Economic Development*, London: Allen and Unwin, 1935, lists an appalling amount of wanton destruction.

[18] For details of Pilsudski's interesting life see D. R. Gillie, ed. and trans., *Joseph Pilsudski: The Memoirs of a Polish Revolutionary Soldier*, London: Faber, 1931; Landau, Rom, *Pilsudski and Poland*, London: Jarrolds, 1929; and W. R. Reddaway, *Marshal Pilsudski*, London: Routledge, 1939.

[19] See Paderewski's *Memoirs*, written by himself with the aid of Mary Lawton, New York: Scribner, 1938. See also Landau, Rom, *Ignace Paderewski, Musician and Statesman*, 1934; and Phillips, C., *Paderewski, The Story of a Modern Immortal*, New York: Macmillan, 1934.

[20] Buell, *op. cit.*, p. 85 ff., and M. W. Graham, *New Governments of Eastern Europe*, New York: Holt, p. 500, show this confusion clearly.

[21] Excellent books on Poland's economic development and natural resources include Roman Górecki, *Poland and Her Economic Development*, London, Allen and Unwin, 1935; Leopold Wellisz, *Foreign Capital in Poland*, London: Allen and Unwin, 1938; *The World Coal Mining Industry*, International Labour Office, *Studies and Reports*, Ser. B, No. 31, Geneva, 1938; and *Poland: Human and Economic Characteristics in Their Geographic Setting*, Birmingham University Service in Slavonic Countries, Monograph No. 1, 1936.

[22] A good book dealing with the peasant is H. Hessell Tiltman, *Peasant Europe*, London: Jarrolds, 1934.

[23] Naturally there were many obstacles to these reforms and none but the fourth was anywhere near completion. The first was hampered by the minority guarantees which exempted the large German estates, located in the western provinces, from subdivision. The second was a difficult matter, contrary to local customs. The third entailed the drainage of the Pripet marshes and their settlement by a surplus peasant population. The nature of the problems involved and the solutions of the government are well described in Humphrey, *Poland Today*, Warsaw: M. Arct Publishing Co., 1935, 112 ff.

[24] Until 1930 Poland solved its population problem by large-scale emigration. Since opportunities for emigrants diminished due to the world depression and worldwide unemployment, Poland began to agitate for colonies. See Buell, *op. cit.*, ch. 8, pp. 220–236, " Emigration versus Colonies."

[25] See Virgilia Sapieha, *Polish Profile*, New York, Carrick and Evans, 1940, also S. E. W. Stokes, " An Escape from Poland in War Time," *Blackwood's*, February, 1940.

SELECTED BIBLIOGRAPHY

Buell, Raymond Leslie, *Poland: Key to Europe*, New York: Knopf, 1939. Perhaps the best single book dealing with Free Poland. Written by the President of the Foreign Policy Association after a visit to Poland in 1938.

Concise Statistical Yearbook of Poland, 1937, Warsaw, 1937.

Dyboski, Roman, *Poland*, London: Benn, 1933. The author, Professor of English Literature at the University of Cracow, maintains the high level of scholarship for which Cracow is famous.

Górecki, Roman, *Poland and Her Economic Development*, London: Allen and Unwin, 1935. A clear treatment by a Polish scholar.

Graham, Malbone W., *New Governments of Eastern Europe*, New York: Holt, 1927. Prints in the Appendix 36 documents on Polish history, 1914–1927.

Humphrey, Grace, *Poland Today*, Warsaw: M. Arct Publishing Co., 1935. A delightful little book written by a keen observer. Very informative.

McBride, R. M., *Towns and People of Modern Poland*, New York: McBride, 1938.

Monographs on Poland, Birmingham University Slavonic Department, 1936–1940, (Nos. 1 and 2, *Poland: Human and Economic Characteristics in Their Geographical Setting*; No. 3, *Poland's New Codes of Law*; No. 4, *National Income of Poland: Basic Statistics*.) A noteworthy and scholarly undertaking.

Patterson, E. J., *Poland*, Modern States Series, London: Arrowsmith, 1934. Clear, factual, popular treatment.

Phillips, Charles, *Paderewski, The Story of a Modern Immortal*, New York: Macmillan, 1934. An outstanding biography written by one who knew Paderewski and Poland.

Reddaway, W. R., *Marshal Pilsudski*, London: Routledge, 1939. One of the latest biographies of the great warrior.

Rose, W. J., *Poland*, London: Penguin Books, 1939. Interesting, informative, and up-to-the-minute.

Smogorzewski, C., *Poland's Access to the Sea*, London: Allen and Unwin, 1934. A clear presentation of one of Poland's serious problems.

Thomas, W. J. and Znaniecki, F., *The Polish Peasant in Europe and America*, 2 vols., New York: Knopf, 1927. A standard work.

Wrzos, C., *Authentic Biography of Colonel Beck*, London: Hutchinson, 1939. Life of Poland's last Foreign Minister.

CHAPTER XX

The Baltic States

"WE HAVE LEARNED THE LESSON OF TIME, AND WE KNOW THREE THINGS OF WORTH;
ONLY TO SOW AND SING AND REAP IN THE LAND OF OUR BIRTH."

— RICHARD LE GALLIENNE, *The Cry of the Little Peoples*

Emergence as National States

Geography. On the eastern shores of the Baltic Sea between the Gulf of
Finland and approximately the Niemen River are located the Baltic states
of Estonia, Latvia, and Lithuania. The geography of the region accounts
for the great similarity in their history and economic activity. They occupy a low glacial plain, which to the east and particularly in the southeastern part of Lithuania is broken by a series of rolling hills from north to
south. The rather sandy soil, cool, temperate climate, and abundant rainfall make the region well adapted to agriculture, especially dairying. Lakes
and rivers are numerous. Important for rafting logs and as a potential
source of electric power, the rivers are not great arteries of transportation.
There are many marshes and bogs which supply a developing peat industry in all three countries. The Baltic states have practically no mineral
resources except extensive oil shale deposits in Estonia. Forests, however,
constitute a major natural resource, 19.6 per cent of Estonia, 29 per cent
of Latvia, and 19 per cent of Lithuania being covered with what literally
amounts to " green gold."

Not only has the location on the Baltic Sea led to important fishing and maritime developments in Estonia and Latvia, and provided
Lithuania and Latvia with rich supplies of amber, but it has also made the
area the *entrepôt* of trade between Russia and the west. The many indentations and the sweeping expanse of the Gulf of Riga provide Estonia with
725 miles and Latvia with 306 miles of coastline. Lithuania is far less fortunate in this respect and without the Memel area was reduced to a stretch of
13 miles of coastline with only one or two small fishing harbors. In addition to her extensive coastline Estonia controlled many islands along the
coast. The chief ports of Estonia, Narva, Tallinn (Reval), Paldiski (Baltic
Port) on the Gulf of Finland and Pärnu (Pernau) on the west coast, the
Latvian ports of Riga, Liepaja (Libau) and Ventspils (Windau), and the
Lithuanian-German port of Klaipeda (Memel), have long been important
commercial centers. Narva is apt to be icebound for a time each winter

---

This chapter by Ernst C. Helmreich, Associate Professor of History and Government, Bowdoin College.

and icebreakers must be used at Tallinn, Paldiski, and Riga. Yet the fact that the Baltic peoples have possessed the only western ice-free ports for the vast Russian hinterland has been fateful for their political independence. Instead of acting as buffers between east and west, Slav and German, Communism and Fascism, the Baltic peoples would have preferred to be a bridge uniting the two cultures.

Area. The three Baltic states have an area about that of England and Wales. Latvia is the largest with 25,409 square miles, or about the area of Belgium and the Netherlands combined. Lithuania comes next with 20,-577 square miles, to which at different times were added the Memel district of 976 square miles with 145,000 people and the Vilna territory of 2600 square miles with 457,500 people. Estonia had an area of 18,359 square miles. Belgium or the Netherlands, however, each exceeded the population of the three states combined. As estimated in January, 1939 the population figures stood: Lithuania 2,572,801, Latvia 1,994,506, and Estonia 1,134,000. Lithuania had, next to Poland, the highest birth rate in northern Europe. All three states were primarily rural, the only large cities being Tallinn, Riga, Kaunas, and Vilna.

Early History. The ethnographic complexity of this borderland can best be explained by a rapid historical survey.[1] From the earliest times the

NATIONALITY AND RELIGION IN THE BALTIC STATES[2]

	ESTONIA		LATVIA		LITHUANIA	
DATE OF CENSUS	1934		1935		1923	
	Number	Per Cent	Number	Per Cent	Number	Per Cent
I. Nationalities						
Estonians	997,923	88.2	7,014	.36		
Latvians	5,632	.5	1,472,612	75.5	14,883	.73
Lithuanians			22,913	1.19	1,701,863	83.88
Germans	16,346	1.5	62,144	3.19	29,231	1.44
Russians	92,656	8.5	233,366	11.97	54,881	2.70
Poles			48,949	2.51	65,599	3.23
Swedes	7,641	.7	292	.02		
Livonians			944	.07		
Jews	4,434	.4	93,479	4.79	153,743	7.58
Others	1,558	.2	7,710	.4	8,771	.44
Total of minorities	128,267	11.8	476,811	24.5	327,108	16.12
II. Religions						
Lutheran	874,026	78.2	1,094,787	56.6	178,549	8.8
Roman Catholic	2,327	.2	476,963	23.7	1,633,322	80.5
Orthodox	212,764	19.0	174,389	8.9	50,724	2.5
Old Believers			107,195	4.8		
Jews	4,302	.4	93,406	4.9	148,115	7.3
Others	24,308	2.2	3,762	1.1	18,261	.9

Esths, Letts, and Lithuanians have occupied the shores of the Baltic. The latter two are today the sole representatives of a distinct Aestian or Baltic branch of the Indo-Germanic family. Today Lithuanian is the closest to ancient Sanskrit of any spoken language. In Latvia there is also a tiny remnant (about one thousand) of the Livonians (Livs) with whom the German merchants first came in contact and after whom they named Livonia, the modern Latvia. The Livs have in the course of time been assimilated by the Latvians, but are racially akin to the Estonians. The latter are of Mongolian origin and belong to the Ugro-Finnish group, like the modern Finns and Magyars.

Germanic Conquests. The early Vikings, who from the ninth to the twelfth centuries pushed trading caravans — in which Baltic amber played an important role — down the river system of Russia to Constantinople and points eastward, were the first to dominate the Baltic natives. The Danes established control over northern Estonia and remained there until 1346, when the last prince sold his territories to the Teutonic Knights. The Germans had originally penetrated the region as merchants and missionaries, and when in 1200 the Pope proclaimed a crusade against the Baltic pagans the German Knights of the Sword (later amalgamated with the Order of Teutonic Knights) responded to the call. They established a base at Riga and gradually extended their territories, primarily to the west, and northward into the land of the Esths. The Lithuanians to the south never really came under the jurisdiction of the Knights, and constituted a sort of wedge between the eastern and western possessions of the Teutonic Order. Only in the region of Memel did the Order make any real conquest of Lithuanians. In the feudal ecclesiastical state of the Teutonic Knights, the Germans became the land-owning class and remained so down to 1919. With the Reformation, the Teutonic Order was secularized and the inhabitants adopted the Lutheran faith. While the native Letts and Esths had been reduced to serfdom by the Teutonic Order, there was no attempt to exterminate or Germanize them. It was to the advantage of the aristocracy to maintain the native population, for German peasants never followed the Knights to this remote colony. The Lutheran clergy, although dominated by the aristocracy, did much to encourage the development of a native written language, for a chief tenet of Protestantism is that the service should be in the language of the people and that they should be able to read and study their Bibles.

The Lithuanians, on the other hand, under the leadership of energetic dukes, created a large independent Grand Duchy of Lithuania, extending from the Baltic to the Black Sea. In 1385 Grand Duke Jagello married Jadwiga, Queen of Poland, and established a personal union between the two countries. Dominant at first, Lithuanian influence gradually receded before the rising might of Poland. Yet the Lithuanians remained intensely conscious of their nationality and this period of subservience largely accounts for their persistent antagonism to Poland. Lithuania, unlike Estonia and Latvia, never acquired a dominant German land-holding aristocracy, nor did the Reformation affect Lithuania, which remained a Catholic country.

The Swedish Period. The Reformation and the difficulty of warding off repeated attacks of the expanding Russian state brought the final dissolution of the Teutonic Order. In 1561 the City of Reval (Tallinn) and the nobility of northern Estonia took the oath of allegiance to the King of Sweden. The Polish-Lithuanian state annexed most of modern Latvia, but was later forced to cede a great part of this territory to the Swedes. Thus Estonia and Latvia were subjected to an extended period of Swedish rule. Protestantism was firmly established, education encouraged, the University of Dorpat (Tartu) founded, and above all the privileges of the German Baltic barons were curtailed. So enlightened was Swedish rule that the phrase " in the good old Swedish times " has become a byword in this region. To this day Swedish communities have maintained themselves on some of the Estonian islands and constitute a minute ethnographic minority. In 1710, as a result of victories in the Great Northern War, Czar Peter the Great occupied Estonia and most of modern Latvia. Lithuania, which throughout this period was subject to the troubled and disorganized rule of Poland, did not come under Russian domination until the partitions of Poland at the end of the eighteenth century.

The Russian Period. The period of Russian domination for the first time brought the three peoples under one sovereign. And yet it did not bring uniformity of rule. The privileged position which was always accorded to the Baltic barons by the Russian government, and the dominance of this aristocracy in the peculiar class system of local government, set Estonia and Latvia apart. Lithuania, because of its historic connection with Poland, shared the vicissitudes of that country. Thus from 1864 to 1904 the Lithuanians were forbidden to print books in Latin characters, and were forced to use the cyrillic alphabet. This attempt to convert Lithuanian into a Slavic language retarded intellectual advance. People were forced to rely even on prayer books smuggled into the country from the Lithuanian press in Germany. In Russia Roman Catholicism was pretty much synonymous with Polish nationalism and treason, and special measures against their religion tried the Lithuanians severely.

In the last decades of the nineteenth century more uniformity was established in the administration of the " Northwestern Provinces " and the whole Baltic territory, not merely Lithuania, suffered under a militant policy of Russification. This policy furnishes the background to the subsequent history of the Baltic peoples. The Slavic settlements and the Orthodox church flourished, the Russian language came into wide use, the railways and the industrial resources of the region were developed in relation to the Russian territories. Industrialization brought a shift of population to the cities of Estonia and Latvia, fostered the growth of a native bourgeoisie, and created a relatively small but nationally conscious proletariat. Socialism, opposition to the Czar, and nationalism were combined with the revolutionary liberal movement in Russia proper. Finally, while serfdom was abolished, no landed peasantry was really created. German, Russian, and Polish nobility still remained the dominant landlords. Thus racial antagonism came to strengthen the antagonism aroused by the demand of the peasantry for more land. The growth of national consciousness among all classes was fanned by intellectuals. Control of municipal councils passed into native hands; schools, cooperatives and banks were organized; and a national press and literature was created.[3]

The Establishment of Independence. The policy of Russification not only failed to obliterate the nationalist movement, but actually stimulated it. The Russian revolution of 1905 aroused vain hopes of autonomy among the Baltic peoples. The defeat and disintegration of the Russian Empire in the First World War brought independence. Lithuania and part of Latvia were overrun by German troops in 1915. The retreating Russians forced many people to evacuate their homes and systematically destroyed property. It was not until September, 1917 that German troops captured Riga. By February, 1918 the rest of Latvia and Estonia was occupied, and in the Treaty of Brest-Litovsk approximately the territory south of Riga was ceded to Germany, while the territory north of it was to be occupied by Germany pending a final settlement. The German occupation, combined with the Russian revolutions, created immense confusion in the Baltic regions. The armistice of November 11, 1918 led to the gradual withdrawal of German troops, although the armistice terms granted to Germany certain temporary rights of occupation. The Bolsheviks again sent troops into the provinces; White Russians organized a counterrevolution; the Baltic Germans recruited their own *Landwehr;* the German forces under von de Goltz and later freebooters under Avalov-Bermondt tried to salvage what they could. In this welter of conflict Estonia, Latvia, and Lithuania at the point of the sword cleared their lands of hostile forces. Their achievements were primarily due to their own efforts, although German aid against the Russians in the beginning, and later some help from an English naval squadron and French support of Poland in the conflict with the Bolsheviks, should not be forgotten.

Estonia. The establishment of independent governments in each country followed somewhat different patterns. Upon the overthrow of the Czar in the spring of 1917 Estonia demanded and received local autonomy. An Estonian Council was elected on July 7–8, 1917, and chose Kon-

stantin Paets as President.   After the Bolshevik revolution, the Estonian
Council proclaimed itself the supreme authority.   The Bolsheviks invaded
the country but were soon forced to withdraw and on February 24, 1918
independence was declared.   The next day the Germans occupied Tallinn
(Reval) and soon Paets and other leaders were again in exile.   The German
plan, sponsored by the Baltic barons, called for the creation of a Baltic
duchy to be ruled by a German prince, and on April 11, 1918 the Kaiser
graciously consented to this arrangement.   Upon Germany's defeat the
Estonian Council reconvened and on November 11, 1918 Paets resumed
direction of affairs.   In April, 1919 a constitutional assembly was elected
and a bourgeois coalition under Otto Strandman came into power.   Finally on February 2, 1920, the Treaty of Tartu was signed with Russia.
On the east, Estonia obtained a maximum water boundary running through
long Lake Peipsi.   Her Latvian boundary was drawn in March, 1920 with
the aid of a British mediator.   The Soviet government promised to restore
many objects which had been taken from the territory, renounced all
rights over real and personal property, and promised to pay Estonia 15
million gold rubles.   It was on the whole a generous settlement, but even
so the monetary payment by no means equalled the bank deposits and
property which had been carried off.

Latvia.   The Russian revolution of March, 1917 did not alter the status
of Latvia, since that country was largely occupied by German forces.
Although some concessions were made, the provisional government at Petrograd refused to grant to those Latvians who were not under German occupation the measure of autonomy which was bestowed on Estonia.   Immediately after the Bolshevik revolution Latvian representatives from the
unoccupied area met at Walk and proclaimed a Latvian National Council.
Within the German occupied territory Karlis Ulmanis already had formed
a Latvian Democratic Bloc.   With the defeat of Germany in November,
1918 a National Assembly was created by the amalgamation of the different
councils, and a provisional government headed by Ulmanis was established.
The Russian advance of a few months later forced this government to
move from Riga to Libau.   What took place in Riga brings home the nature of this Baltic warfare.   The Bolshevik " occupation which lasted from
January till May of the year 1919 cost Riga the lives of 3,632 citizens, all
shot after trial; 1,400 who were killed without any official death sentence
being pronounced; while the deaths from starvation amounted to 8,590.
. . . In addition to this more than twenty thousand people had been removed by the Reds from the Inner City, and placed in concentration camps
on the barren islands of the Daugava [Düna] where they were slowly dying of privation and exposure." [4]   Finally, with the aid of Estonian and
other troops, the Russian forces were ejected.   In April, 1920 elections
were held for a Constituent Assembly and on August 11, the Peace of Riga

was signed with Russia. This was modeled on the Estonian-Russian treaty.

Lithuania. Towards the end of 1915 a group of intellectuals met in Vilna and designated a committee to defend the interests of Lithuanians against the German army of occupation. At the head of the committee was Antanas Smetona, who had been the leader of the nationalist party since 1905, and later was to become the perennial President of Lithuania. In September, 1917 the German authorities, although not permitting an election, encouraged the calling of a conference of Lithuanian leaders which nominated a National Council (Taryba) of 20 members and adopted a resolution favoring the establishment of an independent Lithuanian state. On February 16, 1918 the Taryba proclaimed the independence of Lithuania and a month later, the Kaiser approved an act recognizing an independent state of Lithuania. On October 18 the Taryba adopted a provisional constitution; after the defeat of Germany a government with Smetona as President and Professor Augustinas Voldemaras as Premier was created.

Lithuania played its share in the confused warfare of the next years and on July 20, 1920 signed a peace treaty with Russia at Moscow. There were the usual provisions in regard to restitution of property and Russia agreed to pay 3,000,000 gold rubles. The boundaries as drawn gave Lithuania the city and district of Vilna which unfortunately had been occupied by the Poles since April, 1919. In the summer of 1920, however, the Russian forces drove the Poles from the city and when they in turn were forced to evacuate in August, the Lithuanians, in accordance with the terms of the Treaty of Moscow, occupied the city. Conflict soon broke out with advancing Polish units and Poland also appealed to the League for mediation.[5] The League proposed the so-called Curzon line which would give Vilna to Lithuania, but neighboring territory to Poland. A similar demarcation was agreed to by direct negotiations between Poland and Lithuania at Suvalki on October 7, 1920. Before this agreement could be put into effect, General Zeligowski, ostensibly acting independently but actually under orders of Marshal Pilsudski, entered Vilna and established a regime which later united with Poland.

A complicated series of negotiations involving the League of Nations followed, but in the end the powers recognized the Polish *fait accompli*. This marks the failure of international diplomacy to solve a problem typical of post-war Europe, where historic claims (Vilna was the ancient capital of Lithuania) and the rights of nationalities (the city was overwhelmingly Polish in population) conflicted. Lithuania never recognized the Polish seizure and the boundary between the two countries remained closed until March, 1938. Polish possession of Vilna gave Poland a sort of corridor extending up to the Latvian border, thereby cutting off Lithuania from any direct contact with Russia.

Memel. Lithuania obtained a vital outlet on the Baltic by seizing in 1923 the Memel territory which had been taken from Germany in 1919 and placed under the jurisdiction of the Allied Powers. Conflicting political interests, chiefly due to France's ardent support of Poland, had prevented the Allies from ever carrying out their expressed intention of turning the city over to Lithuania. The Allied Powers in 1924 recognized Lithuania's seizure, but insisted that the Memel territory be given a great measure of local autonomy. With this territory Lithuania obtained an area of about 976 square miles and a population of 145,000, of whom about half were German-speaking and half Lithuanian-speaking. Many of the latter were bilingual and almost all were Protestant. This was a natural result of the fact that "for close upon seven centuries Memel was uninterruptedly under German rule." [6]

Period of Independence

Political Development. With the cessation of hostilities and the conclusion of peace the governments in each of the three states were faced with a multitude of problems. Six years of warfare left farms, homes, and industries devastated. Post-war reconstruction was a difficult task for established governments. In the Baltic states not only was it necessary to formulate constitutions, but virtually a new administrative and judicial service had to be created, for under Russian rule there had not been much opportunity for the "subject nationalities" to participate in government. The different minorities had to be provided for, and complicated problems of foreign affairs dealt with. The large number of landless farm laborers made a liquidation of the large estates imperative. Agriculture and industry had to be fostered, stable currencies and commercial relations established, education and the arts brought to flower.

Constitutions and Parties. All three countries adopted democratic constitutions, containing elaborate bills of rights, and providing for universal suffrage, proportional representation, a ministry responsible to a unicameral legislature, and the wide use of the initiative and referendum. The Weimar constitution in Germany more than any other served as a model, and just as in Germany certain weaknesses soon appeared. Proportional representation, with party lists taking the place of voting for individuals, brought about an absurd multiplication of parties. In 1925, for example, no less than twenty-eight parties presented lists to the Latvian voters. This made coalition cabinets necessary, leading in turn to frequent ministerial changes, and much time wasted in party bargaining. The fear of a strong executive, which in the Estonian constitution even did away with the office of President, had led to the instability of government. Between 1920 and 1934 there were eighteen cabinets in Estonia and sixteen in Latvia, while between 1920 and 1926 there were nine in Lithuania.

In spite of this complexity, it is possible to make certain generalizations on party trends in all three states. In each there were certain Rightist groups, chiefly religious in their affiliations, anxious to support the existing economic order.[7] The agrarian parties were the strongest in point of numbers. They were intensely nationalist in sentiment, hence anti-Russian and anti-Communist. Their chief aim was land reform, and once this was accomplished they tended to become somewhat conservative. Beside these groups stood a number of more liberal bourgeois parties, and radical working-class groups, including government employees and artisans, who favored in greater or less degree moderate state socialization of industry. The Communist Party had no legal existence in any of these states.

Fascism: Lithuania. After the Pilsudski *coup* of 1926 in Poland, parties with Fascist leanings began to appear in the Baltic states. In Lithuania the nationalist party in 1926 engineered the overthrow of the constitutional government in favor of a dictatorship headed by Smetona as President and Voldemaras as Prime Minister. Voldemaras shaped the new constitution of 1928, drove out opposing leaders, and formed a Fascist corps, the " Iron Wolf," to support his regime. Yet the personal prestige of President Smetona was sufficient to oust Voldemaras in 1929, when his intransigence as to Vilna and Poland became inconvenient. He was supplanted by Juozas Tubelis, who managed to remain Premier until 1938. Subsequently Voldemaras was imprisoned for an attempted *coup* in 1934, but was pardoned in 1938.

Meanwhile the National Party became a typical Fascist organization based on the leader-principle, with Smetona as its head. For ten years the legislature was not convened. An electoral law of 1936 reduced the size of the legislature (Seimas) to 49 members and provided for the nomination of candidates by local government councils instead of by parties. Since the local governments were controlled, it is not surprising that the majority of deputies were government supporters. The dictatorship was not affected by the promulgation of a new constitution on May 12, 1938. Under this document the President was still to be indirectly elected for a term of seven years and he was granted wide powers.

Estonia. In Estonia it was not until 1931 that pressure for a stronger executive became marked. The " Liberators," a group originating among ex-service men, favored the creation of an executive with considerable power, and abolition of the system of voting by lists. They were in direct opposition to the Social Democrats, who wanted no President, while between the two stood the Agrarians, favoring moderate reform. The proposals of the Liberators were accepted by a huge majority at a popular referendum in 1933, indicating that the peasants had gone over to their side. A new constitution was proclaimed, and Paets assumed the provisional presidency.

Meanwhile the Liberators swept the municipal elections in January, 1934 and made promises in line with the best Fascist technique in other countries. Already the Liberators were suspected of affiliations with the Nazi Party in Germany and it was on this score that Paets suddenly proclaimed a state of emergency. General Laidoner, the hero of the fight for liberation, was made commander-in-chief with extraordinary powers. Four hundred leaders of the Liberators were arrested and their party was dissolved. Paets, as an official account phrases it, had taken " democracy in safe keeping until political passions had calmed and elections could once more be held on clearly defined points." [8] It was a Pyrrhic victory for the parliamentarians, yet the dictatorship had none of the more forbidding aspects of Fascism. The labor unions continued to function, strikes and lockouts were permitted,[9] no race hatred was proclaimed, and the government did make an effort to retain the forms of democracy. In 1938 a new constitution gave greater legality to the dictatorship, and in some quarters was hailed as a return to democracy.

Latvia. Latvia possessed an extraordinary military organization, known as the *Aizsargi* (Civil Guards), organized in 1918 to maintain order behind the lines, which developed into a powerful, voluntary, unpaid force of men and women. Such an organization bore the germs of Fascism.

As early as 1927 political parties with Fascist leanings appeared. As an antidote, a Social-Democratic armed and uniformed *Workers' Sporting Club* was formed with the support of the government. Nevertheless the nationalist-Fascist society, *Pehr Konkrusts*, acquired more power. Political strife grew in intensity. On May 15, 1934 Premier Ulmanis, the leader of the Peasant Union, a party which had always taken a prominent part in Latvian politics, ordered the dissolution of the legislature and the cessation of all party activity. Strikes and lockouts were forbidden, martial law was proclaimed and renewed from time to time until February, 1938 when it was replaced by a similar institution called " Law for the Defense of the State." Two years after his *coup*, on the expiration of President Kresis' term of office, Ulmanis had himself elected President. It was largely because of the demonstrations of loyalty and aid from the *Aizsargi* that the authoritarian régime could be established so easily.

With the constitution in abeyance, executive and legislative power was concentrated in the hands of Ulmanis and the Cabinet. Two advisory councils, the Economic Council and the State Cultural Council, eventually came into being. The former (reminiscent of the Italian system) was made up of representatives of the corporations — or chambers as they are called in Latvia — of Commerce and Industry, Agriculture, Artisans, and Labor. Some of these were organized as far back as 1935 and played an important part in their respective fields of activity.[10] The Economic Council itself did not meet until January, 1938. The State Cultural Council, consisting of the Chamber of Art and Literature and the Chamber of Professions, was established by a law of May 5, 1938.

The Dictatorships. While influenced no doubt by happenings in other countries, the dictatorships in the Baltic states have been more moderate. In no case were they bolstered by any particular ideology. The state under authoritarian rule extended its influence in the direction of what might be termed state capitalism. Substantial efforts were made to continue democratic forms. Individual ministers were dropped and at times the whole ministry reconstituted, but the new officials governed much as the preceding ones. The free functioning of political parties and the effectual cooperation of a freely elected legislative body, however, remained banned. The tendency developed to rely on advisory corporative bodies. The Baltic dictatorships differed from those in Italy or Germany in that no really new parties or men overthrew the established governments. Paets in Estonia, Ulmanis in Latvia, and Smetona in Lithuania were leaders in the fight for independence, the establishment of democratic governments, and yet were key men in the dictatorial regimes. In many ways their rule was a " dictatorship of the right people " so far as dictatorship can ever fulfill that requirement.

Minority Problems: Estonia and Latvia. Estonia and Latvia made declarations to the League of Nations in 1923 which recognized the right of minorities to appeal to the League Council. Lithuania undertook wider obligations, similar to those assumed by Poland. The generous minority policies as outlined in the first democratic constitutions were indeed later curtailed, but that was equally true of the civil rights of the whole population. The establishment of the System of Chambers in Latvia, for example, meant the dissolution of the old German guilds, which the German minority resented, but it also caused the Latvian businessman to change his ways and conform to the state pattern.

Estonia had the best record in the treatment of minority populations. The Law of Cultural Autonomy of 1925 provided a model in this respect. Any minority of over 3000 persons could establish a Cultural Council which controlled educational, cultural, and charitable institutions in respect to its minority, could collect taxes and also had certain funds from the state treasury at its disposal. Only Germans and Jews established such Councils, since the other minorities, being concentrated in certain localities, felt that they had sufficient voice through their control of local government. This system worked remarkably well.[11] After the evacuation of the German minority in the autumn of 1939 the German Cultural Council was dissolved.

In Latvia, under a law of 1919, German, Russian, White Russian, Jewish, and Polish councils were established to control their respective schools. In 1929 a Cabinet crisis was occasioned when the Celmins ministry decided to grant a subsidy for the erection of a German war memorial. From then on, especially after the establishment of the dictatorship in 1934, the position of the minorities tended to deteriorate. Latvian was made the sole language in the legislature and in many other public institutions, Riga cathedral was removed from the control of Germans, all public and private economic undertakings had to conduct their books and business correspondence in Latvian, and the old German guilds were replaced. With the withdrawal of the Germans in 1939, the most aggressive minority was liquidated.

Lithuania. Lithuania's treatment of minorities was always complicated by political difficulties with Poland and Germany. Starting out, on the whole, with a generous policy, the treatment of minorities grew less liberal. There were periodic anti-Semitic riots, but no systematic persecution. The possession of Memel gave the Lithuanian government no end of difficulty. There can be no doubt that the overwhelming majority of the inhabitants constantly looked forward to reunion with Germany. This alone was a serious enough problem. In addition the Allied Powers in establishing an autonomous regime for that territory devised a fine theoretical scheme, but one that made political strife inevitable. There was to be a governor appointed by the President of Lithuania, who in turn appointed the President of a Directorate composed of five citizens. This directory was made responsible to a chamber elected by proportional representation. The pro-German parties never obtained less than 24 out of the 29 seats in the chamber. In actuality the governor and directory tended to be Lithuanian in sympathy. When a directorate was named that really had the confidence of the chamber, it could not get along with the Lithuanian governor. The constant bickering between administrative and legislative authorities made orderly government impossible. The growth of National Socialism both in Germany and in Memel heightened the problem, and led to a bitter trade war between Lithuania and Germany which reached its height in 1935. The Germans in Memel made constant use of their right to appeal to the Allied Powers who exercised a certain right of supervision over the autonomous regime. It was largely because of pressure by these powers and the vociferous threats of Germany that representative institutions were maintained in Memel even after they had disappeared in Lithuania.

The Germans within Lithuania proper were largely peasants who had no close bonds with Germany and constituted no real minority problem. The constant friction with Poland over Vilna made the situation of the small Polish minority extremely difficult. On the acquisition of Vilna in October, 1939 Lithuania set out to make Lithuanians out of this mixed ethnographic population. The Polish university at Vilna was closed and a Lithuanian one was organized. Lithuanian became the official language even for religious instruction, which aroused the Pope to protest on behalf of the Polish Catholic population.

Foreign Policy. Following the conclusion of the peace treaties with Russia, *de jure* recognition of their independent status was generally accorded to the Baltic states. In September, 1921 they were admitted to the League of Nations. Strong support of the League, however, did not preclude interest in regional agreements in conformity with obligations under the Covenant.

From 1920 to 1925 there were various conferences and attempts to form a large Baltic bloc consisting of Finland, Estonia, Latvia, Lithuania, and Poland. The bitter conflict between the latter two countries over Vilna and the increasing cooperation of Finland with the Scandinavian countries led to the abandonment of these schemes. Instead, closer cooperation between Estonia, Latvia, and Lithuania became a reality. In 1921 Estonia and Latvia reached a temporary agreement which was converted into a definitive defensive Treaty of Alliance on November 1, 1923. Military assistance was promised if either ally were attacked. A separate agreement called for the creation of a customs union, but although there were repeated negotiations, to some of which Lithuania was party, this never materialized. Yet these conferences strengthened the desire for a small Baltic union. Had it not been for Lithuania's difficulties with Poland over Vilna, and with Germany over Memel, greater and more rapid progress would have been made.

In 1934 Estonia and Latvia extended their alliance treaty. Henceforth the two countries were to be represented at all international conferences by a single delegate. The growing international tension brought her isolation home to Lithuania. Proposals were made to Estonia and Latvia, and the result was a Treaty of Good Understanding and Cooperation, a " Baltic Entente " which came into force on November 3, 1934.

Relations with Germany and Russia. From the establishment of independence the Baltic states were faced with the problem of maintaining friendly relations with Germany and Russia. The Memel question in Lithuania, various problems, never acute but omnipresent, in connection with the Baltic barons in Estonia and Latvia, and constant fear of German expansion always prevented a full German orientation of policy. Fear of Russian expansion and opposition to Communism prevented a pro-Russian orientation. The attempt to conclude a Soviet-Baltic disarmament pact in 1922 failed, largely because Russia was only interested in pushing disarmament provisions while Poland and the Baltic states stressed the non-aggression pact which was to accompany the agreement. The Soviet Union also refused to promise that it would terminate its propaganda in the succession states. Russia continued to make overtures, various treaties were formulated and some concluded with individual states, notably a non-aggression pact with Lithuania in September, 1926 and a commercial treaty with Latvia in July, 1927. All three powers eventually signed with Russia the Litvinov Protocol (1928–1929) centering about a regional renunciation of war as an instrument of national policy. In 1932 Latvia and Estonia finally signed the non-aggression pacts which Russia had been angling for. But the negotiations of 1934 and 1935 for an Eastern Pact to guarantee the security of existing frontiers came to naught. The Baltic states, between the hammer of Bolshevism and the anvil of Nazism, insisted that Germany as well as Russia and Poland should join in the guarantee of their frontiers. Germany, while willing to make bilateral non-aggression pacts, refused to enter any agreement which involved the principle of mutual assistance.

Lithuania's claims to Vilna, let alone the dubious foreign policy of Poland, prevented a Polish alignment. Partly as a result of the rise of Nazi Germany, partly because of a new governmental trade policy in Great Britain which led to new trade treaties with the Baltic states, English influence, always strong, was greatly enhanced after 1933. A significant sign was the fact that in 1934 English became the first compulsory foreign language in Estonian and Latvian schools. Following this example, Lithuania in 1935 made English the first compulsory language in boys' schools. *The Baltic Times*, the first international English newspaper in the Baltic states, was founded at Tallinn in 1932. Unfortunately the English connection was of little use to the Baltic states in 1939–1940, when Russia undertook to absorb them.

Economic Development: Land Reforms. Basic for the history of the economic development of all three Baltic states are the agrarian reforms which were enacted in the first years of independence.[12] In 1918, 58 per cent of the cultivated lands in Estonia, 60 per cent in Latvia and about 50 per cent in Lithuania were in large estates. The large estates in Estonia of which there were 1149 with an average size of 5221 acres were largely in the possession of the German Baltic barons. Outside of about fifty Latvians, the estate holders in Latvia were Germans, Russians, and Poles, while in Lithuania, Russians and Poles predominated. Thus when the lands were confiscated, no compensation being made in Latvia and only belated nominal compensation in Estonia and Lithuania, the cry of minority persecution arose. In each case estate owners were permitted to retain some land, not to exceed 330 acres in Estonia, 125 to 250 acres in Latvia, and 200 acres in Lithuania. The forests were declared state property. The confiscated lands were leased or sold under favorable terms to small proprietors, who also received material aid in building new homesteads. These land reform measures have been carried out with surprisingly few exceptions, as is indicated by the following table.

NUMBER AND SIZE OF LAND HOLDINGS [13]

Size of Holdings	Estonia	Latvia	Lithuania
Under 25 acres	46,000	109,000	132,000
From 25 to 50 acres	35,000	51,000	93,000
From 50 to 75 acres	24,000	24,000	34,000
From 75 to 125 acres	22,000	21,000	21,000
From 125 to 250 acres	6,000	18,000	6,000
Over 250 acres	500	2,000	1,000

Agricultural Progress. This redistribution of land at first resulted in a decline in production, for the small farms were not operated as efficiently as the scientifically managed large estates had been. This has been overcome. Cooperatives, notably in the dairying industry, have been active, with government encouragement, in stimulating production and above all in providing better marketing conditions.[14] Agricultural schools were developed, experiment stations established, blooded stock imported, and in countless ways the governments furthered the adoption of more scientific agricultural methods. With the collapse of world markets as a result of the economic depression, the governments undertook more direct aids to the farmer. Notably in Estonia and Latvia, where there was a shortage of agricultural laborers, greater use of agricultural machinery was stressed. Purchase of machinery was subsidized and opportunity provided for renting certain machines from government depots. Under government supervision more acreage was shifted to grain production; cereal imports were no longer important. Yield per acre increased. Much of the regulation of the agricultural industry was accomplished by the government through the fixing of prices for farm products. Since world prices were often lower than fixed prices, exports had to be subsidized. Government inspectors rigorously maintained the quality of the butter, eggs, bacon, and other meat products which were the chief items of export, England and Germany being normally the largest purchasers. Flax, linseed, and potatoes (many used for distilling) are important products in all three states.

Agricultural policy was much the same in the three countries. All three showed the benevolent effect of the active participation of government in directing and stimulating agricultural production. Latvia, so long under the able leadership of Ulmanis, himself an agricultural expert, probably made the greatest advance.

Industry. In order to overcome the lack of native capital many industries were directly developed by the state. A large amount of the income of the governments was derived from monopolies and various state enterprises. Before the establishment of independence Estonia and Latvia had important chemical, metal, shipbuilding, and above all textile industries. The loss of Russian raw materials, and above all of the Russian market, necessitated great readjustments. Attention was first concentrated on industries essential to local requirements. With the onslaught of the depression, the governments took drastic measures to conserve foreign exchange by developing home industries. In Estonia " large investments were made and government controlled companies formed, notably in the oilshale, brick, peat, wood pulp and textile industries. . . . The result was a record year in industrial production for 1939. Large scale industries in 1938 for the first time since Estonia's independence used 53 per cent of domestic raw materials and an even larger per cent is estimated for 1939." This quotation from the report of the American consul in Tallinn of January 25, 1940 indicates the industrial trend not only in Estonia but in Latvia.

Unlike her sister republics, Lithuania did not have an important industrial development before the First World War. In accordance with the universal post-war urge toward self-sufficiency, great efforts toward industrialization were made. With 1929 taken as 100, the aggregate production index of Lithuanian industry rose to 272 in 1937, while world production rose only to 102.5 during the same period.[15] In spite of great progress, Lithuania industry is insignificant compared to agriculture. The loss of Memel in 1939 was a severe blow, for in 1937 27.5 per cent of Lithuanian industry was located in that territory, and 75.5 per cent of the exports and 68.2 per cent of the imports passed through the port of Memel.[16]

In all three states the well-administered state forests furnished the basis of important woodworking industries. Lumber, plywood, and pulp have been important articles of export. Each country obtained a loan from the Swedish Match Monopoly which in return was granted control of the match industry. Peat has been utilized in increasing quantities.

Estonia possesses the only valuable mineral resources. Its oil shale is so rich that it can be used as fuel in the raw state. Production has risen from 46,125 metric tons in 1920 to 1,642,165 tons in 1939. The combined value of shale oil and gasoline amounted to 8,400,000 krones. Estonia also has an important cement industry and phosphate deposits which the state began to exploit for fertilizer. Mention should also be made of the completion in 1939 of the large government dam at Kegums, Latvia.

Foreign Trade. Most-favored-nation treaties, which were formerly the basis of all trading relations, always contained the so-called Baltic Clause which permitted the Baltic states to grant some special concessions to each other. The economy of the three states was similar, each exporting the same products, and trade among themselves was not significant. In recent years, great efforts were made to stimulate exports, and through state propaganda and by means of state regulation a balanced foreign trade was achieved. Departure from the gold standard in Estonia in 1933, and in Latvia in 1936 helped to stimulate exports. Lithuania firmly avoided any official devaluation but had to rely on subsidies. With a somewhat lower standard of living, Lithuanian peasants seemed more willing to accept exceedingly low prices for their products and so exports could be continued.

Trade relations were most active with Germany and England, the former furnishing more of the imports, the latter buying more of the exports. Trade with the U.S.S.R. was always small.[17]

About 18 per cent of the population in Estonia, 13.5 per cent in Latvia, and 6.4 per cent in Lithuania were engaged in industry. Each country adopted various types of social insurance.

Cultural Development. While politically young, each of the Baltic states had an ancient cultural heritage. The folkways have left their imprint in song and legend, and the customs of the peasantry provide a rich field for the student of folklore. Only after 1918 were there national governments to encourage a national culture. Art, literature, and education were for generations closely associated with religion.

Religion. The relation of church to state was solved in Estonia and Latvia with comparative ease. Religious instruction became a regular part of the Estonian school curriculum in 1923. Church and state were theoretically separated, although the law of 1934 maintained a certain amount of cooperation between the spiritual and temporal power. The Lutheran churches until 1919 had been largely supported from their own estates and were under the control of patrons, that is the big landed proprietors. In the new state the churches were directly in the hands of the parishioners, and the clergy were headed by a bishop. The Orthodox church was autonomous, the Patriarch being consecrated at Constantinople.

In Latvia, the Lutheran church had much the same history as the church in Estonia. The Orthodox and Roman Catholics were concentrated in the province of Latgale. In May, 1922 a concordat was concluded with the Papacy. This agreement was mutually respected. Religious liberty always existed under the republic. Church and state were officially separated, although subsidies were paid from the state treasury, and ecclesiastical affairs were subject to some supervision by the Ministry of the Interior. Religious instruction was carried on in all schools, each denomination being entitled to claim special instruction if there were ten pupils of that particular faith in a school.

The Catholic Christian Democratic Party always played an important part in Catholic Lithuania, yet relations between the Vatican and the government were usually strained. This was due to the Vatican's realistic support of Poland's claims to Vilna. In 1925 negotiations for a concordat were broken off when the Vatican in a concordat with Poland placed Vilna under the Polish episcopate. Finally in 1927 a concordat was concluded but this only led to further disputes and protests. In 1931 diplomatic relations with the Vatican were broken off.

Education. Great emphasis was placed by the new states on public education.[18] In Estonia and Latvia attendance at an elementary school for at least six years was obligatory, and a splendid system of secondary, vocational and continuation schools was provided. Lithuania, to start with, was much less advanced educationally than her sister republics. The government, however, made great efforts to build schools and train teachers, but it was not until 1931 that compulsory education could be enforced in all provinces. Primary schools increased from 877 in 1919 to 2,557 in 1936, and a law of that year made attendance compulsory up to the age of sixteen. Secondary schools, gymnasia, and especially agricultural schools have also been organized.

Opportunities for higher education were varied in Estonia and Latvia. In Estonia there was the University of Tartu, founded in 1632 by Gustavus Adolphus, the Technical Institute in Tallinn, two Teachers' Institutes, a music conservatory, and a School of Arts. In Latvia, the University of Riga, various other conservatories in that city, and the Agricultural Academy at Jelgava provided ample opportunity for higher education. In Lithuania a university was founded at Kaunas in 1922 and by 1927 over three thousand students were enrolled.

The figures on illiteracy show some of the effects of this program. In Estonia illiteracy dropped from 5.6 per cent in 1922 to 3.9 per cent in 1934. In Latvia illiteracy fell from 25.7 per cent in 1920 to 7.91 per cent in 1935. In Lithuania it was estimated in 1927 that 35.1 per cent of the population was illiterate.[19] The multiplication of elementary schools and the rapid growth of institutions of higher learning are an indication that here, too, great strides were made.

The Arts. In 1925 a Cultural Fund was created in Estonia, raised by contributions from the national treasury and certain taxes such as those on alcohol, entertainments, and the revenue from the state lottery. Fifty per cent of the fund was earmarked for literature, music, fine arts, drama, physical culture, and journalism; the rest was used by the government mainly to subsidize scientific research and the theaters. Similarly in Latvia a special cultural fund was raised by a 3 per cent tax on railroad fares.

At Riga, as in Tallinn and Kaunas, the opera played to packed houses for a nine months' season.[20] The Riga opera's standards have always been high and Chaliapin liked to sing with its chorus so much that he took it to Berlin for a special performance. The ballet in these opera-houses upheld the best traditions of the old Russian School. Estonian, Latvian, and Lithuanian composers and writers were not lacking, and great progress was made in all fields. Particularly noteworthy was the interest generally displayed in Lithuania in choral singing. Finally, the sculpture in the Latvian national shrine at Riga is so outstanding that it must at least be mentioned.

Submergence in the U.S.S.R.

On March 19, 1938, shortly after Hitler's annexation of Austria, the more or less well-established status quo of the Baltic region was broken. Lithuania was obliged to recognize Polish possession of Vilna and for the first time normal diplomatic, telephone, telegraph, railroad, and postal relations were established between the two countries. On March 22, 1939 Lithuania was forced to cede the Memel territory to Germany. Subsequently Lithuania was granted free port privileges in that city and a payment of $120,000,000 in agricultural machinery as compensation for the Lithuanian state property in Memel.[21] A non-aggression pact between Germany and Lithuania was also signed. Similar non-aggression pacts with Germany were signed by Estonia and Latvia on July 7, 1939.

Russian Mutual Assistance Pacts. Russia meanwhile endeavored to get some sort of guarantee from the Baltic states beyond the existing non-aggression treaties. The Russo-German Pact of August, 1939 and the German-Polish conflict of the following September, provided Russia with a golden opportunity. The Estonian government was invited to send delegates to Moscow to discuss " pressing problems." Subsequently Latvia and Lithuania received similar invitations. Mutual assistance pacts were signed by each country, which were to come into operation only in the event of attack by some great European power.[22] Russia was granted the right to station garrisons at certain points within the Baltic states and to establish naval and air bases there. In each treaty there was an article wherein, " The two contracting parties . . . [undertook] not to conclude any alliance or to participate in any coalition directed against one of the contracting parties." Each of the three countries was free to continue its independent existence, maintain its own army, and Russia promised to supply military materials at favorable rates. Lithuania was ceded the territory of Vilna which Russia had obtained in the recent partition of Poland.

Exodus of Germans. On October 15, 1939, Germany and Estonia and on October 30, 1939, Germany and Latvia signed protocols providing for the " return " of German populations. Movable property as far as possible was to be taken along, although restrictions were placed on certain objects of historical significance and on the transfer of money and jewelry. Other property was placed under a specially created trust organization which was to undertake its sale, transfer funds, and in general represent the évacuées. Under these agreements some 12,000 persons left Estonia, and 50,000 Latvia, settling mostly in East Prussia and the provinces newly conquered from Poland.[23] Just how the liquidation of property was carried out, whether the owners got anything like a fair compensation, and how much they had to pay for their homes, cannot yet be determined.

Further Russian Demands. The installation of Russian garrisons during October and November, 1939 went off without incident. But on May 25, 1940 the Moscow government complained that some Russian soldiers had been waylaid and beaten in Lithuania. Suddenly on June 14, 1940 Russia presented Lithuania with an ultimatum charging her with violating the mutual assistance pact of October, 1939. It was held that Lithuania had joined in a military alliance with the other Baltic states and that the increasing cooperation among them (they were even publishing jointly a new magazine *Revue Baltique*) was a coalition directed against Russia, contrary to the provisions of the pact. The formation of a new pro-Russian government was demanded, along with the right to station a larger number of troops in Lithuania. Armed resistance was impossible; the Russian demands were accepted and Russian troops swarmed into the country on June 15. Similar demands were made on Estonia and Latvia and on June 17 Russian troops occupied these states.

That the Baltic states constituted a serious threat to the security of Russia, when Russian garrisons already were in control of key military points, is difficult to imagine. If it is true that Lithuania did conclude a military alliance with Latvia and Estonia there might be some ground for the Russian charges of violation of the spirit, if not the letter, of the mutual assistance agreements. Such pretexts, however, do not mask Russia's age-old fight for ice-free ports and the desire to strengthen her military position on the Baltic while Germany was fully engaged elsewhere. Germany accepted the new situation and to all outward appearances at least German-Russian friendship remained unaffected.

In accordance with the Russian demands new pro-Soviet governments were formed in each country. In Lithuania President Smetona and other leaders fled to Königsberg where they were temporarily interned, while in Latvia President Ulmanis and in Estonia President Paets remained in office. The elections for the new Parliaments were held on July 14 and 15, and in each country only one party, that of the Working People's Bloc, was permitted. Mass arrests took place on the eve of balloting, threats were made that anyone who abstained from voting would be considered an " enemy of the people," and promises were made to the peasants not to establish collective farming or abolish private property. In spite of the impossibility of registering an opposition vote, the people streamed to the polls. In Estonia 92.9 per cent, in Latvia 97.6 per cent, and in Lithuania 99.19 per cent of the votes cast were for the only choice they had, the Working People's Bloc.

The election was interpreted as a plebiscite in favor of joining the Soviet Union. On July 21 and 22 the new parliaments met, proclaimed their states soviet republics and voted for incorporation into the U.S.S.R. Delegations were dispatched to Moscow and on August 3–6, 1940 Lithuania, Latvia, and Estonia were accepted by the Soviet Supreme Council as the fourteenth, fifteenth, and sixteenth republics of the Soviet Union. Vilna is henceforth to be the capital of Lithuania.

Moscow on August 12 requested all foreign governments to withdraw their diplomatic and consular officials from the Baltic states.

Sovietization. With the establishment of the pro-Russian governments the gradual sovietization of the territories commenced. Many of the former officials were arrested. President Paets and President Ulmanis were forced to resign on the eve of the meeting of the new Parliaments (July 1, 1940) and their fate is uncertain. Student organizations have been dissolved, the important civil guard (*Aizsargi*) in Latvia disbanded, the armies given Russian commanders or commissars. The new land reform permits a peasant to have an estate up to seventy-five acres if he works it himself, but any additional acreage is to be nationalized. This confiscated land is supposedly to be distributed to landless agricultural workers, but there are reports that it will probably be collectivized. As early as July 23, 1940 the Lithuanian government nationalized its banks and the country's principal businesses. This procedure was followed in the other states. The great amount of state capitalism which already existed in each country will make the transition to complete nationalization less difficult than would be the case elsewhere.

The sovietization of the Baltic countries is " being carried out not so much by the local governments, who are mere agents, but by Russians and former Baltic Communists who have spent the larger part of their lives in Soviet Russia and who are now returning to their native countries as commissars in governmental departments and business enterprises." [24] The creation of " Peoples Courts " to deal with " saboteurs," " wreckers," " traitors to the people," indicates that Baltic sovietization is following the established Communist pattern. So far the churches have not been molested and there have been no anti-religious campaigns. The cancellation of the concordat with the Vatican by the Lithuanian government on July 8, 1940, and the institution of compulsory civil marriage and the liberalization of divorce are, however, signposts of future events.

Summary

The cycle is complete. In 1920 the Baltic states negotiated the peace treaties with Russia which recognized their independence; in 1940 they were again brought under Russian domination. Only two decades of freedom, but what progress was achieved! On territories and with peoples suffering from the desolation of war, stable states were created. Primarily agricultural, no one ever questioned their viability, as was the case with Austria. Few states can show such a record of agricultural and industrial expansion and cultural development. The extreme forms of democratic government which were at first inaugurated had to be altered, but the dictatorships, while real, were on the whole moderate.

REFERENCES

[1] For more extended historical accounts see *The Baltic States, A Survey of the Political and Economic Structure and the Foreign Relations of Estonia, Latvia, and Lithuania*, prepared by the Royal Institute of International Affairs, London: Oxford Univ. Press, 1938, pp. 13–28 (great use of this volume has been made throughout and when cited it will be referred to as *The Baltic States*); Albert Pullerits, ed., *Estonia: Population, Cultural and Economic Life*, Tallinn: Kirjastus-Uhisus Press, 1937, pp. 157–172; Alfr. Bihlmans, *Latvia in the Making*, Riga: Times Edition, 1928, pp. 10–33; E. J. Harrison, ed., *Lithuania 1928*, London, 1928, pp. 23–52; Peter Z. Olins, *The Teutonic Knights in Latvia*, Riga: B. Lamey, 1928; Hans Rothfels, " Russians and Germans in the Baltic," *Contemporary Review*, March, 1940, No. 891, pp. 320–326.

[2] Table compiled from *The Baltic States*, pp. 30–38; Pullerits, *Estonia*, pp. 5, 17, 45; and from information furnished by the Latvian Consulate in New York City and the Lithuanian Legation in Washington, D. C. The figures for Lithuania do not include Memel or Vilna.

[3] For further information on the rise of nationalistic movements see Henri de Montfort, *Les nouveaux états de la Baltique*, Paris: A. Pedone, 1933, pp. 48–66.

[4] E. C. Davies, *A Wayfarer in Estonia, Latvia, and Lithuania*, London: Methuen, 1937, pp. 116–117. Walter Duranty in the opening chapters of *I Write as I Please*, New York: Simon and Schuster, 1935, has some interesting comments on Baltic warfare.

[5] For a compact discussion of the Vilna question, including the ethnography of the district, see *The Baltic Question*, pp. 89–93; accounts favorable to Poland are to be found in R. H. Lord, " Lithuania and Poland," *Foreign Affairs*, June, 1923, I: 38–58; R. L. Buell, *Poland: Key to Europe*, New York: Knopf, 1939, pp. 326–328.

[6] Ian F. D. Morrow (assisted by L. M. Sieveking), *The Peace Settlement in the German Polish Borderlands*, London: Oxford Univ. Press, 1936, pp. 419–420. Mr. Morrow has an excellent chapter on the Memel problem. For a more extended authoritative treatment see Thorsten V. Kalijarvi, *The Memel Statute*, London: Robert Hale, 1937.

[7] Malbone W. Graham, " Parties, Political — Baltic States," in *Encyclopedia of the Social Sciences*, VII: 624–626; see also M. W. Graham, *New Governments of Eastern Europe*, New York: Holt, 1927, pp. 305–313, 344–349, 397–408; *The Baltic States*, pp. 46, 52, 56, where tables are given showing the party complexity of each elected Parliament.

[8] Pullerits, *Estonia*, p. 170.

[9] *Year-Book of Labor Statistics*, 1939, p. 208. For further information on the government of Estonia see *Constitution of the Republic of Estonia*, Official Edition, Tallinn: State Printing Office, 1937; Joseph S. Roucek, " Constitutional Changes in Estonia," *American Political Science Review*, June, 1936, XXX: 556–558; Johannes Klesmet, " Reform of Estonian Constitution," *Revue Baltique*, February, 1940, I: 54–67.

[10] See R. Lindenbergs, " The System of Chambers in Latvia," and J. Birznieks, " Latvian Agriculture in the Past Twenty Years," *The Latvian Economist*, published by the Ministry of Finance, Riga: State Printing Office, 1938, pp. 40–71, 103–114.

[11] C. A. Macartney, *National States and National Minorities*, London: Oxford Univ. Press, 1934, pp. 408, 510–513. For further details and additional bibliographical references on the treatment of minorities see *The Baltic States*, pp. 30–38; A. J. Zurcher, *The Experiment with Democracy in Central Europe*, New York: Oxford Univ. Press, 1933, pp. 233–251. For tables showing the number of minority schools in proportion to minority population see *The Baltic States*, pp. 31, 34, 38.

[12] See A. Schwabe, *Agrarian History of Latvia*, Riga: B. Lamey, n.d.; Karl Jeck, *Geschichte der baltischen Landverfassung und ihre Umwälzung durch die Landordnungen in Estland und Lettland*, Würzburg, 1926.

[13] Table compiled from *The Baltic States*, pp. 106–107.

[14] See the *Special Circular* No. 372 1936, issued by the Division of Regional Information of the Department of Commerce, Washington, D. C., on " The Co-

operative Systems of Scandinavia and Baltic States"; also the appropriate annual sections in *The People's Yearbook* published by the publicity department of the British Cooperative Wholesales Society.

[15] *Ten Years of Lithuanian Economy, Report of the Chamber of Commerce, Industry, and Culture*, Kaunas: Vilniaus, 1938, pp. 24–25; see also the summary table on economic figures, pp. 164–165.

[16] *Ibid.*, pp. 31, 127; see also the "Note on the economic position of Memel," *The Baltic States*, pp. 100–102.

[17] For detailed trade figures see the tables in *The Baltic States*, pp. 160–166; *Foreign Commerce Yearbook*, 1938, pp. 39–42, 99–104.

[18] See Joseph S. Roucek, "The Educational Reforms of Estonia," *School and Society*, July, 1937, XLVI: 61–62; P. A. Speek, "Education in Estonia," *School Life*, April, 1939, XXIV: 206–208; Joseph S. Roucek, "The Development of Latvia's Educational System," *School and Society*, May, 1936, XLII: 639–641; Janis Kronlins, "Latvian Schools and Their Attainments," *School Life*, June, 1939, XXIV: 266–268; *Lithuania 1928*, pp. 92–102.

[19] This figure is taken from the official handbook, *Lithuania 1928*, p. 99. In J. F. Abel and M. J. Bond, *Illiteracy in the Several Countries of the World*, Washington: Bureau of Education Bulletin, 1929, No. 4, p. 26, note that 23.36 per cent of the population could neither read nor write; 32.64 per cent is given as the illiteracy figure for 1923 in *The Baltic States*, p. 41.

[20] For example, during the 1938–1939 season at the Riga opera there were 421 performances, 26 original Latvian operas were presented, and the attendance figure totaled 297,520 (*Latvian Information Bulletin*, Washington: Latvian Legation, September 4, 1939). For further material on cultural affairs see Davies, *A Wayfarer in Estonia, Latvia, and Lithuania;* Pullerits, *Estonia*, pp. 26–62; Alla Verdi, "Estonia: Life and Letters," and E. Howard Harris, "Estonia: The Theatre," *Life and Letters To-Day*, August, 1939, XXII: 202–217; Urch, *Latvia*, pp. 15–32, 162–267; B. Vipers, *Baroque Art in Latvia*, Riga: Valters un Rapas, 1939; *Lithuania 1928*, pp. 102–139.

[21] *The Annual Register, 1939*, p. 221.

[22] Unlike the Estonian and Latvian pacts, the Lithuanian pact was not limited to aggression by a great European power, but applied to aggression by any European power. For texts of the agreements and an analysis see Nikolai Kaasik, "Considerations juridiques sur les pactes balto-sovietiques," *Revue Baltique*, February, 1940, I: 84–93, 136–140; the texts are to be found in *The Annual Register*, 1939, pp. 409–412.

[23] For discussions of the treaties see the *Latvian Information Bulletin* of January 31, 1940; *The Baltic Times*, November 15, 1939, January 4, 1940; the chronicle of events in *Revue Baltique*, February, 1940, I: 144–145, 148; N. Politis, "La transfert des populations," *L'Esprit international*, April, 1940, XIV: 163–186. After the formal admission of the Baltic states into the Soviet Union in August, 1940, Germany and Russia initiated discussions in respect to the agreements previously made with Germany by these states. These negotiations also dealt with the return to Germany of the German minority of about 30,000 in Lithuania and the Germans who had previously remained behind in Estonia and Latvia (New York *Times*, August 26, 1940). The agreements reached were signed on January 10, 1941 but the details are not available (New York *Times*, January 11, 1941).

[24] Otto D. Tolischus in the New York *Times*, August 7, 1940. Much of the data on recent events (1940) has been taken from Mr. Tolischus' reports and other news items in the *Times*.

SELECTED BIBLIOGRAPHY

Baltic States: A Survey of the Political and Economic Structure and the Foreign Relations of Estonia, Latvia, and Lithuania, Prepared by the Information Department of the Royal Institute of International Affairs, London: Oxford Univ. Press, 1938. A mine of information and the best single volume dealing with the Baltic states.

Bihlmans, Alfr., *Latvia in the Making, 1918–1928*, Riga: Riga Times Edition, 1928. A handbook containing much information conveniently arranged.

Eichholz, Alvin Conrad, *The Baltic States: Estonia, Latvia, and Lithuania. A Short Review of Resources, Industry, Finance and Trade*, Washington: Trade Information Bulletin, No. 569, 1928. Very informative.

Davies, E. C., *A Wayfarer in Estonia, Latvia and Lithuania*, London: Methuen, 1937. A well-written travel book, especially good for cultural information.

Graham, Malbone W., *New Governments of Eastern Europe*, New York: Holt, 1927, chs. 8–12. Excellent on the establishment of the independent states and the first constitutions.

——, " The Diplomatic Recognition of the Border States," *Publications of the University of California at Los Angeles in Social Science*, 1939, " Part II: Estonia," Vol. III, No. 3, pp. i–viii, 231–398; 1941, " Part III: Latvia," Vol. III, No. 4, pp. i–x, 399–564. Excellent monographs with extensive general bibliographies.

Harrison, E. J., ed., *Lithuania 1928*, London: Hazell, Watson and Viney, 1928. Contains good articles on various aspects of Lithuanian history and life, written by Lithuanian authorities.

Latvian Economist, Prepared by the Ministry of Finance, Riga: State Printing Office, 1938. Nine articles summarizing various aspects of Latvian economic activity, 1918 to 1938.

Montfort, Henri de, *Les nouveaux états de la Baltique*, Paris: A. Pedone, 1933. A general account which also deals with Finland and Poland.

Pullerits, Albert, *Estonia. Population, Cultural and Economic Life*, Tallinn: Kirjastus-Uhisuse Press, 1937. A very informative volume by the director of the Estonian State Central Bureau of Statistics.

Taylor, Stephen, *Handbook of Central and East Europe*, Zürich: Central European Times, 1935.

Ten Years of Lithuanian Economy, Report of the Chamber of Commerce, Industry and Crafts, Kaunas: Vilniaus, 1938.

Urch, R. O. G., *Latvia. Country and People*, London: Allen and Unwin, 1938. A readable book by a correspondent of the London *Times*.

Vitola, H., *La Mer baltique et les états baltes*, Paris: Domat-Montchrestien, 1935. A well-organized treatment dealing largely with the history of the Baltic states before the establishment of independence.

For additional bibliography including books of more technical nature see the sections on Estonia, Latvia, and Lithuania in *The Statesman's Year-Book*, 1940.

Chapter XXI

Sweden

WHERE ODIN RULED OF YORE, — THIS REALM OF WONDER,
THIS STRAND WHOSE LIKE GOD SHALL NOT MAKE AGAIN: —
THERE LIES OUR COUNTRY. SWEDISH SMELL THE FLOWERS,
SWEDISH THE SEEDLAND SINGS ON ISLETS FAIR:
LOVE INEXPRESSIBLE THRO' OUR POOR POWERS
MAKES GLORIOUS LIFE FOR ALL MEN LIVING THERE.

— ANDERS ÖSTERLING: *There Lies Sweden.*

Introduction

While there are many dissimilarities among the Scandinavian states, there are amazingly numerous similarities. They occupy a naturally bounded part of the European continent, equal in area to pre-war France and Germany combined. All are contiguous to each other, except for Denmark which lies on the German frontier.

The people of Sweden, Norway, Denmark, Iceland, Greenland, and a part of Finland are of the same stock: Nordics, with Baltic and Germanic mixtures. Finland's peoples are of Fenno-Ugrian stock except for the 10 per cent Swedish group and the few Laplanders in the north. The Finns, however, have lived so long among the Scandinavians, and have adopted their cultural, religious, and other institutions so completely that the racial differences are more significant on paper than in fact. None of these lands has serious minority problems; and such minority difficulties as those of the Swedes in Finland and the Laplanders in northern Scandinavia are easily adjustable. In the main the Scandinavian peoples are sturdy, healthy, athletic, unexcitable, dignified, industrious, excellent in mechanical pursuits, and fond of outdoor life. They are basically peaceful, but make good warriors, as history testifies. United by a racial bond which goes back to neolithic times, Norway, Denmark, and Sweden have a common history.

The Scandinavian languages are all related. Finnish bears no resemblance to the rest, but the Finns have become accustomed to the Swedish language after hundreds of years of close association with it. Centuries of independent development, dating back to Viking times, has given each language, Norse, Swedish, and Danish, its distinctive form.

The religion of Scandinavia is Lutheran and church services everywhere are alike. Swedish culture was absorbed by Finland, which Russia

---

This chapter by Thorsten V. Kalijarvi, Professor and Head of Department of Government, University of New Hampshire.

left unchanged from 1809 until the institution of the Russification at the end of the last century. The latter was unsuccessful and only served to harden the Finns in their determination to preserve the institutions they had adopted from Sweden. The educational systems of all four countries are similar. The same tendencies and characteristics are noted in art and literature. Costumes and folkways resemble one another. It is not uncommon for the intellectual leaders of these lands to combine their efforts. Thus, for example, the international lawyers jointly publish the *Nordisk Tidskrift for International Ret* and have organized uniform codes of private international law.

The four states had parliamentary governments until the German invasion of 1940. Each was deeply interested in social problems, especially as they pertained to land, cooperative enterprises, and social security. The governments were democratic in nature, posited on a deep respect for freedom and social responsibility. They did not hesitate to enter into business; labor was conscientiously cared for, adult education fostered, and unemployment was successfully combated.

In 1936 the four countries had a combined population of approximately 17,000,000. Their military strength in 1936 may be gleaned from the following table.

Country	Active	Reserves Trained	Total Armies	Budget for Defense
Denmark	8,100	65,700	73,800	$12,390,737
Finland	30,366	345,000	375,366	14,083,872
Norway	15,100	315,000	330,100	8,937,238
Sweden	33,500	838,400	876,000	28,610,357
Totals	87,066	1,564,100	1,655,866	$64,022,204

In combination they could have mustered a peacetime army which would have been the eighth largest in the world.

Sweden

Geography. Sweden, the largest and most important of the Scandinavian states, is located on the southern and eastern parts of the Scandinavian peninsula; her western neighbor is Norway and her northern, Finland. Over half the boundary consists of coastline, for Sweden faces on three bodies of water: the Gulf of Bothnia, the Baltic Sea, and the North Sea, which include both Kattegat and Skagerrak.

Sweden is 978 miles long and 310 miles wide at its longest and broadest distances respectively, and covers 173,296 square miles. A large part of the country is mountainous, especially in the northwest. The mountains level out toward the Gulf of Bothnia, making the whole eastern border and the southern third of the country either rolling plateau or lowland. It is a land of many lakes, rivers, waterfalls, and forests.

Jutting into the heart of northern Europe, the geographical location has been fortunate for Sweden until comparatively recent times. During the last four hundred years it has enabled her to block the advance of the Russians, while every major European conflict has found her, by virtue of her geography and industrial and seafaring life, beset by belligerents from both sides.

Ethnography: Minorities. The people are descendants of a fair, blue-eyed, tall, and long-headed Nordic race who moved into the country at the end of the last glacial period. The migration is estimated to have been completed by the end of the Stone Age, about 4000 years ago. Researches show that the earliest inhabitants were Germanic, and with the exception of the Lapps and the Finns, who came later, there has been no change in racial composition.

In 1937 the population was 6,266,888.

The Swedish influence may be seen all over the continent, because it was the Swedish *Götar*, or Goths, who ravaged Europe during later Roman times. Likewise the Vikings roamed over the European seas during the Middle Ages and left their descendants in most northern European countries, especially France.

There are no minority problems. The Finns and Lapps are few and well treated. Perhaps because they have the same background, cultural institutions, and religion, there can be little or no chance of grievance.

Government. The Swedish government is a parliamentary monarchy, all citizens over twenty-three being permitted to vote. The constitution of 1809 and the succession act of 1810, established a king at the head of the government. He is advised by a council or cabinet of twelve, three without portfolio. The king is also the head of the judiciary and the leader of the bicameral legislature, called the *Riksdag*. The Upper House is the less important and tends to represent entrenched or conservative interests. The real sovereign is the legislature.[1]

Experiences during First World War. In the First World War, Sweden suffered some casualties on the seas and lost a great amount of property, for she was blockaded as though a belligerent. A staunch upholder of international law, Sweden was harassed by both sides. Her exports were not paid for in many instances, and there seemed no possible way of collecting. The food situation at times was so severe that rationing was instituted, while the economic structure of the country was subjected to a violent shock due to the shift in demand and production attendant upon war.[2]

The temporary improvement of economic conditions after 1918 was short-lived. When the Eden ministry, supported by the Liberals and the Social Democrats, fell in 1920, a six-year period began which is known in Swedish history as the Branting period.

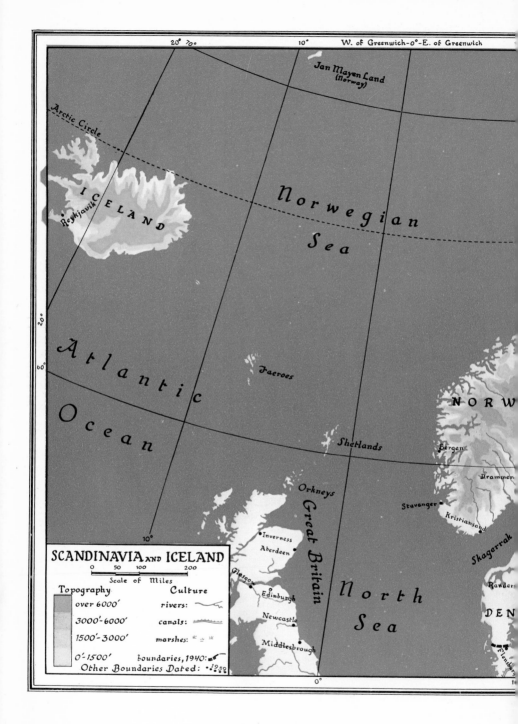

Jan Mayen Land
(Norway)

Arctic Circle

ICELAND

Reykjavik

Norwegian

Sea

20°

60°

Atlantic

Ocean

Faeroes

NORW

Shetlands

Bergen

Orkneys

Drammen

Great Britain

Stavanger

Kristiansand

10°

Inverness

Aberdeen

Skagerrak

SCANDINAVIA AND ICELAND

Glasgow

0   50   100   200

Scale of Miles

Edinburgh

North

Randers

Topography   Culture

Sea

DEN

rivers:

over 6000'

Newcastle

3000'-6000'   canals:

1500'-3000'   marshes:

Middlesbrough

0'-1500'   boundaries, 1940:

Flensburg

Other Boundaries Dated: 1939

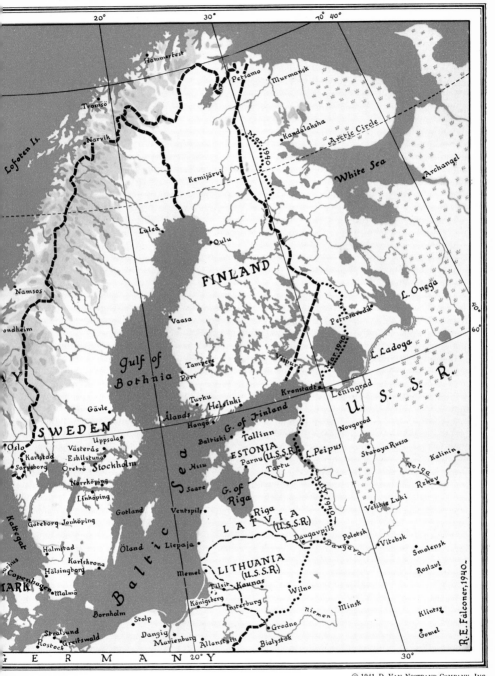

20°   30°   70° 40°

Hammerfest
Tromsö
Petsamo
Murmansk
Lofoten Is.
Narvik
Kandalaksha
Arctic Circle
Mar.1940
Kemijärvi
White Sea
Archangel
Luleå
Namsos
Oulu
ondheim
FINLAND
L. Onega
Vaasa
Petrosavodsk
Mar.1940
Gulf of Bothnia
Tampere
Pori
Viipuri
L. Ladoga
Gävle
Turku
Kronstadt
Leningrad
U. S. S. R.
Ålands
Helsinki
SWEDEN
Hangö
G. of Finland
Oslo
Uppsala
Baltiski
Tallinn
Novgorod
Karlstad
Västerås
Eskilstuna
Hiiu
ESTONIA
(U.S.S.R.)
L. Peipus
Staraya Russa
Kalinin
Sarpsborg
Örebro
Stockholm
Parnu
Tartu
Norrköping
Saare
July 1940
Velikie Luki
Volga
Rzlev
Linköping
G. of Riga
Göteborg
Jonköping
Gotland
Ventspils
Riga
(U.S.S.R.)
Halmstad
Öland
Liepaja
L A T V I A
Daugavpils
Polotsk
Vitebsk
Karlskrona
Daugava
Smolensk
Hälsingborg
Memel
LITHUANIA
(U.S.S.R.)
Roslavl
Copenhagen
Malmö
Tilsit
Kaunas
Wilno
Minsk
MARK
Bornholm
Königsberg
Insterburg
Niemen
Klintsy
Stralsund
Stolp
Danzig
Grodno
Gomel
Rostock
Greifswald
Marienburg
Allenstein
Bialystok
G E R M A N 20° Y
30°

Baltic Sea
Kattegat

R.E.Falconer,1940.

© 1941, D. Van Nostrand Company, Inc.

Domestic Politics. Hjalmar Branting formed Sweden's first Social Democratic ministry in the spring of 1920. Branting endeavored to put into effect a program which called for an extension of labor rights, including a voice for labor in the conduct of industry. This legislation, however, was rejected as too radical by the *Riksdag* — the Communist experiment in Russia was too near and vivid in Swedish minds to permit such an essay — and a marked drift to the Right followed. Branting was forced out of office in the autumn of 1920.

The next two ministries were headed by L. de Geer and Oscar von Sydow respectively and had the sole distinction of extending the franchise to women in 1921. But the country soon tired of the Conservatives, and the Social Democrats joined forces with the Communists to drive the government out of power. In October, 1921 Branting formed his second ministry which remained in power until April, 1923.

The Åland Islands Problem. The question of the strategic Åland Islands, belonging to Finland arose in 1920. Lying within easy distance of Stockholm, possession by an enemy power would have placed the capital of Sweden at its mercy. Moreover the islands had been neutralized and unfortified until the beginning of the war. Thus, when the islanders petitioned for assistance from and union with Sweden, the latter took the side of the petitioners. Finland considered this an act of treason, arrested many islanders in June, 1920, and sent troops into the area. The Swedish government replied by withdrawing its minister to Helsinki, whereupon a crisis was precipitated between the two countries. Great Britain, through Lord Curzon, suggested that the issue be referred to the League of Nations, which decided that they belonged to Finland but ordered them demilitarized.

Unemployment. A problem of far more serious import was the extensive unemployment situation which had arisen because of the post-war deflation. The winter of 1921–1922 was especially severe, and a parliamentary commission was established to study the situation and frame alleviating legislation. The unemployment question was gradually solved; indeed by 1926 unemployment had virtually vanished. The leader in the fight for the improvement of the condition of labor was Carl Ekman, who later became Premier.

Disarmament. Branting resigned in April, 1923 and Ernest Trygges, leader of the Conservatives, formed a new ministry whose special task was to solve the defense question. Demands arose for lowering the period of military service and for reduction of armaments. On October 29, 1923, Foreign Minister Hederstierna advocated in a public address that Sweden should join Finland in a defensive alliance against Soviet Russia. The country split on the issue. The Right supported Hederstierna, while the Social Democrats joined the Communists in opposition; hence nothing came of the proposal. In 1924 the government proposed a reduction of the defense budget, but the *Riksdag* rejected the suggestion. Branting resigned, but was asked to form his third ministry on October 18, 1924. His death in February, 1925 was a great loss to the Social Democrats; leadership of the party went to Richard Sandler. The disarmament issue was finally settled in 1925 by lowering the budget and reducing defense costs.

Prosperity. Sweden enjoyed prosperity from 1926 to 1929. Disarmament still continued to be a topic of discussion. One of the leading small countries in the League, Sweden naturally favored curtailment of arms, because such a program would make the existence of small states less precarious. The situation was complicated by the fact that the armaments limitation clauses of the peace treaties forced the Krupp interests to transfer much of their business to the Bofors plants in Sweden.

The four years were peaceful and progressive for Sweden. Huge industrial developments, including many cooperatives, were developed. The most widely known figure in finance and industry was Ivar Kreuger, the head of Kreuger and Toll, who had begun his career as a construction engineer and ended by dominating the Swedish match trust and its subsidiary companies, owning nine-tenths of the world's match industries.

The Sandler ministry fell in 1926 and was succeeded by a Cabinet formed by Carl Ekman which remained in office until October, 1928. The first major issue before the Ekman government was that of educational reform. In 1921 the school system had been modernized, but the immediate problem was that of higher education for women. Agitation had been carried on for several years and finally in 1927 a law was passed giving women greater opportunities for advanced education.

Labor Legislation. New regulations for labor also became necessary. Good times had spurred unionization and strikes. Peace in the ranks of labor became imperative, for the country was growing alarmed at the disorders which had steadily increased since the end of the First World War, and at the determination of the labor organizations to secure control of the forces of production. Many people believed that the state should pacify labor. The *Riksdag* passed a bill in May, 1928 which provided for the establishment in Stockholm of a labor court to iron out disputes between employers and employees. Supporting laws to enable it to carry out its functions were also passed. This, however, as will be seen, did not terminate the labor troubles.[3]

Coming of Hard Times. Hard times were on the way, heralded by the crash of two savings banks in which the Riksbank was held partly to blame. Per Albin Hansson in the lower house placed the responsibility on the Minister of Finance, Nils Wohlin. Wohlin resigned, but the Cabinet remained in office, and the parliamentary crisis had not abated. The Social

Democrats demanded relief for unemployment (not a dole), higher pensions, health insurance, and other social welfare measures. The most restless element in the population were the peasantry and farmers, whom prosperity had not helped, for rising prices, which had boosted industry and trade, did not appreciably improve their condition. Ekman had finally been forced to regulate the flour industry and make other concessions to the farmers.

In 1931 Sweden began to feel the full impact of the depression. Strikes spread. Uprisings in Sandviken ended in violence and death. The Communists multiplied and in the Ådalen section thousands paraded openly under the Communist banner.

The Kreuger Crash. In 1932 the Kreuger crash imperiled virtually the entire industrial and financial structure of Sweden. As late as February 1, 1932, Kreuger had negotiated a new credit with the Riksbank. He visited New York and from there went to Paris, where he committed suicide. The blow fell like lightning. Thousands lost their life savings in the giant swindle, but Swedish industries and banks survived the shock. Kreuger was symbolic of the times, of the easy money and opulence of the 'twenties, and the harsh reality of the early 'thirties. When references were found in Kreuger's diary to sums paid to Ekman for the support of his party, the Prime Minister was forced to resign (August, 1932).

The Hansson Government. The period from 1932 to 1940 was marked by the leadership of the Social Democrat Per Albin Hansson, who became Prime Minister in September, 1932. Hansson's program provided for extensive social welfare schemes,[4] including unemployment relief, financed partly out of borrowings and partly out of increased inheritance taxes, measures for public works and assistance to the farmers involving regulations for the flour industry and the control of milk and other products.[5] Most of these measures were put into effect. The depression was checked in 1932 and 1933, and conditions improved thereafter.

Rise of Fascism. New issues cropped up as others were settled. The so-called " German epidemic " now visited the land. Hitler had sympathizers in Sweden, and murmurs of anti-Semitism began to be heard. Indeed Fascist and National Socialist agitation was not new. It was anticipated by the teachings of Adrian Molin fifteen years earlier. As early as 1926 Sweden had her Fascist Party, but it was not till the winter of 1932 and 1933 that uniformed Fascisti could be seen on the streets. Parliament was properly disturbed.

The Communists capitalized on the labor troubles, particularly in the building trades, of 1934. The peasant organizations grew steadily stronger, while debate, division, and uncertainty characterized the *Riksdag*. In 1934 the liberal parties joined forces with the independents to check the Nazis. Party realignment and reorganization occurred. The Communists became the Swedish Socialist Party. Each party formed its young people's group to counteract Fascist threats. In December, 1939, as an emergency measure growing out of the Russo-Finnish War, Per Albin Hansson was asked to form his third ministry, heading a Cabinet of national union with Christian E. Guenther, a career diplomat, as Foreign Minister. Hansson continued to command the support of the *Riksdag* and King Gustav throughout the Russo-Finnish War and the invasion of Norway and Denmark when the independence of Sweden was gravely threatened.

Foreign Policy. After the First World War Sweden was confronted with the choice of neutrality or entering the League system of collective security. She chose the latter, and played a leading part at Geneva, where the figure of Hjalmar Branting became familiar.

Due largely to Branting, the Swedish government was given a place on the Council of the League in 1922. While Sweden was on the Council the Corfu incident arose; France invaded the Ruhr; and the Geneva Protocol was debated and finally rejected. Germany's application for admission to the League provided an occasion for many states to demand permanent or quasi-permanent seats in the Council. Sweden voted against these efforts because she believed that the large states were entitled to special consideration. Sweden was not displeased with the expansion of the Council in 1926.[6]

The years from 1926 to 1932 were a period of agitation and unrest in foreign affairs. The stability of the security machinery seemed in danger. When the Nazi revolution occurred in Germany, Sweden began to examine her defense program and rebuild her military establishment.[7]

In the Ethiopian crisis of 1935–1936 Sweden supported the League, and when that effort at collective security ended in complete failure, Sweden lost confidence in the League. The Spanish Civil War revealed that military power, not law and international justice, settled the fates of nations and that the danger to the small states was increasing.

Fear now spread among all the Scandinavian powers, and a movement for a closer union among them could be discerned. The first Scandinavian conference was held in Stockholm in September, 1934. By the end of 1937 three more conferences had been called to devise a way of keeping out of the impending world war. No Scandinavian alliance, however, was formed.

The Russo-Finnish War. When Russia invaded Finland in December, 1939, Sweden offered considerable aid. Volunteers, arms, and supplies flowed across her frontiers. Large sections of the population clamored for an immediate declaration of war on Russia. Indeed, so loud was the outcry that the government was reorganized in December, 1939, and the king made a special plea to the people to remain calm. Pressure from Germany, the friend of Russia, was all too evident. When England asked if she might use Swedish ports for sending troops to Finland, Sweden refused lest she offend Germany. Throughout the war Sweden acted as adviser and mediator.

Germany Invasion of Norway. Meanwhile the greater war continued. The port of Narvik was wrecked and Swedish iron ore from the Kiruna mines had to be shipped to Germany via Luleå, the Bothnian Gulf, and the Baltic. German occupation of Norway (April, 1940) and the possibility of an immediate invasion of Sweden, if she remained obdurate, prompted the latter to permit Germany to use the Swedish railways. Sweden clung to neutrality while Denmark and Norway succumbed to the Nazi forces. Again Sweden experienced the hardships of a blockaded neutral, as during the First World War.

Economic Development. Only 9 per cent of Swedish land is arable. Since metal deposits are of considerable extent and fine quality, and the whole country is pierced by rivers suitable for power and transportation, Sweden has been rapidly industrialized. Only Great Britain, the United States, Germany, and Belgium exceed Sweden in degree of industrialization. About 54 per cent of the population is dependent upon industry in the widest sense of the word. Sweden is in the forefront of scientific discovery and invention, thus insuring the continuance of her present development.

Agriculture. In agriculture, the yield per acre has increased steadily, but the population engaged in this work has declined. Today Sweden is notable for almost complete self-sufficiency in foodstuffs and a wide development of cooperatives. The farmer is both efficient and prosperous. Water power has been extensively developed because of the large number of rivers and falls, and the whole southern part of the country is completely electrified, although the greatest sources are in the north. The state owns about one-third of the power resources, the other two-thirds being in the hands of municipalities and private companies. All power plants are linked into a network of trunk lines.

Industries. Forests, scattered over the larger part of the country, make lumbering, cellulose production, and paper manufacturing important items in Sweden's economy. The extraction of iron ore dates from ancient times, and many valuable minerals are produced. Gustavus Vasa united the country from the proceeds of silver mines; Gustavus Adolphus and Charles XII carried on their wars with the proceeds of the copper and iron mines. Sweden's Kiruna mines are an important element in the conduct of the current war. The Nazi invasion of Norway was impelled, in part, by a desire to safeguard Germany's supply of Swedish iron ore.

The chief Swedish industries are metal and machinery manufacturing, pulp, paper, and chemical production, glass and china, textile weaving, leather working, rubber manufacturing, and food processing.

Commerce and Finance. International commerce and finance are time-honored activities of the Swedes, although they fell into decline until the industrial revolution carried them forward at a rapid pace about fifty years ago. Through Gothenburg, the chief port, the bulk of Swedish iron, wood, and pulp exports pass. Sweden has been able to finance her economic development through her own banking system, which survived the shock of the depression of the early 'twenties, and the disastrous manipulations of Ivar Kreuger and his colleagues.

The growth of Swedish industry and agriculture has meant increased control of business by the government. The state budget is balanced without recourse to loans. Many social welfare measures have been enacted since 1918 in an effort to pacify the dissident elements in the population. Yet, complete harmony has not been achieved, as is seen in the growth of extremist parties during the last few years.

Cultural Developments: Science. Sweden, the home of Celsius and Linné, is in the forefront of scientific progress. Today their work is continued by such men as the geologist Gerhard de Geer, the explorer Sven Hedin, the mathematician Gustaf Cassel, the biologist Herman Nilsson-Ehle, the researchist in radiotherapy Gösta Foresell, the neurologist Herbert Olivecrona, and the chemist Theodor Svedberg. In industry the work of Alfred Nobel and Lars Magnus Ericsson are now carried on by such men as the inventor Gustav Dalen, the ship-owner Dan Broström, and the engineer Sven Gustaf Wingquist.

Literature. Sweden's literature is perhaps the most significant of her cultural contributions. The principal figure of the last generation is Selma Lagerlöf (1858–1940), whose work *Gösta Berlings Saga* (1891) immediately brought her international fame. Other gifted writers include the novelists Sigfrid Siwertz (1882–   ) and Hjalmar Bergman (1883–1931), the poets Per Lagerkvist, Bo Bergman (1869–   ), Anders Österling, Einer Malm, and Hjalmar Gullberg.

Painting and sculpture are less outstanding, but the etchings and portraits of Anders Zorn (1860–1920), the landscapes of Prince Eugen, the animals of Bruno Liljefors, and the landscapes of Karl Nordström (died 1928), Nils Kreuger (died 1930), and Carl Wilhelmson (died 1928) are noteworthy. Carl Milles (1875–   ) is the most eminent of living Swedish sculptors.

Swedish music and drama, although enthusiastically supported at home, are not well known abroad. Sweden has made significant contributions in glass working and in arts and crafts generally. The chief centers of cultural life are Stockholm, Hälsingborg, Uppsala, and Lund.

Summary

Sweden is an old country, with a splendid historical background. Her basic soundness has been demonstrated in many ways during the last generation, when she emerged from political, social, and economic crises with remarkable resilience and power. The long years of peace have not left her soft and enervated, but have given ample opportunity for an enviable cultural, political, and economic development. The social and economic structure is solidly grounded, and the people of Sweden are as free and independent as any in the world.

In the last generation Sweden has been threatened not only by dissident elements at home but by threats of foreign aggressors. Many of the social reforms of the Social Democrats were adopted in fear of the examples set by Russia and Germany. Yet Sweden has demonstrated clearly that social and economic progress are not the possession of totalitarian states alone, that democracies can solve their problems, and that private enterprise may still function fruitfully. Sweden is a living example of what has been aptly called " the middle way."

Growing industry has recently forced Sweden into a precarious position. As the most powerful of the Scandinavian states, she often had to assume political leadership. As a small state, she has been buffeted between the Great Powers, and has preserved her independence by an unswerving determination to remain at peace as well as by a shrewdly opportunistic foreign policy. As a liberal monarchy, she has been forced to combat surrounding Fascist ideologies. Finally, as a maritime state, located in the heart of constantly blockaded areas, she has suffered the depredations of maritime war.

REFERENCES

¹ For excellent and brief discussions in English, see *Sweden — Ancient and Modern*, Stockholm: Turisttraffik — Förbundet, 1938; and Margaret Cole and Charles Smith, *Democratic Sweden*, London: Routledge, 1938, p. 26; also *ibid.*, ch. 2.

² See *Sweden, Norway, Denmark and Iceland in the World War*, edited by James T. Shotwell, published by the Carnegie Endowment for International Peace, New Haven: Yale Univ. Press, 1930, Parts I, II, and III.

³ See Åke Thulstrup, *Reformer och Försvar*, Stockholm: Albert Bonniers Förlag, 1938, pp. 95–99.

⁴ An excellent English summary of the Social Democratic platform is found in *Social Work and Legislation in Sweden*, published by the Royal Social Board, Stockholm, 1938.

⁵ See Arthur Montgomery, *How Sweden Overcame the Depression*, Stockholm: Alb. Bonniers Boktryckeri, 1938.

⁶ See S. S. Jones, *The Scandinavian States and the League of Nations*, Princeton: Princeton Univ. Press, 1939.

⁷ See Eric Cyril Bellquist, *Some Aspects of Recent Foreign Policy of Sweden*, Berkeley, Cal.: Univ. of California Press, 1929.

SELECTED BIBLIOGRAPHY

Scandinavia

Note: For articles of current interest see *The American Scandinavian Review*, 1913–1940.

A list of *Five Hundred Books by Scandinavians and about Scandinavia* is published by the American Scandinavian Foundation of New York, 1938.

Each of the countries publishes official handbooks in English which may be consulted.

Arneson, Ben A., *The Democratic Monarchies of Scandinavia*, New York: Van Nostrand, 1939.   A scholarly study of the governments of Scandinavia.

Franck, Harry A., *A Scandinavian Summer*, New York: Century, 1930.   An interesting and descriptive travelogue.

Jones, S. Shepard, *The Scandinavian States and the League of Nations*, New York: Princeton Univ. Press, 1939.   Based on official documents and original sources, readable and sound.

The Northern Countries in World Economy, Finland: Atava Printing Office, 1939.   Helpful in establishing relationships of the economies of all the northern countries with each other and the rest of the world.

Olson, Alma Luise, *Scandinavia, The Background for Neutrality*, Philadelphia: Lippincott, 1940.   A general work with emphasis upon the political and international relations.

Sweden

Bellquist, Eric Cyril, *Some Aspects of the Recent Foreign Policy of Sweden*, Berkeley, Cal.: Univ. of California Press, 1929.   Helpful and reliable for the first ten years under review.

Childs, Marquis W., *Sweden, The Middle Way*, New Haven: Yale Univ. Press, 1936.   A popular description of Swedish cooperatives.

Cole, M. and Smith, C., *Democratic Sweden*, London: Routledge, 1938.   An excellent analysis of the government, its structure and policy.

Rothery, Agnes, *Sweden, the Land and the People*, New York: Viking, 1938.   Like Miss Rothery's books on other Scandinavian countries this is well written, easy to read, and instructive.

Thulstrup, Åke, *Reformer och Försvar*, Stockholm: Albert Bonniers Förlag, 1938.   A valuable review, from the socialistic standpoint, of the major political events since 1918.

CHAPTER XXII

Norway

" IT IS NOT STRANGE THAT MEN
WHO GIVE SO MUCH TO GRANITE AND THE SEA
SHOULD TAKE THEMSELVES A LOOK OF SEA AND GRANITE.
AND IT IS FITTING THAT SUCH MEN SHOULD BEAR
NAMES QUARRIED FROM THE SOIL: HAUGEN, THE HILL;
MOEN, THE HEATH; STENDAL, STRONG VALLEY;
AND THAT A MAN SHOULD TAKE FOR HIS THE NAME
HIS FARM BEARS. FOR MEN THEMSELVES PERISH,
BUT THE SOIL ENDURES, AND THE SERVICE OF THE SOIL."

— TED OLSON: *Portrait of a People*

Geography. Norway occupies the western half of the Scandinavian peninsula, lying directly north of Denmark and east of the British Isles. It faces the North Sea, the Atlantic and Arctic Oceans, while on its eastern frontier are Sweden and Finland. Like Sweden it has an extremely long and indented coastline; the terrain is mountainous and serrated, and only one-fifth is less than 650 feet above sea level. A straight line drawn from the northernmost to the southernmost tips of Norway would cover 1100 miles, while the greatest width is 270 miles. Norway's total area is 124,556 square miles if the 150,000 islands and skerries are included; if Bear Island, Jan Mayen Land and Spitsbergen are added, approximately 25,000 square miles more.

Climate. The climate of this picturesque land is comparatively mild because the Gulf Stream reaches its shores. Naturally the climatic conditions vary from North Cape to Lindesnes, between the highlands and the sea. Short, rapid rivers and lakes cover about 5000 square miles, and forests about 27,000 square miles. Norway is a land of fjords and waterfalls, of agriculture, mining, manufacturing, electric power production, forestry, and fishing.

Ethnography. The population of Norway was 2,814,194 in 1930 and about 2,908,000 in 1938. The 20,000 Lapps form the only minority element.

The great majority of Norwegians are tall and blond Nordics but there are some interesting mixtures. An Alpine influence accounts for many people with brown eyes and dark hair. Who the original inhabitants were it is impossible to say, but the Alpines and East Balts found in Norway are believed to be descendants of people who migrated early into the area and perhaps were crossed with the survivors of the last great ice age. Anthro-

This chapter by Thorsten V. Kalijarvi, Professor and Head of Department of Government, University of New Hampshire.

pologists believe that they were already in Norway when the Nordic forefathers of the present inhabitants of the eastern countries entered the region during neolithic times. Some of these forebears came by sea from the south and were already mixed with the blond, round-skulled East Balts when they arrived. There is some evidence that a substantial element of Finnish blood flows in the veins of the Norwegian people.

Language. The Norse language is closely related to Swedish and Danish. Old Norse was a highly polished literary language. During the era of union with Sweden and Denmark, and especially during the Reformation, when the Bible was translated into Danish, Norse was split into many dialects. Local dialects, urban vernaculars, a middle-class language, and so-called " solemn language " evolved. When Norway was separated from Denmark in the last century efforts were made to purge the Danish elements and create an independent Norse tongue.

Landsmaal vs. Riksmaal. Knud Knudsen (1812–1895) enthusiastically proposed orthographic changes to purify the language, and his ideas had a marked influence on Ibsen and Bjornson. Another school of philologists headed by Ivar Aasen (1813–1896) asserted that the Norwegian language should not be purified but reconstructed on the basis of the old dialects. Thus in the middle of the nineteenth century there developed a conflict between Aasen's " Landsmaal " and the " Riksmaal " or the Norwegian version of the Danish language which developed during the union with Denmark (1381–1814). In 1892 Landsmaal was allowed to become the chief language of the elementary schools. Later secondary schools and universities were allowed to use Landsmaal. One side of the population has voted for Landsmaal in the primary schools, the rest favor Riksmaal. The two languages differ in pronunciation, spelling, and language forms. Each is used by writers of distinction although Riksmaal is the more literary of the two.[1] The conflict between the adherents of the two languages has had political repercussions.

History. Norwegian history may be traced back eight to ten thousand years. During the Viking period the Norwegians and Danes harried the European coasts, while the Swedes turned their attention to Russia and the east. The Norwegians founded the city of Dublin and settled in large sections of Ireland in the ninth century. Their influence was deeply imprinted on the area when England conquered Ireland in 1170. In the tenth century the Norwegians overran parts of France, while earlier they had accompanied the Danes into England. They discovered Greenland, embarked on expeditions with closely related Icelandic peoples, and explored America about A.D. 1000. The Norwegian colonial empire included the Faroe, Shetland, Orkney, and Hebrides Islands.

The Middle Ages. Civil wars, followed by the Black Death, destroyed from two-thirds to three-quarters of the people in the thirteenth and four-

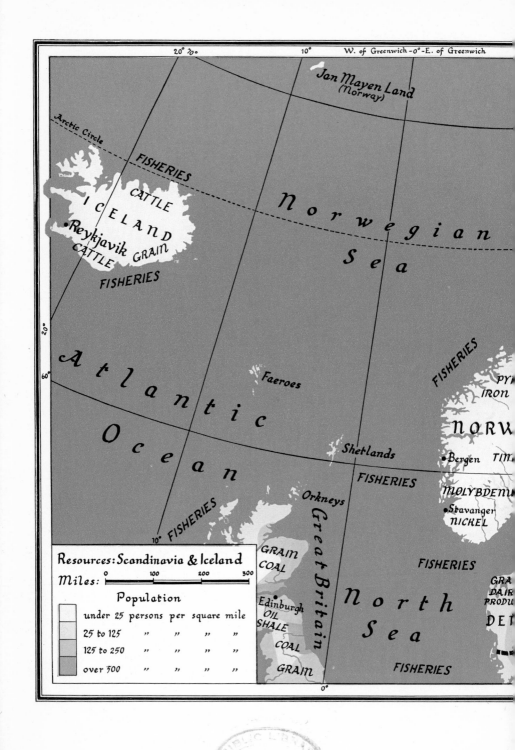

Jan Mayen Land
(Norway)

Arctic Circle

FISHERIES

CATTLE

ICELAND

•Reykjavik GRAIN
CATTLE

FISHERIES

N o r w e g i a n

S e a

20°

60°

A t l a n t i c

O c e a n

Faeroes

Shetlands

FISHERIES

FISHERIES

PY
IRON

N O R W

•Bergen TIN

MOLYBDENU

•Stavanger
NICKEL

FISHERIES

Orkneys

10° FISHERIES

GRAIN
COAL

G r e a t   B r i t a i n

Edinburgh
OIL
SHALE

COAL

GRAIN

N o r t h

S e a

FISHERIES

GRA
DAIR
PRODU

DE

0°

Resources: Scandinavia & Iceland

Miles: 0   100   200   300

Population

under 25 persons per square mile

25 to 125   „   „   „   „

125 to 250   „   „   „   „

over 300   „   „   „   „

teenth centuries, and the empire and colonies were lost. Efforts at colonizing America ceased and contact with Greenland ended. Haakon VI was succeeded in 1381 by his son Olaf V who inherited the Danish throne through his mother, Queen Margreta. When Olaf died in 1387 at the age of sixteen, Margreta succeeded in having a Danish prince elected king of both countries. The Norwegians were forced to submit to the union with Denmark for 400 years.

The Nineteenth Century. During the Napoleonic wars Norway was separated from Denmark, and in 1814 it was transferred to Sweden, while the colonies of Iceland, Greenland, and the Faroes were retained by the Danes. The feeling of nationalism was revived and after long agitation Norway was peacefully separated from Sweden in 1905.

Government of Norway. Norway established a parliamentary monarchy which existed until the German invasion of 1940. The king, Haakon VII, had little power. The Cabinet and Prime Minister were responsible to the Storting, composed of 150 members elected by male and female suffrage according to a system of proportional representation. The Storting met as two bodies, the *Lagting* and the *Odelsting*, and sat, for the most part, as separate chambers. On budgetary and other important measures they deliberated as one body. The President of the Storting took precedence over both the Prime Minister and Cabinet. A Supreme Court headed the judicial system of the realm.

Norway in the First World War. In the First World War Norway, although a neutral, suffered immense losses. Her ships were sunk and her sailors killed. In 1917 she was advised by the Allied Powers to place her population on rations because of the blockade. Yet Norway prospered by selling to both sides, although, in spite of prosperity, the national debt trebled between 1914 and 1919 and commodity prices rose to extraordinary levels. The general collapse of foreign markets in 1921 brought gloom to Norway. In 1923 and 1924 there were financial catastrophes and as a result of hard times Leftist movements arose and parliamentary government received severe tests.[2]

Politics. Between 1918 and 1940 Norway was ruled by coalition governments. Except for the Labor government of Johan Nygaardsvold, which was in power when the Germans entered in 1940, the longest-lived coalitions were those of the Left. The Right and Independent Left were at the helm in 1920–1921, 1923–1924, and 1926–1927. In 1928 Labor, after holding power for 17 days, was forced to yield to the Left. From 1931 to 1933 the government consisted of a Left-Labor coalition and from 1933 to 1935 there was a Labor-Peasant coalition. After 1935 Labor was dominant.

The Communist Movement. The first great post-war problem was to check the Communist movement. The White victory in Finland and the

Weimar constitution in Germany had a moderating influence on the Norwegian Socialists. Yet the extremists gained the upper hand in the party in 1918 and the following year the Norwegian Labor Party joined the Third International, affiliated with Moscow. The moderate Socialists then formed the Norwegian Social Democratic Party. A wave of revolution spread over the land, manifesting itself in the railway strike of December, 1920 and the general strike of May, 1921. Both walkouts were unsuccessful and helped to strengthen the conservative parties. In the autumn of 1923 the Labor Party withdrew from the Third International, but its Left wing remained loyal to Moscow and organized the Norwegian Communist Party. In the elections of October, 1924, the Laborites secured 24 seats in the Storting, the Social Democrats 8, the Communists 6, the Left 36, the Farmers' Party 22, and the Conservative coalition 54. In the elections of 1927 the Labor Party won 59 seats. It lost ground in the 1930 elections, but made impressive gains in 1933 and 1936. The Communists held only 3 seats in 1927 and fewer afterwards.

Prohibition. The prohibition question came to the forefront in 1917. The moderate prohibition law of 1917 injured trade with Spain and Portugal who exchanged their wines for Norwegian fish. When Spain shifted her business to Iceland, Norway's most dangerous competitor, protests were heard on every side and in 1919 a plebiscite was held to determine whether the Norwegian people wanted prohibition. The vote was in the affirmative. Action was taken accordingly, bringing on political crises in 1921, 1923, and 1924. Agitation grew for the complete exclusion of wines with more than 12 per cent alcohol. The Laborites, Leftists, and Socialists advocated prohibition, while some of the other parties opposed it.

During the influenza epidemic agitation against prohibition took on increased proportions. Spain denounced her treaty with Norway, a move which brought heavy losses to Norwegian ship owners and fishing men. The plebiscite of 1919 was declared to have been advisory and not mandatory; and Norway decided in 1931 that she would take wine and liquor from France and Spain in exchange for fish. In 1923 Portugal asked for and received permission to sell her wine in Norway. The Storting thereupon repealed the provisions against strong wines and liquors.

Final Settlement of the Prohibition Question. During 1922 the government placed the sale of liquor in the hands of the Wine Monopoly, a privately organized concern which turned back a percentage of the profits to the state. In 1923 prohibition was partially repealed, an act that was in part made possible by the customary experiences of smuggling, bootlegging, and growing disrespect for law. Another plebiscite was held in 1926 to determine whether complete repeal should be undertaken. In accordance with an affirmative vote the Storting in May, 1927 removed the last obstacles to the sale of liquor. In 1932 the privileges of the Wine Monopoly were extended.

Post-War Depression. The prosperity of 1914–1919 soon gave way, as we noted, to depression. It was necessary for the government to loan the banks 15,000,000 kroner in 1921 and 25,000,000 in 1922. In 1923 the government had to administer some of the weaker financial institutions. The Joint Stock Bank Act of 1924 was designed to reduce the number of banks. Two of the largest institutions, the Centralbanken for Norge and the Foreningsbanken, encountered severe difficulties. In July, 1926 it was discovered that Prime Minister Berge had deposited in the tottering Handelsbank in 1923, with the permission of the Storting, 25,000,000 kroner of government money. Berge was tried and acquitted in 1927.

In other respects, too, the financial picture was clouded. From 1924 to 1934 the Storting was harassed by budgetary quarrels. The Right favored balanced budgets or a " spend as you go " program, while the Left advocated a spend as you please policy with necessary recourse to borrowing. The budgets showed deficits from 1924 to 1927, but in 1927 the elections supported the Left, which meant that the spending and borrowing program was henceforth to be followed.

The elections of 1930 favored the moderates. C. J. Hambro, a Rightist, had been President of the Storting since 1926. Mowinckel was turned out of office and the Agrarians were asked to form a coalition Cabinet in 1931.

The Depression of the 1930's. The depression affected Norway severely, especially the peasant population. As in other countries, hard times increased the power of Labor, while the conservatives, including the Agrarian Party, lost ground. The Communists remained a negligible quantity. In 1933 the first Nazis, led by Major Quisling, appeared. The Nazi movement made little headway, however, and in the 1936 election received only 26,000 votes.

In 1933 the Labor Party challenged the liberal coalition government on the budget issue. The government had recommended a relief budget of 10,000,000 kroner, which Labor insisted should be raised to 50,000,000. The Laborites' slogan was " work for all." Although it was easily the largest party, Labor could not obtain a majority in the country or in the Storting. Mowinckel, who had returned to office, was the object of renewed Labor attacks, because Labor believed that his resignation would give them an opportunity to inaugurate their socialistic program. The Liberal government refused to be driven out. In January, 1934 the Liberals raised the grants-in-aid in their budget to 43,000,000 kroner, with particular emphasis on aid to agriculture.

Advent of the Labor Government. In the 1935 session of the Storting the Agrarians showed dissatisfaction with the government's agricultural policy, while Labor continued to demand expanded grants-in-aid to the unemployed to be paid for by new taxation and loans. The Agrarians joined with the Labor Party to reject the budget of March, 1935, and thereby overthrow the Cabinet. An all-Labor Cabinet was formed with Johan Nygaardsvold as Premier which was still in power in 1940. Once in power the Labor Party introduced a modest budget, abandoned its theoretical and idealistic programs, and embarked upon a course of realistic politics. Between 1935 and 1940 several progressive acts were passed, among them a measure regulating the hours of work and an old-age insurance law covering all people over 70 whose income fell below a certain level. A defense budget of 50,000,000 kroner was voted in 1938.

A quarrel with Denmark over Greenland arose in 1931. The huge Arctic land mass had once been a Norwegian colony, but in 1776 Denmark had claimed it along with other Norwegian possessions. The Norwegians continued to used Greenland's shores for fishing; indeed a Danish-Norwegian agreement of 1923 allowed the Norwegians to " winter, hunt, and fish " there. In July, 1931 the Norwegians explored part of the coast and claimed the entire country. The Danes paid little attention to this expedition but when a second force set foot on Greenland in 1932, Denmark protested to the Permanent Court of International Justice, which upheld Danish claims. Intense bitterness prevailed in Norway.

Better times appeared in 1935 and Norway was well on the way to economic recovery when the Germans invaded the land.

Foreign Affairs. The outbreak of the Second World War in September, 1939 had the same devastating effect on Norway as the First World War. By March, 1940 Norway had lost approximately 3 per cent of her merchant fleet, some 400 seamen, and over 50 ships totaling about 150,000 tons.[3] Protests were made to both belligerents, for ships such as the *Enid*, the *Songa*, and the *Tempo* were sunk by the Germans in clear contravention of international law, and the English blockade with its navicerts and detentions was only slightly less illegal. England replied that she was conducting the war for the sake of the neutrals, and to this the Norwegian Foreign Minister, Halvdan Koht, retorted in a broadcast from Trondheim on February 17, 1930:

" Time after time we hear both from France and from England that it is really for our sakes, for our cause, that they are fighting. Even when they announced that they would prevent neutral ships from carrying goods from Germany or goods manufactured from German raw materials, they stated that it was to help the neutrals. So firmly rooted is the idea that they are protecting us by their war.

" We for our part have, perhaps, more the feeling that the aim is to exploit the neutrals in the struggle itself, and we may get to think — in regard to both sides, if in a very different manner — that the war is not being fought *for* the neutrals, but actually *against* us."

Neutrality. Norway and the other small states had seen the danger gathering momentum long before the actual outbreak occurred. As ardent supporters of the League they had watched the Great Powers, including Germany and England, brush aside the League whenever it suited their purpose. In the summer of 1936, when sanctions had failed against Italy, the small states served notice that the Great Powers alone were to blame for the fiasco. As far as Norway and the rest of the Scandinavian nations were concerned, neutrality was a time-honored and sound policy if only they would be allowed to pursue it. As each crisis occurred, the necessity for combined action in Scandinavia became apparent. When the war finally broke out, the course to be followed — neutrality — had already been agreed upon. Meanwhile a steady and substantial armaments program had been developed.

The Altmark *Affair.* The most serious challenge to Norwegian neutrality prior to the invasion of April occurred on the night of February 16–17, 1940, when a British naval force boarded the German vessel, the *Altmark,* in Josing Fjord. Seven Germans lost their lives and 300 British prisoners were transferred to the British men-of-war. The British admitted a technical violation of Norwegian neutrality, but claimed that Norway should have subjected the *Altmark* to careful search. As the *Altmark* made no call at any Norwegian port, the government insisted that she had the right of passage through Norwegian waters, and was subject neither to the 24-hour rule nor to the necessity of being searched. The Norwegian government vainly protested the British action.[4]

Russo-Finnish War. The Russo-Finnish War affected Norway as much as Sweden. When the League of Nations condemned Russia's attack on Finland, it invited member states to furnish all the " humanitarian help " of which they were capable. When the League failed to provide adequate aid, Finland asked Sweden to become her ally, but Sweden reaffirmed her neutrality. No request was sent by Finland to Norway, who could have rendered little assistance beyond that which she was already furnishing.

Only France and England could have helped Finland materially, but since their enemy, Germany, had a pact of friendship with Russia, their entrance into the war might have brought Germany in on the side of Russia. This would have been an irretrievable disaster for Finland. France and England have since laid the blame on Norway and Sweden for their failure to aid the Finns; but on March 14, just after the Finnish peace had been concluded, Halvdan Koht, in his broadcast, said:

" I do not doubt that the French and British Governments began to discuss this question long before it was taken up in an official manner. But it was not until barely a fortnight ago that we first heard of official support in the form of the despatch of armed forces to Finland. . . .

" Such was the situation when in the afternoon of Saturday, the 2nd of March, the British and French Ministers came to see me with a preliminary inquiry as to whether the Norwegian Government would be prepared to give permission for French and British troops to pass through our country in case the Finnish Government should appeal to France and Britain for military assistance."

The same inquiry was made of Sweden on the following day and was rejected. The Allied request came too late. It would be hard to demonstrate how Norway could have been more scrupulously neutral than she was.

German Invasion. The Germans invaded Norway on April 9 in anticipation, they claimed, of a contemplated British attack. The German-Norwegian War was fought in two main areas: (1) the southern region from Oslo to Trondheim; and (2) around Narvik in the north. On April 11 General Otto Ruge was appointed commander-in-chief and led a desperate retreat with his small Norwegian force for some three weeks, waiting meanwhile for Allied help. An Allied expeditionary force eventually arrived, but failed to check the Nazi advance. By the first week in May the campaign was over, except for the last stand at Narvik. King Haakon and his government had departed. Germany's fast-moving mechanized troops had won a campaign of tremendous strategic importance and Norwegian neutrality was a thing of the past.

Bitter accusations were hurled at Major Quisling, Colonel Sundlo, and other Norwegians because of fifth column and Trojan horse tactics. That their activities were of any vital significance in the collapse of Norway has been firmly denied by Professor Einar Haugen and others.[5] It is pointed out that Norway could not have resisted the German attack in any case. At present the Germans have complete control of the land and what the future holds for the Norwegians will be determined at the peace negotiations that will end the present conflict.

Economic Development. Like the other Scandinavian countries Norway had a progressive social welfare program. Social security and adequate care of the indigent go back to the preceding century. Public health regulations, poor relief, care of mothers and children, schools for the blind, deaf and deformed, continuation schools and psycho-technical institutes, housing, old-age pensions, training of social workers and social education [6] were among the activities of the state. Labor was amply protected by a number of acts which provided for vacations, arbitration of disputes by a Labor Court and Boycott Tribunal, unemployment insurance, accident insurance, and sickness insurance.

Almost one-third of the people live on farms or derive their subsistence from forestry. Norwegian farmers raise cattle, sheep, hogs, goats, horses, chickens, dairy products, wheat, barley, rye, hay, and potatoes. In 1940 a large proportion of the population was engaged in fishing, shipping, mining, and other industries. Spain, Portugal, France, Brazil, and Switzerland furnished markets for Norwegian fish. Norwegian whalers were found everywhere and silver fox pelts were produced in large quantities. These were the most lucrative of Norwegian enterprises. Tremendous opportunities were available for the development of electricity through water power. In 1930 a program for supplying Germany with electricity from the Ulla and Toke falls was undertaken.

Labor was strongly organized and its influence was felt in Parliament. The result was a large number of laws for settling labor disputes. In other ways, too, the Norwegians had learned to live together peacefully. Producer and consumer cooperatives were numerous and embraced agricultural finance, marketing, milk distribution, creameries, meat, pork, eggs, and other agricultural products. Grain was marketed through a state monopoly and cooperation in a modified form was practiced both by fishermen and consuming public. The cooperatives involved private trade credit, health insurance, care of children, sickness insurance, and pensions. Norway had made progress in unemployment insurance, municipally owned apartment houses, public utilities, socialized railways, and state-owned banks.[7]

Cultural Developments. The Nobel Peace Prize, established by the Swede, Alfred Nobel, in 1895, is awarded by a committee of five chosen by the Storting. The award consists of one share of the income of the Nobel fund given " to the person who shall have most or best promoted the fraternity of nations and the abolishment or diminution of standing armies, and the formation and the extension of peace congresses." The four other prizes — namely, in physics, chemistry, medicine, and literature — are awarded by Swedish institutions.

Explorations. The Norwegians have distinguished themselves particularly in marine and Arctic research, in meteorology and weather reporting, which are vital for the fisheries and communications of western and northern Norway. The present tendency is for scientific study and research to concentrate on practical subjects: for example, hydrogen fertilizers. In the last twenty years Norwegian explorations and discoveries in the Arctic and Antarctic regions have probably led the world, and such men as Amundsen, Nansen, Captain K. Mikkelsen, Lars Christensen, and Captain Hjalmar Riiser-Larsen have added enormously to our knowledge of these frozen areas of the earth's surface.

Literature. Norwegian, like the other Scandinavian tongues, has a fertile and varied contemporary literature, much of it translated into English. Perhaps the outstanding figures are the novelists Knut Hamsun (1859–   ), Sigrid Undset (1882–   ), Johan Bojer (1872–   ), and Olav Duun (1876–   ). Hamsun, winner of the Nobel Prize, is probably the most widely read of Norwegian contemporaries. His first novel *Hunger*, the saga of a starving writer, made him known throughout the Norwegian literary world, but his *Growth of the Soil* (1917), an epic of pioneer farm life, spread his fame to all corners of the earth. Madame Undset towers above all Norwegian woman writers and, like Hamsun, is one of the greatest novelists of our time. Her triumph came with the publication of the popular novel of medieval life, *Kristin Lavransdatter*. A prolific author, Madame Undset's favorite theme is the study of woman in marriage. Johan Bojer acquired fame with *The Power of a Lie* (1903). Since then he has written many novels dealing with diverse aspects of Norwegian life, among which *The Great Hunger* (1916) is especially familiar to American readers. Bojer does not have the epic grandeur of Hamsun or Undset, but possesses unusual narrative talent, marred somewhat by a penchant for moral and sentimental discussions. Duun is the most gifted of those authors who write in the Landsmaal. His native Trondheim area is the scene of his novels, of which the six-volume *Juvik Clan*, dealing with the story of a peasant family over a period of two hundred years, is a literary monument of the highest order.

There is no room here to do justice to Norway's many pleasing poets and dramatists, and to numerous charming storytellers, some of whom use the Landsmaal.

Music and Art. In music Norway has produced no major composer since Grieg, although Christian Sinding (1856–) is well known at home and to a lesser extent in the United States, where he has taught.

Norwegian painting, like that of other Scandinavian countries, has an indigenous quality which foreigners are not always able to appreciate. Some of the leading Norwegian painters of the last generation have been Eilif Peterssen (died 1929), Harriet Backer (died 1932), Erik Werenskiold, Gerhardt Munthe, and Edvard Munch (1863–). The last is a genre and landscape painter who revels in gloomy subjects but has a powerful command of color. The chief living Norwegian sculptor is Gustav Vigeland (1869–). His masterpiece is *The Fountain*, a collection of stone groups and smaller bronze figures illustrating the development of mankind.

Summary

Between 1905 and 1940 Norway had shown that, if given the opportunity, she could develop a self-sufficient economy. As a small state, she was a firm adherent of the League of Nations and a staunch supporter of international law and order. With the German invasion she became a tragic example of the weaknesses of small states which lie adjacent to two or more great powers. At the present moment Norway serves as a base for German air and sea operations against England, and until peace is restored the Norwegians can only exist on a day to day basis.

REFERENCES

[1] See G. Gathorne Hardy, *Norway*, London: Bell, 1925, ch. 8, and Agnes Rothery, *Norway Changing and Changeless*, New York: Viking, 1939, ch. 5.

[2] Norway's experiences during the First World War are ably set forth in Wilhelm Keilhau, *Sweden, Norway, Denmark and Iceland in the World War*, New Haven: Yale Univ. Press, pp. 281–411.

[3] An excellent review was given by Minister Halvdan Koht in his speech before the Storting on February 29, 1940.

[4] See the pamphlet *The Altmark Affair*, Oslo: Fabritius.

[5] See Haugen's address delivered on May 17, 1940, in Madison, printed in the Madison *Capital Times* of that date, and reprinted by The American-Scandinavian Foundation.

[6] See Inge Debes, *Social Welfare in Norway*, Oslo: Fabritius, 1939; and *Social Work in Oslo-Norway*, published by the Municipality Oslo in collaboration with Travel Association for Oslo and Environs, 1939.

[7] For a short and interesting review see C. J. Hambro, "Norway Today" in *The American Scandinavian Review*, Spring, 1936, XXIV: 7; also *Norway*, the special number of the *Norwegian Trade Review*, April, 1939, Vol. X, No. 4; *Norway's Export Trade*, Oslo: Blix.

SELECTED BIBLIOGRAPHY

Burchardt, C. B., *Norwegian Life and Literature*, Oxford: Oxford Univ. Press, 1920. The best survey available, but does not cover the last generation.

Elviken, Andreas, *Die Entwicklung des norwegischen Nationalismus*, Berlin: Verlag Emil Ebering, 1930. Reliable and sound.

Grimley, O. B., *The New Norway*, Oslo: Johan Grundt Tanum, 1939. Timely and instructive.

Hardy, G. Gathorne, *Norway*, London: Benn, 1925. A review of Norway in the First World War, the succeeding five years, and the historical backgrounds.

Jorgensen, Theodore, *Norway's Relation to Scandinavian Unionism, 1815–1871*, Northfield, Minn.: St. Olafs College Press, 1935. Useful for a correct perspective for the problem of Scandinavian union.

Olson, Alma Luise, *Scandinavia, The Background for Neutrality*, New York: Lippincott, 1940.

Simon, Sir E. D., *The Small Democracies*, London: Gollancz, 1939. An invaluable work for the political, economic, and social structure of pre-war Scandinavia.

The History of the Scandinavian Literatures, based on the work of Giovanni Bach, with additional sections by Richard Beck, A. B. Benson, A. J. Uppvall, and others. New York: Dial Press, 1938. The most up-to-date work of its kind in English.

CHAPTER XXIII

Finland

" NEVER SHALL OUR NATIVE EARTH
BE WRESTED BLOODLESS BY THE HAND OF TYRANTS FROM HER SONS' POSSESSION.
NEVER SHALL THE WORD GO FORTH
THAT FINLAND'S FOLK BETRAYED THEIR HOMELAND IN THE NORTH.
BRAVE MEN IN THE FIGHT CAN FALL
BUT NEVER SHRINK FROM DANGER'S THREAT OR BOW THE KNEE BENEATH OPPRESSION."

— JOHAN LUDVIG RUNEBERG: *The Tales of Ensign Stal,*

Geography. The sixth largest country in Europe, Finland is situated on a wide neck of land connecting the Scandinavian peninsula with the continent. On the north Finland is bounded by the Arctic Ocean and Norway, on the west by Sweden and the Gulf of Bothnia, on the south by the Gulf of Finland, and on the east by Russia. Finland is the most northerly of civilized lands, with fully one quarter of its surface located within the Arctic Circle. Its total area is 148,000 square miles; there are 1600 miles of coastline.

Finland contains thousands of lakes, rivers, islands, swamps, and bogs. In the east there are a few mountains of approximately 4000 feet. The huge number of lakes and watercourses promises a wide development of water power, the greatest source of which at present is Imatra Falls. The larger part of the country is suitable for agriculture, forestry, and dairying. While not rich in raw materials and metallic resources, Finland has some deposits of granite, gneiss, quartz, sulphide ores, copper, iron, nickel, zinc, aleuvial gold, feldspar, soapstone, graphite, garnet, molybdenum, caoline, lime, and a low grade of asbestos.[1]

Finland is what the Germans call an Anmarschstrasse, or a land through which the armies of one great power may strike at another. It has served in the past as a buffer state and a recruiting ground for Sweden, and as a defensive bulwark for Russia. Today Finland is coveted by Germany and Russia. Socially and politically, Finland is a western nation.

Ethnography. The earliest evidence of civilization in Finland dates back to 4000 B.C. Handicraft objects from this period are fairly numerous, including some excellent ceramics, but skulls and skeletons are lacking to tell what the inhabitants were like. The iron age, which lasted from 500 B.C. to the Christian era, left few artifacts. Authorities have reached the con-

---

This chapter by Thorsten V. Kalijarvi, Professor and Head of Department of Government, University of New Hampshire.

clusion that the Finns wandered into the area between A.D. 400 and 800 from European Russia, between the Urals, Kiev, and the Baltic Sea, pushing the scattered Lapp population northward.[2] Some Swedes may have visited Finland at this time, but they returned to their homeland.

During the twelfth and thirteenth centuries Finland received Swedish settlers, whose descendants occupy the Åland Islands and the Ostrobothnian coast, constituting approximately 10 per cent of the total population of 4,000,000. There are some 2000 Lapps located in the north, mostly in the Petsamo region. With few exceptions the Finns profess the Lutheran faith.

The Finns are descended from an East Baltic race (of the Fenno-Ugrian group) related to the Hungarians and Estonians. The East Balt is a blond European. Only 7 per cent of the Finns have dark complexions, indicating an Alpine influence and intermarriage with the Samian Lapps. Hildén says, " Racially the Finns belong to the rest of the European peoples without sharp demarcations connected more especially to their nearest geographical neighbors." [3]

Languages. Finnish and Swedish are the languages of Finland. The Swedes are the remnants of the old ruling class whose influence has been overpowering for centuries. Swedish was the official language and all transactions of importance were conducted in that tongue. Between the 1840's and 1860's, however, Finnish nationalism awoke and with it came renewed interest in the Finnish language. While Finnish nationalism undoubtedly took its root in the work of the historian Henrik Porthan (1739–1804), the poetry of J. L. Runeberg (1804–1877), and other Swedish as well as Finnish writers, it was Johan Snellman (1806–1881), a Swedish-speaking Ostrobothnian who gave Finnish nationalism its first great impetus. By an Imperial Russian rescript in 1863, Finnish and Swedish were made equal in the eyes of the law. After independence had been achieved in 1917, Finnish rapidly replaced Swedish as the popular tongue. But a bitter language quarrel ensued, and has been going on with lessening intensity as Swedish is pushed into the background.

In spite of this conflict the Finnish Swedes are ardently loyal to Finland. Not even Sweden, except in the case of the Ålanders, can shake that loyalty. During the Russo-Finnish War the two groups united, at least for the time being, in the face of the common peril. Thus the Swedish-speaking Marshal Mannerheim led an army which was overwhelmingly Finnish. The same union of interests is evident in the post-war reconstruction. Perhaps this great crisis has modified the intransigence and stubbornness of both sides.

Historical Background. Europe seems to have become interested in Finland about 1155, when Swedish and Russian expeditions were sent to establish control of the region. The Finns, however, were still in posses-

sion of their fortifications by 1172, but continued attacks from the Orthodox Russians finally forced the Pope to intervene, and the Holy Pontiff
took Finland under his protection in 1228 or 1229. Suzerainty had already
been awarded to Sweden in 1216.

The Finns had not then progressed beyond the trapper stage. After
taking full control, Sweden in 1249 appointed a Swedish bishop to replace
his English predecessor. During the next three hundred years Finland
was loosely joined to the Kingdom of Sweden. A Swedish nobility ruled
the land, while the Finnish nobility was permitted to retain a large amount
of power. Unwisely, the latter revolted in the so-called Mallet War
(1596–1597) and followed Klaus Fleming against the Duke of Söderman-
land (later Charles IX), who had defeated King Sigismund. The Finns
were defeated in two campaigns.

The Finnish nobility thereafter either faded into obscurity or crossed
into Sweden to share in the central government. Finland was now more
closely integrated with the Swedish Kingdom. The rapid rise of Sweden
made Finland a battle-ground and recruiting area for the Swedish army.
The campaigns of Charles XII and the subsequent collapse of Sweden,
when Russia overran the land, entailed dire suffering for the Finns. It was
out of these hardships that Finnish nationalism was born.

Transfer to Russia. The Napoleonic wars resulted in the transfer of Finland from Sweden to Russia (1809). Finland became a Grand Duchy in
the Russian Empire. The beginnings of Russian rule were auspicious because autonomy was promised to the Finns, more territory was added to
the area known as Finland, and the capital was located at Helsingfors (Helsinki). For the major part of the century Russia respected Finnish autonomy, but by 1894, with the advent of Czar Nicholas II, systematic
Russification began. The constitution was nullified, making autonomy
inoperative. In 1904, however, the oppressive measures were modified and
in 1906 a new democratic Parliament was established.

Independence and Civil War. The Russian revolutions of 1917 spread to
all parts of the empire. When the Finns found it impossible to negotiate
with the interim Russian government, the Diet of Finland under the direction of Pehr Svinhufvud on December 6, 1917 proclaimed Finland a free
and independent country. In 1918 Russia and most of Europe recognized
Finnish independence.

There followed a period of bloody civil war. Undisciplined Russians
joined with the Finnish radicals and, supported by the Bolsheviks, seized
Helsinki on January 28, 1918. Immediately a White Guard was formed
which, led by General Mannerheim, counterattacked the Reds, but was
forced to seek reinforcements from Germany. A force of 12,000 German
troops led by General von der Goltz reached Finland in the spring of 1918
and helped the Whites to regain supremacy. The Red Terror was now

succeeded by a White Terror, and altogether about 15,000 Finns were slaughtered. A peace treaty between Russia and Finland was finally signed at Dorpat in January, 1920. The boundaries of the new state were to include the Petsamo region, the Karelian Isthmus, but not Eastern Karelia and the provinces of Olonets and Porajärvi. These boundaries were respected until the Russo-Finnish War of 1939.

The regent of the new state was P. E. Svinhufvud, who was followed by Marshal Mannerheim, the two men holding power until the constitution was adopted in June, 1919. The presidents of Finland since that time have been: Professor K. J. Stålberg (1919–1925), Dr. Lauri K. Relander (1925–1931), P. E. Svinhufvud (1931–1937), Kyösti Kallio (1937–1940), and Risto Ryti (1940–   ).

Domestic Politics. The first major problem of the Finnish government was to suppress the Reds and formulate a constitution. The Finnish constitution is not a single instrument, but consists of the constitution adopted on July 17, 1919, the supplementary Act of Parliament of January 13, 1928, and the Electoral Law of 1935. The government created in 1919 consisted of three separate departments: a President, a unicameral legislature, and an independent judiciary. The last consists of a supreme court, three courts of appeal, and seventy courts of first instance. Judges are appointed for life, on good behavior.

Government. The Diet consists of two hundred members elected by proportional representation. Legislation is a complicated process and the passage of a constitutional law is difficult. The power of initiating legislation is vested in the President and the Diet. The President, chosen for six years, by an electoral college of three hundred members elected by all persons twenty-four years of age or older, has considerable power. He is commander-in-chief of the army and navy, and dominates a Cabinet of thirteen, the Prime Minister acting for the President in his absence. The chief executive may issue administrative edicts, initiate legislation, and dissolve Parliament.

The constitution contains an elaborate Bill of Rights. The Åland Islanders have special privileges. Since gaining independence no single political party has been able to control the Finnish government.[4]

Boundary Problems. A second major problem confronting the new government was the fixing of frontiers, especially in Eastern Karelia and the Åland Islands. The inhabitants of Eastern Karelia are of the same stock as the Finns, but they had fallen under Russian rather than Swedish control. In 1918 they sought independence or a union with Finland, and were in a position to achieve their aim but for the interference of the British. In 1918 General Maynard and Rear Admiral Kemp were despatched to Petsamo and northern Finland. Preventing the Finns and the Karelians from uniting, Maynard determined that Eastern Karelia should belong to Russia. In 1921 the Eastern Karelians vainly rebelled against Russian rule. Russia promised Finland that she would grant the Karelians autonomy, but soon showed that she had no intention of keeping her word. Finland protested against the violation of autonomy provisions, the ejection of Eastern Karelians from their homes, and the oppression of those who remained. In vain Finland appealed to the Council of the League of Nations and to the Permanent Court of International Justice, to whom the Council submitted the question. The court ruled that the Russians were not members of the League, nor of the Permanent Court and for that reason the issue was outside its jurisdiction.[5]

The Åland Islands Problem. Some mention has been made in Chapter XXI of the Åland Islands dispute. The Åland Islands form an archipelago jutting out from the southwestern part of Finland into the Gulf of Bothnia. Their population was of Swedish extraction. By the Treaty of Paris of 1856 the Russians had been forced to demilitarize the Islands because of their strategic value, but during the First World War they began to re-fortify them. When the 1917 revolution broke out, the islanders sought by petition to be united with Sweden. Sweden sent three naval vessels to the Islands and the Finns and the Russians withdrew. When the German expeditionary force under von der Goltz arrived, the Swedes were forced to retire. In the hope of placating the islanders the Finnish Diet granted them local autonomy, but this did not solve the problem. Sweden insisted that the question was of international concern; Finland that it was purely domestic. In June, 1920 they argued their cases before the Council of the League. A commission of three jurists, appointed to investigate, found that a question of international law was involved. A second commission upheld Finland's claim to the Islands but affirmed the autonomous rights granted by the Helsinki Diet.

In October, 1921 a conference was held to determine the future military status of the Islands. Sweden, Finland, Germany, Great Britain, France, Italy, Poland, Estonia, and Latvia were represented. Russia was omitted. It was agreed that the Islands should be demilitarized and receive autonomy. This arrangement worked satisfactorily until the threat of aggression began to press on the Baltic and Scandinavian regions from several directions. Sweden and Finland then sought the right to fortify the Islands, and by the middle of 1939 received assent from all the powers which signed the convention of 1921. Russia, in the capacity of a League member, refused to accede to the request. During the Russo-Finnish War the Islands proved strategically valuable. When the conflict ended Russia affirmed that she had no objection to their re-fortification. Finland has since disarmed the Islands.

Agrarian Reforms. When independence was achieved, a large part of Finland's agricultural land was in the hands of a few people. The Lex Kallio or land law of 1918 ordered radical redistribution of the great estates.

It was not until 1927, however, that a compromise bill was enacted which proved a workable basis of land reforms.   Under this measure provisions were made for the expropriation of large estates with suitable compensation to their owners.   By 1934 900,000 tenant farmers had received full property rights to the land they tilled.

Prohibition.   Like Norway, Finland was forced to deal with the prohibition question.   Prohibition bills were passed in Finland in 1907 and 1909 but these were not enforced until 1919.   The results were similar to our own.   Arrests for drunkenness rose and bootlegging increased.   As early as 1922, a committee of inquiry was appointed to study the prohibition question and acts were passed to prevent smuggling of liquor.   Treaties were signed with the Baltic states to aid in the enforcement of prohibition, and doctors were carefully restricted in issuing prescriptions for alcohol.   Strengthening legislation was passed in 1925 and in 1928 all efforts at correcting the evils of prohibition were abandoned because of divided opinion throughout the country.   After they had been thoroughly discredited — as in the United States — the prohibition laws were repealed in 1932.

The Lapua Movement.   A revival of anti-Communist agitation ruffled the political waters and provided a supreme test of Finnish democracy in 1929–1930.   After 1923 the Communist Party had no official status although it continued to elect deputies to the Diet.   An announcement of the revival of the League of Communist Youth in November, 1929 threw the conservative elements, who visualized a renewal of their struggles with the Reds, into a panic.   The pastors began to preach anti-Communist sermons, and in Lapua Vihtori Kosola, who had spent several years in a Russian prison, organized anti-Communist mass meetings.   The farmers demanded that the government suppress the Communists and announced that unless laws to that effect were passed they would revolt.   By March, 1930 the farmers had organized a powerful Fascist association called the Finnish Lock (Suomen Lukko).   Under pressure from the Lapuans the Diet again suppressed the Communist Party in 1930.   As the disorders continued, however, Kallio resigned as Premier and was succeeded by Pehr Svinhufvud, the Grand Old Man of Finland.   At this juncture Kosola marched into Helsinki at the head of 12,000 farmers on July 7, 1930.   When the government called out troops to meet them, the Lapuans assumed a more pacific attitude.   Immediately afterward Svinhufvud introduced laws which would exclude from Parliament any parties advocating the overthrow of the state, forbid the dissemination of subversive propaganda, and give the government emergency powers.   Led by the Social Democrats the Diet refused to pass these measures and was immediately dissolved.   The Lapuans were ready for civil war, and general turmoil reigned throughout the land.   The Communists, who held 20 seats in the Diet in 1927 and 23 in 1929, were attacked everywhere.   The October elections rejected both the Communists and Social Democrats and the common sense of the Finnish people reasserted itself by returning a government which on November 11, 1930 passed legislation outlawing the Communist Party.

Wallenius and Kosola. The people were satisfied, but some of the Finnish leaders were not, especially the former Chief of Staff, Kurt Wallenius, who was later to be the hero of the battle against the Russians at Lake Kianta. Ex-President Stålberg and his wife were kidnaped. This and other violent acts made it apparent that reactionary elements, consisting of the Civic Guard and remnants of the White Guard, were planning a Fascist *coup* on the pretext that the government was too lenient with the Communists. Wallenius and Kosola incited the people to revolt, but Svinhufvud quieted the masses in a dramatic broadcast, and arrested Wallenius and 400 followers. After a brief trial, Wallenius was released, but by 1939 was back in the army. After the Russo-Finnish War the Fascist movement was naturally enormously strengthened. Every time Russia complains and rants against Finland the Finnish Fascists re-emphasize the dangers of Communism, the threat of the Russian anti-Christ, and the imminent danger of Russian interference in Finnish domestic affairs.[6]

The Depression. Finland encountered a depression from 1928 to 1934. Some authorities have held that the depression brought on by Russian competition was the real cause of the Lapua movement. However that may be, Finland received an economic shock through the cutthroat competition of Russian lumber. The release of money for short-term loans, owing to the crisis in the investment market in 1929, helped Finland to weather the depression. The fact that import prices dropped faster than export prices was of great assistance.

A commission of experts was set up in 1930 to recommend remedial legislation. Grain duties were imposed in September, 1931. Aid to cattle farmers, which had begun in 1929, was increased and grants were allotted to dairy farmers. The prices of farm produce were stabilized. In the process of fighting the depression Finland abandoned gold, lowered the standard of living, made agriculture self-supporting, and freed industry from foreign financial control.[7]

Foreign Policy. Finnish foreign policy upon the achievement of independence was directed towards knitting the Baltic states into a defensive bloc. From 1919 to 1922 Poland, Lithuania, Latvia, Estonia, and Finland discussed their mutual defense problems but, as we have seen in a previous chapter, the Vilna dispute between Poland and Lithuania thwarted collective action.

Toward the rest of Scandinavia Finland maintained a friendly attitude. Norway, Sweden, Denmark, Holland, Belgium, and Luxembourg sought in December, 1930, at Oslo, a common basis for cooperation. In the autumn of 1931 they were joined by Finland.

At first the German influence in Finland was strong, for Germany was an old friend and German culture had entered deeply into Finnish life. Later a trade war between the two governments ensued. Finland began to gravitate toward England, with whom her commerce increased. However, in 1935 the German-English naval pact gave Germany dominance in the Baltic and upset the trend of trade. Finland hastened to adjust herself to the new situation. She rejected guarantees from both Germany and England and followed identical policies of neutrality toward both sides and was doing so when Russia attacked.

Russian Demands. Finnish grievances against Russia go back to 1709, after the defeat of the Swedes at Poltava and the " Great Wrath " which Russia visited upon them.[8] Life under Russian rule, especially after Russification began, filled the Finns with dogged bitterness. After independence had been gained they never imagined that the Russian peril had vanished. Hence, the Finnish preparedness program did not slacken. In 1918 universal military training was introduced and the allotments for military purposes never fell below 12 per cent of the total budget.

After her uninterrupted parade through the Baltic states it was not surprising to anyone, least of all to the Finns, that Russia should make demands upon them. At the end of October, 1939 the Soviets demanded: (1) a thirty-year lease of the Hangö Peninsula and adjoining land; (2) the lease of the Bay of Lappolija as anchorage for Soviet warships; (3) cession to Russia of certain islands and parts of the Karelian Isthmus for defense purposes and the protection of Leningrad; in return the cession of Russia by Repola and Porajärvi north of Lake Ladoga; (4) a neutrality pact; (5) demilitarization of a mutually defended zone across the Karelian Isthmus; and (6) fortification of the Åland Islands by Finland at her own expense.

Finland consulted the other Scandinavian powers and made counterproposals on October 23. Russia was dissatisfied and stated on the same day that she would not give up her demand for Hangö. On November 3 further notes were submitted for boundary changes and Foreign Commissar Molotov suggested that Russia purchase Hangö. When the Finns refused the Russian press began to abuse the Finns and accused them of attacking Russia.

The Russian Invasion. Russian troops invaded Finland on November 30, without a declaration of war. Helsinki was bombed. Since Finland's army of less than half a million was approximately one-fiftieth that of Russia, the world expected a repetition of the German *Blitzkrieg* in Poland. This did not happen. The League of Nations condemned Russia, read her out of the family of nations, and called upon the states to lend every assistance to Finland. Unfortunately for Finland, support was not forthcoming in sufficient quantity for a long war. Some of the most violent critics of

Russia sold her war supplies. This marked the demise of the League and the entire system of collective security.

The war was fought in three theaters which corresponded to its three stages. The first and second, in the northern and middle sections of Finland, were disastrous for the invaders. A combination of heroism, brilliant strategy, and Arctic cold annihilated Russian divisions. Even in the third theater, around Lake Ladoga and the Karelian Isthmus, the Finns held firm against a far superior foe until massed artillery blasted the Mannerheim Line and the Finnish guns were rendered useless.

Peace Terms. The Finns waited in vain for the promised assistance; some of the soldiers had been on the firing line for three weeks. The Slavic tide was ready to flow in and the exhausted army was unable to stem it. There was no choice but to negotiate peace as rapidly as possible. The Red victory on the Summa front led to peace negotiations in Moscow on March 12–15, 1940. Finland lost the Karelian Isthmus, all of Lake Ladoga, and the Ribachi Peninsula, and granted to Russia a thirty-year lease of the Hangö Peninsula and the surrounding land, and the right to build a railway across Finland to Sweden. Finland salvaged her army, self-respect, financial structure, territorial integrity, and independence. But she also acquired a colossal burden of reconstruction and the rehabilitation of a half-million refugees from areas ceded to Russia.

Costs of the War. The war cost Finland $600,000,000; 50,000 were killed, wounded, or lost; 500,000 were left homeless. A capital levy of 10 per cent was made to liquidate these costs and avoid future taxation. In its broader aspects the Russo-Finnish War may be regarded as a move by Russia to bolster her western defenses against a possible conflict with Germany or any other powerful aggressor. Russia won and Finnish security in the future will depend upon the good will of her powerful neighbors. What the future holds for Finland is hard to say: her fate is bound up with that of all Scandinavia. Her security is overshadowed by the vassalage of the Baltic states to Soviet Russia, who has given indications that she is not satisfied with present arrangements.

Economic Development. Finland is essentially an agricultural country. Her climate is like that of Minnesota and the soil is favorable to the raising of oats, rye, wheat, barley, potatoes, timothy, turnips, flax, cabbage, and peas. Livestock consists of cattle, horses, hogs, and sheep. Finland's greatest asset is her forests, consisting chiefly of evergreens, birches, and spruce. The chief products are paper, pulp, and lumber. In addition to sawmills, particularly in the south, there are brickyards, kilns, paper mills, cellulose plants, paint factories, glassworks, porcelain factories, ironworks, cotton mills, linen works, textile manufactories, and leather works. Exports before the present war went to Germany, England, the United States, France, Spain, the Netherlands, and Belgium.[9]

The last twenty years have seen steady and rapid growth in Finnish economic life. A tendency toward industrialization has appeared accompanied by a reduction in the number of people engaged in agriculture. On the other hand, the constant increase in crop yield per acre and in livestock products has been accompanied by a 30 per cent extension of the area under cultivation. The population has increased 15 per cent. Imports of transportation machinery and industrial equipment have risen, and the balance of trade has grown steadily in Finland's favor. Exports have been chiefly paper, cellulose, foodstuffs, and timber. The replacing of foreign capital by domestic capital and the steady accumulation of wealth, accompanied by a scrupulous regard for meeting financial obligations, have given Finland an exceptionally strong place in the economic and financial world in spite of her political and economic problems. The national debt had decreased until the Russo-Finnish War. Finland continues to meet her financial obligations in spite of almost insurmountable hardships. The national budget has steadily risen, but the services performed are growing. Finland's 5000 vessels have brought many visitors to her shores and have tended to make this sub-Arctic region a new vacationland.

The Cooperative Movement. Finland has 7500 cooperative societies embracing every type of economic activity. The most important are the dairy cooperatives, closely followed by credit societies, consumers societies, and other organizations which reach every walk of life, including insurance, flour mills, feeds, sawmills, and welfare organizations. Finland's social and welfare programs have expanded. The state now provides compulsory health and welfare insurance. The cities are slumless and there is little unemployment.

The Finns have shown the most conspicuous success perhaps in labor legislation and in the improvement of the conditions of agrarian laborers. Over 75 per cent of the farm land is now in small holdings.

Cultural Development. The Finns are a highly literate nation. In the eighteenth century most of the young people had been forced to learn to read because a law forbade them to marry or receive holy communion unless they could do so. As a result, there is noted in Finland a veneration for the written word, as well as a certain legal-mindedness.

Education. Elementary education is compulsory. There are 230 secondary schools and numerous professional schools, most of which are state-supported. The University of Helsinki is a state institution while the two universities at Turku are privately endowed. The students enrolled in professional schools and universities number 10,000, including women. There are 2100 libraries and 106 people's colleges engaged in adult education. Great interest is evinced in physical culture as well as in intellectual development.

Music. Finland stands in the forefront of Scandinavian musical and literary life. Jean Sibelius (1865–   ) is a monumental if somewhat inscrutable figure in twentieth-century music. Sibelius' symphonic, orchestral, chamber, and instrumental works have inspired a national school. Played by nearly all the leading orchestras of the world, the music of Sibelius is intensely personal, yet tinctured with the brooding Scandinavian melancholy, and evoking the somber atmosphere of Finland's fens and bogs, of Arctic cold and of a race of men striving for freedom amidst oppression on all sides. Sibelius' tone poem *Finlandia* and his symphonies offer an excellent introduction to this curious world. Amid the galaxy of Finnish composers mention may be made of Armas Jarnëfelt (1869–   ) and Selim Palmgren (1878–   ).

The Finns love singing, and choral societies are to be found everywhere. Concerts are well attended and many people play some instrument or sing.

Literature. There are two literatures in Finland,[11] one in Swedish and one in Finnish. Modern Finnish literature dates from the nationalist revival of the nineteenth century. Of contemporary Finnish writers the works of the novelist Frans Emil Sillanpää (1888–   ), a Nobel Prize winner, are perhaps best known abroad. Sillanpää excels in psychological description and in depicting natural scenes, as evinced in his tragic novel, *The Maid Silja.* Mika Valtari (1908–   ) is a leading novelist using the Finnish tongue. Eino Leino (1878–1926) was a leading poet.

Hjalmar Procopé (1868–1927) was an outstanding Swedish-Finnish poet. The poems of Arvid Mörne (1876–   ) delineate the life and scenery of the Swedish districts on the coast of Finland, those of Bertel Gripenberg (1878–   ) describe the stern beauty of Finland's interior. Runar Schildt (1888–1925), dramatist and storyteller, was one of the greatest of Swedish writers produced by Finland.

Art and Architecture. Elial Saarinen (1873–   ), now head of the Cranbrook Academy in Michigan, has had considerable influence on skyscraper architecture.[12] Vaino Aaltonen is the leading Finnish sculptor; Akseli Gallen-Kallela (1865–1931), Albert Edelfelt, and Eero Järnefelt (1863–1937) are leading painters. There has been an extensive development of Finnish arts and crafts, although accompanied by commercialization and abandonment of some of the earlier skills.

Conclusion. After hundreds of years of agitation, Finland achieved independence in 1917, and after a bloody civil war, began to set her house in order, when Russia wantonly attacked her. Finland was forced to begin anew in 1940, to reconstruct her national life, with much of her best land lost, many of her people ejected from their homes, and her security more menaced than ever.

REFERENCES

1 *The Finland Year Book, 1936,* edited by I. Leiviskä, Helsinki, Oy: The Finland Year Book Ltd., the Nyland Newspaper Company Printing Works, 1936, pp. 13–46.

2 This theory is excellently presented by Kaarlo Hilden, in *The Racial Composition of the Finnish Nation,* Helsinki: Government Printing Office, 1932, especially p. 5 ff.

3 *Ibid.,* pp. 26, 29.

4 An excellent survey of the government may be found in *The Finland Year Book, 1939/40,* pp. 59–79.

5 For a brief summary of the legal aspects of the situation see Thorsten Kalijarvi, "The Question of East Carelia," *The American Journal of International Law,* Vol. XVIII, No. 1, January, 1924, pp. 93–97.

6 For an accurate and readable account of conditions in Finland, see J. Hampden Jackson, *Finland,* London: Allen & Unwin, 1938, p. 153 ff.

7 *The Finland Year Book, 1939/40,* pp. 167–171.

8 A two-page list of these grievances may be found in *The American Scandinavian Review, Finland Number,* Spring, 1940, pp. 26–27.

9 For further details and maps see the excellent *Atlas öfver Finland, 1910,* prepared by Max Alfthan, Onni Ollila, J. J. Sëderholm, J. A. Palmen, E. G. Palmen, and K. R. Willebrand for Sällskapet för Finlands Geografi, Helsingfors: Aktiebolaget F. Tigmanns Bok-och Stentryckeri.

10 Verner Lindgren, *Twenty Years of Economic Reconstruction in Finland,* reprinted in a special brochure from *Unitas,* Helsinki: Keskuskirjapaino, 1938.

11 See Giovanni Bach and others, *The History of the Scandinavian Literatures,* New York: Dial Press, 1938, pp. 291–311.

12 See D. M. Robb and J. J. Garrison, *Art in the Western World,* New York: Harper, 1935, pp. 248–50.

SELECTED BIBLIOGRAPHY

Note: The Finnish Travel Information Bureau, Rockefeller Center, 630 Fifth Avenue, New York City, has an excellent mimeographed bibliography on Finland.

The American Scandinavian Review, Finland Number, Spring, 1940. Contains a series of excellent articles on topics of current interest.

The Finland Year Book, edited by I. Leiviskä, Helsinki, Oy: Suomen Kirja, Ltd., especially 1935/1936, and 1939/1940. A mine of factual and statistical information on most phases of Finnish life.

Gilmour, Kay, *Finland,* London: Methuen, 1931. A reliable descriptive work.

Hannula, J. O., *Finland's War of Independence,* London: Faber and Faber, 1939. A helpful account of the war between the Whites and Reds.

Jackson, J. Hampden, *Finland,* London: Allen and Unwin, 1938. The best general work on Finland in English.

Okkonen, Onni, *L'Art Finlandais aux XIXᵉ et XXᵉ Siècles,* Helsinki: Société Anonyme d'Edition, Second edition, 1938. Attractive, authoritative, and interesting.

Wuorinen, John H., *Nationalism in Modern Finland,* New York: Columbia Univ. Press, 1931. An analysis of the rise of Finnish nationalism with special reference to the language struggle.

Chapter XXIV

Denmark

" SURELY YOU KNOW THAT LOVELY LITTLE LAND,
GIRT BY THE WINDING SEA ON EVERY STRAND,
WHERE BEECH-WOODS ALL THEIR SHADY SHELTER SPREAD
AND THE STRONG WHEAT THRUSTS UP ITS GOLDEN HEAD?

YOU KNOW THE ANCIENT GROUND OUR FATHERS HELD,
RICH IN PROUD MEMORIES AND SONGS OF ELD,
WHOSE SOLEMN VOICES WAKE WITHIN ME YET
SORROW'S DELICIOUS PANG AND YEARNING'S FRET? "

— CHRISTIAN WINTHER: *My Home,*
TRANSLATED BY RICHARD PRESCOTT KEIGWIN

Geography. Denmark and its islands are steppingstones to Scandinavia, lying directly north of Germany, south of Sweden, and due east of England. Until the Kiel Canal was constructed, there was no route to the North Sea and Baltic for Russia and eastern Germany save through Danish waters.

This position enabled Denmark to collect dues from passing vessels and act as a shipping *entrepôt.* In the Middle Ages the coast of Denmark provided a " take off " for Viking raids on Europe.

The Kingdom of Denmark has an area of approximately 16,570 square miles, including the Faroe Islands in the Atlantic. The land is divided into the peninsula of Jutland, which is attached to the continent, and the 500 islands which lie between Sweden and Denmark. Lakes, ponds, and short, slow rivers may be found, but the topography is rolling and flat. The highest rise is at Himmelbjerget, which has an elevation of less than 500 feet. Eighty per cent of Denmark is farm land, while the remaining 20 per cent is covered with forest.

The climate is similar to that of eastern England with slightly colder winters and warmer summers. The length of the Danish summer has made it possible to reduce the indoor feeding of cattle to a minimum in comparison with other Scandinavian countries. This is important because the backbone of the Danish economy is dairying. The soil is fertile and permits of the raising of products essential to the dairy industry, a fact which compensates in part for the lack of mineral wealth.

Ethnography. The Danes are a Gotho-Germanic race, yellow-haired and blue-eyed, who have lived in Denmark since prehistoric times. In stature,

This chapter by Thorsten V. Kalijarvi, Professor and Head of Department of Government, University of New Hampshire.

coloration, and racial composition they resemble the rest of the Scandinavians. Peaceful and genial, their system of independent landholding and small farms makes them a people who cherish freedom and cooperation. The population of Denmark in 1935 was 3,705,000, and of this number 2,058,658 lived in agricultural areas, 759,512 in Copenhagen. Since over 80 per cent of the land is in small holdings, it is hardly likely that there will be any rapid urbanization of Denmark.[1]

When the plebiscite was conducted in Schleswig after the First World War, the Danish-speaking portions were returned to Denmark, while the German part remained in Germany. But since political frontiers seldom mark a racial division, substantial numbers of Danes, especially in Flensburg, were left in Germany, while a substantial number of Germans, especially in Töndern, were left in Denmark. Thus a minority problem was created for Denmark which had not been completely solved up to the time of the Nazi invasion. The two languages being different, many opportunities for complaint arose on both sides.[2]

Historical Background. The history of Denmark is lost in the mists of prehistoric times. The western world first learned of her when the Cimbri, driven out of their homes by floods, migrated southward and reached the passes of the Alps in A.D. 113. Defeated by Marius, Europe was later to hear more of the Cimbri. From 800 to 1042, while the Norwegians explored the northern seas and the Swedish Vikings struck eastward, the Danes swept over large areas of Europe and England. In 1147, Valdemar the Great, the mightiest king in Danish history, succeeded in uniting his forces with those of Bishop Absalon and laid the foundation for a great Danish state. In 1147 Valdemar defeated the Teutonic Knights in Esthonia and thus became the most powerful monarch in Christendom. Through the treachery of one of his nobles Valdemar was forced to abandon most of his lands and never succeeded in recovering them.

The death of Valdemar was followed by two hundred years of internecine wars. In 1396 Margreta, the widowed Queen of Norway, of whom mention has already been made, succeeded by marriage and manipulation in bringing the three Scandinavian countries of Denmark, Norway, and Sweden into a dynastic union called The Kalmar Union, which lasted for thirty years. Finland at this time belonged to Sweden. In 1481, a second union, engineered by Hans, was tried, lasting until 1513. Sweden, revolting against the Danish king, broke away in 1520. This was the end of Scandinavian efforts at union until recent times.

With the Reformation raging along its borders, Denmark succumbed in 1536 to Protestantism. The sixteenth and seventeenth centuries were a period of decline for from 1740 to the end of the eighteenth century peace reigned in the land. Because Denmark had allied herself with Napoleon the Allied Powers forced her to cede Heligoland to England

and Norway to Sweden. In 1858 Denmark lost Holstein. In 1884 Prussia and Austria declared war on Denmark and as victors took Schleswig; and in 1866 Prussia wrested this territory from Austria, retaining control of it until the end of the First World War.

Government. Denmark is the oldest kingdom in the world. The Constitutional Act of June 5, 1849 established the present modern constitution. Democratic parliamentary principles were accepted in the Constitutional Act of June 5, 1915, which included the enfranchisement of women. The legislative and executive powers are vested in the king and the *Riksdag.* Legislation is recommended by a Cabinet of twelve, who also act as the executive for the land. The Riksdag is a bicameral body consisting of an Upper House or *Landsting* of 76 members and a Lower House or *Folketing* of 149 members. The two are elected separately, but an effort to reorganize the Riksdag on the Norwegian basis was barely defeated in 1939. All Danish subjects over 25 years of age are eligible to vote for members of the Lower House, while only those who are 35 years or older may vote for members of the Upper House. The chief political parties before the German occupation were the Liberals, Conservatives, Social Democrats, and Radicals. There were a few minor parties, including the Communists. Since no party could command a majority vote in the Folketing, it was the practice for two major parties to unite to form responsible governments.[3]

In the First World War. This was the form of government under which Denmark lived during the First World War, in which she was treated more severely by both belligerents than Norway or Sweden. Restrictions of all sorts were placed on her foreign and domestic commerce. Her food, dairy products, and meat were rationed, her exchange rates regulated. The German restrictions lapsed with the armistice, but the British and Allied regulations were enforced as long as the blockade of Germany lasted. It was necessary for the Danish government to regulate the production and sale of grain, bread, beer, spirits, pork, butter, milk, cheese, sugar, hides, leather products, fish, coal, coke, firewood, and peat. With the gradual easing of restrictions the Danes entered on a period of prosperity.[4]

The Schleswig Question. While all other nations were striving to aggrandize themselves at the Peace Conference, Denmark distinguished herself by asking for no land, only a plebiscite in North Schleswig. M. Laroche stated that the Danes were actually asking for less than they " deserved." The plebiscite was to be conducted in three zones, but again the Danes, exercising moderation, asked that only the two northern zones should be polled. The plebiscite held in North Schleswig in February, 1920 voted in favor of Denmark, and the area was renamed South Jutland. The inhabitants of the middle zone voted for annexation to Germany. As we have noted, Flensburg was awarded to Germany and Töndern to Denmark.

Agitation for a Republic. Bitter agitation arose in South Jutland, where the people felt that the Danish government had not done all they could to incorporate the area into Denmark. The Zahle ministry was forced out of office in March, 1920,[5] and was followed by the ministries of O. Liebe and M. P. Friis. In addition to the South Jutland agitation the constitutional crisis of the war period helped to unseat the Zahle government. When King Christian appointed the fence-straddling Liebe ministry, the Social Democrats introduced a resolution into the Riksdag calling for the proclamation of a republic. The trades unions simultaneously proclaimed a general strike, and demanded an honest election. The Social Democrats, Radicals, and the Christian Socialists marched on Amalienborg and asked the king for an election which would establish a government that had the support of the people. In the elections the radicals and Social Democrats lost heavily and the Left became the strongest party in the country.

The Neergaard Government. The new government was headed by a former Prime Minister, N. Neergaard, who held office from May 5, 1920 to April 23, 1924.[6] Neergaard proceeded to repeal the Social Democrats' radical measures, raised taxes, instituted widespread economies, and demolished the remnants of the war program. These moves aroused intense opposition, but before the issue could come to a head new economic problems arose to plague the government. Danish prosperity was short-lived and in the fall of 1921 trade losses mounted, unemployment became acute, prices dropped, and industry and agriculture suffered severely. Measures to combat the crisis were introduced by the government, among them tariffs on tobacco and boots. In 1922 the government voted to have the National Bank contribute 3,000,000 kroner to rescue the imperiled Landmandsbank, one of the largest financial institutions in the land.

First Stauning Government. The Neergaard ministry, supported by a combination of Leftists and Conservatives, led a precarious existence, for the alliance was uncongenial to both parties. When a treaty between Denmark and Russia was concluded in 1923, without consulting the Conservatives, the Cabinet was on the verge of defeat in the Riksdag. Only a sudden improvement in economic conditions, due to an exceptionally fine harvest, saved it. But the state finances were still in jeopardy and in the elections of April, 1924 the Coalition government was turned out and the Social Democrats resumed control with Thorvald Stauning as Prime Minister. Stauning [7] was destined to hold office longer than any other Dane in the last two decades.

Stauning, now chief spokesman for the Socialists, secured the support of the Radicals. By 1926 he had stabilized the krone, though prices were dropping at the time. In the fall of that same year the workingmen's organizations asked for an extensive governmental program of public works, import regulations and trade controls. At the same time the farmers sought a reduction of wages and taxes. Since the two programs were in opposition to each other, the government could not support one group without alienating the other. Its position became untenable, and an election was called which gave the Left-Conservative groups a majority of five in the Folketing. The Stauning ministry resigned and was followed on December 14, 1926 by a Left ministry headed by Thomas Madsen-Mygdal.

The new government advocated a reduction of the budget (1927) and lowering of commodity prices. Again the rift between the parties was closed by a good harvest. In April, 1928 the Landmandsbank was taken over by the state and additional regulations were imposed on banking institutions. In the elections of 1928 the Left kept its lead, but soon afterwards the party split with the Conservatives over financial and military issues. The election of April, 1929 returned Stauning to office and except for a short interlude the Social Democrats remained in power until the German invasion of April, 1940.

Second Stauning Government. The disarmament question was the issue of the day when Stauning took office in 1929. The army was reduced to 8000 men and corresponding reductions were made in other services. The general conscription program was impeded. With the breakdown of collective security, however, Denmark sought alliances with other Scandinavian states, for it had long been felt that the nation could offer little resistance if one of the major powers decided to attack her. Therefore, military expenditures would be futile. Yet in 1938 the Riksdag authorized a loan of 50,000,000 kroner for defense. Stauning visited Stockholm to consult with the other Scandinavian premiers who promised support in case of emergency but suggested that each country look to its own defenses and maintain its own air force.

The defense issue was complicated by South Jutland agitations and the advent of National Socialism in Germany. The first measure of protection against Nazi penetration came in the form of a law forbidding any person over 14 years of age to wear an organization uniform. Stauning announced in 1933, with an eye to the Germans in South Jutland, that any resort to force would be met with force; shortly afterward the police raided the Nazi headquarters and arrested Lieutenant Vilfred Peterson.

Disarmament. In 1935 the defense issue came to the fore again. Agitation for rearming the Scandinavian states was heard, and it was widely believed that if the coasts of Sweden and Denmark were amply fortified no major power could break through except at terrific cost. Stauning, however, feared that fortifications might give offense to Germany. Meanwhile matters in South Jutland grew more serious. The Germans in Tönder and nearby districts petitioned Hitler to effect their return to the Reich; the Nazi propagandists began to penetrate farther north and voices of protest and alarm were heard from Jutland. Former minister H. P. Hansen issued a fiery warning to the nation and it was reported that a force of 20,000 young Scandinavians were ready to defend the Danish border against German aggression.

Economic Problems. The Stauning government also had to deal with serious economic problems. The depression attacked Denmark in the autumn of 1929. Prices fell, and Denmark attempted to buy as little and sell as much abroad as she could so as to attain a favorable balance of trade. But economic forces were beyond the control of any country. The duties, quotas, and exchange regulations of her customers brought a slump to Denmark's export industries. Farmers and industrialists suffered alike. When England abandoned the gold standard on September 20, 1931 the exchange in Copenhagen closed in order to prevent a panic. Financial regulations were enacted, and in June, 1932 new laws for the relief of unemployment were passed.

Since Denmark depended upon the British market for the disposal of butter, pork, fish, eggs, and dairy products — her chief produce — the Ottawa arrangements of 1933 for imperial preference threatened to ruin her economy. Not only would Danish farmers suffer, but factories and fisheries would also languish. In December, 1932, 200,000 Danish workers were idle and the rest had to accept wage cuts. Threats of violence were heard and for the first time in Denmark's history fear of Communism was felt. On January 28, 1933 the Riksdag passed a law making strikes and boycotts illegal until February, 1934. A program of planned production was embarked upon.

By spring of 1933 economic conditions had improved. Prices were stabilized and new trade agreements were made with Britain. Recession set in, however, in December, 1933 but an upturn began at the end of 1934 and conditions continued to improve until the outbreak of the Second World War. In 1935 considerable disturbance was made by the Farmer extremists, who were dissatisfied with Stauning's program. An election was immediately ordered which resulted in an unequivocal support for the government.

The Second World War. Denmark's experiences in the Second World War were similar to those of Norway and Finland. Danish ships were sunk and her foreign trade curtailed. Denmark tried hard to maintain neutrality, but feared that, because of her strategic location and because she was the larder of northern Europe, she would be quickly overrun.

German Invasion. The blow came on the night of April 8, 1940 when the mechanized German forces rolled into the undefended land. The attack was so sudden, so completely overwhelming, and so carefully executed that opposition would have been impossible even if desired. Stauning and his predecessors had often stated that Denmark could not resist an invader and now they were proved right. Germany has announced that she will only occupy Denmark until the end of the war, but there can be little doubt that some change in the frontier between the two countries will be made so as to permit the Reich to incorporate the Germans in South Jutland. Meanwhile, Iceland has broken away from Denmark and is under British occupation.

Economic Development. During the closing decades of the last century Denmark abandoned grain production for animal husbandry. Intensive production of bacon, pork, butter, and eggs now characterizes Danish economic life. The many small holdings have made for extensive cooperative enterprises and a far-reaching and effective state control. Denmark also produces beef, lard, poultry, seeds, malt, barley, potatoes, cheese, condensed milk, cream, canned meats, horses, cattle, and pigs, most of which is exported in quantity. Imports consist chiefly of cereals and feeds.

Danish engineering is known the world over. Machinery of all kinds is manufactured, particularly farm equipment, electrical appliances, Diesel engines, and brewery machines. The ship-building industry has assumed substantial proportions. Among industrial exports are paints, lacquers, cement, sulphuric acid, porcelain, medical specialties, and pencils. Danish fishing is a vital part of her economic life, the chief catches being plaice, cod, haddock, herring, eel, mackerel, shrimp, and fish for canning.

Commerce. Danish commerce is under government control and includes an agricultural council, a union of cooperative societies, smallholder societies, a trade bureau for horticulture and market gardening, a council of fisheries, several fisheries associations, a federation of Danish industries, organizations for the control of crafts and industry, a shipping board, and various chambers of commerce.[8]

Socialist Measures. Denmark was a leader in state-supported social welfare measures. Her constitution contains a unique provision guaranteeing every citizen that he shall not starve. The government provides sickness and unemployment insurance, old-age pensions, and other safeguards against indigence. While most of the program is carried on through insurance societies to which the individual contributes, the government appropriates large sums. Thus in 1930–1931 payments by unemployment societies totaled 25,700,000 kroner, of which the state paid 4,900,000. The program was steadily expanding in 1940. These socialistic measures combined with the equable distribution of the national wealth explain why Denmark alone among Scandinavian countries escaped post-war Communist unrest.

Cultural Development. There are many scientific societies in Denmark, among them the Royal Danish Academy of Sciences and Letters, the Carlsberg Foundation, and Rask Orsted Foundation. The most prominent Danish scientist is Niels Bohr, the authority on atoms.

Contemporary Danish literature [9] is perhaps not as well known in foreign countries as the other Scandinavian literatures. The novels of Martin Andersen Nexö (1869–   ), Jens Anker Larsen (1875–   ), and Johannes V. Jensen (1873–   ) are most familiar to Americans. Nexö, author of *Pelle the Conqueror*, is a proletarian novelist whose works have been acclaimed as comparable to Gorki's. Anker Larsen, author of *The Philosopher's Stone*, sounds a mystical note. Jensen, probably Denmark's greatest living novelist, exalts the Teuton, the hard-working inhabitant of the sub-Arctic regions. Of an opposite cast is Emil Rasmussen (1873–   ), who, having lived in Italy, has invested his plays and novels with some of the dazzling warmth and color of the south.

Summary

Danish history in the last generation may be summarized as the quiet existence of an old and well-established country. Without bloodshed or violence, the Danes shaped their economic and social life to meet the demands of the modern industrial age and to provide security for everyone. The German invasion suddenly and ruthlessly interrupted this peaceful existence and enviable economic progress. Once the fiercest of warriors, the Dane has become so pacific that he abhors all resort to force. Like the folk hero, Holge Danske, he is asleep. But will he awake — as it is said of Holge — now that danger is upon him and assert his power? Alone, it is true, he may be helpless, but united with other Scandinavians, whom he once led in union, he may find his long-forgotten strength and vigor.

Conclusion

The first effort at uniting the Scandinavian powers was the gesture of amity by King Erik of Denmark, King Inge of Sweden, and King Magnus of Norway when they met in the year 1101 near Gothenburg and agreed to live in peace with each other. The fourteenth and fifteenth century unions have already been mentioned. The next effort was made in 1857 when King Oscar I of Sweden offered closer union with King Frederick VII of Denmark, but was rejected. Unsuccessful efforts at union have been made since.

An explanation for the current failures was given by Premier Stauning on June 18, 1939, in an address on the " North and Denmark." After dealing with the similarities in culture, language, history, and institutions of the Scandinavian states, he remarked,

"It must, however, not escape our attention that the nations of the North, in spite of similarity of language and culture, are diversified, particularly because the geographic position and economic interests make impossible uniform treatment of the different situations, which can arise."

He then proceeded to show that by no possible arrangement could the Scandinavian powers carry on a trading program which would be mutually beneficial except in a very limited way. They must trade with the other powers in the world. By the same token he showed how each had its peculiar problems of defense, indicating that the frontier problem with Germany was purely Danish and not Scandinavian. Stauning's conclusion was a call for closer relations, especially on the cultural side, but with a simultaneous indication that a union closer than that was out of the question.

The penalty for lack of union has been given twice within the last year. Russia went to war against a Finland without allies. Germany took both Norway and Denmark in the *Blitzkrieg* of April, 1940. The opportunity for union has been shunned several times, and today one of the most significant questions for Scandinavia is, will that opportunity for union come again? Divided, these states were easy prey for stronger neighboring powers, and there is no doubt that they cannot enforce their neutrality as disunited nations. But their combined forces would surely offer greater protection than small individual armies.

For example, each of the Scandinavian powers gave its support wholeheartedly to the League of Nations and the machinery for collective security. When those collapsed, neutrality, so precariously yet successfully followed from 1914 to 1918, was revived. But neutrality was harder to preserve in 1939–1940 than in the previous World War. Embarrassing moments rose for each of the small states when, as Premier Koht said, all that remained for the defense of Norwegian neutrality was to lodge a protest. Neutrality failed and only Sweden has fully survived to date. The *Altmark* case might have been differently treated if the combined Scandinavian powers were involved. The Finnish war might have occurred, but resistance might have succeeded had help from the rest of Scandinavia been forthcoming.

Iceland. No account of Scandinavia would be complete without mentioning Iceland and Greenland. Iceland is now a free state. From 1381 to 1918 it was the second largest possession of Denmark. In 1918 it was granted sovereignty upon condition that it recognize the suzerainty of the King of Denmark and that the Danish Foreign Office conduct its foreign relations. Under the terms of the Act of Union, Iceland had the right to demand a change in status. With the German invasion of Denmark, Iceland became independent but under British protection.

The population of Iceland is approximately 100,000, more than a fifth

of whom live in the capital and only large city, Reykjavik. The Iceland-
ers are descendants of the Viking explorers and colonizers to whom frequent reference has already been made. The chief industries are fishing,
dairying, and sheep raising. From the economic and political standpoints
it is hard to see how Iceland can continue as an independent state. Perhaps, when the new frontiers of Europe are drawn, Iceland may choose to
rejoin Denmark. Her culture and literature, the latter of which is one of
the finest in the world, are so close to the Danish and Norwegian that a
reunion at some future time seems logical.

Greenland. The future of Greenland, too, is in doubt. When Germany
invaded Denmark, the United States announced that it could not permit
this huge territory to be transferred to another European power and almost
a year later sent troops to occupy it. Thus the Monroe Doctrine was extended to Greenland to prevent its being used for hostile air bases by a
strong continental power.

In conclusion, the Scandinavian states have become weaker in relation
to their neighbors during the last century and a half. In 1940 they were,
with the exception of Switzerland, Great Britain, and France, the last great
strongholds of democracy on the continent of Europe. With the changes
of the industrial revolution they grew steadily in population and economic
self-sufficiency. While not rich in comparison with many other lands,
they possess the material resources, the men and brains to recapture the
place they once held among nations.

REFERENCES

[1] See *Denmark, 1934,* Copenhagen: Royal Danish Ministry for Foreign Affairs and the Danish Statistical Department, 1934, pp. 17–41.

[2] Isaiah Bowman in *The New World,* Yonkers, N. Y.: World Book Co., 1928, p. 258, says Danish parishes were forced to adopt German church services in the early 1900's. Both countries profess the same faith, Lutheranism. See the article " Denmark " in the *Encyclopædia Britannica,* eleventh edition, Vol. VIII, p. 23 ff.

[3] See *Denmark, 1934,* pp. 18–41.

[4] See Einer Cohn, *Sweden, Norway, Denmark and Iceland in the World War,* New Haven: Yale Univ. Press, 1930, pp. 411–561.

[5] *Ibid.,* pp. 536–538.

[6] For a list of the ministries from 1848 to 1929 see Poul Engelstoft and Frantz W. Wendt, *Danmarks Politiske Historie,* København, Gyldendal, 1934, p. 444.

[7] For a short sketch of his life see Alma Luise Olson, *Scandinavia, the Background for Neutrality,* Philadelphia: Lippincott, 1940, pp. 166–169.

[8] See *Denmark, 1934,* pp. 60–140, 152–158, 174–248.

[9] Giovanni Bach and others, *The History of the Scandinavian Literatures,* New York: Dial Press, 1938, pp. 355–368.

SELECTED BIBLIOGRAPHY

Note: An excellent bibliography will be found in *Denmark, 1934,* Copenhagen: Royal Danish Ministry for Foreign Affairs and the Danish Statistical Department, 1934.

Birch, J. H. S., *Denmark in History,* London: Murray, 1938. A general survey useful for background purposes as well as for recent history.

Engelstoft, Poul and Wendt, Frantz W., *Haandbog i Danmarks Politiske Historie,* København: Gyldendalske Boghandel, 1934. A general survey of Danish political history.

Goldmark, Josephine, *Democracy in Denmark,* Washington: National Home Library Foundation, 1936. A short account of the operation of the Danish government.

Harvey, William J. and Reppien, Christian, *Denmark and the Danes,* London: Unwin, 1915. Excellent for background purposes.

Stauning, Th., *Norden Og Danmark,* København: Einer Munksgaard, 1939. A short speech valuable because of its correct evaluation of the situation at the time of the invasion.

Westergaard, Harald, *Economic Developments in Denmark,* Oxford: Clarendon Press, 1922. Indispensable for an understanding of the economic revolution in Denmark during the last seventy-five years.

CHAPTER XXV

The Rise of New Ideologies and State Forms

The Nature of the Conflict of Modern Ideologies

Unique Nature of the Present Conflict. The politics of the two decades after the First World War were characterized by the conflict between the democratic and Nazi-Fascist-Communist ideologies, a conflict which resembles the bloody struggle between Catholicism and Protestantism in the sixteenth century. Certain conditions, however, make the present conflict, ever-changing though it is, different from any in the past. Modern education has produced a class of intellectuals well versed in ideologies and able to wage the warfare of ideas on a level never matched before. The intellectual climate is unique, too. We live in an age of speed, of poverty amidst plenty, of Einstein's theory of relativity, of instantaneous communication around the world. Medical, psychological, sociological, and anthropological knowledge have opened new vistas into the nature of society and man. It is important to remember all this in studying the political conflicts of our age, and only in doing so shall we avoid too easy parallels and, consequently, facile conclusions as to the character of the revolutionary ideologies and their practical expressions. We might, for example, see excessive similarities between the present conflict of ideologies and the competition of religions in the later Roman Empire, or of religious sects during the Reformation, or of political doctrines in the eighteenth and early nineteenth centuries. The revolutionary ideologies of today, Communism, Fascism, and Nazism, have their roots in the past, as doctrines always have, but the intellectual atmosphere into which they were born is unique.

Totalitarian Character of the Struggle. One of the sharpest differences between the ideologies of today and of previous eras is the totalitarian character of the intellectual struggle. This can be understood only in the light of the amazing advances in science and technology in the past hundred years which have challenged innumerable traditions and upset many fixed beliefs. Past doctrinal conflicts were usually waged against a background of tradition. The Hussites of the Middle Ages did not question orthodox conceptions of time and causality, nor even the immortality of the soul, or the divinity of Christ. The French Revolution changed the calendar and introduced new weights and measures, but it did not chal-

---

This chapter by George S. Pettee, Instructor in Government, Harvard University.

lenge the essential sovereignty of the state, or the gold standard. Today one cannot name a single premise of thought which is not at issue.

Permutations of Doctrine. The extension of the area of intellectual disagreement carries many implications. On the great doctrines around which war is literally waged today — Communism, Fascism, and Democracy — innumerable opinions have arisen. The spread of education and the advances in the technique of communication permit a greater number of permutations of doctrine than ever before.

In addition to the greater mass of controversial matter with its resulting confusion, there is, as Karl Mannheim [1] has pointed out, an altogether unparalleled use of the weapons of criticism. It is true that in all past ideological conflicts which approached the stage of warfare, one side regarded the other as mad or perverted, but rarely before has the struggle been so bitter and uncompromising. This totalitarian intellectual war must be recognized as one of the basic causes of the Second World War.

Relation of Doctrine and Behavior. It is commonly assumed that there is a direct influence between doctrine and behavior, that those who talk like democrats are democrats, and those who denounce democracy are antidemocrats. In many respects this is true, yet it assumes a degree of rationality which psychology teaches us is an altogether unreliable assumption. We know, also, that history is full of instances where men have continued to recite the verbiage of doctrine long after their loyalties had changed and their behavior had taken new forms. We are familiar with the fact that verbal statements may or may not mean anything, but we all too frequently identify ideas only by the verbal expression given to them in books and speeches, and measure their strength by the noise they make in the world, rather than by their practical effects. This difficulty gives rise to a tendency among many social scientists and historians to neglect ideological factors altogether. Thus many historians turn to the economic interpretation of history, or to an emphasis on social institutions, as a refuge from the uncertain quagmire of the history of ideas.

Role of Ideas. The real role of ideas can be easily demonstrated. We are familiar with institutions and associations of various kinds, from the state and church down to the neighborhood bridge club. In every case, if we examine their origins, we find that some purpose was present in the minds of the founders. What is more, if the organization is perpetuated beyond the lives of its founders, the basic purpose is more or less modified from one generation to another. In a small organization this purpose may never be formally expressed, but in any great association it largely centers around certain expressions or documents. Thus democracy in the United States is perpetuated by a mass of verbal expressions such as the Constitution, the Declaration of Independence, the Gettysburg address, and other documents. We can assert then, that wherever there is a continuous social life, organization, or institution, extending over many generations, there must also be a body of ideas communicated to each succeeding generation, by which its energies are directed into familiar patterns.

This is far from eliminating all the problems in identifying and evaluating the ideologies. It is clear that formal doctrines have a real function in society and that the way in which they function is conditioned by many other factors, such as the means of communication and the system of education. But further, in the case of any social organization as complex as the present United States, the underlying doctrines are often confusing and sometimes antithetical.

Expression of Ideas. Another point needs also to be raised because it is so often neglected, a corollary of the assumption that one cannot assume a perfect correspondence between the verbal expressions of an ideology and its practical application. Any major doctrinal force in the world today, such as Communism, Fascism, or democracy, is far too complex to be defined by any one document. The Communists have not produced any single document which can serve as a guidepost for Marxism. The Fascists have certainly produced no document which can serve the same purpose. Democracy has a richer body of literature, but we do not find in the Declaration of Independence, or in the Declaration of the Rights of Man, any adequate statement of what democracy stands for today. This means that if we wish to understand a political movement from its literature, we must examine a wide range of documents, wide especially in point of time, since statements made at one stage of its development may vary enormously from those made at another time and in other circumstances. This is most obvious in the case of Fascism today. Fascism (in its broadest sense) is often called doctrineless because there is so little uniformity in the declarations of its chief exponents, Mussolini and Hitler. But the same is true of the democratic tradition, as one can find readily enough by examining the works of Tom Paine and *The Federalist.*

Changes in Doctrines. When Mussolini promises a " corporative state " and then requires ten years to work out its form, we know that the term was not entirely clear to him when he first used it. When Stalin promises the most perfect democracy and then secures a unanimous vote for a single-party ticket, we can assume that democracy means something to him which would have baffled Thomas Jefferson and other founders of our republic. When Hitler promises peace, while his cohorts chant a song about conquering the world, we may be forced to suspend judgment until actions make clear to us which is the more significant statement.

One further reservation may be entered before proceeding to a discussion of the ideologies. The books written about the doctrines which have dominated the world in the last twenty years have rapidly become out of date. Those which do not become completely obsolete within a year or two retain a significant position only as contributions to the slowly growing commentary about the ideologies. This could not happen if the doctrines we are concerned with were stable philosophies, clearly and permanently expressed in documents or speeches, and if Mussolini or Hitler, or the leading protagonists of democracy, knew exactly what their principles were and where they must lead.

It is necessary to distinguish preliminary statements from later expressions. We have certainly learned, for example, that Chamberlain and Daladier were victimized at Munich partly because they entertained false notions about the nature of Nazism. We must learn to study Fascism, Nazism, and Communism, not only as seen by their opponents or apologists, but as they are in practice. This is less difficult than it may appear, but also less common than it should be.

Origin of the Nazi and Fascist Ideologies. The desperate struggle between democracy on the one hand and the totalitarian ideologies on the other cannot be understood without some conception of their diverse origins. Just as democracy was born in the revolt against autocratic government, so Communism evolved as a protest against capitalism. Democracy was carried to victory by the middle class in opposition to the feudal aristocracy. Communism is the ideology of the proletariat protesting against the *bourgeoisie* (middle class) which monopolizes the tools of production and the wealth of the land. The victory of democracy in the eighteenth and nineteenth centuries was a victory of the underprivileged middle class against their aristocratic oppressors; the victory of Communism in Russia was similarly a triumph of the expropriated over the expropriators.

Class Basis of Ideologies. Fascism and Nazism cannot be as clearly associated with social classes as democracy and Communism. Indeed, Fascism and Nazism are not yet clearly definable. In a sense, Fascism and Nazism arose because the economic systems of Italy and Germany had become seriously dislocated, and large numbers of people were suffering grievous hardships. Capitalizing on these hardships, Mussolini and Hitler rallied to their standards the disaffected, the unemployed workers who had no jobs and no hopes for the future, the petty tradesmen who were being ground by monopoly capitalism, and the idle youth for whom there was no place in a system which could produce almost illimitable goods but was unable to distribute them for lack of mass purchasing power. These were not the only factors which gave rise to the totalitarian ideologies and permitted them to ride to spectacular success. The economic problems of Italy and Germany which largely inspired the Fascist movements (assuming Nazism and Fascism to be kin) must be viewed as part of a wider picture. Tariff walls and other restrictions on foreign trade combined with the internal weaknesses of the national economic systems to produce the world depression. As each country fell victim to the depression, the anti-democratic forces gained strength, since the failure of the economic system to provide jobs and subsistence for all of the population undermined the democratic concepts of government in both Italy and Germany.

Oddly enough the totalitarian ideologies which are now seen to be Socialist in essence masqueraded as upholders of capitalism. In Italy the conservative propertied interests supported Mussolini because he represented himself as the great enemy of Socialism and the trade unions; similarly in Germany, Thyssen, Stinnes, Schroeder, and other great industrialists and financiers opened their coffers to Hitler because he was opposed to the Communists and the entrenched trade unions. Mussolini did not greatly modify the capitalist structure of Italy, it is true, until he plunged his country into the Second World War. Hitler, however, quickly showed that he intended to gain mastery over the capitalists and in so doing was forced to lead Germany more and more along socialistic lines. The climax came when he made an alliance with Russia in 1939. Competent observers now maintain that Germany is becoming progressively transformed from anything that might be called capitalism.

Democracy

Rise of Democracy after First World War. Immediately following the First World War and the treaty settlements, democracy was the dominant ideology in Europe. The prevalent conception of democracy was clearly a combination of Wilsonian ideals with elements drawn from the governmental systems of England and France. A variety of ideas drawn from Socialism or Syndicalism also entered the picture wherever these seemed to have specific relevance to national conditions.

It is by no means clear how much of true belief or understanding of democracy there was in Europe, how far there was a rush to imitate the political systems of the victorious nations in order to secure more advantageous treatment from the democratic statesmen who determined the broad bases of the peace. For Germany there was little freedom of choice in overthrowing the monarchy and installing a republic, and no basis can be found for analyzing the quantitative roles of these various motives in different countries. The three great victorious powers had parliamentary governments. In the defeated countries there were powerful elements which had long espoused the principles of democracy. There was also Wilson at Versailles, representing the hope, at least, of better treatment for the tardy converts to democracy.

Weaknesses of Post-War Democracies. In some of the countries which adopted beautifully drawn constitutions, democracy was doomed in advance. No democracy has ever been successful in a country without a high level of literacy, relative prosperity, and all the necessary features of society which go with these, such as good schools, universities, highly developed professions, strongly established and broadly based leadership, and a strong and confident middle class. Among the European nations which went through the motions of adopting democratic governments after the war, only Germany, Austria, and Czechoslovakia had the minimum social requisites for democratic life. The results, as we have seen in previous chapters, could easily have been predicted. A narrow clique or oligarchy, comparable to the South American dictatorships of the nineteenth century, took control in countries like Poland, Rumania, and Yugoslavia.

Experience of Democracy in the New Republics. Closely related to the general social background was the degree of past experience with democratic processes in the various nations. Germany, at least, had established parties and the experience of the Reichstag under the Bismarckian constitution. Finland similarly had some experience with representative government under her autonomous status before 1899. In these nations the people themselves had some familiarity with the machinery of parliamentary government and the strategy of party politics based upon popular elections.

Contents of the New Democracy. According to President Wilson, any community which regarded itself as a nation on the basis of a common language, history, and geographical homeland, should have representative self-government. The peaceful cooperation of these sovereign democratic states was to be assured by the League of Nations. One must remember that in those days it was commonly believed that the First World War was caused by the ambitions of the rulers of the non-democratic states and that democracies were incapable of aggression.

The new democracies of the post-war era took their inspiration from the democratic traditions inherited from the preceding century and from the existing parliamentary institutions, in each case reflecting not only faith in the popular will, but also the efficacy of constitutional restraint. Speaking very broadly, one might say that what the victorious democracies expected the new European states to adopt was the whole complex of democracy and constitutionalism, while what they actually could adopt was in most cases only the outward forms of parliamentary government.

Those proponents of democracy in the new states certainly underestimated the importance of certain elements not found in their own countries, which played a major role in the successful operation of the political systems of the United States, Great Britain, and France. France, except for Alsace-Lorraine and Savoy, had been an integrated nation for generations before the Third Republic, and had a tradition of legal restraint dating back to the parliaments of the Middle Ages. Great Britain was a homogeneous state, with only the Irish as a " minority " problem, held together by centuries of tradition and respect for democratic institutions. The United States had been united and indivisible ever since the Civil War.

Imitation of the Older Democracies and Modern Improvements. When it came to writing and adopting democratic constitutions, various other elements entered the picture in the new European republics. There was naturally a tendency to copy the centralized parliamentary system of England or France rather than the American system of checks and balances. The new republics also tended to adopt certain modern improvements, such as proportional representation, as in the Weimar constitution. A strong movement toward industrial democracy found expression in the third house of Parliament in Germany, called the *Reichswirtschaftsrat.*

Unique Circumstances. Because of special circumstances in each state, as many elements of society as possible had to be satisfied in shaping the structures of the new governments. In the Weimar constitution this took the form of various clauses designed to please Socialists and Catholics, landowners, industrialists, and other groups. The idea of federalism, as embodied in the upper chamber, was a concession to the separatist feelings of the German states.

In addition to special conditions which differentiate the problems of democracy in central Europe from those which had been solved in the older democracies, there were national traditions to contend with which survived the defeat of the existing monarchical regimes. Thus, for example, in Germany there was a tradition of economic planning which had continued unbroken from the days of the Teutonic Knights, and which had been strengthened during and just after the war. In other new democracies, such as Hungary, Poland, and Rumania, there were established ideas about the supremacy of one racial group, that created problems with which no democracy had yet successfully dealt.

Difficulties consequently arose out of conditions which had no parallels in the formative periods of American, French, or British democracy. The new republics had to grapple simultaneously with the " minorities problem " and with class consciousness developed by a century of the Industrial Revolution, as well as Marxist propaganda.

The assumption that the state and its boundaries are coterminous may sound obvious, yet this became a major problem in the new democracies of Europe after the First World War. Many Estonians and other Baltic peoples, for example, never felt any deep loyalty to their governments. Many of the inhabitants of Poland and Rumania would gladly have redrawn the map of their countries.

Nationalism. Each of the new democracies was set up on an ostensibly nationalist basis. It is hard to see how this could have been avoided under the circumstances. The assumption was certainly generally accepted that the peoples concerned were in fact nations. It is now apparent that they were not " nations " in the sense in which the word was applied to France or Great Britain. The politics of Poland, Yugoslavia, Rumania, and Czechoslovakia were clouded for twenty years by the bickerings of minorities, and in none could stable national boundaries be drawn. For example, Poland held Vilna, a Lithuanian city, and harbored great numbers of White Russians and Germans; Lithuania was deprived of Vilna, its leading city; in Yugoslavia, the Croats constantly struggled against Serbian domination; Slovak and German tension destroyed the harmony of the Czechoslovak state. Not one of these so-called democracies exemplified the racial cohesion of the Swiss with their great variations of language and religion.

External Dangers to the New Republics. The peaceful cooperation of the democracies of Europe, which was certainly the *sine qua non* for their survival, was jeopardized for many years by the French system of alliances by which the Little Entente of Czechoslovakia, Rumania, and Yugoslavia especially served as a safeguard on the one hand against the possible revision of the peace treaties by Germany, Austria, or Hungary, and on the other against the spread of Bolshevism. At the same time, the United States, which exemplified to the world the conception of a community of democratic, sovereign, and peaceful states, decided not to participate in the League which was designed to implement this conception. Finally, as we have seen in Chapter IV, there were special obstacles to the survival of democracy deriving from the problems of disarmament, reparations, and war debts.

Party Conflicts in Germany. The lack of harmony within the new European democracies is illustrated most clearly in Germany. This topic has been discussed elsewhere, but may be reviewed here briefly. The German electorate was so divided by proportional representation that parliamentary government inevitably had to be based on a bloc system analogous to the French. A certain proportion of the Reichstag was usually available for the construction of a party alliance which might support a cabinet. This included the so-called " Weimar bloc," the Social Democratic Party, the Catholic Center Party, and other political groups which were loyal to the republic but disagreed on innumerable points of policy. Outside this bloc were the Communists on the Left, the Nationalists and National Socialists on the Right, who effectively sabotaged all efforts to strengthen the republic. For ten years these groups sat in Parliament, free to criticize but not to assume responsibility for the formation of alternative cabinets.

As these non-democratic elements grew until they constituted more than 40 per cent of the Reichstag in the depression years, before Hitler came to power, there was a constantly narrower basis for the formation of a Cabinet. The only possible government on truly parliamentary lines came to be one which represented a compromise among the Weimar bloc. This inevitably weakened the republic and strengthened the anti-republican forces.

Antagonism of the Fascists. The weakening of the democratic machinery under adverse economic conditions has been regarded by some as a primary cause for the rise of Fascist movements. Certainly Fascists and Nazis exaggerated the weaknesses of democracy in their propaganda, raising an outcry about too much talk and too little action, about indecision and failure to grapple with the " national tasks." The years of prosperity and hope in the later 'twenties, following Locarno and the Dawes Plan — a prosperity supported by American loans — gave the new European democracies a lease on life. Italy passed under dictatorship by slow stages from 1922 to 1925, but between Locarno (October, 1925) and the beginning of the world depression in 1930, no democracy in Europe was destroyed, and indeed all were strengthened.

Conclusion. In considering the circumstances which made the new European democracies short-lived, we must note the character of the democratic ideology. America, England, and France received the democratic ideology in all its freshness and vigor in the late eighteenth and early nineteenth centuries. The principles of democracy were elaborated by such men as Tom Paine and Thomas Jefferson. At the same time that its libertarian features were developed, its constitutional elements were worked out by such thinkers as Edmund Burke and Alexander Hamilton.

The democracies which were established in Europe after the First World War had their birth in an altogether different intellectual atmosphere. By then, democracy had become a subject of scholastic criticism. Thus it must be recognized that democratic ideas were received in 1919 into a far less favorable environment than was afforded them in the United States, France, and Great Britain, a century and a half earlier. They were received in advance of the process of nation building, before strong and accepted constitutional restraints could be created. Finally, it may be said that the collapse of the new democratic states and of the Third French Republic should contribute much to our understanding of the conditions necessary for the survival of democracy in the modern world.

Communism

Philosophical Origin of Communism. The second great ideology which has shaped the politics of the period 1918 to 1940 is Communism. Communism is younger than democracy, since its first great document, *The Communist Manifesto,* dates only from 1848.[2] Communism has had far less application than democracy, since only Russia since 1917 has offered a proving ground for its theories. The relation between Communist ideas and working institutions is, therefore, less precisely understood. This means that Communism is a doctrine of revolt more than a working system, in spite of Russia, rather more theory than practice.

The major characteristic of Communism perhaps is its assumption of logical consistency. It claims to be a political system posited on a scientific analysis of the social structure. This dogmatic pretension permits of comparatively predictable action by its adherents. The second characteristic of Communism is that its dogmas are based on a foundation of some historical truth.

Marx and Engels. Communism is derived from the social, political, and economic theories of Karl Marx (1818–1883) and Friedrich Engels (1820–1895); in particular from Marx's *Capitalism*, an analysis of capitalist society which contains a closely reasoned prophecy of its collapse and a suggestion of the new order which will rise on its ruins. The exact shape of that new order is unrevealed; its outlines are indicated by Marx only in the broad terms of " economic equality " and the " abolition of the exploitation of man by man." The three major elements of Marxism laid down by Marx and rigidly adhered to ever since, are *Materialism, Dialectics*, and *Economic Determinism* or as it is sometimes called, " historical materialism."

Materialism. The philosophy of Materialism assumes that knowledge and ideas are dependent upon the objective universe, so that matter can be considered as antecedent to thought and not vice versa. Substantially this is the attitude held by scientists contemporary with Marx and it is still regarded as valid in its bare essentials, but the implications given to it by science since the turn of the century are far different from those drawn by Marx. It is implicit throughout Marxism that perfect objectivity of mind had been attained in science and also in Marxism itself, and that, therefore, theories based on a materialistic approach can never be overturned. In this connection it is sufficient to state that, since Einstein's theory of relativity, it has been fully demonstrated that perfect objectivity is exceedingly rare, that nineteenth-century science had not attained it, and that there is no reason whatever to honor the Marxist claim in this connection.

Dialectics. Marx took his conception of Dialectics from Hegel, the only alteration being the shift from Hegel's idealism to Materialism, a shift which Marx characterized as restoring Dialectics from an upside-down position. Marxian (and Hegelian) Dialectics consists of a thesis, such as capitalism, which produces its antithesis, the proletariat, and finally through interaction a synthesis, the *Socialist state*.

Economic Determinism. Economic Determinism is ostensibly derived from Materialism. According to this theory the basic factor in determining all social customs is the " mode of production," a term which includes both the prevailing technology and the forms of organization, such as slavery or wage labor. All aspects of the social system, government, religion, art, science, etc., are determined by the mode of production. To support this argument a great amount of evidence has been collected by Marxist writers.[3] However, all the evidence presented suffices only to indicate a degree of interdependence of all aspects of a culture, and does not substantiate all the conclusions of Economic Determinism.

Other Marxist Tenets. Marxism goes on to define capitalism, social classes, the class struggle, the nature of the state, the coming breakdown of capitalism and proletarian revolution, and the advent of Socialist and classless society. Capitalism is the economic system founded upon the free entrepreneur, the free market, and the free laborer. According to prevailing economic theory at the time of Marx, wages tend to stay at the level of bare subsistence, while production tends to increase. There is, therefore, a wide margin between wages and the value of labor. This margin is called by Marx " surplus value " and measures the degree of the capitalist's exploitation of labor. Capitalism tends constantly toward larger industrial combinations, greater pressure for markets, and overproduction, while the rich become richer and the poor become poorer.

Class Struggle. This is the point at which dialectics plays its most important role in the Marxian system. Capitalism creates the capitalist and proletarian classes. At the same time, it conditions the capitalists to increasing competitive strife and teaches the proletariat the necessity of cooperation. The proletariat, therefore, is the class which not only conceives the possibility of a just economic society, but is ready and willing to organize and fight for its attainment. The leading elements of the proletariat, the most intelligent and energetic, should take the lead and form the Communist Party.

But the state, in spite of any democratic pretenses, is really controlled by the capitalists, through the power of money over press, education, and politics. The capitalists themselves are by no means willing to permit the peaceful abolition of capitalism and thereby of their own wealth. The utmost that can be won by reform are non-essential concessions. Therefore it is necessary for the proletariat to instigate a violent revolution, overthrow the capitalists, and set up the dictatorship of the proletariat as an agency for the creation of the Socialist state.

The Future State. In the writings of Marx and Engels, the concept of the state is by no means clear, since there are contradictory expressions, but to Lenin the case was simple: " The State is the product and the manifestation of the irreconcilability of class antagonisms." [4] Given such a theory of the state, the necessity of revolution follows automatically. Also, Marx's conclusion that the state will wither away after the capitalists have been expropriated is a direct consequence of this theory, since, if the state exists only where there is a class struggle, there can be no state in a classless society.

Scientific Aspect of Marxism. In the Marxist theoretical structure, certain characteristics must be noted. First, the Marxist philosophy based its premises on the most pretentious claim to validity which could be found at the time: namely, that of science. But its claim to scientific truth can no longer be granted. Secondly, Marx's economic and social theories were derived from the works of Ricardo and the early anthropologists, and what Marx selected in most cases turned out to be bad economics and bad anthropology. Thirdly, Marx's political theory, while admirably adapted to the doctrine of revolution, has no relevance in the most advanced industrial countries. In brief, Marxism is a combination of various elements of thought drawn from many sources, and somewhat filtered by the selective faculty of Lenin.

Practical Communism is a combination of two elements, Marxist theory and Russian experience. In this combination it has been hard to estimate the weight that should be given to each component. After all, certain things may be possible or impossible for any government, simply because of given conditions. Russia was 78 per cent illiterate in 1917. Most of the population had never worn shoes. The proletariat, or industrial wage earners, constituted in Russia only one-tenth of the population. With the best will in the world, the Bolshevik government was doomed to play the role of benevolent despot in a country that was not only very backward, but shattered by war.

Role of Russia. Except to devoted Communists, the Russian experience, as we concluded in Chapter XVIII, has been mainly disappointing. Up to 1930 Russia was regarded with sympathy and hope by a great many liberal writers.[5] Solution of the nationalities question was regarded as a triumph; the first Five-Year Plan as highly successful. But gradually, beginning with the famine of 1931, and continuing through the purges and the Soviet Treaty with Germany in 1939, an increasing number of sympathizers have turned away from Russia. During the same years, however, many causes have combined to bring new recruits to Communism, especially the world depression, and the Sino-Japanese and Spanish Civil wars. But Russia today is typified to the world by the inscrutability of Stalin, and the latest books on the Soviet Union advance, more than earlier ones, the claim that Communist policy is, first and last, Russian policy.

Fascism and Nazism

Origin of Nazi-Fascist Ideology. Fascism and Nazism are in many ways the easiest of the great modern ideologies to describe, for they are much the youngest; in many other ways they are the most difficult, because they offer less precise doctrines than either democracy or Marxism. Fascism in its first ten years, from 1919 to 1929, presented a comparatively small and therefore manageable body of ideas. But, even then, there were glaring discrepancies between the promise of one day and the performance of another. In the case of Nazism the same paradox is present in even more marked degree.

The ideology of Italian Fascism and of German Nazism was created in the forum. It is to be found in whatever threads of consistency there are in the speeches and writings of Mussolini and other Fascists, and of Hitler and his followers.

" Fascism is not the nursling of a doctrine previously drafted at a desk; it was born of the need of action, and was action. . . ."[6]

This theory has given rise to at least two interpretations. Some critics have insisted that Fascism and Nazism have no doctrines,[7] that they are basically pragmatic. Such critics necessarily arrive at the most complete nihilistic position, seeing Fascism as the philosophy of men devoted solely to the lust for power.

There is much in the background of modern thinking from which Mussolini and Hitler may have found food for thought. The great Syndicalist, Georges Sorel, claimed that ideologies and doctrines cannot be scientifically valid and, therefore, have no possible merit except as myths: that is to say, as means of inducing faith and action. If they actually generate enthusiasm and energy they have succeeded, and no other test is possible.

Contempt for Fixed Doctrine. Certainly the Fascists have behaved as if they accepted this. The best explanation of the Fascist and Nazi contempt for fixed doctrine is to be found in the biographical background of Mussolini and Hitler.[8] What is clear in the case of Mussolini, as Chapter XIII emphasizes, is that a young Socialist, with rather extreme and violent tendencies, lost faith in Socialism, democracy, and parliamentarism. He remained a revolutionary, but ceased to be a Socialist. All those who regarded Mussolini as a reactionary, because he had deserted the Socialist Party, have had cause to wonder in recent years. Italian conservatives assumed that he was one of them. Historians argued that Mussolini was a conservative nationalist, and this idea lingered until Il Duce finally did what Cavour would never have done, jeopardized the future of his country by entering the war on the German side in June, 1940.

Hitler's Mentality. Hitler, similarly, is a difficult type to define. He has never been what Socialists call a Socialist, nor what Communists call a Communist, nor what conservatives would recognize as a conservative, though conservatives did for a time hold the illusion that they could make use of him. In all the welter of detail, much of it plainly false or obsolete, which clutters his autobiography, *Mein Kampf*, the outstanding fact is that Hitler had no respect or loyalty for the existing order and could find no satisfaction in the Socialist or Communist program of revolt.

Basic Ideas. With these observations in mind, we can examine the actual ideas which have been professed at various times by Mussolini and Hitler. In Italy, from 1919 until the march on Rome in October, 1922, the dominant political forces were anti-Bolshevism, anti-parliamentarism, activism, and national resurgence. Anti-Bolshevism meant, first, a violent reaction against the Syndicalist labor movement which had provoked widespread strikes after the war. Anti-parliamentarism meant denunciations of the democratic regime and party politics. Activism gave the Fascist movement its brutally dynamic aspect, the swift liquidation of opponents. The Fascists had a solidarity, an *esprit de corps* which contrasted markedly with the bickerings and dissension among the democrats.

Nationalism. The emphasis on national resurgence in Fascism and Nazism, together with anti-Bolshevik talk and rearmament, seemed merely an intensified form of the militant nationalism of the nineteenth century. Furthermore, Mussolini first took office in a Cabinet largely composed of nationalists who later became Fascists. On the other hand, Professor Borgese, an eminent authority, believes that Mussolini is not a nationalist but an unprincipled anarchist, with personal power as his sole object. Mussolini, himself, has asserted that the state is the core of Fascist ideology.

" It is not the nation that generates the State, as according to the old naturalistic concept which served as the basis of the political theories of the national States of the nineteenth century. Rather the nation is created by the State. . . ." [9]

In Germany, the Nazis strongly emphasized the national element before and after they took office. Hitler first assumed power in a coalition with Nationalists. Hitler was unable, however, like Mussolini, to woo the Nationalists into his party, but it is obvious that he was regarded as a " nationalist " in the old sense of the term until after the partition of Czechoslovakia.

Fascism and Nazism in Action. Fascism or Nazism can be understood much more clearly by examining it in action rather than by studying its verbal expressions. Italian Fascism before 1925 was an uncertain compound of violence and compromise. When Mussolini had weathered the storm which arose after the murder of Matteotti in 1924, Fascism rapidly developed its institutional form. The Charter of Labor gives a simple if exaggerated statement of the totalitarian position:

" The Italian nation is an organism having ends, life, and means of action superior to those of the individuals, taken singly or in groups, which compose it."

Core of Fascist Doctrine. This and similar statements about the omnipotence of the state reveal the keystone of Fascist doctrine. The corporative institutions which bring all economic organization together and form the basis of the representative system, censorship of the press, the oath of loyalty required in the Italian universities, development of the Ovra or secret police, all these fit the central Fascist doctrine that the state is omnipotent.

Racism. The Nazi slogans voice the emphasis on the Nordic race, or alternatively on the German people. *Blut und Boden* (Blood and Soil), *Deutschland erwache!* (Germany Awake!), the *Völkische Beobachter* (*National Observer*), all point at Germanism as the center of loyalty, at the racial conception of membership which excludes the Jews and non-Aryans.

Non-Nazi writers have universally condemned the racial theories of Hitler. Some regard his anti-Semitism as a demagogic trick useful for gaining power; others believe that the Jews in the Nazi revolution played the same role as the *bourgeoisie* in the Russian revolution. German racism may also be regarded as a myth of the pragmatic type which Sorel described, a means of generating enthusiasm and thereby loyalty to the nation. Whatever may be said of anti-Semitism and anti-Bolshevism — the twin tenets around which Hitler's denunciatory speeches revolved before taking power — they certainly helped to screen the revolutionary character of Nazism from German industrialists and statesmen. Nazi racism, as expounded by its leading exponent Alfred Rosenberg, has no scientific validity whatever. Presumably racism and the myth of Aryan supremacy must be recognized as part of the false front which commonly accompanies a revolution, like the aping of the Roman republic by the Jacobins in France.

The Party and the State. Yet one thing more than any other characterizes Fascism and Nazism and gives us a key to their nature. This is the relation of the party to the state. In both Italy and Germany, a single party is recognized by law. The party militia is an adjunct to the national forces. The party, by means of propaganda and terrorist tactics, secures apparent unanimity in the nation on all issues. The party is carefully recruited from organized and indoctrinated youth. In short, in Italy, Germany, and Russia, the party with its carefully selected and limited membership is the supreme organ of government and the instrument behind which the dictators operate. Not since the French Revolution has such a party dictatorship been seen.

This union of state and party obviously stands at the opposite pole from democracy, which recognizes free discussion and free opinion as the cornerstones of government. It is interesting to note that Communist Russia introduced single-party government and that furthermore it was foreshadowed in England in the days of Cromwell and in France under the Jacobins.

The illiberal and tyrannical nature of the Fascist and Nazi state has aroused the opposition of all types of liberals. " This is the greatest and deadliest and most gratuitous perversion in man's annals," [10] says Borgese of Fascism. Before the Soviet-Nazi Pact of 1939, Communists discussed Nazism and Fascism in equivalent terms, regarding both as extreme forms of capitalism. This belief provided the foundation for the liberal-Marxist alliances known as the Popular Front.

World Revolution. Since the beginning of the Second World War in September, 1939 it has become common to lump Fascism and Nazism together as agents of " world revolution." [11] Certainly the success of the Nazi armies threatens to change not only the map of a large part of the world, but many political and economic structures. Recent statements by leading Nazis and Fascists, especially the speeches of Hitler, have harped upon the idea of a new world order. Yet the question arises, what are the principles of this revolution? Unfortunately a clear answer cannot be given.

Miscellaneous Ideologies

Other Ideologies. In the last two decades a multitude of political movements with more or less pretentious doctrines have arisen in many of the smaller or backward countries. In each case these have been conditioned partly by native circumstances, partly by the generally rising economic tension, and partly by the somewhat accidental choice of elements drawn from the general mass of ideologies. Thus Austria, before the Nazi invasion, was ruled by a government permeated by Fascist doctrines, but with Catholic paternalism replacing revolutionary totalitarianism. Turkey, under Kemal Pasha, was, in the Hellenic sense of the term, a " benevolent tyranny." Kemal sought to develop national strength and not merely aggrandize the " tyrant " or dictator. The Turkish system could hardly be identified with either Fascism or the Austrian Clericalism. Mexico is another interesting example; there, a severe agrarian problem, together with the haphazard influence of Socialist and Communist ideas, has created an anomalous " revolutionary " state.

Small Countries. Many other small countries have had regimes which closely resembled those of Austria or Turkey. Hungary, Rumania, and Yugoslavia have mixed the ingredients of dictatorship and democracy in a fashion reminiscent of Tammany Hall in its palmy days.

A few other states have had exceptional experiences. China has been influenced by the nationalism of Sun-Yat Sen, which was somewhat influenced by Communist ideas of peasant revolution and pre-fascist ideas of absolute national authority. India has had an increasingly strong nationalist movement – still dominated, though precariously, by Gandhi – which seeks a liberal autonomous government.

Decline of Socialism. In spite of the strong influence of the Socialist tradition in certain countries, such as Sweden, and to a lesser degree England, France, and the United States, one of the important features of the period covered by this book has been the decline of Socialist influence. Many factors have contributed to this situation, including the failure of all Socialist parties to oppose the war of 1914, the ineffectual performance of the German Social Democrats in the Weimar republic and of the British Labor Party in its two brief tenures of government. In defense of the Socialists, it must be said that their opponents used every political device to sabotage their program whenever they obtained power.

In France, the Socialists did not become the leading party until 1936 when they took office as leaders of the "Popular Front" government, supported by the Radical Socialists and Communists. Under the guidance of Léon Blum they instituted a number of remarkable social reforms. They were too timid, however, to defy the British appeasers and help the Loyalists in the Spanish Civil War. Moreover, many of their reforms appear to have contributed to the weakness of France in armaments, particularly air power, which became so shockingly conspicuous in June, 1940.

Ideologies in Action

We may conclude this chapter with a rapid survey of ideologies in action, such as the use of propaganda, the regimentation of education and indoctrination of youth.

Revolution in Communication and Education. The success of Fascism, Communism, and Nazism would probably have been greatly hampered without modern communication devices and modern educational systems. Universal literacy was impossible until the productivity of power machines made child labor unnecessary. Because of the tremendous increase in communication facilities, it is easier than ever before to indoctrinate great masses of people with any desired ideology. The telegraph and telephone, combined with the newspaper, make it possible to relay a message to millions at the same time. The radio is an agency of communication *par excellence*, bringing to demagogues virtually world-wide audiences. If, as some maintain, the spoken word is more effective than the written word, the significance of radio in reshaping modern society is even greater than we imagine.

Use of Propaganda. Next to the tremendous change in the means of communication, the systematic exploitation by political leaders of the psychological value of propaganda has had the greatest influence in promoting the ideologies. Name-calling, personification, the skillful playing upon prejudices, the exaltation of leaders, and the everlasting reiteration of the simplest slogans have all been more or less practiced throughout human history, but in the contemporary world they have been exploited to the fullest extent for political purposes. Dr. Joseph Goebbels, the German Minister of Propaganda, for example, has contributed many revolutionary and diabolical devices for controlling public opinion. The new techniques of propaganda, together with the new means of communication and the control of education, have permitted the totalitarian regimes, and the democracies as well, to obtain a firmer grip on the populace than governments ever had before. Changes in popular feeling, which before required a generation, can now be effected in a few months. The new techniques serve for both attack and defense.

Control of Education and Public Utterances. In addition to the changes in political tactics brought about by the development of such devices as radio, opinion polls, and the techniques of propaganda, the dictatorships have reintroduced an ancient political tool — control of education, the press, and all public utterances.

Since the time of Plato, it has been recognized that education is the means by which every generation is taught to accept the existing customs and modes. Certainly the founders of most of the world's universities understood that the function of such institutions is to provide the personnel for civil bureaucracy, the clerical and legal professions, all of which are devoted to the maintenance of the existing order. This was the motive for the creation of local universities in the old German states, as well as Harvard, Yale, and other early American colleges.

The Catholics have never deviated from this theory of education.[12] The Church, by insisting upon its rights to educate the young, has always repudiated the rationalist notion of education as the teaching of unbiased knowledge.

Changes in Education. The dictators have thoroughly overhauled the curricula and purged the teaching personnel. In Germany, which had the most highly developed educational system before the Nazis came to power, enrollment in the universities was reduced by nearly one-half, and in the secondary schools by one-quarter.[13] This reduction at first actually proved beneficial because of the relative crowding of the professions in pre-Nazi Germany, and was in any case useful for the immediate development of military power. As Hitler has said, " the Army is the crowning glory of Nazi education." [14] The Nazis have omitted no device for the shaping of public opinion in the desired direction. The purging of art and music of all " decadent " elements is but one aspect of the process. Burning books unsympathetic to Nazism in the great bonfire of May 10, 1933 was the opening act in the systematic *gleichschaltung* (regimentation) of Germany's cultural life.

Russia and Italy. In Russia and Italy, the picture was quite different for obvious reasons. In Bolshevik Russia, because of predominant illiteracy, there was less a problem of stamping out old beliefs than establishing the minimum basis for collective thinking. Modern dictatorship cannot successfully operate without a literate population since, no matter how much use is made of the radio, the great mass of instructions and orders through which a new order is developed and regulated, are written down. The Fascist regime in Italy has reduced illiteracy from 27 per cent of the population in 1921 to 21 per cent in 1931. At the same time the universities have been purged of anti-Fascist elements, as in Germany.

The Dynamic Aspects of Fascism. In addition to holding the populace in its iron grip by overt and secret means, the Fascist state is featured by a dynamism which is normally absent from all other forms of government. The dictators must continually feed their adherents with sensational victories. The Fascist state cannot stand still. Thus Mussolini, after stabilizing his regime internally, embarked on the Ethiopian campaign; having won this triumph he pledged his country's support to the Rebels in Spain; their success was celebrated in Rome as an Italian victory. Hitler's career since taking power has been even more strikingly dynamic. After consolidating his government and purging the party in 1934 of dissident elements, he embarked upon one sensational move after another: annexation of the Saar, remilitarization of the Rhineland, occupation of Austria, Czechoslovakia, and Danzig, and finally the Polish war. Nazism and Fascism are militant ideologies and the totalitarian states are military states. This fact has altered the whole picture of world politics.

The totalitarian regimes have forced the democracies themselves to become military or semi-military states and to institute many of the controls of economic and social life which are prominent features of the Fascist and Nazi systems. Thus the United States, like England earlier, adopted conscription even in peacetime and began to put her economy on a defense basis. Consciously or not, the mere spending of many billions to match the German armaments will produce vital changes in the organization of American government and in the relation of government to business and social life.

Future of the Ideologies. At the same time, it seems doubtful if any government can ever again allow the freedom of opinion which democracies enjoyed in the past. Even on the most liberal assumptions, government exists to " hinder the hindrances to the good life." It is impossible to foretell the future, but it can hardly be doubted that limitation of free speech and free assembly will be necessary, and that such measures will inevitably affect the political life of democratic countries. The present demand in the United States for the suppression of un-American doctrines reflects the widespread loss of faith in the efficacy of free thought.

The war of ideologies is far from decided today.   Nazism and Fascism are locked in mortal combat with democracy.   Whether the democratic countries can organize themselves for survival in the face of the superior military strength of their adversaries remains to be seen.   Again, whether Nazism contains constructive aspects and is not merely a " revolution of nihilism," as Rauschning maintains, only the future will tell.

REFERENCES

[1] K. Mannheim, *Ideology and Utopia*, New York: Harcourt, Brace, 1936.

[2] The *Manifesto*, and a large selection of other writings of Marx, Engels, Lenin, and Stalin, are given in E. Burns, *A Handbook of Marxism*, New York: Random House, 1935. A smaller selection is given in M. Oakeshott, *The Social and Political Doctrines of Contemporary Europe*, Cambridge: Cambridge Univ. Press, 1939.

[3] For a complete treatment of economic determinism from the strictly Marxist angle, see N. Bukharin, *Historical Materialism*, New York: International, 1925.

[4] Lenin, *The State and Revolution*, New York: Vanguard, 1926, p. 115. This work is reprinted in Burns, and a selection is given in Oakeshott.

[5] For a sympathetic view of the Soviet system, see Sidney and Beatrice Webb, *Soviet Communism, A New Civilization?*, New York: Scribner, 1936.

[6] Mussolini, *Fascism, Doctrine and Institutions*, Rome: Ardita, 1935.
The earliest reasoned statement of Fascist political doctrine is Alfredo Rocco, *The Political Doctrine of Fascism*, republished in translation as an International Conciliation Bulletin, New York, 1926. The first important governmental document is the *Charter of Labor*, of April, 1927, given as an appendix in many of the general works on Fascism, and reprinted in Oakeshott. But the most important single statement is Mussolini's essay written for the *Enciclopedia Italiana*, 1932. It has been issued in several English translations from the Italian press, and is also given in full in Oakeshott. Another useful source is the four speeches by Mussolini on *The Corporate State*, given in the years 1933 to 1937, and published together in English by Vallechi, Florence, 1938.

[7] Outstanding examples of this point of view are G. A. Borgese, *Goliath, The March of Fascism*, New York: Viking, 1937, and H. Rauschning, *The Revolution of Nihilism*, New York: Alliance, 1939. The alternative point of view, tracing the lack of fixed doctrine to the influence of pragmatic philosophy, is examined in W. Y. Elliott, *The Pragmatic Revolt in Politics*, New York: Macmillan, 1928.

[8] See G. Megaro, *Mussolini in the Making*, Boston: Houghton Mifflin, 1938, the only trustworthy account of Mussolini's early life. On Hitler, see in addition to *Mein Kampf*, Konrad Heiden, *The History of National Socialism*, New York: Knopf, 1935, and Heiden, *One Man against Europe*, New York: Penguin Books, 1939.

[9] Mussolini, *Fascism, Doctrine and Institutions*.

[10] G. A. Borgese, *op. cit.*, p. 466.

[11] For interpretations of Fascism and Nazism as the spearheads of world revolution, see Peter Drucker, *The End of Economic Man*, New York: Harper, 1939, or G. S. Pettee, " The Second Civil War of Europe," *Social Science*, September, 1940.

[12] See the article, "Education," in the Catholic Encyclopedia.

[13] See F. Wunderlich, " Education in Nazi Germany," *Social Research*, IV: 347.

[14] Speech to the Reichstag, February 20, 1938.

SELECTED BIBLIOGRAPHY

Albig, W., *Public Opinion*, New York: McGraw-Hill, 1939. The most complete general text on propaganda and related problems.

Ascoli, Max and Feiler, Arthur, *Fascism for Whom?*, New York: Norton, 1938. The best summary account and criticism of both Fascism and Nazism in one volume.

Babbitt, Irving, *Democracy and Leadership*, Boston: Houghton Mifflin, 1924. The classic criticism of demagogic tendencies from the humanist point of view.

Brinton, Crane, *The Anatomy of Revolution*, New York: Norton, 1938. One of the few analytic studies of revolution which have any serious value.

Finer, Herbert, *Mussolini's Italy*, New York: Holt, 1935. The most complete descriptive study of Italian Fascism.

Gilson, Étienne, *The Unity of Philosophical Experience*, New York: Scribner, 1937. The closing chapters give an exceptionally lucid summary of the disintegration of modern philosophy which underlies the present ideological crisis.

Lippmann, Walter, *The Good Society*, Boston: Little, Brown, 1937. An exposition of the faults of totalitarianism from the liberal constitutional point of view.

Loewenstein, K., *Hitler's Germany*, New York: Macmillan, 1940. An exceptionally objective and thorough account.

Lynd, Robert, *Knowledge for What?*, Princeton: Princeton Univ. Press, 1939. A sociologist's examination of the causes and results of intellectual confusion.

Pettee, G. S., *The Process of Revolution*, New York: Harper, 1939. A systematic study of the revolutionary process.

Rappard, W. E., and others, *Source Book on European Governments*, New York: Van Nostrand, 1937. An excellent collection of important documents.

Roberts, S. H., *The House That Hitler Built*, New York: Harper, 1938. The most complete descriptive study.

Trotsky, Leon, *The Revolution Betrayed*, Garden City, N. Y.: Doubleday, Doran, 1937. Still the most significant and formidable criticism of Stalin's regime.

Zurcher, A. J., *The Experiment with Democracy in Central Europe*, New York: Oxford Univ. Press, 1933. The best account of the new European democracies of the post-war period.

Chapter XXVI

The Road to the Second World War
1930–1940

The Diplomatic Background of the War

The opening of the fourth decade of the century found France, largely by virtue of its victory in the First World War, the dominant power on the continent of Europe. The story of international politics in the decade 1930–1940, however, is the story of France's swift decline and the virtually miraculous revival of Germany, culminating in a Second World War which made the Germans lords of almost the entire continent.

In May, 1930 Aristide Briand's plan for European Union was submitted to twenty-six European states who were members of the League of Nations. In June, 1940 the collapse of French resistance to the German army registered the failure of the French search for security, and made even the most indifferent realize that a world order based on military might had emerged from behind the veil of pacts and agreements which had characterized the first post-war decade. The story of this period (1930–1940) is briefly that of rampant nationalism, impelled by economic and political forces, destroying the system of alliances and ententes which had lulled Europe into a sense of false security between 1920 and 1930.

The Situation in 1930. After the dissolution of the Triple Entente which had defeated Germany, France had made a series of agreements with Belgium, Poland, and the members of the Little Entente, thus drawing a ring around the principal losers in the First World War. At Locarno an understanding with Germany had been achieved which was guaranteed by Great Britain and Italy. Dissatisfied Italy had been forced to confine her intrigues to the Danubian and Balkan areas. The aloofness of Great Britain from continental politics and her preoccupation with domestic problems, the disarmament of Germany, and the isolation of Soviet Russia, helped to give France, the richest continental power, pre-eminence.

In the world at large, as in Europe, peace rested chiefly with the League of Nations. Various international pacts dealing with naval disarmament and the distribution of power in various parts of the world were designed to make secure the settlements dictated at the Paris Peace Conference. The League, after its establishment in 1920, had handled rather successfully

---

This chapter by James L. Glanville, Professor of History, Southern Methodist University.

several minor international disputes, such as the Corfu affair of 1923, and seemed in its first decade to be developing a workable system of international administration in many fields. It had busied itself continuously with the problem of armaments and security, although its most ardent admirers could not boast of much progress in either direction. At Washington in 1921, and at London in 1930, some disarmament was effected by stabilizing the ratios of the leading naval powers, Great Britain, the United States, France, Japan, and Italy. Finally, the Four Power and Nine Power Pacts of 1922 constituted a pledge for maintaining the status quo in the Far East.

All these pacts and agreements, however, depended in the final analysis on the weakness of Germany and the strength of Great Britain and France, upon the isolation of the Soviet Union from European affairs, on wise leadership, and on the maintenance by all the major nations of a tolerable amount of political and economic security. Indeed, the " pactomania " 1920–1930 which we described in Chapter III grew principally out of war weariness and exhaustion and depended on the existence of an extremely superficial kind of prosperity. With the spread of the depression every state was faced with increasing economic and political problems. The consequent distress imperiled and in time overturned all the post-war settlements. The vacillating foreign policies of France and Great Britain and the aggressive and truculent policies of Germany, and her ally, Italy, supply the keys to this narrative.

French Diplomacy, 1930–1932. In the period between 1918 and 1939 French statesmen were principally concerned with the problem of security. They realized that the increased number of European states and the insecure social structure which existed in many of them rendered their task most difficult. Unable by herself to preserve the balance of power, France constantly sought the aid of Great Britain. Her primary aim was to erect a powerful coalition to resist the agitation for revision of the peace treaties by the defeated states. Great Britain was unwilling, however, during most of the period to assume continental obligations, and essentially, the weakness of French policy grew out of her effort to exploit the continent and Great Britain in her own interest.[1]

On May 17, 1930 the French government, complying with a request made in the preceding September by the European members of the League, proposed the formation of a federation of European states which would deal primarily with problems of continental security. The Commission on European Union decided, at its first meeting in January, 1931, upon the insistence of Germany and Italy, to include economic problems in its agenda, and to invite the participation of Iceland, the Soviet Union, and Turkey.[2] The economic depression, however, soon threw a formidable obstacle into the path of this body. In March, 1931 Austria and Germany negotiated a customs union. But France, fearing that such a union in the long run would mean Anschluss, succeeded in getting the World Court to declare by a vote of 8 to 7 that the plan was illegal, and used financial and economic pressure to secure its abandonment.[3]

Briand then suggested a scheme for economic cooperation among the nations, involving especially financial assistance to the agrarian states of southeastern Europe. Tardieu went so far as to propose that the Danubian countries establish a preferential tariff system. This proposal was strenuously opposed by the Poles, Germans, Italians, and Austrians, and was supported only by the Czechs, who were interested in ridding themselves of German and Italian commercial competition. Conferences held in April and September, 1932 to consider this scheme thus came to naught.[4]

This failure demonstrated one of the essential weaknesses of France's relations with the nations of eastern and central Europe. Since her well-balanced economy made it impossible to offer markets for their products, her political influence was bound to wane as hard times increased in these states. The cancellation of reparations in 1932, to which France reluctantly consented, may be said to have marked the end of French financial dominance of the continent.

Manchukuo. The first armed challenge to the post-war security system came not from Europe but from the Far East, where Occidental military power was weakest. In September, 1931 the Japanese army, without heeding the Tokyo government, seized every strategic point in South Manchuria. North Manchuria was next occupied by the Nipponese and in March, 1932 the puppet state of Manchukuo was formally established. By 1933 the Japanese had also occupied the province of Jehol.[5]

Up to 1931 the Japanese had always recognized Manchuria as an integral part of China, but had insisted that it was primarily a Japanese sphere of influence. The younger officers, determined to restore the influence of the army in the government, decided to take upon themselves responsibility for the Manchurian adventure. Agrarian discontent in Japan seemed to demand a vigorous foreign policy if Communism was to be forestalled. The Japanese militarists saw that China, after two decades of civil war, was becoming united and would soon be strong enough to challenge the Japanese in Manchuria and Eastern Mongolia. They determined, therefore, to test the system of collective security at the moment when the Western world was in the throes of economic depression, and the Chinese government was busy with a Yangtze flood.

China protested to the League of Nations against the Japanese invasion and the League Council urged both Japan and China to withdraw their troops from the disputed areas. Japan refused and the Chinese declined to negotiate so long as Manchuria was occupied. The League Council, in an effort to break the deadlock, decided to send a Commission of Inquiry. Before the commission reached the Far East the United States, cooperating with the League, in January, 1932 announced that it would not recognize any Japanese gains made in violation of the Kellogg Pact or American treaty rights in China. The Commission of Inquiry, headed by Lord Lytton, reported in the fall of 1932 that Japan was the aggressor in Manchuria and suggested a ten-point compromise program. In the meantime, however, the assassination of Premier Inukai had made it impossible for the moderates in Japan, who opposed the Manchurian adventure, to assert themselves. Consequently, after the League Assembly had adopted the Lytton report, Japan (on March 27, 1933) announced her resignation from the League. This was the first of a series of defections from the League which by and by was to make it helpless.

The failure of the powers to check Japanese aggression was due to many causes. The United States would not take a strong stand without European support. The British, preoccupied with the financial crisis of 1931, apparently hoped that Soviet Russia would check Japan. The French were determined that the League's strength should be conserved to resist Germany. The principal support for stern measures against the Japanese came from small neutrals whose trade with Japan was insignificant, and who needed, for the sake of security, the precedent of strong resistance to a great power which had violated the territorial integrity of a weak state.

This failure had immediate effect upon the policies of Siam and of the Soviet Union, and prepared the way for future happenings. Siam abstained from voting on the Lytton report and prepared to accept economic cooperation with Japan. The Soviet government in May, 1933 offered to sell the Chinese Eastern Railway to Japan.[6] Negotiations for this sale occupied two years, during which period the Russians strengthened their military position in Asia. But they did not challenge the Amau doctrine, which the Japanese Foreign Office proclaimed in April, 1934,[7] declaring that it was Japan's mission to maintain peace and order in the Far East. The application of this doctrine was delayed for more than three years, but its announcement and the failure of Europe and the United States to halt Japan at the gates of Manchuria not only prepared the way for bolder Nipponese moves in the Far East, but set a precedent of a successful aggression which Germany and Italy were later to imitate, with disastrous consequences for the world.

The Failure of Disarmament, 1932–1936. The muddle of international politics in the early 'thirties was clearly revealed in the various meetings of the Disarmament Conference which we have described in Chapter III. The principal reason for the failure of the Disarmament Conference was the fact that each state, fearing decisions that would increase its insecurity or lessen its freedom of action, tried to improve its position at the expense of all the others, or proposed a scheme which suited its peculiar situation. The German watchword was "equality," or disarmament to her level. The French motto was "security." France was willing to disarm if Germany were kept in an inferior position, and if the European powers would guarantee her security, a thing Great Britain, for example, was unwilling to do. The Russians advocated complete disarmament; the Italians the elimination of the more expensive type of weapons; the United States proposed a ban on aggressive arms and a one-third reduction of all armies. The failure of the Disarmament Conference was followed by a gigantic armaments race which must be regarded as one of the primary causes of the Second World War. World expenditures on armaments doubled in the period 1932–1935. By 1938 they were estimated as almost five times that of 1932.[8]

The Four Power Pact and Austria, 1933–1934. The assumption by Adolf Hitler of the Chancellorship in January, 1933, the deadlock of the Disarmament Conference, and Japan's successful challenge of the status quo in the Far East placed the issue of peaceful vs. armed revision of the peace treaties squarely before the powers. The weakness of republican Germany had enabled France, it must be remembered, not only to play a role disproportionate to her resources but to checkmate Italian ambitions. Germany's resurgence violently upset the balance of power. As the Nazis, who loudly denounced the Versailles Treaty, consolidated their position, every European state began to alter its foreign policy in accordance with the situation. The first years of Nazi rule therefore were marked by frantic French efforts to encircle Germany and by Soviet Russia's active return to the European family of nations.

Italy, too, now began to exhibit expansionist ambitions, ambitions which could not be satisfied in a static Europe dominated by the League's principles of the equality of states, disarmament, and arbitration of international disputes. Italian prestige demanded Italy's consultation in all major problems, even where she had no direct interest. Consequently, Il Duce proposed a four power pact providing for the cooperation of Germany, Great Britain, France, and Italy in solving the problems of treaty revision, German rearmament, and non-European issues.[9]

Prime Minister MacDonald's visit to Rome gave Mussolini's scheme the appearance of an Anglo-Italian plan to reorganize southeastern Europe. The Little Entente, already aroused by German rearmament and by the discovery in January, 1933 that Mussolini had tried to ship arms to Hungary, protested that Mussolini's plan assumed that some states could dispose of the rights of others. France was alarmed by the prospect of treaty revision, the possible loss of her eastern allies and by German rearmament. Under such circumstances Mussolini's original proposal was modified until it became simply a pledge on the part of its signatories to consult each other in European crises and to adhere to the procedures of the League in all matters covered by the Covenant. The principal importance of the Four Power Pact, signed in July, 1933, was the promise it gave that critical issues might be settled peacefully by negotiations among the Great Powers. It helped, incidentally, to prolong the Disarmament Conference.

The most pressing revisionist problem which arose in 1933–1934 was that of Austrian Anschluss. A large number of Austrians had long desired union with Germany. The enmity of the Little Entente, and separation from her former markets in the Danubian area by tariff walls, made Austria's economic life extremely precarious. In the last months of 1933 the German Nazis began a determined campaign for Anschluss. But Italy was not yet ready to accede to such a step. France, who saw in Anschluss a grave danger to her ally, Czechoslovakia, as well as an undesirable strengthening of Germany, wanted a European guarantee of Austrian independence. Great Britain, however, refused to make a definite commitment, although on February 17, 1934 she joined France and Italy in declaring her support of the independence and integrity of Austria. In March economic and consultative pacts were signed by Austria, Hungary, and Italy. In July an attempted Nazi *coup* culminated in the assassination of Chancellor Dollfuss, but the despatch of Italian troops to the Austrian frontier forced Hitler to abandon his plans of conquest. Thus, Austria's fate came to depend on the will of Mussolini.[10]

Russia's Return to European Politics. Russia was particularly affected by the resurgence of Germany, since Hitler in his speeches continually hurled fiery bolts at the Bolsheviks. The Soviets also feared the hostility of those bulwarks of capitalism, Great Britain and France. As precautionary measures, therefore, the Soviet Union in the years following Locarno signed the Kellogg Pact, and negotiated commercial, neutrality, and non-aggression treaties with Germany, Italy, and other states.[11]

These agreements, however, did not protect the Soviet Union adequately from a possible German attack in the west or Japanese attack in the east. To strengthen her position Russia sought allies. France was a natural Soviet ally because of mutual hostility to Germany. Soviet participation in the sessions of the Disarmament Conference and the Conference for European Union paved the way for the conclusion of a treaty of neutrality and non-aggression with France in 1932. Increased impetus toward a Franco-Russian rapprochement was provided by the ten-year Polish-German non-aggression treaty of January, 1934, since the Russians, fearing Germany and Japan, were aware of deep-rooted Polish hostility toward them. At the same time, although Poland did not cast off the French alliance, this surprising action increased France's anxiety about her own security and, aided by a Rightist swing in French politics,

Foreign Minister Barthou prepared a counterstroke — an Eastern Locarno — which would be, in effect, a grand alliance against Germany.[12]

The Eastern Locarno, as envisaged by Barthou, would be a treaty of mutual assistance signed by Poland, the U.S.S.R., Germany, Czechoslovakia, Finland, Estonia, Latvia, and Lithuania in which France and Russia would guarantee the boundaries of the various states. But Poland was unwilling to guarantee the boundaries of Lithuania and Czechoslovakia, or to permit her territory to become a battle-ground for Russia and Germany. Germany, against whom the Eastern Locarno was really directed, argued that the question of disarmament must be solved before taking up that of security. She proposed a non-aggression and consultative pact implemented by pledges not to lend aid to an aggressor. Great Britain refused to assume any commitments and took a benevolent attitude towards the scheme, hoping that she and France could reach an agreement with the Nazis which would direct German aggression eastward.

These differences of opinion killed Barthou's project. Instead, a Franco-Russian alliance under the auspices of the League of Nations was effected. The Soviet Union was admitted to the League in September, 1934, after Czechoslovakia and Rumania had been prevailed upon to recognize her. As a sop to Poland for acquiescence in Russia's admission to the League, she was permitted to ignore her treaty obligations to her minorities. In May, 1935 treaties of mutual assistance were negotiated between France and the U.S.S.R., and between Czechoslovakia and the U.S.S.R. Thus Russia was completely restored to the family of nations and provided with potential allies in the event that Hitler's animadversions were implemented by a military move. France, incidentally, did not follow up her pact with a military convention, desiring to use it only to keep Germany and Russia apart.[13]

Italy, France, and the Balkan Entente, 1932–1935. Tension mounted in the Balkan states after 1931, as in western Europe. The Balkan peasants suffered from the drastic decline in agricultural prices, and the feudal ruling classes, allied with foreign capitalists, in fact kept the masses in a state of helotry. Hungary and Bulgaria, amputated by the peace treaties, were dissatisfied powers, threatening to join Germany in her revisionist crusade. German and Italian economic influence was increasing in the Balkans and Italy was trying to encircle Yugoslavia. Amidst these intrigues King Alexander of Yugoslavia hoped to make himself the head of a union of Balkan peoples. A Balkan Entente was indeed created on February 9, 1934 by means of a treaty of mutual guaranty signed by Turkey, Greece, Rumania, and Yugoslavia. This pact was originally intended to weld the Balkans into a bloc which could resist the major powers, but Turkish and Greek reservations converted it simply into a pact against intra-Balkan aggression, pointed at Albania and Bulgaria. The suppression of the I.M.R.O. in Bulgaria during May, 1934, as noted in Chapter XVI, lessened the danger of a Bulgarian attempt to recover territory lost in 1919.[14]

The Balkan Entente harmonized with Barthou's schemes for a Mediterranean Locarno to be signed by Italy, Yugoslavia, Rumania, Greece, and Turkey. The negotiation of such a treaty, however, required the settlement of the quarrel between France, Italy, and Yugoslavia. French overtures to Italy after the Nazi's accession to power, and their viewpoint regarding the need of maintaining Austrian independence were promising factors. But King Alexander, allied with France, was not anxious to come to terms with an Italy which sheltered Croatian terrorists and was seeking to encircle Yugoslavia by agreements with Austria and Hungary. In May, 1934 Alexander negotiated a commercial treaty with Germany.

Had Barthou and Alexander lived, Italy and Yugoslavia might have become reconciled. But when a Macedonian terrorist assassinated both on October 9, 1934 — in a plot aided by Italy and Hungary — the threat of a Balkan war speedily developed. The threat of a Balkan war appeared on the horizon. Rumania and Czechoslovakia were willing to allow Yugoslavia to use this opportunity to square accounts with Hungary. But Great Britain feared the consequences of a Balkan war and France did not want to weaken Italy at the Brenner Pass. The League, however, merely asked Hungary to investigate the conduct of her officials and suggested measures for dealing with terrorism. Many Yugoslavs, consequently, felt that Great Britain and France had betrayed them.

The League's exculpation of Italy, at France's insistence, in the Marseilles assassinations paved the way for the Laval-Mussolini pact of January, 1935. According to its terms, France defined the special rights of Italians in Tunis, added some territory to Eritrea and Libya, and agreed to sell Italy an interest in the Djibouti-Addis Ababa railroad; in return Italy promised to enter a European non-intervention pact, to oppose unilateral armament changes, and to consult with France if Austria's independence were jeopardized. The fact that France seemed, at the time, to have received the best of the bargain led to charges — supported by the turn of events — that Laval secretly promised Mussolini a free hand in Ethiopia. We must not overlook the fact, however, that a friendly France and demoralized Yugoslavia freed Mussolini for the Ethiopian campaign which he had decided upon as early as 1932.

The assassination of Alexander thus had not provoked a Balkan war, as was widely feared, and meanwhile Italy and France had effected a rapprochement. Yet the peace of Europe was by no means secure as the year 1935 opened, for Germany under Hitler was a growing menace. It was thought in London and Paris that Hitler would be peaceful if the Saar Basin were returned to Germany. Accordingly this was done under British leadership and with French cooperation in January, 1935. On the last days of this month Great Britain and France agreed secretly to consult each other if Austrian independence were threatened, to grant equality in arms to Germany if she returned to the League, and to try to negotiate a treaty for the limitation of air forces, which would include all the leading European nations.

But the return of the Saar did not satisfy Hitler. Citing the failure of the disarmament negotiations, France's extension of military service, and the existence of a large Soviet army, Hitler announced the resumption of universal military service, thus repudiating the clause of the Versailles Treaty which limited the German army to 100,000 men. Simultaneously he raised his price for Germany's return to the League to air parity with Great Britain and France and the return of German colonies. Although astonished by Hitler's moves, the British opposed the use of sanctions against Germany at the Stresa conference of April, 1935 and Germany's rearmament consequently drew only a mild rebuke from the League. France thereupon entered into an alliance with Russia and Great Britain. Great Britain surprisingly negotiated an agreement with Germany in June, 1935 which permitted the latter to build a navy up to 35 per cent of British tonnage, excepting submarines. Hitler's first defiance of Versailles was not only successful but created a seeming split in the Anglo-French front.

Mussolini Defies the League. Europe's preoccupation with German rearmament and the ensuing difference of policy between the British and French governments encouraged Mussolini to expedite plans for the conquest of Ethiopia. Economic necessity, the Italian defeat at Adowa in 1896, the practical exclusion of Italy from colonial gains after the First World War, and the Italian desire for prestige gave strong support to his propaganda that Italy should live up to the traditions of her past and must expand or explode.

The blame for the League's failure to settle the Ethiopian problem peaceably should be ascribed to Italian imperialism, Ethiopian stubbornness, French pactomania, and British muddling. The Ethiopians, with an unwarranted confidence in the League and in their own fighting prowess, continued to sabotage efforts looking to amicable settlement of a quarrel which, it must be admitted, Mussolini created. The French were unwilling to alienate Italy and oppose her demands upon Ethiopia so long as Britain refused to guarantee unqualified assistance in the event of German aggression. The British were fully cognizant of Italian designs after Mussolini's speech of March, 1934 envisaging Italy's future in Asia and Africa, and were warned of coming events in January, 1935 by Mussolini's announcement that the time had come to implement the Anglo-Italian agreement of 1925 which had divided Ethiopia into spheres of influence. Since this agreement recognized British interests in Lake Tana and the Blue Nile, however, Italian activities in Ethiopia were not regarded as constituting a threat to imperial interests; the British in fact hoped to satisfy Italy and support the League at the same time. Such a policy proved impossible.[15]

A clash between Italian and Ethiopian forces at Wal-Wal in December, 1934 marked the opening of hostilities between the two nations. From this time until October, 1935 France, England, and the League repeatedly sought to bargain with Mussolini, who demanded annexation of most of Ethiopia and control of the rest. Il Duce was confident that Britain was not in a mood to resist Italian aggression in Africa. Since Ethiopia was careful to avoid provocation and he had gone too far to withdraw, Italy did not assume the offensive until the end of the rainy season in October. The Fascist advance into Ethiopia, however, spurred the League to invoke sanctions against Italy. An embargo on loans, arms, and certain raw materials to Italy immediately went into effect. The British sent their fleet into the Mediterranean. But even as sanctions were being enforced Great Britain and France secretly intrigued to appease Mussolini. In December, the secret Hoare-Laval plan, providing for the sacrifice of Ethiopia to Italy, was inadvertently revealed to an outraged public. Prime Minister Stanley Baldwin was forced to disavow Hoare, who resigned as Foreign Minister. His successor, Anthony Eden, was an enthusiastic supporter of the League and sought to prepare the way for applying oil sanctions, the only vital one, by entering into mutual assistance agreements with France, Greece, Turkey, and Yugoslavia against possible Italian resistance to such a measure. But the French maneuvered the machinery of the League to postpone action, and Mussolini, whose people had rallied to his support under the vexations of sanctions, was able to push the Ethiopian campaign to a successful conclusion. Addis Ababa, the Ethiopian capital, fell early in May, 1936, and sanctions, being of no avail, were lifted on July 15. Great Britain and France did not formally recognize the Italian conquest until November, 1938.

Formation of the Rome-Berlin Axis. Germany, taking advantage of the confusion of international politics during the Ethiopian crisis, remilitarized the Rhineland in March, 1936, in contravention of the Versailles and Locarno treaties. This daring action had been foreshadowed by the German protest in May, 1935 against the Franco-Soviet pact as a violation of Locarno. With an unprepared army, Hitler had gambled on the possibility of Anglo-French retaliations, but as before, France and England were in disagreement, and the remilitarization of the Rhineland went unpunished. Hitler now offered to re-enter the League, sign air and non-aggression pacts, and set up a demilitarized zone on Germany's western frontier if France and Belgium would do likewise. The British helped the German cause by drawing a distinction between the remilitarization of the Rhineland and an actual attack, thereby persuading France to accept merely a League condemnation of the German action.

The way was now open for common action by the great dissatisfied powers, Italy, Japan, and Germany. A mutual agreement on the status of Austria provided a basis for cooperation. Italy assented to the Austro-German pact of July, 1936, whereby in return for Hitler's promise to respect Austrian independence Chancellor Schuschnigg relaxed the ban on the Nazi Party. In October Hitler recognized Italy's acquisition of Ethiopia, and the two powers agreed to form a united front against Communism, especially in Spain. Thus the Rome-Berlin Axis was forged. On November 6, 1937 Italy joined the anti-Comintern pact which Germany and Japan had concluded a year earlier.[16] The three Fascist powers were now embarked on parallel courses of aggrandizement.

The creation of the Rome-Berlin Axis caused the insecure smaller states to scurry for cover and delivered a fatal blow to the French system of alliances. The Belgians, mindful of 1914, forsook the French alliance in October, 1936 and later joined the Oslo group of powers, consisting of Norway, Sweden, Denmark, Finland, and Holland. While remaining in the League, these states proclaimed strict neutrality. Rumania also turned away from France, and Yugoslavia showed a willingness to patch up her differences with Bulgaria and Italy. Poland, since France had refused to wage a preventive war against Germany after Hitler had defied the Versailles Treaty, determined to adhere to the bargain of 1934 with Germany. Czechoslovakia, however, stood firmly by her alliances and together with the U.S.S.R. worked to strengthen the League Covenant.[17]

The Ethiopian conquest aroused the fears of the Mediterranean littoral states and, after the lifting of sanctions had nullified the pledges of mutual assistance made by Great Britain, Greece, Turkey, and Yugoslavia, steps were taken to organize resistance to future Italian aggression. As early as 1933 the Turkish government had broached the matter of fortifying the Straits which had been demilitarized ten years earlier. The combination of Italian and German aggression, plus the British desire to create an example of peaceful treaty revision, persuaded the Conference of Montreux in the summer of 1936 to grant Turkey the right to fortify the Straits and control the passage of warships from the Black Sea into the Aegean. The Italian threat also impelled the Egyptians and the British to strike a bargain in August, 1936, whereby Egypt was to be rid of capitulations, join the League, and obtain a larger share in the control of the Sudan, while the British were permitted to garrison Suez and offer military aid if Egypt were attacked. In September the French and Syrians (as noted in Chapter XVII) agreed to arrange their relations on the model of England's 1930 treaty with Iraq and to divide Syria into two republics.

At the same time Turkey, Iraq, Iran, and Afghanistan drew closer together with the benevolent approval of the U.S.S.R. and Great Britain.[18]

Spain, 1936–1939. The Rome-Berlin Axis' first joint move of great international consequence was its role in the Spanish Civil War. In July, 1936 the inevitable revolution of the vested interests — the army, the Church, the landlords and the industrialists — against the liberal Spanish republic broke out. The Rebel leaders had been in contact with Mussolini and Hitler for years and had with their help carefully prepared the *coup* which was to destroy the republic. Leftist elements throughout the world sympathized with the Loyalists, as did the U.S.S.R., but their influence was not sufficient to offset the prejudice of the British and French governments against the Republicans. Like Premier Blum of France, the British ruling classes feared an international war if they insisted upon the legal right to sell munitions to the Loyalists, and therefore adopted a policy of non-intervention which was supposed to shut off the flow of arms to both sides. This policy, intrusted to a Committee representing twenty-seven powers, was, however, sabotaged by Germany, Italy, and the Soviets. The Rebel government, headed by General Franco, was recognized by Germany and Italy on November 18, 1936, and British and French efforts to extend non-intervention to stop the flow of " volunteers " from Germany and Italy failed. British pressure, however, compelled the Italians to pledge themselves to respect the territorial integrity of Spain and to maintain the status quo in the Mediterranean. Early in 1937 the British and French, alarmed at reports of German and Italian activities around Ceuta and Tangier, increased their naval forces in the Mediterranean. Following clashes between Loyalist and German and Italian ships, the latter states withdrew from the patrol. Sinking of neutral ships by " unidentified " submarines caused the British and French to take a firm stand, and a nine power conference at Nyon in September, 1937 established a patrol which terminated such piracy for a time.

But non-intervention was totally ineffective. Efforts were made in the summer of 1938 to reach a detailed agreement for the evacuation of foreign " volunteers," but General Franco rejected the scheme. This rejection foreshadowed the final collapse of the Loyalists early in 1939. France thus acquired a hostile neighbor on her Pyrenees border, while Germany and Italy obtained paramount influence in the western Mediterranean, a vital spot in case of an Axis war with France and Britain.[19]

Austrian Anschluss. Hitler made another daring move in November, 1936 by denouncing the international control of German rivers as provided in the Versailles Treaty. In 1935 Germany had embarked upon an unparalleled rearmament program with the consequent effect of creating a war economy. After 1936 Hitler's demands became increasingly bolder as the implements were piled up to wrest by force what he could not obtain by diplomacy or threat. The leading role in alteration of the European status quo passed into his hands, but Mussolini vigorously tried to keep pace. Their first joint move — as we have seen — was in Spain, where the defeat of the Loyalists meant in reality a defeat of England and France, although the latter governments did not seem to realize it. Even as the Spanish conflict raged Hitler took another large step forward — the rape of Austria. Mussolini's visit to Berlin in September, 1937 was significantly followed by renewed Nazi activity in Austria. It is likely that Lord Halifax, in the course of visits with Goering and Hitler during November, led the Germans to believe that Great Britain would not oppose their adventures in central Europe, so long as this was not accompanied by war and if British colonial and commercial interests were unmolested.

Whatever the secret understandings among the Great Powers, the fate of Austria was decided when Mussolini, after joining the Rome-Berlin Axis, withdrew his support from Schuschnigg. Austria by itself was in no position to oppose Germany. By crushing the Socialists in February, 1934 the Clerical government of Austria, as we indicated in a previous chapter, had lost popular support. Divided internally, and menaced by Germany, Schuschnigg was called to Berchtesgaden in February, 1938 and forced virtually to renounce Austrian independence by admitting Nazis in his government. As a last-minute gesture Schuschnigg tried to call a plebiscite on the question of Anschluss but this was countered by a German ultimatum demanding his resignation. Neither England, France, nor Italy offered assistance in this, Austria's darkest hour, and the Germans occupied the country on March 13. France, in the midst of a ministerial crisis, remained silent and Chamberlain, who had succeeded Baldwin the preceding December, confined himself to a mild protest, remarking that without available forces nothing could be done to save Austria. An Austrian plebiscite, held under duress, on April 10, 1938, marked the ratification of the first important territorial seizure of Hitler's regime.[20]

Anglo-Italian Rapprochement, 1937–1938.   British behavior in the Austrian crisis was closely connected with the British Cabinet's decision in the fall of 1937, during the non-intervention farce, to appease the Rome-Berlin Axis, a decision which led to the resignation of Anthony Eden as Foreign Minister. This decision was in part due to dislike of France's Soviet alliance, to the retardation of British rearmament, to fear of Italian aggression in the Mediterranean, and to a desire for peace at almost any price. The first open avowal of appeasement, however, was the Anglo-Italian agreement of April 16, 1938.

This treaty provided for British recognition of the Ethiopian conquest. The Italians in return agreed to withdraw from Spain and to support the status quo in the Mediterranean. The British hoped to effect a similar agreement between France and Italy, thus weaning Mussolini from Hitler.

But Mussolini tried to wring excessive concessions from the French, and moreover he delayed even a token withdrawal from Spain until the Loyalists were doomed. The Anglo-Italian agreement went into effect after this token withdrawal on November 16, 1938. By this time Czechoslovakia had been partitioned and the hopes of a settlement in the Mediterranean disappeared to the tune of cries for Tunis, Jibuti, Nice, and Savoy in the Italian Parliament.[21]

Dismemberment of Czechoslovakia. With the Anschluss of Austria Czechoslovakia was placed, a glance at the map will show, within the pincers of Germany. As we have seen in Chapter XI, the Sudeten Germans now began to make louder demands for autonomy in the Prague government through the German Party led by Konrad Henlein. Prague felt that concessions to its German minority would pave the way for German domination of southeastern Europe, but knew that without foreign assistance it could not resist Hitler. Great Britain, France, and the U.S.S.R. were the possible sources of assistance, the last two being allies of Czechoslovakia. But Czechoslovakia's geographic isolation rendered military aid difficult, and the British had never felt inclined to defend the territorial arrangements of post-war central Europe. Chamberlain, because of faith in his appeasement policy and because the Sudeten question involved the principle of self-determination, decided as early as May, 1938 that revision of Czech frontiers would be necessary to accommodate Hitler. The French leaders also realized the strength of rearmed Germany and moreover dared not hazard war since the desire for peace among the French people was as great as among the English.

Now that Austria had fallen into his lap, Hitler ruthlessly determined to destroy Czechoslovakia and eliminate the last barrier to Germany's *Drang nach Osten* (March toward the east). Using the Henleinists as his agents, he sought by familiar Nazi strategy to weaken the Czech state from within, to provoke civil war and then take the German districts under his wing. Negotiations carried on in the summer of 1938 between the Sudetens and the Czechs under the mediatory auspices of Lord Runciman broke down in August. Germany thereupon threatened to invade Czechoslovakia if the Sudetens' terms were not met by Beneš. Military preparations were thereupon taken by all the powers allied with Czechoslovakia, but at the last minute Chamberlain, in order to avert war, flew to Berchtesgaden and there secured Hitler's promise to refrain from attacking the Czechs, if the principle of self-determination were applied to the Sudeten land. But almost immediately Hitler raised his demands to include similar treatment for Polish and Hungarian Czech minorities — in order to encircle Czechoslovakia further — and demanded occupation at once by the Nazis of strategic territories. It seemed for a moment in September, 1938 that in spite of Chamberlain's appeasement, war would result — a war which would embroil France, England, and Russia. France ordered partial mobilization, England put its fleet in battle order, and the Soviets promised military assistance to the Czechs. But amidst world-wide appeals for peace, and the influence of Mussolini, Baron von Neurath and Marshal Goering, Hitler was persuaded to attend a conference at Munich (September 29, 1938) of the four Western powers — the Czechs were not even invited — at which the peaceful dismemberment of Czechoslovakia was agreed upon.[22]

The Munich Settlement. Chamberlain and Daladier agreed in effect at Munich that Germany should dispose of Czechoslovakia according to its will, although the details were left to the determination of an international commission. This commission obeyed Hitler's wishes, and Germany immediately secured one-fifth of Czechoslovakia, including the principal industries and fortifications, and a military highway across the land. Poland occupied Teschen and Bohumin during the crisis. Part of Ruthenia was awarded to Hungary by a German-Italian commission in November. Great Britain and France made consultative pacts with Germany, but appeasement had won the day. Czechoslovakia, the bastion of democracy in central Europe, was shamefully destroyed, and Anglo-French prestige reached its nadir.

The Italians, seeing the hesitancy of the democracies to go to war, were not slow in capitalizing on the situation. On November 30, 1938 the Italian Chamber of Deputies resounded with cries for Tunis, Nice, Corsica, and Savoy, and on December 17 the 1935 agreement with France was denounced. But after Munich, which cast a terrible onus on the democracies, appeasement became unpopular in England and France. Premier Daladier vehemently denied Italy's claims to French territory. Mussolini apparently realized that the game of blackmail and bluff was over, since France and England seemed determined to resist by resort to war any new demands of the dictators.

Hitler, however, having annexed Austria and acquired the Sudetenland of Czechoslovakia, quietly prepared for the next stroke. Since 1934 the Polish-German treaty engineered by Pilsudski had been more or less faithfully complied with. But on October 24, 1938 Foreign Minister von Ribbentrop, in the midst of the Polish-Czech-Hungarian negotiations, demanded the return of Danzig to Germany and the right to build a road across the Corridor, offering various guarantees and privileges to Poland in exchange. The Poles ignored Ribbentrop's demands, and renewed their non-aggression agreement with the U.S.S.R. Repeated German hints concerning the Corridor only revealed the Poles' firm determination not to yield; Poland, said her leaders, would fight rather than give up territory. The colossal German war machine did not frighten them.

On March 15, 1939 Hitler took advantage of a Nazi-manufactured

Czech-Slovak quarrel to declare a protectorate over Czechoslovakia, graciously permitting Hungary to occupy a strip of Czech territory.[23]

Jockeying for Position. German occupation of Prague and Memel (March 22) made a European war inevitable, for it revealed to the world the boundless appetite of the Nazis, and their determination to alter the map of Europe almost as they pleased. Both France and Britain now realized that they had been deceived at Munich and that appeasement had been futile. At Munich Hitler had said that, if granted the Sudetenland, he would make no more territorial demands in Europe. The destruction of Czechoslovakia emphasized the utter worthlessness of his promises. Appeasement was now dead in France and England, both of which girded themselves for war. To Germany's demands upon the Poles Chamberlain replied by announcing on March 31, 1939 that England had guaranteed the territorial integrity of Poland. France did likewise, thus creating a situation in which a German attack on Poland would immediately involve France and England. Indeed a heated exchange of notes between Colonel Beck and Ambassador von Moltke over Danzig on March 23 showed that the Franco-British guarantees sooner or later would mean war unless Hitler or the others backed down.

Moves and counter-moves soon set the stage for such a *denouement.* Countering Hitler's acts in northern Europe, Mussolini occupied Albania on April 7, 1939 in violation of the Anglo-Italian agreement of 1938. The British, fortifying their diplomatic position in eastern Europe, countered with a pledge of assistance to Rumania and Greece; in May and June, Great Britain and France made arrangements for a mutual assistance pact with Turkey. President Roosevelt, following up a theme he had emphasized since 1936, and in order to give Britain and France time to prepare for war, proposed that if Hitler would sign non-aggression agreements he would call a world conference on disarmament and trade. Mussolini poked fun at this appeal; Hitler replied on April 28 by denouncing the Polish pact of 1934 and the Anglo-German naval agreement of 1935, and pointing to some weak points in the United States' Latin-American policy. Germany signed non-aggression agreements with Estonia, Latvia, and Denmark, principally to forestall the possibility that the Oslo group, the Baltic states, and Poland might find common ground. In May, 1939 the Rome-Berlin Axis was transformed into a military alliance.

The Russo-German Pact. It is possible that by this time Hitler had already decided upon a rapprochement with Russia. The Anglo-French-Polish front made it advisable for Germany to seek an understanding with the U.S.S.R., a move that was supported by the Reichswehr which strove to avoid fighting on two fronts. Hitler omitted the usual disagreeable references to Russia in his April speech, and the replacement of Foreign Commissar Litvinoff by Molotov in May lent confirmation to reports that the

Soviet Union, weary of the failure of the League and angered at having been excluded from the Munich negotiations, was ready to abandon the policy of collective security and cooperate with Germany. The Soviet leaders did not trust the French and British ruling class, although inviting their representatives to come to Moscow to negotiate an alliance. Since the British and French hesitated to support the Soviet's paramount interests in the Baltic states, these negotiations fell through, and the Russians, secretly bargaining with Hitler, announced to a stunned world on August 22, 1939 the conclusion of a Russo-German non-aggression pact.

This momentous treaty not only freed Germany from the possibility of war on two fronts but secured access to invaluable Russian raw materials. Throughout the summer the German newspapers truculently calumniated and vilified the Poles, as a year before they had calumniated and vilified the Czechs. The Germans paid no attention to British and French warnings that they would support Poland against German aggression. On August 23, with Russia safely neutralized, Hitler announced that he would solve the problem of Danzig and the Polish Corridor as he saw fit. Two days later a mutual assistance pact was signed by Great Britain and Poland; but the British insisted that Poland should avoid provocation and seek direct conversations with Germany. At the same time they suggested to Hitler that a settlement with Poland reached in a peaceful manner would have international guarantees, but that war would follow if Germany attempted forcibly to annex Danzig or the Corridor. Since the Poles were adamant while Hitler's demands became more arrogant the world knew that the long-expected European war would not be long delayed.

On the last day in August Germany demanded the immediate appearance in Berlin of a Polish delegate to accept her terms. When he did not appear, Hitler ordered his troops to invade Poland on September 1, 1939; at the same time Danzig, ruled by Nazi sympathizers, proclaimed its return to the Reich.

The tedious exchange of notes between Germany, France, and England during the last days of August simply meant that each side was preparing its case for the bar of public opinion. The attack on Poland made general war inevitable, unless the French and British should back down. The British public was in a belligerent mood. France, already mobilized, accepted the British decision to go to war. The Italians were shocked at Hitler's determination to fight so soon. France and Great Britain on September 1 sent notes to Berlin demanding the cessation of hostilities in Poland. When Hitler declined to honor them, England and France declared war on Germany on September 3. Italy proclaimed her non-belligerency.[24] The armistice years had come to an end. Armageddon had returned.

The Second World War: Act One

The Polish Phase. Probably the most impressive change in foreign policy during the first months of the Second World War was that of the U.S.S.R. For years the Soviet Union had followed a course of non-aggression which had been climaxed by the pact with Germany. But once the dogs of war were let loose, Stalin embarked upon a course of imperialism, designed primarily to safeguard Russian frontiers and strengthen Russia's military position.

The first fruit of the new Russian imperialism was the occupation of eastern Poland, a move foreshadowed by Moscow's refusal to supply Poland with war materials. A Russian note of September 17, 1939 — when the Germans had crushed Polish resistance — announced that Poland had ceased to exist and that Russia must protect the White Russians and the Ukrainians dwelling in Poland. Russian troops occupied the region. This action, probably agreed on during the German-Soviet negotiations, was ratified in a Russo-German treaty of September 28, 1939 which assigned to the U.S.S.R. the mainly Ukrainian and White Russian territory lying to the east of an irregular line drawn across Poland from southern Lithuania to Hungary and Rumania.

The Baltic States. At the same time, the Germans in the Baltic states were ordered to return to the Reich. Estonian and Latvian pacts of mutual assistance with the U.S.S.R., signed on September 29 and October 5 respectively, gave the latter naval and air bases in these two areas. A Soviet-Lithuanian mutual assistance treaty of October 10 which ceded Vilna to Lithuania completed the Russian domination of the Baltic states. Finland was next approached. But as we have seen, the Finns, clinging to neutrality, defied Soviet demands for a naval base at Hangö and territorial cessions near Leningrad and in the Gulf of Finland. War broke out between Russia and Finland on December 1, 1939, and an enraged public opinion forced the League of Nations to expel Russia. Finland secured some war supplies from France, Great Britain, Italy, and Sweden. But active military aid was unobtainable owing partly to the reluctance of France and Great Britain to add the Soviet Union to enemy ranks, and partly to the refusal of Norway and Sweden to allow supplies to cross their territories. Finland surrendered and gave Russia a lease on the Hangö peninsula, territory around Lake Ladoga, and a railway route to Sweden.[25]

The Collapse of Western Europe. Finland's fate was a warning of what soon would befall the four members of the Oslo group, Belgium, Holland, Norway, and Denmark. Allied policy apparently aimed at regulating their commerce and at trying to convert their antipathy toward Germany into active opposition. The Germans coveted their territory as bases of operation against England and France. The little nations hoped that strict neutrality would enable them to escape the horrors of war, and bore their increasing losses of shipping with remarkable patience.

These hopes were futile. On April 9, 1940 the Germans, alleging that the Allies were conniving to extend the war to northern Europe, invaded Norway and Denmark. Denmark offered no resistance; by May the Norwegian campaign was terminated.

The collapse of the Allied forces in Norway foreshadowed a greater disaster on the western front. The Germans started a *Blitzkrieg* on May 10 with a simultaneous invasion of Holland and Belgium. Four days sufficed to force the Dutch to surrender, eighteen to destroy Belgian resistance. On May 15 the Germans broke through the French line at Sedan, and the Allied armies were rapidly rolled back in Flanders. Several hundred thousand British soldiers were evacuated with extreme difficulty from Dunkerque and other coastal towns by the British navy as the Germans seized the Channel ports from Abbeville northeastwards. Churchill (who had replaced Chamberlain as Prime Minister), Reynaud, and General Weygand (who had succeeded Daladier and General Gamelin respectively), were unable to organize adequate resistance. Both Great Britain and France were pathetically deficient in airplanes, tanks, and mobile units to match the Germans. France, rent by internal dissension, proved a fertile ground for the operations of defeatists and "fifth columnists." As a consequence, two weeks of well-coordinated German attacks and the entrance of Italy into the war on June 10 were enough to bring her capitulation on June 17.

Armistices signed with Germany and Italy placed the northern and western parts of France under German occupation and provided for the demobilization of the French army, the immobilization of the French fleet, and the demilitarization of French naval bases in southeastern France, Tunis, and French West Africa. The Italians received permission to occupy Jibuti and use the connecting French section of the Djibouti-Addis Ababa railroad. The destruction or seizure of a large part of the French fleet by the British in July served to lessen some effects of the French collapse.[26]

War in the Mediterranean. The entrance of Italy into the war extended the conflict to the Near East and the Balkans, despite her promise not to attack Egypt, Greece, Yugoslavia, Turkey, or Switzerland. The disintegration of the Little Entente in 1936–1937 had induced Yugoslavia to try to strengthen the Balkan Entente and to pacify her neighbors. Accordingly she signed pacts with Italy and Bulgaria, and in 1938 recognized the right of Bulgaria and Hungary to rearm. The collapse of Czechoslovakia permitted Germany to increase her influence in the Balkans. Thus, Hungary adhered to the anti-Comintern pact in February, 1939. British and French attempts to head off German and Italian influence in eastern Europe by means of generous trade agreements and pledges of military assistance — in the case of Turkey implemented by a formal alliance signed in October, 1939 — failed because of their own military weakness and inability to cope with Germany's economic advantages in the area. Indeed Germany was now vitally dependent on Rumania's oil and the cereals of Hungary and Yugoslavia. Both Italy and Germany tried to preserve peace in the Balkans in order not to interrupt the steady flow of supplies. In November, 1939 Bulgaria and Turkey agreed to demobilize their frontier forces. In March, 1940 " tourists " were expelled from the Balkan states as suspected spies and the riparian powers determined to patrol the Danube without German help. With the collapse of France, his nominal ally, King Carol of Rumania veered toward collaboration with Germany. He was forced, however, to acquiesce in the Russian seizure of Bessarabia and northern Bukovina. Axis pressure also forced Rumania in August to return the Southern Dobrudja to Bulgaria, and negotiations which gave nearly one-half of Transylvania to Hungary were carried on under Axis auspices. On September 6, Carol abruptly abdicated upon demands of the Nazi-controlled Iron Guard. The Axis thus removed its last major enemy in the Balkans.[27] Hungary and Bulgaria were meek followers of Hitler; Yugoslavia was expected to succumb to German pressure and Greece to Italian coercion. How both nations failed to live up to these expectations will be explained in a subsequent chapter.

Japan and the Changing World Scene. The European crisis had repercussions on all continents. In the Far East Japan saw glittering opportunities for aggrandizement at the expense of the European powers. The Japanese moderates gradually gained power from 1932 to 1936. But in 1936 the militarists persuaded many capitalists to support their plans for aggression on the mainland of Asia, and the next year Japan resumed its offensive in China which, after years of civil war, was being united under the leadership of General Chiang Kai-shek. The League thereupon resurrected its Far Eastern Advisory Committee, and President Roosevelt called for a quarantine against aggressors. But the powers interested in China failed to agree upon common action at the Brussels Conference of November, 1937 and meanwhile Italy and Germany drew closer to Japan. Great Britain and the United States lent military and financial assistance to the Chinese. But the march of the Japanese continued until they were in possession of all the chief cities of eastern China and the Chiang Kai-shek government had retreated to Chungking.

The denunciation by the United States on July 26, 1939 of its commercial treaty of 1911 with Japan and the signing of the Soviet-German non-aggression pact in August checked Japanese extremists for a time. But the collapse of France was the signal for Japan to reaffirm her intention of establishing a " new order " in eastern Asia. Japan forced France to close the Indo-Chinese supply route to Chungking on June 20, 1940 and on July 17 obtained Great Britain's consent to a three-month closure of the Burma route. But Chinese resistance was not broken and the Sino-Japanese War, of which Japan was heartily weary, continued. A militaristic government under the direction of Prince Konoye assumed control at Tokyo and threats, overt or implied, were made to oust the British from Singapore, to occupy French Indo-China and attack the Dutch East Indies. Britain replied by opening the Burma road, the United States, whose interests were affected, by sending its fleet into the Pacific.

The Sino-Japanese struggle continued, a struggle which was sapping the strength of Nippon and which the indomitable Chinese were determined to continue until their life blood was spent.[28]

Thus the first act of the Second World War ended with Germany dominant in western Europe, France a vassal of the Nazis, the neutral Oslo states overrun by Germany, Italy an active belligerent, and Japan threatening to extend her conquests into the rich islands and peninsulas of the South Pacific.

REFERENCES

1 The best survey of British and French policy after 1919 is Arnold Wolfers, *Britain and France between Two Wars*, New York: Harcourt, Brace, 1940.

2 For an explanation of the European Federal Union plan, see Edouard Herriot, *The United States of Europe*, New York: Viking Press, 1930. The text and replies of European states are in *International Conciliation, Documents for the Year, 1930*, New York: Carnegie Endowment of International Peace, 1930, pp. 325–346, 653–749. On the problem of economic collaboration, consult Vera Micheles Dean, "European Efforts for Economic Collaboration," *Foreign Policy Reports*, New York: Foreign Policy Association, August 19, 1931.

3 The best documented account of Austrian foreign relations is M. Margaret Ball's *Post-War German-Austrian Relations*, Palo Alto, Cal.: Stanford Univ. Press, 1937.

4 Robert Machray, *The Struggle for the Danube and the Little Entente, 1929–1938*, London: Allen & Unwin, 1938, provides a convenient outline of the meetings and utterances of officialdom. The best documented account of the foreign policy of Czechoslovakia is Felix John Vondracek, *The Foreign Policy of Czechoslovakia, 1918–1935*, New York: Columbia Univ. Press, 1937.

5 There are many books on the Manchukuoan question. The documents can be found in John W. Wheeler Bennett and Stephen Heald, *Documents on International Affairs, 1932*, London: Oxford Univ. Press, pp. 240–398. Nathaniel Peffer, *Must We Fight in Asia?*, New York: Harper, 1935, Joseph Barnes, *Empire in the East*, Garden City, N. Y.: Doubleday, Doran, 1934, and C. Walter Young, *Japan's Special Position in Manchuria*, Baltimore: Johns Hopkins Press, 1931, furnish a suitable background. For American policy, see Henry L. Stimson, *The Far Eastern Crisis*, New York: Harper, 1936, and William Starr Myers, *The Foreign Policies of Herbert Hoover*, New York: Scribner, 1940, ch. 9. Consult for Japanese policy Hirosi Saito, *Japan's Purposes and Policies*, Boston: Houghton Mifflin, 1935, and Tatsuji Takeuchi, *War and Diplomacy in the Japanese Empire*, Garden City, N. Y.: Doubleday, Doran, 1935.

6 T. A. Bisson, "Soviet-Japanese Relations, 1931–1938," *Foreign Policy Reports*, February 1, 1939.

7 Arnold J. Toynbee, *Survey of International Affairs, 1934*, New York: Oxford Univ. Press, 1935, pp. 650–651.

8 William T. Stone, "Economic Consequences of Rearmament," *Foreign Policy Reports*, October 1, 1938. On the general question of rearmament, consult Ewald Banse, *Germany Prepares for War*, New York: Harcourt, Brace, 1934; Henry Liddell Hart, *Europe in Arms*, New York: Ryerson, 1938; Hanson W. Baldwin, *The Caissons Roll*, New York: Knopf, 1938.

9 Maxwell H. H. Macartney and Paul Cremona, *Italy's Foreign and Colonial Policy*, New York: Oxford Univ. Press, 1938, ch. 10. This should be consulted as the best analysis in English of post-war Italian policy.

10 Ball, *op. cit.*, chs. 10 and 11, also Macartney and Cremona, *op. cit.*; for a vivid description of the decline of Austrian morale, see Willi Frischauer, *Twilight in Vienna*, Boston: Houghton Mifflin, 1938.

11 On Russia and the Baltic states, see Michael T. Florinsky, *The World Revolution and the U.S.S.R.*, New York: Macmillan, 1933, chs. 5 and 6; Malbone W. Graham, "The Peace Policy of the Soviet Union" in Samuel N. Harper, ed., *The Soviet Union and World Problems*, Chicago: Univ. of Chicago Press, 1935; T. A. Taracouzio, *The Soviet Union and International Law*, Toronto: Macmillan, 1935.

12 The situation Barthou found in Europe is described in Vera Micheles Dean, "Toward a New Balance of Power in Europe," *Foreign Policy Reports*, May 9, 1934.

13 John W. Wheeler-Bennett and Stephen A. Heald, *Documents on International Affairs, 1935*, I, London: Oxford Univ. Press, 1936, pp. 116–140, 252–261. Short discussions of the movement which brought Russia into the League and into European politics are found in John T. Whitaker, *And Fear Came*, New York: Macmillan,

1936, p. 182 ff.; Sir Arthur Willert, *What Next in Europe?*, New York: Putnam, 1936, p. 143 f.

[14] The best treatments of the Balkan Entente are Robert J. Kerner and Harry N. Howard, *The Balkan Conferences and the Balkan Entente, 1930–1935*, Berkeley, Cal.: Univ. of California Press, 1936, and Norman J. Padelford, *Peace in the Balkans*, New York: Oxford Univ. Press, 1935. The undocumented biography, Stephen Graham, *Alexander of Yugoslavia*, New Haven: Yale Univ. Press, 1939, provides an interesting analysis of Yugoslav policy under Alexander.

[15] Ernest Work, *Ethiopia, A Pawn in European Diplomacy*, New York: Macmillan, 1935, furnishes a competent study of the documents published prior to the crisis of 1935–1936. On imperialism, see Grover Clark, *A Place in the Sun*, New York: Macmillan, 1936; on imperialist ideology of Fascist Italy, James L. Glanville, "Colonialism in the New Italy," *Arnold Foundation Studies in Public Affairs*, II, No. 4, Dallas: Arnold Foundation, 1934. The best account of the Ethiopian crisis is George Martelli, *Italy against the World*, New York: Harcourt, Brace, 1938. See also Macartney and Cremona, *Italy's Foreign and Colonial Policy*, ch. 14; M. F. Bonn, "How Sanctions Failed," *Foreign Affairs*, January, 1937. For a criticism of French policy in this crisis, see Jean Bastin, *L'Affaire D'Éthiopie et les Diplomates*, Paris: De Brouwer, 1937.

[16] Ball, *op. cit.*, ch. 12. For the various agreements, see John W. Wheeler Bennett and Stephen Heald, *Documents on International Affairs, 1936*, London: Oxford Univ. Press, 1937, pp. 297–299, 320–327, 341–349. For an anti-British view, consult Toto Ishimaru, *Japan Must Fight Britain*, New York: Telegraph Press, 1936.

[17] Royal Institute of International Affairs, *Southeastern Europe*, New York: Oxford Univ. Press, 1939, p. 35 ff.; Raymond L. Buell, *Poland, Key to Europe*, New York: Knopf, 1939; Machray, *Struggle for the Danube*, ch. 7.

[18] Stephen Heald, *Documents on International Affairs, 1937*, London: Oxford Univ. Press, 1939, p. 443 ff.; Royal Institute of International Affairs, *Great Britain and Egypt*, New York: Oxford Univ. Press, 1936. The student of Mediterranean problems should know the following books: Margret Boveri, *Mediterranean Cross-Currents*, New York: Oxford Univ. Press, 1938; Elizabeth Monroe, *The Mediterranean in Politics*, London: Oxford Univ. Press, 1938; George Slocombe, *Dangerous Sea*, New York: Macmillan, 1937.

[19] The diplomacy of the Spanish Civil War can best be followed through the *Foreign Policy Reports* of December 1, 1936, January 15, 1937, April 1, 1938, and May 15, 1940. For background and various aspects, see J. Alvarez del Vayo, *Freedom's Battle*, New York: Knopf, 1940; Allison Peers, *The Spanish Tragedy*, New York: Oxford Univ. Press, 1936; Vincent Sheean, *Not Peace But a Sword*, Garden City, N. Y.: Doubleday, Doran, 1939. Note the bibliography at the end of the chapter on Spain in this book.

[20] G. E. R. Gedye, *Betrayal in Central Europe*, New York: Harper, 1939, and M. W. Fodor, *Plot and Counter Plot in Central Europe*, Boston: Houghton Mifflin, 1937, provide the details and background.

[21] Texts of the Anglo-Italian agreements may be found in *Il Popolo d'Italia*, April 17, 1938. For Italy and France, see Vera Micheles Dean, "Italy's African Claims against France," *Foreign Policy Reports*, June 1, 1939. For discussion of appeasement, see Churchill, *While England Slept*, pp. 381–383; Neville Chamberlain, *In Search of Peace*, New York: Putnam, 1939, pp. 50–58, 106–115. A thoughtful survey of the British-German situation, always associated with the British-Italian relations, can be found in A. L. Kennedy, *Britain Faces Germany*, New York: Oxford Univ. Press, 1937.

[22] *International Conciliation, Documents for the Year, 1938*, New York: Carnegie Endowment for International Peace, 1938, pp. 399–484. For the background of this Hitler-promoted struggle, see Elizabeth Wiskemann, *Czechs and Germans*, London: Oxford Univ. Press, 1938, pp. 235–283; J. S. Roucek, ch. 9, "Czechoslovakia and Her Minorities," pp. 171–192, in R. J. Kerner, ed., *Czechoslovakia: Twenty Years of Independence*, Berkeley, Cal.: Univ. of California Press, 1940.

[23] For the Hungarian background, see C. A. Macartney, *Hungary and Her Suc-*

cessors, New York: Oxford Univ. Press, 1937. French policy toward Italy is stated in Edouard Daladier, *In Defense of France,* Garden City, N. Y.: Doubleday, Doran, 1939, pp. 151–194. At this point official documents begin to be of value. The published Polish and German documents add little to our knowledge, but the French documents, especially the dispatches of the French ambassador at Berlin, are well written and penetrating. See France, *The French Yellow Book,* New York: Reynal & Hitchcock, 1940, pp. 69–108; Germany, *Documents on the Events Preceding the Outbreak of the War,* New York: German Library of Information, 1940, ch. 1; Poland, *Les relations polono-allemandes et polono-soviétiques au cours de la periode 1933–1939,* Paris: Flammarion, 1940, pp. 72–86.

²⁴ Poland, *op. cit.,* pp. 95–169; France, *op. cit.,* pp. 109–403; Germany, *op. cit.,* chs. 2, part C, 3 and 4. The British Blue Book, *Documents Concerning German-Polish Relations and the Outbreak of Hostilities between Great Britain and Germany on September 3, 1939,* London: H. M. Stationery Office, 1939, argues that Great Britain sought security; the German thesis is that Britain sought to encircle her. The most convenient reference for the United States' policy is Joseph Alsop and Robert Kintner, *American White Paper,* New York: Simon & Schuster, 1940. On Hitler, see the contrasting opinions in Neville Henderson, *Failure of a Mission,* pp. 182–183 and Herman Rauschning (a former Danzig Nazi), *The Voice of Destruction,* New York: Putnam, 1940, pp. 117–135.

²⁵ Finland, *The Finnish Blue Book,* New York: Lippincott, 1940, presents Finland's legal case against Russia and gives the terms of the treaty of peace. For Russian policy before and after the attack on Finland, see the pro-Soviet W. P. Coates and Zelda K. Coates, *World Affairs and the U.S.S.R.,* London: Lawrence, 1939, and Vera Micheles Dean, "Russia's Role in the European Conflict," *Foreign Policy Reports,* March 1, 1940; Rauschning, *op. cit.,* p. 124 ff.; Poland, *op. cit.* pp. 211–221.

²⁶ For a survey of literature about the opening phases of the Second World War and the changing interpretations of recent historical events, see J. S. Roucek, "World War II – A Survey of Recent Literature," *The Educational Forum,* May, 1940, Vol. IV, pp. 465–477. Since the outbreak of the war, as before, much reliance may be placed in such newspapers as the New York *Times,* the New York *Herald Tribune,* and the *Christian Science Monitor.* Carl J. Hambro, *I Saw It Happen,* New York: Appleton-Century, 1940, is a moving record of the Norwegian invasion by the President of the Norwegian Parliament.

²⁷ Robert G. Woolbert, "Italy's Role in the European Conflict," *Foreign Policy Reports,* May 1, 1940; Philip W. Ireland, "The Near East and the European War," *ibid.,* March 1, 1940; John C. de Wilde, "The Struggle for the Balkans," *ibid.,* December 15, 1939; Helen Fisher, "Cross Currents in Danubian Europe," *ibid.,* July 15, 1937; Royal Institute of International Affairs, *The Balkan States,* New York: Oxford Univ. Press, 1936, pp. 39–56.

²⁸ T. A. Bisson, *Japan in China,* New York: Macmillan, 1938; "Japan's Position in the War Crisis," *Foreign Policy Reports,* November 1, 1939, and "Soviet-Japanese Relations 1931–1938," *ibid.,* February 1, 1939, and David H. Popper, "The Western Powers and the Sino-Japanese Conflict," *ibid.,* August 1, 1938 are well informed and reliable. W. W. Willoughby, *Japan's Case Examined,* Baltimore: Johns Hopkins Press, 1940 is hostile to Japan. A number of good accounts of the Chinese revolt are available, among which may be mentioned James G. Bertram, *First Act in China,* New York: Viking Press, 1938 and Edgar Snow, *Red Star over China,* New York: Random House, 1938.

SELECTED BIBLIOGRAPHY

Armstrong, Hamilton Fish, *When There Is No Peace,* New York: Council of Foreign Relations, 1939. An excellent account of 1938 which should be read for its discussion of the Czechoslovak crisis.

Brown, J. J., Hodges, Charles and Roucek, J. S., *Contemporary World Politics,* New York: Wiley, second edition, 1940.

Chamberlain, William Henry, *The Confessions of an Individualist*, New York: Macmillan, 1940. Interesting for his opposition to the usual opinions about British and French policies in 1939. A pleasant book with an unpleasant outlook toward the future.

Dean, Vera Micheles, *Europe in Retreat*, New York: Knopf, 1939. A well-written survey of the period since 1933 by an authority.

Ford, Guy Stanton, ed., *Dictatorship in the Modern World*, Minneapolis: Univ. of Minnesota Press, 1939. In view of much prevailing hysteria this dispassionate examination of dictatorship should be read by every student of history.

Gathorne-Hardy, G. M., *A Short History of International Affairs, 1920–1938*, New York: Oxford Univ. Press, 1938. A very successful attempt to balance facts and interpretation.

Gunther, John, *Inside Europe*, New York: Harper, 1940.

——, *Inside Asia*, New York: Harper, 1939. These volumes admirably meet part of the need of the student of international affairs for the information which lies outside diplomatic documents. However, one should not take his analyses of personalities too seriously.

Hutton, Graham, *Is It Peace?*, New York: Macmillan, 1937. An excellent and thoughtful examination of the international problems of Great Britain and the world.

Millis, Walter, *Why Europe Fights*, New York: Morrow, 1940. An excellent and sane survey of the period since 1919 by the author of *The Road to War*.

Penguin Political Dictionary compiled by Walter Theimer, London: Penguin Books, 1940.

Roucek, J. S., *The Politics of the Balkans*, New York: McGraw-Hill, 1939. A compact introduction to the internal politics of the Balkan states in relation to their foreign policies.

Schuman, Frederick L., *Europe on the Eve*, New York: Knopf, 1939. An impassioned and well-documented study of foreign policies of European states from 1933 to 1939. Simonds, Frank H. and Emeny, Brooks, *The Great Powers in World Politics*, New York: American Book Co., 1937. This interpretation of international affairs from the economic point of view should be read by every student, although the authors base too much of their interpretation on the narrow " have vs. havenots " theory.

Swing, Raymond Gram, *How War Came*, New York: Norton, 1939. The approach of war after March, 1939, as described from day to day by one of the best radio commentators.

Thompson, Dorothy, *Let the Record Speak*, Boston: Houghton Mifflin, 1939. To be read for its point of view, not as factual material. Important as part of the reaction of many to the activities of Hitler.

Tolischus, Otto D., *They Wanted War*, New York: Reynal and Hitchcock, 1940. A hostile examination of totalitarian policies.

Young, A. Morgan, *Imperial Japan, 1926–1938*, New York: Norton, 1938. A hostile but well-informed account of Japanese developments since 1926.

CHAPTER XXVII

Grand Military Strategy on the Stage Set by European Geography

War consists of an attempt by one nation to impose its will forcibly upon another. This accounts for the existence of armies and navies, which are the instrumentalities of national will to resist aggression or dominate by aggression. Elsewhere in this book examination is made of the factors producing war in so far as Europe is concerned. The subject matter in this chapter has to do with its execution, remembering that war is not a contractual affair. It can be caused by one party alone, regardless of the desires of the other parties concerned.

Once resort is had to arms the basic objective on each side is to reduce the will to resist of the other party concerned. This condition may be brought about (a) directly, by destruction of the opposition's armed forces, (b) indirectly, by throttling the normal means of existence, thus making life unbearable for the opposition, or (c) by combination of both. Specific modern example of (a) is the recent destruction of the French army in the field by Germany. Britain's present naval blockade of the Axis Powers is clear-cut illustration of (b). For definite example of (c) we must look back at what we shall term for brevity, although incorrect historically, the First World War. In 1918 the German defeat was brought about by a combination of blockade and military operations. Starvation at home produced disintegration of the will to win, while the American drive through the Meuse-Argonne cut the lifeline of the German armies in the West, forcing a general retirement and consequent disruption. The armistice of November 11, 1918 forestalled the complete destruction of the German military forces. Within this bracket are contained all elements of success in war.

Modern wars are never haphazard affairs in so far as the aggressor is concerned. Their operation begins in accordance with a basic policy and a plan for the furtherance of that policy. Both policy and plan call for certain combinations to carry them out. For want of a better name we shall call these combinations " grand strategy." Basically, strategy is that branch of the art of war concerned with the moving of troops in the theater of war in order to enforce the national objective. In its higher aspect strategy embraces study of what Jomini terms *politique de la guerre* (di-

---

This chapter by R. Ernest Dupuy, Lieutenant Colonel, Field Artillery, United States Army.

plomacy and power politics) and *politique militaire* (military intelligence). The first of these includes knowledge of physical geography in the light of specific military operations (military geography) and the second, of the political groupings involved (geopolitics).

Wars are waged on land, in the air, upon and under the surface of the sea. Critical analysis of war must then include discussion of avenues of, and barriers to, invasion. Man to live must eat, and to fight must have weapons. Since no nation of Europe is totally self-sustaining for either purpose our examination must include all channels of supply. The fact that the airplane, with certain limitations of time and space, can leap physical barriers, does not affect this consideration, since man lives on the land, although he utilizes the water and — to a much lesser degree — the air for transport. Furthermore, until such time as the airplane becomes capable of landing anywhere, or of hovering indefinitely over any one point, its use in war is as a weapon, a member of the combat team, and must be supported in the end by surface troops who will take permanent possession of the terrain desired. This condition will remain until the day arrives when tanks can roll, fly, and float indefinitely. That day may come, but has not yet arrived.

Since time immemorial man has traveled, for trade and for conquest. Naturally, he has always sought the easiest way. On the surface of the earth this has been over the plains, along the river valleys, through the mountain passes and the bottlenecks to and from the ocean. The advent of the airplane has to some degree eliminated physical obstacles. However, the air lanes in general also follow the easiest way, since the airplane is limited in the amount of fuel it can carry and must therefore rely on bases; must seek the gaps in mountain ranges, or go around the peaks to avoid danger of crashing. In military operations the shortest air route can be followed, it is true, but this is always dependent upon the radius of action of the machine: that is, the amount of fuel it can carry. Like the ship on the sea it must at some time return to a base for refueling.

Thus the age-old paths of conquest by land and by sea are all-important to grand strategy. The pattern of invasion in Europe has always followed them. It is a definitely recurring one.[1]

Europe's Physical Geography. Let us glance at the physical geography of Europe. Beginning at the Scandinavian peninsula, we find the highlands — rugged mountainous masses — sweeping down its western side, splitting Norway from Sweden. The Skagerrak and Kattegat, dividing Scandinavia's southern tip from the Jutland peninsula, afford a tortuous water channel from the Black Sea to the Baltic and the Gulfs of Bothnia and Finland.

From the North Cape east to the Urals, and south roughly to latitude 60° North, the character of the land itself — the plains of tundra which in summer are marshy, lake-spotted and soggy, in winter snow-covered and wind-swept, and which are forested in part — becomes an obstacle to movement. An inhospitable, unfertile land this, in which military operations can be carried out only with extreme difficulty.

On the remainder of the continent, from west to east, we find first the Pyrenees, barring the northern entrance to the Iberian peninsula, with the Sierra Nevadas to the south. Southernmost spurs of the latter are Tarifa and Gibraltar, northern gateposts of the Mediterranean bottleneck. North of the Pyrenees lies the plain of France, part of the Great Lowland Plain of northern Europe — flatlands bordering on the sea all the way to the Gulf of Finland, and thence to the Urals. First major obstacle east of the Bay of Biscay is the Massif Central of France. Then comes the Rhone valley, bordered on the east by the great Alpine masses and their spurs stretching southward to enclose the fertile Po valley in Italy and the Adriatic Sea.

North of the Alps come the Vosges and the Ardennes forming the west boundary of the Rhine valley. To the east again the mighty Danube flows from the Black Forest generally southeast through the Hungarian plain to the Black Sea. North and east of the Danubian headwaters the Elbe rises in the Bohemian plateau to drain into the North Sea. Eastward is the Oder flowing north to the Baltic. The Bohemian plateau is itself fringed by the Erzgeberg and Sudeten mountains on the north, the Bohmer Wald on the south, to form a spearhead jutting westward. On its easterly side the Carpathians and the Transylvanian Alps swing in a rough semicircle like an inverted C to enclose the Hungarian plain and the Danube valley between their respective points and the Alpine masses to the northwest, the Balkans to the south. East again we find the successive valleys of the Vistula and Duna flowing north, the Dniester and the Dnieper flowing south. Still further east the Don and the great wandering Volga drain the rich Russian lowland plain to the Black Sea, while to the north the Dvina drains the tundras to the White Sea. South and east of the jumbled hill-masses of the Balkans the Dardanelles, Sea of Marmara and Bosphorus bar Asia Minor from Europe, afford channels from the Mediterranean via the Aegean into the Black Sea. The tableland of Asia Minor is itself sealed to the south and east by the Taurus mountains, the Armenian highlands and the Caucasus.

Swinging up northwest to the British Isles, we find them separated from the mainland by the English Channel and the North Sea. The major terrain obstacles in Great Britain are her chalk cliffs to the south, the Pennine chain with the top-bar of its T at the Scotch border, the Grampians in the north of Scotland, and the Welsh mountains. Across the narrow Irish Sea lies Ireland, with its coastal highlands and central plain.

It is axiomatic that wherever the land be washed by the sea potential landing places are afforded. This is of course modified greatly in fact by

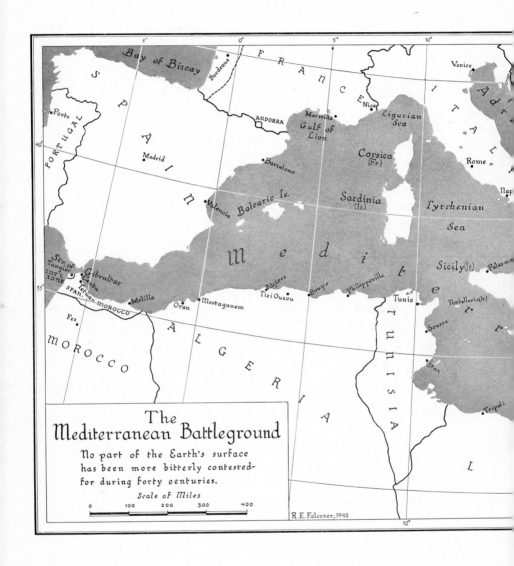

The
Mediterranean Battleground

No part of the Earth's surface
has been more bitterly contested-
for during forty centuries.

Scale of Miles

| 0 | 100 | 200 | 300 | 400 |

R.E. Falconer, 1940

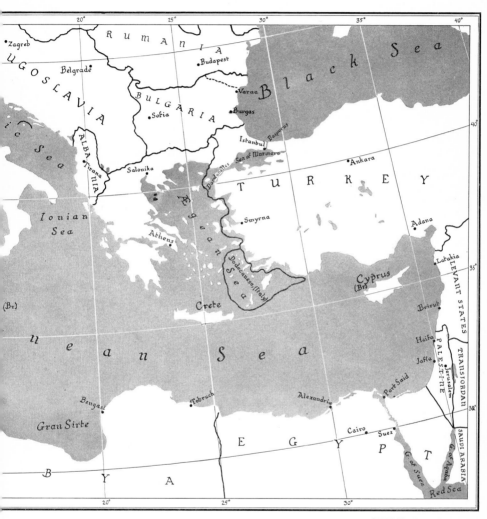

climatic conditions, and by the actual topography of the coastal terrain which may hinder or assist the safe approach of vessels. Arctic Ocean ports, for instance, are ice-locked during the long winter except at the North Cape tip of Scandinavia and a short distance eastward, where the Arctic current has influence. In winter also the Gulfs of Bothnia and Finland are both ice-locked. Prevalent fog in the North Sea at times hinders navigation both surface and aerial. And depth of water and shelter determine in general the location of safe anchorages and ports.

However, other considerations affect navigation. These are bottlenecks that nature has placed on interior waterways. And these are important militarily since they can be controlled by exercise of land, air, and sea power.

So, looking at the map, we can say in general that except for climatic and coastal conditions the sea offers no obstacle to approach to the Atlantic edge of the Scandinavian peninsula, to the British Isles, to the western coasts of France and of Spain. All other water-washed ports in Europe are entered only through bottlenecks. Egress from the Baltic is through the Kattegat-Skagerrak straits and the Kiel Canal in Germany which are themselves more remotely controlled by the Dover straits of the English Channel to the south, and the northern exit of the North Sea. Black Sea ports can be entered only through the Dardanelles. But that itself, as we have said, debouches into the Aegean Sea and thence to the Mediterranean. And there are but two entrances to the entire Mediterranean area — the Straits of Gibraltar to the west, and the Suez Canal to the east.

These bottlenecks are controlled either (a) by the countries contiguous to them or (b) through the use of sea power operating from bases within the radius of action of warships.

Thus, it can be seen, any nation possessing a superiority of sea power, in the form of capital ships — battleships, capable of keeping the sea and fighting in all weathers; together with cruisers to overhaul commerce, and all the necessary auxiliaries — can not only assure the flow of supplies to its own country, but can deny sea-borne supplies to any other nation. This was England's position when the First World War came to a close, and this position she has thus far maintained. Since modern ships are dependent on fuel — the sailing vessels of old were not so dependent — a chain of bases is necessary. Battle fleets today are limited to an approximate 3500 mile radius of action. Air power is today attempting to usurp the place of sea power as a blockade agency. Its physical limitations, plus sensitivity to atmospheric conditions, have so far presented obstacles to complete success as an independent operating force, but it is essential as an adjunct of sea power.

Geography in Relation to National Boundaries and Ethnic Groupings.
The same barriers of physical geography — mountain ranges, broad rivers,

seas and gulfs — which canalize and restrict the flow of traffic also have greatly influenced national boundaries and race groupings.[2] At the opening of the First World War most of these boundaries had been of long standing. The Treaty of Versailles and other contingent treaties of peace at the end of that war brought about a tremendous shifting of boundaries — some of them entirely new, some reversions to older boundaries changed long before by conquest, and some hodgepodges following no set pattern, melanging mutually alien societies and ideologies, restricting on the one hand, opening new doors to commerce on the other.

Since these new boundaries have been among the causes of the Second World War, their influence on present-day conditions is all-important, and deserves some study. Incidentally, it must be borne in mind, as noted in earlier chapters, that when the new lines of national demarcation were set up, the powers imposing them had mixed objectives in view. Outwardly clamoring for the liberation of small nations, the Allies had also mutually selfish motives, seeking by the new groupings to set up a series of buffer states through which both Germany and Russia could be curbed.

On the Baltic Sea the creation of Finland, Estonia, Latvia, and Lithuania as independent nations definitely restricted Russian influence. One seaport — Leningrad, with its fortress of Kronstadt — became Russia's only Baltic outlet. In addition, so long as a neutral Turkey held the Dardanelles, blocking the Black Sea, and ice conditions partly hindered Russian egress from the White Sea to the Atlantic, Russia in Europe, with the additional double check of the Skagerrak-Kattegat strait and of British sea power in the North Sea, was bottled up from a naval viewpoint.

Germany, by use of the Kiel Canal, could maintain communications of her own between the North and Baltic Seas, but the re-creation of Poland set up a pro-Ally buffer state between Germany and Russia, potential check to German eastward and Russian westward moves. To give Poland an open door for trade, the Polish Corridor was created, dividing East Prussia from Germany proper. It must be admitted that this was, in German eyes, an intolerable condition. This narrow strip of Polish land, unprotected by any physical barrier, faced on both sides by an irate people, made one of the finest tinderboxes ever to be set in any European political powder keg. The free city of Danzig — solitary return to the political concept of the Hanseatic League — created an island of unrest from which, as it turned out, sparks would fly into the tinderbox.

Geographically, Poland had little protection against invasion except on her southern border — where the passes were in Czech control, and for the Pinsk marsh area in the east which canalized possible military moves from the north in the general line, Warsaw–Minsk, and from the south, Lwow– the Ukraine.

The creation of Czechoslovakia had good political as well as military reasons behind it. The old kingdom of Bohemia was an ethnological entity, which, overrun by conquest, had become an unwilling part of the loose-knit Austro-Hungarian Empire. East of the Waag River, Slovakia and Ruthenia belonged originally to the Hungarian plain grouping. The people of all three had fought the Dual Monarchy; a synthetic Czechoslovakia had been set up during the war as a backfire which accomplished much in the disruption of Austro-Hungary; the Czech Legions had fought for the Allies, and recognition of these things was due.

Militarily Czechoslovakia was of the utmost importance in checking a post-war Germany. The Bohemian plateau, protected by its mountain ranges, was an arrowhead pointing into the heart of the Reich, and controlled the Danube valley. From the viewpoint of German strategy, the elimination of Czechoslovakia was hence essential. The fact that the Czech army was a good one, that the mountain barriers had been fortified, delayed reduction of the country until such time as the bloodless capture of an emasculated Austria assured possibility of a pincers blow against Czechoslovakia from both north and south if necessary. Political considerations, as we know, eliminated the necessity for a capture by force.

The Achilles heel of Czechoslovakia was its own geographical situation. A landlocked nation, she was dependent upon the good will of her neighbors for international commerce, on allies for military assistance. Her defensive geographical strength lay in the fact that nearly all the passes through the Bohmer Wald, Erzgeberg, and Sudetens lay *inside* her territorial domain, permitting fortification. If Czechoslovakia's allies would fight with her, Germany faced a two-front war. Once the Sudeten area was ceded to Germany, the defensive barriers of the Bohemian plateau were breached. She lost further value to the allies who had forced this first surrender.

The war treaties had given to Rumania Transylvania, once part of Hungary, and — in the Middle Ages — debatable ground, claimed by both the Hungarians and the Patzinaks occupying Rumania and the Don valley. This placed Rumania in control of the eastern Carpathians and the Transylvanian Alps and of the northern bank of the Danube at the Iron Gate, whence it debouches into the Rumanian plain and flows to the sea. The Danube also, bounding Rumania and Bulgaria, was further protected by the earlier cession of the Dobruja to the former, thus placing its mouths in Rumanian hands. Cession of Bessarabia to Rumania, to include the south bank of the Dniester River, gave Rumania on the north and south defensible river lines, but the western boundary, adjoining Hungary, was open. Behind it, however, lay the Carpatho-Transylvanian Alps mass, a region offering many difficulties to military penetration. All the passes, of which the Predeal is the most important, thus lay entirely in Rumanian territory (except the Iron Gate mentioned above). Both the Transylvania and Bessarabian acquisitions, however, were weaknesses to Rumania in that they included alien minorities antagonistic to the new overlords.

The little kingdom of Serbia became Yugoslavia, or the kingdom of the Serbs, Croats, and Slovenes. The Dinaric Alps protected its new western coastal boundary, although Italy had been given some and had later taken other strategic ports along the Dalmatian coast enabling her to control the Adriatic Sea. There is, however, one principal gateway to Yugoslavia, which must be considered as of major importance. This is the Pear Tree Pass [3] just northeast of Trieste, on the Italo-Yugoslav border. Through this gorge lies the main highway from the Po valley to the Save valley and it is a key to the Balkan region. The Drava and the Danube on the north and east of Yugoslavia, and the Balkan hill-masses to the south are all defensible barriers, particularly since the new political setup brought under Yugoslav domination the major portion of the only main arteries cut by nature through the Balkans — the Morava-Maritza and Morava-Vardar corridors.[4]

The Morava, rising in the mountains near Skoplje, flows north to empty into the Danube. Its valley thus becomes the north-south highway. The Maritza, rising slightly to the east, flows down southeastward to touch the Turkish plain, thence south into the Bay of Samothrace. The Vardar, rising south and west of Skoplje, flows from that place south into Greece to empty also into the Aegean Sea, at Salonika. From Italy into Greece or vice versa the road runs thus: Valley of the Po — Pear Tree Pass — Save valley to the Danube — Morava valley — Vardar valley. From Italy to Istanbul one takes the same route south to Nis, thence southeast into the Maritza valley.

Italy in the shuffle gained some territory to the north and east, part of it with alien population. She was thus enabled to command the Pear Tree Pass into Yugoslavia. The Izonzo minor passes — the Bacha and Predil and the Pontebbo leading into the Tagliamento valley, still lay on the Austrian border. West of these comes the most important gate — the Brenner Pass, opening into the Adige valley. This also lies on the Austro-Italian border, and all border passes are debatable gateways, since they may be fortified by both sides concerned, and — in theory at least — may be seized by either through a sudden coup.

West of the Brenner lies the Reschen Pass [5] at the junction of the Italo-Austro-Swiss border, another opening from Austria into the Adige valley, and like the others mentioned above, a border gate.

Between Italy and Switzerland the Stelvio Pass, running east-west, is in Italian hands. Leading directly to Milan via the Lake Como valley we find the Bernina, in Swiss territory; and the Spulgen, a border pass. Further west lie the St. Gotthard, well inside the Swiss boundary; the Simplon Pass (Swiss) and tunnel (crossing the border), and finally the Great St. Bernard, a border gate.

Italy's western boundary was unchanged by the First World War. From north to south the gateways are the Little St. Bernard, Mt. Cenis, Mt. Genevre, Larche, Tende and the Mediterranean littoral.[6] All these are border passes.

In considering Italy's position from the viewpoint of military geography, however, it must always be remembered that all inward-bound paths converge finally into the Po valley, the heart of northern Italy; diverge on leaving Italian territory. Invaders of Italy using more than one route may expect that their columns will be mutually supporting. The reverse is not true, although the passes into France do open eventually into the Rhone valley, but not within supporting distances. Thus future Italian territorial objectives might well be expected to include demands for French territory to the east bank of the Rhone inclusive, with the objective the securing of all western portals. The situation of the Swiss and Austrian fronts is another matter; and Italian aggrandizement would affect Germanic aims adversely. The acquisition of Slovenia, Croatia, and Slavonia by Italy would open wide the path for domination of the entire Balkan area south of the Danube. And for some years past a certain school of thought in southern Europe has held the opinion that the mutual relationships of the Axis Powers would end with an agreement whereby the Danube, south of the Hungarian border, would be the eventual line of demarcation of their respective hegemonies.

Switzerland offers no highways for war. The only entrance to it not through a defended mountain pass is north of Zurich, where the Rhine may be crossed. Her territorial boundaries were unchanged by the First World War.

While France's eastern boundaries were temporarily changed for the better following the First World War, the later relinquishment of the Rhineland to Germany placed her, from the viewpoint of military geography, in the same situation as before the Treaty of Versailles, since Germany was in potential position to move through any of the three natural gateways. These, from south to north, are the Belfort Pass, between the Vosges and the Jura; the Stenay Pass through the Ardennes, and the flatlands of Flanders north of the Ardennes to the sea.[7]

In so far as Germany's western boundary was concerned, the step-by-step reacquisition of her former territory to include the Saar was of tremendous advantage. It gave her the entire Rhine valley as a channel of communications, together with the terrain west of it not only to protect that valley once it debouched from the Schwartzwald highlands, but also for use as a springboard for offensive moves into the Ardennes and, further north, into the plain. The Maginot Line — no line at all but a highly organized defensive zone — reinforced France's natural barriers from the Swiss border to the Belgian Ardennes only. The Flanders plain was wide open to any invasion which pierced Belgian defenses, and these in turn were bare to a thrust directed through the Netherlands. On the German side the so-called Siegfried Line, another barrier, defended with iron grip the Rhine valley.

Theoretically, the Maginot and Siegfried zones were of equal strength defensively, and might be expected to provide springboards for offensive action. Either could be used as a pivot for such moves. Actually, let us see what happened. Germany, prepared for offensive action, her left resting on the Siegfried Line, gobbled up Holland, turned the Belgian defenses, overran the Flanders plain. Simultaneously she pierced the Ardennes. France and Britain, unprepared for offensive action, were caught flat-footed. The Maginot Line crumbled as the offensive north of it swirled into its rear areas. In football parlance, the Allied left end and secondary defense were neatly mousetrapped by what turned out to be a cleverly timed spinner play through Corap's French army, playing a very poor defensive tackle position.

Here we might remember that so long as one party in war respects the rights of a neutral nation, the physical position of that neutral becomes an artificial barrier, regardless of the neutral's strength or weakness, geographical or military. One offensive move only was open in theory to France at the outset of the war – a thrust duplicating Napoleon's 1805 campaign, in the direction of Metz–Karlsruhe–Ulm–Munich. Such a thrust departing from the shelter of the Maginot Line, would have as natural obstacles the Rhine and the Schwartzwald hill-mass. Given a potent Czechoslovakia as an ally, it would have a chance for success. To block this move Germany had done two things: she created the Siegfried Line, she eliminated Czechoslovakia. France, as we know, was not prepared for an offensive action, but even if she had been, such a move would have been suicidal after the Pact of Munich.

No better example of successful long-range planning in grand strategy, and of the close alliance between diplomacy and war in furthering national objectives, can be found than in the progressive moves of Germany during the period 1937 to 1940. On the other hand it would be hard to find a more glaring example of futile political fumbling in disregard of national self-defense than the amateurish appeasement policy of the Allies both prior to and during the same period.[8] Certainly one cannot believe that all British and French military men could have been blind to indications patent to other military observers. But, as remarked at the opening of this chapter, national armed forces are instrumentalities of national policies, and are not normally directors of those policies. They may advise; they cannot – except in military dictatorships – control.

This brings us to the Iberian peninsula – Spain and Portugal – unchanged territorially by the First World War. The Pyrenees form the natural barrier between France and Spain, with main passes the littoral on both Atlantic and Mediterranean and four additional minor passes between them. At the southern tip of the Iberian peninsula, Gibraltar, in English hands, blocks the Mediterranean bottleneck, so long as it may be utilized as a base for sea power to operate from. The eastern Spanish coast and the Balearics offer potential bases for sea and air power operating in the western Mediterranean. The western coast of Spain and Portugal offers the same advantages for operation. Operation against what? Against the sea lanes between the English Channel and the Suez Canal, and down the African coast around the Cape of Good Hope. These factors and no altruistic consideration as to the relative merits of Republican (Communistic) and Nationalistic (Fascist) Spanish factions led to the active interest of the various powers during the Spanish Civil War. They all needed Spain as a potential ally. That is, they needed Spanish territory to which if necessary they could move units of sea and air power for operations furthering their own ends.

Elsewhere in this book the ideological and economic factors leading to the clash of national aims and ambitions in Europe are fully discussed. For the purposes of this chapter we may assume that this clash of ideologies existed, that the national objectives of Germany and Italy ran counter to those of Great Britain, France, and the smaller powers, and that those of Russia were adverse to both. Success on each side was dependent first upon the success of diplomatic and economic moves and later upon the success of the extension of diplomacy — war. Hence in the formulation of national policies the military, as an instrument of national policy, would be consulted, so that the political coat could be cut according to the military cloth available.

Germany's Expansionism. Given a German national policy to dominate Europe, the essential elements of success depend on the sea, in obtaining (a) free and uninterrupted access to the Atlantic Ocean — that is, domination of the English Channel and the North Sea; (b) domination of the Baltic by control of the Skagerrak-Kattegat channel. On land, control of the Bohemian plateau — by means of which thrusts north of the Carpathians toward the Ukraine might be safeguarded, and access to the Hungarian plain and the Danube valley attained. This means control of Czechoslovakia, Poland, Austria, Hungary, and Rumania. Control of the entire Balkan region would be still better; however, such control might run counter to Italian objectives (which will be taken up later). These German objectives fit into the greater German plan of domination of southern Europe and Asia Minor — the Berlin to Bagdad line — long dreamed of prior to 1914, which would place under Teutonic control the fertile Hungarian plain, the Anatolian plateau and the oil fields of Rumania and of Iraq.

Since attainment of all these objectives hinges upon the elimination of the British Empire as a sea power, the cooperation of Italy in the control of the Mediterranean would be necessary.

Let us see how many of these objectives have been reached. Austria and Czechoslovakia fell, opening the Danube valley; Hungary and the Balkans have been conquered or peacefully overrun. Poland fell, which resulted immediately in Russian countermoves, to save the latter's share of the Baltic, protect the Ukraine, and ensure a better hold on the Black Sea.

It is pertinent to mention here that in so far as central Europe is concerned the Russian mouthful of Poland which includes the territory north of the Ruthenian border is of some importance. Three passes exist in the Carpathians along this border — from east to west the Uzok, Beskid, and Jablonika. Hungary snapped up Ruthenia when Czechoslovakia was thrown to the wolves. These border gates open three subsidiary routes of invasion through the otherwise Germanic seal, into the north marches of the Danube valley. However, since they are flanked from the west by terrain offering no difficulty to a German move from her share of Poland, their value is minimized. But they would be of assistance to an anti-German or anti-Hungarian move by a Russo-Rumanian alliance, and this was a factor in the Hungarian desire to wrest Transylvania from Rumania. That Transylvania, including its mountains, was once Hungarian, lends some logical ethnic reasons for the demand; but it is, basically, one of grand strategy and has resulted in additional protection to the Hungarian plain.

To return to our discussion, Denmark and Norway fell, Sweden is dominated. Germany thus has a toehold on the northern reaches of the North Sea. The Netherlands, Belgium, and France fell, placing the southern littoral on the English Channel in German hands.

The fall of France places Germany in touch with the Iberian peninsula. The elimination of British sea power is still essential, however, before the outer gates can be opened — from the Arctic to Gibraltar. This can be eliminated only by removal of British bases: that is, by the subjugation of the British Isles. Had the fall of France brought the French fleet into German hands, the combined German-Italian fleet would have been sufficient, on paper, at least, to contest this sea power on equal basis. Hence the almost instantaneous action of the British in destroying part of the French fleet and seizing another part, thus offsetting any advantage that Germany had obtained by capturing what was left.

Italy's Strategy. From the Italian point of view possession of the Mediterranean is essential for the consolidation of her African empire; the lanes between Italy and North Africa must be open. Unless Italy controlled the Suez Canal or the Anglo-Egyptian Sudan, Italian East African forces were definitely cut off from supply from the homeland, except by British permission. Until and unless Italy controls the Straits of Gibraltar, she is blocked from the Atlantic Ocean. That is, Italy must look to the continent of Europe for foodstuffs and munitions. Hence Italy also seeks to eliminate British sea power. Italian contact with the Balkans depends upon (a) Yugoslavia, through which the highways run; (b) Greece whose shore line affords protection to Italian craft plying between the Adriatic, the Aegean, and the Black Sea, and where land routes offer a by-pass. Italy holds Albania, but there are no real highways through that mountainland either to Yugoslavia or Greece. These might be built — Italians are good road builders and three tenuous trails exist through the Pindus range and Macedonia — but this costs in time, man power, and money.

Italy would be in a far better condition if she controlled the Balkans, but a permanent Italian hold on the Aegean blocks Russian ambitions. Russia has already seized Bessarabia as a buffer against Pan-Germanic moves in the Danube valley. She is thwarted in the Black Sea area whether Britain holds the Mediterranean exits, or Italy the inside lines. In somewhat similar manner must Turkey, possessor of the actual water barrier cutting Europe from Asia Minor and constituting the maritime highway to the Black Sea, look on the future. Axis domination of Greece which came to pass at the end of April, 1941 constitutes the most pressing threat against Turkey.

Britain's View. A glance at the European strategical situation from the British viewpoint must close this discussion. Up until a few years ago, Britain's naval superiority in warships, and her outlying bases throughout the world from which she could utilize that sea power, had been her offensive weapon, permitting blockade. For defense the same sea power prevented any invasion of the British Isles.

Today, from the angle of defense, England's situation has changed to some degree. Hostile air power from bases within range hammers directly upon the British Isles. But in the long run England cannot be conquered until a hostile army lands and successfully overruns England. That this air power alone can actually transport sufficient men and material across the English Channel remains to be proved, although it is certain that it can be of assistance in such an expedition. To transport troops by water across the English Channel in sufficient numbers will require surface craft in large numbers. But such surface craft cannot move safely until and unless Axis air power can defeat British air power and also overthrow British sea power.

In the meantime superior British sea power is carrying on an effective blockade of Axis ports. Superior Axis air power is attempting a counterblockade, each side striving to bar the highways of the earth's surface to the other, since neither England nor her adversaries can long carry out warfare without ability to use the international sea lanes. Look at it from whatever angle one may, this fact emerges: the only belligerent cargo-vessels using the outer international sea lanes today are British. This traffic may be restricted, it may be suffering heavy losses, but nevertheless it is still moving. Axis Power cargo vessels are not plying the Atlantic. They are not plying any of the outer sea lanes of any continent. Sea power is once more proving its ability to impose indirect reduction of the will to win; air power has not yet proved equal potency.

To sum up, we thus find that the waging of successful war depends upon possession or domination of the paths of conquest by water, land, and air, and that the physical conformation of the earth's surface radically affects world politics. Hence the study of military geography is an essential element of all grand strategy.

REFERENCES

1 For a condensed discussion of the routes of past European invasions, see R. E. Dupuy and G. F. Eliot, *If War Comes*, New York: Macmillan, 1937, pp. 231–239.

2 For further research into this subject, see W. R. Shepherd, *Historical Atlas*, seventh edition, New York: Holt, 1929.

3 The importance of the Pear Tree Pass is discussed at length in W. W. Johnson, *Battlefields of the World War*, New York: Oxford Univ. Press, 1921, pp. 542–544, 560.

4 Balkan topography in general and the corridors mentioned in particular are subjects of exhaustive study in *Battlefields of the World War*, pp. 573–632.

5 An interesting survey of this area is contained in " Trento to the Reschen Pass," by Griffith Taylor, University of Toronto, in *The Geographical Review*, April, 1940, pp. 215–237.

6 The value of the Franco-Italian Alpine passes in the sixteenth century is entertainingly discussed in " An Itinerary for Morisco Refugees from Sixteenth-Century Spain," by J. N. Lincoln, *The Geographical Review*, July, 1939, pp. 483–487.

7 Complete and comprehensive geographic analyses of all the western battlefields of the First World War are contained in *Battlefields of the World War, passim*. Such study is essential for comprehension of the economic disagreements between France and Germany, and the probable territorial demands of the latter following her present conquest of France.

8 See *If War Comes*, pp. 247–281, 297–309.

SELECTED BIBLIOGRAPHY

Dupuy, R. E., " Checkerboard of Mars," *Today*, Vol. VII, No. 5, p. 12 *et seq.*, Nov. 21, 1936. An article discussing the geographic importance of the Iberian peninsula.

——, " Nations at War," ch. 5, *Contemporary World Politics*, Brown, Hodges and Roucek, New York: Wiley, 1940.

——, *If War Comes* (collaboration with George Fielding Eliot), New York: Macmillan, 1937. A survey of modern war, its methods and probabilities.

——, *World in Arms*, Harrisburg: Military Service Publishing Co., 1940. A study of military geography.

Johnson, D. W., *Battlefields of the World War*, New York: Oxford Univ. Press, 1921. An exhaustive critical analysis of the terrains of the First World War.

Lincoln, J. N., " An Itinerary for Morisco Refugees from Sixteenth-Century Spain," *Geographical Review*, July, 1939, pp. 231–239.

Mahan, A. T., *The Influence of Sea Power upon History*, *1660–1783*, 1890.

——, *The Influence of Sea Power upon the French Revolution and Empire, 1798–1812*, New York: Little, Brown, 1892. In these two volumes are contained comprehensive analyses of the effect of naval strength in the past.

Mitchell, W. A., *Outline of the World's Military History*, Washington, D. C.: National Service Publishing Co., 1931. A textbook formerly used at West Point and prepared by a West Point professor.

Shepherd, W. R., *Historical Atlas*, 7th ed., New York: Holt, 1929. A textbook. Essential to fundamental study of geopolitics.

Taylor, Griffith, " Trento to the Reschen Pass," *Geographical Review*, April, 1940, pp. 215–237. A geographic discussion of the Italo-Austrian frontier.

Note: The opinions expressed and conclusions drawn in this chapter are those of an individual, and should not be construed as being official War Department views, nor as necessarily reflecting those of the services at large.

CHAPTER XXVIII

Science and Technology

Pure science is inherently international. This is true of both its major aspects: research, the quest for new knowledge and for mastery of nature's secrets, and the great storehouse of facts, principles and power thus accumulated. Both are obviously the property of humanity as a whole. But applied science, the use of this method and knowledge in the service of society or of individuals, is selfish in origin and is valued as a private asset, a powerful weapon in competition and a bulwark of nationalism. In this dual nature of science lies its contradictory meaning in the life of today and in the history of Europe. It is because in these two aspects men of science serve both God and Mammon, that they stand in an anomalous position, holding in the one hand the hopes of humanity for a better life, and in the other wielding the most fearsome instruments of destruction. Contemporary Europe reveals the contrast more poignantly than does any other period of history.

The ordeal of the war of 1914–1918 forced every nation to utilize its resources to the utmost and therefore to examine its own capacity for the mastery of science and technology for economic, cultural, and military ends. When the war began the Germans had achieved acknowledged leadership in almost every branch of pure science and the demands of the war forced them to utilize that knowledge and skill for national and military purposes. They did so with impressive success. The Haber process for the manufacture of nitrates, and hence explosives, from the atmosphere made Germany independent of Chilean nitrate. Consummate skill provided not only new weapons of aerial, submarine, and chemical warfare but countless satisfactory substitute materials for civilians, to replace those eliminated by the blockade. The Allies, too, lacked many materials formerly obtained from Germany so that the needs of defense led to a host of good resolutions among them for the greater support of scientific research and for its organized exploitation in the national interest.

But the Peace of Versailles, resting with apparent certainty on military, political, and economic dominance, caused most of these resolutions to be forgotten. In the 'twenties each nation reverted to its economic and cultural habits. But the great resource left to the Germans was the one they treasured most, yet the one habitually ignored in the education and culture of all other nations: namely, the brains, the trained intellectual

This chapter by Gerald Wendt, formerly Dean, School of Chemistry and Physics, Pennsylvania State College.

power of its technical men. This they developed. Without resources they were yet resourceful. Thus arose the present situation.

To understand the wide divergence in standards of quality and in productiveness among the different nations of Europe it is necessary to examine the underlying motives, in each nation, of the men who devote themselves to a life of science. There are no inherent biological differences between the men of different nations, which lead to such different results. There is also no essential difference between creative power in science and in art or even in industry or politics. The social background, however, does determine the outlet for this creative power.

In England the educational system has for generations made a radical distinction between the gentlemen and others. The traditional emphasis in the training of gentlemen has been on the use of language and on the handling of people. Technical training was not included. At Oxford, for instance, there were in the late 'thirties 27 professors of science but 79 in the arts; at Cambridge the proportion was 23 to 46; in all the universities of Great Britain the proportion was 262 to 555. In 1935 the number of full-time advanced students in all the sciences in all the universities of Great Britain was only 1107 men and 111 women.

On the other hand a gentleman might with impunity become an amateur in any field and thus England has produced many of the world's greatest amateur scientists. Always, however, there has been a great gap between them and the much larger number of engineers and technical assistants, while both of them stood apart from the normal ken of government and of industrial and commercial leaders. The English social structure gave no spiritual rewards to scientific achievements except the mutual esteem of the scientific men themselves. The motivation of English science has thus been the creative instinct of the isolated amateur gentleman.

In France the cultural tradition was republican and philosophical. The achievements of pure intellect at any social level were fostered. The universities rated philosophy, mathematics, and science as clear and beautiful structures of rationalism, so that membership in the Academy of Sciences was a national distinction. Thus a French scientist earned prestige and honor which could be achieved through the democratic universities without any handicap of social origin. Yet here again was an élite group set apart from the national life among the poets and artists. If the government encouraged research and the growth of science it was primarily for the sake of culture and not primarily for the sake of national, industrial, or commercial advantage.

In Germany, however, the industrialized feudalism, the yearning for power, and the conscious need of the masses for expression and progress, together with a belated and somewhat forced upsurge of the industrial revolution, made the study of science an all but universal part of education and, second only to the army, provided countless careers of steady advance and distinction. To adopt a military metaphor, the scientific forces of France and England were composed almost entirely of officers while German society has for two generations encouraged the development of a complete, highly organized and fully equipped army of science with an adequate complement of trained men in all ranks. Even prior to 1914 they performed their function throughout the educational, industrial, and political systems. It is significant that more than 40 per cent of the Nobel Prizes awarded in chemistry have gone to Germans — 41 per cent in the years 1901–1919 and an actual increase to 43.5 per cent in the years 1920–1939. But this is a measure of originality and creative power; even more important are social esteem and economic power. The prestige of a *Herr Doktor* or of a *Herr Geheimrat* had no equivalent in any other nation. It was an accepted commonplace to address the head of a great industrial corporation by his proper title of *Doktor* a generation ago, when elsewhere professors, especially professors of science, were lampooned as absent-minded, impractical creatures who spoke only in a ridiculous technical jargon.

As for the other nations of Europe, in them the position of men of science was honored, but in a remote international sense, much like the reverence paid to Shakespeare, Leonardo da Vinci and Socrates. Of the Nobel Prizes awarded in physics and chemistry in the years 1901–1939 nearly one-fourth were awarded to Swedes, Danes, Dutch, Austrians, and Italians, a relatively large number, but the recipients were isolated individuals not supported by large fertile research institutions. The scientific community in each of the nations, including Russia, was too small to create standards of its own. Thus most of Europe joined together to provide a large body of distinguished and original men who were true internationalists and did little to serve the special interests of their nations either in government or in industry.

The Treaty of Versailles and the League of Nations greatly strengthened the international point of view. International congresses were organized in most of the sciences so that leading men of science throughout the world not only read and studied the work done in other countries but became personally acquainted with their fellow-scientists across the barriers of language and thus enhanced the fruitfulness of research everywhere. In all fields, but particularly in the great new science of atomic physics and of nuclear chemistry, the cross-fertilization and cooperation, irrespective of national boundaries or interests, thrived as never before. The new international fellowship among scientists even included close relations with many individual Germans, although German scientific societies were not generally admitted into the new international congresses and scientific unions. Gradually but surely the rancors of the war were forgotten, and its lessons too, so that by 1933 most scientific men were probably almost unconscious of national feelings.

An exception must be made in the case of the Soviets since the devotion of their scientists to the superior cause of the state itself seemed incompatible with the disinterested search for truth and was therefore suspect. Nevertheless great credit was awarded to the Soviets for the handsome support given to pure science and for the unquestionably competent creative work done by the new generation of previously unknown men.

All this relates to the world of pure science which is small though immeasurably important in the progress of humanity. Behind this growing internationalism of science dark forces of national competition and struggle were at work, as is shown in the other chapters of this book. Yet outside of the U.S.S.R. and of the National Socialist Party in Germany probably no one suspected the phenomenal growth of nationalism that was to come. Competition was keen but it was competition for profits and for foreign markets. England, France, and Germany strove to bear in mind the services of science during the war and made efforts to encourage research in industry and to support a program of research by and for the government.

In England, a Department of Scientific and Industrial Research was organized to improve the competitive position of British industry and to operate such governmental institutions as the National Physical Laboratory and the governmental investigations of problems relating to fuel, food, building, forest products, and stream polution. In the year 1937–1938 this department spent about 3 million dollars and received about one million dollars in fees. Much of the net expenditure was contributed to research associations formed by firms in a score of industries. The original intent was that once the government established such research by subsidy, the fact that research is profitable in industry would be proven. But this conviction never materialized. In addition to the Department of Scientific and Industrial Research, the British government also established an Agricultural Research Council and a Medical Research Council. The three agencies spent about 4 million dollars a year on scientific research. Other departments of the government spent another 4 millions and a like amount was spent on scientific research concerned directly with military problems. J. G. Crowther estimates that the total expenditure by British corporations and industry on research has been about 8 million dollars a year with possibly another 4 million in the universities, so that the entire expenditure in Great Britain was less than 25 million dollars a year.

In France, the confidence in the political and financial power of the state was so great that the impetus given to science by the war was soon spent. Even in industry reliance was placed on the purchase of patents developed in other countries rather than on research. It was not until 1933 that a Council of Scientific Research was established and in 1935 Madame

Irene Curie-Joliot was appointed Under-Secretary of State for Scientific Research. This was an unprecedented gesture toward the recognition of science, yet it was empty, since this distinguished Nobel-prize-winning daughter of Nobel-prize-winning parents was expected to, and did, continue her esoteric work in atomic physics as her major occupation. The expenditures of the French Department of Scientific Research as late as 1938 were only a million dollars a year.

The inadequacy of the programs in England and in France is best shown by the comparison with the similar expenditures in the United States. American industrial research laboratories alone, exclusive of government and university laboratories, spent at least 200 million dollars a year. Even so, progress has been much too slow in view of the impending international crisis, yet the expenditure per person in the United States was about twelve times the expenditure per person in the British Empire and incomparably greater than in France.

These figures express the relative importance attached in Great Britain, France, and the United States to the value of creative work in industrial and commercial competition. Obviously in Britain and in France there was confidence that national prosperity and economic power rested on other factors than the creation of new industries, the increase of production, and the decrease in costs. These other factors in the international rivalry did not however include recourse to a major war. It is common knowledge that in military, naval, and aeronautic science, both Britain and France forged slowly and complacently ahead without that desperate pressure for advantage which the year 1939 made necessary. But when the military situation did suddenly call for supreme effort neither the equipment nor the trained men were available. Both nations had failed to incorporate the power of science into their resources and hence, as in 1914, were unable to call upon that resource. And the illusory internationalism of the scientific world itself had, quite innocently, been content.

The post-war record of science in the smaller nations shows a motley pattern. In Italy and in Poland the intensification of national sentiment hampered research by giving higher value to political and military achievement and by preoccupation with local pride, the native language and history. But it did not compensate by a program of modernization and by calling upon science to produce and to serve the national cause. Science was in general ignored, though new industries were developed and technical training thus became more of an asset. The great Snia Viscosa synthetic textile works at Milan are an outstanding example of a new industry based almost wholly on imported science.

In the Balkans, nationalist pride seized on every asset as a talking point and many a gesture was made toward recognizing men of science as benefactors. Lack of wealth made any real support impossible. Efforts were, however, made to capitalize natural resources, such as the Rumanian petroleum, with foreign capital and foreign technologists. International scientific congresses were entertained at great expense both to publicize these resources and to fertilize local potentialities by direct contact with leaders in science, but the results were small. In Czechoslovakia, however, a very rapid industrialization in terms of modern low-cost quantity production took place.

In the northern lands — Scandinavia, Denmark, the Netherlands — liberal and international ideals thrived, untouched by politics, nationalism, or militarism. The universities at Uppsala, Copenhagen, Leyden, and Utrecht developed scientific departments of real distinction. In Denmark occurred the unique bequest of an entire large firm to the support of scientific research and art — the Carlsberg Breweries, so bequeathed by its founders, J. C. and Karl Jacobsen. In the Netherlands, the Philips Lamp Factory at Eindhoven supported one of the finest industrial research laboratories in the world, with notable results in both applied and pure science. In the Netherlands, too, the entire educational system was enriched by absorbing in its teaching staff large numbers of university graduates and holders of the Ph.D. degree in science. In these countries, and to a lesser extent in Norway and in Switzerland, science became an accepted and respectable aspect of human culture, yet quite without ulterior purpose or nationalist bias.

The story is obviously very different for the Soviets and for Germany. The primitive development of applied science in Russia in 1918 and the high goals set for social achievement by the Soviets required emphasis in the past twenty years on the growth of an elementary technology and on an immediate utilization of machinery and practices that were long established elsewhere in solving the broad problems of the new society. The task was more one of educating a great body of engineers and technical experts to operate a modern mechanized society than it was to create new ideas or invent new processes. Merely to catch up with the American scale in the use of power and of raw materials would have required most of the tremendous energy and emphasis that was given to technology.

The highest scientific body in the U.S.S.R. is the Academy of Science. It is directly responsible to the elected Supreme Council. It operates numerous laboratories directly but its chief function is the coordination of the scientific activities of all the Commissariats, with a special view toward the programs of the State Planning Commission. The Commissariats of Education, of Health, of Agriculture, of Light Industry, and of Heavy Industry all have ambitious programs in science. The last-named not only operates innumerable factories, each with control laboratories, but its Technical Education Sector controls the technical colleges and their research laboratories, while the Industrial Sector operates a number of excellent industrial research institutes such as the Nitrogen Institute of Moscow. In addition a separate Scientific Sector of the same Commissariat operates several research laboratories in fundamental or pure science, such as the Physico-Technical Institutes at Leningrad, Kharkov, Dnieprope-trovsk and Sverdlovsk and the Karpov Institute of Chemistry at Moscow.

But, in theory at least, all this expenditure, planning, and study for the benefit of the production program is not so important as the broad effort to make science permeate the general life, to inculcate a scientific outlook in the oncoming generation and thus to abolish the gulf that elsewhere separates the scientific community from the people. The Stakhanov movement, a surge of rationalization and efficiency which comes from the masses, not from above, is one very significant result of the gradual conviction of the masses that it pays to think. The place of science in the Communist ideology is important, indeed fundamental. Handsome appropriations and new government laboratories express this intent. But the time has not been sufficient to determine whether a nation trained in this ideology can create new values and maintain leadership in a competitive world. While much credit must be given to the realistic education of Soviet youth, there has not been opportunity to demonstrate what social power science can exert under the Communist theory.

In Germany the traditional leadership in science had long been considered a prime national asset. In the sorry years after 1918 it was prized as never before. In spite of poverty and dissension the great universities and research institutions were given every possible support in money and in morale. Science blossomed. The theory of relativity and the quantum theory, together comprising the greatest advance in science since the days of Isaac Newton, both came from German universities during those years. Synthetic vitamins, motor fuel and lubricants from coal, carbohydrates from wood, plastics without number, synthetic textiles, all poured from the industrial laboratories. Thousands of doctors of philosophy found places at low pay in industry or lived on almost nothing in teaching careers. Maximum production by optimum intelligence was the cultural as well as the industrial ideal. But salvation by this means was too slow and the Nazi ideology took over.

This political religion, this fanatic worship of the corporate state, immediately set every resource to work for competitive national advantage — not merely by harnessing all to the production of wealth, as in the U.S.S.R., but also, or even especially, toward the specific goal of military power. The production of synthetic motor fuels was improved and greatly enlarged. Synthetic rubber, originally American, was made practical and large production from coal was assured. Above all, every effort was made toward radical improvements in military aviation. Never have latent resources been so swiftly and so completely developed and coordinated toward a common national goal. The one prized resource, untouched by defeat or reparations — competent scientific research together with almost universal scientific education — was commandeered *in toto* by the National Socialist Party for use as the overpowering weapon of a nation that was supposedly unarmed. Never has the inherent power of science been so dramatically revealed — nor so cruelly perverted. It marks a new era in history, for the same power can, of course, be wielded for humanitarian purposes, for construction as well as for destruction, for the production of ample food, clothing, shelter, comfort, and leisure. It is safe to say that after this revelation of the power of science no nation, no society, can survive in the future without primary and maximum use of scientific intelligence for peace and plenty just as effectively as for war.

The Nazi revolution, like that in Russia, eliminates all motives for scientific research except service to society. As has been pointed out in the chapter on Germany, science, like all other forms of action and thought, is there wholly subservient to the state. As a social ideal this is valid. But in practice it inevitably means subservience to a small group of dominant governmental officials. When, as in Germany now, the state is able to command the services of all technical and scientific men it will no doubt be able to achieve the maximum immediate results in the application of science. It takes little intelligence to appreciate the tremendous value of such application, whether it be in destruction or construction, and it may be assumed that any government which once bases its effectiveness on the maximum use of science will find it wise to continue appropriations for laboratories and for technical training. However, when immediate advantage is thus sought, emphasis is invariably on technology rather than on research, on exploiting present knowledge rather than on the creation of new knowledge. It requires intelligence of a high order, vision, and courage, to create wholly new values. Such intelligence and vision are conspicuously lacking in all government circles. Thus a regime of science which is under the direct command of politicians is likely to be shortsighted and sterile after a preliminary period of mere exploitation.

This lesson may be drawn from the record of research in industry. Among successful corporations in any country the pressure for immediate profits and for competitive advantage is a strong support for science and technology. But any research program that must be justified year by year, or even day by day, through increased profits or by valuable patents, and is therefore under the immediate direction of businessmen who have those goals ever in mind, is almost invariably profitable only in the immediate and temporary sense. It exploits the advances in pure science made elsewhere by men of long vision to whom financial profit is meaningless. So long as the endowed research institutions continue, in which the direction of research is under the control of unhampered scientists themselves, so

long does the flow of new knowledge continue to be successively and repeatedly exploited in the laboratories of applied science. The creative
instinct is essentially artistic and the highest type of mind is essentially
immune to material rewards. Profit is seldom a motive for creation.
Hence businessmen can seldom direct creative research or even encourage it.

It should be added, of course, that there are numerous strong corporations whose function is based upon science and who are able to project
their own existence many decades into the future, which are notably far-
sighted in the support of pure research. Among them are the Philips
Lamp Factory at Eindhoven, Holland, the Siemens-Halske works and the
I. G. Farbenindustrie in Germany. It is only when success is unquestioned
that the scientific staff can thus be permitted to dwell on the remote future
and to direct its own course without the control of executives whose burden of responsibility is the day-to-day balance sheet.

For such reasons no industrial research institution and no laboratory
under a corporate state could have produced our present knowledge of
science. The greed for gold rendered the medieval alchemists futile. It
was Priestley, a clergyman, who discovered oxygen and Lavoisier, an aristocratic amateur, who became the " father of chemistry " by explaining
combustion. Since then a century and a half of uncontrolled research in
the universities of the world has uncovered radioactivity, relativity and
atom-smashing, X rays and electrons, synthetic materials and thermody-
namics, genes and chromosomes, bacteria, vitamins, viruses, and hormones.
None of these, it is safe to say, would be known today if science had in the
past century been under the strict control of " practical " politicians.

For the same reasons the limitation of science in Germany to the high
ideal of social service has actually been a disaster of the first order. When
the broad-minded, far-seeing national government became a corporate
state passionately devoted to immediate practical advantage, it assumed the
weaknesses of an industrial corporation and became narrow-minded and
shortsighted. The loss of such men as Haber and Einstein would not be
irreparable if the next generation were allowed free thought. But so long
as that freedom is denied and research is regimented for immediate objectives there is no hope for the emergence of genius and no hope for any
but a minor and opportunist role for German science. No future for the
nation can be built on mere imitation and exploitation and no leadership is
possible under strict orders from political headquarters.

This is not to say that the ideal of service to society is itself inadequate.
It may be that the totalitarian order will become so successfully established
that it need not confine its efforts to desperate emergencies and that it can
in time undertake a fifty-year plan of development instead of a five-year
plan. It may be that in that case freedom can be restored to creative minds.

Such a confidence in the new order would reverse our prognosis, but it is certain to be possible only if the social ideal embraces not a party, a nation, or a race, but all of humanity.

In sum, this means a return to the international point of view and a recognition that research in pure science cannot be partisan or competitive. It means that the increasing nationalism of the past decade must be transcended. It also means that the international and humanitarian nature of science, as formerly exemplified in nearly all the smaller nations of Europe, and as expressed in the Nobel Prizes, was the right, indeed the only, atmosphere in which science can thrive and from which humanity can benefit. The present perversion of science to destructive uses and the sterilization of science for immediate partisan advantage are both high crimes against the human spirit. Creative power is the most precious of all human resources, and the tragedy of the past two decades in Europe is that they have ignored that power and hence man's power to make the world a good place to live in and to make life worth living.

SELECTED BIBLIOGRAPHY

Bernal, J. D., *The Social Function of Science*, New York: Macmillan, 1939. A full study of the present place of science in society, education, war, manufacturing, and international relations and a bold outline of what science could do in the service of man under more far-sighted organization, financing, and training, including copious factual and statistical appendices.

Crowther, J. G., *The Social Relations of Science*, New York: Macmillan, 1941. A history of the development of science in relation to social conditions since ancient times with emphasis on the motivation and consequences of scientific discovery at present, especially in England.

Leonard, J. N., *Tools of Tomorrow*, New York: Viking Press, 1935. A description of recent developments in industrial research and technology, full of optimism on their value in future utilization.

Levy, Hyman, *Modern Science*, New York: Knopf, 1939. A philosophical discussion of the fundamental concepts and methods of science today with a constant eye to social significance.

Soddy, Frederick, and others, *The Frustration of Science*, New York: Norton, 1935. A series of brief essays on the failure of society to take advantage of the inherent possibilities of research in agriculture, aviation, medicine, industry, and other fields, all from the point of view of the situation in Great Britain.

CHAPTER XXIX

Philosophy, Religion, and Literature

Popular and Abstract Philosophies

European Maladjustment. In many European faces we see today the tormented features of an old and harrassed civilization. The gargoyles of Gothic architecture seem serene compared with the distorted physiognomies of many Europeans.

The basic cause of harrassment and sorrow is the evil that has been let loose upon Europe. Neither Rousseau's view that happiness consists of the successful functioning of the emotions nor Stendhal's belief that one can attain happiness by the application of reason to the problems of conduct is any longer practical for great numbers of men. The central problem of thinking Europeans is how to act intelligently in an exhausted and maltreated world; how to be human in an inhuman age. Maladjustment is therefore the keynote of the era. The philosophy, religion, and literature of the last two decades amply reflect this maladjustment.

Dominant Philosophical Schools. The dominant philosophical schools of contemporary Europe are Positivism, Determinism and Indeterminism, Experimental Humanism and Integrated Humanism, Dialectical Materialism, Individualism, and Collectivism. We shall very briefly survey each of these.

Positivism is concerned with knowledge based solely on experience and rejects everything that is speculative or metaphysical. Its champions maintain that in the interpretation of life the accent should be placed on science. Positivism is a monistic philosophy: that is to say, it recognizes the unity of spirit and matter. Contemporary positivism has rendered some service to sociology; it also furnishes ideas to certain literary schools, mainly to the realists and naturalists.

Determinism is a variety of Positivism. Whereas the Positivists believe in progress, the Determinists hold that life is meaningless. Indeterminism is a metaphysical branch of Positivism; it, too, interprets life in terms of scientific data, but assumes that a force, not human, rules the world. The Indeterminists' chief contribution to philosophy is the place they have made, in a scientific world, for free will.

Experimental Humanism is a revival of Greco-Roman and Renaissance ideas, modified, however, by the subtle consciousness of modern man. It accents man's struggle with man, and underlines the indifference of destiny.

This chapter by Joseph Remenyi, Assistant Professor of Comparative Literature, Western Reserve University.

It differs from Integrated Humanism in that the latter posits a belief in God and the need of religious experience as a criterion of conduct.

Dialectical Materialism is derived from Hegel's philosophy of history. It assumes that for every concept (or thesis), there is an opposite concept (antithesis), and that both are finally united in a new concept (synthesis). Marxism is based on this syllogism.

Individualism is a form of Humanism. It asserts the supremacy of the individual over the mass, and the rights of the ego over that of society. Collectivism repudiates Individualism. It upholds the supremacy of the mass over the individual, of society over the ego. Its greatest influence has been in political theory, where it has created blueprints for the collectivist, utopian society of the future.

Exponents of Contemporary Philosophies. Let us examine for a moment the fate of these philosophies in the contemporary world as expressed by their leading proponents.

Positivism underwent considerable change in post-war Europe. Auguste Comte, father of Positivism, dogmatically accepted the validity of knowledge and experience. Bertrand Russell, who might be called a modern Positivist, grounded his philosophy on scientific data, but his conclusions are far from dogmatic. Rather he reflects the *relativistic* modern attitude toward experience and knowledge.

The Determinism of the nineteenth century has been rejected by many modern thinkers, most notably, perhaps, by Henri Bergson, author of *Creative Evolution.* By stressing intuition and creative evolution as the substance of life, Bergson made the transition from nineteenth-century Determinism to the Indeterminism of the twentieth century. This indeterministic philosophy has been greatly influenced by the new conception of the physical universe unfolded by physicists like Albert Einstein, Sir Arthur Eddington, Sir James Jeans, and Max Planck. Their cosmology has helped to restore free will to the realm of philosophy.

Experimental Humanism, which is more or less in the blood stream of European philosophy, has found a prominent protagonist in Johan Huizinga, the Dutch historian. Huizinga has refused to accept both the philosophy of intuition of Bergson and the pessimism of Oswald Spengler. As a genuine humanist, a sort of twentieth-century Erasmus, he believes in the supremacy of reason and the progress of civilization.

The Integrated Humanism of the great Catholic philosopher Jacques Maritain represents an attempt to transcend the limited horizon of Positivism. Thus, according to Maritain, man's fate is determined not only by his relations with his fellow men, but his relations with God.

Popular Reception of the Philosophies. It would be preposterous to assume that in modern Europe ordinary people ascended to such heights of intelligence that they could understand the above philosophies. Yet abstract philosophy makes greater headway in our generation than in former periods not only because there are more educated people, but because they are interpreted by publicists in terms which the uninitiated can understand. The spread of books, magazines, and newspapers has made this possible.

Thus the philosophies of Dialectical Materialism, as well as Individualism and Collectivism, have been accorded a warm welcome by large numbers of people; sometimes as blind emotional responses, sometimes as intelligent and percipient reactions. The main reason for the abounding interest in abstract philosophies was their social character. Dialectical Materialism forms the philosophical basis of Socialism, Communism, and other political philosophies seeking social and economic justice. Similarly, Individualism is the philosophical root of *laissez-faire* capitalism. Collectivism is the official philosophy of Communist Russia, and may be discerned in the intellectual atmosphere of Fascist Italy and Nazi Germany.

Numerous minor political movements drew their ideologies from the various philosophical schools, but since they played only an insignificant role in the cultural history of post-war Europe, we cannot stop to discuss them here.

A word might be said about the influence of psychoanalysis, discussed in a previous chapter. Without ignoring the Spenglerian dogma that Western civilization is at the end of its tether, or the Marxist prophecy of social reconstruction, the psychoanalysts seem to believe that not only the social, political, and economic systems of Europe need overhauling, but the European individual, so to speak, requires nervous reorientation. Europe, they say, is suffering from general nervous disturbances; indeed its nervous system is on the verge of collapse, and psychoanalytical treatment is prescribed. The psychoanalysts have had profound influence not only on the creative minds of Europe but on the average man as well. Besides psychoanalysis, other psychological schools enjoyed popularity, and thus affected the cultural character of Europe. Wilheim Dilthey's conception of the significance of the various components of a work of art led to a new and complicated interpretation of the creative spirit.

Religion in Post-War Europe

The Religious Revival. Post-war Europe enjoyed a religious revival. The search for supernatural solace became more imperative after the disillusionment of war. The philosophical Indeterminists gave intellectual support to those who reached out for God. There was a notable rebirth of religion in western Europe, as well as in northern, eastern, and southeastern countries. According to the Russian mystic, Nicholas Berdayev, even in atheistic Soviet Russia the religion of absolute immaterialism asserted itself from time to time. The effectiveness of religion as a balancing agent of the human mind and society impressed many post-war intellectuals. Catholic and Protestant thinkers, artists, and poets found comfort and support in the mystic veneration of Christ. By means of spiritual faith many of them found purgation for their emotions and a happy outlook on life. It suffices in this respect to refer to Karl Barth, the pioneer of the dialectical-theological movement in the German Protestant Church. Here and there new sects were organized.

Among writers who drew sustenance from religion we may mention Lucian Blaga, the Rumanian playwright, T. S. Eliot, Paul Claudel, Giovanni Papini, Franz Werfel and Sigrid Undset. The pacifists should be included in this group of religionists because their dream of political, social, and economic harmony derived its strength from a religious and ethical temperament. The religious revival of the post-war period was probably an escape from madness, but it was also an anchor of contentment.

Progress of Atheism. Amidst the religious revival atheism flourished, a continuation and, in certain social stratas, an expansion of nineteenth-century agnosticism. Contemporary atheism echoes Georges Sorel's credo of violence and Schopenhauer's pessimism and Nietzsche's " superman " complex. Many prosperous philistines and intellectual élite resented the tenets and allegories of religion. Many proletarians and agrarian workers as well as *petit bourgeois*, partly influenced by Marxism, saw in the representatives of organized religion agents of capital exploitation. Religion was regarded by many of the better educated as meaningless romance; the less educated saw in religion and its exponents an attempt to distort their social and economic lives. The renunciation of religion gave them some kind of inner peace.

Literature at the Crossroads of European History

Political, social, and economic upheavals as well as the sensational discoveries in theoretical and applied science naturally affected post-war writers and poets. Amidst the chaos, no literary school became dominant; art for art's sake, however, or pure literature, was of less importance than in previous generations.

Breakdown of Tradition. The breakdown of traditional values was shown in the short-lived prominence of most literary schools. Much of post-war European literature may be regarded as bizarre offshoots of nineteenth-century romanticism. Expressionism, Futurism, Unanism, Activism, Illusionism, and Surrealism often disagreed with one another. With few exceptions, the literary movements preached a doomsday philosophy; indeed most post-war literature had a sardonic humor born of profound pessimism, as in the plays of Luigi Pirandello and the novels of L. F.

Celine.   There was also an exaggerated worship of craftsmanship, particularly in the 'twenties.   This was manifested, for instance, in the settings and designs for the stage, in the ingenious, sophisticated or fantastic search for novel theatrical effects.   Indeed, every creative art related to literature was affected by what has been called the " transvaluation of social values," and by the lust for unique and exotic pleasures to stimulate a satiated palate.

Humanist and Humanitarian Writers.   Yet amidst the feverish experimentation the traditions of European literature were maintained by many illustrious practitioners.   There were writers and poets who abjured formlessness and who enriched the heritage of literature by traditional techniques, as in the humanistic works of Georges Duhamel, Roger Martin DuGard, Jules Romains, and Paul Valéry in France, Richard Aldington and E. M. Forster in England, Hans Carossa and Thomas Mann in Germany, Rainer Maria Rilke in Austria, Mihaly Babits in Hungary, and Karel Čapek in Czechoslovakia.   These men more or less synthesized the absurd contradictions of contemporary European culture.   For example, the English characters in Forster's *Passage to India* belong to a civilization that is found in every section of the globe.   The novelists who imaginatively recreated the First World War and the Spanish Civil War made contributions not only to literature but to social thought.   Erich Maria Remarque, for example, cannot be compared with Tolstoi, but his anti-war novel *All Quiet on the Western Front* is a monument of pacifist, humanitarian literature.   Among humanitarian writers belong Marxist novelists like André Malraux.

Besides the humanists and humanitarians, we must mention the writers who drew their inspiration from the soil and from the simple peasants. This trend is observed in the works of Frederico Garcia Lorca in Spain, Jean Giono in France, Aron Tamasi the Transylvanian Hungarian, Sillanpaa the Finn, Ramus the Swiss, Wladyslaw Reymont the Polish novelist, and others.   The regionalists found their inspiration in nature, in local customs and folkways, and in simple peasant life.   In strange contrast with regionalism was the very popular literature of escape, the historical novels, poems, plays, and bibliographies in which those who found contemporary life hectic and unbearable sought surcease from anguish.   The exotic and scientific novels and plays, like Aldous Huxley's *Brave New World* and H. G. Wells' *Fantastic Stories*, served pretty much the same purpose.

The stream of consciousness novels were unique attempts at depicting the complicated motives of individual behavior and the decadence of contemporary society, as in James Joyce's *Ulysses*, Proust's *Remembrance of Things Past* and the novels of André Gide and Virginia Woolf.   D. H. Lawrence brought to light in his stories undiscovered aspects of the pure and vital sensuous world.   The bitterness, loneliness, and dullness of post-war European life were delineated with the same supersensitive indignation by the novelists of northern, central, eastern and southeastern Europe. Sorrow, joy, and courage are not less interesting in Finnish, Hungarian, Estonian, Lithuanian, Polish, Latvian, Czech, Slovak, Yugoslav, Rumanian, Greek, or Bulgarian than in, let us say, Irish, English, or French literature. The poetry of William Butler Yeats has its counterpart in countries without the background of Celtic folklore. Distinguished spirits face life and death everywhere with fortitude and nobility. It is noteworthy, incidentally, that in the past two decades of rampant nationalism the most effective internationalists were those who translated into their native language the popular literary works of " enemy " nations.

Effect of Totalitarianism on Literature. In the totalitarian states, philosophers, writers, poets, or men and women of independent ideas had to accept the ruling ideology or observe silence. The most trivial notion of liberty was interpreted as a violation of totalitarian standards. No wonder that this pressure intimidated even those who were preoccupied with the universal values of mankind. Some went into exile, where they launched attacks on totalitarianism. Some could not bear the strain and ceased to write. Others, however, accepted the status quo and wrote in conformity with Fascist, Nazi, or Communist demands. Such conformist literature naturally partook of the nature of propaganda.

Granted that the writers who remained in the totalitarian states could not reject the dominant ideology without endangering their lives, the fact remains that all over Europe the conflict between integrity and unscrupulous adaptability to conditions became one of the most dominant cultural trends.

Summary

Spengler's prophecy of the collapse of western culture and the Communist emphasis on the class struggle found innumerable echoes in post-war religion, philosophy, and literature. The *Communist Manifesto* appeared in 1848; the final edition of Spengler's huge work in 1922. Despite the three-quarters of a century which separated them, their ideas are intrinsically interwoven in the activities and reflections of post-war Europe. Cultural trends showed that an age was dying but that fresh forces were rising to combat the old, and in this one could find hope for the future.

The artists and thinkers were acutely aware of the miseries of their age. But not many undertook to reconcile conflicting forces and help to create an international, peaceful society. Jingoistic nationalism speeded decay. Social, political, and economic evils fostered revolutionary activities and undermined the traditional concept of cultural unity. Not only in the totalitarian countries, but in the more or less liberal nations, nationalistic intolerance grew apace.

All strata of society were in flux and conflict. Peasants and proletarians tried to wrest more economic and social privileges from the aristocrats, gentry, and middle class. The younger generation relentlessly opposed the incompetence and complacency of the older generation. In these conflicts much energy was wasted and valuable time lost. The " pure in heart " and the " men of good will " were sadly reduced in numbers, and the evil and brutal spirits multiplied prodigiously.

To reconcile cultural conflicts must be the ultimate aim of European civilization. Only when this task is successfully accomplished will the " good society " arrive. Without this, Europe will remain a slaughter-house. As long as Machiavellian techniques in politics and economic life direct the destiny of Europe, the cultural efforts to unify peoples and nations will be paralyzed.

SELECTED BIBLIOGRAPHY

Benda, Julien, *The Treason of the Intellectuals*, New York: Morrow, 1928.
——, *Belphegor*, New York: Payson and Clarke, 1929.
Berdyaev, Nicholas, *The End of Our Times*, New York: Sheed and Ward, 1933.
——, *The Bourgeois Mind*, New York: Sheed and Ward, 1934.
Bertaux, Felix, *A Panorama of German Literature*, New York: McGraw-Hill, 1935.
Bettex, A. W., *The German Novel of Today*, Cambridge: Bowes and Bowes, 1941.
Borgese, C. A., *Goliath*, New York: Viking, 1937.
Croce, Benedette, *An Autobiography*, Oxford: Clarendon, 1927.
Dickinson, Thomas H., *The Theatre in a Changing Europe*, New York: Holt, 1937.
Duhamel, Georges, *In Defence of Letters*, New York: Greystone, 1939.
Eastman, Max, *Artists in Uniform*, New York: Knopf, 1934.
Eliot, T. S., *After Strange Gods*, New York: Harcourt, Brace, 1939.
——, *The Idea of a Christian Society*, New York: Harcourt, Brace, 1940.
Fernandez, Ramon, *Messages*, New York: Harcourt, Brace, 1927.
Freud, Sigmund, *Civilization and Its Discontents*, London: Jonathan Cape, 1930.
Hansen, Agnes Camilla, *Twentieth Century Forces in European Fiction*, Chicago: American Library Association, 1934.
Huizinga, Johan, *In the Shadow of Tomorrow*, New York: Norton, 1936.
Huxley, Aldous, *The Letters of D. H. Lawrence*, New York: Viking, 1932.
Jeans, Sir James, *The Mysterious Universe*, New York: Macmillan, 1935.
Keyerling, Count Herman, *The World in the Making*, New York: Harcourt, Brace, 1927.
Maritain, Jacques, *Freedom in the Modern World*, New York: Scribner, 1936.
——, *True Humanism*, New York: Scribner, 1938.
Marx and Engels, *The Communist Manifesto*, New York: International Publishers, 1930.
Massis, Henri, *Defence of the West*, New York: Harcourt, Brace, 1928.
Ortega y Casset, José, *The Revolt of the Masses*, New York: Norton, 1932.
——, *The Modern Theme*, New York: Norton, 1933.
Problems of Soviet Literature, Reports and Speeches at the First Soviet Writers Congress, New York: International Publishers, 1935.
Reavey, George and Slonim, Marc, *Soviet Literature*, New York: Covici-Friede, 1934.
Richards, I. A., *Science and Poetry*, New York: Norton, 1926.
Rose, William and Isaacs, J., *Contemporary Movements in European Literature*, New York: Dial Press, 1929.
Siegfried, André, *Europe's Crisis*, London: Jonathan Cape, 1933.
Spender, Stephen, *The Destructive Element*, London: Jonathan Cape, 1935.
Spengler, Oswald, *The Decline of the West*, New York: Knopf, 1926.
——, *The Hour of Decision*, New York: Knopf, 1934.
Tradition and Experiment, Address delivered at the London Literary Institute, New York: Oxford Univ. Press, 1929.
Wilder, Amos N., *The Spiritual Aspects of the New Poetry*, New York: Harper, 1940.
Wilson, Edmund, *Axel's Castle*, New York: Scribner, 1931.
Woolf, Leonard, *Quack! Quack!*, New York: Harcourt, Brace, 1935.

Illustrious examples of post-war literature which reveal the cultural trends of the age.

Aldington, Richard, *Collected Poems*, New York: Covici-Friede, 1928.
——, *Death of a Hero*, New York: Covici-Friede, 1929.
Auden, W. H., *Poems*, New York: Random House, 1934.
——, *Ascent of F6*, New York: Random House, 1937.
Čapek, Karel, *R.U.R.*, New York: Doubleday, Page, 1923.
Carossa, Hans, *Rumanian Diary*, New York: Knopf, 1930.
Celine, L. F., *Journey to the End of the Night*, Boston: Little, Brown, 1934.
——, *Death on the Installment Plan*, Boston: Little, Brown, 1938.

Claudel, Paul, *Three Poems of the War*, New Haven: Yale Univ. Press, 1919.
DuGard, Roger Martin, *The Thibaults*, New York: Viking, 1939.
Duhamel, George, *Pasquier Chronicles*, New York: Holt, 1938.
Eliot, T. S., *Murder in the Cathedral*, New York: Harcourt, Brace, 1935.
——, *Collected Poems*, New York: Harcourt, Brace, 1936.
Forster, E. M., *Passage to India*, New York: Putnam, 1924.
Garcia Lorca, Federico, *Poems*, New York: Oxford Univ. Press, 1939.
Gide, André, *The Counterfeiters*, New York: Knopf, 1927.
——, *The Immoralist*, New York: Knopf, 1930.
Giono, Jean, *Song of the World*, New York: Viking, 1937.
——, *Harvest*, New York: Viking, 1939.
Gorki, Maxim, *Lower Depths*, New York: Brentano, 1923.
——, *Mother*, New York: Appleton, 1923.
Hasek, Jaroslav, *Good Soldier Schweik*, Garden City, N. Y.: Doubleday, Doran, 1930.
Huxley, Aldous, *Point Counter Point*, New York: Literary Guild, 1928.
——, *Brief Candles*, Garden City, N. Y.: Doubleday, Doran, 1930.
——, *Brave New World*, Garden City, N. Y.: Doubleday, Doran, 1932.
Joyce, James, *Ulysses*, New York: Random House, 1934.
——, *Collected Poems*, New York: Viking, 1937.
——, *Finnegan's Wake*, New York: Viking, 1939.
Kafka, Franz, *The Castle*, New York: Knopf, 1930.
Lawrence, D. H., *The Lost Girl*, London: Secker, 1920.
——, *Women in Love*, New York: Knopf, 1920.
——, *Collected Poems*, London: Cape and Smith, 1929.
Malraux, André, *Man's Fate*, New York: Smith and Haas, 1934.
——, *Man's Hope*, New York: Random House, 1938.
Mann, Thomas, *Magic Mountain*, New York: Knopf, 1929.
——, *Stories of Three Decades*, New York: Knopf, 1936.
Papini, Giovanni, *Life of Christ*, New York: Harcourt, Brace, 1923.
——, *Life and Myself*, New York: Brentano, 1930.
Pirandello, Luigi, *Each in His Own Way*, New York: Dutton, 1923.
——, *The Late Mattia Pascal*, New York: Dutton, 1923.
Proust, Marcel, *Remembrance of Things Past*, New York: Random House, 4 vols.
Remarque, Erich Maria, *All Quiet on the Western Front*, Boston: Little, Brown, 1929.
——, *The Road Back*, Boston: Little, Brown, 1931.
Reymont, Wladyslaw, *The Peasants*, New York: Knopf, 1928.
Rilke, Rainer Maria, *Later Poems*, London: Hogarth, 1938.
Romains, Jules, *Men of Good Will*, New York: Knopf, 1933–1941.
Sillanpaa, F. A., *Maid Silja*, New York: Macmillan, 1933.
——, *Meek Heritage*, New York: Knopf, 1938.
Undset, Sigrid, *Gunnar's Daughter*, New York: Knopf, 1938.
Werfel, Franz, *Emberfled Heaven*, New York: Viking, 1940.
Woolf, Virginia, *Mrs. Dalloway*, New York: Harcourt, Brace, 1925.
Yeats, William Butler, *Collected Poems*, New York: Macmillan, 1933.
——, *Collected Plays*, New York: Macmillan, 1934.

CHAPTER XXX

The Arts and Music

Introduction

Art and Culture. Whether or not the artist will have it so, art is invariably the product of a culture. The cultural influence varies to the extent that the artist has striven to embody in his work the values which his society considers important. Even when such social expression is far from the conscious object which he sets for himself, the artist's work is best understood as the product of reaction, indifference, or conformity, in relation to the prevailing culture.

We are able to see, for example, how characteristically modern functional architecture has arisen out of the needs and possibilities of the machine age, and how such inventions as radio and motion pictures have broadened if not deepened cultural activity.

Effects of War. We might expect, then, that the tremendous social disturbances caused by the First World War will be reflected in post-war art. Wars are crises not merely because they cause sorrow and death, but also because out of this chaos there arises a questioning of those features of society which made such destruction necessary. Disillusionment follows despair, and there comes a striving for new methods, a searching for new goals, and a spiritual reconstruction to correspond to the material one. We shall see how this was the case after 1918; but first let us take a glance at the spiritual atmosphere in post-war Europe, so that we may better understand the hurricanes and blizzards and the sunshine and blue sky as well.

Trends in Post-War Art. Out of the disorganization of intellectual life, certain important tendencies appeared. In the first place, the search for new values and methods of expressing them, the influence of modern science, and the example of pre-war modernists led to an increasing experimentalism in the arts. Ever since the middle of the nineteenth century, artists had been searching for new forms and techniques. This movement, encouraged by the post-war intellectual reaction, assumed greater strength in the last two decades. Modern science and the development of new industrial techniques led to an increase in the effect of the machine on the arts — a tendency toward industrialization. With the rise of democracy in Europe and the possibility of making the finer features of civilization available to greater numbers of people, a gradual democ-

This chapter by Roland L. Warren, Assistant Professor of Philosophy, Hofstra College, and Margaret H. Warren, Ph.D. in History of Art, Heidelberg, Germany.

ratization of art was becoming apparent. Art in its various forms was affecting more people than ever before. Finally, the growth of nationalism had an effect not only on the subject matter of art, but in some countries on the life and fortune of the artists themselves. These four tendencies — experimentalism, industrialization, democratization, and nationalism — will make a convenient outline for the study of post-war art.

The Scope of Art. This is not the place to attempt a theoretical analysis of the differentia of art.[1] Suffice it to say that recent thought on the meaning of art has indicated a growing tendency toward an extension of the term to include many factors not formerly emphasized. The folk dance, industrial arts, handicrafts, city planning, photography, the motion picture, radio, even the design of such lowly things as kitchen utensils and sewing machines, are embraced within the meaning of " art." Lewis Mumford and John Dewey have been of great service in bringing into prominence this broader conception which considers art continuous with all phases of life.

Experimentalism

The tendency of the artist to experiment with subject matter and style is an outstanding characteristic of modern art. The war of 1914–1918 certainly did not initiate this wide experimentation, which had been a dominating force in art since the middle of the last century. If anything, the war interrupted its pace, and the resulting chaos increased the search for new values and new means of expressing them. The younger artists felt that all had been said and done only too often in the traditional manner. Painters and sculptors searched for new techniques, and as a result an almost uncountable number of " isms " sprang up in the last fifty years,[2] most of them short-lived, but a few continuing to influence artists today.

The Critics. The critics and art dealers — the " agents " between the artist and the public — were influenced by the new art and in turn influenced the artists. New undiscovered values were found in primitive and Negro arts, in the art of children and psychopaths. Older experimenters were rediscovered; El Greco, for example, hitherto unclassifiable, was hailed as the patron saint of the moderns. The Impressionists who were once denounced were now lauded, more than was their due in some cases, until struggling artists seemed to conclude that to be misunderstood is to be great. Often they seemed deliberately to surprise, even insult, the public.

Branches of Art Widened. In their attempts to discover new meanings, artists revived branches of the arts which had fallen into disuse. Lithography and other graphic arts, stained glass, tapestry, and batik became very popular. Photography had by the time of the First World War, progressed enormously from the posed portrait stage. The scientific improvements in the camera led to wider use and experimentation, and photographers learned to select and emphasize subject matter and to produce pictures of great beauty, heightened by the use of unusual angles and new lighting effects.

New life was instilled into painting and sculpture by freeing the artist from the conventional modes of expression. The Dadaists showed that to produce a work of art it was not necessary to be bound to mere paint and color. They introduced rope, yarn, buttons, bits of newspaper and colored paper and mechanical objects into their paintings. Nor did sculptors limit themselves to the conventional wood, plaster, stone, and metal; they employed wire, springs, screws, and other mechanical devices. Indeed artists experimented widely and recklessly. To work in one medium, or even one art, was no longer satisfying. Picasso, for example, practiced sculpture, stage design, and the graphic arts, as well as painting. The attempt was occasionally made to fuse several branches of the arts, to achieve a successful *mélange*. Belling, for example, tried to convey in sculpture the audible impressions of musical chords. Archipenko's *Peinture changeante* is a mechanized " painting " that goes through a series of successive forms and thus approaches the motion picture. The cinema itself incorporates photography, drama, and music into an artistic whole. Pare Lorenz's films, *The River* and *The Plough That Broke the Plains*, are outstanding examples of the fusion of drama, photography, and poetry.

Choice of Subject Matter. There is hardly a phase of life or any period of history from which the modern artist did not derive inspiration. He painted laborers and factory workers, cripples and social misfits, buxom nudes, religious subjects,[3] self-portraits, still life, animals, and landscapes. All periods of art, from the primitive cave drawings through the pre-Christian civilizations, the medieval, and the present, not omitting the cultures of Africa and Asia, were copied, assimilated, and reinterpreted in modern art. Only the outstanding influences can be mentioned here, but it should be borne in mind that never was subject matter so comprehensive and techniques so bewildering.

Treatment of Subject. The traditional manner of presenting the subject was felt by many artists to be stale and overworked. From Impressionism (the impression made by the subject on the observer at a given instant) artists progressed to Expressionism (a movement originating in Germany, which attempted to express the inner nature of the subject regardless of its outward appearance) and Cubism (which sought to interpret nature in terms of the significant geometric forms, in various combinations). Rhythm and balance were stressed in a type of painting which was design rather than illustration. Indeed, post-war painting and sculpture became somewhat of a puzzle for the observer to figure out. Abstract art went to such an extreme that the subject was often no longer recognizable, as for example, in Marcel Duchamp's famous painting, *Nude Descending the Staircase*. Some artists abandoned tangible subject matter and painted such ideas as Man Ray's *Admiration of the Orchestrelle for the Cinematograph*. The numerous abstract modernistic paintings labeled *Composition* profess to be nothing more than balanced arrangements of line, mass, and color.

The Layman and the New Art. The tendency to reorganize subject matter in such drastic fashion that it is no longer recognizable by the unsophisticated tended to alienate art from the layman. The ordinary mortal was bewildered by the esthetics of the new art. He could not link it up with the rest of his experience, and therefore it seemed strange, unappealing, and often ludicrous. Parallels might be cited in the realm of literature, as in James Joyce's *Finnegan's Wake* or Gertrude Stein's writings, which scorn the very meaning of language. The cult of the unintelligible can be seen in architecture, in Le Corbusier's plans for " artistically ideal " buildings and cities, wholly unadapted to human needs.

This general shift of emphasis from the simple to the complex and from the familiar to the esoteric and incomprehensible has been defended by many esthetic theorists. Clive Bell and Roger Fry, two of the most penetrating writers in esthetics in the last generation, agree on the unimportance of subject matter and its subordination to pure form. The Spanish philosopher José Ortega y Gasset is even more emphatic in his essay *The Dehumanization of Art:*

" Even if pure art is impossible there is no doubt room for a tendency to purify art. This tendency will lead towards a progressive elimination of the human, all too human elements, which dominate romantic and naturalistic production. In this process the point will be reached when the human element of the work of art will be so scanty that it will be hardly visible. . . . It will be an art for artists and not for the masses of the people." [4]

Influence of Freud. The influence of Freud and other psychologists assumed great importance just after the war. There was pronounced interest in sex, in the psychology of dreams and their interpretation, and in the inner workings of the psychopathic mind. The employment of symbolism in art, sometimes obscure and sometimes logical and obvious, became widespread.

The Surrealists, like Salvador Dali and Giorgio di Chirico commonly used dreams as subject matter, perhaps as a form of escape from a troubled world. Objects were chosen at random, metamorphosed and placed in outrageous connotations, as in the wanderings of the mind in sleep or in the illogical and uninhibited brain of the insane.[5] The artist tried to probe the furthest recesses of the subconscious. Disinterested in bridging the gap between his subconscious paintings and a conscious, inhibited public, he created a storm of protest, or exposed himself to the criticisms of the rationalists.

Music. Similarly, in music, an increasing number of composers concluded that the older forms, scales, and rhythms had been fully exploited, and that if music was to translate the complexities of the modern world it must blaze new trails and disentangle itself from the major traditions of the past.[6]

As already suggested in previous chapters, modern music is characterized by a greater emphasis on color and texture than on melody, a radical departure from the older rhythms, and a new harmony. Far more sophisticated than the music of the nineteenth century, it is written in protest against romanticism, abjures sweet and soft melodies, and reveals a critical and skeptical spirit, more intellectual than emotional, often bitter and ironic.

Harmony. In the field of harmony, three new departures were apparent. Led largely by Arnold Schönberg, many illustrious composers experimented with atonality, or the absence of tonal center or " key." The chief characteristic of this music is the free employment of all the tones of the scale in their relationship to one another, rather than in their relationship to the predominating tonic and dominant. Polytonality, with which the name of Igor Stravinsky is most often associated, employs simultaneously two or more keys in order to produce a wide variety of harmonic color.

Even more radical departures were made by those who discarded the twelve half-tones of the familiar diatonic system and created an entirely new scale based on the quarter-tone or other intervals. The Czech Elois Haba (1893–   ), for instance, composed in quarter-tones and sixth-tones and gave recitals on a specially constructed quarter-tone piano. In short, composers, like plastic artists and men of letters, struck out in all directions.

Rhythm. The traditional rhythmic pattern also underwent drastic revision by the experimentalists, as for instance in American jazz music, with its high degree of syncopation. The lack of a regular " beat " was particularly apparent, and instead the individual beat of each note was emphasized. In addition, Asiatic and African rhythms were used. For subject matter, composers often reverted to folk songs, but these works frequently showed great incongruity between the simplicity of the folk tunes and their sophisticated treatment.

Effects of Industrialization

The effect of industrialization was twofold: (1) technological inventions and improvement of materials brought new forms and methods in architecture, decoration, and the industrial arts. (2) The choice of subject matter and its treatment in sculpture and painting showed the direct influence of the machine.

Architecture. The plasticity of poured concrete, the strength and lightness of structural steel, and the development of glass as a building material opened new vistas in architecture. The use of structural steel revolutionized the construction of industrial and public buildings, just as the Gothic arch had revolutionized church building in the twelfth century. In both Gothic and modern architecture the sustaining walls could be reduced to a minimum and the window space enlarged to admit a maximum of light. Public buildings, factories and warehouses, department stores, railroad stations, and theaters were the first to apply the new principles because there the need was greatest and space was at a premium in the large cities.

Functionalism,[7] as a reaction against the overornateness of the last century, was the new force in architecture. Decorations on the façade, which became so unsightly with dirt and dust, were largely eliminated and masses of light and shadow became the decorative forces on the exterior.

City-Planning. The industrial revolution changed the faces of cities and for decades the need was felt to make urban life healthy and enjoyable. Individual efforts were occasionally made to achieve these goals, but in general public authority brought about the greatest reforms in slum clearance and housing for the underprivileged. Instead of just one block or a small section, regional planners now took into consideration the industries, the geographical location, and the size of the community in attempting to coordinate over a long period of time all aspects of city life into an efficient and esthetic whole.[8]

Furniture. The design of furniture and the decorative arts took lines of development similar to that of architecture. The functional superseded the Victorian and other period styles. A new interest arose in materials. Beautiful grains in wood and highly polished surfaces became popular; fine leathers, new textiles, and exotic materials were used to upholster the simple frames.

Art in the Factory. Whereas in the latter part of the nineteenth century factory-made goods and the arts and crafts were completely irreconcilable, recently a reconciliation has been brought about. It is necessary only to mention the benefits to the artists in the form of better tools and improved materials. More important still was the fact that artists and manufacturers worked in closest collaboration. Artists were employed by manufacturers to design textiles, glassware, ceramics, and furniture, even machines, packages, and containers, and to see that the designs were carried out with the greatest possible artistic effect.

Machine Forms in Art. Painting, sculpture, and the graphic arts showed the increased importance of the machine in shaping our daily lives. Social conditions of laborers and factory workers provided subject matter for some decades before the war. Now the influence of the machine itself became more significant. Geometric forms, important in industry, were utilized by the new schools of art, as, for example, in Cubism, Rondism, Vorticism, and Constructivism. Men trained as engineers and architects became successful painters.[9] The new " isms " were reduced to a formula not unlike the specifications for a machine-made product. Even the more conservative artists conventionalized still-life objects to look as though they had been produced by a machine. Pure machine forms were apparent, particularly in sculpture. Duchamp-Villon, for example, depicted the horse as a representation of its mechanical forces. Moholy-Nagy used wires, springs, screws, and rope in his sculptured creations. Marcel Duchamp created a panel which included a real bicycle wheel, bedsprings, a corkscrew and a wire ice-box cleaner. Sculpture, as well as painting, showed a perfection of technique and machinelike precision of finish, as in Archipenko's geometric, flamelike torsos, and Brancusi's *Bird in Flight*.

Music. In music, the influence of the machine on rhythm as well as subject matter was pronounced. Arthur Honegger described the movements of a locomotive in *Pacific 231*. George Antheil's *Ballet Mécanique* made use of airplane propellers and typewriters in its instrumentation. Even harmony itself did not escape the influence of machine culture.

Democratization of Art

A growing tendency to bring the masses in contact with the arts can be attributed to three forces: the industrial revolution, the rise of a collective spirit, and more recently, the growth of conflicting political and social ideologies.

The Artist. Art was now regarded as an integral part of life. It was to be found wherever one looked: in household furnishing, clothing, even in tools and kitchen utensils. Art in return took its subject matter from all aspects of life. The attitude toward the artist also changed. Instead of being regarded as a social misfit, he was accepted as a normal human being pursuing his chosen occupation. Patronage by art dealers,[10] governmental agencies, individuals, and the mutual help and strength provided by the newly formed artists unions, all aided in giving the artist security and permitting him to live a more normal and settled life.

The artist took as subjects people at work and play, and was relatively little interested in landscape. The painter and sculptor exalted the lower classes and depicted children, animals, healthy youths, and people of all ages who were interested in living and enjoying life. Their manner of portrayal was often simple and naïve, and sometimes consciously childlike.

Popularization also took an ideological turn, partly as a result of nationalistic fervor and partly through encouragement by the governments. Legends and folk tales were more than ever subjects for paintings, drama, and music. Folk songs were assiduously collected. Peasants were painted in their native costumes doing native dances or following the traditional customs of their districts.

Industrial Arts. Progress in machine production was instrumental in bringing art to the homes of the common people. Articles of everyday use: chinaware, glassware, textiles used by the interior decorator and by the dressmaker, rugs, and innumerable other articles, including good photographic reproductions of masterpieces of painting, were produced in such variety and so cheaply that even the laborer was able to afford them. Popular books and magazines helped to elevate standards of taste by giving simple instruction in methods of production of one or another of the arts and at the same time stimulating interest in and appreciation of art.

Statues that were pure works of art and not memorials to statesmen and generals were erected in parks, on bridges, and in other public places. In conjunction with architecture, mural painting became an important form of public art. Murals, mosaics, and sculptured reliefs are the chief interior decorative feature in the modern architecture of flat surfaces and plain building materials.[11]

Architecture and Decoration. Functional architecture not only eliminated the nonessentials but was, at its best, also considerate of the persons who were to occupy the buildings. The flat surfaces of interiors and furniture were easily cleaned and did not catch dirt and germs. Furniture was often built into the room, and served, as simply as possible, the purpose for which it was designed. Furniture in England, on the whole, followed the traditional styles, and English interior decoration was also more conservative than on the continent. The use of color in interior decoration underwent a profound change. Interest in psychology led to experiments on the effect of color on mood and personality, and color schemes were often chosen for their practical as well as artistic value.

After the war thousands of families were left homeless, hence the great interest in erecting homes for middle-class families, both apartments and private dwellings. The need to raise the standard of living was great, but since economy was also an important factor space had to be conserved. Rooms were put to more uses and arranged more efficiently for easier housekeeping. Space conservation was evident also in the outdoor recreational facilities. The chief criticism of middle-class construction was its monotony of design, where the factor of economy was doubtless the reason for such unromantic simplicity.

Motion Pictures. The motion picture has had probably greater influence on contemporary life than any other popular art. It has developed its own canons and techniques, especially since the introduction and perfection of the sound film.[12] The cultural contributions of the motion picture are incalculable, for it has brought cinematic versions of literature and art to people all over the world who would otherwise have no contact with the theater or the world of fiction. The United States, France, Russia, England, and pre-Nazi Germany have been the leaders in cinematic progress.

Radio. Radio entertainment has had even more phenomenal growth. It, too, had to develop its own techniques, and has enriched the lives of great masses of people, by bringing into their homes symphonic programs and operas which they otherwise would not hear. Radio dramas widened the possibilities of cultural enjoyment for those to whom the legitimate stage was intellectually, financially, or geographically remote.

Nationalism in Modern Art

Two types of nationalism in art must be mentioned. One was the result of tradition and history, as exemplified in the Balkan countries where an intense nationalism was engendered by the difficult struggle for survival of many small racial groups. This type of nationalism expressed itself chiefly in literature and folk arts. The second type of nationalism arose out of the ideological movements in Russia, Germany, and Italy analyzed in Chapter XXV.

Folk Arts. Cheaply produced manufactured goods and the changing economic conditions after 1918 threatened the folk arts of eastern and central Europe. Immediately steps were taken to preserve and encourage the crafts which the peasants had practiced for centuries, and which were recognized for their artistic and nationalistic value. Systematic studies were made of all aspects of peasant crafts, such as rug and tapestry weaving, pottery, wood carving and cabinetmaking, embroideries, and laces. The festivals, old customs, folk dances, folk drama, legends, and songs were recorded and their observance and cultivation were encouraged. Publications aroused national pride in this heritage of the past.

Graphic and Poster Art. In another realm, the graphic arts became an effective means of advertisement and nationalist propaganda. After the First World War cartoons and illustrated periodicals became increasingly popular and stimulated the renewed interest in the graphic arts, which lent themselves well to representation of subject matter and were easily reproduced on the printed page.[13]

During the First World War and again in the present conflict nationalist posters spurred the participation of the people on the home-front in the various aspects of the conflict. Following the war, poster art was widely developed in all European countries by railway, steamship, and travel companies. These posters with their excellent composition, striking use of masses and flat color, and their strong draftsmanship had definite artistic value.

Sculpture and War Monuments. Countless sculptural monuments were erected after the war. In the victorious countries these statues glorified the noble sacrifice of youth for a just cause and the support of the heavenly powers. In spirit they were not distinguishable from the memorials of any other war. Germany's war monuments, however, were in a more pessimistic, disillusioned strain, severely simple to the point of ugliness. Sadness and great restraint characterized even the Tannenberg memorial, which commemorated Germany's outstanding victory. Instead of a triumphant winged victory or gloating Mars, a sorrowing father, mother, or sister was depicted. This strain of sorrowful pessimism is noticeable in other forms of post-war German art, as in Käthe Kollwitz's drawings and sculptures.

Statues of generals, liberators, statesmen, and historical heroes are to be found in increasing number in all countries, particularly in Russia and the eastern European countries. Germany, recalling a more heartening period in her history, erected many statues of Bismarck.

New faith was placed in youth, who, it was hoped, would not make the same mistakes as the older generation. Sculptors portrayed nude youths and young women of strapping vigor, greeting the future with brave hope. Russia produced the same type of work. The Russian buildings at both the Paris International Exposition of 1937 and the New York World's Fair formed pedestals for colossal figures of youths.

Painting. Most of the leading painters of the period might be called international. Paris, as in the nineteenth century, attracted artists from all parts of the world, and became the home of most of the experimental schools. Recently New York has also become an artistic center, due to increased opportunity in this country for remunerative artistic expression and the political and social unrest in Europe. The most celebrated artists of our generation have thought less of national characteristics than of esthetic forms and goals. It is difficult, for instance, to consider a bullfight by Picasso in cubist style as glorifying an old Spanish custom. Those artists, however, whose subject matter was nationalistic tended also to adopt a more conservative style. For instance, Uprka's paintings of peasant life and customs, Vladimir Dimitroff's pictures of Bulgarian villages, and Sorolla's canvases in the library of the Hispanic Society in New York City depicting the various phases of Spanish life, sprang from nationalistic feeling but were not propagandistic in nature.

The Totalitarian Countries. The totalitarian countries were quick to realize the tremendous political value of art. Communist Russia, Fascist Italy, and Nazi Germany were unified in at least one important sociological viewpoint: namely, that the arts always serve some class interest, consciously or not. Prince, church, and *bourgeois* have, at times, dominated the arts which, in turn, have reflected their interests. What was more logical, therefore, than to place art in the service of the state, to further its ideals and help establish its ideological dominion?

Russia. Soviet Russia's use of the arts to disseminate Communism was more difficult than Germany's or Italy's for three reasons: (1) the widespread illiteracy and unfamiliarity with the arts; (2) the attempt to place the country's art on an entirely new ideological basis with little precedent and tradition; and (3) the self-imposed or enforced exile of practically every well-known artist of Czarist days during or after the revolution. Russia's greatest cultural achievement has probably been in the field of education. The Russians realized that they could develop neither art nor technology without reducing illiteracy and increasing scientific knowledge.

The Soviets set out to create an art which would really belong to the people. Paintings which showed the people healthy and happy under the Soviet regime were most popular. At the same time, Russia was not so hostile to foreign schools as Germany and Italy.

Gradually a new generation of artists sprang up to replace those who had left. The best and most original opposed the stifling instructions of the RAPP (dissolved in 1932) which dominated art and literature under Stalin. Under the Trade Union of Art Workers which supplanted the RAPP, however, it soon became impossible for a non-member artist to secure recognition of his work or even assurance of personal safety.[14]

Musicians did not suffer from censorship as much as writers and painters, whose ideological leanings could be easily detected. Yet even Dimitri Shostakovitch, the most brilliant of young Soviet composers, was censored by the Russian government for the sensationalism of his *Lady Macbeth of Mzensk*.

Italy. Fascist Italy also regimented its artistic production for nationalistic purposes. The Arts and Professions Guild included lawyers, architects, journalists, musicians, craftsmen, and art dealers. The guild set prices, stimulated demand, and carried on many activities besides that of making its members aware of their cultural mission and national obligations.[15] These obligations consisted of emphasizing Italian customs and traditions, commemorating the achievements of the Fascist state, and reminding the people of the glories of ancient Rome.

The *Dopolavoro* (*After Work*) movement, created in 1925, organized the leisure of workers along nationalist lines. The section devoted to culture and art brought art, music, and drama to the masses. In 1937 there were 21,695 Dopolavoro centers with a total membership of 3,180,000. Members were admitted to museums, concerts, plays, and movies at reduced prices. Competitions were held regularly in painting, sculpture, and architecture.[16]

Germany. In Nazi Germany artistic activities have been regimented by the Reich Chamber of Culture, organized by Joseph Goebbels' Ministry of Propaganda. As early as 1924, Hitler in *Mein Kampf* deplored the existence of such international movements as Cubism, Dadaism, and Surrealism, associating them with Judaism and Bolshevism. When Hitler came to power he purged the Reich of all creative talent not in harmony with the Nazi spirit or of non-Aryan origin.

Nazi Germany also had its *Strength through Joy* movement, similar to the Italian Dopolavoro. This organization was devoted to the popularization of national art through inexpensive performances of drama and concert and reduced admission to museums. Native costumes and crafts were encouraged and the old German festivals were observed. There was a campaign against jazz and foreign music and the older German dance forms were encouraged.

It is still too early to evaluate the results of Germany's crusade against non-Aryan art. The loss of artists, scholars, and men of science for political or racial reasons was a heavy blow to Germany. Architecture, in which Germany was outstanding, did not suffer so much, although Hitler, who studied architecture, dictated an impressive modern classic style for national buildings.

Among the leading composers, Richard Strauss remained in Nazi Germany; Paul Hindemith fled. The work of Hans Pfitzner, an enthusiastic nationalist, became popular after 1933.

The Wagner Festivals continue at Bayreuth, and the Passion Plays at Oberammergau. German concert orchestras still excel under such conductors as Furtwängler; well-known singers like Hans Herrmann Nissen and Albert Schlussnuss and a host of others still appear. Interest in classical music has increased, if anything. But the works of German Jews like Mendelssohn and Mohler are taboo.

Music of Other Countries. Nationalism in music was not limited to Germany, Russia, and Italy. A host of influential composers from all parts of Europe reverted to more or less nationalist ideals. Zoltan Kodaly, as mentioned elsewhere, zealously collected Hungarian folk music and incorporated it in his compositions. The Rumanian, Georges Enesco, has written a famous *Rumanian Poem* as well as highly nationalistic *Rhapsodies*. The music of the Czech Leos Janacek is thoroughly nationalistic, while Weinberger cleverly wove Czech folk tunes into his celebrated opera, *Schwanda the Bagpipe Player*. Spain produced a great nationalist composer in Manuel de Falla, who, without drawing directly on folk music for his melodies, developed a style which gained international acclaim.

Without founding a " school," Jean Sibelius created in his tone poems and symphonies truly Finnish music, drawing upon nature legends for inspiration. His tone poem *Finlandia*, an early work, helped greatly to heighten Finnish national consciousness.

Conclusion. What can be said of the future of the arts in Europe? Perhaps the only safe conclusion is that the future of art, like that of European civilization in general, is indeed uncertain. Periods of social conflict create restlessness and change in intellectual life. Yet certain trends can be seen.

In the first place, the tendency away from naturalism has gained a permanent foothold. Once and for all, the realization has been attained that art is not a mere copy of nature. Dadaism and Surrealism may come and go, but the artist will retain the privilege, except in totalitarian countries, of depicting in his subject matter something " closer to the heart's desire," whatever that may be for the individual.

Secondly, the influence of industrialization will probably increase, unless the folly of national pride and international hate result in the destruction of Western civilization. Democratization of art — even in the Fascist countries — will doubtless continue. At best it will be a conscious striving of the people for a broader, enriched life. At worst, it will be the portioning out to the people of trumped-up nationalistic art.

But whatever its course, the current of artistic change will continue to flow, and that is perhaps the safest speculation of all.

REFERENCES

[1] The student interested in such an investigation can benefit from Melvin M. Rader's *A Modern Book of Esthetics*, New York: Holt, 1938, a collection of the more important contributions to esthetic theory in the twentieth century.

[2] Western European countries sponsored most of the " isms " — Italy with Futurism, England Vorticism, France Cubism, Dadaism, Surrealism, Purism, Verism, Constructivism, and Rondism — to mention but a few. The art of most of the eastern European countries has been freed from constraining influences, both religious and national, only within the last century. Eastern artists have begun to imitate the western Europeans but their art still remains behind that of western Europe. This is, of course, not true of those international artists who were trained in Paris, Berlin, and Rome.

[3] A wave of religious revival swept over Europe after the war. The Polish sculptor Swiecinski, who imitated Gothic forms, and Eric Gill (1882–   ), an English sculptor, both embraced Catholicism and executed many religious works. The Hungarian Livia Kadar was a religious mystic.

[4] Melvin M. Rader, *op. cit.*, p. 346. Compare this theory with the purpose of art in the totalitarian countries.

[5] Salvador Dali is said to have remarked in a newspaper interview, " The only difference between my art and the art of a madman is that I am not mad."

[6] " It is impossible to count the composers who invent their own conventions, but it is safe to say that never in the history of Western music has there been such diversity of methods as during the first part of the twentieth century," from " The Early Twentieth Century " by Arthur Mendel in Waldo Selden Pratt's *The History of Music*, New York: Schirmer, 1935. The student will find a brief but excellent account of the major trends in modern music in the last chapter of this book.

[7] Louis Sullivan and Frank Lloyd Wright, American architects, were leaders in developing the new styles. While the United States led the world in the use of the skyscraper it lagged far behind Europe in other branches of functional architecture.

[8] Excellent work has been done under governmental authority in England, Finland, Sweden, Germany, and Holland. For an excellent account, see Lewis Mumford's *The Culture of Cities*, New York: Harcourt, Brace, 1938, see chs. 5, 6, 7.

[9] For example, Fernand Léger, a French artist, and Archipenko, a Russian.

[10] C. J. Bulliet, *The Significant Moderns*, New York: Halcyon House, 1936, p. 131.

[11] A typical expression of the democratic trend in architecture was formulated in the competition for the design of the Palace of the Soviets in Moscow:

" It should be a people's architecture and, as such, basically humane, rich with details which should appeal to the people. It should have much sculpture and painting."

T. F. Hamlin, " Style Developments in Soviet Architecture," *American Quarterly of the Soviet Union*, April, 1938, p. 19.

[12] A good survey of the development of the motion picture in Europe and the United States is found in M. Bardèche and R. Brasillach, *The History of Motion Pictures*, translated by Iris Barry, New York: Norton, and The Museum of Modern Art, 1938.

[13] Periodicals devoted mainly to cartoons were popular, as well as the cartoons and caricatures which appeared regularly in newspapers and magazines, as for example, in England *Puck*, *Punch*, and in Germany *Simplizissimus, Jugend, Fliegende Blätter,* and *Klatteradatsch*.

[14] For a thorough treatment of Soviet art see Max Eastman, *Artists in Uniform*, New York: Knopf, 1934. Eastman is less enthusiastic than such historians as Harry Elmer Barnes regarding Soviet educational and cultural achievements. Mention should be made of such exiles as the composers Sergei Rachmaninoff, Alexander Glazunow, Alexander Gretchaninoff, and Igor Stravinsky.

[15] " In the totalitarian guild State as we have defined it, which seeks to harmonize, coordinate, and stimulate all the energies of the nation, directing them towards the

ends it has in view, the arts and professions cannot stand aside, indifferent to the political and civic progress of the nation.

Professional men, writers, artists, must acquire a sense of their national responsibilities." Mario Missiroli and Olivia Agresti, *The Organisation of the Arts and Professions in the Fascist Guild State*, Rome: Laboremus, 1938, p. 21.

¹⁶ Organizations for the utilization of leisure and encouragement of art and culture were not limited to totalitarian countries. Rumania, for instance, had its *Strajeri* movement.

SELECTED BIBLIOGRAPHY

Bardèche, Maurice and Brasillach, Robert, *The History of Motion Pictures*, New York: Norton, 1938 (translated and edited by Iris Barry). A good account of the development of motion pictures in Europe and America.

Barnes, Harry Elmer, *An Intellectual and Cultural History of the Western World*, New York: Corden Co., 1937, ch. 26.

Barr, Alfred H., Jr. and Hugnet, Georges, *Fantastic Art, Dada, Surrealism*, New York: Museum of Modern Art, 1936. A sympathetic and historical handling of Dadaism and Surrealism. The large collection of reproductions includes many examples of fantastic art produced by older masters.

Bulliet, C. J., *Apples and Madonnas*, New York: Covici-Friede, 1933. Bulliet gives a sane explanation of the purposes and results of modern art from the middle of the last century to the present.

——, *The Significant Moderns*, New York: Blue Ribbon Books, 1936. A good supplement to *Apples and Madonnas*.

Craven, Thomas, *Modern Art*, New York: Simon and Schuster, 1934. Craven's treatment of modern art is up to date and ties up contemporary American art with European movements. He includes architecture and his illustrations are well selected.

Dyson, George, *The New Music*, London: Oxford Univ. Press, 1926. A helpful book for music students; of lesser value to those lacking the technical knowledge necessary to follow the discourse.

Eastman, Max, *Artists in Uniform*, New York: Knopf, 1934. Max Eastman, a disappointed Communist, demonstrates the suppression of creative thought in Russia.

Mumford, Lewis, *Technics and Civilization*, New York: Harcourt, Brace, 1934.

——, *The Culture of Cities*, New York: Harcourt, Brace, 1938. The last three chapters deal with the problems of modern cities and how they are being solved in the United States and abroad.

Pratt, Waldo Selden, *The History of Music*, New York: Schirmer, 1935. (Chapter on " The Early Twentieth Century," by Arthur Mendel.) Mendel's chapter affords the student with little technical knowledge a brief but comprehensive picture of music in the twentieth century.

Rader, Melvin M., *A Modern Book of Esthetics*, New York: Holt, 1938. Well-chosen selections from the writings of estheticians who have influenced the contemporary scene.

Richards, J. M., *An Introduction to Modern Architecture*, New York: Penguin Books, 1940. The author treats the purposes and requirements of modern architecture and the effects of industrial developments.

CHAPTER XXXI

The Social Sciences and Education

A survey of European social sciences and education today can be much less chaotic than it would have been thirty years ago. In the earlier period virtually every writer approached social phenomena in his own way. In recent times, however, these paths have tended to merge into streets or even avenues, although of course no general plan of the city can yet be discerned.

It will be necessary to devote perhaps disproportionate attention to "sociology," since sociology embraces many fields of research which will ultimately achieve independent status, but which until now have not been graced with distinctive names.

Political Science

The science of politics can be divided into two basic categories: (1) studies of particular fields of governmental practice (called "social technology"), and (2) studies of the nature and function of the state. The second division concerns us most.

One of the earliest post-war developments was the continued growth of a "pluralist" philosophy of political science in which the state is viewed as a super-arbiter among independent associations or groups. The state, in this essentially anti-totalitarian view, exists in order to adjust the differences between social groups. Pluralist views are expounded in the early works of the Englishman Harold Laski,[1] and (to some extent) that of G. D. H. Cole.[2] Using a different concept to carry out the same purpose, the German Hugo Krabbe [3] expounds a theory of the state in which law is sovereign, political agencies being controlled by legal systems.

Marxian Political Theory. The outstanding exposition of Marxian political theory in English-speaking countries is that of Harold Laski and John Strachey. After considerable journeying through the realms of political philosophy, Laski finally arrived at the conclusion that capitalist institutions must be overthrown if a Socialist society was to emerge. According to Professor Catlin, Laski's main function in recent years has been to act as the "broker of Marxism to the middle-class intelligentsia." [4] Laski feels that democratic institutions are perhaps not at present under the

---

This chapter by Howard Becker, Professor of Sociology, University of Wisconsin, and William L. Kolb, Instructor, Department of Sociology and Rural Life, Oklahoma Agricultural and Mechanical College.

complete control of the capitalists. Strachey has taken a more orthodox Marxian position: namely, that the state is an instrument of exploitation, and that the crisis in capitalism is at hand. Fascism to Strachey represents the last gasp of decadent capitalism.

On the continent, the most significant trend in Marxian political theory is represented by Georg von Lukacs in his *Marxismus und Klassenbewusstsein* (*Marxism and Class-Consciousness*). Abandoning the attempt to jam the whole cosmos within the framework of the Hegelian-Marxian dialectic, Lukacs limits this dialectic to the realm of social phenomena. Moreover, he strongly stresses Lenin's theory that Marxism can become a potent force only when class consciousness has been engendered by the skilled professional revolutionists.

Fascist Political Theory. The Fascist theory of the state is expounded by Alfredo Rocco and Giovanni Gentile.[5] According to Rocco the fact that man cannot exist without society implies that the ends of the society are superior to individual ends, and the basic problem is to harmonize the rights of the state with the duties of the individual. Gentile's conception of Fascism revolves around the national state, which is held to be antecedent to the individual, and is a wholly spiritual creation. Fascism itself is neither a philosophy, a religion, nor a political theory; it is a way of life in which the state is identified with the consciousness of the individual, and this in turn is molded and shaped by the leader.

The National Socialist theory of the state, minus anti-Semitism, is expounded by Werner Sombart in *A New Social Philosophy*.[6] It must be remembered, however, that Nazi political science is based on the dogma of racial superiority, as elaborated by Alfred Rosenberg and others.

Among contemporary theories of the state which are associated neither with Communism, Fascism, nor Nazism one in particular is worthy of note: that of R. M. MacIver.[7] In contrast to the totalitarian theories which identify the state with society, MacIver distinguishes between spontaneous social groupings, which he designates as " communities," and the state, which is an organization formed for particular purposes. MacIver emphasizes the importance of spontaneous groups in controlling the behavior of men, thus limiting the actual influence of the state.

One fact emerges from this very brief survey of political science: namely, theories of the state are derived either from the ancient assumption that the state and society are identical, or from the hypothesis that the state is limited in the scope of its operations.

Economics

Economics during the last two decades has chiefly derived from the theories of " marginal utility " (goods have value only in proportion to the satisfaction they yield, the margin of utility being the margin of value). Thus there appeared a " mathematical economics," " economics of imperfect competition," and " welfare economics," among others. Economics is a study of the processes by which men secure the material objects they value; its basic postulate is a working fiction: namely, the " economic man " who is motivated solely by a desire to increase his income to the fullest extent. Not that any individual is completely an economic man, but by means of this concept a certain amount of prediction and control of economic behavior can be obtained.[8] Given certain conditions, the economic man will attempt to increase his income and thus produce and consume up to a point that can be determined mathematically.

By using this type of analysis Joan Robinson and others have accounted for the fact that the monopolistic producer will sometimes produce more, and sometimes less in order to derive the greatest profit and manipulate prices accordingly, while the smaller producer operating in a purely competitive market, must sell at the price set in the total industry [9] or not sell at all. Using the same method, the " social welfare economists " have demonstrated that to raise the income of the producer either in free or monopoly competition does not necessarily increase the income of society, since in both cases too much or too little may be produced. That is, industry may be using resources which might be employed more economically elsewhere. Thus the theory upon which *laissez-faire* economics is based — " free competition " — has been used to explain why such a policy will not automatically improve the lot of all men.[10]

Werner Sombart made a thorough analysis of capitalism in *Modern Capitalism.* It is in his other writings, however, that he began as a Marxian and wound up with a philosophy akin to National Socialism.[11]

This cursory discussion of contemporary economic theory cannot be concluded without mentioning the influence which Marxian theories — the labor theory of value, the doctrine of class struggle, and the prophecy of the ultimate fall of capitalism — exerted on a large number of non-Nazi economists, such as Franz Oppenheimer, Hans Zeisl, Alfred Braunthal, and Carl Landauer.[12]

Sociology

Historical Sociology. When the sociologist turns to the study of historical materials, rather than contemporary phenomena, it is usually in an attempt to answer one of four questions:

" (1) What was the earliest condition of the creatures we call human, and how are those conditions changing with the lapse of time?   (2) Can there be discerned an all-encompassing drift toward a single goal, in spite of the baffling maze of changes?   (3) Are there any sequences or stages in societal development that when discovered will enable us to estimate the varying speeds at which the differing sections of mankind have approached the goal? (4) Can it be said that ' History repeats itself ' in any fundamental sense? " [13]

In the late nineteenth and early twentieth centuries, scientists attempted to prove, by a crude illustrative method, that mankind was evolving through fixed stages which were basically the same throughout the world. Today this doctrine, called " social Darwinism," is virtually dead.

" Anthropo-sociology " (sociology of preliterate man), a branch of historical sociology, has moved in two main directions. In the first, called " functionalism," largely an American product, anthropologists have attempted to account for similarities in social development by man's biological uniformity. In this type of analysis every culture trait is regarded as intimately associated with all others, making the comparison of cultures almost impossible. In the second, as exemplified by Thurnwald, the anthropologist is interested in the processes of man's development rather than in his origins. Thurnwald is interested in discovering generalizations that will illuminate this development. [14]

If the sociologist hopes to answer the four basic questions, he must study literate as well as preliterate groups. One of the most significant attempts to explain the genesis and growth of civilizations has been made by Arnold Toynbee, an English historian. [15] Despite the fact that one can discover a religious transcendentalism in his work, and that he has fallen into error which knowledge of recent sociological literature might have avoided, Toynbee has used a comparative method far superior to that of the older evolutionists. Realizing that historical data cannot be torn from their full contexts, Toynbee has not forced his material into " timeless " categories. By intensive study of historical periods, he has accounted for the genesis and change of several civilizations either by the challenge of a hostile natural environment, or by forces within society itself.

Discussion of Toynbee's work leads us into the consideration of the second question: viz., the goal toward which mankind is moving. Suffice it to say that Toynbee believes that mankind moves toward a predestined goal; other sociologists, such as Kurt Breysig, maintain that there is a goal toward which humanity *should* strive; while Ernst Troeltsch [16] reconciles " historical relativism " with the belief that all cultures have a common basis of reconciliation.

The German sociologist Max Weber has demonstrated that the trend of man's social development has been toward the growth of rational habits of thought. Weber refused, however, to indulge in prophecies about the future. His method is as important as his conclusions, since for the first time we encounter the use of types as a means of discovering historical generalizations. These types, constructed from available data, are never found in their pure state, but are dealt with " as if " they were pure in order to systematize the material and make scientific predictions possible.[17]

The attempt to find stages that are generally applicable to social development seems to have gone out of fashion with the older type of evolutionary hypothesis. Of recent studies of social stages, three main types can be discerned, but only that variety which involves no postulate of genetic continuity, as do the others, need be mentioned here.[18]

In determining whether or not history repeats itself, it is necessary to distinguish between small-scale and large-scale cycles. Most studies of small-scale cycles since the First World War are the work of Americans, but one of the best examples of the search for large-scale cycles is that of Oswald Spengler.[19] It is widely agreed that Spengler's morphology of cultures was arrived at by distorting historical material, although there is some value in his analysis of industrial-urban and peasant cultures.

Systematic Sociology.[20] Sociologists have met with considerable difficulty in attempting to establish their subject as an independent science, partly because they have so often intruded into fields of research which other investigators of social phenomena have pre-empted. The other social sciences, however, study chiefly the goals toward which human beings direct their activity and the purposes for which they are associated in groups. Hence those sociologists who have defined their science as the study of interhuman relations as such, with only a secondary emphasis on goals and purposes, have partially avoided the charge that they are encroaching on the territory of others.

Systematic sociology goes back to the early work of the German, Ferdinand Tönnies.[21] His chief contribution was the analysis of the concepts of " community " and " society." Emphasizing the close relationship between the personality and the social structure, Tönnies dealt mainly with social processes. The " community " is that type of social structure, illustrated by preliterate groups and some peasant societies, in which human behavior is determined by the non-rational, sometimes unconscious, acceptance of established customs. In " society," of which modern urban life is an example, behavior is largely the result of individual calculation and choice. Although the germs of systematic sociology are found in the writings of Tönnies, it remained for Georg Simmel [22] to define sociology as the science of " interhuman " relations. His conception of sociology was that of a science which studied the uniformities of human behavior but was not restricted to any particular social group, period, or culture.

Simmel's work, which was done prior to 1910, greatly influenced Leopold von Wiese,[23] one of the post-war leaders in systematic sociology. Starting with Simmel's conception of sociology, and drawing on the writings of contemporary Americans and Europeans, Wiese developed a system of sociology centering around the basic concepts of " social process," " social distance," " social space," and " social structure." Social processes, according to Wiese, are of two types: (1) those which are relatively un-influenced by social structures, and (2) those which take place between social structures or within them. These processes can be studied as inde-pendent units, or as part of a social pattern, and in either case must be studied through " ideal types." It is in the use of types and the search for insights by imagining the standpoint of his subjects, that Wiese is most indebted to Max Weber.[24] By using these methods, social processes can be classified as: (1) associative, or a tendency for human beings to come together, (2) dissociative, or the opposite tendency, and (3) tendencies in both directions. In this fashion Wiese analyzes social relations and then proceeds to study social structures, which he divides into " crowds," " groups," and " abstract collectivities."

Although the system described above may seem forbiddingly abstract, a great deal of research has been carried on in this realm at the University of Cologne. The most satisfactory results have been achieved in the study of crowds, organized groups, and the locality patterns of villages and small towns.[25]

Although in Europe systematic sociology has been largely restricted to Germany, significant work in this field has been done in other coun-tries. In Holland, P. Endt [26] has dealt with social processes in a manner closely approximating that of Wiese, and in Greece Panajotis Kanellopou-lous [27] has also developed a similar analytic sociology. Systematic sociol-ogy has made some progress in France, under the leadership of Gaston Richard [28] and Maunier, who made a systematic classification of social groups. Duprat in Switzerland and Morris Ginsberg [29] in England have also contributed to this branch of sociology. Thus, although the activity of the German systematic sociologists has declined since the advent of Hitler, the basic tenets of their theory have been diffused to other coun-tries, so that further developments along this line can be expected.

The Sociology of Knowledge.[30]   Of the various branches of sociology perhaps none has greater significance for the future of Western civiliza-tion than the " sociology of knowledge." In grappling with one of the most subtle problems of human behavior — namely, the relation of thought to the social milieu — the sociologist may develop a theory that can be used in dealing with the problem of conflicting ideologies.

Most of the research in the sociology of knowledge since 1918 em-anated from France and Germany. French sociologists have worked in the " sociologistic " tradition of Émile Durkheim, who died during the war. As the term " sociologistic " implies, Durkheim attempted to prove that the basic categories of thought, such as space and time, are derived from the nature of society.[31]

Among the studies made by Durkheim's followers, perhaps the most important is the investigation of memory by Maurice Halbwachs.[32] Halbwachs attempts to prove that memory is a product of group life. An- other of Durkheim's disciples, Marcel Granet,[33] adds other cultural items as determinants of thought. Not only did Granet explain the fundamental categories of Chinese thinking with Durkheim's concepts, but he pointed out that the monosyllabic language and ideographic writing of the Chinese has perpetuated a medium of communication unfitted for abstract thought, since it is associated so closely with action. Jane Harrison has used Durkheim's analysis to explain the development of Greek religious myths out of earlier tribal practices.[34]

Lucien Lévy-Bruhl has attempted to demonstrate that the preliterate peoples are " prelogical." Lévy-Bruhl has described a " primitive mentality," dominated by mysticism. This sharp contrast of preliterate and civilized peoples has been severely criticized partly because it was falsely believed that Lévy-Bruhl claimed that preliterate society is biologically inferior to literate groups.[35]

German sociologists have been influenced to some extent by Durkheim, but have devoted themselves mainly to exegetical exercises on Marxian concepts. Max Scheler,[36] considered by some the founder of the sociology of knowledge, is a disciple neither of Durkheim nor Marx, but has been influenced by both. According to Scheler, there is an absolute realm of ideal objects. These " ideal " factors, however, can only restrain and guide cultural development, for the latter is essentially based on " real " factors concerned with elemental drives such as hunger and reproduction. Thus Scheler has developed a theory of " historical relativism," which he in turn circumvents by postulating a transcendental realm of ideal religious, metaphysical, and scientific factors.

The Marxian formula that " It is not the consciousness of men that determines their being, but their being that determines their consciousness " has been amplified by Karl Mannheim.[37] Mannheim contends that there are two types of ideologies: (1) the " particular ideology," which may lead to self-deception but can be thrown off, and (2) the " total ideology " under whose influence one can never think impartially. This leads Mannheim to the conclusion that all thought, including utopian, is relativistic, except that of a small élite who are " socially unbound." Mannheim also holds that the truth of a utopian theory lies in the role it plays in social change, which involves an assumption that the meaning of the historical process is knowable.

Other social scientists could be profitably discussed here, including those who have modified Mannheim's theories to some extent, but enough material has been presented to indicate the direction in which this branch of the science is moving. The sociology of knowledge has become nonexistent in Nazi Germany, but research goes on in other parts of the world.

Social Psychology.[38] Very little progress in social psychology has been made in England, but one of the earliest attacks upon the orthodox theory of instinct was made by Morris Ginsberg in his *Psychology of Society.*[39] One of the outstanding French works in social psychology is Charles Blondel's investigation of insanity. He views " loss of mind " as a desocialization of the mental framework, which is societal in origin. The " loss of will " is viewed as another result of " desocialization," since it is society which presents to the individual the motivating values without which human will cannot exist.[40] One of the most interesting contributions to social psychology is the study of the " forms of sympathy " by Max Scheler.[41] Scheler finds that under the concept of sympathy is included at least four different phenomena: sharing the same emotion with others, rejoicing in another's joy or having pity for his sorrow, emotional contagion, and complete emotional identification. Scheler maintains that the careless use of the word " sympathy " can only result in disaster for the social scientist.

Along with these essentially individual contributions to social psychology, there have developed in Europe two important schools of systematic social psychology. The first, as embodied in the work of Kurt Lewin,[42] centers around the *Gestalt* school of psychology, but adds " topology," which is a form of non-metrical mathematics.

The second can be broadly classified as psychoanalysis. It has three branches, that devised by Sigmund Freud, Alfred Adler, and Carl Gustav Jung.[43] Each of these men attempts to explain the characteristics of human personality by the development of a single basic factor: Freud by the sexual libido; Adler by the drive for power, and Jung by the *élan vital*. These psychologists stress the individual, and pay little attention to the influence of society on the development of personality. The attempts of the psychoanalysts to analyze social and cultural phenomena in terms of their own psychology have shown the effects of this bias. Nevertheless a great deal of psychoanalytical theory will ultimately find a place in social psychology, chiefly the studies of the unconscious and of the irrationality of human behavior. Despite the fact that the psychoanalytic idea of the unconscious contains theories of racial memory which contradict the biological assumption that acquired characteristics cannot be inherited, the psychoanalysts have shown that considerable human behavior is dominated by impulses which lie in the unconscious. The work of Otto Rank,[44] a psychoanalyst with a broader cultural and social perspective than Freud, Adler, or Jung, is invalidated in part by the unproved assertion of racial memory. Recently cultural factors have been stressed so that, except for fanatical adherents, both orthodox and analytic psychology are gradually working toward a common ground.

Social Statistics.[45]   The use of quantitative techniques is one of the most recent developments in the social sciences, and is derived from the work of the Britons Francis Galton and Karl Pearson and the Frenchman Frédéric LePlay. In recent years many quantitative studies have been made by British students, the most important under the leadership of Victor Branford and Patrick Geddes.

With the exception of Halbwachs, who made an intensive study of German labor statistics and budgetary data which was published in 1913, and Simiand, the social economist, French sociologists have made little use of the statistical method. The same is largely true of German sociologists.

Italy has produced several social statisticians, L. Bodio, C. Gini, R. Benini, C. B. Turroni, F. Coridore, and F. Savorgnan. Without reviewing all their work, we may mention the important conclusion of Gini: namely, that the sociologist must not seek more refined measuring instruments — social data being usually too rough to allow the satisfactory use of the refined techniques now available — but rather develop a statistical " intuition " which will enable him to select the proper instrument for measuring the data in hand.[46]   This seems to be the main direction in which quantitative social theory is moving today. The application of refined statistical techniques, the results of which are largely meaningless, is being abandoned on all fronts.

Population Studies.   The scientific study of population became prominent after the First World War. Sir George H. Knibbs [47] pointed out that the rate of increase in world population could not long be maintained without lowering the standards of living, since those portions of the earth's surface still uninhabited could not support the growing surplus of population on the overcrowded continent. Renewed interest in Malthusianism study of the relation of population to the food supply made it necessary to discover the biological laws of population growth.

G. U. Yule and Raymond Pearl attempted to solve the problem on a mathematical basis. Pearl postulated the theory that the birth-rate declines with the increase of population density, using domestic fowl and the fruit fly to prove his contentions. Gini,[48] whom we have mentioned above, has adopted the theory that entire populations, as biological entities, pass through periods of youth, maturity, and senescent decay. These theories imply that populations grow in an uncontrolled manner, but Carr-Saunders claims that when a seemingly optimum number is reached attempts are made by social groups to regulate the size of population. All of these hypotheses tend to ignore the actions of individuals, resulting in restriction of the birth-rate, a common phenomenon in sophisticated cultural groups.

Education

The study of educational processes in Europe has centered to a great extent on the problem of training the individual in a manner which will insure his effective participation in social life. We have seen in various chapters of this work that different demands are made on the individual in a democratic society and in a totalitarian state, making it necessary to emphasize different aspects of education. This trend can be demonstrated in all countries, but limitation of space forces us to concentrate our attention here on those countries which illustrate this phenomenon most clearly. Although the struggle between Protestantism and Catholicism in Ireland and Catholicism and anti-clericalism in France exemplify the impact of social forces in education, it is in Germany and Czechoslovakia that we note most forcibly how political movements have affected education.

With the advent of the republic, the various branches of the German educational science attempted to discover the best methods of inculcating democratic beliefs and forms of behavior in youth and adult alike. Czechoslovakia undertook the same task. President Masaryk believed that the schools should emphasize moral education rather than " a barren intellectual grooming." [49] This conception of education was elaborated by Frantisek Drtina, Frantisek Krejci who made the first Czech systematic study of educational psychology, and Frantisek Cada founder of Czech genetic psychology. After the partial dismemberment of Czechoslovakia in 1938 there was strong criticism of the moral education and internationalism which Masaryk had advocated.[50]

The Nazi revolution brought a complete upheaval in German education, as already indicated. There was an attempt to change the whole outlook on life, and the science of education was directed to finding methods for the propagation of the Nazi *Weltanschauung* (world-view). Even the history of education in Germany was reinterpreted, as by Herbert Freudenthal,[51] to suit the Nazi regime, while the work of reorienting educational practice in the light of the fantastic theories of blood and soil, the leadership principle, and Aryan supremacy was carried out by Ernst Krieck [52] among others. The Nazi philosophy of education rejects any conception of knowledge which does not make allowance for basic presuppositions, and maintains that learning has meaning only when it grows out of racial consciousness. Müller-Freienfels [53] and Hansen have written works on child psychology acceptable to the Nazis, while problems in education for war have been dealt with by Altrichter, Picht, and others.

Educational Psychology.[54] Since educational psychology is still vaguely defined, students in several fields have made independent contributions to the subject. Of those who have written about social pedagogy, Paul Natorp, Paul Bergemann, Paul Barth, and Otto Willman have been most influential. Assuming that education of the individual is inadequate for solving the problems of society, they maintain that a " social attitude " is necessary, that education is not only an affair between pupil and teacher, but between the pupil and the social milieu. Although these men have different philosophical views (Natorp is a Neo-Kantian, Barth a pantheist, and Willman a Thomist), they all arrive at the conclusion that education " serves the conservation and perfection of society," and hence all members of society rather than a few should be educated. Similar ideas are advanced by Saverio de Dominicus, whose views are based on the doctrine that the progress and retrogression of society are intimately connected with its educational system, and by Siegfried Kawerau, who suggested that Socialism could be attained through educational reforms.

While Masaryk and Beneš made many contributions to educational sociology, the Czech I. A. Blaha in his *Sociology of the Intelligentsia* argued that the intelligentsia, cutting across class lines, helps to unite and integrate society by creating the spiritual essentials of social life. The present crisis in the " spiritualization function " of the intelligentsia results, in part, from the unsatisfactory educational systems in all countries.

The most definite attempt to develop a " sociology of education " was made in Poland under the leadership of Florian Znaniecki, who is interested in creating a science which will deal with the cultural aspects of education, and would be separated from applied sociology.

Conclusion. What is the future of the European social sciences and education? Clearly, the social sciences are closely associated with the social structures within which the scientist lives and works, and particularly with the educational system. This " relevance to social structure " does not mean, however, that the validity of science derives from its correspondence with the educational aims of any political or economic group. Science is not a political matter, nor can it function effectively, in the long run, when subjected to totalitarian dogmas. The continued existence of the social sciences depends upon the survival of societies with a sufficient measure of free thought and free speech.

" We cannot remain free from the biases of lore if we do not foster a bias in favor of science. . . . Only when and if we transcend the relative, only when and if we uproot . . . the seeds of limited and partial logics, the entangling biases of nation and class, and the cherished illusions by which we have tried and failed to live with our fellows, can we find sociological theories valid for all men as men." [55]

REFERENCES

¹ Harold J. Laski, *Authority in the Modern State*, New Haven: Yale Univ. Press, 1918.

² G. D. H. Cole, *Self-Government in Industry*, London: Bell, 1919. A brief description of this type of political thought can be found in Paul Ward, *A Short History of Political Thinking*, Chapel Hill: Univ. of North Carolina Press, 1939, pp. 101–105.

³ Hugo Krabbe, *Modern Idea of the State*, New York: Appleton-Century, 1922, trans. by G. H. Sabine and W. J. Shepard.

⁴ George Catlin, *The Story of Political Philosophers*, New York: McGraw-Hill, 1939. These theories of the state are to be found in Laski, *Democracy in Crisis*, Chapel Hill: Univ. of North Carolina Press, 1933, *The State in Theory and Practice*, New York: Viking Press, 1934, and Strachey, *The Nature of the Capitalistic Crisis*, New York: Covici-Friede, 1935.

⁵ Alfredo Rocco, *The Political Doctrine of Fascism* (*International Conciliation Bulletin*, No. 223), New York, 1926, and Giovanni Gentile, " The Philosophical Basis of Fascism," *Foreign Affairs*, 1928, VI: 290–304.

⁶ Werner Sombart, *A New Social Philosophy*, Princeton, N. J.: Princeton Univ. Press, 1937.

⁷ R. N. MacIver, *The Modern State*, Oxford: Clarendon Press, 1926.

⁸ For an excellent discussion of economics as a deductive science, see J. N. Keynes, *Scope and Method of Political Economy*, New York: Macmillan, 1930.

⁹ Joan Robinson, *Economics of Imperfect Competition*, London: Macmillan, 1933. See J. R. Hicks, " Annual Survey of Economic Theory: The Theory of Monopoly," in *Econometrica*, Menasha, Wis., 1935, III: 1–20.

¹⁰ A. C. Pigou, *Economics of Welfare*, London: Macmillan, fourth edition, 1932.

¹¹ Werner Sombart, *Der moderne Kapitalismus*, Munich: Duncker and Humblot.

¹² See Erich Roll, *Spotlight on Germany*, London: Faber and Faber, 1933, pp. 206–213.

¹³ Howard Becker, " Historical Sociology," in H. E. Barnes, Howard Becker, and Frances Becker, eds., 1940, *Contemporary Social Theory*, New York: Appleton-Century, pp. 510–513.

¹⁴ *Ibid.*, pp. 500–501.

¹⁵ Arnold J. Toynbee, *A Study of History*, London: Oxford Univ. Press, 1934–1939; six volumes have appeared to date and others are forthcoming.

¹⁶ Ernst Troeltsch, *Der Historismus und seine Probleme*, Tübingen: Mohr, 1922.

¹⁷ The best discussions of Max Weber's method are found in Theodore Abel, *Systematic Sociology in Germany*, New York: Columbia Univ. Press, 1929, pp. 140–156, and Talcott Parsons, *The Structure of Social Action*, New York: McGraw-Hill, 1937. A good elementary description is L. J. Bennion, *Max Weber's Methodology*, Paris: Les Press Modernes, 1931.

¹⁸ L. T. Hobhouse, *Social Evolution and Political Theory*, New York: Columbia Univ. Press, 1922; Gustav Schmoller, *Grundriss der allgemeinen Volkswirtschaftslehre*, Leipzig: Duncker und Humblot, 1900; Georg von Below, *Probleme der Wirtschaftsgeschichte*, Tübingen: Mohr, 1920.

¹⁹ Oswald Spengler, *The Decline of the West*, New York: Knopf, 1939.

²⁰ This section on systematic sociology is based largely on the materials dealing with German sociology in Barnes and Becker, *Social Thought from Lore to Science*, Boston: Heath, 1938, pp. 878–933.

²¹ Ferdinand Tönnies, *Fundamental Concepts of Sociology*, trans. by C. P. Loomis, New York: American Book Co., 1940.

²² The best work on Simmel in English is N. J. Spykman, *The Social Theory of Georg Simmel*, Chicago: Univ. of Chicago Press, 1925.

²³ Barnes and Becker, *op. cit.*, pp. 915–920. Wiese's chief work is the *System der Allgemeinen Soziologie*, 1933. This work, in essentials, has been presented by Howard Becker, *Systematic Sociology on the Basis of the Beziehungslehre and Gebildelehre of Leopold von Wiese*, New York: Wiley, 1932.

24 Wiese has also taken over to some extent Weber's belief that the scientist has no right to make judgments, since ultimate decisions as to what is right and wrong are arbitrary: i.e., they cannot be made on the basis of reason alone. One still can find such judgments, however, in Wiese's writings.

25 Studies in crowd psychology have been made by Wiese, Edward Fueter, Georg Sieber, Gerhard Colm, Wilhelm Vleugels, and Gerhard Lehmann. Willy Latten and Willy Gierlichs have studied the sociology of locality patterns.

26 P. Endt, *Sociologie*, 1931.

27 Barnes and Becker, *op. cit.*, p. 1097.

28 Gaston Richard, *L'Evolution des moeurs*, Paris: G. Doin, 1925.

29 Morris Ginsberg, "Recent Tendencies in Sociology," *Economica*, February, 1933, pp. 21–39.

30 For a more detailed discussion of the writers mentioned in this section see Barnes and Becker, *op. cit.*, pp. 829–844, 848–850, 864, 921–927, and H. Otto Dalke, "The Sociology of Knowledge," in Barnes, Becker, and Becker, eds., *Contemporary Social Theory*, pp. 64–89.

31 For further consideration of Durkheim see Talcott Parsons, *The Structure of Social Action*, New York: McGraw-Hill, 1937.

32 Maurice Halbwachs, *Les Cadres sociaux de la memoire*, Paris: F. Alcan, 1925.

33 Marcel Granet, *Chinese Civilization*, New York: Knopf, 1930.

34 Jane E. Harrison, *Themis*, Cambridge: Cambridge Univ. Press, second edition, 1927.

35 Lévy-Bruhl has written five books on primitive mentality: *Les Fonctions mentales dans les sociétés primitives*, Paris: Alcan, 1923; *La Mentalité primitive*, Oxford: Clarendon Press, 1925; *L'Âme primitive*, 1927; *Les Surnaturel et la nature dans le mentalité primitive*, 1931; and *La Mythologie primitive*, 1935.

36 Max Scheler, *Die Formen des Wissens und die Bildung*, Bonn: Friedrich Cohen, 1925; *Die Wissenformen und die Gesellschaft*, Leipzig: Der Neue-Geist Verlag, 1926; "The Future of Man," trans. by Howard Becker, in *The Monthly Criterion*, London, February, 1928; *Die Stellung des Menschen im Kosmos*, Darmstadt: Otto Reichl Verlag, 1928; *Mensch und Geschichte*, Zürich: Verlag der Neuen Schweizer Rundschau, 1929.

37 Karl Mannheim, *Ideology and Utopia*, trans. by L. Wirth and E. Shils, New York: Harcourt, Brace, 1936.

38 Alexander Goldenweiser discusses the psychoanalytic schools in "Some Contributions of Psychoanalysis to the Interpretation of Social Facts," in Barnes, Becker, and Becker, eds., *Contemporary Social Theory*, pp. 391–429.

39 Morris Ginsberg, *Psychology of Society*, London, 1921.

40 Charles Blondel, *La Conscience morbide, essai de psychopathologie generale*, 1913. Also, *Introduction à la psychologie collective*, 1928.

41 Max Scheler, *Wesen und Formen der Sympathie*, Bonn: F. Cohen, 1926.

42 Kurt Lewin, *A Dynamic Theory of Personality*, New York: McGraw-Hill, 1935, and *Principles of Topological Psychology*, New York: McGraw-Hill, 1936.

43 Cf. Freud, *New Introductory Lectures on Psychoanalysis*, New York: Norton, 1933, and W. Healy, A. Bronner, and A. Bowers, *The Structure and Meaning of Psychoanalysis*, New York: Knopf, 1930.

44 See Otto Rank, *Art and Artist: Creative Urge and Personality Development*, New York: Knopf, 1932.

45 A review of the development of social statistics is given in George Lundberg, "Statistics in Modern Social Thought," in Barnes, Becker, and Becker, eds., *op. cit.*, pp. 110–141. See also Helen M. Walker, *Studies in the History of Statistical Method*, Baltimore: Williams and Wilkins, 1929.

46 This conclusion is drawn by Gini in an article on Italian statistics. C. Gini, "Contributions of Italy to Modern Statistical Methods," *Journal of the Royal Statistical Society*, July, 1926, pp. 703–724.

47 George H. Knibbs, *The Shadow of the World's Future*, London: Benn, 1928.

48 C. Gini and others, *Population Lectures on the Harris Foundation*, Chicago: Univ. of Chicago Press, 1930.

[49] Joseph S. Roucek, "Concepts of Education in Czechoslovakia," *Review of Educational Research*, October, 1939, IX: 377–380.

[50] Roucek, *ibid.*, p. 379.

[51] Herbert Freudenthal, *Die deutsche Volkschule*, Langensalza: Julius Beltz, 1938.

[52] Walter M. Kotschnig, "Educational Changes in Germany, 1936–1939," *Review of Educational Research*, October, 1939, IX: 372–376.

[53] Richard Müller-Freienfels, *Kindheit und Jugend*, Leipzig: Quelle and Meyer, 1937.

[54] For a brief discussion of educational sociology see Joseph S. Roucek, "Trends in Educational Sociology Abroad," *The Educational Forum*, May, 1939, III: 488–494, and Roucek, "Some Contributions of Sociology to Education," ch. 22, in Barnes, Becker, and Becker, eds., *Contemporary Social Theory*, pp. 793–833.

[55] Barnes and Becker, *op. cit.*, pp. 1177–1178.

SELECTED BIBLIOGRAPHY

Barnes, H. E. and Becker, Howard, *Social Thought from Lore to Science*, 2 vols., Boston: Heath, 1938.

Barnes, H. E., Becker, Howard and Becker, Frances Bennett, *Contemporary Social Theory*, New York: Appleton-Century, 1940.

Catlin, George, *The Story of the Political Philosophers*, New York: Whittlesey House, 1939, pp. 649–744.

Healy, W., Bronner, A. and Bowers, A., *The Structure and Meaning of Psychoanalysis*, New York: Knopf, 1930.

Heimann, Edward, "Literature on the Theory of a Socialist Economy," *Social Research*, 1939, VI: 88–113. This article covers some writers who were not considered in this chapter.

Hicks, J. R., "Annual Survey of Economic Theory: The Theory of Monopoly," *Econometrica*, 1935, III: 1–20. A good article, but requires some familiarity with economic theory.

Homan, Paul T., *Contemporary Economic Thought*, New York: Harper, 1928.

Lowie, Robert E., *History of Ethnological Theory*, New York: Farrar and Rinehart, 1937.

Rice, Stuart A., ed., *Methods in Social Science*, Chicago: Univ. of Chicago Press, 1931.

Seligman, Edwin R. A., Editor-in-Chief, *Encyclopedia of the Social Sciences*, New York: Macmillan, 1934. See especially the sections on economics, political science, anthropology, and sociology.

Spahr, Margaret, *Readings in Recent Political Philosophy*, New York: Macmillan, 1935, pp. 516–701.

Spann, Othmar, *The History of Economics*, trans. by Eden and Cedar Paul, New York: Norton, 1930.

Suranyi-Unger, Theo, *Economics in the Twentieth Century*, trans. by Noel D. Moulton, New York: Norton, 1931.

Ward, Paul W., *A Short History of Political Thinking*, Chapel Hill: Univ. of North Carolina Press, 1939, pp. 99–117.

CHAPTER XXXII

Europe in World Affairs

The Significance of the First World War. The end of the First World War closed a chapter in the history of Europe and in the history of mankind. It brought to the European continent the realization, although necessarily imperfect, of all the noblest dreams and aspirations of the nineteenth century. The great process of the spiritual and social liberation of peoples and individuals, of their growth to autonomy and maturity, which had started in the eighteenth century and had been anticipated in its promise of full realization in the middle of the following century, in 1848, seemed now consummated. At the beginning of the nineteenth century, at the Congress of Vienna, the forces of reaction had tried to erect a dam against the two great forces which were to dominate the nineteenth century, against liberalism and national self-determination, to which a few decades later a third movement, Socialism with its demand for the emancipation of the fourth estate and for social reform, was added. Now, at the end of the First World War and as its result, the forces of liberalism, national self-determination, and Socialism seemed triumphant in Europe. The great conservative empires of central and eastern Europe crumbled, democratic republics on the basis of national self-determination took their place. Suffrage became everywhere general, and included workers and women; social reforms were introduced in all countries; Socialist parties came into power for the first time. This spectacular democratization of Europe in the wake of the First World War overshadowed another and perhaps more fundamental result of the war: the change of the position of Europe in world affairs.

Role of Europe in World History. Until the First World War, Europe had been, politically, economically, and culturally, the dominant and decisive factor in world politics. Its influence had grown during the nineteenth century, both in extent and in scope. On an unprecedented scale, tens of millions from all parts of Europe migrated across the oceans and populated vast territories in the New World and in the South Seas.[1] The dark continent of Africa was opened up by European explorers, mapped and divided up among European powers. The Far East, secluded until then in its own mysterious and ancient civilizations, was brought into the comity of nations. The dynamic economic system of Europe, increasing its productive capacity by leaps and bounds with each new discovery

---

This chapter by Hans Kohn, Sydenham Clark Parsons Professor of History, Smith College.

and invention, demanded ever larger dependencies which had to supply its ever-growing needs for industrial raw materials and for foodstuff, and to serve as markets for the ever-growing flow of its manufactured goods.

During that period, European history was world history, European affairs were world affairs. All recognized great powers were European powers. European civilization, not only in its material and economic aspects, was on the way to become the universal civilization of mankind. This European or modern civilization had originated in the seventeenth and eighteenth centuries in northwestern Europe, especially in England, France, and the Netherlands. It was based upon the belief in man's perfectibility and in human progress. Man was regarded as a rational being who had the right and the ability to subject existing institutions and traditions to the scrutiny of his mind, to inquire into causes and consequences of social relations, and to change existing conditions for the furtherance of the common weal. A new emphasis upon the equality of all men before the law and of equal opportunities for all, upon the dignity of each individual and upon his liberty to think and to speak according to his own conscience, upon a common destiny for mankind, had increased the self-reliance and the spirit of activism of the individual. This new attitude toward life expressed itself in the writings of Milton and Locke, of Voltaire and Condorcet. It was the foundation of the Bill of Rights and of the Declaration of the Rights of the Man and of the Citizen. In its name the people claimed and received the right to participate in legislation; government by laws replaced government by men; arbitrariness and inequalities before the law were abolished.

During the nineteenth century this new evaluation of man and of his place in society spread, in spite of much resistance, from western Europe to central and eastern Europe. At the beginning of the twentieth century it was accepted even beyond the boundaries of the European races. Revolutions in China, Persia, and Turkey destroyed the ancient theocratic monarchies with their Oriental despotism and tried to introduce modern constitutional reforms. Japan accepted, although haltingly, the Western outlook of government and of individual rights. Throughout Asia, even in Africa, the non-European peoples demanded liberties and national self-determination, after the example and under the influence of nineteenth-century Europe. This whole era of the growth of liberal institutions all over the world was under the influence of Anglo-Saxon traditions of representative government and individual rights. Progressive statesmen and thinkers in the eighteenth and nineteenth centuries looked to British institutions as a guidance and a norm; the industrial and maritime leadership of the British went hand in hand with the spread of Anglo-Saxon ideals.[2]

The Function of Imperialism. European imperialism in the second half of the nineteenth century fulfilled not only an economic task on behalf of the European nations, it fulfilled also a most important educational mission in bringing to the non-European populations the fundamental message of liberty and equality underlying Western civilization. Sometimes intentionally, more often as an unsought but unavoidable by-product of its impact, British imperialism carried with it the liberal attitude and the message of liberty embodied in the tradition of all the centuries from the Magna Charta to Gladstone.[3] From the example set by individual Englishmen and from the reading of English texts, a new feeling of individual dignity, a new appreciation of civic and personal liberty, a new sense of social responsibility began to change the thought and feeling of the educated classes of the native populations, and to imbue them with new ideals and aspirations.[4] The message of modern civilization, as developed in the Anglo-Saxon and French revolutions, has from the beginning been universal in its scope, destined on principle for all classes and all races, and therefore carrying a powerful appeal, to all those who still were excluded from its full benefits, to claim their equal share. Thus European domination, as long as it rested on liberal foundations, carried with it the seeds of its own gradual destruction, replacing, at least in theory, domination and exploitation by trusteeship and partnership.

The wave of democratization, of a new feeling of social responsibility, and of rising demands of the masses, brought about by the First World War, did not remain confined to Europe. It produced even greater changes among the non-European peoples. The masses in Egypt and in Turkey, in India and in China, awakened for the first time from their age-old lethargy, from the narrow bounds of their traditionalism, and under the leadership of men like Saad Zaghlul in Egypt, Mustafa Kemal in Turkey, Mohandas Gandhi in India and Sun Yat-Sen in China organized themselves for political action and reforms. As a result of the new activity, of this revolt of the East, the political and economic domination of Europe was shaken off in the Near and Far East. The undisputed hold of Europe over Asia and Africa began to crumble. Even more important than the struggle for political independence was the effort of the non-European countries for a gradual modernization of their economic and social life, so as to put them on a footing of equality with the European countries. The four years of the First World War had broken the flow of economic goods between Europe and the non-European continents; many of the non-European countries had started a process of industrialization to make themselves economically independent of Europe and to retain the gains derived from manufacturing raw materials for their own national economy. This process of a transformation of backward agrarian countries into modern industrialized nations went ahead, with great differences in speed and energy, in the vast and semi-Oriental regions of the Soviet Union [5] as well as in Turkey, in China as well as in Latin America. This beginning of the economic reorganization of the world destroyed the equilibrium between highly industrialized and mainly agricultural countries, as it had developed in the late nineteenth century, a system which had benefited the European countries which possessed large industrial plants, a trained stock of skilled workers, and sufficient reserves of capital for investment abroad.

World Powers: Old and New. Of the six great European powers which had made history before the First World War, only five remained; but most of them were far surpassed in strength and importance, in man power and resources, by the two new great powers that the war, in which they had participated, brought to the fore: the United States and Japan. Both had profited by the war in their military, diplomatic, and above all economic strength. The United States, a debtor nation before the World War, had become the leading creditor nation; the financial center of the world had shifted from London to New York; the United States, whose navy had occupied only the fifth position in the world, built a fleet second to none and equal in strength to the British fleet; [6] in the councils of the nations, the voice of the United States could speak with exceptional authority. From a continental power the United States has grown into a world power. Even more spectacular was the rise of the small island kingdom of Japan at the extreme limit of Asia into a great military and economic empire, claiming the hegemony over the whole Far East and the western Pacific.[7] The emergence of the United States and Japan as world powers gave a new significance to the Pacific area, which until then had been of little importance compared with the Atlantic Ocean or the Mediterranean.

Effect of Technological Developments. Thus the First World War broadened the area of world political decisions. The economic relations of the different countries and continents became more and more complex; with the rising standard of living of the masses all over the earth and with the greater intensification of production, the economic interdependence of all peoples grew to an unprecedented stage. At the same time new means of communication, unknown in the nineteenth century, changed all traditional concepts of time and space even more strikingly than railroads and telegraph had done one hundred years ago. Railroads had integrated individual nations into closely knit administrative and economic units; the telegraph had made the fast transmission of news possible. After the First World War, airplanes began to perform for the globe the task of close connection and fast communication which in the nineteenth century railroads had performed for individual countries; the radio broadcast news and views with an immediacy and a width of territory covered infinitely surpassing all performances of the printing press and the telegraph.

Whereas the discoveries of the fifteenth and sixteenth centuries had widened the earth to such an extent that it gave to contemporary mankind the feeling of an infinite and unending adventure, whereas even in the nineteenth century frontiers remained open for expansion, the period after the First World War witnessed a fast shrinking of the earth as the result of the new inventions. The globe became finite and completely mapped out, formerly unknown deserts were easily crossed by motorcar and plane, man conquered the mysteries of the air, thus realizing one of the oldest and most daring dreams of mankind — all the frontiers for expansion were closed. This unprecedented and fantastic situation required as its necessary corollary the establishment of some new form of world order, to maintain peace among the nations and continents, and to assure to all peoples freedom and equality.

The Need for a New World Order. The outcome of the First World War had established the foundations on which a world society based upon democracy and peace could be built. The victory of the three great Western democracies over the conservative monarchies of central Europe; the great promise which at that time many saw in the Russian Revolution; the introduction of democratic constitutions to almost all countries in central and eastern Europe and even to Asia; the rejuvenation of life and the rise of freedom in long oppressed and stagnant nations like Mexico and Ireland, Spain and Egypt, Poland and Bohemia, Turkey and China: all that pointed in the direction of the fulfilment of the hopes which had animated many people in the Western democracies in 1918 — for a lasting peace and for a secure growth and spread of democratic institutions. The League of Nations, the most important contribution which the United States under the leadership of Woodrow Wilson has made in the twentieth century to the development of political thought (the idea had first been suggested and discussed among English liberal statesmen and writers, but had found its most powerful spokesman in the President of the United States), seemed destined to become the instrument of a " universal dominion of right by such a concert of free peoples as shall bring peace and safety to all nations and make the world itself at last free." It was upon the insistence of Woodrow Wilson that the Covenant of the League of Nations became not only an integral part of all the peace treaties concluded after the World War, but occupied the place of honor at their beginning, thus turning them into a great promise for the future which might compensate for their shortcomings.

Woodrow Wilson expressed in many addresses in 1918 and 1919 his conviction that in this closely knit world of the twentieth century the peace of all countries, including the United States, depended upon the establishment of a League of Nations which would be able to protect all countries, weak and strong, against aggression, by a system of collective security.[8] He made it clear that the two great aims animating the soldiers on the Allied side in 1918, to end wars and to make the world safe for democracy, could be secured only through the creation of a firm international order and through the close cooperation of the democratic nations. One of the most clear-sighted political thinkers and pacifists of our time, Norman Angell, put forward as early as 1917, in a book called *The Political Conditions of Allied Success*, the necessary conditions for the survival of democracy after a victory of the Western powers:

The survival of the Western democracies, in so far as that is a matter of the effective use of their force, depends upon their capacity to use it as a unit, during the War and after. That unity we have not attained, even for the purposes of the war, because we have refused to recognize its necessary conditions — a kind and degree of democratic internationalism to which current political ideas and feelings are hostile; an internationalism which is not necessary to the enemy, but is to us. He can in some measure ignore it. We cannot. His unity, in so far as it rests upon moral factors, can be based upon the old national conceptions; our unity depends upon a revision of them, an enlargement into an internationalism.

The greatest obstacles to a permanent association of nations by which the security of each shall be made to rest upon the strength of the whole are disbelief in its feasibility and our subjection to the traditions of national sovereignty and independence. Were it generally believed in, and desired, it would be not only feasible but inevitable. Return to the old relationships after the War will sooner or later doom the democratic nations, however powerful each may be individually, to subjugation in detail by a group, inferior in power but superior in material unity — a unity which autocracy achieved at the cost of freedom and human worth.

The hopes for the establishment of an international order to end wars and to make the world safe for democracy did not come true; the fault was not in the peace treaties, but in the fact that the nations refused to join the League of Nations or to work it in earnest.[9] For this failure the people themselves, not the governments, were primarily responsible; they had not yet understood that a system of collective security was absolutely necessary to them if they really wished to maintain democracy at home and peace abroad. They sought security and happiness in the old and by now obsolete notions of national sovereignty, they withdrew into isolation and took refuge in wishful thinking and were disillusioned when their hopes were not fulfilled, not realizing that they themselves had refused to establish the necessary conditions.

The Liberal Decade of World Politics. The period between the First and the Second World Wars can be divided roughly into two parts: the first, comprising the 'twenties, seemed an age of mingled confusion and consolidation; the second, comprising the fourth decade of our century, brought the consequences of the lack of cooperation among the democratic nations into the open, and resulted in new wars and in violent assaults upon the democratic form of life.

The Role of Japan. The hopes of the 'twenties were best expressed in the progressive liberalization of the British Empire and in the Washington Conference of 1921–1922 on the limitation of naval armament. At Washington in 1922, Great Britain, who before the World War had insisted upon a navy equal in strength to the combination of any other two navies, agreed to naval equality with the United States and thus renounced the British domination of the seas which had lasted for more than three centuries. Japan's new position as a great power was recognized in her right to build the third largest fleet, strong enough to control the seas around her islands in the western Pacific, but not powerful enough to menace the eastern Pacific, as long as the British fleet controlled the Atlantic Ocean and thus allowed the American fleet to concentrate on the protection of the Western Hemisphere in the Pacific. At the same time Great Britain, to stress her amity for the United States, renounced her treaty of friendship with Japan. This treaty, originally concluded in 1902 for a duration of ten years and renewed in 1912, had helped Japan to defeat Russia in the war of 1904. During the First World War Japan had attempted to gain a strong position in China and to turn the vast empire into a Japanese protectorate. This ambition was, at least temporarily, checked at Washington. With regard to China the Washington Conference laid down the principle of strict maintenance of China's territorial integrity and national sovereignty, and thus promised the Chinese people security and freedom in their process of adaptation to the conditions of the modern world.

The New British Empire. The Chinese struggle for emancipation and modernization [10] was only one example of a world-wide effort on the part of all the non-European and " backward " or " colonial " peoples to acquire the foundations of modern civilization and thus to make their independence from European control as secure as possible. This process of " decolonization," as it has been sometimes called, was helped by the attitude of the British government, which gradually promoted the growing liberties of the peoples under its sphere of influence. The Statute of Westminster in 1926 sanctioned the complete independence of the self-governing dominions. The former colonies became full sovereign nations, not only in their domestic affairs, but also in their foreign relations. No fixed and visible sign of interdependence remained among the members of this British Commonwealth of Nations except the nominal allegiance to the monarch. Britain's foreign policy was no longer binding upon the dominions. If Great Britain were involved in war, the dominions could decide of their free will whether and how far they wished to support the mother country.

This far-reaching reconstruction of the relations between Great Britain and her dependencies in the spirit of democratic progress and growing liberty was applied in many directions. The long-standing and painful Irish question was solved by granting Ireland dominion status. Egypt, which had been occupied by British forces in 1882, was given complete independence. India, the largest and most important British colony, received a constitution which assured the participation of elected representatives of the Indian people in legislation and transferred some branches of the administration to the control of Indians, responsible to the elected assemblies. This constitution was proclaimed as a step towards India's attainment of full dominion status and of equal partnership in the British Commonwealth of Nations.[11]

The "Softening" of Democracy. This growth in liberty and peaceful adjustment which expressed itself also in the slow gathering strength of and confidence in the League of Nations, and in the spirit of the Locarno agreement, led in the great democratic nations, Great Britain, the United States and France, to a neglect of their armaments. Although disarmament was theoretically not accepted, a far-reaching demilitarization was carried through, psychologically even more than in a military sense. The democracies, who had refused to lay the firm foundations of an international democratic order, were not animated by a determined resolution of defending it; the masses had no understanding of the necessity of collective security; they lived in the illusion that the spirit of dominion and conquest was dying out everywhere in the twentieth century, and that all men had begun to realize that " wars do not pay." Thus they remained unaware of the dangers of the Fascist way of thought and life which denied the foundations of democracy and rejected the faith underlying the Anglo-Saxon and French revolutions of the seventeenth and eighteenth centuries, that all men are created equal and that they are endowed with certain inalienable rights, among which are life, liberty, and the pursuit of happiness. This new way of life derided the idea of the possibility or desirability of peace, and glorified war and the martial spirit. It proclaimed openly the inequality of men and nations and the right of the stronger to dominate and ruthlessly exploit the weaker. Democracy was regarded as decadent, the people under its influence were judged to be softened by their desire for comfort and security, considerations for human rights and individual liberty were scorned.

This disregard for democracy and for all efforts at peaceful solutions of international disputes was deepened by the denial of all generally applicable standards of truth and justice. The " new way " of life regarded itself as destined to become the general way of life in the twentieth century and to destroy everywhere the achievements of the Anglo-Saxon and French revolutions. To that end it had to make the world safe for aggression. It succeeded as a result of its own determination and purposefulness, and of the isolationism and illusions of the democracies.

The Fascist Decade of World Politics. The first aggressive move of Fascism was taken in the Far East by Japan in 1931. Different from China, where the family and not the nation has always formed the center of loyalty and where the scholar and not the soldier has been honored as the example and model for civic life, Japan has always cultivated and glorified the military virtues of a feudal warrior caste.[12] In Japan all individuals have been closely welded together in an absolute devotion to the nation represented by the Emperor, whose divine origin was accepted by all his subjects as the fundamental article of faith.

In this exaltation of military discipline and virtues as the model way of life, and the concentration of all moral energies upon the regimentation of its citizenry, Japan resembled Prussia. As Prussia had done after her crushing defeat by the revolutionary armies of Napoleon in 1806, so Japan, faced in 1868 by the superior strength of the Western world, accepted in a most methodical and efficient manner the technique of modern rational and industrial civilization, and applied it to army and education, in science, organization, and administration. But she adapted it, as Prussia had done, for the purpose of strengthening her own feudal pre-industrial tradition, rejecting the spirit of Western civilization with its liberalism and individualism. With the spread of democratic institutions all over the earth at the turn of the century, Japan, like Prussia, introduced gradually legal and constitutional reforms after the Western model.

Towards the end of the 'twenties, " patriotic " organizations of young Japanese officers and related elements started a drive for the integral resurrection of the ancient Japanese military spirit, for the heroic and absolute devotion of every citizen to the Emperor, and against Western, above all American, influences which were characterized as materialism, Mammonism, and soft living. These " patriotic " organizations agitated against " plutocracy " and parliamentarism, they terrorized and assassinated leading Japanese statesmen, editors, businessmen and intellectuals who tried to lead Japan on the road towards a more liberal and democratic regime. These young officers and " patriots " proclaimed the need for Japan to dominate the whole Far East and the South Seas and thus to fulfill the Imperial mission of the race. Conquest and the preparation for it appeared to them the most efficient way of strengthening their influence in domestic affairs and of transforming Japanese society completely according to their ideals.[13]

Japanese Aggression. As an outcome of this policy, Japan committed in September, 1931 the first act of overt aggression, which started a decade of violence and disregard for treaties and solemn promises, of lawlessness and invasion, which were finally to lead to the Second World War. The precedent set by Japan in her attack against China was faithfully followed in many later instances. Japan used an " incident " as a pretext for the occupation of Manchuria, the large and rich northern part of China which she had coveted for a long time; she declared herself offended or threatened by the alleged incapacity of the Chinese government to maintain law and order; she proclaimed herself the protector of conservative interests; she acted without any formal declaration of war, and stressed from time to time, for outside consumption, her peaceful intentions; she played upon the sentimental credulity of large circles in the democracies by stressing her " poverty " and overpopulation, forgetting about the much greater poverty and overpopulation of China; she did not annex Manchuria, but " liberated " the inhabitants of Manchuria by creating an " independent " Manchukuo which in reality was nothing but a helpless puppet in Japanese hands; finally she showed her contempt for the League of Nations and its humanitarian and equalitarian tendencies by renouncing her membership in that body which Woodrow Wilson had intended as a shield against aggression everywhere.

At that time opinion in the democratic countries was largely convinced that Japan would be satisfied with Manchuria. At the root of this belief was the erroneous conviction that Fascist imperialism of the twentieth century was the same as the liberal imperialism of the nineteenth century, and that Fascist nations wished to expand in order to gain definite and limited objectives, especially in the economic field. It was then difficult to understand that Fascist imperialism is not motivated economically, but by pre-democratic heroic ideals of power and by an irrational urge towards domination and unlimited expansion. To make that possible, Fascist nations had to act in disregard of traditional economic tenets, or, to use a famous German phrase of recent years, to prefer guns to butter, privations to comfort. They did it because they hoped to become thereby strong enough to impose their will upon vast populations, less trained in and prepared for war, and to live then as the dominating master race from the toil of the multitudes of helots. Fascist expansion does not know any limits, except those imposed upon it by superior strength; its dynamism admits of no saturation point, of no standstill. Each conquest is but a link in a plan which encircles the earth, a new strategic position to make further expansion possible.

Some people in the democratic countries viewed the Japanese move without great concern because they believed that Japan had occupied Manchuria as a point of strategic importance for a struggle with the Soviet Union. In reality, however, Japan did not turn north against Russia; similarly as Germany was to do at a later time by turning west instead of east, Japan turned south, gained in 1933 and 1935 control of North China, and started in 1937 a war for the subjugation of the whole of China. The

League of Nations was as unable or unwilling to protect China as were the powers which had concluded the Pact of Washington, of which the United States had been the sponsor and a chief signatory, and which had guaranteed the territorial integrity and independence of China. The heroic struggle which the Chinese people have waged against Japanese aggression and against the great superiority of Japan in armament and in military training, for more than four years now, has so far prevented Japan from controlling the whole of the vast Chinese territory. This has not stopped Japan from wishing to extend her empire further south into the Dutch, British, French, and other territories north and south of the Equator.

The New World Politics. The Far Eastern policy of Japan, although remote from Europe, was nevertheless of immediate importance to European politics; not only because it helped to undermine the system of collective security upon which the peace of Europe as well as that of all other continents was based, but also because Japan soon proceeded to close cooperation with the two leading Fascist powers of Europe, with Germany and Italy. Germany concluded in 1937 a treaty of friendship and cooperation with Japan. This treaty, the principal sponsor of which was Herr von Ribbentrop, then German ambassador in London and later German Foreign Minister, was broadened in 1938 into the so-called triangle which included Germany, Italy, and Japan, and which was then known as the anti-Comintern pact. Bound together by this pact, the Fascist powers followed a long-range world policy with great determination and concentrated effort. Their cooperation made itself felt in Africa as well as in the Far East, in Latin America as well as in the Mediterranean. Thus the connection of European and world politics became more intimate than ever before. The plans of Japan for the control of the Far East and of the South Seas, of Italy for the control of the Mediterranean and of northern Africa, of Spain for control of the southern Atlantic and all those lands which in the golden century of Spain had formed part of her political and cultural empire, of Germany for the control of Europe and the northern Atlantic — all these plans were coordinated into a vast effort of world politics, aiming not only at a re-distribution of power and resources, but above all at the world-wide triumph of the Fascist way of life over the democratic principles of individual liberty and human equality. In this world-wide struggle Germany, on account of her economic and military strength, assumed the leadership. By that leadership in the " re-ordering " of the world, Germany declared her task to be to restore to a Europe molded and living according to Fascist principles the decisive role in world politics.

This new turn in world politics halted the movement of decolonization which had aimed at the liberation and equality of the non-European subject peoples. The Fascist doctrine of the inequality of men and races, its glorification of ruthlessness and mastership, its derision of "sentimental humanitarianism" — all these fundamental traits of the new trend in international relations mark an attitude toward weaker, backward, or less military races which tends to re-establish the rights of conquest in their ancient and primitive forms.

The treatment meted out by Fascist Italy to the Arabs in Libya and to the Ethiopians after the conquest of their country in 1936, and by National Socialist Germany to Poles and Jews are only the first examples of this new trend of an imperialism entirely different from that which characterized the first decade after the First World War. This Fascist imperialism acts often under the cover of slogans which seem borrowed from the thought of the liberal era, but the real meaning is the very opposite of liberalism and of national self-determination. Thus the Japanese in proclaiming "Asia for the Asiatic" mean in reality Asia for the Japanese, with the complete subordination of the Asiatic peoples as serfs and tools to their self-appointed superior masters. The "New Europe" which Germany and Italy promise to the European peoples has a similar meaning.

The Coming of the Second World War. This new turn in world politics found the democratic peoples not only in a semi-demilitarized state as regards armaments, but above all completely unprepared, in their habits of thought and in their emotional reactions, to meet the challenge. The new heroic and dynamic conception of history and the world-wide character of Fascist aspirations seemed to the democratic mind so fantastic as to be unbelievable and not to be taken seriously. The people in the democracies continued to act as if they lived in the conditions of the period which had produced and witnessed the First World War; this absorption in the immediate past through which the older generation had lived, and about which the younger generation had been taught, closed their minds to a real understanding of the preparations which the Fascist nations were making for the Second World War. As the First World War had brought about a world-wide triumph of the democratic way of life, so the Second World War, for which the nations for many years prepared feverishly and with complete coordination of all their resources for its coming, was to bring the total and world-wide victory of the Fascist way of life. The democratic nations after the First World War, following a shortsighted and egoistic policy, had not been willing to maintain the new democratic order which they had helped to create. The growing complexity of life on this shrinking earth with its new, fast means of communication made the establishment of a world order imperative. The isolationism of the democracies and the breakdown of the League of Nations gave the Fascist powers the opportunity to try to establish, by their close cooperation and their readiness to sacrifice, a world order according to their own ideals of power and inequality and under their leadership.

Fascist Warfare. In the struggle which the Fascist powers started in the fourth decade of the twentieth century in their effort to establish a world-wide control, they did not observe the old rules of international relations, of warfare and of economics. War was waged by the traditional and by new military equipment which the Fascists had perfected with untiring energy, but even more by economic pressure and by an entirely new use of propaganda which exploited the love of peace and the generous impulses of the peoples which were to be brought into submission and whose will to resistance was to be broken.[14] The military, mental, and moral unpreparedness of the democracies made possible the rise of the legend of the higher efficiency and invincibility of the Fascist powers, a legend eagerly fostered by Fascist propaganda and used to disseminate terror in the hearts of its adversaries. This alleged superiority was, however, not due to any intrinsic strength of Fascism — as the British rout of the Italian armies demonstrated — but only to the slowness of the democracies to understand the situation. The example of the Chinese resistance to the far superior military equipment and organization of the powerful Japanese military machine also shows clearly what the democratic energies of an even very poorly prepared and technically backward people can accomplish. With resolute understanding and courage, and in the spirit of cooperation, the democratic way of liberty and equality may prove again its superiority over the way of authoritarianism and inequality, as it has done in the long struggle for freedom in the last three centuries.

Conclusion. In September, 1939 the war between Germany and Great Britain began. It seemed to many observers a European conflict, a struggle which was to decide the hegemony in Europe. As the war went on, the people learned to understand that it was not only a conflict of two powers, but of two opposite and completely incompatible ways of life and scales of human values. Still, however, the results of this struggle seemed confined to Europe. But soon it became apparent that at the present stage of history no dividing line can be drawn any longer between European and world politics. The outcome of the struggle between Great Britain and Germany will not decide the fate of Europe alone; its immediate effects will be felt all over Africa and Asia, in the South Seas, and throughout the Western Hemisphere from Labrador to Patagonia. The future destiny of all non-European peoples will be determined as much by the events in Europe as events in Asia or America have today a determining influence upon the life and fate of European peoples. At the present stage of history, European and world politics are indissolubly linked in a community of life and destiny from which no part of mankind is excluded or can keep itself separated.

REFERENCES

1 *The Encyclopaedia of the Social Sciences*, Vol. 10, p. 433 ff., says of the modern phenomenon of migrations: " Modern mass migration, a voluntary movement of free wage earners, tenants and small farmers, began in Great Britain with the industrial revolution in the second half of the eighteenth century and lasted until the World War. The early part of this period, preceding 1850, must be distinguished from the later part, which was marked by revolutionary changes in transportation and by the rapid technical development of large scale industry. . . . Intercontinental migration between 1800 and 1924 totaled approximately 60,000,000. . . . Between 1800 and 1930 the population of Europe rose from 180,000,000 to 480,000,000 and the number of persons of European stock in the oversea countries reached 160,000,000."

2 On the Anglo-Saxon foundations of modern civilization, see George Catlin's *Anglo-Saxony and Its Tradition*, New York: Macmillan, 1939; on France's contribution to the common Western civilization, see D. W. Brogan's *France under the Republic*, New York: Harper, 1940, the best introduction to the modern history of France. The latest brief but excellent book on the foundations of American civilization is Ralph Barton Perry's *Shall Not Perish from the Earth*, New York: Vanguard Press, 1940.

3 On Gladstone as the representative figure of English liberalism in the nineteenth century, see Paul Knaplund's *Gladstone and Britain's Imperial Policy*, London: Allen and Unwin, 1927, and J. L. Hammond's *Gladstone and the Irish Nation*, New York: Longmans Green, 1938.

4 The most important steps in this process of the westernization of the Orient was Lord Macaulay's famous memorandum of 1835, in which he proposed to make English the language of instruction for Indian education and thus to open to the Indians full access to the British tradition of liberty. He foresaw the consequences when he wrote in his memorandum, " It may be that the public mind of India may so expand under our system that it may outgrow that system, and our subjects having been brought up under good government may develop a capacity for better government, that having been instructed in European learning, they may crave for European institutions. I know not whether such a day will ever come, but if it does come it will be the proudest day in the annals of England." Fifty years later, in 1885, the Indian National Congress was founded, under the influence and upon the suggestions of liberal Englishmen. At its first meeting the president acclaimed British rule for having brought to India " the inestimable blessing of Western education. But . . . the more progress the people made in education and material prosperity, the greater would be their insight into political matters and the keener their desire for political advancement." These predictions were fulfilled. The Indian National Congress, the first political and representative body to arise in any Asiatic country, became the mouthpiece for the political demands of the Indian people. See on this development Hans Kohn, *A History of Nationalism in the East*, London: Routledge, 1929, chs. 2, 5, 11 and 12.

5 This tendency was expressed in the resolution of the sixteenth congress of the Communist Party of the Soviet Union in July, 1930, which read: " The Soviet Union is changing with enormous speed from a backward country, an agrarian country, into a progressive country of large scale industry." See on the Russian Revolution Hans Kohn, *Revolutions and Dictatorships*, Cambridge, Mass.: Harvard Univ. Press, 1939, ch. 4, and Hans Kohn, *Nationalism in the Soviet Union*, London: Routledge, 1933.

6 According to *A Statesman's Yearbook* for 1930, the total tonnage of steamers and motor ships of the leading countries for June, 1914 and for June, 1929 were as follows:

Country	June, *1914*	June, *1929*
Great Britain	18,892,000	20,046,000
Germany	5,185,000	4,058,000
U.S.A. (seagoing)	2,027,000	11,036,000
Norway	1,957,000	3,218,000
France	1,922,000	3,303,000
Japan	1,708,000	4,187,000
Italy	1,480,000	3,215,000
Netherlands	1,472,000	2,932,000

By far the greatest increase was to be noticed in the fleets of the United States and Japan.

⁷ On the rise of Japan, see E. Herbert Norman, *Japan's Emergence as a Modern State*, New York: Institute of Pacific Relations, 1940; Mary A. Nourse, *Kodo: the Way of the Emperor*, Indianapolis: Bobbs Merrill, 1939; A. E. Hindmarsh, *The Bases of Japanese Foreign Policy*, Cambridge, Mass.: Harvard Univ. Press, 1936.

⁸ It is worthwhile to reread at the present moment the addresses which President Wilson made on his Western tour in September, 1919. There are several easily accessible collections of *The Messages and Papers of Woodrow Wilson.*

⁹ On the attitude of the United States toward the League of Nations in the early years, see the two books by Denna Frank Fleming, *The United States and the League of Nations, 1918–1920*, New York: Putnam, 1932, and *The United States and World Organization, 1920–1933*, New York: Columbia Univ. Press, 1933. The latest best books on the League of Nations are William Rappard, *The Quest for Peace*, Cambridge, Mass.: Harvard Univ. Press, 1940, and Viscount Cecil, *A Great Experiment*, New York: Oxford Univ. Press, 1941.

¹⁰ On China, see Lin Yu-tang, *My Country and My People*, New York: John Day, 1935; Arthur N. Holcombe, *The Chinese Revolution*, Cambridge, Mass.: Harvard Univ. Press, 1930; George N. Steiger, *China and the Occident*, New Haven: Yale Univ. Press, 1927; Nathaniel Peffer, *China, the Collapse of a Civilization*, New York: John Day, 1930; H. F. MacNair, *China in Revolution*, Chicago: Chicago Univ. Press, 1931.

¹¹ On the new developments in the British Empire, see William Y. Elliott, *The New British Empire*, New York: McGraw-Hill, 1932, and Albert Viton, *Great Britain: An Empire in Transition*, New York: John Day, 1940.

¹² On the differences between Japan and China, see Harley Farnsworth MacNair, *The Real Conflict between China and Japan*, Chicago: Univ. of Chicago Press, 1938, an analysis of the opposing ideologies and mentalities of the two Far Eastern nations.

¹³ See on the recent developments in Japan Westel W. Willoughby, *Japan's Case Examined*, Baltimore: Johns Hopkins Press, 1940, A. Morgan Young, *Imperial Japan, 1926–1938*, New York: William Morrow, 1938, and Edgar Snow, *The Battle for Asia*, New York: Random House, 1941.

¹⁴ On the use of propaganda as a new weapon in this war, see Edmond Taylor, *The Strategy of Terror*, Boston: Houghton Mifflin, 1940, and Hermann Rauschning, *The Voice of Destruction*, New York: Putnam, 1940.

SELECTED BIBLIOGRAPHY

Agar, Herbert and others, *The City of Man*, New York: Viking, 1940. The book discusses the present world chaos, its causes and its possible remedies.

Alsop, Joseph and Kintner, Robert, *American White Paper*, New York: Simon & Schuster, 1939. A journalistic explanation of the recent foreign policy of the United States.

Cobban, Alfred, *Dictatorship in History and Theory*, New York: Scribner, 1939. A scholarly, readable history of dictatorship from traditional monarchy to the different forms of the modern totalitarian state.

Earle, Edward Meade, *Against this Torrent*, Princeton: Princeton Univ. Press, 1941. An excellent analysis of the world situation in 1941 by a leading American historian.

Kohn, Hans, *Western Civilization in the Near East*, New York: Columbia Univ. Press, 1936. A study of the effects of the impact of Western civilization and imperialism on the development of the countries of the Near East.

——, *Revolutions and Dictatorships*, Cambridge, Mass.: Harvard Univ. Press, 2nd ed., 1941. This book, together with its predecessor, *Force or Reason*, Harvard Univ. Press, 1938, and the later volume, *Not by Arms Alone*, Harvard Univ. Press, 1940, analyzes the historical and philosophical background and the implications of the present world-wide struggle between Fascism and democracy.

Rauschning, Hermann, *The Voice of Destruction,* New York: Putnam, 1940. One of the most revealing and important books about the world-wide aims of the National Socialist regime.

Schuman, Frederick L., *International Politics,* New York: McGraw-Hill, 3rd ed., 1941. An extremely well-written survey of international politics for the period between the two World Wars.

Staley, Eugene, *World Economy in Transition: Technology vs. Politics, Laissez Faire vs. Planning, Power vs. Welfare,* New York: Council on Foreign Relations, 1939. A penetrating analysis of the most recent world economic trends.

Stimson, Henry L., *The Far Eastern Crisis,* New York: Harper, 1936. The former Secretary of State under the Hoover administration relates the diplomatic history of Japan's move into Manchuria.

Toynbee, Arnold J., *Survey of International Affairs,* published yearly from 1924 to 1938 by the Oxford Univ. Press. A detailed, impartial, scholarly, and most reliable survey of international affairs, by the Director of Studies in the Royal Institute of International Affairs. From 1928 on, a separate volume, *Documents on International Affairs,* edited by John W. Wheeler-Bennett, was published as a supplement.

CHAPTER XXXIII

The Second World War: Act Two

The Second Year of War

The Armistice. Marshal Pétain, the aged World War hero who had succeeded Daladier as French Premier, requested a truce from the victorious Germans on June 17, 1940. The peace to which Pétain was forced to accede did not become effective until an armistice with Italy was negotiated on June 24. Terms included German occupation of all of northern France, plus the western coast — with a Nazi promise that the western coast would be evacuated after the war with England. Local French officials remained in power in the occupied zone, with the understanding that they were to cooperate with the German military governors. The French were permitted to keep only enough soldiers under arms to " maintain order " in the unoccupied territory. The new government chose Vichy in central France as its capital. The Germans occupied Paris.

To the British the swift capitulation of France was a stunning blow. Determined not to yield, they were intent on preventing the very considerable French fleet from falling into the hands of the Germans, and on July 3 attacked the French navy at Oran, Algeria, capturing or sinking five battleships, two cruisers, a plane-carrier, ten destroyers and several submarines. On July 15 the British put a blockade around French warships at Martinique, West Indies and the next day took possession of another unit of the French fleet at Alexandria, Egypt.

Thousands of civilians and soldiers fled from France rather than submit to Pétain's peace, and these General Charles de Gaulle organized into an army on English soil. De Gaulle sent agents to stir up rebellion in France's African colonies, and the governors of some of these went over to the British standard. An attempted landing at Dakar, French West Africa, on September 23 failed however.

Causes of the French Collapse. Taking advantage of France's impotence Japan forced the cession of military bases in French Indo-China, then staged a partial invasion. Meantime, at home, famine threatened a country systematically stripped of supplies by the Nazis. A new French state was formed on July 8, 1940 whose Parliament named the venerable Marshal "Chief of State" — with dictatorial powers — and voted itself out of existence. Thus died the Third Republic, born out of the travail of the

---

This chapter by Joseph S. Roucek, Associate Professor of Political Science and Sociology, Hofstra College.

disastrous Franco-Prussian War and crushed to death by the German defeat of 1940.

On October 18, France became a semi-Fascist state by setting up concentration camps for aliens and " Jews." Already the government had arrested a score of its former leaders, among them General Gamelin, Reynaud, and Blum, on charges of treason, neglect of duty and fomenting war when they knew the nation was unprepared. The arrests brought into sharp focus the charges that France's downfall was due to incompetent commanders, and lack of economic preparation for the war, particularly under the Blum regime.[1] Naturally, this was a tremendous oversimplification, since many other causes, moral, diplomatic, and military, as well as economic, must be reckoned as causes of defeat. The Vichy government in casting the blame on the former rulers of France ignored the inadequate mobilization due to economic depression and social strife as well as sabotage by the propertied classes.[2] Moreover Germany had been preparing for war since 1933 and found it easy to shift to actual war conditions; her inevitable economic and military superiority was evident.[3]

The majority of the French people had lacked sufficient faith in their government to fight for it. Many ascribe this to the patient work of Nazi " Fifth Columnists " whose effective propaganda demoralized the French " sacred union." France also failed to realize in the years of appeasement (1935–1938) that Germany was determined to overthrow the peace settlements of 1919–1920.[4] With discontent in high and low circles Communist and Nazi agents found ready listeners. The masses were basically pacifistic and listened eagerly to those who promised peace.[5] Naturally, the lack of unity was reflected in France's vacillating diplomatic policy in the years before the war.[6] The advent of the Popular Front government in 1936 had isolated the French from the English and antagonized the Conservatives, who refused to cooperate with Blum. Thus, when Daladier came to power, France had no internal solidarity. A strong leader to weld these discordant elements was required, but Daladier lacked the qualities of a great statesman.[7]

Although the Finnish debacle forced Daladier out of the Premiership, Reynaud had to keep him and his clique in the Cabinet. By the time he was able to drop Daladier it was too late.[8]

The victories of Hitler's armies can be attributed to numerous causes, and especially to the misguided pacifistic policies of Europe's democracies as well as to their suicidal appeasement. But from a more direct point of view, the German successes between 1939–1940 were attributed to the fact that Nazi Germany succeeded in establishing the superiority of the machine over the man.[9] If the decisive weapon of the First World War was the machine gun, which greatly increased the strength of the defense, the decisive weapons of the Second World War were the tank and the

airplane, which had again tipped the balance in favor of offensive warfare.[10]   The German military leaders possessed imagination and foresight.
The French General Staff clung to outdated weapons and defensive
strategy with the result that the French armies were helpless before the
superior mechanized forces of the invaders.   Deficiencies in the Anglo-
French military system were not remedied, despite the eight months' respite from September, 1939 to April, 1940.[11]   All these factors contributed
to the downfall of France.

The Battle of Britain.   The Battle of France ended in June; the Battle of
Britain began on August 8, 1940 when hundreds of German bombers
raided British towns.   A new era in human warfare was inaugurated —
the merciless aerial bombardment of peaceful cities and towns, the
slaughter of innocent noncombatants and the woeful destruction of property which in no conceivable way could be regarded as of military value.
Thus war reverted to its primeval stages, when tribes fought each other
until annihilation, and the victors razed settlements to the ground.   " Civilized warfare," a phenomenon of modern centuries, with its etiquette
and sportsmanship, was totally discarded.   Introduced by the Germans,
the challenge of " total war " was perforce taken up by the British.   The
bombing of English cities brought retaliation upon Germany and the
occupied areas.   New and heavier bombers, more deadly bombs and
torpedoes were invented.   Because of their great aerial superiority, and
because the British Isles offered a compact target, the Germans inflicted
much the greater damage.

London had its first aerial attack on August 25, Berlin on September 10,
1940.   " All-out " bombing of London began on September 7, with hundreds of German raiders coming over by night and day, causing indescribable havoc.   Life in London, as in Liverpool, Manchester, Bristol,
Birmingham, Belfast, Coventry, Plymouth — in every industrial or port
city or town — became a nightmare, as in the most ghoulish novels of
H. G. Wells.   The British were able to cope rather successfully with the
day raiders, whose presence could be easily detected; as many as 185
German planes were shot down over Britain in one day.   When day raid-
ing proved too costly, however, the Germans confined themselves largely
to night raids.   Against night raids, with the deadly bombers flying at
stratosphere altitudes, there was almost no protection.   Anti-aircraft guns
could only make lucky hits.   The bombers dropped their lethal cargoes
almost at their leisure.   The populace scurried to air-raid shelters, to
basements, and subway tubes.   Throughout the late summer and autumn
of 1940 a large part of the population of London was sleeping in unsanitary
subways.   Nights were made hideous by the screeching of sirens, zooming
of airplanes, and the rat-a-tat-tat of anti-aircraft guns.   Scores of fires
burned simultaneously.   Nothing in human history ever foreshadowed the

destruction caused by the Germans in England in the memorable summer, autumn, and winter of 1940–1941. Thousands of people were killed monthly; thousands more were mangled and scarred. But the endurance of the British was beyond the power of words to describe; the determination to see this most ghastly of ordeals through to the end became stronger as the fiendish destructiveness of the enemy increased.

From the sporadic bombardment of many areas in one night German aerial tactics changed to the concentrated attack of one city at a time. On November 14 the industrial city of Coventry was almost wiped out by several hundred Nazi bombers. Later Liverpool, Manchester, Plymouth, and London were subjected to this intensified fury. The art of warfare and the destructive ingenuity of man seemed to have reached perfection. Henceforth a new word was added to military terminology, " coventrated," meaning the utter devastation of a peaceful, slumbering metropolis by dropping several hundred thousand tons of fire bombs upon it in a few hours.

The British too participated in this savagery. Hamburg and Bremen and the French ports of Boulogne and Calais were coventrated. Berlin was repeatedly harried. But the British suffering and losses were far greater than the German. As the British air force, however, was augmented by American bombers and the increasing output of its own factories, the ruin caused by British night bombers over enemy territory was multiplied. At the end of the first nine months of full-scale aerial bombardment the property losses from this finest technique of war was beyond human estimation. A large part of London was in ruins; several provincial cities were partially annihilated. Two or perhaps three German cities were largely reduced to rubble. A few hundred thousand human beings were dead from aerial destruction. Hundreds of thousands of homes were obliterated. The record of havoc caused by the First World War was easily surpassed. Civilization in Europe had reached a nadir, and the gloomiest prophecies of pessimists had come true.

Japan's " New Order." Japan now announced the advent of a " new order " in the Far East. Its right to the Asiatic empire, Japan has repeatedly said, must neither be questioned nor interfered with, and just as repeatedly have the questions and the interferences come. In 1940 Japan coveted the Dutch East Indies and French Indo-China, although the war with China was far from ended. The biggest fly in the Japanese ointment, however, was the United States, whose fleet hovered menacingly in Pacific waters.

The traditional policy of the United States of maintaining the status quo in the Far East was given concrete form in September, 1940 by establishing a scrap iron embargo on Japan, and loaning China $25,000,000. Britain on October 8 reopened the Burma road.

Japan's "diplomatic" drive into Indo-China was highly successful, for by March, 1941 she was virtually in control of the economic and military systems of the country, thus controlling an important source of Chinese supplies, with an advantageous position for a military descent into the East Indies.[12]

Thailand, taking advantage of Vichy's plight, demanded territorial concessions in Indo-China and attacked the French forces. With the cooperation of Japan, Thailand wrested from the French favorable concessions in the eventual peace negotiations.

With virtual possession of Indo-Chinese ports, naval bases and airfields, Japanese ships entered the Gulf of Siam and her soldiers were at the borders of Burma and British Malaya. Being on the outskirts of the Dutch East Indies, all that was needed was the necessary stimulus and the psychological opportunity for expanding farther into the Pacific.

America Prepares. The United States launched a gigantic preparedness program in the summer of 1940, and in September inaugurated, for the first time in its history, peacetime conscription. The Burke-Wadsworth Bill, signed by President Roosevelt on September 16, required every civilian between 21 and 36 to register for service, provided "deferments" for certain public officials, workers in key industries, and those physically unfit or with dependents to support. The act limited the draft army to 900,000 and specified it be not sent out of the Western Hemisphere, except to an American possession. The training period was fixed at twelve months, subject to extension if Congress declares the national interest imperiled. A two-ocean navy bill, boosting the fleet by 70 per cent, was enacted on June 6, 1940, and by the end of the year 17 battleships, 12 aircraft carriers, 166 destroyers, and 81 submarines were in the process of construction. Navy personnel was increased from 134,892 officers and men to 196,000, Marine Corps officers and men from 23,035 to 49,643. More than half of the 250,000 National Guardsmen were called up for training.[13]

On August 18 a Permanent Joint Board on Defense for the United States and Canada[14] was set up with five members from each country to "co-ordinate defense by the armed services, and to supply them with the necessary material."

To supervise the rearmament program, President Roosevelt appointed a National Defense Advisory Committee headed by William S. Knudsen, former General Motors president. A priorities board was established to help iron out difficulties arising from the defense program and the nation's policy of offering all possible aid to Britain.[15]

That the United States intended to help Britain to its fullest extent was revealed when a bill, H. R. 1776, was introduced by the President to Congress on January 7, 1941. This measure gave the President virtually unlimited power to " sell, transfer, lease or lend " any defense article to any friendly power. Although such a bill had only wartime precedents, it was defended by democratic leaders in terms of speed and efficiency, and was passed after acrimonious debate on March 11. Several months earlier the United States had traded to Great Britain fifty " over-age " destroyers for leases on air and naval bases in British territory in the Western Hemisphere.

The rearmament program did not stop with the mobilization of man power and industry in the United States. The year 1940 saw closer " rearmament " relations between the United States and South and Central America. Meeting in Havana in July, 1940 representatives of twenty-two American republics voted to share the defense of this hemisphere, establish a neutrality belt around the Americas, and issued a strictly hands-off order to the Axis Powers. Secretary of State Cordell Hull attended the conference and signed the pact in behalf of the United States.[16]

By the end of 1940 America was rapidly discarding the attitude of " neutrality " and " isolation " which had dominated its thought and action for the last twenty years.[17]

Germany, Italy, and Japan Divide the World. In spite of the victories of the Axis in Europe, England was still in the war. On September 27 the Fascist diplomats assembled in Berlin and signed an alliance between Germany, Italy, and Japan to partition the various continents. To Japan went East Asia, to Germany and Italy Europe and Africa. To the United States went, according to the Italian press, the Western Hemisphere, pending good behavior. In October Hitler sent his forces quietly into Rumania and later into Bulgaria.

Unable to strike a telling blow at England itself, the Axis brought increasing pressure to bear on Spain, Greece, and Yugoslavia in the expectation of cutting England's communications at Gibraltar and the Suez Canal. Mussolini's Greek campaign, inaugurated on October 28, was to have been the prelude for a much larger Axis drive into the Near East. The Italian thrust into Egypt, begun on September 14, even if not successful in capturing Suez, was at least to occupy Britain's full strength in the Near East while other Axis victories were won northeast of Suez.

The " New Order " Expands. Meanwhile Hitler was having trouble with his other partners. Mussolini's Greek campaign was a failure. What had presumably been planned as a quick and easy war had brought few laurels to the Fascist legions. They had been ejected from Greek soil and were fighting in the inhospitable region of southern Albania.

But the most obstreperous partner was France. Marshal Pétain, head of the Vichy government, accused Germany of violating the armistice terms by expelling Frenchmen from Lorraine. The Germans had ordered the 800,000 Frenchmen in Lorraine to choose between moving into unoccupied France or into the bleak plains of Poland. No warning was given in advance. The French were allowed a few hours to pack what few belongings they could carry with them. No one was permitted to take more than $40. Stunned by the suddenness of the order, the exiles chose France. Farms, homes, and business were left behind, as German settlers moved in, intent not only on taking over the industries and rich iron mines of Lorraine, but wiping out all traces of French civilization. By November 27, 1940 evacuation of about 60,000 French-speaking inhabitants from Lorraine had been completed and about 120,000 Germans, including many who lost their homes in the war, were moving in. On November 30, Lorraine was combined with the Saar region as Germany's " Westmark " (western province).

France under Pétain. That Pétain was supreme in France, however precariously, was revealed in the Laval affair.

On December 16 Marshal Pétain, in a broadcast to the people of France, announced that Pierre Laval was no longer a member of the government, and that Pierre Flandin had received the portfolio of foreign affairs. He ascribed this action to reasons of internal policy which would have no effect on relations with Germany. Hitler was officially notified by telegram.

Connections between Vichy and the outside world were severed, and when they were resumed the story was current that Laval had intrigued to unseat Pétain and made himself head of a Fascist regime.[18] In the reorganized cabinet, Minister of Interior Peyrouton emerged as strong man. Pétain announced his intention of creating a consultive assembly to be composed of delegates from the provinces.

Upon the insistence of Otto Abetz (the German representative) Pétain allowed Laval to leave unoccupied France and take up residence in Paris. Negotiations between the French and Germans were resumed after a lapse of two weeks. Admiral Darlan and later Ferdinand de Brinon were named official negotiators. Little is known of the demands Germany made upon France except that the negotiations lasted for seven weeks. The impasse was broken on January 20 when Pétain and Laval met.

On January 25 Pétain designated a national council — a consultive group of 188 — replacing Parliament, Clergy, Arts, Science, Industry, Agriculture, and Labor, giving the body a corporative basis.[19] Pétain further increased his power on January 28 by passing a constitutional act making all ministers and public officials responsible to him. A national body to replace political parties, called *Rassemblement Nationale* was created on January 30.

The Germans retaliated by reporting the formation in Paris of a new political organization known as the *Rassemblement Nationale Populaire* with a program calling for the reconstruction of France based on collaboration with Germany.

On February 4, 1941 Pétain seemed to capitulate to Hitler's demands and agreed to reinstate Laval to Cabinet rank. The terms which Laval submitted for reconciliation, however, would have made him Premier, with far-reaching powers. Pétain agreed only to restore him as Minister of State. But, on February 9, Pierre Laval declined the offer which " was made in the spirit of European collaboration outlined by the Marshal and Hitler at Montoire." On February 9 pro-Nazi Flandin resigned and was replaced by Admiral Jean Darlan who will retain his position in the navy, direct the information services and preside at Cabinet meetings as Vice-President.

By steering France through this crisis Pétain showed himself a statesman able to cope with superlatively cunning politicians.

The Balkans. Hitler's ability to add new recruits to his cause produced the signature of Hungary to his " new world order." On November 20, 1940 Hungary signed the Pact of Berlin. To drag at the coattails of her powerful neighbor had been Hungary's foreign policy since the country signed the anti-Comintern pact in February, 1939.

The Hungarian move was, however, only part of the diplomatic web Hitler had been weaving in the Balkans. On November 23, 1940 Rumania, once the keystone of the Little Entente and the most strident satellite of France and Britain in southeastern Europe, " formally " pledged her allegiance to the Berlin-Rome-Tokyo alliance in which she had already been a silent partner for many weeks through German military occupation.

For Rumania, as for Hungary, there was no other choice left. Rumania had begun to swing toward the Axis soon after the fall of France in June, 1940. Until then, the country, fattened by territory acquired as a result of the Allied victory in the First World War, was bound diplomatically to Great Britain and France, although her commercial ties with Germany were rapidly increasing. France's capitulation to the Axis marked a turning point. Then Soviet Russia moved to reclaim Bessarabia. Unable to resist, Rumania acceded on June 27 to Russia's demands. In July a pro-Nazi government was installed in Rumania and the British guaranty was renounced. As British influence waned, Axis influence mounted. Hungary pressed her demands for Transylvania. On July 28 Hitler met with Rumanian and Hungarian representatives and told them to settle their territorial differences in order to insure peace in the Balkans. When these negotiations stalled, Hitler, impatient with the delay, summoned representatives of both nations to Vienna and awarded a part of Transylvania to Hungary; Germany guaranteed Rumania's shrunken frontiers.

King Carol was forced to abdicate on September 6 under Iron Guard pressure, and fled into exile, leaving the throne to his son, Michael, and control of the state to General Ion Antonescu, who later proclaimed himself Chief of State.

Antonescu issued a decree on September 15 setting up a state on Nazi lines. It designated the totalitarian, pro-Nazi Iron Guard as the sole Rumanian political party. Under his rule, Rumania moved still closer to the Axis. On October 12 the vanguard of German troops rolled into Rumania — to " train " the Rumanian army and protect Rumanian oil wells from the British, the Germans said.

By the end of February, 1941 events were moving fast in the Balkans. Bulgarian newspapers reported the infiltration of Germans. Hitler's procedure followed the well-established pattern. He was methodically clearing the road to the East by " softening up " Bulgaria and Yugoslavia, after bloodlessly conquering Rumania. The German tactics consisted of promises, threats, internal demoralization, " peaceful " penetration, the encouragement of national antagonisms — with a powerful military machine on the border ready to move if " the strategy of terror " should fail.

On March 2, 1941 Bulgaria was brought into the tri-partite military alliance of Berlin, Rome, and Tokyo, the seventh nation to join the group. Hitler's purpose was twofold; (1) to use Bulgaria as a base for operations against the Greeks and, if need be, the Yugoslavs; and (2) to bring Germany closer to the Mediterranean in case she should decide to attempt to dislodge the British from the Near East.

Yugoslavia. Yugoslavia, of course, was now in a difficult position, since she was encircled by the hostile Germans and Italians whose protecting advances she had hitherto declined. As the Germans and Italians advanced eastward the position of Turkey became more precarious.

The Mediterranean Countries. Even though the Mediterranean countries are poor in material resources, and almost completely lacking in heavy industry, the Mediterranean is one of the greatest commercial highways in the world. Nearly 2300 miles long, averaging 300 miles in width, this narrow, almost tideless sea washes the shores of three great continents — Europe, Asia, and Africa — and its basin contains the cradles of three great religions — Judaism, Christianity, and Islam. To Italy, Yugoslavia, Greece, and Turkey, the Mediterranean provides the only outlet to the high seas. To Russia, Rumania, Bulgaria, and to unoccupied France, it offers the best outlet. For France and Italy it serves as a link to territories in North Africa. To Great Britain it is one of the most important life lines of empire, providing a short cut to East Africa, India, Australia, New Zealand, Malaysia, and Hong Kong.

Sea control has special importance in the Mediterranean Basin because neither on the African shore nor in the islands is there industry sufficient to provide munitions for an army. A great part of the African littoral, notably that held by Italy, is likewise deficient in food production and much of it is waterless. All operations involving these areas are therefore dependent on maritime communications.

But to Italy, this sea has been the core of her ambitions. " If for others the Mediterranean is a route " Mussolini once said, " for us it is life itself." In normal times, 86 per cent of Italian imports come through the Mediterranean; of these only a quarter originate within the Mediterranean area, the rest come through the narrow bottlenecks of the Dardanelles, Suez, and Gibraltar. To the Italians it has been a considerable source of irritation that the three narrow entrances to the Mediterranean are controlled by other powers — by Britain at Suez and Gibraltar, and Turkey at the Dardanelles. To remedy the situation, Italy seized the Dodecanese Islands off the Turkish coast after the First World War; to weaken Britain at Suez, Mussolini's legions invaded Ethiopia in 1935, and at Gibraltar by backing a Spanish uprising in 1936; in the spring of 1939 Albania was seized, and finally, war was declared by Rome on Britain and France on June 10, 1940.

Italy's African Campaign. Even after four months of war, Italy was still, however, not in control of the Mediterranean. Although France had fallen, Italy was cut off from a good part of the world by the British blockade. A drive toward the Suez Canal had begun. The attack from the south succeeded in ejecting the British from British Somaliland, a barren strip of East African coast of no commercial value, but possession of which permitted Italian aircraft and submarines to operate against British troop and supply ships passing through the Indian Ocean, the Gulf of Aden, and the Red Sea.

In the meantime an Italian force of about 270,000 troops, with from 600 to 1000 aircraft, had been moved south across the Mediterranean into Libya under the command of Marshal Rodolfo Graziani. The task of the greatly outnumbered British was not only to prevent Graziani's Libyan army from pushing on to the fertile and populous lands of the Nile delta, but to prevent another large force, 80,000 to 100,000 strong, from striking into Egypt from Ethiopia in the south.

Egypt and the Moslem World. Mussolini, although his forces aimed to reach Egypt, was, however, cautious in dealing with King Farouk, assuring him that Italy's aim was only to drive the British from Egypt, and that Egyptian troops would be engaged only if they attacked. War was not declared on Egypt. Under the provisions of the Anglo-Egyptian Treaty of Alliance of 1936, however, Britain was permitted the use of Egyptian airdromes and sea bases and could move troops through certain areas in defense of the Suez Canal.

Mussolini's caution was promoted by the fact that Egypt with its more than 15,000,000 Arabs is the leading Moslem country. An embroilment with Egypt might, therefore, incur the enmity of a good part of the world's 200,000,000 Moslems, from northwest Africa to Java.

The Battle for Greece. Meanwhile the Greeks valorously held off the Italians. The Italian strategy was to drive south, parallel to the west coast, to take Jannina. From there they would turn almost due east toward the plains of Thessaly, to cut off the entire Greek peninsula. The Italian army moved slowly forward, through mud and canyons, blasting the Greeks out of solid rock, but after two weeks they had not taken Jannina, for the Italian flank had been severely but not fatally slashed by General Papagos. At the far northern end of the Italian line, strong Greek forces claimed to have surrounded an Italian division in the bed of the Aos River. The Italian invasion, admittedly planned without thought of Greek resistance, had come to grief in the Pindus mountains, where bad weather and rough terrain aided the men of Hellas.

That the Greeks, a nation of less than 7,000,000 people, could resist Italy with its 43,000,000 for long, had seemed impossible when the war began. That they had been able to defeat the Fascist legions in the first month of fighting appeared to result from a combination of circumstances: (1) British aid in the air and at sea, with a consequent threat to Italian communications; (2) inadequate Italian preparation for the campaign; (3) overextension of Italian lines; (4) unwise use of mechanized equipment in mountain country; (5) insufficient use of the Italian navy and air corps; and (6) Greek ability to make the most of Italian errors.[20]

Rated as a helpless underdog, the Greeks " handed the invading army of Fascist Italy a defeat as shameful as those other Italian nightmares of Adowa, Caporetto and Guadalajara." [21] After six weeks of war, they had not only repulsed the Italian invaders but had captured 7000 Italians and much equipment.

British Successes in Africa. Meanwhile the British had landed in Crete, only 50 miles from Italian bomber bases in the Dodecanese Islands. The British fleet tried to coax the Italian fleet into battle. On November 12, Admiral Sir Andrew Cunningham sought the enemy at Taranto, a harbor within the boot-heel of Italy. There the Italian fleet, at anchor, was bombed by British planes, putting several major ships out of commission. On November 27 the British fleet drove other Italian ships into port at Sardinia.

The effects on the Italian supply line and morale were so great that in the middle of November General Archibald Wavell was able to launch an attack from his stronghold in Egypt with a force far inferior in numbers to the Italians. Marshal Graziani's army, which had advanced 60 miles along the coast into the Egyptian desert, spread into small camps over an area extending 30 miles inland, since their coastal positions could be shelled by British warships offshore. Moreover, their supply line from Italy to Libya was extremely vulnerable the moment the British occupied Crete.

On December 15 General Wavell's forces pounced upon the Italians on the Libyan escarpment and across the desert " in one of the most successful surprise attacks of this or any war," [22] opening up a wide gap in the Italian defenses. A whole Italian corps was captured or destroyed.

Moving with the aid of the Royal Navy and the Royal Air Force, British troops captured Sidi Barrani in three days. On January 5 they were in Bardia, where 25,000 prisoners were taken. Marching westward, Wavell's mechanized forces invested and occupied Tobruk on January 22; Derna fell on January 30; Benghazi, capital of Cyrenaica, was captured on February 6. Altogether the British took about 150,000 prisoners. Fascist Italy's military pretensions were completely shattered and the British had won their first land campaign in the war, a victory that was, however, to be reversed but two months later when the Germans took up the task of the hapless Italians in North Africa.

Early in 1941 the British successfully invaded Eritrea and Ethiopia. On February 1 they captured the town of Agordat in Eritrea; two months later they were in possession of Cheren. Simultaneously British forces advancing from Kenya into Italian Somaliland occupied Chismaio on February 15 and the capital Mogadiscio on February 26.

Everywhere in Africa the Italians retreated before the British. Ethiopia was invaded by several British columns aided by native tribesmen under the command of the ex-Emperor Haile Selassie. The chief Fascist strongholds in Ethiopia were gradually subdued, Burye on March 5, Harar on March 27, Diredawa on March 31, and finally the capital Addis Ababa at the end of April. On May 5, 1941, five years after the entry of Italian troops into Addis Ababa, Haile Selassie returned in triumph, emphasizing again the impotence of the Italian armies and the hollowness of Mussolini's pretensions.

The Fall of Greece and Yugoslavia. The successive failures of the Italian armies left Hitler no choice but to rescue his Axis partner. It was even rumored that the Germans had taken control of the Italian government and that Italy was permeated with Gestapo agents and German soldiers, in order to prevent the Italian people, who overwhelmingly opposed the war, from making peace with the British.

At any event, as spring approached the German armies in the Balkans were being primed for a great offensive. With his troops in Rumania, Bulgaria, and Hungary, the familiar diplomatic " squeeze play " was attempted on Yugoslavia. Early in March Prince Paul and Premier Stoyadinović duly visited Germany and secretly negotiated a pact which was to bring Yugoslavia into the Axis. Signing of the pact, however, was repeatedly postponed, for the Yugoslav people, especially the Serbian element, were violently opposed to Germany. At length, on March 27, General Šimović engineered a *coup d'état,* deposing the Regent Prince Paul, and putting on the throne young King Peter, son of Alexander who had been assassinated in 1934. This surprising event doomed the pact with Germany, and announced to the world that Yugoslavia, unlike Hungary, Rumania, or Bulgaria, would fight for her freedom. Germany quickly prepared for the assault, and on April 5 the Nazi hordes invaded Yugoslavia and Greece simultaneously. The Yugoslavs, with the exception of the treacherous Croats, fought bitterly but, like the Poles, their antiquated army and want of air power doomed them to quick defeat. Within ten days Yugoslav resistance was broken.

In Greece the Germans were held back for more than three weeks. Reinforced by a few divisions of Australian, New Zealand, and British troops, the brave men of Hellas inflicted terrific casualties on the Germans. The fighting took place in cloud-capped mountains and along rugged passes. Hopelessly outnumbered, the Allies retreated steadily, and by the end of April the Germans hoisted the dreaded Swastika on the ancient Acropolis of Athens. Hitler thus added two more countries to his long roll of conquests; the cost in German lives, according to journalistic accounts, was tremendous, but since the Nazi regime holds human life very cheaply, this did not trouble the victors. The British were now completely ejected from the continent of Europe, and Nazi arrogance mounted to new levels. Yugoslavia was partitioned between Italy, Germany, and Hungary. Bulgaria was rewarded with part of Greece.

Blitzkrieg on the Desert. Flushed with their easy victory over the Italians, the British halted their drive in Libya at Benghazi, and withdrew a portion of their army to bolster the Greeks on the mainland of Europe. Meanwhile Germany managed to sneak through the British blockade of the Mediterranean several divisions of mechanized troops, and with Tripoli as a base began an effective counterattack. On March 26 the Axis troops recaptured El Aghelia and thereafter made a speedy advance, forcing the British back toward Egypt, taking Benghazi, Derna, Bardia, and finally Sollum. Tobruk remained in British hands, its 25,000 defenders undergoing a long siege. At Sollum the Axis counterattack was halted. With Greece and strategic Aegean islands in their hands, the Axis strategy was to launch, in due time, a pincer movement toward Suez, from the Sollum front on the west and by way of Syria (where the Germans were obtaining secret control) or Turkey, perhaps, on the east.

Europe Under Nazi Rule

Hitler's New Order. By June, 1941 Germany (with her satellite Italy) through military, political, or economic influence, controlled the whole continent except Russia, Switzerland, and Sweden. Hitler's New Order, slowly imposed on the conquered nations, promised to divide Europe among the dominant races into large regional areas.[23] He used the pro-Fascist native leaders as his instruments of government in the conquered nations whose industries were reorganized and adapted to the German economy. Foreign trade payments between Greater Germany and Belgium, the Netherlands, Sweden, Finland, France, Switzerland, Italy, Bulgaria, Yugoslavia, and Greece are cleared through Berlin. Finally, to insure Nazi dominance, propaganda or force was used to subjugate the intellectual leaders of the conquered territories.[24]

Eastern Europe. Poland when conquered in September, 1939 was divided among Germany, Slovakia, and the Soviet Union. Germany acquired 36,242 square miles; Russia acquired the western Ukraine and western White Russia. Conditions in Poland foreshadow the New Order wherever the Nazi legions are planted. Germany's conviction that the Poles were an inferior race led them to reduce the Poles to the status of agricultural workers and deport thousands to farms in the Reich.[25] The farmers who remained were required to turn over a portion of their crops to Germany. The minority issue was settled by mass exiles. Approximately 60,000 Poles were brought together in nationality groups in sharply defined geographic areas. This hectic disorder was increased by the influx of Germans from the Baltic region and the Reich. Germany's intention to transform Poland into an agricultural region prompted her to reduce Polish participation in trades and professions, and close and demolish factories. The standard of living was reduced; food was severely rationed, while many starved. Any appearance of resistance by the Poles was harshly suppressed. Tens of thousands of men and boys perished in mass murders or died of starvation and cold in prison camps.[26] Although Germans were forbidden to intermarry with the Poles because of their inferior status, young girls were constantly abducted, imprisoned with prostitutes, or deported to German brothels.

Czechoslovakia. On October 1, 1940 Germany announced the adjustment of the Bohemian-Moravian economy and price structure. Elaborate tariff agreements between industries in the protectorate and Germany were, however, necessary. Industries depending upon foreign materials were forced to close down. Unemployed workers were sent to the Reich as farm laborers. The Czechs, however, had a greater degree of political freedom than the Poles, as evidenced by Reich's Protector von Neurath's announcement that a declaration of loyalty to Berlin was required by Czech organizations which were still permitted to exist. Systematic exploitation was carried on by Nazi troops paying for Czech supplies in German money, which Czech banks were obliged to redeem.[27] All signs pointed toward the full incorporation of Czechoslovakia into the German Reich. Czech factories, industries, and universities were discriminated against, and approximately 80,000 laborers were sent to labor on German farms.[28] The Czechs refused to reconcile themselves to German domination, and accordingly strove to shake it off by political conspiracy within the existing Protectorate and under the leadership of Dr. Edward Beneš in London. The German Gestapo seemed unable to eliminate the underground, secret organizations, despite their attempt to break the people's resistance. By the end of August, 1940, 854 persons had been convicted of " political crimes "; 9,613 were under protective arrest, and 43,284 were in concentration camps. The National Solidarity Party was dissolved because of its identification with Czech nationalism, rather than with the totalitarian party. The group chosen by Hitler to rule was unimportant because the Czechs did not consider them their leaders. Sabotage was common, as the frequent wholesale arrests of workers attested. Hitler could not imprison, exile, or execute all the living Czechs; hence his power was limited.

The Balkans. Within the space of three years the Germans and Italians had conquered or annexed by " peaceful means " all the Danubian countries, commencing with Austria in 1938; then Czechoslovakia, Hungary, Rumania, Bulgaria, Yugoslavia, and Greece. Each nation was given the choice of struggling against overwhelming odds or giving up its independence. Those who refused to succumb to threats, like Yugoslavia and Greece, went down fighting gloriously.

Turkey. After talks with Foreign Minister Anthony Eden and Sir John Dill, Chief of Imperial Staff, the Turkish government closed the Dardanelles to all ships without special permits, and on March 3, 1941 announced that Turkey would stand by the British alliance. Turkey's final decision, however, depended upon the attitude of the Soviet Union, and although Greece, Bulgaria, and Yugoslavia were overrun, Turkey remained on the side lines.

Denmark. Denmark was suffering perhaps less than the other countries because the Germans needed their produce and consequently sought to co-operate with them. Although the Scandinavians are, according to the Nazis, racial kin, the Danes, like the Norwegians, scorned the conquerors. Although the Germans tried to please the Danes, unrest grew as Denmark's food supply began to diminish, despite trade agreements. Danish farmers paid exorbitant taxes, and unemployed seafaring men were sent to Germany. Germany had also taken control of Denmark's foreign trade in her drive to reorganize the economic life of conquered countries.

Norway. At the end of the Norwegian campaign in May, 1940 a Norwegian Administrative Commission, headed by Ingolf Christensen, was created temporarily to handle the country's affairs. However, on September 25 a State Council was formed, supported by one political party, the National Union of Major Quisling. The Norwegians hated Quisling because he was considered an arch traitor. On December 4 the supreme court was wiped out when the Reichkemmessar Terboven stated that it had no authority over the orders issued by the acting heads of the governments. Thereupon a German "People's Court" was set up under German military judges. Death was the penalty for communication with the British government or exiled royal family. The Norwegian church protested vigorously, citing the systematic violence of the storm troopers, the interference with the preacher's "sworn secrecy" and the registration of Norwegians fifteen years and older. The Norwegians refused to resign themselves to German domination. Sabotage was common, as well as daily demonstrations against the regime. Regimentation and censorship of the press resulted in publication of illegal pamphlets which circulated throughout the country.[29]

Sweden. Through its neutrality Sweden attempted to escape domination by Germany or the Soviet Union. Cooperation with Germany was supported by a majority in the elections of September 15, 1940, owing partly to fear of the Soviet Union's expansion in case of German defeat, although the Swedes held no illusions about the effect of a German victory on Sweden's independence. Sweden knew that she had to cooperate with Germany or suffer a German invasion; long-drawn-out hostilities would eventuate in economic starvation. Cut off by the blockade from customary markets, she was forced to readjust her economy to please Germany as well as the Soviet Union. Germany conducted the trade agreements with Sweden on behalf of Belgium and the Netherlands, claiming that such indirect arrangements were necessary, since the Dutch government in London controlled Dutch financial resources in foreign countries.

Belgium.[30] Belgium is one of the occupied territories which has no native organization. The government in exile, sitting in London, controlled the Belgian Congo with its vast resources of copper, tin, radium, and gold. Belgium is governed by minor native officials, supervised by Germans under General von Falkenhausen, Governor of Belgium and the north of France. The German conquest radically disorganized the economic life of Belgium, a country which had formerly imported 50 per cent of its foodstuffs. Rations were allotted since the Germans systematically looted the country. Unemployment became serious as one million out of a population of 8 million were out of work. The number increased as the hordes of refugees who sought shelter in France during the war returned to their homes. To liquidate the situation the Germans instituted compulsory registration of workers for labor in Germany and 50,000 men were deported for this purpose. Further restrictive measures were the inflation of Belgian currency by unbacked occupation marks, amalgamation of Belgian and German firms and control of all production of foreign exchange.[31] Jews were required to wear arm bands. However, despite German attempts to foster Nazi sympathy among either Walloon or Flemish groups, Belgian distrust of the conquerors was not diminished. A huge army of occupation was kept in Flanders.[32]

Holland. Direct responsibility for governing Holland was delegated to a Dutch Administrative Committee. Government bureaus were formed to control distribution of raw materials. The chief problem was the reestablishment of foreign trade, half of which was cut off by the blockade. Even much of the rationed goods was unobtainable. Relations between the German authorities and the Dutch population were very strained. The Germans controlled the press, introduced anti-Jewish legislation, dissolved all political groups, and transferred trade union funds to Nazi organizations. They also "purified" all the libraries and book-shops. About 250,000 laborers were sent to work in German armament factories. The Dutch, however, continued to indulge in acts of sabotage, despite severe reprisals. About 2000 Hollanders were in German prisons; fines upon cities were common; hundreds were sent to concentration camps, including such distinguished groups as the entire law faculty of the University of Utrecht, two or three hundred civil servants and other prominent persons.[33]

France. The armistice, as we have seen, divided France into two sharply separated areas. The boundary between the occupied and unoccupied zones was closely guarded with no radio or postal communication between except for official purposes. Pétain was not permitted to make any important decisions without consulting the Franco-German Armistice Commission or the German Ambassador to Paris, Otto Abetz.[34] France was in a deplorable state after the armistice. There was a shortage of fuel, trains, and communications. As the food situation grew worse in the occupied area, fats, soap, and milk becoming almost unobtainable, the plight of the government grew. German spoliation and the cost of $8,000,000 a day for maintaining German troops in occupied France drained the national exchequer. Furthermore the exchange was set by the Germans at the low figure of 20 francs to the mark. The German troops and civilians in occupied territory bought consumers' goods and foodstuffs with their cheap francs, and sent them to their families in the Reich. Thus France was bled white. Yet Marshal Pétain, although an ardent patriot, believed in cooperating with the Nazis. Moreover, France was powerless to reacquire about 1,500,000 French prisoners of war still languishing in German camps, hostages for the Vichy government's good behavior. Unem-

ployment was prevalent, since the government had no money for reconstruction. The social structure was adapted to the new Fascist system.
Individuals in public office or the professions had to prove French citizenship. Youth groups were formed; anti-Semitic legislation and sweeping
powers over production and trade, as well as regulatory laws for industry,
agriculture, and commerce, were adopted. Pétain declared that the old
order was to be utterly abolished, that the slogan of " Liberty, Equality
and Fraternity " would be replaced by " Community Discipline, Labor
and Family." That many Frenchmen did not agree with the Marshal was
indicated by the numerous fines imposed by the Germans in the occupied
zone, such as 1,000,000 francs for wire cutting, and 20,000,000 francs for
" *lèsé majesté*." Efforts to suppress pro-British sentiments were unavail-
ing. The contents of safety boxes and bank deposits were being examined
so that the Germans might estimate the liquid capital of the country and
levy due indemnity. To this pitiful state had France, the mother of liberty, fallen one year after its military collapse.[35]

REFERENCES

1 M. Fagen, "Lesson of France," *New Republic*, September 2, 1940, Vol. CIII, No. 10, pp. 296–299; "America, Learn from France!" *ibid.*, September 9, 1940, Vol. CIII, No. 11, pp. 341–344. These two well-documented articles refute the Vichy government's declaration that the reforms of the Popular Front hindered the nation's industrial preparation and caused its defeat by the Germans. Fagen proves that financial interests retarded armament preparation by refusing to advance credit whenever the government launched a defense program. André Simone, *J'Accuse*, New York: Dial Press, 1940, elaborates upon the same theme. Simone reveals the unwillingness of the conservative moneyed classes to cooperate with the Popular Front.

2 D. Popper and J. C. deWilde, "Wartime Economy of Britain and France," *Foreign Policy Reports*, July 15, 1940, Vol. XVI, No. 9, pp. 119–124; J. C. deWilde, "German Wartime Economy," *ibid.*, June 15, 1940, Vol. XVI, No. 7.

3 C. Dreher, "Why Hitler Wins," *Harper's*, October, 1940, Vol. CLXXXI, No. 1085, pp. 61–76.

4 Hamilton A. Fish, *A Chronology of Failure*, New York: Macmillan, 1940, shows that France's morale was weakened by her failure to act decisively in such crucial moments as the Rhineland invasion; her refusal to stop Italy's Ethiopian venture; and the rotten financial policy before the Blum regime. Fish reveals how past political events alienated both the Right and the Left factions of the government to such a degree that German agents found ready listeners among the discontented people for their fifth column work, one of the causes of France's downfall. Heinz Pol, *Suicide of a Democracy*, New York: Reynal & Hitchcock, 1940, stresses the effective propaganda technique of the Germans in associating Communism with the Popular Front so that certain elements hated social democracy and wished for an authoritarian regime. He classified Pétain, Weygand, and Flandin as Fascists and claims that if they had not hated democracy they would not have surrendered so rapidly to the Germans.

5 Peter Muir, *War without Music*, New York: Scribner, 1940, claims that during the last ten years the French masses had become profoundly pacifistic; individualism had run wild; when war came there was no unity and most of the soldiers and officers tried only to save their skins; this lack of leadership made the confusion which followed inevitable.

6 Jules Romains, *The Seven Mysteries of Europe*, New York: Knopf, 1940, is a superficial and rather glamorous treatment of the downfall of France, emphasizing the point that the totalitarian state gained confidence in the effectiveness of violence in international relations when Laval failed to apply sanctions to Italy during the Ethiopian crisis and incidentally antagonized many nations who did cooperate.

7 William H. Chamberlin, "Daladier: The Tragedy of France," *The American Mercury*, August, 1940, Vol. L, pp. 477–483, describes Daladier's inability to act decisively in a crisis and thus his hindrance of French efficiency. From the commencement of the war Daladier was burdened by heavy responsibility. The pace was too hard, especially since he was unable to delegate authority and responsibility, in order to keep his mind clear for momentous decisions.

8 René de St. Jean, "The Failure of France," *Harper's*, October, 1940, Vol. CLXXXI, pp. 449–460, explains the power of the ineffectual bureaucracy. When Reynaud became Premier the military clique as represented by Daladier and Gamelin was so strong that he could not dislodge them without destroying himself politically. Reynaud fully realized their defects and errors, but the average Frenchman did not.

9 H. W. Spiegel, "Wehrwirtschaft: Economics of the Military State," *American Economic Review*, December, 1940, Vol. XXX, No. 4, pp. 713–723, explains the pattern of total war and demonstrates that there is no line of demarcation which separates war from peace; war production and warfare are simple and well-defined objectives of economic policy in the military state; and there is no unused capacity since all resources are placed in the service of war. G. Stolper, *German Economy: 1870–1940*, New York: Reynal & Hitchcock, 1940, presents an impressive and enlightening survey of Germany's economic development.

[10] H. Foertsch, *Art of Modern Warfare*, New York: Oskar Piest, 1940, is a fascinating work which analyzes the strategic and tactical tenets of the German army. Particular emphasis is laid on the new weapons, such as the mechanized forces, motorized infantry, and air power. S. L. Marshall, *Blitzkrieg*, New York: Morrow, 1941, is a comprehensive study of Germany's total war, which traces the historical development of the *Blitzkrieg* and shows how all social forces are coordinated for the purpose of conquest.

[11] A. Geraud, " Gamelin," *Foreign Affairs*, January, 1941, Vol. XIX, No. 2, pp. 310–332, shows the astounding backwardness of the General Staff which underestimated completely the ability of the German army and ignored the political and psychological weapons.

[12] T. A. Bisson, " America's Dilemma in the Far East," *Foreign Policy Reports*, July 1, 1940, Vol. XIV, No. 8, and T. A. Bisson, " Indo-China: Spearhead of Japan's Southward Drive," *Foreign Policy Reports*, October 1, 1940, Vol. XVI, No. 14.

[13] At no other time since 1917 has the topic of " militarism " received so much attention as since May, 1940. Among recent excellent studies, most of them designed for the general public, consult Major General H. Arnold and Lt. Col. Ira Eaker, *Winged Warfare*, New York: Harper, 1941; modern fighting planes, aerial warfare, future developments, and national defense are some of the topics treated by these authors; Col. Hollis Miller, *Technique of Modern Arms*, Harrisburg: Military Service Publishing Company, 1940, presents an excellent description of army organization and techniques of strategy.

[14] James Frederick Green " Canada at War," *Foreign Policy Reports*, Vol. XVI. No. 12, September 1, 1940, maintains that whatever the outcome of the present war, the close collaboration of Canada and the United States will have far-reaching implications. It is also an excellent survey of Canada's military and economic mobilization.

[15] H. J. Trueblood, " Economic Defense of the Americas," *Foreign Policy Reports*, August 1, 1940, Vol. XVI, No. 10, is a fine description of the problems which must be considered: i.e., inter-American trade problem, geographical problem, the United States import potential; problem of surplus products, before a solution is drawn up. J. C. deWilde and George Monson, " Defense Economy of the United States; Problems of Mobilization," *Foreign Policy Reports*, November 1, 1940, Vol. XVI, No. 16, describes how the defense commission met the problem of bottlenecks in defense production; of insuring raw material supplies; of stock-piling and the necessity of revising the board for the centralization of authority.

[16] H. J. Trueblood, " The Havana Conference of 1940," *Foreign Policy Reports*, September 15, 1940, Vol. XVI, No. 13. A. R. Elliott, " European Colonies in the Western Hemisphere," *Foreign Policy Reports*, August 15, 1940, Vol. XVI, No. 11, lays before us a more detailed analysis of the problem of the European colonies.

[17] Malcolm Wheeler-Nicholson, *Battle Shield of the Republic*, New York: Macmillan, 1940; here a one-time army officer writes an excellent criticism of the deficiencies of the army, contending that both personnel and strategy need modernization, citing a variety of specific reforms. Whitney Shepardson, *The United States in World Affairs*, New York: Harper, 1940, is a compact review of our role in international affairs.

[18] New York *Times*, December 15, 1940.

[19] New York *Times*, January 25, 1941.

[20] New York *Times*, " Review of the Week," December 1, 1940.

[21] *Life*, December 23, 1940, Vol. IX, No. 26, p. 20.

[22] Major George Fielding Eliot, " Britain Tries to Knock Italy Out," *Life*, December 23, 1940.

[23] John Wheeler-Bennett, " Hitler's New Order: Slavery," *New Europe*, January, 1941, Vol. I, No. 2, pp. 25–26. Each country under German domination will consist of two classes, masters and slaves. Economic exploitation in countries which the " New Order " has taken are cited to verify this thesis.

[24] Vera Micheles Dean, " Europe under Nazi Rule," *Foreign Policy Reports*, October 15, 1940, Vol. XVI, No. 15, treats in great detail the political and economic reorganization, as well as ideological changes in all the countries which have come

under the "New Order," viz.: Poland, Czechoslovakia, the Balkans, Rumania, Norway, Denmark, Sweden, Belgium, the Netherlands and France.

[25] New York *Times*, January 15, 1941. A dispatch said there were 1,391,000 foreign laborers working on German farms. These include 650,000 Polish, French, and Belgian prisoners of war, 180,000 Polish prisoners working voluntarily in Germany, and other nationalities.

[26] New York *Times*, November 27, 1940.

[27] *News Flashes from Czechoslovakia under Nazi Domination*, Release No. 54, October 22, 1941, Chicago: Czechoslovak National Council of America.

[28] New York *Times*, December 8, 1940.

[29] New York *Times*, January 18, 1940.

[30] Lars Moen, *Under the Iron Heel*, Philadelphia: Lippincott, 1941, is an eyewitness account of life in Nazi-controlled Belgium from May until October, 1940.

[31] New York *Times*, January 18, 1941.

[32] Jean Peters, "A Nation in Jail," New York *Herald Tribune*, Magazine Section, March 9, 1941, pp. 12-29, presents a graphic account of life in Belgium.

[33] New York *Times*, December 15, 1940.

[34] Vera Micheles Dean, *op. cit.*, October 15, 1940.

[35] *All Gaul Is Divided*, Greystone, 1941.

Index

Aaland Islands, 32, 41, 459, 479, 481, 482, 485

Abyssinia. *See* Ethiopia

Action Française. See France

Adler, Alfred, 604

Affairs, world, Europe in, 611–626

Africa, 25–26

British successes in Second World War, 637

campaign, Second World War, 636

German successes in Second World War, 639

modernization, 613

Aggression, definition of, 48

Agreements, trade. *See* Trade

Agriculture. *See* names of countries

Air power, and sea power, 560; limitations of, 549, 551

Albania, 42, 310, 311, 350, 363

and Italy, 311

annexation by Italy, 314, 364, 538

foreign affairs, 369

Zog, King, downfall of, 364

Albert, King of the Belgians, action in the war, 168–169

Alexander, King of Yugoslavia, 529; assassination, 313, 358, 530

Alexandretta, Sanjak of, 383, 384

Alfonso XIII of Spain, 276, 277, 278, 281, 282, 289

Alsace and Lorraine, 125, 129, 192, 193, 211, 320, 325

autonomy question, 135

expulsion of French from Lorraine, and union with the Saar, 632

religious question, 130

Altmark affair, 473, 498

Amau Doctrine, 526

Amber Route, 224, 253

America. *See* United States

Americas, South and Central. *See* Latin America

Angell, Norman, quotation from, on association of ideas, 616

Anglo-French naval accord, 56

Anschluss (union of Austria and Germany), 27, 78, 209, 228, 230, 328, 366, 368, 528; effected, 534–535

" Anthropo-sociology," 600

Anti-Comintern pact (1939), 367, 533, 621, 634

Anti-Semitism. *See* Jews

" Appeasement," 537, 555; failure of, 538

Arabia, 29, 30

Arabia, Saudi, 374, 381; oil, 386

Arabs. *See* Palestine

Architecture. *See also* names of countries

and decoration, 589

functionalism, 587, 589

modern, 587

Armaments

disarmament, failure of, 526

limitation of, 52–62

MacDonald plan, 61

mechanization, German, 628

naval building program, British, 99

naval, limitation, Washington Conference (1922–1923), 52, 617, 621

neglect by United States, Great Britain, and France, 618

parity, naval, 59

Armenia, 29

Art (*see also* names of countries)

abstract, 585–586

and music, 582–596

Constructivism, 588

critics, 583

Cubism, 584, 588

cultural influence, 582

Dadaism, 584

democratization, 582, 588–589

encouragement of, 588

effect of war, 582

experimentalism and industrialization, 582–588

expressionism, 584

folk, 590

Freud, Sigmund, influence of, 585

graphic and poster, 590

human elements, elimination of, 585

Impressionism, 583, 584

industrial, 589

industrialization, 586, 587

murals, 589

nationalism, 583, 590

new, 583; and the layman, 585; defense by critics, 585

political use, in totalitarian countries, 591

Rondism, 588

scope, widening of, 583

education, 264, 606
geography, military, 552–553
German seizure and domination, 78, 210, 254, 265–270, 537–538, 640
independence, 255–256
Jews. *See* Jews
labor and agriculture, 262
literature, 263
Masaryk, Thomas Garrigue, 254, 255, 256, 257, 260, 261, 263, 264, 265
minorities, 41
music and art, 264
party system, 257–260
peoples, 253
policy, foreign, 261
protectorate by Germany, 268, 537–538
republic, " second," 266
revival, national, 254
revolutionaries abroad, 269
Slovakia, 258, 342; secession, 268, 269
sokols, 264
Sudeten Germans. *See* Sudeten Germans

Daladier, Edouard, 137, 149, 628
d'Annunzio, Gabriele, 41, 297, 309
Danube River, 553, 555
Danubian Union, 366
Danzig, 25, 72, 209, 210, 537, 538, 539, 554
Dardanelles. *See* Straits
" Darwinism, social," 600
Dawes Plan, 208, 212, 222, 509
Debts, international. *See* Finance
Debts, war; French default, 137; to the United States, 46
Declaration of Independence quoted, 618
Decline of the West, by Spengler, 11
" Decolonization." *See* Colonies
Decoration, interior, 589
Deflation. *See* Finance
Defoe, Daniel, quotation from, on Englishman, 84
Democracy, 502, 503
American and European, 507
bases of, essential, 505, 506
criticism of, 509
essence of, 403
experience with, 506
expression in words, 502, 618
false, 4
Fascist antagonism, 504, 509, 618
new, contents of, 506; external dangers, 508; weaknesses, 505
rise after First World War, 505
safety for, 3
" softening," 618
victory of, 504
Democratization, 611, 613

Denmark, 25, 211, 490–499
and Germany; non-aggression pact, 538
commerce, 496
cultural development and literature, 496–497
disarmament, 494
dispute with Norway over Greenland, 472
during the First World War, 492
during the Second World War, 495
economic development, and problems, 495, 496
Fascism, 494
government, 492
history, 491
invasion by Germany, 495
minority problem, 491
people, 490
politics, 493–495
republic, agitation for, 493
Schleswig question. *See* Schleswig
science, 567
Socialist measures, 496
Stauning governments, 493–495
under German rule, 641
Depression, economic, 7, 75
Determinism, 573, 574; economic, 510
De Valera, Eamon, 107, 108
Dialectical materialism, 574, 575
Dialectics, 510
Dictatorships, 4, 9. *See also* names of countries
Disarmament. *See* Armaments
Disarmament Conference, General, 59
Doctrine and behavior, 502
Doctrines, changes in, 502, 503
Dollfuss, Engelbert, 231; assassination, 210, 233
Dominions, British. *See* British Empire
Drexler, Anton, 203, 231
Druses, country of, 381, 383
Dual Monarchy. *See* Austria-Hungary
Dunkerque, evacuation by British, 541
Dutch East and West Indies, 185
Duties. *See* Tariffs

East, Far. *See* Asia; Near East and Far East
East, Near. *See* Near East
Eastern Europe under Fascist rule, 640–641
Eastern Locarno, 529
Ebert, Friedrich, 199–200
Economic Conference, Geneva (1927), 73
Economic determinism, 510
" Economic law," 6
" Economic man," 6